Teaching in the Secondary School

An Introduction

Fifth Edition

David G. Armstrong
The University of North Carolina at Greensboro

Tom V. Savage
Santa Clara University

Merrill
Prentice Hall

Upper Saddle River, New Jersey
Columbus, Ohio

D1530635

Library of Congress Cataloging in Publication Data

Armstrong, David G.
  Teaching in the secondary school—an introduction / David G. Armstrong, Tom V. Savage.—5th ed.
    p. cm.
  Includes bibliographical references (p.) and index.
  ISBN 0-13-028766-0
  1. High school teaching—Unites States. 2. Education, Secondary—United States.   I. Savage, Tom V. II. Title
LB1737.U6 A75 2002
373.1102—dcl   00-052686

Vice President and Publisher: Jeffery W. Johnston
Managing Editor: Allyson P. Sharp
Editorial Assistant: Penny S. Burleson
Production Editor: Kimberly J. Lundy
Design Coordinator: Robin Chukes
Photo Coordinator: Nancy Harre Ritz
Cover Designer: Linda Fares
Cover Image: SuperStock
Production Manager: Pamela D. Bennett
Electronic Text Management: Marilyn Wilson Phelps, Melanie N. Ortega, Karen L. Bretz
Director of Marketing: Kevin Flanagan
Marketing Manager: Krista Groshong
Marketing Services Manager: Barbara Koontz

This book was set in Transitional 511 by Prentice Hall. It was printed and bound by R. R. Donnelley & Sons Company. The cover was printed by Phoenix Color Corp.

Photo Credits: Michelle Bridwell/PhotEdit, p. 25; Andy Brunk/Merrill, p. 356; Scott Cunningham/Merrill, pp. 72, 164, 196, 232, 235, 276, 321, 336, 377, 393, 406, 425, 452; Tony Freeman/PhotoEdit, p. 0; Larry Hamill/Merrill, p. 134; Will Hart/PhotoEdit, p. 434; Anthony Magnaca/Merrill, pp. 101, 314; Jeff Maloney/PhotoDisc, Inc., p. 5; National Education Association of the United States, p. 465; John A Rizzo, p. 214; Barbara Schwartz, pp. 88, 124, 142, 294; Anne Vega/Merrill, pp. 37, 137, 175, 359; Tom Watson/Merrill, pp. 252, 263; Todd Yarington/Merrill, p. 422.

Prentice-Hall International (UK) Limited, *London*
Prentice-Hall of Australia Pty. Limited, *Sydney*
Prentice-Hall Canada, Inc., *Toronto*
Prentice-Hall Hispanoamericana, S.A., *Mexico*
Prentice-Hall of India Private Limited, *New Delhi*
Prentice-Hall of Japan, Inc., *Tokyo*
Prentice-Hall Singapore Pte. Ltd.
Editora Prentice-Hall do Brasil, Ltda., *Rio de Janeiro*

10 9 8 7 6 5 4 3 2
ISBN 0-13-028766-0

Merrill
Prentice Hall

PREFACE

Good teaching helps your students deal with two competing needs. On the one hand, it gives them a sense of efficacy that allows them to respond to present realities. On the other hand, it gives them confidence as they adapt to a world where frequent change challenges them to look beyond traditional ways of doing things. Your task is to help young people acquire knowledge in ways that will not commit them permanently to patterns that may not serve them well in future years.

History tells us that even bright people sometimes convince themselves that present assumptions are unerring and that those who would challenge them express views not meriting serious consideration. Look over some of these now-amusing predictions by people who were willing to go public with their own versions of unalloyed "truth."

- "There are defects about the electric light which, unless some essential change takes place, must entirely prevent its application to ordinary lighting purposes."[1]

- "Jupiter's moons are invisible to the naked eye, and therefore can have no influence on the earth, and therefore would be useless, and therefore do not exist"[2] (Comments made by Aristotelian professors who were Galileo's contemporaries).

- "The actual building of roads devoted to motor cars is not for the near future, in spite of many rumors to that effect."[3]

- " . . . The advancement of the arts from year to year taxes our credulity and seems to presage the arrival of that period when further improvements must end"[4] (Comments by Henry L. Ellsworth, U.S. Commissioner of Patents, 1844).

- " . . . It was argued that inoculation of the kind employed by Jenner would produce a cow-like face; that those who had been vaccinated . . . would grow hairy and cough like cows. . . . "[5] (Reaction of some members of the English medical establishment in 1796 to Dr. Edward Jenner's efforts to develop a vaccine for smallpox).

[1]Select Committee on Lighting by Electricity. (1879). Remarks of Mr. Keates. *Report from the Select Committee on Lighting by Electricity* (p. 146). London: House of Commons, 1879.
[2]Williams-Ellis, A. (1930). *Men who found out* (p. 43). New York: Coward-McCann, Inc.
[3]*Harpers Weekly.* (1902, August 2). *Harpers Weekly.* p. 1046.
[4]Woods, R. L. (1966, October). Prophets can be right and prophets can be wrong. *American Legion Magazine.* p. 29.
[5]Butler, R. R. (1947). *Scientific discovery* (p. 100). London: English Universities Press, Ltd.

- "'Knife' and 'pain' are two words in surgery that must forever be associated in the consciousness of the patient. To this compulsory combination we shall have to adjust ourselves"[6] (Comments of Alfred Velpeau, a famous surgeon, in 1839).

- " . . . That any general systems of conveying passengers would answer, to go at a velocity exceeding 10 miles an hour, or thereabouts, is extremely improbable."[7]

These statements reflect the views of individuals who were imprisoned by learning rather than liberated by it. It was not the case that they failed to master what they were taught. Neither did their teachers fail to impart the best available wisdom. Instead, the culprit was a faulty assumption. These people mistakenly concluded that their teachers' interpretations appropriately explained reality for all time. They could not deal with a world in which confounding new information could successfully challenge tradition.

As you work with students, you need to encourage a perspective that inclines them to remain open to new ideas. If they leave your care convinced that education is a life-long process of personal growth and development rather than something that is bounded by their experiences in the school, you will have done your job well. At the same time, you, too, need to guard against the luring appeals of the presently known and familiar. Times change. Patterns that make sense given your situation today may be ill-suited to meet demands you will confront later in your career. Build on your experiences, but don't be held hostage by your own educational history.

Organization

Students in both undergraduate and graduate courses have successfully used earlier editions of *Teaching in the Secondary School*. We have designed the book for introduction to secondary education classes, introduction to teaching classes, foundations of education classes, secondary curriculum classes, issues in education classes, and problems in education classes. In addition, much of the material will be useful to you as a reference once you begin your career as a secondary-school educator.

Part 1 is titled "The Setting Today." Chapter 1 illuminates many changes influencing secondary school teaching today. You will also have an opportunity to engage in a self-diagnostic activity related to some of your personal beliefs about teaching. Chapter 2 introduces material related to student diversity, development, and potential for alienation as well as content related to types of secondary schools and characteristics of those that are especially effective. Chapter 3 provides a sound overview of principles associated with reflective teaching. In Chapter 4 you will encounter material dealing with legal issues that concern both students and teachers.

Part 2, titled "Planning," features three chapters that include information you can use to plan instructional programs. Chapter 5 provides guidelines that are useful in selecting content. Chapter 6 includes a comprehensive discussion of practical

[6]Gumpert, M. (1936). *Trail-blazers of science.* (p. 232). New York: Funk and Wagnalls Company.

[7]Tredgold, T. (1835). *Practical treatise on rail-roads and carriages* (2nd ed.)(p. 119). London: J. B. Nichols and Son.

approaches for matching instruction to special needs of students from varied cultural, linguistic, and ethnic backgrounds. Chapter 7 introduces practical approaches to planning both instructional units and lessons.

The title of Part 3 is "Instructing." Chapter 8 presents basic information relating to direct-instruction approaches. In Chapter 9 you will learn techniques for implementing various small-group and cooperative learning models. Chapter 10 features an emphasis on individualized instruction. Chapter 11 introduces ways to develop lessons that will promote students' higher-level thinking skills.

Part 4, "Assessing and Managing," includes two chapters. Chapter 12 introduces approaches to authentic instruction, as well as models for preparing a large number of formal and informal teacher-prepared assessment devices. Chapter 13 includes content that will help you discharge your important classroom management and discipline responsibilities.

Part 5, "Teachers' Performance and Growth," focuses on your career-long needs as an educator. Chapter 14, "Evaluating Teacher Performance," introduces specific approaches you can use to monitor your work in the classroom with a view to improving your instructional practices. Chapter 15 explains that your education as a teacher is a process that will continue throughout your years in the field. You will find material here that is useful for designing a long-term professional development plan.

Special Features of This Text

- **More From the Web** (*NEW!*) features in each chapter. These provide opportunities for you to enrich your understanding of new content by going to listed sites on the World Wide Web.

- **Bulleted objectives** at the beginning of each chapter draw your attention to important chapter content.

- **Links to the Companion Website** (*NEW!*), located at http://www.prenhall.com/armstrong, are embedded at various points throughout the text and will help you derive more value from the text.

- **Introductions** at the beginning of each chapter set the stage for information to be presented.

- **Graphic organizers** (*NEW!*) at the beginning of each chapter provide a convenient graphical summary of chapter content.

- **For Your Portfolio** (*NEW!*) sections, included in chapters in Parts 2, 3, and 4, provide you with opportunities to embed new information in your own professional-development portfolio.

- **Figures** in each chapter provide opportunities for you to reflect on issues that are introduced.

- **Critical Incidents** in each chapter provide opportunities for you to engage in higher-level thinking as you reflect on situations faced by teachers today.

- **What Do You Think?** features provide opportunities for you to examine your personal convictions and consider your positions on key issues.

- **Cartoons** (*NEW!*) appear periodically to remind you that education, while a serious business, need not be grim.
- **Key Ideas in Summary** sections at the end of each chapter will help you to review important information.
- **Reflections** (*NEW!*) sections at the end of each chapter will engage you in critical thinking about various issues that have been raised.
- **Learning Extensions** (*NEW!*) material at the conclusion of each chapter will suggest things you can do to apply and extend what you have learned.
- **References** at the end of each chapter direct you to source materials used by the authors.
- **A Glossary** (*NEW!*) at the end of the book provides you with a convenient way to review your understanding of meanings of specialized terms.

New to This Edition

- A new introductory chapter titled "**The Changing World of Teaching**" (Chapter 1)
- A new chapter titled "**Accommodating Diversity**" (Chapter 6)
- A new chapter titled "**Small-Group and Cooperative Learning**" (Chapter 9)
- Important information about **Interstate New Teacher Assessment and Support Consortium (INTASC) Standards** and **National Board for Professional Teaching Standards (NBPTS)**
- New content on **homeschooling**
- Continued and broadened coverage of topics associated with **Managing and Controlling Students** in a chapter titled "Management and Discipline" (Chapter 13)
- Expanded coverage of **portfolios** both for assessing students and for self-monitoring your own development as a teacher
- New content associated with **standards-based education**, **service learning**, and **parent involvement**
- Greatly expanded coverage of issues associated with **school violence** and **characteristics of outstanding schools** in a chapter titled "Students and Schools" (Chapter 2)
- Useful and appealing new chapter features, including **Graphic Organizers, More from the Web, Reflections, What Do *You* Think?, Learning Extensions, Critical Incidents, For Your Portfolio,** and **Merrill Education's Link to General Methods Resources**

Instructor's Guide

The **Instructor's Guide** provides a variety of useful resources, including chapter overviews, teaching strategies, and ideas for classroom activities, discussions, and assess-

PREFACE

vii

ment. All supplements are available free of charge to instructors who adopt this text. To request an Instructor's Guide, contact a Prentice Hall representative or visit our website at http://www.merrilleducation.com. (If you do not know how to contact a Prentice Hall sales representative, please call faculty services at 1-800-526-0485 for assistance.)

Companion Website

The Prentice Hall Companion Website builds on and enhances what the textbook already offers. For this reason, the content for each user-friendly website is organized by topic and provides the professor and student with a variety of meaningful resources. The Companion Website includes includes features that benefit both instructors and students.

For the Professor

Every Companion Website integrates **Syllabus Manager**™, an online syllabus creation and management utility.

- **Syllabus Manager**™ provides you, the instructor, with an easy, step-by-step process to create and revise syllabi, with direct links into Companion Website and other online content without having to learn HTML.
- Students may log on to your syllabus during any study session. All they need to know is the web address for the Companion Website and the password you've assigned to your syllabus.
- After you have created a syllabus using **Syllabus Manager**™, students may enter the syllabus for their course section from any point in the Companion Website.
- Clicking on a date, the student is shown the list of activities for the assignment. The activities for each assignment are linked directly to actual content, saving time for students.
- Adding assignments consists of clicking on the desired due date, then filling in the details of the assignment—the name of the assignment, instructions, and whether or not it is a one-time or repeating assignment.
- Links to other activities can be created easily. If the activity is online, a URL can be entered in the space provided, and it will be linked automatically in the final syllabus.
- Your completed syllabus is hosted on our servers, allowing convenient updates from any computer on the Internet. Changes you make to your syllabus are immediately available to your students at their next logon.

For the Student

These Companion Website features include resources that enhance course content, along with interactive features that connect students with their peers and instructors:

- **Topic Overviews** outline key concepts in topic areas
- **Web Links** give users access to a wide range of websites that provide useful and current information related to each topic area
- **Lesson Plans** provide links to lesson plans for appropriate topic areas
- **Projects on the Web** link to online projects and activities in relevent topic areas
- **Education Resources** contain links to schools, online journals, government sites, departments of education, professional organizations, regional information, and more
- **Electronic Bluebook** sends homework or essays directly to your instructor's e-mail in a paperless form
- **Message Board** serves as a virtual bulletin board to post—or respond to—questions and comments to or from a national audience
- **Chat** feature allows real-time chat with anyone who is using the text anywhere in the country—ideal for discussion and study groups, class projects, etc.

To take advantage of these features and other resources, please visit the Companion Website for *Teaching in the Secondary School: An Introduction, Fifth Edition*, at

www.prenhall.com/armstrong

Acknowledgments

Some outstanding professionals participated in the development of this fifth edition of *Teaching in the Secondary School*. We are pleased to acknowledge contributions of the following individuals who reviewed preliminary versions of the chapters: James L. Alouf, Sweet Briar College; Leigh Chiarelott, Bowling Green State University; Katherine R. Robinson, Southern University at New Orleans; Patricia M. Ryan, Otterbein College; and Betty R. Tutt, William Woods University. In addition, we particularly want to express our appreciation to Debbie Stollenwerk, our editor at Prentice Hall, for the careful attention she devoted to this project. Her well-reasoned suggestions contributed significantly to the substance of the final version of the manuscript. Finally, we extend a special "thank you" to our families for their unwavering support while we were working on this revision.

BRIEF CONTENTS

Contents

Note: Every effort has been made to provide accurate and current Internet information in this book. However, the Internet and information posted on it are constantly changing, so it is inevitable that some of the Internet addresses listed in this textbook will change.

I

The Setting Today

1

The Changing World of Teaching

The aim of this chapter is to

- show you that change is a constant of life for secondary school teachers;
- describe the term *systemic reform* and point out features of school reform proposals that have attempted to address problems from this perspective;
- point out some claimed advantages and disadvantages of *standards-based education;*
- describe the rationale behind *school-to-work* initiatives and *school-business partnerships;*
- suggest reasons that some people have advocated replacing coeducational schools with single-sex schools;
- point out some claimed advantages of *homeschools;*
- describe some approaches to school choice initiatives such as *voucher plans* and *charter schools;*
- explain some characteristics of typical *service-learning programs;*
- point out some ways *parent/guardian involvement* occurs at the secondary-school level; and
- describe some ways the *Interstate New Teacher Assessment and Support Consortium (INTASC)* and the *National Board for Professional Teaching Standards (NBPTS)* hope to improve the quality of teachers in the nation's classrooms.

Introduction

Does change excite you? Do you reject the dull and routine? Are you energized when you confront novel situations? Can you commit to a profession that may place quite different demands on you in 2025 or 2030 than it will when you start teaching? "Yes" answers to questions such as these suggest that you have qualities that will serve you well as a newcomer to the dynamic world of secondary education.

Secondary schools today are caught up in waves of innovation that will transform our entire society in the future. As an educator, you will confront and respond to changes of a magnitude and character that educators in years past could barely imagine would affect their professional lives. As an example, consider cellular phones and secondary school students.

Half a decade ago, educators worried about designer pagers. These tiny beepers, marketed with bright colors and equipped with a huge variety of accessories, appeared suddenly in the hands of hundreds of thousands of students. Many teachers found their in-class beeps to be enormously disruptive. They, along with many administrators and parents, also believed that some students were using pagers to arrange for sales of illegal substances. As a result, many school districts banned them from school property.

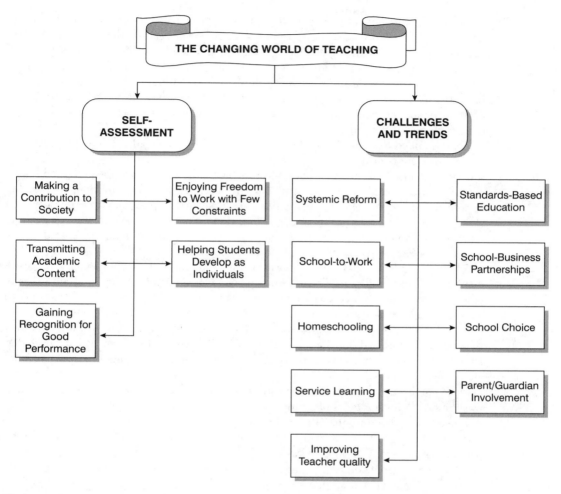

Figure 1–1
Graphic Organizer

Today, the age of the designer pager has given way to the epoch of the cellular telephone. Technological innovations have reduced the sizes of these devices almost to the size of pagers, and monthly access charges have fallen to levels low enough to bring cell phones well within the budgets of many students and their families. A recent survey found that the cell phone ranked behind only the home phone and the radio as a device that teenagers consider to be most valuable in their everyday lives (Verkler, 2000). Teachers who dislike pagers in the classroom tend to be even more passionate haters of cellular phones. The phones not only provide disruptive rings but also encourage students to engage in conversations with calling parties. In response, some schools have adopted regulations forbidding their use on school property.

What are your opinions on this issue? Framing a defensible response is not as easy as you might suppose. In addition to being an electronic gadget that confers a certain standing to status-seeking secondary students, many adults want children to have cell phones. Many parents and guardians particularly want their children to have them when they are in the car or on a date so they can call home if there is a problem. Some parents and guardians also point to instances where students have used their cell phones to call the police or their parents or guardians to seek help when something dangerous has happened at school.

You also need to think about some education issues associated with cell phones. Most objections from educators center around phone rings and follow-up conversations as lesson interrupters. Is it possible that educators in the future may see the cell phone as an ally rather than as an enemy of instruction? In thinking about this question, you need to appreciate that, soon, cell phones will be equipped with screens that permit instantaneous access to the Internet (Hempel, 2000). When this happens, you may well come to view the cell phone as an important instructional aid rather than simply a student toy with high potential to disengage students' attention from what you are teaching.

There is evidence that other innovations have resulted in social changes that were little anticipated by developers and initial users. Consider this example. A century ago, when a much higher percentage of people in the U.S. lived on farms, there was concern about how to get farm produce quickly into the cities. In those days, few roads were paved. Travel in rural areas meant contending with deep ruts and, in rainy weather, mud. A farmer in Missouri invented a device known as the King Road Drag that allowed back-country roads to be quickly graded (and, hence, made more passable) after a heavy rain (Gladwell, 1999). Use of this new tool helped create conditions that made it much easier to move goods from rural to urban areas. Following this innovation was the quick development of a proposal for a parcel post system that would allow farm produce to be taken into the cities to be sold.

Helping farmers to sell their goods was the driving force behind development of the parcel post system; yet, once it was established, the new system had an effect on society that developers had not imagined. Delivering produce continued to be problematic because of somewhat undependable timing of deliveries and spoilage of agricultural goods. However, what the system did accomplish was to provide farmers opportunities to order goods from the cities. Instead of being an innovation that resulted in a great increase in the volume of goods shipped from country to city, parcel post created a scheme that resulted in a huge increase in the flow of non-perishable items from city to country (Gladwell, 1999).

If you study the history of social change, you will quickly come to appreciate the folly of making premature judgments about the ultimate "good" or "bad" effects of individual innovations. However, what you *can* count on as a secondary school educator is that change will be your constant companion, and that your life in the classroom will be greatly influenced by political, economic, social, and technological trends developing in the world beyond the school. Throughout your career, you will confront unexpected changes of many kinds. To prepare for this, you might begin by evaluating your own attitudes toward schools and schooling. In addition, to gain context for the professional world you will be entering, you will want to keep abreast of important issues that challenge secondary school teachers and administrators today.

Self-Assessment

What are your motives for seeking a career as a secondary-school teacher? How do your priorities square with the realities of teaching at this level? These are interesting questions. In order to gain a personal perspective on these issues, spend a few minutes completing the "Self-Assessment Ranking Exercise." (See Figure 1-2). Your answers may tell you something about your priorities.

Now, let's look briefly at the five presumed characteristics of teaching noted in Figure 1-2 that, many people believe, help attract newcomers to the profession:

- Making a contribution to society,
- Enjoying freedom to work with few constraints,
- Transmitting academic content,
- Helping students develop as individuals, and
- Gaining recognition for good performance.

Making a Contribution to Society

Did you rate this option high on your list? If so, you have lots of company. Many people are motivated to teach because they believe they will be doing "something important." Certainly, few people challenge the point that education is critical to social survival. However, this by no means suggests that educators are members of a profession that enjoys an especially high status. In fact, you may be surprised at the number of your friends and acquaintances who will willingly assert that teaching demands quite low levels of sophistication and skill. Others actively challenge this view. As a prospective teacher, you need to understand that not everyone will recognize the importance of the contributions you will make as a professional educator.

Individuals' reasons for choosing a career in secondary teaching vary. A few reasons that people sometimes mention are included in the statements that follow. What priority would you assign to each?

Hi	Priority Medium	Low	
_____	_____	_____	Making a contribution to society
_____	_____	_____	Enjoying freedom to work with few constraints
_____	_____	_____	Transmitting academic content
_____	_____	_____	Helping students develop as individuals
_____	_____	_____	Gaining recognition for good performance

Figure 1-2
Self-Assessment Ranking Exercise

Enjoying Freedom to Work with Few Constraints

As a classroom teacher, you will enjoy a certain freedom of action. For example, rarely (if ever) will someone interrupt your class and challenge you while you are presenting a lesson. On the other hand, there are limitations on what you can teach. You may teach in a state or school district that requires teachers to follow a detailed curriculum. Even if these conditions don't exist, the increasing use of standardized tests and pressures on schools to produce high test scores may require you to spend more time on content that will be tested rather than on content you personally feel is more important. There is a clear trend for teachers increasingly to be held accountable for what they do in the classroom and what their students learn. These expectations, while they do leave you some freedom of action, will influence your classroom practices.

Transmitting Academic Content

Are you excited about the subject or subjects you want to teach? If you are, you will find your enthusiasm to be a great asset in the classroom. Enthusiasm conveys to students that you believe what you are teaching is valuable and, even more importantly, that you derive some real satisfaction from knowing what you know. Your personal interest can ignite a commitment to your subject even among students who, initially, may express little enthusiasm for what you are teaching.

On the other hand, when you begin working with a class of students, you need to understand that many of them may not share your interest in the subject. Part of your role as a teacher is to motivate initially reluctant students to extend themselves to master the material. To do this, you need to develop ways that help students respond "yes" to the Is-this-material-something-I-should-bother-learning? question. Motivated students *do* learn. The self-confidence that accompanies mastery of content often becomes a potent motivational force. In time, it can engender an enthusiasm that matches your own.

Helping Students Develop as Individuals

Sometimes debates about school issues seem strangely disassociated from the real human beings the schools serve. Prescriptions for "improvement" tend to focus on test scores and other issues tied closely to the content-transmission goal of public education. The students, as human beings, when mentioned at all, often appear to be members of an undifferentiated species who sit passively waiting to be "improved" by the latest reform initiative.

When you begin to teach, you quickly learn that any suggestion that "students are pretty much the same" is a statement having no basis in reality. In fact, students represent as broad a diversity as exists in our entire society. Members of your classes will bring incredibly different sets of assumptions about "how the world is" with them to school, and they will vary hugely in terms of attitudes, aptitudes, and physical characteristics. One of your tasks as a teacher is to diagnose and respond to characteristics of students *as individuals*. Your challenge will be to find a suitable balance between the need to provide instruction tailored to characteristics of each student and the need to meet requirements to provide some common instructional experiences to all.

Gaining Recognition for Good Performance

If you expect to work hard when you begin teaching, you will not be disappointed. Interacting with students, planning for instruction, participating in meetings, conferring with colleagues, and assuming other responsibilities will give you ample opportunity to demonstrate your commitment to the profession. You will find many students, parents, guardians, and members of the general community to be highly appreciative of your efforts. However, it is a mistake to assume that everyone will applaud what you do.

People vary enormously in their beliefs about what constitutes "good" educational practice. For example, you may be a strong believer in the worth of educational simulations as a way of engaging students' higher-level thinking skills. You might encounter a parent who thinks you should focus on preparing students for standardized tests by using the lecture method to cover a variety of factual material. No matter how hard you work developing and implementing high-quality simulations, this parent may not regard you as an effective teacher. What all this means is that different people apply different criteria in determining whether the job you are doing is acceptable. You need to understand that people who define quality instruction differently than you do may not be impressed by your instructional practices, no matter how hard you work to perfect them.

Challenges and Trends

Regardless of your personal priorities concerning teaching, you will come face to face with a number of key challenges and trends that are affecting virtually all secondary schools today. Some examples include changes associated with:

- Systemic reform,
- Standards-based education,
- School-to-work initiatives,
- School-business partnerships,
- Homeschooling,
- School choice,
- Service learning programs,
- Parent/guardian involvement, and
- Improving teacher quality.

Systemic Reform

Systemic reform centers on a simple but powerful idea. It recognizes the complexity of the educational enterprise. It appreciates that real change for the better will result only when multiple and concurrent changes occur in all the variables that contribute to the quality of the educational experience.

The logic supporting systemic reform is compelling. Suppose, for example, that you are teaching in a middle school where leaders of the school improvement team have decided to "improve" the mathematics program. Leaders in your school might believe it sufficient to adopt a well-researched new mathematics program, purchase the necessary support materials, and train the teaching staff to use it. This course of action would go forward on the assumption that the "cause" of previously unsatisfactory mathematics achievement scores has been a deficient mathematics curriculum. But, other variables may also have influenced performance levels of at least some students in your school. Perhaps family problems at home, lack of time or place to study, health problems, nutritional deficits, lack of parental interest in mathematics, peer pressure not to be "a teacher's pet," and other factors affected students' mathematics achievement scores.

What all this means is that diverse forces impinge on students. A reform proposal targeted only at changing the curriculum may not produce the hoped-for results. That is why educational experts support the idea of systemic reform, which recognizes and attempts to respond to a variety of needs at the same time.

Systemic approaches to reform have attacked many kinds of problems. Two examples of reform proposals that have evolved out of this effort include the following:

- Development of full-service schools, and
- Encouragement of site-based management.

Full-Service Schools

Performance of students results not just from their aptitudes, interests, and commitments. Young people also are greatly affected by their family situations, their mental health, and their physical health. School leaders who have seen negative consequences from the erosion of the traditional family and social support systems increasingly appreciate this reality. One response has been to gather together a number of human-services support activities in the same building where young people are taught. The term that has been applied to institutions that provide comprehensive educational and social support services is *full-service school*.

The full-service school traces its roots from the eighteenth century when schools began to serve as centers for immunization against smallpox and other dread diseases (Dryfoos, 1994). The need to broaden the range of human support services available in schools was recognized in the 1970s by the Bicentennial Commission of the American Association of Colleges of Teacher Education (Howsam, Corrigan, Denemark & Nash, 1976). Later, in the Children's Defense Fund publication, *The State of America's Children* (1994), a strong case was made in support of applying the expertise of multiple human-services professions to problems facing students.

The total number of full-service schools in the country is small but growing. The most common social support activity is the implementation of school-based health clinics. These clinics provide services for young people from impoverished environments and render services and assistance for problems that can affect students' academic performance such as pregnancy, drug abuse, and violent and suicidal behaviors.

Not everyone agrees that full-service schools are desirable. Critics argue on two key grounds. First of all, they fear that full-service schools will assume responsibilities that properly belong to students' families. Second, some fear that the proliferation of multiple services at schools may result in scarce educational dollars being diverted to support health care and other non-instructional services, which could lead to reduced levels of student achievement.

Though some of their critics are vocal, at the present time the tide seems to be flowing in support of the idea expanding the number of full-service schools. If this trend continues, as supporters hope it will, there are important implications for you as a future secondary school teacher. You may well find yourself working alongside professionals from other human-support services. You may find a need to have quite specific information about the professional functions of social services physicians, social workers, public health workers, and juvenile law enforcement officials.

Site-Based Management

Site-based management, sometimes also known as *school-based management,* presumes that education can be improved if decisions are made by those most likely to be affected by them. Supporters of this idea believe that the multiple variables influencing student learning vary importantly from school to school. Hence, a one-size-fits-all management approach that features policy and curriculum decisions made by distant central school district authorities will not result in arrangements well suited to meet the needs of all students. Many supporters of systemic school reform strongly support site-based management and its decentralization of decision-making power. This approach is supposed to provide benefits that include:

- taking advantage of the expertise of people working in individual school buildings who recognize what needs to be done to improve learning,

- improving the morale of teachers by giving them more authority over decisions affecting their professional lives,

- promoting greater creativity in school program design,

- directing resources to meet special needs of individual schools, and

- developing a larger sense of ownership in the individual school on the part of parents, community members, and others involved in school management councils.

The word *site* in the phrase *site-based management* refers to an individual school. Site-based management approaches provide principals and teachers (and often parents, guardians, students, and community members as well) with greater control over the schools' programs. This is accomplished by giving site-based management councils authority over budgets, personnel, and curriculum. These school management councils always involve administrators and teachers. In many places, parents and guardians, students, and community members also serve as regular members.

Today, there are hundreds of schools being managed according to the principles of site-based management. It is highly probable that you will work in a school with this type of management and governance arrangement. Exactly what you and members of the school management council can do will vary depending on the policies in place in your school district. For example, in some school districts, individual school-based management councils make budgetary authority and many personnel decisions, but the central district office maintains considerable control over the curriculum. In other school districts, almost all decision-making authority, including responsibilities associated with the school curriculum, has been vested in school-based management councils.

Not everyone endorses the idea of site-based management. Sometimes site-based management councils have had difficulty in handling the responsibilities assigned to them. In part, this seems to have resulted because teachers, parents, guardians, and others involved in school-based management councils have sometimes been unfamiliar with their roles as policy-makers. In such cases they have deferred to the leadership of principals and others who traditionally made these kinds of decisions. Problems of this kind are diminishing. For example, you and other prospective teachers typically now receive much more information about teachers' responsibilities for policy-making, budgeting, and management in your preparation programs than teachers who were prepared 10 or more years ago. Parents, guardians, and other community members also are becoming more accustomed to discharging school-leadership responsibilities which, in the past, largely were left in the hands of professional school administrators.

Standards-Based Education

Standards-based education seeks to provide clear, concise descriptions of what students should glean from your instruction. Interest in establishing rigorous standards accelerated with the publication of the famous 1983 report of the National Commission on Excellence in Education titled *A Nation at Risk*. The modern standards movement owes much to the ideas of Diane Ravitch, a former U.S. Assistant Secretary of Education, who promoted the approach in her 1995 book, *National Standards in Education: A Citizen's Guide*. In this volume, Ravitch argued that "standards can improve achievement by clearly defining what is to be taught and what kind of performance is expected" (Ravitch, 1995, p. 25).

One argument that supporters of standards-based education make is that this approach places the focus on what students actually learn. Measurements of these educational *outputs*, in turn, provide a way to make meaningful comparisons among schools. Parents, guardians, and citizens can use this information to make judgments about individual schools and to apply pressure to improve those that do not prepare students well.

Proponents of standards-based education argue that, too often in the past, schools have been judged on the quality of *inputs* such as learning resources (textbooks, computers, laboratories, and so forth) that are provided to encourage students to learn. Critics of comparisons based on this kind of information contend that these measures fail to shed light on the all-important "what-are-students-learning" question.

National professional organizations have developed standards for large numbers of secondary-school subjects. Often these standards feature descriptions of goals to be reached or levels of proficiency to be attained (Noddings, 1997). Some standards take the form of *performance standards* that identify levels of proficiency that students are expected to attain. Others take the form of *content standards*. These describe what you are supposed to do in the classroom to help your students master specific kinds of content.

Content standards describe what teachers are supposed to teach and what young people are to learn (Noddings, 1997). Though establishing specific content standards has prompted considerable debate, the approach has gained momentum in recent years. For example, many national subject-area organizations have developed a set of content standards defining what the organizations believe to be essential learning outcomes for their subjects. National content standards have been developed for such subjects as mathematics, English-language arts, history, civics and government, science, and geography. In addition, many states have developed content standards that are to guide curriculum development and assessment of learners' academic progress.

Not everyone endorses standards-based education. In recent years, the approach has drawn considerable criticism from individuals who are wary of standards developed nationally. Many Republican members of Congress have been especially hesitant to support an initiative that, to some people at least, seems to challenge the tradition of vesting authority for school policies in the hands of state and local authorities. You may want to think about who should determine what the content standards ought to be for schools. Should this be a group appointed by politicians such as Congress, the President, or a state governor? Should they be decided by business leaders or, perhaps, by academic professors from higher education? How might standards established by varying groups differ, and how might your life as a teacher be affected if you had to follow standards favored by different groups?

There have also been difficulties in creating standards that teachers will actually follow. One problem has been that national professional organizations have not always been careful about limiting the number of standards they have adopted and the length of the descriptive prose that accompanies them (Schmoker & Marzano, 1999). If you have an opportunity to view some standards developed by certain national subject-specialty organizations, you may well feel intimidated by the number and kinds of expectations for students these appear to be advocating.

One of the more significant changes brought about by standards-focused education is an emphasis on testing. Once standards are established, then it is possible to develop assessment tools for measuring the attainment of the standards. There has been a large increase in the volume of assessment, and in almost every grade level and in nearly every subject learner achievement is being assessed (Stake, 1999). Much testing associated with standards is what is known as *high-stakes testing*. This means that the results of the assessment have important consequences. They may influence promotion and graduation of learners, funding of the school, evaluation of teachers, and the autonomy of the local school. Because of the high stakes associated with assessment, you probably will spend more of your instructional time preparing students for testing than you would have had you entered the profession years ago.

The testing associated with standards-based assessment presumes that the testing program will be well matched to the instructional program. In reality, this has not always been the case. In California, for example, the state adopted a highly regarded set of standards for language arts programs and then went on to adopt an assessment system bearing little relationship to the standards. Clearly, in this kind of situation, using test results as a valid measure of what students learned about content referenced in the standards makes little sense.

In summary, you may find that you have mixed reactions to standards-based education. You will need to weigh the advantages of having clearly identified "targets" for your instruction against some possible negatives associated with (1) assessments that may not relate well to the content you teach, (2) concerns about turning over responsibility for establishing content priorities to people who may not have a good understanding of your students' needs, and (3) worries about the accuracy of school-to-school comparisons that may be made easier when standards-based programs are in place.

 CRITICAL INCIDENT

Unintended Consequences of Supporting a New Magnet School

Rosetta Sanchez cornered her long-time friend, Victor Orsola, during the social session following the business part of the monthly beginning teachers' meeting. Rosetta and Vic were graduates of the same teacher-preparation program. Both had accepted positions with the Larsen City Public Schools after graduation. Rosetta was teaching physics at Iskerdahl Senior High School and Victor was teaching English to 7th graders at Montgomery Middle School.

"Vic, I'm in a bind." Rosetta said.

"What's up?" Vic asked.

"Well, you know I got assigned to the district planning group. That's the one that Dr. Marshall, the Deputy Superintendent, chairs."

Vic nodded. "Yes, I think you'd told me that earlier."

"Well, anyway," Rosetta continued, "when I came on board this group was in the middle of a feasibility study for a new magnet science high school. You remember when we learned about these magnet schools back at the U? They're designed to draw students from the whole district with aptitude for a high-powered program. The one we're thinking about for Larsen City will draw bright science students and expose them to the kind of science content most kids don't get until they go to college. I would have killed for such a program when I was in high school. If this thing goes through, I would really like to be one of the teachers."

"Sounds great," Vic said. "So what's the problem?"

"I'm getting to that," Rosetta replied. "As I was saying, this district planning group has been working on this idea for some time. I let it be known early on that I knew a little bit about the magnet school approach and that I was *really* enthusiastic about starting one here with a focus on science. Well, to make a long story short, the group selected me as one of the people to make a formal pitch for the project at our next school board meeting. The Deputy Superintendent will do most of the talking, but he feels board members will be impressed if the plan is also enthusiastically supported by a science teacher."

"You're not afraid of speaking in front of the school board, are you?" asked Vic.

"No way. That's not the problem. What I'm worried about are the people at my own school. Some of my science colleagues at Iskerdahl have really been on my case since they've heard about the plan for a magnet school and, particularly, since they've learned I have been tapped to push for the plan at the school board meeting."

"What's their beef?" asked Vic.

"They've got several concerns. Their biggest worry is that the magnet school will skim away what little 'academic cream' we have at Iskerdahl. The few really top science kids we have in our classes will not be there. They're almost sure to seek enrollment in the new magnet science high. When they go, there won't be any real academic leadership left in our science classes. My colleagues feel these bright kids push along some of the less talented ones. When they're gone, the kids who remain will not do as well as they do now when these sharp kids are there in our classes."

Rosetta paused, then continued, "The folks in my science department are also afraid that the district will want to make the new science magnet school a showcase operation. They're afraid lots of money will be diverted to buy supplies and equipment for the new school. This may result in less support for the science program at our school."

"Anything else troubling your colleagues?" Vic asked.

"One more thing, Vic. They've picked up on my interest in moving to the new magnet school if and when it's built. I'm sure some of them see me as a traitor to Iskerdahl who'll be abandoning what will become an under-funded program to work in a spanking new, well-supported science program at the new school.

"All of this stuff is coming down heavy on me," Rosetta continued. "I can't tell you how 'chilly' the atmosphere becomes when I come in to sit down at our weekly science department meetings. I'm really distressed about this. On the one hand, I respect my colleagues and don't want to do anything to hurt them. On the other hand, I think many students in our district would really benefit from a magnet school. What bothers me most of all is worrying about what the future will hold for me at Iskerdahl if the district decides not to go ahead with the magnet school. I'm feeling incredibly stressed by all this, and I don't know what I should do."

■ ■ ■

What values are suggested by proposals endorsed by the district planning committee to establish a magnet science high school? Which elements of the community are likely to endorse these values and, hence, this proposal? Which elements are likely to oppose it? What values are implicit in some of the concerns raised by Rosetta's colleagues at Iskerdahl High School? Are Rosetta's fears about the future of her relationship with her fellow science teachers at Iskerdahl justified? Are there other people Rosetta should consult about her situation? What do you think Rosetta's next steps should be?

School-to-Work Initiatives

How can you best help your secondary students who will not go on to complete baccalaureate programs in colleges and universities? This question has concerned thoughtful educators for years. After World War II, there was much discussion about how schools should best serve the students in the middle. In those days, there was a concern that school resources were overbalanced in support of students who were either at the top or at the bottom academically. Too often, critics alleged, students in the middle group were not well-served.

Today, the concern for serving these students has taken a slightly different turn. The argument is not so much that these students are not being served by present secondary school programs but that the programs they experience do not connect well to the realities of today's job market. In particular, there is a belief that many entry-level positions do not require four-year degrees but require sound technical skills instead. In response to this need, many secondary schools now are participants in *school-to-work programs*.

Initially, the term *tech prep* was used to describe the kind of rigorous, integrated experiences needed to make students' transition from school to work a smooth one. A key piece of federal legislation supporting this effort was the Carl D. Perkins Vocational and Applied Technology Act of 1990 (P.L. 101–392). This act identified these features of a tech prep program:

- Leads to an associate degree from a community or junior college or to a two-year certificate;
- Provides students with technical preparation in at least one field of engineering technology, applied science, mechanical, industrial, or practical art or trade, or agriculture, health or business;
- Builds students' competence in mathematics, science, and communication (including applied academics) through a sequential course of study; and
- Results in students' employment.

The initial Perkins Act and modifications authorized by the Carl D. Perkins Vocational and Technical Education Act of 1998 (P.L. 105–332) have resulted in a proliferation of different approaches to preparing students for the world of work. To encourage the spread of school-to-work programs and to ensure sound program planning, the federal School-to-Work Opportunities Act was passed in 1994 with strong bipartisan support. This legislation is administered jointly by the U.S. Department of Labor and the U.S. Department of Education and provides states with planning grants to develop comprehensive plans for statewide programs.

Most school-to-work programs follow a 2+2 model. This means that participating students are involved in the transition to work during the last two years of high school and during an additional two years, usually at a community college or a junior college. Many of these programs feature extensive on-the-job kinds of experiences for participating students. The idea is for students to see the workplace as a legitimate learning environment, to appreciate the need to master important technical and mathematical skills, and to see connections between what they learn in school and what they will have to know in order to earn a living.

If you and your school are involved in a school-to-work program, you will be expected to maintain close working relationships with both employers and community/junior college personnel. You quite probably will be involved in program planning that will include a much larger group of people than traditionally have planned secondary school curricula. This implies a need for you to be sensitive to multiple perspectives, to have good negotiating abilities, and to be skilled in making decisions in group settings. These skills should be part of the "professional baggage" you take to your first teaching position.

School-Business Partnerships

As is the case with school-to-work programs, *school-business partnerships* have resulted from concerns about a disconnection between what goes on in school classrooms and what employers expect of graduates when they enter the workplace. Many of today's partnerships feature quite intensive business-school relationships. These tend to be aimed at achieving fundamental changes that will result in new ways of teaching and new and better approaches to promoting student learning. Large numbers of secondary schools are involved in business-school partnerships, and their number continues to grow. You may well find programs involving partnerships with schools already in place in the school where you begin your teaching. If not, you almost certainly will encounter discussion of such programs early in your career.

The spread of school-business partnerships has generated controversy. On the one hand, supporters appreciate the attention to schools and their problems that often has resulted from these initiatives. Some of these relationships have generated high levels of public interest in helping the schools. More specifically, funds from businesses in some places have provided individual schools with up-to-date computers and other technological equipment that they simply could not afford given available money from traditional tax sources. These contributions have enabled these schools to improve their capacity to deliver high-level instructional programs. Many teachers, too, have benefited from training and development opportunities made available by school-business partnerships.

Critics, on the other hand, argue that school-business partnerships provide access to impressionable students that allow members of the business community to promote their own political and economic agendas. This is done, some allege, by emphasizing aspects of school program improvement that respond to the needs and biases of business. For example, some critics wonder whether a new economics curriculum, developed with money from private businesses, would treat issues such as corporate tax rates and labor unions fairly. There are also concerns that private-sector support for schools might lead legislatures to reduce the level of state financial support for schools and divert scarce tax dollars to highways, prisons, and other needs.

Homeschooling

More and more parents and guardians are choosing to remove their children from schools and teach them at home. Most young people who are homeschooled are in the elementary grades, but increasing numbers are in the secondary school grades as well. Today, well over one million young people are being taught at home. The growth in homeschooling has been accompanied by a parallel increase in the number or organizations devoted to promoting this approach to education and in the number of businesses producing materials for purchase by parents and guardians who homeschool their children.

Several periodicals are being published that are devoted exclusively to homeschooling. One that is widely circulated is *Practical Homeschooling*. (For information, write to Practical Homeschooling Home Life, P.O. Box 1250, Fenton, MO 63026, or contact this website: http://www.home-school.co/). Another helpful source is *Home Education Magazine*. (For information, write to Home Education Magazine, P.O. Box 1083, Tonasket, WA 98855, or contact their website: HEM-Info@home-ed-magazine.com). You can obtain more information about homeschooling by writing to the National Coalition of Alternative Community Schools (P.O. Box 15036, Santa Fe, NM 87506).

 WHAT DO *YOU* THINK?

Single-Sex Schools

Some people who believe that the achievement levels of young people in secondary schools should be higher argue that single-sex schools deserve more consideration. Supporters of this idea tend to make arguments such as these:

- Younger secondary school students come to maturity in a world saturated with sexual imagery. As a result, they develop interests in the opposite sex at too young an age. They will do better in single-sex schools where their attention will not be diverted from academics by daily contact with members of the opposite sex.

- Female students in co-educational schools resist competition with male students in mathematics and science. This situation does not occur when females and males attend different, single-sex schools.

- Some research shows that teachers spend more time with male than with female students when teaching mathematics and more time with female than with male students when teaching reading. This kind of teacher sex-bias will be eliminated in a single-sex school.

Questions

1. How compelling do you find the above arguments?
2. What groups in the community would be most supportive of single-sex schools? What groups would be least supportive?
3. Would setting up single-sex schools increase or decrease school costs? Why do you think so?

Today all states allow homeschools. Regulations about how they must operate vary. Interestingly, many states have no requirements at all related to the educational background of the people (usually parents or guardians) who will be doing the actual teaching. When such requirements exist, they tend only to require homeschool teachers to have graduated from high school. The following features are typical of state legislation governing homeschooling:

- All required school subjects must be taught to homeschooled students.
- Homeschoolers' classes must meet for the same minimum number of days each year as public school classes.
- Records of daily attendance must be maintained for each student.
- No state financial support can be expended in support of homeschooling.

Homeschooling places heavy demands on the parents and guardians who undertake it. They must abide by numerous state regulations. They have to commit huge blocks of their time every day to teaching their children—something that makes it all but impossible for them to hold full-time jobs outside the home. They are obligated to become familiar with all subjects taught in school and to provide the young people they teach with appropriate learning materials. Taken together, these responsibilities comprise a daunting set of obligations. Why, then, are so many adults willing to take on these duties?

Reasons vary. Some parents and guardians complain that public school programs have become so driven by standardized testing that, in the effort to raise average test scores, the needs of individual students have been overlooked. They believe that individual differences of their children can be better addressed by teaching them at home. Other parents and guardians object to certain features of the required state curriculum. For example, they may find fault with a high school English program that fails to expose students to as much traditional English and American literature as they would like. Other parents and guardians have religious orientations that they believe might be undermined by programs and experiences available in public schools. They believe that homeschooling can reinforce the religious convictions they deem appropriate and prevent their children from falling into religious error. Other parents and guardians have still other motives for homeschooling their children.

The growth of homeschooling presents some interesting issues to you as a prospective secondary school teacher. For example, you may well ask, "What will be the effect on regular public school budgets if proponents of homeschooling convince legislators to divert some state support money to parents and guardians who educate their children at home?" Many people who are committed to homeschooling are keenly interested in educational issues. Given this reality, "What will be the impact on leadership of school boards and other bodies responsible for influencing public school policy if ever larger numbers of adults lose interest in public education?" In many parts of the country, citizens are asked to vote periodically on school bond issues and on other legislation affecting schools (often local property tax levies). "Will people who have little connection with and commitment to public schooling be willing to vote for tax increases to support public education?" All of these are vexing issues that you may well confront early in your teaching career.

School Choice

Several challenges facing educators fall under the general heading of *school choice*. Proponents of school choice argue that bureaucratic school district regulations that require students to attend particular schools provide no incentives for schools to improve. These regulations ensure a guaranteed supply of students even to extremely poor schools. School choice supporters want parents, guardians, and students to be free to select schools the young people will attend. In theory, more students will select "good" schools than "bad" schools. The possibility that a weak school may lose students to a strong school will act as an incentive to the weak school's administrators and teachers to improve. This is true because individual public schools typically receive money based on the size of their enrollments. If a school loses enrollments, its budget could go down, something that could have extremely adverse effects on personnel employed at that particular school.

Supporters of school choice also point out that views about what constitutes "good" schooling vary tremendously. It is quite possible that the specific kind of school programming individual parents or guardians desire may not be available at schools in the attendance zone where they reside. School choice would allow the children of these parents to enroll in schools outside of their assigned attendance zone where programming is more in line with the preferences of the parents or guardians.

People who advocate school choice point out that affluent citizens always have been able to choose the schools their children attend. They have the financial capacity to either send their children to private schools or to pull up stakes and purchase a residence in the attendance zone of a school they like. However, people of more modest means lack the ability either to pay for private school education or to move to areas where the schools are better. They are prisoners of their places of residence who have no choice but to send their children to the schools in their designated attendance zones. A school-choice system would allow these parents to send their children to better schools that might be located outside of their attendance zones without requiring them to move. It is argued that this approach would equalize educational opportunity for all children.

There have been many approaches to implementing the general idea of school choice. Two that have drawn considerable attention are (1) voucher plans, and (2) charter schools.

Voucher Plans

You may have heard something about the *voucher plan* for improving schools that has been discussed widely, and sometimes implemented, for at least twenty years. To understand how this approach works, you first need to appreciate that state and local governments expend a certain dollar amount to support instruction of each student enrolled in public schools. In a voucher plan, a check or voucher in this amount is provided to parents and guardians for each school-aged child in the household. (Only a school can cash the voucher.) Parents and guardians are supposed to study programs available in various schools. When they make a decision about where they want their child enrolled, they turn the voucher over to this school. The money it represents becomes part of the school's operating budget.

The voucher plan seeks to promote competition among schools. Proponents point out that schools will gain more operational money if they attract more students. They will get more students if their programs are good and large numbers of parents and guardians elect to send their children there. If a given school begins to lose students, there will be tremendous pressure on administrators and teachers to implement changes to improve programs. If this does not happen, more students will leave, diminishing budgets even further. In time, some schools may even have to close their doors. This possibility does not dismay supporters of voucher plans. They argue that schools with programs too weak to attract students should not survive.

Opponents of voucher plans argue against some of proponents' assumptions. For example, they doubt that the threat of losing students and accompanying governmental support money will result in improved school programming. They contend that many of the problems so-called poor schools face is a result of their being under-funded. As evidence, they point out that per-pupil expenditures are much lower in many inner-city schools than in schools in affluent suburban areas. If so-called poor schools are already having a difficult time doing a responsible job given present levels of funding, critics of voucher plans argue that it is not reasonable to expect them to "improve" when they begin to lose students and find themselves with even less money to work with.

Charter Schools

Some critics of American education argue that public schools' alleged failures are a result of the fact that they are organized according to a highly centralized, monopolistic, bureaucratic model. One suggested remedy is the *charter school*. Charter schools are schools that state and local authorities exempt from many regulations affecting other schools. The idea is to provide them with more flexibility. Most charter schools are organized to pursue some specific objectives. These are approved by the chartering agency, which typically is part of the state government.

Supporters of charter schools argue that, freed from burdensome regulations, charter schools will develop outstanding instructional programs. The hope is that they may develop approaches that will be good enough to be modeled by other schools. Some charter schools have been established to serve the needs of particular categories of learners. For example, in places with heavy populations of Latino students, charter schools have been set up to provide exemplary programs for students who are not fully proficient in English.

People who favor charter schools argue that they have the potential to be exceptionally cost effective. This is true, they suggest, because many regulations imposed on regular schools—but not on charter schools—are costly. Supporters also believe that outstanding teachers will seek to work in charter schools where they will be free to develop innovative and exciting programs without having to worry about bureaucratic guidelines.

Some critics of charter schools are concerned that they may drain scarce education dollars away from other schools. Any improvements at charter schools, they feel, may come at the expense of program quality in other schools. This problem has been recognized in some state legislation that authorizes charter schools. Often these laws limit the numbers of charter schools that can be established.

Many people continue to be enthusiastic about charter schools. The United States Department of Education recently established a Charter Schools Demonstration Program that seeks to gather and disseminate information about effective charter schools. Charter schools are still too new for there to have been long-term studies of their effectiveness. The attraction of schools that are encouraged to innovate in environments freed from heavy regulation is considerable. As a result, you may well encounter interest in this approach to improving the schools when you enter the teaching profession.

Service-Learning Programs

Do you think secondary schools have an obligation to help students develop a sense of responsibility for improving their own communities? If you do, you will join many other educators and community leaders who have supported *service-learning programs* in the schools. Service learning "is a teaching methodology that enriches instruction by providing thoughtfully designed opportunities for students to use their skills and knowledge in service to and with the community" (Texas Center for Service Learning, 1997). Service-learning programs have been increasing in number. In part, this growth has been prompted by the passage of the National and Community Service Trust Act of 1993 (P.L. 103–82). This legislation established the Learn and Serve America Program, administered by the Corporation for National Service. Support funds are provided in the form of grants to states and certain national organizations. They, in turn, are passed along to school districts and individual schools.

Though each service-learning program has its own special characteristics, most feature the following three general phases:

- Planning and preparation,
- Delivery of services, and
- Analysis of results.

Planning and Preparation
The initial phase of a service-learning program or project involves students, as directed and assisted by their teacher, working with community representatives to identify community needs. Involvement in activities and lessons associated with this aspect of service learning adds to students' knowledge and understanding of their local community. Part of the agenda during this phase is to help pinpoint needs that students, themselves, can help to meet. Kinds of service-learning activities that can be identified span a wide range of possibilities. In various places, students associated with service-learning programs have been involved in projects such as these:

- Cross-age tutoring with at-risk learners (for example, high school and middle school students may work with at-risk pupils in elementary schools),

- Working in community gardens alongside low-income community residents in an effort to improve their nutritional needs,
- Assisting health professionals in clinics and hospitals,
- Participating in community-history projects,
- Assisting law enforcement officials to prepare and deliver drug-education and safety-education lessons to younger members of the community,
- Interning with officials in local and regional governments, and
- Working to improve the local environment with projects to plant and maintain decorative vegetation and to clear debris from waterways.

Delivery of Services

After the diagnostic and information-building activities in phase one are completed, students in service-learning programs begin their volunteer work in the community. Typically, they spend several hours a week outside of the school building doing the community work to which they have been assigned. The amount of time individual students spend varies tremendously. Educators who manage service-learning projects should strive for a reasonable balance between the need to allow students enough time

The high school senior at the right, as part of a cross-age tutoring project in her school's service-learning program, helps the middle school student with her homework

to complete their regular academic tasks at school and the need to allow them enough time to make contributions to the community that "will make a difference."

Analysis of Results

If you were in charge of a service-learning project at your school, during the third phase of the program you typically would involve your students in some serious analyses of what they had learned and done. The purpose of this phase of a service-learning program is to help them develop the kinds of reflective powers that good citizenship requires. Further, there is a hope that discussions will help students understand that their work has had a positive impact on their community. If students draw this conclusion, prospects increase that they will develop a broader "sense of ownership" in the community and be more inclined to get involved in important community service work in the future.

How Effective?

Though service-learning programs are increasing in popularity, relatively few studies have been made of their effectiveness. One important large-scale study of the national Learn and Serve America Program was recently completed by the Center for Human Resources at Brandeis University (*Summary Report: National Evaluation of Learn and Serve America,* 1999). Among other findings, writers of the report noted that students who participated in such programs developed better attitudes toward school and, in most of their subjects, had higher achievement levels than students who were not involved in service learning.

Immediately following their participation in the service-learning program, students indicated a higher willingness to participate in volunteer community service than students who were not involved in the program. However, after one year, those who had experienced service-learning activities no longer showed a higher-level of commitment to volunteer work than those who had not been involved in service learning. Writers of the report suggest that, to maintain the positive impact on attitudes toward volunteer work, there need to be provisions that allow students to continue to participate in volunteer community activities after they have concluded their membership in a formal service-learning project.

Parent/Guardian Involvement

Do you believe involvement of parents and guardians is important at the secondary-school level? When most people discuss this issue, they refer to programs in elementary schools where parents and guardians often are frequent visitors at the school. Parent/guardian involvement programs are much less common at the secondary school level. The North Central Regional Educational Laboratory (2000) suggests that there are three key reasons for this pattern:

- Many secondary school students do not feel comfortable having their parents or guardians in school, and they often discourage them from coming.
- Parents and guardians tend to be unsure of exactly what they can do to help their children when they are old enough to enroll in secondary schools.

- Secondary schools, particularly high schools, have not given parent and guardian involvement a high priority.

There has been growing interest in promoting more contacts between parents/guardians and public schools. Many states now have laws on the books that mandate parent/guardian involvement. At the federal level, interest in this area has been increasing. For example, a Center on Families, Communities, Schools, and Children's Learning now is conducting systematic studies of relationships between schools, homes, and communities. In part, dissemination of important research findings has renewed secondary-school leaders' interest in programs of this kind. Among other things, researchers have found that well-designed parent/guardian-involvement programs:

- lead to higher student achievement (Parent News, 1997),
- reduce student use of alcohol and patterns of antisocial behavior (Parent News, 1997), and
- increase the likelihood that high school graduates will complete a program of study leading to a baccalaureate degree at a college or university (Engle, 1989).

Characteristics of parent/guardian involvement programs vary greatly from school to school. Many of them promote involvement that occurs in two distinct settings: (1) the home, and (2) the school or community.

In the Home

Contributions parents/guardians make at home center around basic nurturing and communicating with teachers and other school personnel. With respect to nurturing, parent/guardian involvement programs emphasize the importance of providing students with a good diet, attending to their health needs, assisting them with school work, and giving them emotional support to build their sense of personal efficacy and self-esteem. Communication obligations associated with these programs are designed to promote a free flow of information from parents/guardians to teachers and others at the school. For example, if you were teaching in a well-functioning involvement program, you might receive a call from a parent or guardian to alert you to an upsetting experience one of your students had at home that might result in this person acting in atypical ways during the day.

New technologies are making it easier for parents/guardians to communicate with schools. Some school systems are now putting students' daily and weekly grades, attendance records, lesson plans, disciplinary reports, and other information on special Web sites (Newton, 2000). Parents and guardians are given special passwords they can enter that provide access to this information. These computer-based systems also allow parents to send information from home to school electronically.

In the School or Community

Activities of parents and guardians in the school encompass much more than assisting students in classrooms. In fact, because many secondary students are not comfortable

"Friday night you stayed out until almost 9:00, yesterday you had cola instead of milk and this morning you forgot to floss. Your father and I are afraid you're getting too wild."

having parents or guardians in the classroom with them, it is rare for parents and guardians to function in the kinds of teacher-assistant roles that are common in elementary schools. Assistance with course work tends to take less intrusive forms. For example, parents or guardians may talk to teachers privately to gather information about required reading and homework assignments so they can provide some assistance to their children at home. School-based activities also frequently feature involvement in parent/guardian-teacher organizations. In these settings, parents and guardians work closely with professional educators to make policy decisions and to advocate for school improvements of various kinds. Often discussions in these settings lead to links with businesses and governmental agencies in the local community. The work that parents and guardians do with local community leaders often provides a potent force in support of actions that will improve the overall quality of the secondary school experience.

Improving Teacher Quality

Few people challenge the proposition that quality education demands good teachers. To encourage talented people to enter and remain in the profession and to assure that teachers have the knowledge and skill they need to be effective in the classroom, educational leaders and reformers have proposed several approaches to achieving these twin purposes. Your own teacher preparation program may well include components that have been added in response to some of these improvement initiatives. Ideas put forward by the Interstate New Teacher Assessment and Support Consortium (INTASC) and the National Board for Professional Teaching Standards (NBPTS) have been particularly influential.

Interstate New Teacher Assessment and Support Consortium (INTASC)

The Interstate New Teacher Assessment and Support Consortium (INTASC) was established about 15 years ago as an alliance among state education leaders, colleges and universities, and national groups with interests in promoting educational improvement and development of high-quality educators. INTASC has pushed hard for teacher preparation programs that assure that teachers leave their preparation programs knowing both the subjects they will teach and methods for transmitting content that will enable all students to learn. To achieve this end, INTASC has developed a guiding set of principles that are known as the *INTASC Model Core Standards*. They represent features of teaching and teacher performance that should be present regardless of subjects taught or age and grade-levels of students. Increasingly, teacher preparation programs incorporate experiences that seek to provide new teachers with skills consistent with the ten *Model Core Standards*.

The *Model Core Standards* are listed in Figure 1-3. At the end of each chapter in Parts 2, 3, and 4 of this text, you will find an exercise titled "For Your Portfolio." This provides you with an opportunity to put information you have learned into a professional-development portfolio. You will be asked to cross-reference materials you include to one or more of the *Model Core Standards*. To do this, you will want to refer back to the standards provided in Figure 1-3.

At present, INTASC leaders are engaged in the development of additional standards for individual school subjects. They are also exploring new ways to assess teachers' performances that feature extensive use of evidence assembled in professional portfolios.

National Board for Professional Teaching Standards (NBPTS)

In 1987, the Carnegie Forum on Education and the Economy supported establishment of the National Board for Professional Teaching Standards (NBPTS). NBPTS's governing board includes teachers, administrators, members of the public, and other stakeholders in education. The organization operates as a private, nonprofit group that receives financing from foundations, grants from large businesses, and certain federal sources.

NBPTS seeks to improve education by promoting the development of teachers who:

- are committed to students and their learning,
- know the subjects they teach and how to teach those subjects to students,
- are responsible for managing and monitoring student learning,
- think systematically about their practice and learn from experience, and
- are members of learning communities. (NBPTS, 1999)

STANDARDS

S1   The teacher understands the central concepts, tools of inquiry, and structures of the discipline(s) he or she teaches and can create learning experiences that make these aspects of subject matter meaningful for students.

S2   The teacher understands how children learn and develop, and can provide learning opportunities that support their intellectual, social and personal development.

S3   The teacher understands how students differ in their approaches to learning and creates instructional opportunities that are adapted to diverse learners.

S4   The teacher understands and uses a variety of instructional strategies to encourage students' development of critical thinking, problem solving, and performance skills.

S5   The teacher uses an understanding of individual and group motivation and behavior to create a learning environment that encourages positive social interaction, active engagement in learning, and self-motivation.

S6   The teacher uses knowledge of effective verbal, nonverbal, and media communication techniques to foster active inquiry, collaboration, and supportive interaction in the classroom.

S7   The teacher plans instruction based upon knowledge of subject matter, students, the community, and curriculum goals.

S8   The teacher understands and uses formal and informal assessment strategies to evaluate and ensure the continuous intellectual, social and physical development of the learner.

S9   The teacher is a reflective practitioner who continually evaluates the effects of his/her choices and actions on others (students, parents, and other professionals in the learning community) and who actively seeks out opportunities to grow professionally.

S10   The teacher fosters relationships with school colleagues, parents, and agencies in the larger community to support students' learning and well being.

Figure 1–3
INTASC Model Core Standards

MORE FROM THE WEB ━━━━━━━━━━━━━━

Trends

You have been briefly introduced to examples of trends you will encounter as a secondary school teacher. Many Web sites contain information related to issues associated with these developments. We have selected examples you may wish to visit to broaden your understanding of these topics.

Systemic Reform

http://www.nap.edu/readingroom/books/techgap/systemic.html

- This site presents a useful historical perspective on the development of interest in systemic reform of schools. There is a particularly good discussion of emerging technologies and the trend toward establishing performance standards as drivers of the effort to approach school improvement systemically.

Preventing Youth Violence: Full-Service Schools

http://www.uncg.edu/edu/ericcass/violence/docs/skoolfu3.htm

- Material at this site focuses on the demonstrated value that good full-service schools have in preventing school violence. You will find excellent descriptions of social changes, inadequate learner health, and poor nutrition as establishers of conditions that can lead to violent behavior at school. Full-service schools seek to help young people overcome these circumstances, and the material presented at this site includes numerous examples of individual full-service schools that are serving students well.

Standards Resources: National Links

http://www.mdk12.org/practices/good_instruction/standards_resources.html

- Numerous national groups and organizations have developed content and performance standards for students. This site provides a useful compilation of links to these groups. There are also links to general information about standards-based education.

To Be Effective, School-Business Partnerships Should Boost Student Learning and Educate the Community

http://www.asbj.com/achievement/sbsa/sbsa5.html

- Anne L. Bryant prepared material at this site. It includes excellent examples of existing school-business partnerships. Bryant points out that these relationships provide benefits not only for students in the schools but for the adults representing the partner businesses as well.

Homeschooling

http://homeschooling.about.com/education/homeschooling/mbody.htm?once=true&

- You will find dozens of sites on the Web with information about homeschooling. The example cited here provides outstanding links to useful information about implementing homeschooling programs. For example, you will find suggestions for preparing mini-units, developing lessons about a state, and using curriculum guides. There are also links to books and other general information about homeschooling.

National Service-Learning Clearinghouse

http://www.nicsl.coled.umn.edu/home.htm

- This address takes you to the home page of the National Service-Learning Clearinghouse, located at the University of Minnesota. There are links to many other sites with information about service learning. In addition, you can download excellent resources related to service learning. For example, one available document, titled *Service-Learning and Assessment: A Field Guide for Teachers*, includes marvelous information about planning, implementing, and evaluating service-learning experiences.

The National Coalition for Parent Involvement in Education (NCPIE)

http://www.teacherlink.usu.edu/Tlresources/1999-06/ncpie.html

- As the title suggests, this site is maintained by a national group with interests in promoting more parent and guardian involvement in the schools. You will find links to other information related to promoting productive relationships among parents, schools, and communities.

Much of the work of NBPTS has been dedicated to identifying high standards related to what teachers should know and do to help students achieve. NBPTS has established a certification process for the purpose of identifying teachers who meet these standards. If you seek a National Board Certificate after beginning your career as a teacher, you will undergo a rigorous set of assessments. You will be observed in your own classroom and in special situations that are developed for candidates at NBPTS assessment centers. You will also be required to prepare an extensive portfolio to document your instructional procedures and their effectiveness with learners.

National Board certificates do not replace teaching credentials, certificates, or licenses that states issue. What they do is provide formal recognition of teachers who have met much higher standards. National Board certificates provide evidence that holders have met rigorous criteria that clearly identify them as outstanding classroom practitioners.

Not everyone approves of NBPTS. A few critics argue that the practice of applying national standards and awarding certificates to people who meet them challenges the tradition of certifying teachers at the state level. Even though National Board certification does not replace state certification, some people suggest that it is a step in that direction. Supporters point out that the high NBPTS standards may encourage states to adopt more rigorous certification requirements that, in time, will improve the quality of teachers everywhere.

For additional information, you may wish to visit the National Board's Web site. The URL is: http://www.nbpts.org/

Key Ideas in Summary

- New challenges and trends are changing the face of secondary education. If you want to play a role in shaping your profession, you need to become familiar with arguments of both proponents and opponents of school change and reform proposals.
- Systemic reform refers to the idea that what goes on in schools results from the interaction of multiple variables. School improvement cannot result from changing a single variable. True reform requires simultaneous attention to all the variables that, collectively, affect the quality of the school program.
- Standards-based education seeks to provide clear descriptions of what teachers should teach and students should learn. The idea is to provide clear "targets" for instruction and to assess students' performance once their teachers have completed an instructional cycle. The approach is driven by a desire to hold educators accountable for students' learning through assessment systems that tie in clearly to what has been taught.
- School-to-work programs are designed to bridge the gap between the world of the school and the world of work. Many of these are 2+2 programs. Students begin during the last two years of high school and continue for two more years of additional training, often at a community or junior college. Students gain competence in a well-defined technical or practical arts field and gain employment in this area at the conclusion of the program.
- In many parts of the country, school-business partnerships have been established to address what many see as an inappropriate lack of connection between what goes on in school and what graduates will have to do when they enter the work force. Partnerships take many forms. Some are limited to the provision by business of speakers or of scholarships and other student incentives. Others feature more direct business involvement and seek to help schools upgrade the overall quality of teaching and programming.
- In recent years there has been a tremendous increase in homeschooling, which means educating students at home. This approach places huge demands on parents. Nevertheless, because of dissatisfactions with public schools, more and more parents are making this commitment. Legislation authorizing homeschooling is in place in every state. Journals serving homeschoolers and companies offering learning materials have appeared. Proponents are now pressuring legislatures for some financial assistance. This attempt worries public school officials who fear that scarce education dollars, potentially, may be diverted from public school support to homeschoolers.
- Some critics of present educational practices argue that educational quality is undermined because our school system has become too centralized. They allege that distant bureaucrats stifle initiative at the individual school level. Further, they deny parents and guardians a choice as to where their children can go to school. What is needed, according to school choice proponents, is a school system that allows parents and guardians to seek out the best schools and that allows individual schools to take aggressive action to improve their own programs. Voucher plans and charter schools are examples of responses to the desire for school choice.

- Service-learning programs are designed to provide students with experiences that help them develop a sense of responsibility for their own communities. Many such programs feature these three phases: (1) planning and preparation, (2) delivery of services, and (3) analysis of results.

- Parent/guardian involvement programs are less common in secondary than in elementary schools. However, because of studies revealing that such programs may have a beneficial impact on older students as well, parent/guardian programs are being adopted by increasing numbers of middle schools, junior high schools, and senior high schools. Often they feature suggestions regarding how parents and guardians, teachers, and community members can work collaboratively to help young people. Many of them include suggestions for how parents and guardians can work effectively with students in the home and additional suggestions regarding how they might make contributions in their own schools or in the general community.

- Two important efforts to improve the competence of classroom teachers have been mounted, respectively, by the Interstate New Teacher Assessment and Support Consortium (INTASC) and the National Board for Professional Teaching Standards (NBPTS). INTASC has identified a list of capabilities that new teachers should have. Many teacher preparation programs now are designed with a view to preparing candidates who meet these standards. NBPTS has developed a system of issuing National Board certificates to experienced teachers whose performances measure up to rigorous standards.

Reflections

1. You may be doing an outstanding job of teaching according to standards that are important to you; yet, others may feel your performance is not particularly noteworthy. How do you explain differences in how different people might assess a given teacher's performance?

2. What is meant by the term *systemic reform,* and what arguments have been used to support it?

3. What do you see as strengths and weaknesses of *standards-based education*?

4. Are school-business partnerships desirable? Why, or why not?

5. Homeschooling places very heavy demands on parents and guardians. What motivates them to take on these responsibilities given the availability of tuition-free public schools?

6. Some critics of present school practices assert that many schools face problems today because they are organized as highly centralized, regimented bureaucracies. They favor a variety of school-choice initiatives that vest more authority in the hands of parents and local leaders and remove it from the hands of centralized school program managers. What are some examples of school-choice initiatives, and what arguments have been made both in support of and in opposition to them?

7. Good service-learning programs require careful planning and preparation. Are the benefits worth the time and effort needed to plan and implement them?

8. What are some kinds of things parents or guardians of secondary school students might be asked to do at home to help their children derive as much benefit as possible from the school program?

9. Look at the Model Core Standards developed by INTASC (see Figure 1–3). Which ones do you think will be most difficult for you to meet? What might you do to prepare for these especially challenging standards?

10. Some critics of the National Board for Professional Teaching Standards suggest that National Board certification represents a first step toward displacing state-issued certificates with an official national certificate. If this were to happen, would this benefit or hurt the quality of education in the nation's schools? Why do you think so?

Learning Extensions

1. Together with several others in your class, organize a symposium on this topic: "The 10 Most Likely Changes in Secondary Education During the First Quarter of the 21st Century." Present findings to your class, and invite follow-up comments at the end of the presentation.

2. Invite some administrators and teachers from a local secondary school who are involved in site-based management to visit your class. Ask them to discuss how site-based management works in their building. Ask teachers how their roles have changed since site-based management was implemented and for suggestions on how you might prepare yourself to serve on a site-management team.

3. Review professional journals for articles focusing on standards-based education. Share your findings with members of your class in the form of an oral report.

4. Organize a debate on this topic: "Resolved that school districts should pay teachers who hold National Board certificates an extra $10,000 a year." Invite comments from members of the class as a whole following the debate.

5. Prepare a formal paper in which you describe three to five examples of voucher plans. Consider using the *Education index* to locate information. Go to the World Wide Web, locate a search engine, and enter the phrase *voucher plan* to get a listing of available articles. In your paper, be as explicit as possible with regard to (a) the legal authority for individual plans you discuss, (b) specific features of the plans, and (c) numbers of students involved. Conclude your paper with a personal view of voucher plans as a means of improving secondary education.

6. Go to Merrill Education's Link to General Methods Resources site at this URL: http://www.prenhall.com/methods-cluster/. At the bottom of the page select "curriculum" as your topic and click the "begin" button. This will take you to the "Overview" page. On the left side, click on "Web Links." On the Web Links page, click on "Reform and Improvement Movements and Issues." Follow links that will provide information about curriculum reform efforts and prepare a brief oral presentation on "Three Curriculum Reform Proposals and How They Will Affect Secondary Schools and Teachers."

References

Children's Defense Fund. (1994). *The State of America's Children*. Boston: Beacon Press.

Dryfoos, J. G. (1994). *Full-service schools: A revolution in health and social services for children, youth, and families*. San Francisco: Jossey-Bass.

Engle, E. (1989, May). *Socioeconomic status, family structure, and parental involvement: The correlates of achievement*. Paper presented at the annual meeting of the American Educational Research Association, San Francisco.

Gladwell, M. (1999). Clicks & mortar. *The New Yorker, 75*(37), 106–115.

Hempel, C. H. (2000, February 4). World's coming unwired: Cell phones augur future with info everywhere, all the time. *The Commercial Appeal (Memphis)*, p. F1. [http://www.newslibrary.com/deliverppdoc.asp?SMH=274511]

Howsam, R. B., Corrigan, D. C., Denemark, G. W., & Nash, R. J. (1976). *Educating a profession: Relating to human services education*. Washington, DC: American Association of Colleges for Teacher Education.

Interstate New Teacher Assessment and Support Consortium. (1999). *Interstate new teacher assessment and support consortium*. Washington, DC: Council of Chief State School Officers. [http://www.ccsso.org/intasc.html]

National Board for Professional Teaching Standards (NBPTS). (1999). *The five propositions of accomplished teaching*. San Antonio, TX: NBPTS.

[http:/www.nbpts.org/nbpts.standards/five-props.html]

National Commission on Excellence in Education. (1983). *A nation at risk: The imperative for educational reform*. Washington, DC: U.S. Department of Education.

Newton, C. (2000, February 21). Parents give online grades an "A." *Greensboro, North Carolina News and Record*, pp. A1, A5.

Noddings, N. (1997). Thinking about standards. *Phi Delta Kappan, 79*(3), 184–89.

North Central Regional Educational Laboratory (2000). *Parent involvement at the secondary school level*. Oakbrook, IL: NCREL. [http://www.ncrel.org/sdrs/areas/issues/envrnmnt/famncomm/pa1lk36.htm]

Parent News. (1997). *National PTA releases standards for parent involvement*. [http://npin.org/pnews/pnew797/pnew797e.html]

Ravitch, D. (1995). *National standards in American education: A citizen's guide*. New York: Basic Books.

Schmoker, M., & Marzano, R. J. (1999). Realizing the promise of standards-based education. *Educational Leadership, 56*(6), 17–21.

Stake, R. (1999). The goods on American education. *Phi Delta Kappan, 80*(9), 668–672.

Summary report: National evaluation of Learn and Serve America. (1999). Waltham, MA: Center for Human Resources, Brandeis University.

Texas Center for Service Learning. (1997). *What is service learning?* [http://www.txserve.org/servlrn/general/aboutsl.html]

Verkler, E. (2000). *Teens reaching out to use cell phones*. [http://wwihigh.com/cell_phones.html]

2

Students and Schools

This chapter will aim to

- point out some racial and ethnic characteristics of today's student population;

- describe some relationships between poverty and academic success;

- identify some characteristics of special-needs students and some policy debates that have surrounded proposals to provide them with high-quality school services;

- suggest ways in which families influence what students do at school;

- explain some patterns of pre-adolescent and adolescent behavior and how they influence the behavior of secondary school students;

- point out how the *comprehensive high school* developed, and describe some challenges to this model;

- explain competing views of the purposes of schools designed to serve students in the 10-to-14-year-old age group;

- describe how schools are funded and some approaches designed to ensure that money is distributed fairly;

- point out some issues associated with the topic of school violence; and

- explain qualities of good schools as described by such authorities as William Glasser and William Watson Purkey.

Introduction

Here is today's puzzler: "Give me a one-word description of secondary students and schools today." If your reply is "diversity," take a bow. Young people enrolled in middle schools, junior high schools, and senior high schools mirror the variation within our society today. Individual students differ in their physical characteristics, aspirations, intellectual abilities, interests, and values. Similarly, the schools they attend range in size from tiny operations scattered in rural areas across the continent to gigantic complexes of buildings in metropolitan areas. Regardless of important place-to-place differences, today most secondary education takes place within three broad categories of schools: senior high schools, junior high schools, and middle schools.

Secondary-school buildings vary tremendously in quality. Some are ill-maintained relics with interiors and instructional support features that would appear little changed to a graduate who returned for a reunion after a 50-year absence. Some are magnificent architectural statements that embrace the latest technologies and present a well-scrubbed, even elegant, face to their communities. Many other buildings have some sections that have been modernized and others that remain much as they were 20, 30, or even more years ago.

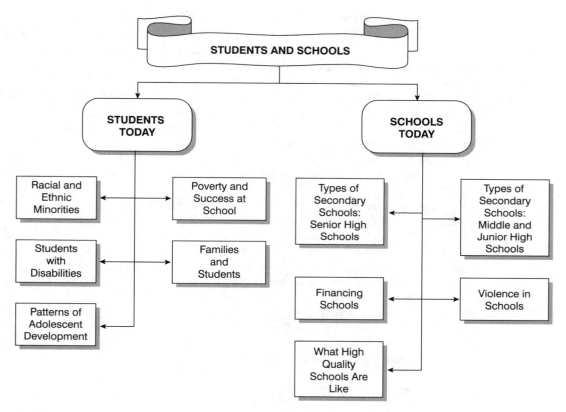

Figure 2–1
Graphic Organizer

Conditions of schools differ, in part, because of variations in wealth from community to community. They differ also because of the nature of relationships that have developed over time between community members and school leaders. Both local wealth and local attitudes influence decisions that affect school budgets.

Schools also vary because of community characteristics that go beyond the issue of wealth. For example, families greatly influence attitudes of their children toward schools and school programs. When parents and guardians are positively disposed toward the school and supportive of its agendas, students tend to adjust better to school than in places where this kind of support is lacking. The local community context can also affect the safety and security of the school environment.

Students Today

The population of secondary school students is growing larger and more diverse. You can expect this trend to continue for much of the first decade you will spend in the profession. Experts project that secondary schools will enroll about 13 percent more students by the year 2009 than in school year 2000–2001 (Gerald & Hussar, 1999). Total public school enrollment in grades 5 through 12 will increase during this period from 25.2 million to 28.9 million students. There will be important differences from one region of the country to another. Enrollment growth will be much less dramatic in the Northeast and the Midwest than in the South and the West (Gerald & Hussar, 1999). Some states that are likely to experience high percentage increases are Illinois, Florida, Georgia, Tennessee, Texas, North Carolina, Arizona, California, Colorado, Hawaii, and Idaho. Among states likely to see fairly large declines in numbers of secondary students in fall 2009 as compared to fall 2000 are Maine, North Dakota, West Virginia, and Wyoming (Gerald & Hussar, 1999). See Figure 2-2 for projections of changes from 2000 to 2009 by grade level.

The young people you will teach will be a very mixed group. In your classes, you may well have students from many ethnic and racial backgrounds. Large numbers may not speak English as their first language. Some will have physical, emotional, or behavioral disabilities of various kinds. Students' families will reflect a cross-section of patterns found in our society as a whole. Because of family and other outside influences, individual members of your classes will bring with them multiple perspectives on the "worth" of schools and schooling. In economic terms, students will range from those who have lived their entire lives in a culture of poverty to those who have never known anything but affluence. Some of your students will expect the school to be a continuation of a world that they believe, in the main, is a calm, well-ordered, predictable place. Others will see it as a part of an unstable reality where violence and unpredictability are among life's only constants.

Numbers of Students (in Millions)							
Year	Grade 5	Grade 6	Grade 7	Grade 8	Grade 9	Grade 10	Grade 11	Grade 12
2003	3.68	3.79	3.86	3.75	4.12	3.62	3.20	2.91
2004	3.64	3.72	3.85	3.81	4.20	3.71	3.27	2.92
2005	3.62	3.68	3.78	3.80	4.27	3.79	3.35	2.98
2006	3.60	3.66	3.74	3.74	4.26	3.85	3.42	3.05
2007	3.58	3.64	3.72	3.69	4.19	3.84	3.48	3.11
2008	3.57	3.62	3.70	3.68	4.14	3.77	3.47	3.17
2009	3.57	3.61	3.68	3.66	4.12	3.73	3.41	3.16

Figure 2–2
Projected Changes in Enrollments of Middle School and High School Students through 2009*

*Data are from D. E. Gerald and W. J. Hussar (Eds.), *Projections of Education Statistics to 2009*.
Washington, DC: National Center for Education Statistics, 1999, p. 183.

In addition to the multiple backgrounds of students you will face as a teacher, you will also be working with young people at a time when they are going through important personal developmental changes. You need to recognize these maturational patterns and seek ways to respond to students that are sensitive both to these "growing up" challenges and to the unique background characteristics each student brings to school every day.

Racial and Ethnic Minorities

Regardless of where your first teaching position is located in the country and regardless of whether your school is in an urban, suburban, or rural area, chances are high that many of your students will be members of racial or ethnic minority groups. Looking at the nation as a whole, nearly 40 percent of all students today are members of minority groups. Minority populations are growing at a more rapid rate than the general population. If present trends continue, minority-group students will comprise an even larger percentage of the secondary school population in the years ahead. Today, especially high percentages of minority students are found in central cities. In one recent year, African-American students comprised about one-third and Latino students about one-fourth of the central city student population (Wirt & Snyder, 1999).

You may be aware that many educators believe our increasingly multicultural society will be well-served by a school system that brings together young people from diverse racial and ethnic backgrounds. However, as a result of the rapid increase in the total population of students who belong to racial and ethnic minorities, a pattern has developed which shows that, within some schools in a given area, numbers of students from a single racial or ethnic group grow significantly higher than numbers of students from other groups. Looked at as a whole, it appears that the schools are becoming more racially diverse, when it may also be true to say that large numbers of individual schools are becoming less diverse. This pattern acts to increase isolation of members of one racial group from another. Recent data suggest, for example, that African-American students in the Border States and the South have less exposure to white students in their schools than they did 10 to 15 years ago. Similarly, Latino students in the schools have less exposure to white, non-Latino students in the South and the Northeast than they did 10 to 15 years ago (Wirt & Snyder, 1999).

You may be aware that African-American and Latino students have experienced more academic difficulty in school than white (non-Latino) students. Many explanations for this have been proposed. The poor economic circumstances of many African-American and Latino families seems to be a contributing factor. There may be unintended cultural biases in modes of instruction and in testing procedures that fail adequately to measure what young people from ethnic minorities have learned. For some students who learned a language other than English as their first language, problems with English may contribute to difficulties at school.

One problem that seems likely to concern you throughout your career is the school dropout rate. Traditionally, members of some ethnic minorities, particularly African-Americans and Latinos, have dropped out of school at much higher rates than white students. A survey issued recently identified the percentages of school dropout rates for individuals aged 16 to 24. In one recent year, 7.6 percent of the white students, 13.4 percent of the African-American students, and 25.3 percent of the Latino students had dropped out (Wirt & Snyder, 1999). Over the last 30 years, dropout rates of African-American students, though still higher than those of white students, have declined significantly; however, the number of Latino students dropping out remains very high. Dropout rates of Latino students who were born outside of the United States are especially high—38.6 percent (Wirt & Snyder, 1999).

What can be done to improve this situation? There is some evidence that today's school programs are responding better to needs of ethnic minorities than in the past. One measure of this change is a record of improvement of minority students' scores on National Assessment of Educational Progress tests. Scores of African-American and Latino students have greatly improved over the past 20 years on tests of reading, writing, mathematics proficiency, and science performance. While these scores still lag behind those of white (non-Latino) students, the gap has become much smaller. These differences in achievement levels greatly affect the rate at which minority students take sophisticated courses. For example, the percentage of white students taking calculus courses in high school is almost twice that of African-American and Latino students (Snyder, 2000).

You may find that many of your students whose first language is not English experience academic difficulties. Numbers of students with limited English proficiency are increasing. Today, they account for approximately eight percent of the total school population (National Clearinghouse for Bilingual Education, 1998). However, because many of these young people drop out of school before completing their secondary school years, there tend to be fewer students with limited English proficiency in secondary than in elementary schools. For example, one survey reported that about two percent of 12th graders are students with limited English proficiency (Mazzeo, Carlson, Voelkl, & Lutkus, 2000). There are especially large numbers of these students in the states of California, Texas, Florida, and New York.

When you think of students with limited English proficiency, you may be inclined to think of students whose first language is Spanish. While Spanish is the most common first language among students with a home language other than English, schools today enroll students who speak many other languages at home as well. In fact, there are often more than 20 languages other than English spoken at home in even medium-sized school districts. In metropolitan school districts, the number often exceeds 60.

For information on specific approaches you might wish to consider in working with students from racial and ethnic minorities, see Chapter 6, "Accommodating Diversity."

Poverty and Success at School

Chances are that many students you teach will come from families living below the poverty level. Today, the percentage of school-aged young people living in poverty exceeds 20 percent (National Center for Children in Poverty, 1999). This figure represents a modest decline from a high of 22 percent in 1993. However, today's child poverty rate is still much higher than the rate of 14 percent thirty years ago (National Center for Children in Poverty, 1999). African-American students and Latino students are much more likely than white (non-Latino) students to come from economically deprived families.

Young people from poor families face many challenges during the years they are in school. Among other things, these students are greatly at risk of dropping out before finishing high school. Note some of these other differences between poor young people and non-poor young people:

- Poor young people are much less likely to enjoy excellent health than non-poor young people.
- Poor young people are twice as likely as non-poor young people to be in the lowest 20 percent of the student population in terms of their height.
- Poor young people are more likely to have a learning disability than non-poor young people.
- Poor young people are twice as likely to have repeated a grade in school than non-poor young people.
- Poor young people who are female during their teen years are nearly three times as likely to give birth to a child out of wedlock than a non-poor female teenager. (Brooks-Gunn & Duncan, 1997)

Students with Disabilities

More secondary students with disabilities of all kinds are now enrolled as members of regular middle school, junior high school, and senior high school classes. Federal legislation and supportive laws and regulations enacted by individual states have increased a commitment to *inclusion* which means that these young people are included in regular class activities and that instructional services need to be delivered to them in an appropriate manner by regular classroom teachers. For more detailed treatment of this issue, see Chapter 6, "Accommodating Diversity."

Federal legislation requires states each year to report numbers of special education students falling within each of the following 13 categories:

1. specific learning disability,
2. speech or language impairment,
3. mental retardation,
4. serious emotional disturbance,
5. multiple disabilities,
6. hearing impairment,
7. deafness,
8. orthopedic impairment,
9. other health impairment,
10. visual impairment or blindness,
11. autism,
12. traumatic brain injury, and
13. deaf-blindness.

Today, more than two million secondary students fall into one of these two categories. The number of special education students has been growing as a percentage of the total population of secondary-school learners. The specific-learning-disability category has been growing fastest of all.

One policy issue you will face as an educator has to do with costs of services provided to special-needs students. As numbers of special education programs have increased, so have costs associated with supporting them. To pay for these programs, it has been necessary for many school districts to divert funds from accounts traditionally used to support the general education program for all students (Parrish, 2000). The issue raises two questions: (1) How much money can be reallocated from general education to special education without undermining the quality of services provided to general education students? (2) Given the growth of special education programs and the need to support them, is it possible to increase the total amount of money available to support education so that increased costs of special education programs will not result in decreased support for general education? At present, there is little consensus on issues implied by these questions. You are certain to encounter arguments in support of many approaches to responding to these difficulties during your years in the profession.

Families and Students

Have you ever seen reruns of television shows from the 1950s? You know, the ones that feature a "typical" happy family with a stay-at-home mother, a couple of kids, and a father who is welcomed happily into the group as he returns from a hard day at the office. All fathers on those shows seemed to be well-situated professionals. All families seemed to live in white houses in nicely maintained neighborhoods on tree-lined streets. All families seemed to have children who, if they had problems at all, tended to suffer from nothing so serious that it could not all be nicely resolved within a single half-hour episode. For the most part, the portrait these shows presented of a "typical" American family was quite a stretch even in the 1950s. However, the depiction of two-parent families, including a stay-at-home mother, closely mirrored the national reality in the middle of the 20th century. Today, this kind of family arrangement is the exception, rather than the rule.

Recent surveys reveal that mothers of over two-thirds of school-aged children are employed. About 30 percent of children live as members of families headed by a single parent. This single parent is six times as likely to be the mother than the father (Wirt & Snyder, 1999). The nature of your students' families may have an effect on their performance in school.

One validated finding is that students with mothers who have more than a high school education perform better in school than students whose parents have received less formal education. Over the last three decades, there has been a tremendous increase in the educational-attainment levels of students' mothers. For example, in the early 1970s, only about 18 percent of the mothers of these women had some college or university work or a college or university degree. Today, this figure has risen to about 49 percent (Wirt & Snyder, 1999).

Another interesting fact is that fathers' involvement in schools is closely associated with their children's academic performance. Fathers who do not live with their children

	Fathers with *Low Levels* of Involvement in School	Fathers with *High Levels* of Involvement in School
Percentage of Students Getting Mostly As	34.1	50.4
Percentage of Students Saying They Enjoy School	33.0	49.8
Percentage of Students Participating in Extracurricular Activities	79.3	94.5

Figure 2–3

Relationship Between Fathers' Involvement and Their Children's Behavior in School

*Data are from U.S. Department of Education, National Center for Education Statistics, *National Household Education Survey*. Washington, DC: NCES, 1996.

tend to have very low levels of involvement with their children's schools. Fathers in two-parent families are much more likely to volunteer in schools, attend class events, participate in parent-teacher conferences, and go to general school meetings. The highest involvement levels at all are found among fathers who head households as single parents. However, single-parent households headed by males are very few in number. (Wirt & Snyder, 1999). Some "pluses" for students with fathers who are highly involved in schools are reflected in these data for fathers from two-parent households:*

Taken together, research on the influences families have on students' performance underscore a key point. That is, you need to take time to know your students well. The instruction you provide does not occur in a vacuum. Students' family situations vary greatly from individual to individual, and you need this kind of contextual information as you plan instructional experiences with the potential to respond to each student's particular circumstances.

Patterns of Adolescent Development

Though circumstances of your individual students impart a unique set of characteristics to each of them, there are developmental patterns associated with young people as they go through their secondary-school years. An understanding of these developmental changes can help you understand and respond to behaviors you will see in your classroom. However, you need to appreciate that descriptions of sequences of adolescent development are not meant to imply that all students experience exactly the same thing or that there is an iron-clad sequence of life events that assures every person will experience the same emotional, physical, and social changes at precisely the same age. These patterns are *general* ones, and there are enormous person-to-person differences in terms of when they occur and how much they influence individual young people.

"At your age, Tommy, a boy's body goes through changes that are not always easy to understand."

You will see more profound physical differences among younger secondary-school students than among older ones. Size differences among individual seventh-, eighth-, and ninth-graders sometimes startle visitors to their classrooms. Some girls may look little different from much younger fourth- and fifth-graders. Some boys may not yet weigh 80 pounds, while others will have the height and bulk found more typically among high school seniors. Younger secondary students are notorious for having unpredictable behavior patterns.

If you are teaching seventh graders, on some days you will find a student acting as a mature adult might act. On other days, you may well see the same person doing something that would (or should) embarrass a fourth-grader. As young people in this age group strive to establish personal identities, they engage in a lot of behavioral experimentation. As this process develops, their behaviors swing wildly between surprisingly adult to disturbingly childish patterns. In general, these are some patterns you might expect to see if you're assigned to teach younger secondary school students:

- Students experience tension as they seek to establish a balance between a need to find their unique personal identities and a need to be an accepted member of a group.
- Students tend to shift their focus from their parents to their friends as they seek cues regarding acceptable attitudes and patterns of behavior.
- Students tend to place great emphasis on physiological changes they are experiencing and to worry whether their own rate of development is consistent with what others in their age group are experiencing.

- Students begin to develop more sophisticated patterns of thinking; one consequence is that they begin to see their parents and other adults as less than perfect—a realization that leads to some disappointment and to an increase in a willingness to challenge adult authority.

Many secondary students, as they begin to develop their abilities to engage in more sophisticated, abstract kinds of thinking, develop an intense interest in the nature of their own personal identity. Sometimes this results in an excessive concern about what others think about them. David Elkind (1981), a leading authority on developmental psychology, suggests that many adolescents behave as if an "imaginary audience" was closely observing their every action. Young people who have this attitude think others are closely watching everything they do. You can sometimes see reflections of this attitude in shy students who fear to speak up because they feel their "audience" will find their performance wanting, or in the slavish way in which some secondary-school students follow clothing fashions—a behavior testifying to their fear about wearing something that the "audience" would not like.

As students progress through their secondary school years, they tend to become more personally secure, more confident in their thinking abilities, and more accepting of the physiological changes that they have experienced (or are continuing to experience). High school students, particularly juniors and seniors, begin to reflect quite adult patterns of thinking and behaving. Though they continue to place a high value on attitudes of friends the same age, typically, they are able to understand and appreciate the perspectives of people outside their own friendship group to a much greater extent than students in the early middle school years. Here are some characteristics you might expect to see among students if you are teaching at the high-school level:

- Students often develop serious and intense relationships with members of the opposite sex.

- Students tend to begin reconnecting and recommitting to values and traditions of their own families and cultural groups, even when these may be at variance with views of their school friendship groups.

- Students' capacities for setting and pursuing long-term goals increases.

- Students develop more tolerance for accepting compromises and for delaying gratification of immediate wants.

- Students develop a strong sense of who they are—a pattern that is accompanied by more emotional stability and more self-reliance.

Schools Today

When you begin your career as a secondary teacher, you will probably teach in one of three broad categories of schools: senior high schools, junior high schools, and middle schools. Schools in one of these categories, the junior high schools, are declining in numbers. The middle school is displacing this school type in many parts of the country.

Whether you teach in a middle, junior high, or senior high school, you are certain to confront issues related to school financing early in your career. What is your own opinion on the all-important "Are-we-spending-too-much-money-on-our-schools" question? Ask almost any audience about this issue, and you will find a division of opinion. Some people will argue passionately that the answer to the question is "yes." Others will just as strongly affirm their commitment to a "no" response. As a professional, you need to know something about how schools are funded and about issues that play a role in debates about how much money is allocated and spent to support school programs.

Numerous other broad issues will come to your attention early in your teaching career. One of these has to do with assuring that schools are physically and emotionally safe places for students. If they are not, there can be highly negative effects on students' overall personal development and academic achievement. You will want to get involved in efforts designed to assure a safe and secure school environment. You and others perhaps will pursue this goal in the context of a larger concern for developing sets of conditions in your school that act to enhance its overall quality.

Types of Secondary Schools: Senior High Schools

The Boston English Classical School, established in 1821, was the first public high school in the United States. Its curriculum emphasized useful and practical subjects. The curriculum devoted less attention to subjects lacking a clear connection to the demands of daily living.

Interest in the high school as an institution developed slowly. Even as late as 1860, there were only about 40 public high schools in the country (Barry, 1961). Concerns about money contributed to a lack of popularity of public high schools. The principle of using tax money to support elementary schools can be traced all the way back to early colonial times. However, for many years the legality of using tax money to support secondary schools remained questionable. A key decision that clarified this situation was handed down in the famous Kalamazoo case of 1874 [*Stuart v. School District No. 1 of the Village of Kalamazoo,* 30 Mich. 69 (1874)], which supported the right of state legislatures to pass laws permitting local communities to levy taxes to support secondary as well as elementary schools.

Once the legality of financing of high schools was ensured, their number increased rapidly. By 1900, there were over 6,000 high schools serving more than half a million students. Today, between 15 and 16 million students attend the nation's high schools (Gerald & Hussar, 1999).

Seeking a Purpose
During the latter years of the nineteenth century and the first decades of the twentieth century, there was a great debate about the curriculum of the high school program. This argument focused on whether the high school's primary role should be to prepare students for the world of work or for the academic world of the university.

In the 1890s, the National Education Association's Committee of Ten issued a report recommending that the high school curriculum should be designed almost exclusively for the purpose of preparing students for college-level work. The committee recommended that all high school students take (1) Latin, (2) Greek, (3) English, (4) a modern foreign language, (5) mathematics, (6) sciences, including physics, astronomy, and chemistry, (7) natural history, (8) history, civil government, and political economy, and (9) geography (National Education Association, 1893; Tanner & Tanner, 1980).

 WHAT DO *YOU* THINK?

The Sophomore Year in High School as Proposed by the 1893 Committee of Ten

In 1893, the Committee of Ten proposed that all high school sophomores should take these subjects:

- Latin
- Greek
- English Literature
- German (continued from the freshman year)
- Algebra (could be replaced by bookkeeping or commercial arithmetic)
- Botany
- English History to 1688

Questions

1. How would citizens today react if a local school board attempted to implement this program?
2. How would today's students fare if this were the established program of study?
3. How would you have felt if you had faced this program of study as a high school sophomore?

Those who had noted the tremendous enrollment growth of high schools challenged this view by arguing that high schools were serving many students who would enter the work force immediately after graduation. For these students, a purely academic program would not adequately prepare them for survival in the world of work. Positions of these critics were reflected in the final report of the National Education Association's Committee of Nine issued in 1911. The Committee of Nine argued that high schools had a responsibility to produce "socially efficient" individuals, by which it meant people who were committed to basic American values and who were capable of making contributions to the technical and social development of the country.

The Comprehensive High School and the Cardinal Principles

In 1918, a grand compromise was struck that bridged the gap between those favoring a college-preparatory high school and those favoring a practical, world-of-work-oriented high school. The report of the National Education Association's Commission on the Reorganization of Secondary Education of 1918 is a seminal document in the development of the American senior high school. It took the position that the public high school should be "comprehensive."

In using the term *comprehensive,* the commission implied that the senior high school should serve multiple purposes. This broad view was expressed in the description of these *cardinal principles* of secondary education:

- Health,
- Command of fundamental processes,
- Worthy home membership,
- Citizenship,
- Worthy use of leisure time, and
- Ethical character.

The comprehensive high school and its associated cardinal principles have been guiding assumptions of senior high school education for three quarters of a century. The promise to provide something for every kind of student usually has allowed school leaders to maintain working majorities in support of this general approach. Not everyone agrees, however, that the comprehensive view of senior high school education continues to be in our nation's best interest.

Challenges to the Comprehensive Senior High School

Although the comprehensive high school continues to be the dominant form of the American high school, you may have heard about some challenges to this approach to formatting the high-school program. Critics' concerns span a broad spectrum of issues. Some of them contend that the comprehensive high school "dilutes" the secondary experience by presenting students with too many choices. As a result, they fail to achieve depth of understanding in some important areas of knowledge. Others claim that the comprehensive high school, rather than being a means to meet individual differences of students, presents educators with a way to provide weak courses to students from politically impotent groups and, at the same time, reserve high-powered electives for sons and daughters of economically powerful and influential citizens. Still others point out that many high schools never have had a wide enough variety of programs to meet the real needs of all students and, consequently, students too often still are required to select from among alternatives that are not well matched to their individual characteristics.

Some school reformers who have concerns about the quality of education provided to students enrolled in comprehensive high schools want to place more emphasis on certain aspects of the curriculum. A few have proposed alternative models for the high school that would completely eliminate the comprehensive high school as we know it. Let's look at some of these ideas.

Theodore Sizer and the Coalition of Effective Schools

Theodore Sizer has mounted one of the strongest challenges to the comprehensive high school. Sizer, a former headmaster of Phillips Academy in Andover, Massachusetts, and a former dean of the Graduate School of Education at Harvard helped to found the *Coalition of Essential Schools* at Brown University in Providence, Rhode Island. Three of Sizer's books, *Horace's Compromise* (1984), *Horace's School* (1992), and *Horace's Hope* (1996), have prompted spirited discussion among those interested in redesigning the high school.

Sizer argues that the comprehensive high school presents students with disjointed academic courses and that this arrangement stands in the way of deep and coherent learning. He points out that large high schools allow many students to go through their entire high school program without ever becoming well acquainted with individual teachers who could mentor them. Sizer also notes that present practices of evaluating students place a premium on displaying learned information on tests rather than on using learned information in ways that make sense in the world beyond the school.

In his book, *Horace's School,* Sizer (1992) proposes some remedies. Here are some principles that Sizer believes should characterize a worthy successor to the comprehensive school:

- *All students would follow the same curriculum.* Sizer argues that the present high school program with its multiple electives is designed to classify students. That is, so-called able students take college-preparatory work, and so-called less able students take less challenging courses. Sizer contends that high schools should be about the business of providing a strong substantive education for all learners.

- *Less is more.* The comprehensive high school offers so many different subjects that students often sacrifice depth of preparation to breadth of exposure. Sizer contends that a program requiring students to take a smaller number of subjects and pursue them in more depth would better serve their needs. He favors organizing the curriculum around three key subject areas: (1) mathematics/science, (2) the arts, and (3) history/philosophy. Faculty members in all three areas would share responsibility for developing students' language proficiency (reading, writing, speaking), developing their inquiry skills, and promoting productive study habits.

- *"Exhibitions" as evidence that knowledge can be used.* As a replacement for conventional tests to show evidence that learning has taken place, Sizer proposes the use of what he calls *exhibitions*. These would be complex presentations of the products of learning that would demonstrate to students and to others in a highly convincing way that they could use newly gained knowledge. Students would be encouraged to keep portfolios of work indicating their progress toward preparation of presentation of their exhibitions.

- *High schools subdivided into houses.* Sizer (1992) argues that "everyone at school should be accorded the respect of being well known" (p. 143). To ensure that no student goes through high school without being known and appreciated as an individual human being, high school student bodies would be subdivided into "houses" of between 200 and 220 students. Twelve to 16 faculty members would lead each house, getting to know each student well and serving as academic and personal mentors.

- *Extend the school year.* To provide adequate time for serious learning, the school year should be extended from 36 to 42 weeks.

Sizer's ideas are not just abstract discussion prompts. They are foundations for a serious high school reform initiative promoted by a group called the Coalition of Essential Schools. Several hundred schools are members. Here is some contact information:

Coalition of Essential Schools
Brown University
Box 1969
Providence, RI 02912
Phone: (401) 863-3384
Web site: http://www.ces.brown.edu

Advanced Placement Program

The College Entrance Examination Board has sponsored the Advanced Placement (AP) program since 1955. The program was initiated to provide additional opportunities for academically talented high school students. It gives hundreds of thousands of participating capable and motivated students opportunities to take rigorous college-level courses while still in high school. Nearly 14,000 high schools offer AP courses, and almost 3,000 colleges and universities give students college credit or award advanced academic standing based on AP examination grades. In one recent year, 700,000 students took more than one million AP exams (Advanced Placement Program, 2000). The American Council on Education (ACE) accredits the Advanced Placement program.

If you teach approved Advanced Placement Program courses, you will have access to many special AP publications and will be eligible to attend AP summer teaching institutes that provide additional preparation for your work with AP students and academic subjects. The Advanced Placement program has some resources available to provide financial support for some teachers who attend these professional development sessions.

For further information about the Advanced Placement Program, contact:

AP Publications
Box 6670

Princeton, NJ 08541-6670
Web site: http://www.collegeboard.org/ap/

The International Baccalaureate

The term *baccalaureate* in the phrase *International Baccalaureate* is not used in the American sense of a university degree awarded after a minimum of four years of college or university study. Rather, it is used in the French sense of an examination taken at the conclusion of a rigorous secondary school program, the results of which are heavily weighed in college and university admissions decisions. The program evolved over a number of years, beginning in the early 1960s. It was designed as a program for students in different countries that, if completed successfully, would qualify them for entry to top universities throughout the world. Today, International Baccalaureate programs are offered in more than 800 secondary schools in over 100 countries, including the United States. Instruction, depending on the location, is generally in English, French, or Spanish.

Students attending high schools that offer the International Baccalaureate program take a special set of courses during their last two secondary school years. These are selected from the areas of (1) their first language, (2) a second language, (3) individuals and society (including history, geography, economics, philosophy, psychology, social anthropology, organization, and management studies), (4) experimental sciences (including biology, chemistry, physics, and environmental studies), (5) mathematics, and (6) one of the following: art/design, music, Latin, classical Greek, or computing studies. In addition to these areas, students in International Baccalaureate programs take a course called *Theory of Knowledge* that challenges them to reflect critically on all experiences gained inside and outside of the classroom. To qualify for the International Baccalaureate diploma, the student must also pass a series of rigorous examinations.

If you are interested in obtaining more information about the International Baccalaureate program, contact:

International Baccalaureate Organization
North American and the Caribbean Region
200 Madison Avenue, Suite 2301
New York, NY 10016-3903
Phone: (212) 889-9242
E-mail: ibna@ibo.org
Web site: http://www.ibo.org/

Types of Secondary Schools: Junior High Schools and Middle Schools

For nearly a century, debates raged over how best to serve needs of young people in the transition years between the elementary school and the senior high school. Two basic orientations developed concerning what schools serving preadolescents and early adolescents (generally young people in the 10- to 14-year-old age group) should empha-size. Some contended that since high school work is academically rigorous, schools stu-dents attend after completing the elementary school program should emphasize acade-mic content to prepare students for the intellectual challenges they will face in high school. Others pointed out that young people in this age group have special personal, social, and emotional needs and that schools that serve them should have programs that respond to their special developmental characteristics.

The first type of school developed to serve students after they completed the ele-mentary school program was the junior high school. The birth of the junior high school represented something of a victory for those who saw the primary function of a school for pre-adolescents and early adolescents as preparation for the academic demands of the high school. Today, the junior high school is rapidly disappearing and is being replaced by the middle school. The ascendancy of the middle school suggests that opinion of many education decision-makers has shifted in favor of school programs for pre-adolescents and early adolescents that pay particular heed to the personal develop-mental characteristics of young people in this age group.

The Junior High School

Junior high schools did not appear until the early years of the twentieth century. The movement to establish them began late in the nineteenth century when large numbers of public high schools were being built. Academic programs offered in the high schools were much more demanding than those in elementary schools.

The first junior high school appeared in Berkeley, California, in 1909. By 1925, there were 880 of them in the country. By the middle 1930s, their number had grown to nearly 2,000. Their popularity continued to grow for the next several decades, peaking at a high of about 8,000 around 1970 (Lounsbury, 1992). The school organizational plan developed in Berkeley was copied by many school districts throughout the country. This 6-3-3 scheme featured a six-year elementary school, a three-year junior high school, and a three-year senior high school (Popper, 1967). Most often, the junior high school was designed to serve students in grades 7, 8, and 9. However, some junior high schools included other grade-level groupings.

From the beginning, junior high schools drew teachers from college and university preparatory programs that were oriented toward the senior high schools. With few exceptions, junior high school teachers were expected to have secondary rather than elementary teaching certificates. Large numbers of junior high school teachers saw teachers in high schools as their professional role models. Many of them hoped to teach at the senior high school level. Ever sensitive to negative comments that might come their way from teachers in the senior high school, many junior high school teachers worked hard to demonstrate that there was nothing "academically soft" about junior high school programs.

One consequence of all this was to divert attention away from the personal needs of junior high school students. This situation had always prompted criticism from people concerned about growth and development issues. These critics became more numerous in the years following the end of World War II. Drawing on the work of developmental psychologists and physiologists as an intellectual rationale, critics of the junior high school recommended the establishment of a new kind of school to serve preadolescents and early adolescents. They proposed that the new school be called a *middle school,* a term borrowed from European education.

The Middle School

The middle school concept began to catch on in the 1960s. In general, middle schools spanned three to five grades, always including grades 6 and 7 (Lounsbury & Vars, 1978). Though some middle schools include grade 9, many today do not. The presence of grade 9, in the minds of some critics of the traditional grades 7 to 9 junior high schools, led many junior high schools to model practices of high schools rather than develop programs more responsive to the developmental needs of preadolescents and early adolescents.

Grade 9 was considered one of the high school years when the Carnegie Unit system of awarding credits toward high school graduation was established in 1910 (Toepfer, 1992). This scheme required students to spend specified amounts of the day in separate classes in subjects such as mathematics, history, English, and science to earn high-school graduation credits. This system closely linked grade 9 to organizational and instructional patterns common in the other high school grades (10, 11, and 12). It also placed pressure on teachers of seventh and eighth grades to adopt instructional patterns that would prepare students for what they would confront as ninth-graders.

There continues to be evidence that middle schools that include grade 9 tend to take on more characteristics of high schools than those that have no grade higher than grade 8. This information about grade 9 needs to be approached with caution. There are great school-to-school variations among institutions serving preadolescents and early adolescents. Some institutions called junior high schools are highly oriented toward serving students' developmental needs. Some institutions called middle schools (including those that end at a grade no higher than grade 8) organize the school day and provide instruction in ways that are close to prevailing high school practices.

Leading proponents of middle schools suggest that, ideally, middle schools should have a character that is unique—one that can be differentiated clearly from what goes on in either elementary schools or senior high schools. Program recommendations reflect a concern for providing an appropriate environment for young people between the ages of about 10 and 14. Typical suggestions for good middle school programming include the following:

- Providing instruction that connects to the real lives of students;
- Organizing learning experiences in ways that allow students to move and otherwise become physically engaged in what they are doing;
- Developing learning experiences that build student self-confidence by enabling them to achieve success;
- Grouping practices that feature cooperative learning;
- Giving instruction that features interdisciplinary teams and lessons drawing on multiple disciplines;

These students are enjoying some free time during lunch in a middle school cafeteria. Today, middle schools are the schools most students attend between their elementary and senior high school years.

- Having flexible scheduling;
- Organizing students into teacher advisory groups for the purpose of providing them with academic, social, and personal support;
- Providing programs for at-risk learners that maximize their potentials for success; and
- Providing an extensive activities program designed to involve students in both recreational and service opportunities.

Middle schools have gained tremendous popularity over the past 30 years. Today, there are many more middle schools than junior high schools. Our country's predominant school organizational pattern has become the 5–3–4 (5 elementary grades, 3 middle school grades, 4 high school grades).

Though middle schools have become common, specialists in the education of preadolescents and early adolescents recognize that many problems remain to be solved.

These schools seem to be doing a better job of providing environments that are sensitive to the social and emotional needs of the young people they serve. However, recommendations that middle schools provide instruction that is heavily interdisciplinary in nature have not been implemented as widely as some would hope. Another troubling area has to do with changes in the self-concept of female learners through their middle school years. Several studies have pointed out that eighth grade girls rate themselves lower than sixth grade girls on (1) their sense of self-confidence, and (2) the pride they take in their school work.

These problems are among the challenges that professionals working in the nation's middle schools will address in the years ahead. Despite these difficulties, most believe the middle school arrangement has proved its mettle and that it will be the institution of choice for serving young people between their elementary school and senior high school years.

Financing Schools

Schooling is big business. In one recent year, approximately $8,000 was spent for every enrolled student in the country (Snyder, 2000). This means that billions of dollars are expended each year to support public school programs. You may well ask, "Where does the money come from?"

Judging from the rhetoric of federal officials and campaign speeches from people seeking national office, you would think that the federal government plays a large role in financing public schools. It does not. In fact, the federal government is very much a minor player in this arena. In recent years, total federal support has accounted for only around 7 percent of total public expenditures on education. Further, the percentage of federal support has generally declined over the past 30 years. Today, state and local governments pay for most expenses associated with public education. In one recent year, states, on average, paid 48 percent of these costs, and local governments paid about 45 percent (Snyder, 2000).

Most money, about 60 percent, allocated to support schools goes to pay for instruction. This includes regular teaching in traditional classrooms as well as instructional services for learners with special needs. You may have heard people comment that "too much money is spent on school administration." In fact, administrative costs account for just a little over 8 percent of the costs of operating schools (CPRE, 1999).

One issue related to school financing you will encounter repeatedly throughout your career is that of equity. As the term relates to financial support of schools, the equity principle means that the financial resources to support students should not vary tremendously among school districts. In recent years, there have been contentious debates and court cases related to contentions that distributions of funds to schools in different school districts have not observed the equity principle.

Equity problems stem from a traditional delegation by state governments of authority to local school districts to raise money for schools by levying taxes on property. The problem is that the value of taxable property within different school districts often varies tremendously. Hence, when a school district with large numbers of students and a relatively low level of taxable property within its boundaries uses this approach to raise money, difficulties arise. If the tax rate is kept at a modest level, too little money comes in to provide adequate support for school programs. If a higher tax rate is set, then local citizens complain because they are taxed at higher rates than their neighbors in districts that have a higher value of taxable property. The politics of this situation means that low-wealth school districts have to keep their tax rates reasonably competitive with those of their more affluent neighbors. As a result, they often are strapped for cash, and students in these districts do not receive educational services as varied and of as high a quality as those fortunate enough to live in wealthier school districts.

State governments have tried to respond to this situation in several ways. One involves the establishment of something that often is called a *foundation program,* where the state provides additional funds to less wealthy school districts to enable them to improve the quality of their educational services. In practice, many state foundational programs have established support levels that are too low to provide the kind of help the poorest school districts require.

Another plan a few states have considered is the *guaranteed tax base* (GTB) approach. This scheme requires a state government to treat all taxable property in the state as part of a state-wide pool. The value of this property is allocated among individual school districts according to their enrollments. The idea is to put an equal amount of taxable property behind each learner in the state, regardless of where he or she lives.

Making changes in school funding practices is difficult. Almost any proposal for change requires funding arrangement that, if implemented, will drain resources from some school districts. What results is a political war between public representatives of districts that will gain and districts that will lose revenues. School districts that will potentially lose resources often have powerful legislators aligned with their interests. As a result, securing passage of legislation to achieve more equitable distributions of funds to support schools is extraordinarily difficult.

Violence in Schools

In recent years, images of schools as safe havens for students and teachers have been shattered by several tragic shootings. Deaths of students and teachers have focused unprecedented attention on the issue of violence in the schools. Today, people in all parts of the country are engaged in efforts to identify and implement workable solutions to this problem.

As you think about this issue, it's important to keep the problem in perspective. While everyone wants to make schools safer places, you need to understand that, despite the high profile school shootings that have been so widely reported in recent years, most people who spend their days in schools are not nearly so much at risk of experiencing violent behavior as are many others. Still, numbers are large enough to be of concern. In one recent year, about 149,000 teachers experienced an episode of violence at their work site (Warshol, 1998).

Your chances of being a victim of a violent crime in school are much less than the chances of people who work in retail sales. Police officers, taxi drivers, bartenders, gas station attendants, convenience store clerks, and mental health professionals are at more risk of experiencing a violent attack at work than are teachers at any level. Among teachers, middle school and junior high school teachers are at greatest risk. High school teachers are attacked at school only about half as often. Elementary school teachers experience the fewest attacks of any teacher group (Office of Safety and Health Administration, 1999). Though you should be concerned about the school violence issue, you also want to keep in mind that about 90 percent of the nation's schools that were recently surveyed reported that no violent crimes were committed on their campuses during the past school year (National Center for Education Statistics, 1998).

The type of violence a secondary school student is likely to experience at school is a physical fight. One recent survey found that over one-third of students nationwide were involved in a physical fight one or more times during a single year. Students during the last two years of high school were much less likely to be involved in fights than younger secondary schools students. (American Medical Association, 1999)

Fears stimulated by physical fighting and other concerns have prompted some students to bring weapons to school. A recent study found that almost one-fifth of the nation's students had brought a gun, knife, or club to school during the 30-day period preceding the survey (American Medical Association, 1999). There are particular concerns about young people who feel it necessary to carry guns for their own protection. They have been found to be three times more likely to commit a crime than students who do not own guns for the purpose of protecting themselves (Howell, 1998).

The fears some students experience lead them to seek safety by joining gangs. The culture of many gangs, in turn, supports physical confrontation and other approaches to violence (Howell, 1998). The paradox is that, in an effort to find safety and security by joining a gang, a young person often ends up embracing a subculture that prizes violence. Gang membership, too, increases the probability that a young person will have access to and abuse illegal drugs. Drug use, among other things, decreases the influence of traditional social controls, a circumstance that makes it psychologically easier for an individual to see violence as an acceptable behavioral option.

In response to concerns about weapon-bearing students, gang membership, and other conditions that increase the probability of violent behavior occurring in schools, educational leaders are developing plans to combat the problem. Indeed, an active national organization, the National School Safety Center, helps schools in this country and elsewhere create safe school environments. For more information, contact:

National School Safety Center
141 Duesenberg Drive, Suite 11
Westlake Village, CA 91362
Phone: (805) 373-9977
Web site: http://www.nssc1.org

MORE FROM THE WEB

Students and Schools

If you are interested in learning more about some of the issues raised in this chapter, you will find dozens of excellent information sources on the Web. Some examples are provided here.

American Academy of Child & Adolescent Psychiatry

http://www.aacap.org/

- This site includes a tremendous number of links to information related to emotional, behavioral, and intellectual development of young people. There is an entire section titled "Facts for Families and Other Resources" that treats topics such as mental illness symptoms in teenagers, violence, and the psychiatry of adolescents.

National Center for Children in Poverty

http://cpmcnet.columbia.edu/dept/nccp/index.html

- The National Center for Children in Poverty (NCCP) supports initiatives designed to reduce the poverty rate among young people and, thereby, to improve their life chances. You will find information here related to families and family support, welfare reform, and research on poverty. There is also an extensive listing of articles and newsletters that feature information about child poverty.

Adolescents and Violence

http://www.ama-assn.org/adolhlth/special/school.htm

- The American Medical Association (AMA) maintains this site. You will find here an extensive array of information sources featuring content related to youth safety and violence. Links allow you to easily access material from these sites. You will find content related to such issues as suicide, gun violence, early indicators of potentially violent behavior, and how you can help young people cope with disasters.

School Reform Networks and Associations

http://www.ed.gov/pubs/Idea_Planning/resource_6.html

- At this site you will find an extensive listing of organizations and groups with interests in improving schools. Material here is especially useful because there are thumbnail sketches of each group that outline its general areas of interest and scope of activity. In addition, you will find Web site addresses for each cited organization and group.

United States High Schools

http://www.edunet.ie/links/ushigh.html

- Hundreds of high schools now maintain their own Web pages. At this site, you will find direct links to home pages of high schools all over the country. You may be interested in seeing what individual high schools have chosen to say about themselves. If you visit a number of these sites, you may find some categories of information that most include and others that seem important only to a few schools.

National Middle School Association

http://www.nmsa.org/

- This is the home page of the National Middle School Association (NMSA). Members of this group are dedicated to improving middle schools and supporting the development of young adolescents. If you are interested in working with younger secondary-school students, you will find many links to additional useful information here.

Adolescence Directory On-Line

http://education.indiana.edu/cas/adol/adol.html

- This site provides an outstanding electronic guide to information related to adolescents. You will find links to topics including conflict and violence, mental health issues, health and health risk issues, and information for counselors of adolescents.

The *Safe Communities-Safe Schools* model developed in Colorado is typical of approaches taken in many parts of the country to create violence-free school environments. This model recommends that schools take actions related to five basic categories (Safe Communities–Safe Schools, 1999):

1. *Establish a Safe School Planning Team.* The idea here is to involve a broad spectrum of people from the community in the process of planning for a safe school environment.
2. *Conduct a School Site Assessment.* This activity seeks to identify any problems related to the school climate that might be negative enough to provide fertile ground for outbreaks of violent or unsafe behaviors.
3. *Develop Strategies and Implement Violence Prevention Problems to Address School Safety Concerns.* This component is the heart of the model. It requires implementation of approaches designed to do such things as (a) ensure opportunities for all students to be involved in positive, rewarding activities, (b) identify students who may be at risk of engaging in violent behaviors, (c) establish guidelines for behavior

that spell out rights and responsibilities of all members of the school community, (d) identify procedures that students and others can use to quickly and anonymously report impending outbreaks of violence, and (e) identify and implement procedures for controlling access to the building and for screening visitors.

4. *Establish a Social Support Team.* The purpose of the Social Support Team is to improve the social climate of the school. Members may include parents, teachers, administrators, students, counselors, mental health workers, and law enforcement officials.

5. *Develop a Crisis Response Plan.* This plan describes precisely what teachers and staff members should do if an emergency situation develops. The idea is to prevent panic and help education professionals deal quickly, efficiently, and appropriately with a serious problem when it arises.

What Are High-Quality Schools Like?

What are the characteristics of a high-quality school? If you asked a cross-section of people, you might or might not find patterns of agreement. If respondents spoke only about very general characteristics of good schools, you quite probably would find wide agreement on a number of points. For example, you might hear comments such as these:

- "Good schools respect and respond to the dignity of individual students."
- "Good schools help students develop tolerance for others."
- "Good schools produce students who are committed to democratic decision-making."
- "Good schools promote the idea that citizens should work together for the good of the total community."

On the other hand, if you pressed people to elaborate on the meaning of phrases contained within these broad statements, you might be surprised at the different, and often conflicting, answers you would get. People with different life experiences, with different cultural backgrounds, and from different social groups bring widely varied perspectives to bear when they consider qualities associated with good schools (Oakes, Quartz, Ryan, & Lipton, 2000). Conflicting views about what constitutes excellence mean that different people apply different standards when they are asked to rate the relative excellence of a program at a particular school. These disagreements result because large numbers of people subscribe to one of two incompatible conceptions of the reality of the school. These are:

- the consensus view of schools, and
- the conflict view of schools.

The Consensus View

You will find that people who commit to this position believe that most Americans subscribe to a common set of values. They contend that people in this country agree about more things than they disagree about. The notion that our present way of doing things is fair, good, and worthy of maintaining underpins the thinking of people who subscribe to this position. In their view the purpose of the school is to provide the intellectual talent needed to keep social institutions going in their present form.

There is an assumption that individuals start their school programs with relatively equal opportunities to succeed. Differences in their success as students come from individual effort. Economic rewards and high social status are thought to come to students who get good grades, qualify for admission to good colleges and universities, and develop the kinds of expertise our society appreciates. Good schools encourage students to achieve the kinds of academic success that, in their later years, will allow them to contribute to the nation's economic growth. Their success will help the entire country and result in improved standards of living for all.

Strong supporters of this position evaluate proposals for change in terms of their ability to promote and maintain existing social arrangements. For example, if there is evidence that more rigorous science, mathematics, and technology courses will provide better workplace opportunities for graduates, then such innovations are likely to be supported. If there is a suspicion that an innovation may be directed at altering basic social arrangements, then individuals who commit to the consensus view will be less likely to support it.

The Conflict View

Those who subscribe to the conflict view reject the assumption of the consensus position that there is broad agreement that present social arrangements are good and should be maintained. They argue that many present arrangements act to benefit some groups and to disadvantage or marginalize others. They tend to see our society not as a harmonious collection of individuals sharing common values but rather as an arena where competing groups compete for benefits. This situation tends to produce winners and losers, whose fate tends to be largely predetermined by the particular social, ethnic, or economic groups to which they belong.

People who subscribe to this position often see present school programs organized in ways that clearly provide more benefits to students from some groups than others. For example, secondary schools that offer classes in advanced mathematics may have adopted these programs to better serve the sons and daughters of highly educated parents who want to prepare them for positions in elite colleges and universities. Because school resources are limited, supporters of the conflict position contend that curricular decisions too often divert money away from needs of students from groups with little political or economic power. When this happens, school programs tend to perpetuate social differences across generations.

Proponents of the conflict position can be both receptive and resistant to change. Because of their view that many existing school programs do not deal fairly with all students, they often will listen attentively to suggestions for change. However, because their view of schools conditions them to look for ways in which programs advantage some students and disadvantage others, they are inclined to look carefully at change proposals to see whether, when implemented, they will provide more benefits to some students than to others.

CRITICAL INCIDENT

Would a High-Quality School
Support This Approach to Teaching?

Pam Estaban, principal at Mossman Middle School, believes that she heads a particularly outstanding school. She believes her teachers do an excellent job of presenting content in ways that engage students' interests and build their general enthusiasm for learning. She is especially pleased with the work of teachers in the math department.

However, not everyone shares her pleasure. Rose Larsen, mother of sixth grader Judith Larsen, made these comments recently during a conversation with Edwin McKenna, one of Mossman's math teachers":

> Mr. McKenna, I'm quite unhappy about what is going on in your classroom. I have to admit that Judith doesn't share my concerns. In fact, you're one of her favorite teachers . . . and, I'll have to agree, you have done a good job of helping her develop a good attitude about mathematics.
>
> But your approach bothers me. I keep hearing about all the time students spend working in groups and helping one another. Now, I know Judith is capable, and I think she likes being looked at as "the expert" when you involve the class in cooperative work. But, I don't think this is good either for Judith or for the other students in the long run. It is making the slower kids too dependent on the brighter ones. It tends to hold back the bright people because they have to spend too much of their time assisting those who "just don't get it."
>
> As you know, I'm an engineer. I hope Judith will think about this career when the time comes. I had to struggle through sophisticated mathematics courses to get my degree. Frankly, I had to do this by myself. In high school and college there is none of this group-hand-holding business. I'm afraid that Judith is going to lack the personal study habits she is going to need once she gets to high school. In addition, because this group arrangement fails to encourage her to master content beyond what is expected of everyone in the group, she's not going to enter high school as intellectually equipped as she should be.
>
> I'm here to ask you to give up this cooperative business and get back to teaching these students as individuals. This emphasis on process at the expense of substance has got to go. These kids need more "meat."

■ ■ ■

What are some values that are especially important to Judith's mother? How do these values shape her views of what should go on at a high-quality school? What things do you think are highly important to her? Given her priorities, do her comments make sense?

What are some priorities that you can infer from the decision of Mr. McKenna to use a lot of group work in his classes? What might his motives for this approach be? What do his actions suggest about the kinds of things that are important to him?

Are there ways in which differences in perspectives of Rose Larsen and John McKenna can be bridged? Is there an accommodation that might be made that takes into account important values of each? What are some of your suggestions for responding to this situation? What do your proposed solutions reveal about your own values and priorities?

Attempts to Describe High Quality Schools

In spite of difficulties associated with bridging widely divergent views about what constitutes excellent education, there have been several attempts to describe characteristics of high-quality schools. These descriptions have attempted to identify features that individuals who identify with both the consensus-view of schools and the conflict-view of schools will support. Two examples of these proposals are (1) the *Quality School* approach, based on the work of William Glasser (1998a; 1998b), and (2) the *Invitational Education* approach, based on the work of William Watson Purkey (1992; 1999).

Glasser's approach stresses the importance of building trustful, respectful relationships among all in the school. There is an emphasis on promoting learning at a high enough level to assure that students have a grasp of material that goes beyond the merely competent. Every student does some truly outstanding work each year. They are taught to think carefully about their choices and to recognize that consequences that come to them directly relate to decisions they have chosen to make. Further, students in high quality schools perform well on standardized tests and on university entrance examinations, and the school emphasizes their importance. Finally, teachers, students, parents and guardians, and administrators see the school as a joyful place.

Glasser's ideas are being implemented in many schools not only in the United States but in many foreign countries as well. If you are interested in learning more about Glasser's Quality School Program, contact:

The William Glasser Institute
22024 Lassen Street, Suite 118
Chatsworth, CA 91311
Phone: 1-800-899-0688
e-mail: wginst@iearthlink.net
Web site: http://www.wglasserinst.com/quality.htm

William Purkey's (1992, 1999) Invitational Education approach derives from *invitational theory.* Purkey points out that schools operate as a sophisticated signal system. Teachers and administrators generate signals that students "read." The building itself (how it is organized, the state of upkeep, and so forth) sends messages to students. The policies that the school has adopted are received and interpreted by students in ways that affect their reactions to the provided educational program. The nature of school programs . . . their purposes, their organizational structure, their assumptions about students and their lives . . . also communicate important messages to students. Finally, the processes a school adopts to manage students, programs, and other aspects of its operation collectively convey important information to students.

The Invitational Education approach encourages schools to look simultaneously at the kinds of messages being sent by people, buildings, policies, programs, and processes. The intent is to assure that students see these communications as welcoming and positive. When this happens, they see the school environment as supportive, and they are likely to respond better to the school program and to value it more highly. Many schools around the country have attempted to implement principles associated with Invitational Education. The International Alliance for Invitational Education supports these efforts. If you would like to know more about this initiative, contact:

International Alliance for Invitational Education
School of Education, The University of North Carolina at Greensboro
P.O. Box 26171
Greensboro, NC 27402-6171
web site: http://www.invitationaleducation.net/

Key Ideas in Summary

- The word *diversity* applies well to today's secondary schools. Today's students reflect the spectrum of differences found throughout our society. Students vary in terms of their physical characteristics, aspirations, intellectual abilities, interests, and values.
- Today nearly 40 percent of students in the schools belong to racial or ethnic minorities. Percentages tend to be much higher in central cities. Educators today are challenged to develop school programs responsive to the needs of students in these groups who, traditionally, have not done as well at school as white, non-Latino students. The number of students whose native language is not English is increasing in secondary school classrooms. Though their achievement scores relative to white, non-Latino students have been improving, educators still have much work to do to close the gap.
- Young people from economically impoverished families face many difficulties during their school years. They are less likely than other students to enjoy good health. They are more likely to have a learning disability. They are twice as likely to repeat a grade in school than non-poor young people.
- Today, more than two million secondary school students fall into one of 13 special education categories identified by the federal government. The category with the largest number of students includes young people with specific learning disabilities.
- Characteristics of students' families have changed over the years. Today, mothers of over two-thirds of the total school population are employed. Nearly one-third of the nation's children live in households headed by a single parent, usually the mother. The nature of families greatly influences how students perform at school. For example, young people with parents or guardians with more than a high school education do better than young people whose parents have had less formal schooling. Involvement of parents in school activities influence students' grade levels, general level of enjoyment of the school program, and level of participation in the extracurricular program.
- As they mature, secondary students experience sequential changes that affect their attitudes, interests, and personal concerns. For example, at certain stages of their lives, secondary students are greatly concerned about how their rate of physiological change compares to that of others in their group. Over time, their abilities to engage in sophisticated levels of thinking and to seek long-term goals increases.
- Through the years, there have been debates over whether the high school should be primarily a college-preparatory institution with a heavy emphasis on traditional academic subjects or whether it should be a "more practical" institution dedicated to

preparing young people for the world of work. A grand compromise to bridge these two perspectives was offered in the 1918 report of the National Education Association's Commission on the Reorganization of Secondary Education. This report laid out a number of cardinal principles that, collectively, became the basis for what has come to be known as the *comprehensive high school*. This term implies that the senior high school should be an institution directed at serving multiple purposes, including both traditional academics and preparation for the world of work.

■ Not everyone likes the comprehensive senior high school model. Theodore Sizer and his followers have organized the *Coalition of Essential Schools*. Sizer argues that the comprehensive high school presents students with fragmented, disjointed academic experiences. He makes a case for less is more, arguing that students should pursue a more limited number of subjects in much more depth. Another program designed to improve the comprehensive senior high school is the *Advanced Placement* program. Students enrolled in this program take rigorous college-level courses while still in high school and many colleges and universities give these students college credit or award them advanced basic academic standing based on this work. The *International Baccalaureate* is an established program that enables students from different countries to qualify for entry into top universities throughout the world.

■ For many years, people have debated about what kinds of schools and experiences are best for preadolescents and early adolescents (basically young people from about age 10 to about age 14). During the last part of the nineteenth century, more and more people recognized that there was a gap between the kinds of expertise students had at the end of their elementary school years and what they were expected to have as beginning high school students. The first new school type to arise out of this concern was the junior high school. In response to a belief that 10- to 14-year-old learners were not being well served by some junior high schools, interest in a new kind of school, the middle school, began to catch on in the 1960s. Proponents of middle schools have suggested that this school devote itself to programming that is specifically designed for young people in the transition-years between elementary school and senior high school.

■ Billions of dollars are spent each year on public education. Most money comes from state and local governments. Though federal officials often speak about improving the nation's schools, the federal government provides only about seven percent of the money required each year to support the schools.

■ Many people recognize that there are more dangers associated with public schools today than there used to be. Though incidences of school violence draw well-deserved attention, in general, violent crimes occur much less frequently in schools than in other places, for example, retail establishments. The most common kind of violence that occurs in school is the physical fight.

■ It is difficult to define qualities of a "high-quality" school. This is true because people have different beliefs about what schools should do. For example, some people suggest that most Americans subscribe to a common set of values and that it is the job of the schools simply to pass them on intact to subsequent generations. Others contend that conflict rather than consensus more properly describes our society. People with this orientation tend to look somewhat suspiciously at individual school programs because they may serve the narrow interests of one group more adequately than another. Despite these difficulties, there have been attempts to define general characteristics of excellent schools. William Glasser and William Watson Purkey have done important work in this area.

Reflections

1. What are some characteristics of today's diverse student population?

2. What are some special problems facing students whose first language is not English?

3. Name some particular patterns often observed among children from economically deprived families that you are not so likely to see among students from more affluent families.

4. There is evidence that family backgrounds of students affect their attitudes toward school as well as their academic performance. Individuals you will teach have no choice in the matter of families. Given this reality, what are some things you might do, for example, to work with students from families where no parent or guardian has even a high-school level education?

5. What are some patterns of development of young adolescents? How do you think they should affect practices of teachers who are employed in middle schools and junior high schools?

6. Describe alternative purposes for senior high schools that have been debated over the years. What are your own feelings on these issues, and what personal experiences have helped shape your attitudes?

7. What explains the rapid growth in the number of middle schools and the parallel decline in the number of junior high schools over the last two decades? Do you expect this trend to continue? Why, or why not?

8. Candidates for important positions often make strong public commitments to "improving education." Is the federal government a major player when it comes to providing financial support for public schools? Would you expect the federal government to play a larger or smaller role in the future, and why do you think so?

9. How dangerous are public schools, and what are some actions schools and school districts have taken to respond to this problem?

10. Why is it so difficult to describe a "high-quality" school? What are some of William Glasser's and William Watson Purkey's suggestions to develop these kinds of schools? Do you agree with their recommendations?

Learning Extensions

1. To help you learn more about today's diverse student body, invite a secondary teacher to your class who teaches a course that draws a typical cross-section of students. (Classes that are required for high school graduation tend to do this.) Ask the

teacher to describe the variety of interests, abilities, and attitudes of individuals in one of his or her classes. You might also wish to ask this teacher about specific instructional modifications that are made to respond to the needs of diverse learners.

2. Go to the Web, find a good search engine, and enter the term *school violence*. Prepare a paper for your instructor that focuses on examples of what individual school districts are doing to respond to this problem. If you uncover evaluations of these efforts, include this information in your paper as well.

3. Organize a group of students in your class who are interested in working with middle school students. With others in the group, seek out as much information as you can find about development of early adolescents. Based on this information, prepare a group presentation on this topic: "Promoting Success in the Middle School: Needed Characteristics of Teachers and Promising Instructional Approaches."

4. For most of this century, there have been debates over how responsibilities of teaching learners in grades K to 12 should be divided among different school types. Many schemes have been devised. Some of these have been based on developmental levels of learners. Others have been designed with a view to optimizing learning of academic content. Frankly, too, some have been created simply as a matter of administrative convenience. Suppose you had an opportunity to devise a system of schools to instruct learners in grades K to 12. How many school types would you have? What grade levels would each serve? What would be your rationale for making these choices? Prepare a paper that includes your responses to these questions.

5. Do some additional reading on Theodore Sizer's ideas for reforming secondary education. Your library will have some information. You might also consider writing to the Coalition of Essential Schools. (The address is provided in the chapter.) Once you feel you have a good understanding of Sizer's ideas, interview a secondary school principal. Ask him or her to comment on difficulties that might be encountered in an effort to incorporate Sizer's ideas into his or her school. Present a report of your interview to your instructor or to the class.

6. Go to Merrill Education's Link to General Methods Resources site at this URL: http://www.prenhall.com/methods-cluster/ At the bottom of the page select "parents and the community" as your topic and click the "begin" button. This will take you to the "Overview" page. On the left side, click on "Web Links." On the Web Links page click on "general." Follow links that will give you information related to: "Building Parent-School Partnership." Use information you gather as the basis of a paper you prepare focusing on this topic.

7. Go to Merrill Education's Link to General Methods Resources site at this URL: http://www.prenhall.com/methods-cluster/ At the bottom of the page select "policies and handbooks" as your topic and click the "begin" button. This will take you to the "Overview" page. On the left side, click on "Web Links." On the Web Links page, click on "school security." Take notes, and use the information you find as the basis for a chart you prepare titled "Things Schools Can Do to Make Schools Safer Environments."

References

Advanced placement program. (2000). [http://www.collegeboard.org/ap/]

American Medical Association. (1999). *Back to school: Safe schools and violence prevention.* [http://www.ama-assn.org/adolhlth/special/school.htm]

Barry, T. N. (1961). *Origins and development of the American public high school in the nineteenth century.* Stanford, CA: Unpublished doctoral dissertation, Stanford University.

Brooks-Gunn, J., & Duncan, G. J. (1997). The effects of poverty on children. *Children and Poverty*, 7(2), pp. 55–71.

Consortium for Policy Research in Education at the University of Wisconsin-Madison (CPRE). (1999). Traditional resource reallocation and use: Uses of the educational dollar-expenditure patterns. [http://www.wcer.wisc.edu/cpre/Finance/Finance/tradresource.htm]

Elkind, D. (1981). *Children and adolescents: Interpretive essays on Jean Piaget* (3rd ed.). New York: Oxford University Press.

Gerald, D. E., & Hussar, W. J. (Eds.). (1999). *Projections of education statistics to 2009.* Washington, DC: National Center for Education Statistics.

Glasser, W. (1998a). *The quality school: Managing students without coercion* (3rd ed.). New York: Harper Perennial.

Glasser, W. (1998b). *The quality school teacher: Specific suggestions for teachers who are trying to implement the lead-management ideas of the quality school in their classrooms* (rev. ed.). New York: Harper Perennial.

Howell, J. C. (1998, August). Youth gangs: An overview. *Juvenile Justice Bulletin*, pp. 1–16.

Lounsbury, J. H. (1992). Perspectives on the middle school movement. In J. L. Irvin (Ed.), *Transforming middle level education: Perspectives and possibilities* (pp. 3–15). Needham Heights, MA: Allyn & Bacon.

Lounsbury, J. H., & Vars, G. E. (1978). *Curriculum for the middle years.* New York: Harper & Row.

Mazzeo, J., Carlson, J. E., Voelkl, K. E., & Lutkus, A. D. (2000). *Increasing the participation of special needs students in NAEP.* National Assessment of Educational Progress. [http://nces.ed.gov/nationsreportcard/pubs/main1996/2000473.shtml]

National Center for Children in Poverty. (1999, September 30). *New census data show that child poverty rate continues to lag behind other key economic indicators.* [http://cpmcnet.Columbia.edu/dept/nccp/cps99pr.html]

National Center for Education Statistics. (1996). *National household education survey.* Washington, DC: NCES.

National Center for Education Statistics. (1998). *Violence and discipline problems in U.S. public schools: 1996–1997.* Washington, DC: NCES. [http://www.nssc1.org/studies/studies/nces98.htm]

National Clearinghouse for Bilingual Education. (1998). *Summary report of the states' limited English proficient students and available education programs and services, 1996–1997.* [http://www.ncbe.gwu.edu/ncbepubs/seareports/96–97/part1.htm]

National Education Association. (1893). *Report of the Committee of Ten on secondary school studies.* Washington, DC: National Education Association.

Oakes, J., Quartz, K. H., Ryan, S., & Lipton, M. (2000). Becoming good American schools: The struggle for civic virtue in education reform. *Phi Delta Kappan*, 81(8), pp. 568–575.

Office of Safety and Health Administration. (1999, August). *Workplace violence.* [http://www.osha.gov/oshinfor/priorities/violence.html]

Parrish, T. B. (2000, Winter). Special education—At what cost to general education? *CSEF Resource*, pp. 2–3, 6.

Popper, S. H. (1967). *The American middle school: An organizational analysis.* Waltham, MA: Blaisdell.

Purkey, W. W. (1992). An introduction to invitational theory. *Journal of Invitational Theory and Practice, 1*(1), pp. 5–16.

Purkey, W. W. (1999). *What students say to themselves: Internal dialogue and school success.* Thousand Oaks, CA: Corwin Press.

Safe Communities–Safe Schools. (1999). [http://www.Colorado.EDU/cspv/safeschools/model/htm]

Sizer, T. (1984). *Horace's compromise: The dilemma of the American high school.* Boston: Houghton Mifflin.

Sizer, T. (1992). *Horace's school: Redesigning the American high school.* Boston: Houghton Mifflin.

Sizer, T. (1996). *Horace's hope: What works for the American high school.* Boston: Houghton Mifflin.

Snyder, T. D. (Ed.). (2000). *Digest of education statistics, 1999.* Washington, DC: National Center for Education Statistics.

Tanner, D., & Tanner, L. N. (1980). *Curriculum development: Theory into practice* (2nd ed.). New York: Macmillan.

Toepfer, Jr., C. F. (1992). Middle level school curriculum: Defining the elusive. In J. L. Irvin (Ed.), *Transforming middle level education: Perspectives and possibilities* (pp. 205–243). Needham Heights, MA: Allyn & Bacon.

Warshol, G. (1998, July). Workplace violence, 1992–1996. *Bureau of Justice Statistics: Special Report.*

Wirt, J., & Snyder, T. (Eds.). (1999). *The condition of education, 1999.* Washington, DC: National Center for Education Statistics.

3

Reflective Teaching

This chapter will aim to

- define *reflective teaching*;

- define *constructivism*;

- describe the four elements of the decision-making processes of reflective teachers;

- point out how the following affect a teacher's classroom performance: *pedagogical personality*, *pedagogical assumptions*, and *pedagogical repertoire*;

- describe strengths and weaknesses of various sources of information about effective teaching and learning;

- point out some limitations of learning theories as sources of information teachers can use as bases of lessons for students in specific classes;

- describe how teachers' expectations of students may influence their instructional practices;

- define *fluid planning*, and state why it is necessary; and

- explain how *professional-development portfolios* can help teachers to be more effective.

Introduction

Since you are interested in a career as a secondary school teacher, let's focus on teaching. Suppose you have just been employed to teach tenth grade world history (or math, English, or science—choose your own subject). Where will you begin? How will you approach your task?

Some of you may smile and say to yourself, "I'm a history major. In high school, I had an outstanding world history teacher. I'll begin by following his/her example." Being knowledgeable in the subject is certainly an important prerequisite for teaching success, but it doesn't help you make decisions about where to start, what to include, and how to make your subject meaningful to a particular group of students. What if they don't share your interest?

Your intent to follow the example of one of your own outstanding teachers may be a good start, but this approach presents you with certain problems. For one thing, you and your model teacher are different people. You do not share the same experiences, personality, or knowledge of this individual. In addition, the students in your classroom may be quite different from those taught by your model. Even in the unlikely event that you were able to follow patterns established by this teacher perfectly, students you teach may well not react to your instruction as you remember yourself and others reacting to your model's instruction.

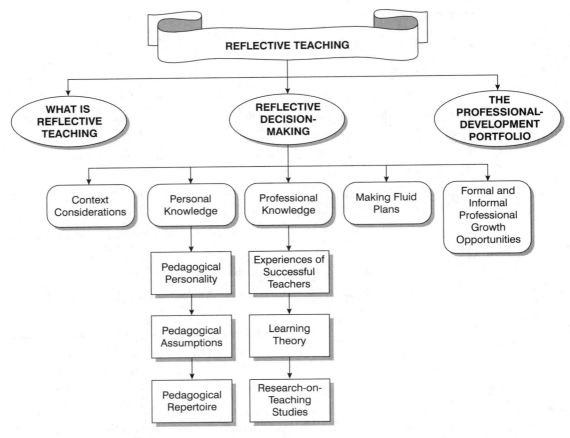

Figure 3–1
Graphic Organizer

If you decide not to follow the example of one of your own teachers, you may decide to simply follow suggestions provided in the teacher's guide that accompanies the text you are using. This approach presumes that teaching is simply a matter of finding the right "recipe." Once it is located, all you need to do is follow the steps, and all your students will learn. Not true. Teaching has little in common with work on an assembly line. Students are not inert raw materials who will eagerly and passively await your attempts to "mold" them into predetermined final products.

If teaching were like manufacturing, you would reject raw materials (students) with flaws that prevented them from benefiting from your actions. That is not how education functions. As a teacher, you have to accept all students. It is a violation of professional ethics to deny instruction to anyone who fails to conform to an expectation you might have that they should come to your classes enthusiastic about your subject and eager to learn. If the motivation is not there, it is your responsibility to do whatever you can to ignite student interest and provide conditions that give every member of your class a legitimate chance to achieve success.

Because of differences among students and because of your obligation to respond to the needs of all of them, simply following suggestions in a teacher's guide will not suffice. Recommendations typically will have been developed by people who do not know your personal characteristics and who also lack information about your students and your community. In spite of these difficulties, there have been numerous attempts throughout educational history to develop "teacher proof" programs or prescriptions that, if followed religiously by teachers, would all but guarantee high-levels of student learning. Not surprisingly, educational history is also replete with multiple examples of failures of these attempts to ignore differences among teachers, students, and settings.

What you need to recognize is that teaching is not a technical act but a professional one. It requires you to engage in decision-making based on knowledge that takes into account unique circumstances. You must consider the nature of the students you are teaching, their previous knowledge, aspirations, motivations, and attitudes. You need to know your own attitudes, beliefs, and level of knowledge of your subject. In addition, you need to understand alternative approaches to teaching and when and how to use them. Finally, you need to be sensitive to the context of your teaching. You need to ask yourself some important questions:

- What are the goals of the curriculum?
- What are the expectations of parents?
- What are the norms and values of the community and the school? (Henderson, 1996)

The need to respond to these questions points out the importance of your becoming a *reflective teacher* who can synthesize multiple variables into a workable plan.

What Is Reflective Teaching?

Reflective teaching is based on the psychological model of *constructivism*. Constructivism holds that human beings build knowledge. Knowledge does not consist of a set of facts or concepts waiting to be discovered. It is created when people seek to bring meaning to their experience (Zahorik, 1995). This means that learning how to teach cannot be reduced to a set of procedures that you can apply effectively in all situations. You bring a set of personal experiences and beliefs to the task of learning how to teach. How you interpret information about teaching will be different from those around you. What you see as relevant may be perceived as irrelevant by another. In order for you to develop as a professional, you need to be able to reflect on your beliefs and theories and check their validity.

Preparing to teach, then, does not involve collecting a list of "how tos." Rather, your task is to master techniques that will help you make sense out of your experiences. New information you learn should present you with alternatives and should challenge you to test your assumptions and beliefs. If you are open to new information and are willing to engage in reflection, then professional growth is possible.

Because humans construct knowledge, it is conjectural and fallible and grows through exposure. This means that knowledge is never stable. Indeed, it is constantly changing. Your understanding of teaching will be continuously altered as you learn from new experiences. This process of non-stop professional renewal energizes teachers. Members of our profession never "know all there is to know" about teaching.

Reflective teaching builds on the concept of *reflection*. As applied to education, reflection refers to your ability as a teacher "to reflect thoughtfully on the conditions at hand and respond appropriately in the best interest of the learner" (Rogers & Freiberg, 1994, p. 349).

James Henderson (1992), a leading proponent of reflective teaching, points out that good reflection takes the form of a spirited internal debate. This internal debate leads you to hypothesis formulating. As you weigh and debate alternative approaches to responding to an instructional task, you formulate a hypothesis concerning what you predict will work with your students. The results of your thinking become your teaching plan. Henderson (1996) suggests that decision-making processes of reflective teachers include these four elements:

1. *Decisions are sensitive to the context of the situation.* Learning does not take place in a vacuum. It occurs in the context of a specific school in a particular community during a certain time of the year. Schools and parents have expectations. Your students may come from families with few resources or abundant resources. The peer groups within the school have certain norms and sanctions for those who choose to ignore them. The students may be concerned in the fall with trying to become a part of a group while in the spring they might be consumed with thinking about summer vacation. Their moods change according to things they are experiencing in their personal lives. They simply do not leave all of their experiences and emotions at the classroom door.

2. *Decisions are guided by a cycle of fluid planning.* As a teacher, you face an interesting dilemma. On the one hand, you have to plan to achieve success. On the other hand, you are working with unpredictable human beings. Even your best plans, those that worked last period, may not necessarily work this period. What is the solution? It is certainly not to give up planning. Rather, you have to engage in fluid planning. This means that you have to be ready to modify plans when unexpected conditions arise. It sometimes is difficult to see that this is something excellent teachers do routinely. What you are likely to see in a visit to their classrooms is a seamless flow of orderly instruction. What you ordinarily don't see are the minute-by-minute decisions that the teacher is making.

3. *Decisions are informed by professional and personal knowledge that is critically examined.* In order to make good decisions, you need to have a good knowledge base. You need to be aware of the possible reasons learning occurs. You need to know about alternative approaches to teaching your content and the possible consequences of these approaches. However, beyond just having a lot of background about teaching and learning, you have to constantly reflect on or examine your decisions. What were your reasons for making a particular decision? Were they valid? Did you overlook important information that should have been considered?

This means that you subject your personal and professional knowledge base to an ongoing critical examination.

4. *Decisions are enhanced by both formal and informal professional growth opportunities.* As a reflective teacher, you function as a lifelong learner who is constantly seeking new knowledge. You need to discover sources of information that will help you to grow professionally. These might be formal opportunities such as additional coursework, or they might come to you in informal ways. For example, you might gain important insights into your local community by cooperating with area residents on an important neighborhood project.

Judy Eby (1998) proposes a model of reflective teaching based on Dewey's ideas (1933) of reflective thinking. This model focuses on active, persistent, and careful thinking that takes into account evidence that is synthesized into action (Eby, 1998, p. 8). Specifically, Eby suggests that successful reflective teachers are:

- *Active* people who energetically seek solutions to problems rather than passive people who ignore them or rely on tradition and imitation as guides to their instructional practices;
- *Persistent* people who are undaunted in their search for successful responses to instructional challenges and who are not satisfied with superficial or simple solutions;
- *Careful* practitioners who reflect a commitment to the ethical and moral dimensions of teaching as they keep an unwavering focus on students' needs rather than their own;
- Individuals who give *thoughtful consideration to evidence* as they review, study, and reconsider what has occurred in the classroom for the purpose of revising practices in ways that will better serve students' needs.

As a reflective teacher, you function as a hypothesis-tester. Based on your own past experiences and your knowledge and intuition about capacities of your students, you devise an instructional strategy. As you implement it (and after), you check the accuracy of your assumptions. You might ask yourself questions such as these:

- Were my pre-conceptions about what might be effective correct? If not, why not?
- Were there parts of the lesson that worked particularly well? If so, how might I capitalize on these successes in preparing other lessons?
- Were there a few weak spots in a generally good lesson? If so, how might I fix them?

This kind of systematic review helps you keep focused on student understanding. Researchers have found that effective teachers spend considerable time thinking about impact-on-student issues as they reflect on their own instructional practices. Less effective teachers tend to focus on issues associated with relatively superficial events that interrupt the flow of their instruction (for example, announcements coming in unexpectedly over a speaker system) rather than on components of classroom instruction that provide important learning benefits to students (Reynolds, 1992). In other words, effective teachers use more important, student-learning-related criteria as they assess the adequacy of their instruction.

A key to your development as an effective reflective teacher is to "do something" with your conclusions once you have thought carefully about how well a lesson has served your students. You want to put new insights to work as you plan new learning experiences for members of your class. It does no good whatsoever to think carefully about what has happened and then simply repeat instructional practices that did not work particularly well the first time. A department head one of the authors knows mentioned a comment she made to a particularly ineffective teacher who went through the motions of thinking about how her lessons were being received by students (generally not well), carefully diagnosing problem areas, and then making absolutely no modifications in her instructional program. In a conversation with the department head, the teacher said: "I should be getting better. After all, I've had five years' teaching experience."

The department head replied, "No, you haven't. You just repeated your first year of teaching five times!" This comment may have been a bit harsh, but it underscores the point that simply *thinking* about how your lessons have gone is not enough; to grow as an effective, reflective practitioner you have to *act* on your conclusions. Such action over time adds to your professional knowledge base and is a key element in your professional growth (Reynolds, 1992).

Reflective Decision-Making

Combining James Henderson's (1996) reflective-teaching decision-making processes with Judy Eby's (1998) reflective-teaching dimensions results in a framework for putting reflective teaching into action. This framework suggests that, as you seek to become a more effective reflective teacher, you need to commit to:

- using context considerations,
- using personal knowledge,
- using professional knowledge,
- making fluid plans, and
- committing to formal and informal professional growth opportunities.

Context Considerations

In order to achieve success, you need to actively and carefully consider elements of the context that will influence how you teach and how your students learn. Successful teaching requires more than just walking into a classroom and implementing a generic set of lesson plans. The most significant variable of all is the nature of your students.

Students are not empty vessels or blank slates who walk into your classroom eager to be filled with knowledge (Henderson, 1996). Young people in a typical classroom are incredibly diverse. You can expect some who are eager to learn, and some who are not. Certain individuals will have a previous history of success, and others a history of failure. Many students will view your subject as relevant; some others may view it as boring. Some students may come from homes where they have been provided with considerable support and assistance; others will come from homes where indifference seems to rule. You may have some students for whom English is a second language.

As you begin planning, you need to think about answers to these questions:

- What are your students' hopes, dreams, and aspirations?
- What is their history of success?
- What is the previous knowledge of the students?
- What are their attitudes toward the subject?
- How powerful are the peer groups and what are the prevailing norms of the peer group about education in general and this subject in particular?
- What are their interests, and what motivates them?
- What are their cultural backgrounds?

Actively pursuing the answers to these questions means that you must spend considerable time and energy observing students, speaking to them, diagnosing their previous knowledge, conducting interest surveys, reviewing records, and talking with other professionals in the school. You will not be able to gather all of this information before you begin teaching. You will need to continue gathering this information throughout your career. Your students will change from year to year. You are likely even to see important student differences in the various classes you might teach during a given year.

 CRITICAL INCIDENT

Somehow, I'm Not Connecting

Jared North, a first-year social studies teacher at Cotton Mather Senior High School, poured a cup of coffee and slumped into a chair in the departmental office. He looked wearily across the room at Ramona Reyes, the long-time head of the social studies department.

"Rough day?" Ramona asked.

"Not one of my greatest," Jared admitted. "You just wouldn't *believe* some of the answers I got on my short essay question."

"Right," Ramona acknowledged with a grin. "I'm sure my shock will be utter, total, complete. Nothing like you've seen has ever before been witnessed in the annals of public education. If these answers are made public, *surely* the very foundations of our civilization will be at risk! Come on, Jared, get real. All of us get strange answers from kids all the time."

"Well, OK," admitted Jared, "this may not be all that unusual. But, damn, it's discouraging. We've been studying the Civil War and the campaign leading up to the Battle of Gettysburg for a solid week. I just can't understand where some of these kids are coming from. Some of their answers don't make any sense at all."

"Give me a 'for instance'," asked Ramona. "Maybe that will shed a little light on what's going on."

"OK," Jared replied. "I asked a pretty straightforward question: 'Why did Lee take the army into Pennsylvania?' I got some just crazy answers. One kid said that Lee went there because the other Confederate generals were busy elsewhere. Another one said Lee knew that Quakers who opposed war had settled Pennsylvania and that he felt no one there would fire a shot at his troops once they crossed the Pennsylvania border. Another person said that Lee might have had relatives in Pennsylvania and that he had personal reasons for going there. Someone else actually wrote that fodder for horses was known to be good in Pennsylvania and that's why Lee took his men there."

"And, I take it," Ramona asked, "that these answers don't have much to do with what you were discussing in class?"

"Absolutely nothing!" replied Jared.

"OK, let's think about these answers. But, first of all, tell me something. How did you give your students the question? I mean, did you give it to them orally, or was it written on the board or on a paper that you gave to each student?" asked Ramona.

"I wrote it on the board. The students wrote their answers in class on paper I gave them," answered Jared, shaking his head and wondering why Ramona was interested in this issue.

"All right, let's think about this," Ramona continued. "You know, Jared, written language doesn't communicate as clearly as spoken language. It lacks the inflections and emphases we give individual words when we speak that add to the clarity of what we're trying to say. When your students read your question, they probably put their own inflections on your written words. These could have given your question a different meaning than you had intended. There are many ways your question might have been spoken. Let's look at some of these. Now help me out, the exact wording of your question was 'Why did Lee take the army into Pennsylvania?' Is that right?"

"Yes," Jared acknowledged. "That's exactly what I put on the board."

"Here are some different ways individual students might have read your question: '*Why* did Lee take the army into Pennsylvania?' A student who read the question this way, probably would have focused on the reasons, motives, and so forth for Lee's actions. This is probably what you wanted.

"But, another student could have read the question as 'Why did *Lee* take his army into Pennsylvania?' Read in this way, the question seems to be asking why Lee as opposed to someone else took the army into Pennsylvania. A student who interpreted the question in this way would tend to focus on other people who might have taken the army and why, in the end, Lee led the army to Pennsylvania.

"Still, another student could have read the question as 'Why did Lee take his army into *Pennsylvania?*' Read in this way, the focus of your question seems to focus on special characteristics of Pennsylvania that convinced Lee to take his army there. Again, this interpretation would prompt a student to answer your question in a certain way."

"That just blows me away, Ramona. I thought I was asking a really simple question. So how do I keep this kind of problem from happening again?"

"There's no simple answer. There is no 'silver bullet' out there that will slay every instructional problem. In fact, that's one of the difficulties we've had in this business. People keep forgetting that we deal with individuals and keep looking for a one-fits-all approach to teaching. What you need to keep in mind is that each of your kids has a special set of prior experiences. You need to be careful about dismissing an answer that you get that seems 'strange,' 'bizarre,' or 'totally off base.' Often there is an internal logic to what students tell us in their answers. But, we can't know what this logic is until we really know our students well. That's the real key. Know your kids, how they think, what is important to them, and how they 'make sense of the world.' When you do that, you'll be a lot less astounded by the responses you get on your tests."

■   ■   ■

What steps should Jared take next? How can he go about finding out more about each of his students? Are some students likely to have values that lead them to think some things not so important (or, in some cases, more important) to them as they are to Jared? If so, what use might Jared make of this information? What does he need to do to make his instruction more responsive to his students' needs? Where should he seek information about possible instructional responses he might make? Who are some other people whose advice he might seek?

You must carefully consider the information and evidence you gather from these inquiries. Is the information reliable? Are you making unfounded assumptions or stereotyping certain types of students? Gathering data is only the first step. Thoughtful and careful consideration of the information is required if it is to be of value.

Another key context variable is the school itself. Characteristics of individual schools vary enormously. Even those in the same district with similar student populations might often provide quite different contexts for teaching and learning. One way to understand these differences is to think about each school as having a unique culture. Individual schools have their own norms, values, and sanctions that influence both the teachers and the students.

The culture or environment of your school can affect your success as a teacher. To gain some insight into the special culture of your school, you might seek answers to questions such as these:

- How good are relationships between teachers and administrators?
- Are teachers and administrators generally optimistic or generally pessimistic?
- Do teachers in the school believe that they can achieve success with their students?
- Do teachers in the building work comfortably together?
- What kinds of non-academic programs does the school have in place for the students?
- Do students take pride in the school?
- Is the physical plant kept in good order?
- Is the school a place where individuals feel safe, both physically and psychologically?

- What resources are available for teachers to use to supplement and support their classroom instruction?

Clearly, some answers to these questions will highlight conditions that may make it difficult for you to be successful. For example, it is hard for students to concentrate on learning if they are worried about their safety. If access to the Internet is difficult, then there are constraints on teachers' abilities to plan lessons that depend on information available only on the World Wide Web. The physical environment of the school can also undermine your well-intentioned efforts to serve students well. In places where there are out-of-date textbooks, leaking roofs, poor lighting, and overcrowded classrooms, students' performance levels are likely to suffer. Finally, if faculty members do not get along or if there is tension between teachers and administrators, issues associated with smoothing difficult interpersonal relations problems may divert attention from providing optimal learning experiences for students.

An additional element of the school context that you should consider has to do with what school leaders expect of teachers. What are you supposed to achieve with your students? How will your success be measured? What support will be provided to you if you need help? What and how you teach will be influenced by the school's expectations and by its processes for evaluating your effectiveness. If your success is going to be measured by how well your students perform on certain standardized tests, you will probably feel constrained to prepare lessons that provide content knowledge that has a high probability of being assessed on these exams.

In summary, school contexts affect both students and teachers. For example, differences in school cultures mean that practices that may bring you a great deal of praise in one school because they are highly consistent with the school's culture may not be appreciated at another school with a culture that values different patterns of teacher behavior.

In addition to the student context and the school context, you also need to be aware of how the community context might affect what you do. In general, teachers tend to be most successful in settings with a tradition of positive, supportive community-school relationships. In places where community members for the most part take pride in their schools, teachers tend to feel more validated and appreciated than in settings where many people are inclined to either be indifferent or even somewhat disparaging in their view of local educators and their work.

Community priorities and values affect the entire educational enterprise. In response to this reality, it makes sense for you to learn as much as you can about the community where your school is located. This task will require some real effort, particularly if you find yourself teaching in an urban school that may be located in an area far removed from your personal residence. Students attending your school may manifest behavior patterns and reflect attitudes that will make sense to you only if you understand the residential patterns, demographics, religious preferences, norms, values, and other characteristics that go together to create the local community culture. You might begin by seeking answers to questions such as these:

- What is the ethnic and socioeconomic composition of the community?
- What are the major opportunities and challenges in the community?
- What are the hopes and desires of the community for the children?

- What opportunities are provided in the community for the students to be involved in local activities?
- What are the expectations of the community for the school?
- Do community members view the school as supportive or threatening?
- What specific examples are there of community involvement in the schools?

Careful consideration of these questions can contribute to understandings that will help you understand some of the student attitudes and behaviors you will see in your classes. This information can assist you in the process of making instructional decisions that are appropriate to the needs of your students. Instructional decisions that are made in light of information about community characteristics enhance students' chances for learning. In turn, students who learn feel good about themselves, reflect positive attitudes back to the community, and act to enhance your credibility as a professional educator.

Personal Knowledge

Decisions you make as a teacher are filtered through your own beliefs and understandings. Some of these you will have developed as a consequence of your fundamental personal values. Others will be associated with some of your general personality characteristics. Still others will tie closely to the particular store of knowledge you have acquired through formal academic training and in other ways.

What should you know about yourself as you consider your role as a teacher? One authority who has investigated this question suggests you should think about information related to these three categories (Millies, 1992):

- Pedagogical personality,
- Pedagogical assumptions, and
- Pedagogical repertoire.

Pedagogical Personality

Pedagogical personality is a term used to refer to your self-concept, confidence, and bias in terms of how these characteristics affect your interactions with students. To gain an appreciation of your pedagogical personality, ask yourself these questions:

- What do I believe about myself and my abilities as a teacher?
- How well do I know my subject?
- How confident am I in my ability to control members of the class?
- What are my biases regarding what a teacher "ought to be like"?

Pedagogical Assumptions

The phrase *pedagogical assumptions* refers to the basic values and beliefs that guide teachers' practices in the classroom. Questions that you might answer as part of a self-diagnostic exercise focused on this dimension include:

- What is the purpose of education?
- What do I believe about teaching?
- How do I feel about students from different social, economic, and ethnic groups?
- What learning principles are most important and should guide my instruction?

Answers to these questions will help explain how you organize for instruction and interact with students.

Pedagogical Repertoire

The term *pedagogical repertoire* refers to teachers' knowledge of and appreciation for alternative approaches to managing students and introducing content. Questions such as these provide insights into the nature of your own pedagogical repertoire:

- What are the best approaches to managing students in the classroom?
- What alternatives are available to me to teach this content?
- In which instructional approaches do I have the most confidence?
- What are some of my ideas for motivating members of this class?
- With which instructional techniques am I not comfortable?
- Of the instructional approaches I know and value, which one (or ones) make the most sense given what I must do next?

The act of answering questions associated with pedagogical personality, pedagogical assumptions, and pedagogical repertoire can help you think through alternative approaches to teaching specific content to specific students. Thinking about possible responses challenges assumptions and encourages thought about choices you might make when several options seem to have promise. The hope is that, over time, this process will broaden your willingness to try new things. The problems some teachers face are a result of the untested assumptions they hold that prevent them from choosing potentially successful instructional and management approaches.

Professional Knowledge

In addition to personal knowledge, reflective teaching requires you to have professional knowledge related to basic principles of teaching and learning. There are several sources of information about this kind of professional knowledge. These include:

- Experiences of successful teachers,
- Learning theory, and
- Research-on-teaching studies.

Experiences of Successful Teachers

You can sometimes learn about these experiences by consulting directly with a successful teacher. This kind of exchange may well take place during your student teaching semester when you are likely to have opportunities to work with one or more especially effective teachers. Information about practices of outstanding teachers sometimes is reported in printed materials. One particularly good title is *Teacher Lore: Learning from our Own Experiences* (Schubert & Ayers, 1992).

While you can learn much from reports of experiences of successful teachers, it is a mistake to rely *only* on professional judgment as you seek to broaden your knowledge of teaching. For example, some outstanding teachers have developed patterns gradually over the years that have become so embedded in their own personalities that they may be unable to tell you how they operate in the classroom. In response to the question "Why did you do that?" they may just respond, "I can't really tell you; it just felt right."

Another obvious limitation on professional judgment as a source of information is that each person has a unique personality and style. Something that works splendidly for another teacher may be a disaster when you try it.

Finally, professional judgment sometimes is just plain wrong. Behaviors that may seem right to a given individual and that may even have a lot of intuitive logic behind them may be undesirable. For example, common sense would seem to dictate that the more praise a teacher gives to a student, the better that student's academic performance will be. Researchers have found that this is not true. In fact, praise that is not tied clearly to a specific correct accomplishment with a given academic task may have little or no impact on students' learning (Good & Brophy, 2000; Levin & Long, 1981).

Learning Theory

Learning theory is another source you can go to for information on teaching and learning. Individual learning theories explain relations among variables in the teaching-learning process. Thinking about the implications of a given learning theory for a particular instructional problem can help you develop a feel for what might work.

However, learning theory is not always as helpful as you might suppose. The theories themselves are grounded in a huge body of research and analysis that attempt to frame general principles that are consistent with this scholarly work. However, they make no guarantees that these general principles provide guidelines that will fit *every* instructional situation. Hence, it is quite possible that you will find some instructional approaches that are completely compatible with a given learning theory do not produce expected results with your students.

Research-on-Teaching Studies

Individual research studies represent another source of information about teaching. There has been an enormous increase in research focused on classroom instruction over the past two decades. Organizations such as the American Educational Research Association publish reviews of research in specific areas. One journal that sums up great quantities of research on topics of interest to teachers in each issue is the *Review of Educational Research*. It is available in most university libraries and many public libraries as well.

Regrettably, research rarely speaks with a united voice on a given issue. It is not uncommon for several studies of the same question to come up with quite different results. You need to be especially wary when someone prefaces a defense of a particular instructional practice with the phrase, "Research says." Research rarely *says* just one thing. It is important to know how much research has been done, and what the general trend of the findings is. (Generally, a trend is all you can hope to find. All studies of a given question almost never yield common results.)

In spite of frustrations you may encounter as you try to find consistent patterns of findings, we highly recommend that you become familiar with professional research literature. Researchers on teaching apply rigorous analyses to their work, and other experts in the field subject their methodologies and findings to thorough reviews. Further, as professionals dedicated to adding to the knowledge base of the profession, they often have less vested interests in the worth of a particular innovation than sometimes is the case when information comes to us from enthusiastic users. To give you some sense of trends uncovered by specialists who conduct research on teaching, we have selected some findings that can provide you with information that will aid you in making sound instructional decisions. Information in this section has been divided into these five categories:

- Beliefs about students,
- Stimulating student interest,
- Using student contributions,
- Making wise use of time, and
- Presenting good lessons.

Beliefs About Students
The most important variable teachers work with is student characteristics. It makes no sense for you to plan instruction without good information about the backgrounds, abilities, interests, and general behavior patterns of your students. Decisions you make in response to this information will greatly influence the overall impact of your instruction.

Teachers' expectations of individual students are strongly tied to their beliefs about what students can do (Good & Brophy, 2000). These findings suggest that students for whom you hold high expectations will achieve more than students for whom you have lower expectations.

Teachers' expectations have been found to result from their analyses of several key variables. These include student appearance, intelligence and achievement test scores, and behavior patterns. Some evidence suggests that some teachers even form opinions about how an individual student will perform based on how their older brothers and sisters did in school. If you are not aware of these perceptions and their limitations, you may find yourself interacting with some class members in ways that do not support their maximum personal and intellectual development. Braun (1987) has described a cycle of behavior that some teachers develop as a result of their beliefs about what individual students can do.

1. The teacher establishes a level of expectation for a student based on what he believes to be true of this individual.

2. Student behaviors are interpreted in light of this expectation.

3. As a result of how the teacher reacts, the student begins to develop a self-concept that is consistent with the teacher's beliefs.

4. As a result, the student's performance begins to reflect the teacher's expectation. This means students for whom the teacher has higher expectations do well, and students for whom the teacher has lower expectations do poorly.

How should you deal with the possibility that your perceptions of individual students may affect how you interact with them? There is no easy answer. It is human nature to make certain inferences about others. However, self-monitoring efforts can help you check on the accuracy of the inferences you are making and ensure that you are not prompting irresponsible patterns of behavior. Periodic efforts to take stock of what is going on often are helpful. As part of ongoing reflection, you need to think seriously about any biases you might have that are resulting in unproductive patterns of working with certain individuals.

WHAT DO *YOU* THINK?

Have a Teacher's Expectations Ever Influenced You?

Without realizing they are doing so, teachers sometimes communicate to some students that they have little confidence in their abilities. At the same time, they may communicate to others in the class that they expect great academic work from them. Reflect on some of your own experiences as a secondary school student as you respond to these questions.

Questions

1. Can you recall times when a teacher's actions prompted you to do more? To do less? What happened in each case?

2. Do you recall any students who could have done better work but were turned off by what they perceived to be lack of teacher confidence in their abilities?

3. If you remember times when teachers seemed to have preconceived notions about what individuals could do, how do you think their impressions affected these students' abilities?

Stimulating Student Interest

Disinterested students tend to misbehave and disrupt learning of others. The key to prompting student interest, according to Henderson (1992), is to plan learning experiences that connect students' past experiences and views to what is important in the school curriculum. This implies a need for you to know your students well. You also must know your subject matter well enough so you can adapt and explain it to students in an understandable way (Reynolds, 1992).

It is important to remember that planning for motivation does not occur only at a lesson's beginning. You need to plan for motivation during three distinct phases of a lesson: (1) at the beginning, (2) as the new material is introduced, and (3) at the conclusion of the lesson.

Motivation often results when students' curiosity is aroused. Frequently this happens when they are introduced to something unique or novel (at least unique or novel to them). Sometimes students react positively to information regarding the personal importance of mastering the content that is about to be introduced. Variety during the lesson also tends to prompt continued student interest. The same can be said about encouragement. It is especially important for you to take time at the end of a lesson to highlight what students have learned.

Students' confidence grows as they realize they have encountered and understood substantial amounts of new material. Feelings of success and accomplishment build students' levels of self-esteem. As a result, they become more highly motivated to study material introduced in subsequent lessons.

Reflective teachers work hard to stimulate students' interest in learning. This teacher provides students with some hands-on prompts as a lesson motivator.

Additional information related to motivation is introduced in Chapter 8, "Models of Direct Instruction."

Using Student Contributions

How should you use student contributions? No answer to this question fits every occasion. The key principle is that your reaction to students' contributions should encourage their continued participation, provide them with appropriate feedback, and, at the same time, ensure that you do not lose the central focus of the lesson (Emmer, Evertson, Sanford, Clements, & Worsham, 1989).

When should you challenge students' ideas? In general, if a challenge to an idea will cause the student to do more thinking about the issue and develop more sophisticated reasoning skills, the challenge may make sense. However, if the student is likely to see your challenge as a put down, little good will come of it, and you ought to consider another approach. When you decide challenge is appropriate, you want to deliver it in a tone of language that implies, "I may disagree with what you have said, but I still think highly of you as a person."

Making Wise Use of Time

Time available for instruction is limited. As a result, you need to use it wisely. It is particularly important for you to allocate sufficient time for students to work on academic tasks. Unless you plan carefully, administrative tasks such as roll taking, distributing and collecting materials, and making announcements can significantly reduce the time students spend on learning tasks. A reduction in learning time, not surprisingly, results in reduced levels of academic performance (Good & Brophy, 2000). Carefully planning administrative tasks so that you spend only a few minutes each day on them will provide you with many additional hours of instructional time over the academic year.

Time decisions you make can be sorted into these three distinct categories:

- allocated time,
- engaged time, and
- academic learning time.

Allocated Time refers to the amount of time you set aside for students to learn specific material. Researchers have found that different teachers allocate very different quantities of time for teaching the same content (Good & Brophy, 2000). Why is this so? In part, this situation arises because of class-to-class differences in students. Interestingly, another determinant seems to be the teachers' varying levels of personal interest in and feelings of competence with the topic being taught. Teachers tend to allocate more instructional time to topics they like and about which they believe themselves to be particularly well informed.

It is possible that some students may be educationally disadvantaged by time-allocation decisions based on your personal preferences. To properly make time-allocation decisions, you also need to consider the relative importance of each topic as it relates to the major aims of the course. You need to provide sufficient time for students to learn material associated with each topic, but not so much time that they become bored and you are faced with motivation problems. Just because you allocate a given amount of time for students to work on an assigned task does not guarantee they will do so. The term *engaged time* refers to that proportion of allocated time when your students are actually studying assigned material. There are great classroom-to-classroom differences in proportions of engaged time (Good & Brophy, 2000). In general, your intent should be to increase the total amount of engaged time. More engaged time correlates with more student learning (Berliner, 1984). Engaged time can be increased when you are well organized and attend efficiently to tasks such as roll taking, clear explanations of assignments, and monitoring students as they work.

Academic learning time is that portion of engaged time when your students are not only working on the assigned task but also are experiencing success. Research has found that increased academic achievement accompanies an increase in academic learning time (Berliner, 1984). If you want to increase academic learning time, you must know your students well. Your assignments need to be well matched to students' prior levels of knowledge, aptitude, and (to the extent possible) interests. You also need to monitor students carefully and to help them with any problems they may encounter (Reynolds, 1992). When you see they are having difficulty, you may need to re-teach part of the lesson, modify it, or take other actions to ensure that student learning gets back on track.

Presenting Good Lessons
Good planning is a hallmark skill of the effective secondary teacher. Well-planned lessons feature:

- clarity,
- variety,
- good modeling of appropriate practice,
- feedback to students, and
- appropriate pacing.

Clarity requires a clear and precise use of language and a presentation style that moves logically and smoothly from point to point. There are many threats to clarity. For example, your students may be confused if you use vague and ambiguous terms. Vague terms fall into a number of categories, including: (1) approximations (*about, sort of, roughly,* and so forth); (2) probability statements (*frequently, generally, often,* and so forth); (3) possibility statements (*chances are, could be, maybe,* and so forth); and (4) bluffing (*everybody knows, it's a long story,* and so forth).

These phrases have become so much a part of ordinary speech that they cannot be eliminated entirely. However, overuse of these statements can cause confusion. Students' understanding is enhanced when you use more specific terms and phrases. For example, the phrase "20 years ago" communicates much more effectively than "some time ago."

Clarity can also be undermined when you use false starts and verbal mazes. *False starts* occur when a teacher starts a lesson, gets diverted, and then starts again. If you do this too often, your students will stop paying attention when you begin your lessons. They will have learned that you will be going over the same material a second time.

Verbal mazes are explanations that fail to communicate information in a clear, concise manner. Sometimes information provided fails to tie meaningfully to other things you may have told students (at least no tie is evident in the minds of your students). Most secondary students find it very difficult to derive coherent meaning from a teacher presentation that follows an excessively meandering course. They do far better when information moves smoothly from point to point and when you pause periodically to highlight key ideas.

Digressions are another threat to clarity. Sometimes you may be tempted to insert high-interest digressions into lessons as a means of capturing student interest. Some research evidence suggests that this practice fails to have the intended effect and actually can reduce what students otherwise would learn (Hidi, 1990).

Your clarity can be enhanced if you use *advance organizers*. An advance organizer is a brief overview or organization of important content to be presented. It provides students with a map they can follow as a lesson progresses. In addition, it gives them a way to pinpoint key points and to relate them to previously learned information.

Internal summaries also enhance clarity of lesson presentation. These are stopping points during a lesson when you pause to recapitulate with students what you have already covered. These summaries help students to focus on key points and to see interrelationships among important ideas.

Marker expressions draw students' attention to important ideas. These are verbal cues you can use to help students appreciate the importance of what is to follow. These are some examples: "This is important." "Write this down." "I want you to remember this." "Listen carefully to this point."

Clarity is improved when your lessons feature a well-organized conclusion. A good conclusion summarizes what you have covered and draws students' attention to important ideas. You often will want to repeat key content ideas during this phase of a lesson. This kind of repetition will help your students retain the new material.

Feedback to students involves specific action you provide to students that communicates information to them about the appropriateness or correctness of their responses. This information helps people in your classes avoid errors and to focus on important dimensions of content.

Praise is often used as part of feedback. Researchers have found that effective praise is specific and genuine. Further, you need to use it in moderation (Good & Brophy, 2000). The term *specificity*, as applied to appropriate use of praise, means that you need to tell your students what they have done that you have found praiseworthy. The praiseworthy behavior you cite should relate to content you are teaching. If you give general praise that has no clear connection to a desirable academics-related behavior, this action will have little impact on student performance.

Criticism also has its place when you provide feedback to students. Proper criticism focuses on helping a student resolve an academic difficulty. It is designed not simply to indicate student errors, but rather to suggest appropriate ways of correcting mistakes. Good criticism never demeans students as people. It focuses on enhancing their self-esteem by helping them master content.

Your grades of student work are also a form of feedback; however, they often are not as effective as some other approaches. One reason for this is that grades tend to represent a summary judgment over a considerable quantity of work. Hence, they do not provide specific information to a student about exactly what he or she has done that was either "excellent," "average," or "poorly done." Written comments you provide to accompany letter grades often provide more useful feedback information for students. Your written words help them understand why you awarded a given grade. They also help students focus their attention on how well they have mastered certain elements of content.

Providing a model for learners during a lesson acts to improve student performance. For example, your personal enthusiasm for a topic often is catching and most likely will increase levels of student interest. Students also benefit when you model thinking processes that are appropriate for a particular task. For example, you might solve a problem similar to ones your students will be asked to solve by thinking out loud with members of the class. ("Now if I found myself faced with this situation, the first thing I would look at would be. . . . Next, I would compare _____ and _____. If they seemed consistent, I probably would decide to. . . . ")

You sometimes may find it useful to develop an example of a product of learning similar to what you expect to receive from students. For example, if you want your students to write a short paper comparing and contrasting positions of two individuals, you might prepare a sample of such a paper. When making your assignment to the students, you can share this material, drawing their attention to various features you hope to see in the papers they will be preparing. An example of this kind greatly reduces the possibility your students will fail to understand your expectations.

Lesson pacing refers to the general speed of presentation you adopt in introducing students to new material. Researchers recommend that your lessons move at a brisk pace, but one that is accompanied by high levels of student understanding (Good & Brophy, 2000). This does not mean you should race to cover the material. Rather, you need to move along as quickly as possible given the abilities of your students to keep up and profit from your instruction.

Pacing decisions place heavy demands on you as you work with your students. You have to make them at the same time you are teaching a lesson. This requires you to monitor student understanding closely to ensure that they are grasping the new material. To accomplish this task, you need to pause frequently to ask questions. This allows you to make periodic judgments about how well your students are following your instruction.

Making Fluid Plans

Armed with thoughtful information carefully gathered about the context and your personal and professional knowledge, you will be ready to make fluid plans. *Fluid plans* are flexible and responsible. They are general designs that you prepare carefully, but they do not lay out an inflexible instructional path. They function as guides you will use to begin your lessons and that you will be expected to modify, as needed, as your teaching unfolds. As a user of flexible plans, your teaching is adaptive. It does not consist of a set of preplanned, totally scripted instructional acts.

Walter Doyle (1986), an expert on research-validated teaching practices, strongly supports fluid planning. He notes that classrooms are unpredictable, multidimensional places where many things happen simultaneously and where you may be called upon to make unanticipated adjustments. Often you will have to make changes as you attempt to make reasoned responses to several challenging things that are occurring at the same time. In these circumstances, you cannot plod relentlessly through a set of preplanned activities. You have to deal with these situations immediately. If you fail to do so, you run the risk that a minor difficulty will grow into a major crisis.

Formal and Informal Professional Growth Opportunities

Your preparation for teaching does not end when you are awarded an initial teaching certificate or license. You need to continue developing your personal and professional knowledge throughout your career. You can best do this by pursuing activities that will help you learn what you need to know. Your specific actions will vary depending on your own diagnosis of your personal professional needs. For example, if you need additional knowledge in your content area, you might decide to take additional courses in your subject. If you need to develop a better understanding of your community, then you might consider one or more informal approaches to gaining this information. For example, you might think about volunteering for some community events or taking other actions that will bring you into closer contact with local people, organizations, and neighborhoods.

MORE FROM THE WEB

Developing Your Personal and Professional Knowledge Base

The following Web sites provide you with places you can visit as you work to add to your personal and professional knowledge base. These Web pages will give you opportunities to interact with others, locate notices of professional development opportunities, find current research, and see examples of lesson plans.

Teachers Helping Teachers

http://www.pacificnet.net/~mandel

- This site is regularly updated with new information. Among other things, you will find advice posted for newcomers by experienced teachers. Lesson plans are available. There are excellent links to other educational resources. In addition, a chat room is available.

Discovery School

http://discoveryschool.com/schrockguide/

- This is an excellent beginning site that features links to many kinds of resources for teachers. For example, you will find ties to sites dealing with topics as varied as: (1) tips for teaching individual school subjects, (2) evaluation tools, (3) locations of reference information, (4) special education resources, and (5) upcoming professional development seminars and workshops.

The Awesome Library

http://www.neat-schoolhouse.org/awesome.html

- This site features links to content that is organized in ways that should allow you to locate desired information quickly. One scheme features ties to other Web sites that have been gathered together under names of individual school subjects. Another organizes sites according to their probable interest for people playing different professional roles in the school (teachers, principals, counselors, school nurses, for example). In addition, you will find good links to sites that feature information about using technology to support your instruction. Lesson plans are also available here.

New Teachers

http://www.new-teacher.com

- This site focuses on needs of prospective teachers and new teachers. You will find an abundance of useful material here. Among topics treated are: (1) mentoring new teachers, (2) finding a teaching position, (3) substitute teaching, and (4) professional books of interest to teachers. You will find additional links to and Web addresses of many other topics that are relevant to concerns of newcomers to the profession.

Adolescence Directory On Line

http://educ.indiana.edu/cas/adol/adol.html

- As the name implies, this site features information related to problems and development of adolescents. Among the many links you will find here are those related to (1) conflict and violence, (2) mental health issues, (3) health and health-risk issues, and (4) resources for school counselors.

The Professional-Development Portfolio

By definition, reflective teaching demands reflection. As a means of organizing information to consider as you engage in serious thought about teaching and learning, you
may find a *professional-development portfolio* useful. This kind of a portfolio often
includes ideas and thoughts about information or instructional techniques you would
like to include in your lessons. In addition, you may also want to include materials you
actually use in lessons along with your thoughts about how effective individual lessons
were and what you might have learned that will improve your teaching of subsequent
lessons. Keeping a professional-development portfolio can be an important aid to your
development as a teacher.

Professional-development portfolios can be formatted in a variety of ways. Often,
they include (1) information or materials that prompt you to reflect, and (2) written
summaries of your reflections.

Individual teachers vary in terms of specific items they put in professional-development portfolios to prompt reflection. After considering your options, you might decide
to include entries such as these:

- descriptions of procedures for implementing new instructional techniques;
- explanations of special features of your teaching context (nature of the students,
  noise levels in your classroom, adequacy of learning materials, and so forth);
- copies of lesson plans you have developed;
- general information from a variety of sources that you think might facilitate your
  development as an effective teacher;
- comments of any observers who may have seen you teach; and
- examples of student work.

Written summaries of your reflection may take different forms. For example, you might
decide to frame your written reactions as answers to questions you might pose, such as:

- How might I actually incorporate some new instructional techniques into my
  lessons, and what is my rationale for wanting to do so?
- To what extent have context variables helped and hindered the effectiveness of my
  lessons, and how might I change what I have been doing in light of this information?
- Do lesson plans I have used really emphasize what I want to highlight with my students and is the presented information optimally organized and sequenced to facilitate learning of all of my students? What specific changes would I want to make in
  teaching these lessons again?
- How can I move from a knowledge-level understanding of new information I have
  learned about effective teaching to converting this information to part of my active
  teaching repertoire?

- How congruent are comments noted by people who have observed my teaching with my own perceptions about how I have been performing? What thoughts do I have about changing what I have been doing as a result of thinking about their observations and suggestions?
- How pleased am I with the quality of work I am getting from students? What can I do to increase the numbers of students who are achieving high levels of academic success and deriving personal satisfaction from their involvement in my lessons?

Whether you decide to use questions to prompt written summaries of your reflections or to use a different approach to recording your thoughts is a matter of personal preference. The critical point is that a professional-development portfolio must include some record of your own reflections about the basic information that is included. Otherwise, preparation of the portfolio amounts to little more than construction of a scrapbook. To have real value as an aid to your professional development, you need to engage the content, mull it over carefully, and give written expression to your reflections. It is the intellectual engagement, not the simple gathering together of included materials, that makes professional-development portfolios credible vehicles for developing teachers' expertise.

You may wish to start a professional-development proposal as you work through this text. At the end of each chapter in Parts 2, 3, and 4 of this text, you will find a "For Your Portfolio" exercise. This provides you with an opportunity to put information you have learned into a professional-development portfolio. Once you have started a portfolio, you need to review it regularly. You might ask yourself some general questions as you conduct these periodic status checks. Some examples include:

- Does my portfolio reveal that I have been actively engaged in seeking answers for questions and in growing professionally?
- Have I been persistent in seeking knowledge and in finding ways to respond to the challenges of teaching?
- Have I been thoughtful and careful in drawing my conclusions, and have I considered the moral and ethical dimensions of my actions?
- Have I adequately considered the impact of my ideas on my students?
- Are criteria I have been using to judge my success as a teacher worthwhile and important?
- Does my portfolio reflect changes I have made as I have learned new things about my students, my teaching context, and my subject?

Professional-growth portfolios can provide you with a basis for understanding yourself and for promoting your professional development. You may find yourself looking back at sections of your portfolio completed early in the academic year and observe with real satisfaction some of the changes you have made in working with your students. Portfolio-based documentation of your increasing expertise as a teacher can be a tremendous confidence builder. A record of past successes will function as an excellent motivator as you begin thinking about ways to become more effective in areas that, you believe, still need work.

Key Ideas in Summary

- *Reflective teaching* is an orientation to instruction that will call on you to reflect thoughtfully on the conditions at hand and to vary your teaching responses so as best to serve the needs of students. Henderson (1996) claims this process requires you to conduct a kind of "internal debate" that involves you in considering the many variables that affect your teaching. Your teaching plans will evolve out of this thinking exercise. Eby (1998) points out that the reflective teacher needs to be active, persistent, careful, and to consider available evidence while engaging in reflection. The foundations of reflective teaching are found in *constructivism*, the idea that knowledge does not exist in any abstract sense but that it is "constructed" by individuals as they interact with and attempt to make sense of their environment.

- Reflective teaching involves (1) a sensitivity to content, (2) a willingness to be informed by personal and professional knowledge, (3) an understanding that good instruction is best guided by fluid planning (planning that quickly adjusts to changing circumstances in the classroom), and (4) a commitment to career-long informal and formal professional development.

- Your decisions as a teacher will be influenced strongly by your own personality, biases, and general world view. This means that you need to develop an awareness of your own personal perspectives. Such an awareness will help you avoid making decisions that are too strongly tied to your biases—decisions which, in some cases, may not be best for your students.

- Researchers have found an important connection between teachers' expectations of students and students' levels of performance. In general, your students will do better when you hold high expectations for them.

- When you teach, you may find yourself gathering information for decision-making from many sources. Personal experiences of other teachers may provide some useful information. However, because of differences in individual teacher personalities, students to be served, and other variables, these experiences may not be wholly useful to you. Learning theory offers some guidance. However, principles derived from learning theory may not be applicable in every instructional situation. Individual research studies also provide some useful information. Again, studies may yield insights that may not be applicable to the special features of your own teaching setting.

- Relating the school curriculum to students' needs and interests enhances their levels of interest. Ideally, motivational activities should occur during three distinct phases of a given lesson: the beginning, as new information is presented, and at the end. Researchers have found that using student ideas during a lesson helps to maintain student interest and involvement. Ideally, you should react to students in ways that (1) encourage their continued participation, (2) provide them with appropriate feedback, and (3) help them maintain a focus on the central content of the lesson.

- Effective teachers manage time wisely. It is particularly important to maximize the amount of classroom time actually devoted to instruction. Researchers who have looked at the issue of teachers' use of time have identified three important time concepts. *Allocated time* refers to time set aside for instruction. *Engaged time* refers to the time students are actually working on an assigned task. *Academic learning time* is when students are both working on an assigned task and experiencing success. Increases in academic learning time tend to correlate with improved achievement levels.

■ Good lessons do not happen by accident. They tend to feature recurring patterns of effective teacher behavior. These include (1) efforts to ensure clarity of communication, (2) attempts to enhance student achievement through provision of appropriate feedback and modeling, and (3) attention to establishing an appropriate lesson pace.

■ Understanding your teaching context requires you to gather information about your students, the culture of your school, and the nature of your community. Information about these dimensions can help you reflect on the opportunities and challenges you face in the classroom and assist you as you seek to design more successful lessons.

■ Continued professional growth is a characteristic of successful teachers. This professional growth is best enhanced when you actively pursue formal and informal professional development opportunities.

Reflections

1. What do you see as the critical elements of *reflective teaching*?

2. Do you consider yourself a reflective person? If not, how might that affect your teaching?

3. What personal knowledge do you have about yourself that you think is related to your potential success as a teacher? How can you check that knowledge to make sure it is accurate?

4. How can you best use findings of instructional researchers as you plan your instructional program?

5. What is meant by the term *pedagogical personality*? How would you describe your own pedagogical personality?

6. Describe some things you can do to enhance the clarity of your communication in the classroom.

7. In what ways do teachers' beliefs about students affect levels of student performance?

8. What areas of research on teaching do you find especially useful and important?

9. In what ways can the culture of your school impact your performance as a teacher?

10. What are some approaches you might take to continue your professional development throughout your career as a classroom teacher?

Learning Extensions

1. Several books have been compiled that relate teachers' classroom experiences. A particularly good one is *Teacher Lore: Learning from Our Own Experiences* (Schubert & Ayers, 1992). Read several teachers' accounts from *Teacher Lore* or another source. As you read these accounts of classroom teachers, consider how they

address the context, the personal and professional knowledge base, fluid planning, and professional growth. Prepare a report on your reading to share with your class.

2. Much is being published today about reflective teaching. Read four or five journal articles that focus on this subject. Summarize your findings in a short paper. Include comments comparing and contrasting information from these articles to information about reflective teaching introduced in this chapter.

3. Do an informal needs-assessment of your personal and professional knowledge. Identify what you want to know about yourself and what you want to know about teaching and learning. Use this assessment to guide you as you proceed through this book and your teacher preparation program.

4. Teach a lesson to other members of your class and arrange to have someone video-tape your presentation. Review the videotape privately. Identify aspects of your lesson that you think could have been done better. Prepare a written summary explaining precisely what you would do another time to improve your overall presentation.

5. Spend some time as an observer in a secondary school. Try to identify and characterize the elements of the school culture. How does this culture seem to influence both teachers and students?

6. Go to Merrill Education's Link to General Methods Resources site at this URL: http://www.prenhall.com/methods-cluster/ At the bottom of the page select "discipline/classroom management" as your topic and click the "begin" button. This will take you to the "Overview" page. On the left side, click on "Web Links." On the Web Links page, click on "General" and follow links there. Then, return to the Web Links page and follow links under the heading "secondary." If you are similar to many others who are preparing to teach in secondary schools, you have concerns about managing students. As you pursue your own professional-development agenda, you may well be in the market for information about how to handle challenges associated with student behavior and classroom control. Use these links to find information of interest to you that relates to classroom management and discipline. Prepare a brief oral report for others in your class based on what you find. You may also be interested in including some of this information in your professional-development portfolio.

References

Berliner, D. C. (1984). The half-full glass: A review of research on teaching. In P. L. Hosford (Ed.), *Using what we know about teaching* (pp. 51–77). Alexandria, VA: Association for Supervision and Curriculum Development.

Braun, C. (1987). Teachers' expectations. In M. Dunkin (Ed.), *The international encyclopedia of teaching and teacher education* (pp. 598–605). New York: Pergamon Press.

Dewey, J. (1933). *How we think* (rev. ed.). Lexington, MA: D.C. Heath.

Doyle, W. (1986). Classroom organization and management. In M. Wittrock (Ed.), *Handbook of research on teaching* (3rd ed., pp. 392–431). New York: Macmillan.

Eby, J. W. (1998). *Reflective planning, teaching and evaluation K–12* (2nd ed.). Columbus, OH: Merrill.

Emmer, E., Evertson, C., Sanford, J., Clements, B., & Worsham, M. (1989). *Classroom management for secondary teachers.* Upper Saddle River, NJ: Merrill/Prentice Hall.

Good, T., & Brophy, J. (2000). *Looking in classrooms* (8th ed.). New York: Longman.

Henderson, J. G. (1992). *Becoming an inquiring teacher: A caring approach to problem solving.* New York: Macmillan.

Henderson, J. G. (1996). *Reflective teaching: The study of your constructivist practices,* (2nd ed.). Columbus, OH: Merrill.

Hidi, S. (1990). Interest and its contribution as a mental resource for learning. *Review of Educational Research, 60*(3), pp. 549–571.

Levin, T., & Long, R. (1981). *Effective instruction.* Alexandria, VA: Association for Supervision and Curriculum Development.

Millies, P. (1992). The relationship between a teacher's life and teaching. In W. Schubert & W. Ayers (Eds.), *Teacher lore: Learning from our own experience* (pp. 25–42). New York: Longman.

Reynolds, A. (1992). What is competent teaching? *Review of Educational Research, 62*(1), pp. 1–35.

Rogers, C., & Freiberg, H. J. (1994). *Freedom to learn* (3rd ed.). Upper Saddle River, NJ: Merrill/Prentice Hall.

Schubert, W. H., & Ayers, W. C. (Eds.). (1992). *Teacher lore: Learning from our own experiences.* New York: Longman.

Zahorik, J. A. (1995). *Constructivist teaching (Fastback 390).* Bloomington, IN: Phi Delta Kappa Educational Foundation.

4

Legal Issues Affecting Students and Teachers

This chapter will aim to

- describe some rights and responsibilities of students and teachers;

- state some conditions under which officials may place controls over the contents of student publications;

- explain basic principles that have tended to guide courts in cases involving freedom of conscience;

- differentiate among different types of teaching contracts;

- point out teachers' responsibilities in reporting suspected cases of child abuse;

- define different types of teacher negligence;

- explain some limitations that legally can be placed on teachers' out-of-school behavior; and

- describe some implications of copyright law for teachers.

Introduction

If you had begun your career in teaching 30 years ago, you would have entered a professional world where legal issues related to schools and schooling rarely impinged directly on educators' work. Years ago, courts heard few challenges to teachers' and administrators' authority over students. As a teacher, you would have been expected to make and enforce rules, and students would have been expected to follow them. If they failed to do so, they could be summarily dismissed. Even if students felt they had been treated unfairly, courts typically rejected attempts of complaining students to mount legal challenges to decisions of school authorities.

Times have changed. Today's legal environment makes it possible for students to carry challenges to the courts concerning a wide range of dissatisfactions they might have with educators' decisions. For example, in recent years cases brought against schools have focused on such diverse topics as curriculum content, books included in the library, required reading materials, school assemblies, access to the Internet, censorship of student publications, student dress, condom distribution, student discipline, and even what can be duplicated for use in the classroom. As a teacher, you need to know something about patterns of court decisions in cases focusing on these issues. You also should have an understanding of other issues that can affect you personally, for example (1) legal principles associated with teacher contracts, (2) your authority in areas relating to retention and promotion of students, and (3) constraints on your own personal behavior (both in-school and out-of-school).

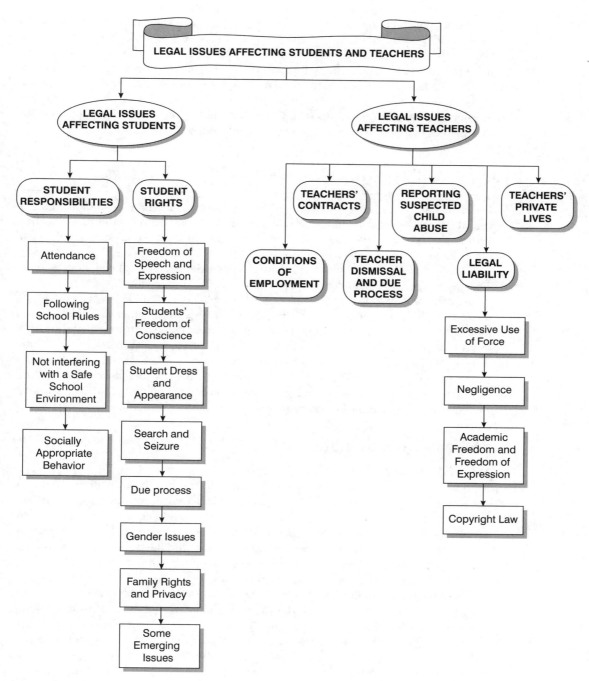

Figure 4–1
Graphic Organizer

It is not our intention to cover all of the possible legal issues that may confront you as a teacher. There are whole volumes of books that address this topic. Nor is it our intention in this chapter to delve into the legal issues relating to the establishment and operation of a school district. For those topics, we recommend you seek more comprehensive sources. Rather, our intent is to focus on some of the legal issues that may be of immediate interest to you, even as you begin your career. To accomplish this purpose, we have developed a section relating to issues that may affect your students and another that treats issues that pertain more directly to you and your teaching colleagues.

Legal Issues Affecting Students

Few issues in secondary education generate as much controversy as student rights. In recent years, the legal relationship between students and school authorities has been greatly altered. Since the 1980s, students have enjoyed legal rights generally comparable to those extended to all adult citizens.

Contrary to what some believe, legal decisions have not just defined student *rights*. They have also defined student *responsibilities*. In fact, in recent years, because of incidents such as the violence at Columbine High School, more attention has been directed to the area of student responsibilities. A few people have gone so far as to suggest that student rights should be severely limited in order to prevent tragic occurrences such as these.

As a beginning point, you need to understand that most legal issues result because of conflicts among different sets of rights. For example, dealing with school violence brings into play disputes about (1) rights of students in areas such as freedom of dress, expression, and association, and (2) the rights and obligations school districts have to establish a safe educational environment.

Student Responsibilities

School Attendance

An educated and informed citizenry is essential to the health of a nation. Therefore, students have a duty to participate in educational experiences. Courts have consistently upheld this principle. However, there have been many recent cases regarding the meaning of regulations requiring students to get an education. Recent cases have tended to suggest that society's interest in promoting the development of knowledgeable citizens requires each young person to get an education, but it does not necessarily imply that the only place this can occur is in a school.

There have been numerous legal challenges to compulsory attendance laws. In general, court decisions have reflected the view that the interest of the state is in promoting a satisfactory education of the person, not in the place or the manner of education. This has raised some legal questions concerning what constitutes a satisfactory education and what is required in order to satisfy compulsory attendance provisions. Because of an increased interest in homeschooling, this issue has received considerable legal attention.

The legal responsibility students have to participate in educational experience results from decisions arising out of a potential conflict between two sets of interests.

On the one hand, parents have a right to direct the upbringing of their children. On the other hand, society, in order to survive, depends on a supply of educated young people who, as they mature, will move into positions of responsibility. Because most parents lack the breadth and depth of knowledge required to prepare young people for the complex roles they will face as adults, the courts have typically supported rights of the state to insist that young people receive an education, either by attending a state-supported school or by pursuing an *acceptable alternative*.

What constitutes an acceptable alternative varies from state to state. In a typical situation, an acceptable alternative must be equivalent to what is provided in the public school curriculum. These alternatives might be private schools, or they might be schools taught by parents or others in home schools. Some states require that a qualified individual teach students who enroll in acceptable alternatives to regular public schools. In some places this means that the people discharging the teaching function hold regular teaching certificates. In some locations, other evidence of expertise may be presented to establish qualifications.

A few challenges have been made to mandatory schooling regulations on the grounds that school conditions put students in physical or emotional danger. Court decisions in these cases have not followed a consistent pattern. In some cases, the courts have recognized that protection of their children is a valid reason for parents or guardians to ignore compulsory attendance laws. However, judges usually have placed a heavy burden of proof on the parents to prove their contention that the school environment is unsafe (Valente, 1994).

Another challenge to these regulations has been made based on the claim that school attendance can have a negative impact on religious beliefs. Most challenges of this type have not been successful. An interesting exception to this pattern was a ruling made in response to a challenge brought by Amish parents in Wisconsin (*Wisconsin v. Yoder*, 1972). These parents refused to send their children to school beyond the eighth grade. They contended that the general emphasis of secondary schools was contrary to the basic tenets of their religion and way of life. The Supreme Court ruled in their favor, holding that the Amish way of life constituted an acceptable alternative to formal secondary education. However, the court was careful to note that this did not set a precedent for other groups who wished to challenge compulsory education laws (Fischer, Schimmel, & Kelly, 1999).

Following Reasonable School Rules

School officials have the right to establish reasonable school rules. Students have the responsibility to obey them and to submit to the authority of teachers. For example, the California School Code states that every teacher in a public school has an obligation to hold each student accountable for conduct on the way to and from school, on the school grounds, and during breaks from classroom activities. Any certified employee is given the right to exercise reasonable control over a student in order to protect property, ensure safety for others, or to maintain conditions conducive to learning. Willful violations of teacher authority by students is grounds for suspension or expulsion (California Teachers Association, 1992).

The operative word, however, is *reasonable*. Arbitrary rules or regulations that have nothing to do with establishing a safe school or a climate conducive to learning are not legally protected. If a school district attempts to impose and enforce rules that fail to meet the "reasonableness" test, these rules are unlikely to survive a legal challenge.

Not Interfering with the Maintenance of a Safe School Environment

School officials have an obligation to protect the health and safety of those who are present in the schools and to maintain a school environment that is conducive to learning. Students have a responsibility to refrain from bringing weapons or controlled substances to school that might endanger the health and safety of others. Most states provide for immediate suspension if students violate this responsibility. The increased fear of violence in schools has led many school districts to establish a *zero tolerance policy*. This means that students do not get a second chance. Any violation results in immediate suspension.

Similarly, threatening violence or harm to another person is also grounds for suspension or expulsion. Thus, a student who threatens you or who threatens another student can be immediately suspended. You need to be sensitive to the fact that taunting and name calling can often lead to violence. One of your obligations is to ensure that students understand their responsibilities in this area and that such behavior will not be tolerated.

Socially Appropriate Behavior

When political and social leaders suggest that one of your jobs as a teacher is to inform young people about the boundaries of socially acceptable behavior, they assume there are restrictions that can be placed on student behavior. Further, this perspective implies that behavior that might be appropriate in other settings may not be acceptable in school. Several court cases have endorsed this view.

In one case, a high school student who was nominating a friend for a school office gave a speech that was filled with sexual metaphor and innuendo. Although the student did not use explicit language, he was suspended from school for three days. The student sued, claiming that his First Amendment rights to freedom of speech had been violated. The court upheld the actions of the school district, ruling that the rights of this student were outweighed by society's interest in educating young people within the bounds of socially appropriate behavior (Zirkel & Richardson, 1988). Findings in this case suggest that students must accept that they have responsibilities to behave in ways that permit schools to maintain a productive environment for learning.

To summarize, your students *do* have certain responsibilities that you can require them to discharge. However, you and others in your school must recognize that you face certain constraints in establishing expectations related to student behavior. For example, courts will not be sympathetic if your school adopts and attempts to enforce capricious regulations. Rules and expectations must be reasonable and consistent with defensible educational purposes.

Student Rights

Legal actions relating to student rights focus on the idea that students are citizens who enjoy a legal status that the United States Constitution guarantees to all citizens. Court cases have centered on two key areas. First, there has been litigation concerned with the limits of school authorities' power to interfere with students' actions. Second, there have been cases that have considered the appropriateness or fairness of procedures school authorities have used to make decisions affecting students.

In reviewing information related to students' rights cases, you need to keep in mind that each case is considered by the courts on its own merits, as well as in light of laws and decisions in previous, related cases. Laws and precedents change over time. Hence, you cannot always presume that, when courts consider new cases, they will follow the same course of action they have tended to take in the past. For reasons we cannot discern today, future courts may take quite different views of some issues related to students' rights.

Freedom of Speech and Expression

One of the fundamental rights guaranteed by the Constitution is *freedom of expression*. This issue has caused school officials considerable concern. In the past, school officials were quite free to limit students' freedom of expression. School officials took the position that these restrictions were necessary to promote an orderly school environment. This situation began to change dramatically in the late 1960s and the early 1970s. One of the landmark freedom of expression cases was *Tinker v. Des Moines Independent Community School District* in 1969.

The *Tinker* case evolved out of a situation that developed in Des Moines, Iowa. Children from several families who opposed the Vietnam War decided to express their protest to the war by wearing black armbands to school. When school officials discovered this was going to happen, they quickly adopted a policy forbidding the wearing of these armbands in school. According to this policy, a student who came to school wearing an armband would be asked to remove it. Failure to comply would result in suspension.

Three students defied this regulation, arrived at school wearing armbands, refused to remove them, and were suspended. Suit was brought on behalf of the students, and the case ultimately worked its way up to the United States Supreme Court. In its decision in the *Tinker* case, the High Court ruled that students do not leave their constitutional rights at the classroom door. The wearing of armbands to school as a protest was viewed as symbolic speech. The Court, arguing that the First Amendment to the United States Constitution protects free speech and expression, ruled that the wearing of armbands was protected. Hence, the school authorities had erred in passing and enforcing the regulation. This decision means that if you and your colleagues wish to limit students' freedom of expression, you have to demonstrate that unrestricted student speech would lead to a material and substantial disruption of the educational process. For example, if you could demonstrate that the exercise of unrestricted free speech would result in disruptions such as fights among students, then the courts might be sympathetic to a regulation limiting certain kinds of student expression.

Another freedom of expression issue that has prompted much interest over the years concerns the authority of school officials to limit what is printed in official student publications as well as in "underground" or unauthorized student newspapers. In many places, school officials have censored student publications and have forbidden unauthorized publications. Some of these actions have been challenged in court.

In general, the courts have determined that school administrators' power to regulate a publication depends on whether the publication in question is sponsored by the school in some official way. Courts have tended to support more administrative control over student newspapers that are written by students as part of a regular journalism course than publications that are not officially connected with the school. An important precedent in this area was established in 1988 in the case of *Hazelwood School District v. Kuhlmeier.*

The *Hazelwood* case focused on the actions of a school principal who deleted two articles from the school newspaper. One article referred indirectly to some pregnant students. Though names in the article had been changed to mask the true identities of these students, the principal felt that many readers might be able to identify them. In the second article, a student had written a complaint about her father, but the father had not been given an option to respond. The principal felt the treatment was unbalanced and, hence, unfair. In its decision, the court upheld the right of the principal, noting that educators have the authority to exercise considerable control over school-sponsored publications.

The courts generally have supported educators' rights to reject articles that are poorly written, insufficiently researched, clearly biased, vulgar, or otherwise unsuitable for immature audiences. They may prohibit articles that advocate unacceptable (and often illegal) social practices such as alcohol or drug abuse and irresponsible sexual activities. Control can be exercised when actions taken by school leaders are undertaken to ensure some consistency with the ongoing instructional responsibilities of the school.

Authority to limit the content of school publications does not extend to censorship of controversial issues or of views that may be unpopular with administrators, teachers, or parents. If you and others in your school want to place limitations on what students can print in school publications, you must be prepared to demonstrate that your actions are for valid educational reasons, not for capricious, convenient, or punitive reasons.

Underground and other publications that are produced without formal school recognition and support generally lie outside the control of school officials. These publications ordinarily cannot be regulated unless their contents can be challenged on grounds that would invite legal actions against publications of any kind. Though you and your colleagues may find some of these articles to be highly irritating, you generally lack legal grounds for barring publications containing them from the school campus or for punishing the writers. However, school leaders generally have been found to have the legal authority to place some limits on practices associated with the distribution of underground publications. These guidelines cannot be so restrictive that they actually bar distribution.

 MORE FROM THE WEB

Legal Concerns of Educators

Because the legal climate is constantly changing, you need to review new information as you seek to keep up to date on rulings and interpretations of the law. There are several Web sites that will enable you to do that as well as gather information to supplement what you will find in the chapter.

Students' Rights

http://www.aclu.org/issues/student/hmes.html

- This site, maintained by the American Civil Liberties Union, focuses on such important rights issues as freedom of expression and church and state separation. There are excellent links to additional resources related to the topic "Students and Their Rights."

Trends And Issues: School Law

http://eric.uoregon.edu/issue/law/index.html

- You will find excellent articles here focusing on (1) sexual harassment, (2) copyright law, (3) school discipline, and (4) religion in the school. The ERIC Clearinghouse on Educational Management has compiled this information.

Supreme Court Collection

http://www4.law.cornell.edu/cgi-bin/fx?DB=SupctSyllabi&TOPDOC=0&P=education

- The Legal Information Institute at Cornell University maintains this site. You will find an extensive listing of Supreme Court cases that have focused on education-related issues.

Sexual Harassment: It's Not Academic

http://www.ed.gov/offices/OCR/ocrshpam.html

- The United States Department of Education's Office of Civil Rights maintains this site. You will find extensive information here about Title IX and the general topic of sexual harassment. There is an especially useful question-and-answer section.

Copyright for Educators

http://falcon.jmu.edu/~ramseyil/copy.htm

- This site includes a tremendous number of links to Web pages featuring information about copyright. You should definitely go here if you have questions or concerns about this important issue.

Internet Free Expression Alliance

http://www.ifea.net/

- An emerging legal issue facing educators has to do with whether students should have a right to unrestricted Internet access when using computers at school. A group committed to the view that restrictions on Internet access are an improper infringement on free speech rights maintains this site. You will find good links here to legislative and court actions related to this issue.

In considering freedom-of-expression-and-speech cases, the courts have tended to look carefully at special circumstances surrounding the situation being litigated. For the most part, decisions have supported the idea that students enjoy constitutional free-speech and free-expression rights. If you become involved in a situation where there may be an attempt to limit students' free-speech rights, you need to be sure that the contemplated action is being taken because of a legitimate educational concern and not in response to a desire to limit student abilities to (1) criticize school officials, or (2) discuss controversial issues.

Students' Freedom of Conscience

Legal questions focusing on the issues of separation of church and state and the place of religious expression in schools have generated much controversy. Two basic First Amendment principles often have been involved in these disputes. One principle guarantees the right to free exercise of religion; the other bars the government from establishing any religion.

Courts have consistently affirmed the idea that freedom of religion cannot be abridged unless the state and its officials demonstrate an overwhelmingly compelling need to do so. This means that school officials cannot arbitrarily require all young people in the school to do something that may interfere with the fundamental religious principles of some students. For example, court cases have upheld the right of individual students to refrain from participating in daily pledge of allegiance exercises on the ground that their participation conflicts with their religious beliefs. In pledge-of-allegiance cases, the courts have taken the position that a refusal to recite the pledge does not threaten any major public interest; hence, the state has no compelling interest in compelling *all* students to participate in this activity.

However, suppose you encountered a situation in which a religious group claimed that teaching students to read was contrary to the group's fundamental religious convictions. It is doubtful the courts would excuse students who belonged to this group from reading instruction. The state probably would be able to demonstrate that there is a compelling public interest in teaching future citizens to read.

Courts often have ruled that your students' religious views may excuse them from certain parts of the school program. For example, courts sometimes have upheld students' rights to refrain from dancing and viewing films, based on the students' religious convictions. In recent years, there have been challenges by parents to ban the teaching of literary works such as *The Wizard of Oz* and *Macbeth* on the grounds that they promote witchcraft. For the most part, courts have supported school officials' contentions that familiarity with these works is essential to the complete educational development of students, something in which the state has a compelling interest.

The issue of prayer and meditation as forms of religious expression has drawn lots of attention and has been the subject of considerable dispute. To understand this complex issue, you must remember that the First Amendment states that Congress shall make no law respecting the establishment of religion, or prohibiting the free exercise of religion. Therefore, the schools, as governmental bodies, cannot seek to further a religious belief or impose a religious practice on students. However, neither can the school prohibit a student from exercising his or her own religious freedom.

Suppose you were asked, "Is school prayer against the law?" In considering your answer, you need to look back at the First Amendment to the United States Constitution. What you will discover is that the Amendment prohibits state support or sanction for a particular religious practice, for example prayer, Bible readings, or posting the Ten Commandments. This means that courts are unlikely to support school policies that might seem to advance a particular religion. Though a few public schools continue to allow prayers to be recited over loudspeakers and at required educational events, legal precedents suggest that these practices will not be supported if suits are brought on behalf of students who complain about them. There continues to be some ambiguity in this area. For example, are athletic events such as football games educational experiences? Are prayers at such events legal or illegal? These and other questions are still being asked, and patterns of court decisions continue to evolve.

Student Dress and Appearance

The topic of student dress and appearance has resurfaced in recent years as some school districts have considered requiring all students to wear a uniform. (This idea even received positive mention from the President of the United States in a recent State of the Union address.) Proponents claim that uniforms will result in a decrease in discipline problems. Many students, along with their parents and guardians, have not found this idea appealing, and there have been court challenges to the authority of schools to place restrictions on what students can wear to school.

Though many court cases have dealt with this issue, a review of decisions reveals only a few consistent patterns. Basically, courts have recognized that schools do enjoy some rights to govern what students wear to school (Fischer, Schimmel, & Kelly, 1999). However, school officials do not enjoy unrestricted power in this area. In the case of *Bannister v. Paradis* (1970), the court ruled that a school can exclude students whose clothing is unsanitary or whose clothing violates obscenity standards. However, this logic by no means suggests that school leaders have blanket authority to ban wearing of blue jeans or other clothing on the grounds that they are too informal for school wear.

What the courts seem to be saying is that dress standards established by a school district cannot be capricious or arbitrary. Standards must bear a reasonable relationship to the educational process or to the health or safety of students. For example, if your school adopts a regulation barring students from wearing floppy clothing that might conceal a weapon, this restriction might be defended on safety grounds. Similarly, courts probably would be inclined to uphold regulations your school might adopt forbidding students to wear shirts with slogans that could lead to a disruption of the instructional process by prompting fights or other unrest. In recent years, the courts have tended to uphold school regulations banning the wearing of clothing associated with gang membership such as certain kinds of caps, earrings, jewelry, and other emblems.

In the absence of compelling data indicating that uniforms or strict dress codes are necessary for maintaining an orderly and safe education environment, it is questionable whether such standards will survive legal challenges. Many schools have instituted voluntary uniform policies. That is, they adopt an official uniform, encourage students to wear it, but do not punish individuals who choose not to do so. This policy places compliance in the hands of parents or guardians and students. These voluntary programs have met with some success.

Hairstyle and grooming standard regulations have been the subject of numerous court cases. Some courts have held that hairstyle is a more fundamental right than clothing style. The argument has been that a restriction on hairstyle represents an unacceptably intrusive invasion of individual privacy. Where hairstyle regulations have been supported when they have been legally challenged, courts have found that regulations were developed either with (1) a clear focus on students' health and safety, or (2) as a response to prevent a clear and documented interference with the educational process. In general, schools today give students much broader latitude in the area of personal grooming and dress than was the case a quarter of a century ago.

Search and Seizure

Concerns about drugs and weapons on school campuses have prompted much interest in the issue of search and seizure. For example, school officials have often wished to conduct searches of school lockers, automobiles parked in student lots, possessions of students, and, sometimes, students themselves. The need to search for drugs, weapons, and other illegal items that potentially can threaten the general student population has had to be weighed against Fourth Amendment guarantees against unreasonable search and seizure.

In general, court decisions in this area require school officials to apply four basic tests as they attempt to decide whether a proposed search is appropriate. The first test relates to the *nature of the material or object* they will be looking for. The greater the potential danger to the health and safety of students, the stronger the justification for the search. For example, a gun or bomb poses a tremendous danger to all students in a school, and a search certainly could be justified in response to this potential threat to safety. However, a stolen book generates no immediate threat. As a result, a highly intrusive search probably cannot be justified.

The second test used in determining the potential legality of a proposed search has to do with the *quality of the information* that has led to the search decision. In deciding the issue of information quality, the reliability of individuals providing supporting evidence must be weighed. If several reliable people provide similar information, a stronger case for a search can be made than if information comes in the form of a tip from an anonymous caller. If a search is to be particularly invasive (that is, if it involves a search of a person, a student's clothing, or a student's private possessions, such as a purse or a wallet), then school officials must demonstrate *probable cause*. This calls for a very high standard of evidence as a justification for the search and is equivalent to what courts require before issuing a search warrant.

The third test concerns the *nature of the place to be searched.* If this is an area where there is a high expectation of privacy, school officials need extremely reliable information to justify the search. This would apply if you intended to search a student's person, a student's clothing, or a private possession, such as a purse or wallet. However, there is much less of an expectation of privacy for an area such as a school locker. A search of a locker can be justified on slimmer evidence than a search of a student's person.

The fourth test concerns the *nature of the proposed search.* Highly intrusive searches that may result in an invasion of privacy require considerable evidence before a search can be justified. However, minor searches that involve little invasion of privacy need less supporting evidence.

The case of *New Jersey v. T.L.O.* (1985) set some important search and seizure precedents. In this case, a vice principal questioned a girl suspected of smoking, a behavior not permitted by school rules. At the principal's request, the girl opened her purse. It contained not only cigarettes but also drug paraphernalia. This led the principal to do a thorough search of her purse. The girl challenged the search as unjustified and alleged that it violated her rights to be free of unreasonable searches. The case ultimately ended up in the U.S. Supreme Court.

In its decision, the Court stated that the initial suspicion that the girl had been smoking and might have cigarettes in her possession was sufficient reason to ask her to open her purse. Once this was done, the physical evidence of drug paraphernalia provided sufficient justification for the extensive search of her purse that followed.

The ruling in *New Jersey v. T.L.O.* seemed to give school officials considerable latitude in search and seizure situations. However, there are important limits on this authority. For example, if you want to conduct a search of a student, you must have *reasonable suspicion* that the individual has violated a specific rule. Reasonable suspicion refers to evidence that is sufficiently compelling to convince a prudent and cautious individual that some criminal or illegal activity has occurred. General "fishing expeditions" are not permitted, and, when undertaken in the absence of reasonable suspicions, they are likely to be viewed by courts as illegal invasions of students' privacy rights.

To summarize, case law relating to search and seizure does not provide you with absolutely clear guidelines. In general, our advice to you is not to attempt searches on your own initiative. Responsibility for searches should be left in the hands of school administrators who are in a better position to check on the legality of search and seizure procedures.

Due Process

Discussion of student rights and responsibilities inevitably leads to the issue of *due process.* Due process is a principle requiring that certain procedures and safeguards must be followed when accusing students of failing to comply with rules or regulations.

Until the late 1960s, school attendance was widely regarded as a *privilege* to be enjoyed by those who were willing to live by the established rules. Because schooling was not seen as a fundamental *right* protected by the constitution, students had no legal recourse if they were removed from school for violating any school rule. In this earlier era, absence of schooling or possession of a high school diploma was not seen as imposing any serious hardships on an individual.

However, after World War II, it became evident that literacy and the possession of a high school diploma were important for the future economic well being of individuals. Thus, to deprive an individual of an education had serious consequences. This view, coupled with the fact that public schools were tax-supported institutions, soon led to the idea that education was much more than a privilege extended to those who were willing to conform to the desires of school officials. It began to be regarded as a substantial right. This right merited due-process protection.

A legal precedent extending due-process safeguards to public schools was established in the *Goss v. Lopez* case in 1975. In its decision, the court noted that while the United States Constitution does not require states to establish public schools, once they are established, a student's right to attend them is a constitutionally protected property right. Therefore, efforts to deny students access to schooling through such measures as expulsion and suspension must be accompanied by due-process procedures in conformity with the Fourteenth Amendment to the Constitution.

There are two basic components of due process. The first, or *substantive component,* consists of the basic set of principles on which due process is based. The second, or *procedural component,* delineates procedures that must be followed to ensure that due-process rights have not been violated.

The following are included in the substantive component of due process:

- Individuals are not to be disciplined on the basis of unwritten rules.
- Rules must not be unduly vague.
- Individuals charged with rules violations are entitled to a hearing before an impartial body.
- Identities of witnesses are to be revealed.
- Decisions must be supported by substantial evidence.
- A public or private hearing can be requested by the individual accused of a rule violation.

The following steps are consistent with guidelines to be followed by schools to ensure compliance with the procedural component of due process:

- Rules governing students' behavior are to be distributed in writing to students and their parents/guardians at the beginning of the school year.
- Whenever a student is accused of a serious violation of rules that can lead to the loss of a right, charges must be provided in writing to the student and to his or her parent/guardian.
- Written notice of the hearing to consider the alleged violation must be given, with sufficient time for the student and his or her representatives to prepare a defense. However, the hearing must be scheduled in a timely manner (usually within two weeks).
- A fair hearing must include the following:
    - Right of the accused to be represented by legal counsel,
    - Right of the accused to present a defense and to introduce evidence,
    - Right of the accused to face his or her accusers, and
    - Right of the accused to cross-examine witnesses.
- The decision of the hearing board must be based on evidence presented and must be rendered within a reasonable time.
- The accused must be informed of his or her right to appeal the decision.

The need to comply with due-process requirements means that you and others in your school need to exercise great care in initiating actions against a student who is suspected of having violated an important rule or regulation. Due process requirements, for example, must be carefully followed when your school administrators take actions to suspend or expel students.

Suspension is defined as a temporary separation from school. A suspension of less than 10 days' duration is considered to be a *short-term suspension*. When students face a potential short-term suspension, only minimal due-process guidelines must be observed. In such cases, they must receive (1) at least an oral (preferably a written) notice of the specific charges that led to the suspension decision, (2) an explanation of the evidence supporting these charges, and (3) an opportunity to provide their version of facts relevant to the situation. When the result of action by school officials is to be short-term suspension, it is not required that legal counsel be present to represent the students' interests when they are apprised of the relevant charges and provided with an opportunity to challenge their accuracy.

A suspension exceeding 10 days in length is considered to be a *long-term suspension*. Long-term suspension has the potential to seriously interfere with a student's ability to profit from school instruction. Hence, school officials are obliged to follow all of the guidelines noted under the procedural component of due process.

Expulsion is serious. It permanently separates a student from the school. In situations when expulsion is likely to be the end result of actions initiated against a student by school authorities, strict due-process procedures must be followed. Usually, you and the administrators at your school do not, by themselves, have the authority to make an expulsion decision. This tends to be a prerogative of the highest governing officials of the school district. The policy of referring this kind of decision to higher authorities helps ensure that procedures are followed that adequately protect and represent the student's interests. If they are not, the student or his or her representatives may initiate potentially expensive legal actions against the school district and the school board.

There are important implications of due process for you as a teacher. First, you need to recognize that your students have been legally defined as citizens whose rights are protected by the United States Constitution. This means you must proceed in a fair and appropriate manner in making and enforcing school rules. However, the need to observe due-process guidelines by no means diminishes your authority to control students in the classroom. The courts have affirmed your rights, as a teacher, to establish and maintain a safe and orderly educational environment for students.

The following are some guidelines you may find useful in considering whether rules you develop are fair and appropriate:

- Is the purpose behind the rule clear?
- Is the rule consistent with local, state, and federal laws?
- Is the rule stated in clear and precise language?
- Does the rule bear a clear relationship to the need to maintain an orderly educational process and to prevent disruptions?
- Do all students know that the rule has been established?

Gender Issues

Gender discrimination has been a topic of great interest in recent years. Title IX of the Education Amendments of 1972 stands as landmark legislation in this area. Title IX provides that any educational program or activity that receives federal financial assistance cannot exclude individuals from activities on the basis of gender. Following adoption of this federal regulation, many state legislatures enacted equal rights acts of their own to cover general gender discrimination issues in their respective states.

As a result of Title IX, related legislation, and court decisions, it is no longer permissible to exclude individuals from any part of the school curriculum on the basis of their gender. However, this does not mean that students may not be separated for instruction in some particularly sensitive topics. When this is done, however, school officials must be prepared to respond to potential court challenges that would require them to provide strong reasons in support of such a decision.

In recent years, the issue of separate schools for students of different genders has occasionally come up. In general, schools for single sexes have been found to violate gender discrimination laws. There are exceptions, however. In one case, a school system maintained one high school for academically talented boys and another one for academically talented girls. Because attendance at either school was voluntary and the two schools were genuinely equal in terms of their size, prestige, and quality of academic programs, the courts allowed the arrangement to continue (*Vorcheimer v. School District of Philadelphia*, 1977).

The biggest impact of Title IX has been in the area of athletics. Both genders must have equal access to non-contact sports. There may be separate teams for each gender if a school is able to fund two teams. If only one team can be funded, students from both genders must be eligible to participate. Although funding for teams of different genders does not need to be equal in terms of dollar amounts allocated, team schedules, equipment, and support must be roughly comparable.

Another gender issue that, at one time, was the source of considerable controversy concerned school policies that barred married or pregnant students from attending the same schools as other students (or even from attending school at all). Years ago, many schools required these students to attend alternative schools or to stay home and continue their studies through correspondence courses. Over the years, these regulations have been struck down. Typically, the courts have argued that the presence of married or pregnant students has not been demonstrated to have an adverse impact on the overall educational environment of the school.

Rights of married students to participate in extracurricular activities have generally been supported by the courts. In one Ohio case (*Davis v. Meek*, 1972), a local school district adopted a policy barring married students from participating in school-sponsored athletic events. This policy was challenged. In its decision, the court affirmed that participation in these activities was an important part of students' overall educational opportunities and that a policy excluding married students represented an illegal deprivation of their rights.

To summarize, court decisions, by and large, have greatly reduced the number of school policies and practices that discriminate against students on the basis of gender. This by no means suggests that no such policies or practices remain. In our legal system, there are no "educational police" going about the country checking to see that procedures everywhere are consistent with what courts have decided. A practice or policy in a given location may continue until it is challenged in a court of law. Only then may local officials be obliged to bring their policies into conformity with what courts, generally, have found to be legally defensible practice. Policies that discriminate against students on the basis of gender are likely to remain in place for a long time in places where school leaders believe there is little likelihood that such policies will be challenged in court.

Family Rights and Privacy

Since the 1960s, concerned citizens have raised questions about potential misuses of school records. Much of the discussion has focused on long-term damage to students that might occur as a result of their being stigmatized by comments made about them in school records.

In 1975, Congress passed the Family Educational Rights and Privacy Act in response to this concern. This legislation requires schools to protect students' privacy rights by denying access to their files to anyone except individuals immediately concerned with their education. Files can be opened to others only with the consent of students' parents or, in the case of students who are 18 years old or older, the students themselves. The law also gives parents free access to school files and records pertaining to their children. Students who are 18 years of age and older have similar rights to see this information. After parents have viewed files and records of their children (or after students who are 18 years of age and older have viewed their records), they may request to amend any record they believe to be (1) inaccurate, (2) misleading, or (3) a violation of their privacy rights.

The access to student records by parents and by students 18 and older authorized by the Family Educational Rights and Privacy Act means that you need to exercise care when placing information in these files. Your comments should be descriptive rather than judgmental. It is particularly important to avoid malicious or other kinds of general statements that might be construed as a negative summary judgment about a student. Such comments may subject you to legal action (Connors, 1991).

You also need to be careful about the kinds of comments you make to others about individual students. A person who knowingly spreads false information that hurts another's reputation (for example, that of a student) has committed slander, a punishable offense.

Some Emerging Issues

There are several new topics that have recently received considerable attention. It is likely that they will be the subject of some future court decisions that will influence educational practice.

One of the issues relates to school responsibility for student-to-student sexual harassment. It has become increasingly clear in recent years that school officials have legal responsibility to stop sexual harassment among students. The exact nature of this responsibility has yet to be clearly defined (Fischer, Schimmel and Kelly, 1999). However, you may place yourself in potential legal jeopardy if you become aware of student-to-student sexual harassment and choose to ignore the behavior.

Limiting control of students to content on the Internet is another issue that promises to become the focus of numerous legal actions. In recent years, computers and Internet access have become a regular feature of secondary schools. However, certain risks have accompanied the educational benefits these electronic wonders bring to the classroom. In addition to enabling young people to access important knowledge, they also allow easy accessibility to websites containing material that many educators, parents, and guardians find objectionable. There continue to be interesting legal questions regarding the authority of school officials to block access to this kind of information. Another concern has to do with ease of copying and printing material from Internet sites. There is potential here for students to violate copyright regulations, and we may expect to see an increased number of legal actions in the years ahead focusing on this issue.

Other issues that are likely to result in court decisions in the next few years relate to such issues as protecting the rights of homosexual students, the legality of hate speech codes, and a clarification of dress codes.

Legal Issues Affecting Teachers

Legal issues concerned with schools and schooling do not pertain only to students. There also are important legal dimensions related to your rights and obligations as a teacher. These include such areas as conditions of employment, contracts, freedom of expression, academic freedom, drug and alcohol abuse, copyrights, and professional performance of duties.

Conditions of Employment

Generally, you must possess a valid *teaching certificate* as a condition of employment. Some states prohibit school districts from paying salaries of teachers who do not hold a valid certificate. Several court cases have declared that people who sign contracts and perform teaching duties without possessing valid certificates are "volunteers" who have donated their services to the district.

Most school districts will require you to register your certificate with the personnel office of the school district prior to the issuance of a paycheck. Some states prohibit payment by a school district until proof of certification is provided. It is important for you to accurately represent your certification status when you seek employment as a teacher. If you suggest that you have a certificate when, in fact, you do not, this misrepresentation may eliminate your future prospects not only in the district where you have sought employment, but elsewhere in your state as well. The significance of this issue highlights the importance of determining your certification status prior to leaving your preparation program.

Certification is a state responsibility. Each state has its own requirements for people who wish to teach in its schools. Because teaching requirements vary from state to state, when you complete a teacher preparation program and receive a teaching certificate in your state, you may not necessarily have met all the certification requirements of other states. If you are interested in teaching in another state, you should contact the Teacher Certification Office in the State Department of Education in the state where you wish to seek employment. This office will be able to provide information about procedures you need to follow to qualify for a certificate.

Teaching certificates are not guaranteed for the life of the holder. They may be terminated for a variety of reasons, and states can establish conditions that must be met to renew them or keep them in force. In many states, certificates have fixed expiration dates. For example, you may find regulations that require you to meet renewal conditions such as taking college or university courses or participating in other professional development opportunities. Certificates may be revoked for conviction of a felony, public displays of immorality, incompetence, or extreme examples of socially unacceptable behavior.

CRITICAL INCIDENT

Completing the Employment Application

Rodney Harte started a business after he graduated from college. The business prospered, but his day-to-day routines did not satisfy his need to be involved in more service-oriented work. Rodney always had enjoyed being around young people and, after talking to several of his friends who were high school teachers, he started taking courses at a local university to qualify for a teaching certificate.

Rodney proved to be an excellent student. He completed the required course work, and he did his student teaching. As a result of his outstanding performance, he received excellent recommendations from his supervising teacher and from the university professor who worked with him during the student teaching semester. At this point, he made an official application for a teaching certificate.

When he was completing the application form, he noted a question asking for information about any prior legal problems. Many years earlier, Rodney had been convicted of shoplifting. He noted this information on his application, being careful to explain the circumstances and that many years had passed since this unhappy episode. After some follow-up correspondence regarding this matter, the state department of education granted Rodney a teaching certificate. He began looking for a teaching position.

During his job search, he was interviewed for a position that he felt was ideal. It was in a good school district, not too far from his home, and offered opportunities to teach and assist coaches in the school's athletic program. During the interview, he was asked whether he had ever been convicted of a felony. He reflected on this matter before answering. He considered the state department of education's review of his situation and its decision to award him a teaching certificate. As a result of these deliberations, he concluded that there was no need for the school district to know about his prior conviction, and he told the interviewing official that his record was clear.

He was hired for the position and began teaching at the beginning of the fall term. At the end of September, he received a note from the school district's central office requesting him to report immediately to the director of personnel. When he arrived, he was told that his employment was being terminated. The school district had learned of his felony conviction, and he was being dismissed for failing to report this information.

■ ■ ■

What should Rodney Harte do? Did the district have a right to ask him questions about a possible felony conviction? Did he have an obligation to provide this information given that the matter had not resulted in denial of a teaching certificate by the state? Was it fair for him to be held accountable for something that had occurred many years ago? What do you think a court of law might decide were Rodney Harte to hire an attorney and contest the dismissal action?

Teachers' Contracts

Teachers' contracts are important documents. They contain information related to such issues as conditions of employment, salary levels, sick leave policies, insurance provisions, and grievance procedures. For a contract to be valid, it must include these four basic features:

- Language that reflects a meeting of the minds of the signatories,
- Signatories who are competent parties,
- Obligations from each of the signatories to the other(s), and
- Definite and clear terms delineating what is to be done and by whom (Fischer, Schimmel, & Kelly, 1999).

The phrase *meeting of the minds* means that all parties must agree on the contents of the contract. One party must offer the contract and the other must accept it. (There may be some negotiation of provisions before acceptance occurs.) In the case of teaching contracts, the formal process of offer and acceptance is not officially over until the contract is approved by action of the school board.

For a contract to be between *competent parties*, the individual signatories must be of legal age and be legally and intellectually able to engage in and conclude needed negotiations. As a prospective teacher, you must have a teaching certificate (or be eligible to receive one before you begin work) to be competent to enter into a contract.

Teaching contracts are legal documents. A contracting party who breaks a contract may face legal action. For example, a school district may sue to collect monetary damages from you if you break a signed and approved contract. Likewise, you could take a school district to court if it failed to observe the terms of a valid contract.

There are circumstances that make it possible for contracting parties to agree to dissolve their agreement in an amicable fashion. If you have a compelling reason to be released from a signed and approved contract, the appropriate procedure is to make a formal request to the school district to be released from the contract. There is no legal obligation on the part of the school district to agree to your request, but often it will be honored. As a practical matter, school districts do not want people working for them who would really prefer to be doing something else.

There are several types of teachers' contracts. Typically, new teachers are offered a *term contract*. A term contract offers employment for a specified term, usually for one school year. At the conclusion of the term, a decision is made about renewing the contract. The term contract allows either party (the school district or the teacher) to negotiate new terms of employment or to terminate the relationship at the end of the contract period. No reason for terminating the relationship needs to be provided. In some places, term contracts are issued to all teachers. In others, regulations require that term contracts be issued only to new teachers. Usually, after they have taught for a given number of years, teachers must be offered a different type of contract.

A second type of contract is the *continuing contract*. Unlike term contracts, basic employment provisions of continuing contracts do not have to be renewed after a specified term. (Ordinarily there are allowances for adjustments of salaries.) This kind of a contract is automatically renewed at the end of each year. Before a district can make a decision not to renew a continuing contract, it must provide specific and legal reasons for the termination, and it must follow strict procedural guidelines. This means that teachers holding continuing contracts enjoy more security of employment than teachers holding term contracts.

A third type of contract is the *tenure contract*. Like a continuing contract, a tenure contract remains in force from year to year. Usually teachers holding tenure contracts can be dismissed only when they have been found guilty of violating state statutes governing behavior of teachers. The school board has the burden of proving that there is legal cause for dismissing a teacher.

 WHAT DO *YOU* THINK? ▬▬▬▬▬▬▬▬▬▬▬▬▬

Should Tenure Contracts Be Banned?

Tenure is an issue that has attracted much attention in recent years. Some policy makers, such as governors and state legislators, impatient with the rate of change in schools, view tenure as a significant obstacle to educational innovation.

A member of a state legislature made these remarks during a hearing of a committee considering education legislation.

> "We should repeal present teacher-tenure legislation. All tenure does is keep marginal teachers on the job. People in other lines of work don't have this protection. Teachers need to be held accountable for their performance and dismissed if it does not measure up. There is no place for these sort of lifetime guarantees in an area as important as educating the youth of our nation.
> "Good teachers should not be afraid of these changes. They don't need this kind of legal safety net. It only casts suspicion on all teachers that they are incompetent and need this type of protection."

Questions

1. Do tenure laws make it impossible to hold teachers accountable for their actions?
2. Would the quality of teaching improve if tenure laws were removed? Why or why not?
3. How would you respond to the position reflected in this legislator's remarks?

Tenure contracts tend not to be awarded to teachers until they have worked success-fully in a given district for several years. A typical probationary period is three years. During their initial years of service, teachers are issued term contracts. Laws that established tenure contracts were passed, in part, to protect teachers from political interference on the part of parents or others who might take issue with what they were teaching in their classrooms and try to get them dismissed. Tenure laws also repre-sented attempts to provide more stability to the group of teachers working a particular school by offering teachers considerable employment security.

Some critics have attacked tenure contracts because they seem to guarantee lifetime employment for teachers. This is a misconception. Tenure does not guarantee perma-nent employment. What it does guarantee is that due-process procedures will be fol-lowed in any proceedings that might lead to a dismissal and that dismissal will occur only when certain conditions have been met. Some reasons for firing tenured teachers include: (1) evidence of gross incompetence, (2) physical or mental incapacity, (3) neglect of duty, (4) immorality, (5) unprofessional conduct, and (6) conviction of a crime.

Teacher Dismissal and Due Process

There is no general answer to the question of whether you, as a teacher, always have the right to challenge non-renewal of your contract or actions undertaken to dismiss you from your position. Legal discussions of this matter have focused on two basic rights, liberty rights and property rights.

Liberty rights free individuals from having personal restraints imposed on them. These rights give them, among other things, opportunities to engage in the common occupations of life (*Meyer v. Nebraska*, 1923). Some court decisions in this area have established that school districts cannot use unconstitutional reasons to deny teachers employment. As a result, you cannot be dismissed for such things as gender, age, or religious beliefs.

Property rights, among other things, give individuals rights to enjoy benefits associ-ated with their employment. Courts have wrestled with the question of whether teach-ing, as defined in a teacher's contractual agreement with a school district, is a property right. In general, the answer depends on the kind of contract a teacher holds and the specific language it contains. Sometimes this issue becomes murky. For example, term contracts ordinarily terminate a teacher's employment on a given date. On the surface, it appears that the teacher has no property right to employment by the district after the termination date of the contract. However, in places where it has become customary for districts to almost automatically reissue new term contracts to teachers, teachers may enjoy some property rights to employment going even beyond the strict terminology in their contracts. The courts tend to weigh questions about such matters in terms of the specifics of the particular cases they consider.

In circumstances where there is agreement that teachers have either liberty rights or property rights that merit legal protection, actions undertaken by school districts to interfere with these rights (typically actions taken to dismiss teachers) must follow strict due-process guidelines. If you were in such a situation, you would have to be given notice of charges against you, provided with an opportunity to state your position in a hearing, given a chance to respond to charges made against you, and allowed to have your position represented by legal counsel. Some states with stricter procedures would also require the school district to provide you with an opportunity to remediate any deficient behaviors before initiating a formal dismissal proceeding.

Reporting Suspected Child Abuse

Public concern about child abuse continues to grow. As a result, all 50 states now have legislation requiring people in certain positions to report suspected cases of child abuse. You, as an educator, are included among the group of people with special legal obligations to file these reports.

No state requires a teacher to know beyond a reasonable doubt that a child is being abused before reporting suspicions to the authorities. All you need is a reasonable suspicion of abuse (Monks & Proulx, 1986).

Each state has a set of specific procedures that are to be followed when reporting cases of suspected abuse. Some states have established a 24-hour telephone hot line to make it easier for suspected cases to be reported. In most cases, there is a requirement that an oral report be followed by a written report within a few days (often from about one to three days). Many school districts provide teachers with forms they can use in preparing reports of suspected cases of abuse.

All states provide teachers with some immunity from lawsuits for reporting suspected child abuse. This offers protection to individuals who may, otherwise, hesitate to file a report out of fear of reprisals. Immunity from lawsuits is not unlimited. Immunity is guaranteed only when reports are filed in good faith. For example, if you are found to have filed a report maliciously for the purpose of harming the child's parents, you may find yourself facing a lawsuit.

Many states have established penalties for individuals who suspect a child is being abused but fail to report it. Penalties range from fines up to about $1,000 to jail terms of up to one year. These penalties and the long-term negative consequences of abuse on a student's development make it imperative for you to recognize signs of potential abuse and to become familiar with proper reporting procedures.

Legal Liability

The volume of litigation involving teachers has increased in recent years. One major category of liability you can face as a teacher is tort liability. A *tort* is a civil wrong against another that results in either personal injury or property damage. There are many categories of torts, including negligence, invasion of privacy, assault, and defamation of character. The areas that result in the largest number of lawsuits against teachers are (1) excessive use of force in disciplining students, and (2) negligence.

Excessive Use of Force

Many court cases have centered on the issue of using physical punishment as a means of disciplining students. In the case of *Ingraham v. Wright* (1977), the United States Supreme Court ruled that teachers could use reasonable but not excessive force in disciplining a student. The justices further noted that corporal punishment did not constitute cruel and unusual punishment, and, therefore, did not violate students' constitutionally protected rights.

Some individuals mistakenly conclude that this makes the use of corporal punishment legal. This is not the case. Because of the concern for child abuse and the message that is conveyed by hitting students, numerous states and school districts have prohibited corporal punishment. Even where corporal punishment is technically allowed, often teachers must follow strict guidelines before administering such discipline. For example, they may be required to ask an administrator or some other designated person to act as a witness. Even then, legal action is possible if the punishment worsens a student's preexisting health condition. This can be the case even if the person administering the punishment was unaware of the condition. In addition, allega-

Note the safety goggles and the teacher watching closely as the student transfers chemicals from one glass container to another. This kind of careful monitoring greatly diminishes the chance that this teacher would face a misfeasance complaint in the event of an accident.

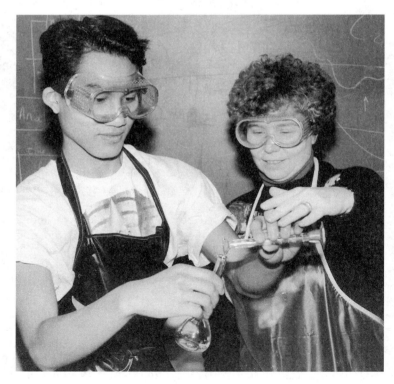

tions of excessive force by students or their legal representatives may result in criminal assault and battery charges being filed against the teacher. In such situations, juries often decide cases on whether or not, in their view, the teacher acted as a prudent parent would have acted.

Corporal punishment is an extremely controversial topic. In light of recent concerns about child abuse and the possibility of legal action against teachers who are deemed to have gone too far in administering corporal punishments, we subscribe to the view that the risks associated with corporal punishment outweigh potential benefits. It is a practice you should avoid.

Negligence

Negligence is a failure to use reasonable care and/or take prudent actions to prevent harm from coming to someone. These are the three basic types of negligence:

- Nonfeasance,
- Misfeasance,
- Malfeasance.

Nonfeasance occurs when an individual fails to act when there is a responsibility to do so. Many lawsuits filed against teachers fall into this category. Ordinarily they stem from a situation when something bad has happened to a student and the teacher has been absent from his or her assigned place of responsibility. For example, if a student is injured in your classroom while you have slipped out to have a quick cup of coffee across the hall, you might be found guilty of nonfeasance. Another nonfeasance suit might result if you have information that a fight is about to occur between two students, fail to act to stop it, allow the fight to go on, and a student is hurt.

By no means does this imply that there are no circumstances that can justify your absence from your designated area of responsibility. There can be compelling reasons for being out of the room. For example, if someone in the hall lights a fire in a wastebasket, you leave your room to put it out, and a student is injured in the room while your are away, you probably would not face a nonfeasance suit. Even if one were filed, there would be little likelihood you would be found guilty.

Misfeasance occurs when an individual fails to act in a proper manner to prevent harm from coming to someone. In the case of misfeasance, the person acts, but the action taken is not proper or correct. Misfeasance suits against teachers often result from their failure to take appropriate precautions when having students work with potentially dangerous equipment or materials or when they engage in potentially harmful activities. Misfeasance suits often are the result of an injury in a shop or a physical education class. For example, one high school teacher was charged with misfeasance as the result of an injury to a student during wrestling practice. It was alleged that the teacher did not exercise appropriate supervision and had not informed the wrestlers about potential dangers of particular holds.

To avoid misfeasance suits, you have to provide clear and specific instruction to your students regarding such issues as equipment safety and proper uses of chemicals and equipment. You also must provide proper supervision when they work with potentially dangerous equipment and materials or engage in other activities, which, if not performed properly, have the potential to harm them.

Malfeasance occurs when a person deliberately acts in an improper manner and, thereby, cases harm to another. For example, you might be charged with malfeasance in a situation at school when, in an effort to stop a fight, you used too much physical force and injured a student.

Academic Freedom and Freedom of Expression

Academic freedom issues often involve conflicts between (1) teachers' rights to conduct their classes according to their best professional judgment, and (2) school authorities' responsibilities to see that the authorized curriculum is taught. Court decisions in this area do not reflect a consistent pattern.

One principle that has often been supported by the courts is that school officials have the right to impose some limitations on teachers' academic freedom. For example, your school district has the right to require you to teach the subject-matter content of courses to which you have been assigned. If your responsibility is to teach mathematics, you cannot avoid teaching this content and, instead, promote your personal political views on the grounds that such instruction is an expression of your academic freedom.

However, the courts usually have decided that school districts cannot require you to avoid dealing with controversial issues in their classes. In one case focusing on this issue, the right of an American history teacher to use a simulation exercise that evoked strong racial feelings was upheld (*Kingsville Independent School District v. Cooper,* 1980). In another case, the court supported a teacher who challenged an administrative ruling that forbade her from using a particular book. In this decision, the court ruled that the book was appropriate for high school students, contained nothing obscene, and that the decision to ban its use had violated the teacher's academic freedom rights (*Parducci v. Rutland,* 1979).

In the *Parducci* case, the court noted that the right to teach, evaluate, and experiment with new ideas is fundamental to a democratic society. In other cases, however, courts have upheld the rights of school boards to prohibit use of certain books, even literary classics. Decisions in this area have tended to be responsive to specific characteristics of the work in question, the age and sophistication of the students, and the nature of the local community.

Freedom of expression refers to the rights of individuals to state their views on a subject without fear of reprisal. Court cases in this area that have involved teachers often have resulted from situations in which school authorities have attempted to punish teachers for out-of-classroom speech.

A landmark freedom-of-expression case is *Pickering v. Board of Education of Township School District 205, Will County* (1968). Pickering, a teacher, wrote a letter to the editor of the local newspaper criticizing the way school funds were being allocated. Members of the school board were outraged. They claimed Pickering had made untrue statements in the letter and, thereby, had damaged the reputations of school board members and leading school administrators. The board took action to dismiss Pickering. Pickering disagreed with this decision and challenged it in court. The case ultimately made its way up to the United States Supreme Court.

In arriving at its decision in the *Pickering* case, the High Court considered two key issues. The first centered on whether a teacher can be dismissed for making critical comments about the school district and its policies in public. On this issue, the Court ruled that teachers have a right to speak out on school issues as part of a general effort to provide for a more informed public. The second issue the Court considered had to do with whether a teacher can be dismissed for making false statements. In this particular case, the Court found that Pickering had made only one false statement in his letter. In the absence of any information that Pickering had knowingly or deliberately made the false statement, the Court decided in favor of Pickering. In other cases, dismissal actions taken against teachers have been upheld when evidence has been presented that they knowingly made false statements with a clear understanding they were recklessly disregarding the truth.

However, these rulings by no means suggest that, as a teacher, you have a right to complain publicly about *everything*. There are some activities of schools and school districts that may not be seen as matters of public concern by the courts. In addition, the style and the manner of your complaint is important. Complaints cannot be made at a time or in a manner that interferes with the operation of the school or the responsibilities of administrators to perform their assigned responsibilities.

Copyright Law

Copyright law seeks to protect the works of authors and artists. Federal copyright law covers use of materials copied from books, journals, computer programs, and videotapes.

The doctrine of *fair use* is an exception to copyright law that has implications for you as a teacher. Fair use seeks to balance the rights of a copyright owner with the public's interest in having easy access to new ideas and information. The fair use doctrine makes it permissible for you to make single copies of book chapters, articles from journals, short stories or poems, or charts and graphs for your own scholarly research or as part of your preparation for teaching lessons. Multiple copies (not to exceed one for each student in a class) may be made if guidelines related to (1) brevity, (2) spontaneity, and (3) cumulative effect are met (Committee on the Judiciary, 1976).

Brevity (as the term applies to fair use) for different kinds of materials is defined as follows:

- A complete poem may be used if it is not more than 250 words and not more than two pages in length.
- An excerpt from a longer poem may be used consisting of no more than 250 words.
- A complete article or story may be used that is less than 2,500 words long.
- From a longer work, an excerpt may be used that is less than 1,000 words in length or that consists of no more than 10 percent of the length of the total work, whichever is less.
- One chart, diagram, picture, or cartoon per book or periodical may be used (Committee on the Judiciary, 1976).

The issue of *spontaneity* refers to situations when your need to use the work is so close to the time it must be provided to students in your class that it would be unreasonable or impossible to request and receive permission to use it before this time.

Criteria applied to meet the cumulative effect standard include the following:

- The material is used for only one course.
- Not more than one short poem, article, short story, or essay or two excerpts from works by the same author and not more than three excerpts from the same collective work or periodical volume may be used without permission.
- There are not more than nine instances of such multiple copying for one course during one term.

Unless these fair use guidelines can be met, you are obligated to secure permission from authors, artists, or other copyright holders before making and distributing copies. If you fail to do so, you may face legal action brought by the copyright holders or their representatives.

It is also important to note that computer software programs are not covered by the fair use doctrine. It is illegal to make copies of commercially produced programs and to use them on different computers in the classroom unless specific permission has been granted. Many software vendors will sell a site license to a school or business authorizing the purchaser to make and distribute a given number of copies of a specific program.

There are special copyright provisions that apply to videotaping for educational purposes. A copyrighted program may be videotaped, provided that you use it for instructional purposes within 10 days and keep the videotape for no more than 45 days. The only legal use that can be made of the videotape between the tenth and the forty-fifth day is evaluating its contents. If you wish to keep a given program for some time and to use it repeatedly in your classes, you need to secure written permission from the copyright holder.

Failure to abide by provisions of copyright regulations can result in significant penalties. There may be an award to the copyright holder equivalent to a loss of profits resulting from the infringement or an amount of money determined by the court ranging between $500 and $20,000. If the court determines that the violator acted willfully, it can increase monetary damage to an amount as high as $100,000. However, if the violator can prove the infraction was unintentional, the court can scale back damages to a figure as low as $200.

Teachers' Private Lives

The case of *Board of Trustees v. Stubblefield* (1971) helped establish the principle of higher standards of behavior for people in certain professions, such as teaching. The argument is made that, because teachers work with impressionable young people, they should be held to especially high personal standards.

There have been many cases involving allegations of immoral teacher behavior. Typically, the courts have dealt quite harshly with teachers who have been found to be "immoral." The difficulty in deriving general principles from a review of these cases is that the terms *moral* and *immoral* tend to take on different meanings from place to place.

A theme that runs through many of these cases has to do with the perceived impact of a given teacher's behavior on his or her classroom performance and standing in the local community. When a teacher has been dismissed for alleged immoral behavior and there is evidence the behavior violates prevailing community standards, the courts have tended to support the dismissal action. However, when the alleged immoral behavior has been shown to have little if any impact on the teacher's ability to teach effectively and has elicited little negative reaction in the community, the courts have often held for the teacher and against the school officials who initiated the dismissal action.

Consequences have been severe for teachers whose immoral behaviors have involved students. Courts have upheld dismissals of a male teacher who was found playing strip poker with a student in a car, of another teacher whose offer to "spank" two female students was interpreted as a sexual advance, and of a teacher who tickled and used suggestive language to female students on a class field trip.

In still another case, a teacher was dismissed when a high school girl he had been dating became pregnant. He admitted to having an affair with the student, but contended that since the girl was not a student at the school where he taught there was no adverse impact on his teaching. The teacher felt he should be reinstated. The court that heard his case disagreed, arguing that no evidence of interference with the classroom performance of this individual was needed (*Denton v. South Kitsap School District No. 402*, 1973). The court found that the relationship between the teacher and any student constituted sexual misconduct that was inherently harmful to the school district.

Other cases in which teacher dismissal actions have been upheld have involved situations in which teachers have been arrested for public intoxication, convicted for drunk driving, shoplifting, lying about being sick to collect sick leave pay, allowing students to drink in the teachers' homes, taking school property, and engaging in welfare fraud. Conviction for any serious crime, such as a felony, ordinarily is grounds for dismissal.

To summarize, because of the sensitive role you play as a nurturer of young people, as a teacher you are expected to reflect standards of personal behavior that are higher than those expected of average citizens. Hence, you have to be a careful monitor of your own behavior. In particular, you have to avoid personal behaviors that interfere with your ability to function as an effective leader or that clearly conflict with standards of morality prevalent in your community.

Key Ideas in Summary

- Students have certain responsibilities. These include attendance, following reasonable rules and regulations, refraining from the possession of unsafe articles such as weapons and controlled substances, and behaving in socially responsible ways.
- Students enjoy considerable freedom-of-expression rights. Administrators have limited rights to oversee contents of student publications that are produced as part of the regular school program, but they may not censor materials simply on the grounds they are controversial or on other grounds that clearly violate students' constitutional rights. Administra-

tors have even less authority over student publications not produced under the auspices of the school. Students' oral speech behaviors are also constitutionally protected.

▪ In general, the courts have allowed students' religious beliefs as grounds for excusing them from school activities that cannot be shown to be essential to students' health or welfare or essential to the general society. In practice, this has meant that religious beliefs have been viewed as grounds for excusing students from pledge of allegiance ceremonies, but not as grounds from excusing them from instruction in a basic school subject as reading (viewed as an essential survival skill in our society).

▪ Regulations regarding dress and appearance have been supported most frequently when courts have found a demonstrable connection between a student's dress or appearance and (1) safety or health of the student body, or (2) disruption of the instructional process. Recent cases have also supported decisions to ban items of dress associated with gang membership.

▪ The Fourteenth Amendment to the United States Constitution guarantees due-process rights to citizens. These provide that certain procedures and safeguards be in place whenever decisions are considered that might result in negative consequences for students. There are two key components of due process, the substantive component and the procedural component. The substantive component identifies basic principles on which due process is based. The procedural component delineates procedures to be followed to ensure that due-process rights have not been violated.

▪ Title IX of the Education Amendments of 1972 banned gender discrimination from school programs receiving federal support. In general, state legislation and other actions have now extended this protection to all school programs. Today, schools usually cannot ban students from school programs based on gender.

▪ Search and seizure cases have considered the authority school officials have to search students, students' property, and such areas as school lockers. In determining whether a given search has been warranted, courts generally have considered (1) the nature of what is being looked for, (2) the quality of evidence leading to the decision to conduct a search, (3) the degree of expectation of privacy associated with the place to be searched, and (4) the nature or intrusiveness of the search.

▪ The federal Family Educational Rights and Privacy Act gives parents and students who are 18 years of age or older rights to look at school records. Further, the law prohibits records from being shown to anyone not immediately concerned with students' education. Parents (or students who are 18 or over and who ask to see their files) can request that records be amended to change information that they believe is (1) inaccurate, (2) misleading, or (3) in violation of privacy rights. Teachers can be sued if parents (or students 18 or over) believe they have written defamatory information in a record.

▪ Teachers' contracts are documents that establish a legal working relationship between teachers and the districts that employ them. Typically, contracts include the obligations of both teachers and the employing districts. To become valid, the school board of the employing district must approve a contract. There are several kinds of teaching contracts. Among them are term contracts, continuing contracts, and tenure contracts.

▪ Dismissal procedures must be followed when a school district decides to release a teacher with a continuing or a tenure contract. Dismissal actions against a teacher with a term contract cannot be initiated for reasons that are inconsistent with constitutional guarantees of citizenship. Processes to be followed when there are concerns about teachers' academic performance or other issues thought to impair their effectiveness vary somewhat depending on the types of contracts the individuals have and the specific language these contracts contain.

- All states have laws requiring teachers to report suspected child abuse. These laws provide some legal protection against reprisal for teachers who make such reports in good faith. There are penalties in many states for teachers who recognize a potential child-abuse situation and fail to report it.
- Teachers may be held liable for certain types of actions. Many teacher liability suits have resulted from charges of (1) excessive use of force when disciplining students, or (2) negligence. Negligence cases often have focused on issues related to nonfeasance (a failure of the teacher to act when he or she had a responsibility to act), misfeasance (a failure of the teacher to act in a proper manner to prevent harm from coming to a student), and malfeasance (a deliberately improper action of the teacher that causes harm to a student).
- In considering academic freedom issues, courts have weighed both teachers' rights to conduct their classrooms according to their own best professional judgment and needs of school district administrators to see that the prescribed curriculum is taught. In general, courts have supported actions of administrators to ensure mandated content is taught. However, courts have supported teachers in cases involving administrative attempts to stifle consideration of embarrassing or controversial issues in the classroom.
- Copyright regulations are designed to protect the interests of the developers of intellectual property such as books, journal articles, works of art, computer programs, and radio and television programs. In general, teachers need to request and receive written permission for making and distributing multiple copies of these materials. Fair use guidelines allow some limited classroom use of copyrighted material without securing permission; these guidelines must be adhered to strictly.
- Actions teachers take in their private lives sometimes come to the attention of the courts. The courts have declared that, because of their potential influence on young people, teachers can be held to higher moral and behavioral standards than citizens in general. Dismissal actions against teachers have frequently been upheld when courts have found their actions to undermine their credibility in the community and to make them ineffective as instructional leaders.

Reflections

1. What is your reaction to the balance of student rights and responsibilities? Do you think that circumstances dictate severely limiting student rights?

2. What are some implications for teachers of the due-process protections that students enjoy today?

3. What is your position on church-state issues? Have the rulings gone too far in limiting religious expressions such as the posting of the Ten Commandments in schools?

4. What position should the schools take on the use of textbooks or library books that a religious group finds objectionable?

5. What types of policies do you think need to be established to govern student use of the Internet?

6. Do you agree with the idea that teachers should be held to higher standards of personal conduct than the citizenry at large?

7. What is your response to proposals that tenure be eliminated because it protects incompetent teachers?

8. Is it fair for teachers to be legally bound to report incidences of suspected child abuse? Why, or why not?

9. What are the implications of the fair use doctrine for teachers? Do you think it is an appropriate standard for education?

10. Why are restrictions on use of software so strict? What might result if these restrictions were not in place? Would such a change increase or decrease the availability of high quality educational software? Why do you think so?

Learning Extensions

1. Review newspaper articles that have appeared over the past several months dealing with legal issues related to education. Organize articles into groups according to the issue addressed. Write a short summary of issues being litigated. Present your information to the class in a brief oral report.

2. Interview a high school principal about procedures followed in his or her school when it becomes necessary to expel a student. In particular, ask the principal to share information regarding due-process guidelines that are followed. Prepare a short summary of your interview for your course instructor.

3. Invite a personnel officer from a local school district to visit your class. Ask this person to bring an example of a teaching contract and to discuss its provisions with the class.

4. Organize a symposium on the topic: "How gender-equity initiatives over the past 15 years have changed school athletic programs." Gather information from journal articles and other sources (perhaps including interviews with school district directors of athletics). With others in your symposium group, present your findings to the class. Follow up with a general discussion of this issue.

5. Obtain information regarding laws in your state pertaining to reporting child abuse. Your instructor may be able to suggest where this information is available. Share your findings with others in the class.

6. Go to Merrill Education's Link to General Methods Resources site at this URL: http://www.prenhall.com/methods-cluster/ At the bottom of the page select "policies and handbooks" as your topic and click the "begin" button. This will take you to the "Overview" page. On the left side, click on "Web Links." On the Web Links page click on "internet access." Follow some of the links that will provide information about this issue. Prepare a brief oral presentation to your class on how schools are responding to parents' and other school patrons' concerns.

7. Go to Merrill Education's Link to General Methods Resources site at this URL: http://www.prenhall.com/methods-cluster/ At the bottom of the page select "policies and handbooks" as your topic and click the "begin" button. This will take you to the "Overview" page. On the left side, click on "Web Links." On the Web Links page click on "sexual harassment." Follow some of the links and, using the information you find, prepare a short paper that outlines issues associated with this topic that educators face today.

References

Bannister v. Paradis, 316 F. Supp. 185 (d. N.H. 1970).

Board of Trustees v. Stubblefield, 94 Cal. Rptr., 318, 321 (1971).

California Teachers Association. (1992). *Guide to school law*. Burlingame, CA: California Teachers Association.

Committee on the Judiciary, H.R. No. 94–1476, 94th Congress, 201 Sess. 68–70 (1976).

Connors, E. (1991). *Educational tort liability and malpractice*. Bloomington, IN: Phi Delta Kappa.

Davis v. Meek, 344 F. Supp. 398 (n.d. Ohio 1972).

Denton v. South Kitsap School District No. 402, 516 P.2d 1080 (Wash. 1973).

Fischer, L., Schimmel, D., & Kelly, C. (1999). *Teachers and the law* (5th ed.). New York: Longman.

Goss v. Lopez, 419 U.S. 565 (1975).

Hazelwood School District v. Kuhlmeier, 484 U.S. 260 (1988).

Ingraham v. Wright, 430 U.S. 651 (1977).

Kingsville Independent School District v. Cooper, 611 F.2d 1109 (5th Cir. 1980).

Meyer v. Nebraska, 262 U.S. 390, 399 (1923).

Monks, R., & Proulx, E. (1986). *Legal basics for teachers*. Fastback No. 235. Bloomington, IN: Phi Delta Kappa.

New Jersey v. T.L.O. 105 S. Ct. 733 (1985).

Parducci v. Rutland, 316 F. Supp. 352 (m.d. Ala. 1979).

Pickering v. Board of Education of Township School District 205, Will County, 225 N.E. 2d 1 (1967); 391 U.S. 563 (1968).

Tinker v. Des Moines Independent Community School District, 393 U.S. 503 (1969).

Valente, W. (1994). *Law in the schools* (3rd ed.). Upper Saddle River, NJ: Merrill/Prentice Hall.

Vorcheimer v. School District of Philadelphia, 531 F.2d 880 (3rd Cir. 1976); aff'd, 430 U.S. 703 (1977).

Wisconsin v. Yoder, 406 U.S. 205 (1972).

Zirkel, P., & Richardson, S. (1988). *A digest of Supreme Court decisions affecting education*. Bloomington, IN: Phi Delta Kappa.

II

Planning

5

Choosing Content

This chapter will aim to

- describe some issues you need to consider when selecting content to introduce to students;

- distinguish between single-subject and integrated-subjects content-organization patterns;

- point out how rules and regulations, curriculum guides and textbook guides, standardized tests, and availability of support materials can influence your content-selection decisions;

- explain some of the issues you should consider when making content-breadth and content-depth decisions;

- point out how the structure of knowledge can help you decide what content to include and exclude in your instructional programs;

- point out some things that you must consider when you attempt to match your instructional programs to specific needs of your students; and

- identify several ways content can be sequenced.

Introduction

Norman Daly, a new world history teacher at Carpenter High School, expressed these feelings at the end of his first few weeks of teaching:

"Three weeks of school are behind me. I have a few battle scars showing, but nothing major. My enthusiasm remains high. I know I can control my classes. I'm beginning to think a little more about *what* I am teaching. It is nice to have moved beyond an elemental concern for physical survival.

"My classes and I are tromping our way through Ancient Greece. Six notebooks crammed with university lecture notes on the topic are on my desk at home. I have also gathered together some good reference books. The subject is just so deep.

"The text we're using is one of these 'gems' that compacts 3,000 years of historical truths into 600 pages. It purports to *do* Ancient Greece in ten pages. It seems so irresponsible. We flit by something and then dash madly on to something new. I just don't feel this quick 'once-over-lightly' approach is producing much learning.

"To make matters worse, the text is too difficult for many students. Beyond problems with the book, many of them don't have much context for a lot of the material. I mean, some of them don't know where Greece is. One of them asked me the other day if Greece is in South America!

"I know I should be providing more, but I just don't know exactly what I should expect these students to be able to do. I'd like to be doing better by them, but I'm not sure where to begin."

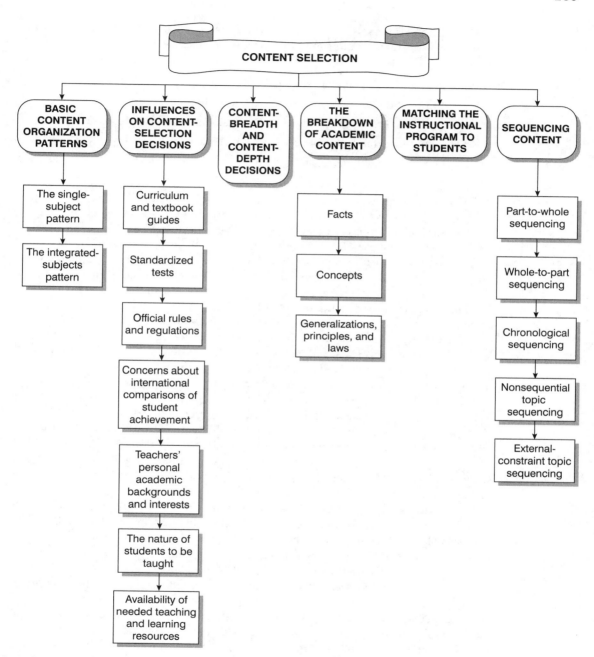

Figure 5–1
Graphic Organizer

The issues Norman raises are typical of those you may ask as a new teacher. Don't be surprised if you find yourself wondering about issues such as these:

What should I be teaching my students?

What do I do if the textbook coverage is inadequate?

How can I transform my university notes into material suitable for people in my classes?

What should I do if my students can't read the textbook?

How concerned should I be about what my students will be asked on standardized tests?

These difficult questions vex even many experienced teachers. How to select important content that is well matched to students' capabilities is one of the challenges you will face throughout your career. As noted in Chapter 4, "Reflective Teaching," achieving a "proper fit" will require you to think seriously about such issues as (1) the nature of the content you wish to teach, (2) the kinds of expertise you expect students to take away from your lessons, (3) the general interests and backgrounds of your students, and (4) the nature of support material available to support your instruction.

In recent years, the influence of content selection on learning has gained in popularity as a research topic. International comparisons of student achievement have prompted much of this interest. Many of them reveal that American students score lower on standardized tests than students in other nations. The Third International Mathematics and Science Study (TIMSS) was one of the most extensive and rigorous international comparisons of student achievement ever undertaken. Data were collected on academic achievement of fourth graders, eighth graders, and students in their last year of secondary schooling. In grade 4, U.S. students were found to be achieving above the international average in both mathematics and science (*Pursuing Excellence*, 1997). In grade 8, U.S. students were above the international average in science, but below the international average in mathematics (*Pursuing Excellence*, 1996). High school seniors in the United States performed below international averages in both mathematics and science (*Pursuing Excellence*, 1998).

The TIMSS study data reveal a disturbing trend: as U.S. students progress through school, their performance compares less favorably with students in other countries in later school years than in earlier school years. What explains this pattern? Some people have argued that too little money is being used to support school programs. However, others have presented compelling evidence that the United States pays more money for the education of each enrolled student than the vast majority of other countries (Walberg, 1998).

Others suggest that, particularly at the high school level, schools in the United States enroll a higher percentage of age-eligible young people than many other countries. Careful examination of this issue has revealed that this pattern was true years ago. However, today, the percentage of age-eligible young people completing secondary schools in the United States differs little from that in the other countries that were part of the TIMSS study (1999). In addition, amount of homework assigned, amount of instructional time devoted to science and mathematics, and amount of television watching do not seem related to performance of U.S. students compared to those in the other nations (*TIMSS, 1999*).

Two variables that do seem to account for some of the performance differences continue to be studied. First of all, the TIMSS results revealed that a high percentage of American middle school and senior high school teachers were familiar with research-validated methodologies associated with effective mathematics and science instruction. However, relatively few of them were implementing these approaches. These techniques were found to be much more prevalent in classrooms of countries where students outscored their U.S. counterparts. Second, the content of the curriculum, particularly the mathematics curriculum, at grades 8 and 12 in U.S. schools was found to be less sophisticated than that in schools of many nations whose students' achievement scores were higher (*TIMSS, 1999*).

Some authorities argue that reports of poorer performance of U.S. students do not necessarily mean teaching in U.S. schools is inferior. Many of these scholars have focused on a variable called *opportunity to learn* to explain lower scores of American students. Researchers who have studied opportunity to learn have concluded that student achievement tends to go up when (1) a given aspect of content is treated, and (2) sufficient time is allocated for students to master this aspect of content (Good & Brophy, 2000).

The opportunity-to-learn variable sometimes has been found to be a logical explanation for failure of American students to do as well as students in other countries on tests of comparative performance. One such study compared mathematics achievement of 11-year-olds in California and England (Barr, 1987). Students in England achieved higher scores than students in California. Close analysis of backgrounds of students who took these tests revealed that much of the achievement test focused on topics that were treated in English schools one or two years earlier than in American schools. In this case, differences in scores could be explained by content-selection differences rather than by lower quality teaching in California schools.

As you prepare for a career in education, does it really make sense for you to be concerned about international comparisons of student performance? Yes, it does. For one thing, the issue of relative performance of students as compared with those in other countries promises to be a hotly debated topic for years to come, and you need to be prepared to respond to critics who argue that "schools should get less public financial support, because we aren't getting good value for our money."

As you begin studying this issue, you may find yourself sympathizing with those who suggest Americans lack a society-wide commitment to "do something" to improve the level of American students' academic performance. They argue that we are more inclined to identify a problem than to take meaningful action to deal with it. For example, compared to Japanese students, American school children seem unable to get consistently strong support from parents and guardians for rigorous academic programs. When you begin teaching, you may find yourself agreeing with many teachers who wish that students' families would take a more active role in encouraging learners to establish a high personal standard of performance and to support teachers who expect this kind of student work (Burns, 1996; Whitford, 1996).

What you can influence more directly than parent involvement is selection of content. This is an important power that tremendously influences achievement of those you will teach. Students cannot learn what they are not exposed to and what they are not encouraged to learn. You may think that people writing textbooks and preparing curriculum guides have already made the key content selection decisions. This is not the case. Characteristics of students in every class you teach and other variables associated with your specific teaching will differ from the assumptions of the textbook and curriculum document writers. Further, if you examine several textbooks in a subject you want to teach, don't be surprised if you find that textbook authors do not agree on how the content should be divided and sequenced. Further, you will probably find that the individual texts vary considerably in terms of the depth of treatment given to individual topics.

If you can't rely on textbooks to do the content organization and selection process, how about notes from your college courses? A nice thought, we agree, but this, too, is no solution. For one thing, the scope of many college and university courses is narrower than the typical secondary school course you will teach. For example, only a small portion of the content presented in a university-level comparative anatomy course is relevant for students in an introductory high school biology course. Further, the intended audience for university professors' lectures differs considerably from the students enrolled in typical secondary school classes.

In the end, *you* are responsible for making important content decisions. You will want to make them after reflecting carefully on the nature of your students, your intended purposes, specific state and local requirements, and other elements of your own instructional setting. The idea is for you to select content that represents a good fit between what you teach, what legal and setting requirements demand, and what students in your classes need.

Basic Content-Organization Patterns

Many arrangements of courses in secondary schools have been around so long that you may never have thought about the content-organization logic that led to their adoption. Two basic patterns dominate in middle schools, junior high schools, and senior high schools:

- Single-subject pattern
- Integrated-subjects pattern

The Single-Subject Pattern

This familiar design is the basis for the traditional arrangement of secondary school courses. Courses with titles such as *Biology, Mathematics, Auto Mechanics, Bookkeeping,* and *Economics* are examples. Lessons and courses reflecting this orientation take findings from a single area of knowledge and modify them so they are suitable for transmission to secondary-school students.

The single-subject pattern is popular. One reason is that most scholarship in universities is organized in this way. Hence, this arrangement makes it convenient for new knowledge generated by leading scholars to be incorporated within secondary-school courses that focus on individual subjects. As a teacher, this scheme makes it relatively easy for you to find information to use in your lessons.

Consider, for example, the relative difficulty you might face in searching out information to enrich instruction in a course titled *United States History* compared with a course called *The Character of Americans*. Huge quantities of information have been organized under the heading *United States History*. However, although material on *The Character of Americans* certainly exists, it is fragmented. You would have to do a lot more digging to uncover information about this subject than about United States history. This is not to say a course titled *The Character of Americans* might not be worthwhile; however, such a course would place heavier preparation demands on your time than a course called *United States History*.

Parents and others interested in the schools are familiar with courses organized according to the single-subject pattern. In addition, the long-history of these courses has resulted in some reasonably standardized expectations about what students should be expected to learn as a result of their exposure to them. For example, there is more consensus about what students should be able to do after a year's instruction in a course titled *Geometry* than in a course titled something like *Special Topics in Quantitative Issues*. Some supporters believe the single-subject arrangement encourages accountability. There is likely to be much more place-to-place similarity in what is taught than in situations where courses include contents drawn from multiple subjects. This may pose problems for people who want to make judgments about the relative effectiveness of teachers and programs at different schools.

The Integrated-Subjects Pattern

Not everyone agrees that the single-subject pattern is well suited to meet students' needs. They argue that the packaging of learning into individual subjects is an artificial arrangement that may help scholars do their work, but may not provide young people with what they should know to cope with the "real world." Supporters of integrated school subjects argue that, in their everyday lives, people do not encounter information as *biology, mathematics, political science,* or *chemistry*. Rather, life experiences require them to draw simultaneously on content from many different fields. Because of this, proponents of integrated-subjects courses contend that school programs should strive to break down barriers separating individual subjects. The idea is to help students encounter the world as one piece, not just as separate parts of a puzzle that they are left to put together on their own.

Courses that reflect an integrated-subjects pattern do not carry the name of just one subject. They treat content that cuts across a wide domain of knowledge to embrace information drawn from many different subjects. Examples include integrated mathematics and science courses, general industrial and technical arts courses, and humanities courses. Often, a broad-fields course such as humanities will be organized around a guiding theme, for example *Technological, Social, Political, Economic, Literary, and Artistic Accomplishments through Time*. Because themes guide planning and instruction, the terms *thematic teaching* and *interdisciplinary teaching* sometimes are used to describe teaching integrated-subjects courses.

If you undertake to develop an integrated-subjects program, you will face important challenges. Once a general theme has been identified, you may find it difficult to decide exactly which elements of content should be included to support it. Further, you may be asked to explain how the issue of accountability will be handled. Accountability can be a problem for teachers of integrated-subjects programs. For example, a course titled *Humanities* taught in one school may feature content that is quite different from content in a similarly named course taught at another school. This situation makes it difficult to make place-to-place quality judgments about integrated-subjects courses. (See Figure 5–2, below.)

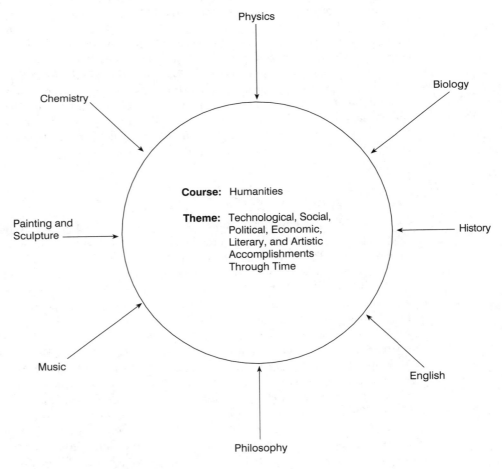

Figure 5-2
The Integrated Subjects Pattern

Some Influences on Content-Selection Decisions

Although, as a teacher, you will have a great deal of discretion about selecting and teaching content, there are important influences that will encourage, and sometimes require, you to make certain decisions. These influences include the following:

- Official rules and regulations,
- Curriculum guides and textbook guides,
- Standardized tests, and
- Availability of support materials

Official Rules and Regulations

Some states have rigid regulations that require certain kinds of content to be included in individual secondary school courses. Some local school districts have similar requirements. These legal guidelines place limits on your decision-making authority. Some of your actions may also be influenced by decisions of district- and building-level curriculum committees. Decisions of committee members sometimes bind all teachers in a district or a school. In other situations, these decisions are presented in the form of suggestions that individual teachers are invited to accept, modify, or reject. Even if you teach

These teachers must consider local rules and regulations as well as state-level guidelines and standards as they proceed with their curriculum-revision work.

in a place where guidelines require you to do certain things, you still will retain much autonomy in deciding the relative emphasis on mandated elements of content and in selecting content beyond the scope of what is required by state or local regulations.

Curriculum Guides and Textbook Guides

Many school districts today make curriculum documents of various kinds available to teachers. Curriculum guides most often are produced by teams involving individuals from several schools within a district or by people from departments within individual schools. There are many types of these documents, and they vary greatly in terms of the kind and quality of information they provide. For example, *general scope and sequence* documents may provide little more than a listing of topics to be covered in a given course, with some possible reference to the relative importance of each.

Curriculum guides (sometimes known as *course guides*) provide more explicit information. Although formats vary, many of these documents include (1) lists and descriptions of units to be covered; (2) important generalizations, principles, and concepts to be mastered by students; and (3) very general descriptions of suggested instructional approaches and evaluation procedures.

Instructional unit documents are designed to provide you with explicit, practical information about individual instructional units in a course. Formats of these documents differ, but many of them include focus generalizations and concepts for the unit, lists of learning intentions or instructional objectives, suggestions for sequencing lessons in the unit, lists of needed materials and equipment, recommended instructional techniques, and detailed suggestions for evaluating students' progress. Sometimes they even include examples of daily lesson plans.

Another form of packaged content that you may encounter is the *textbook guide*. Today, it is a universal practice of commercial publishers to provide these as guides to using the adopted school text. Textbook guides provide overviews of the material to be taught, suggestions for sequencing content, ideas for introducing material, evaluation recommendations, and other information. Sometimes they include detailed sample lessons.

Curriculum guides and textbook guides may influence some instructional decisions you make. You need to take care, however, not to rely too heavily on the provided recommendations. Even the best-informed, best-intentioned writers of these materials know much less about your students and teaching circumstances than you do. Information in curriculum guides and textbook guides should be viewed as important planning resources. Your own thinking about instruction that will best serve your students' needs should determine what to incorporate into their programs.

Standardized Tests

Results of standardized tests are often reported in local news media. Schools and teachers whose students score poorly on these tests may come under public criticism. As a result, administrators in your school district or building may urge you to think about types of information assessed on standardized tests as you make decisions about which content to emphasize. Students' standardized test scores are likely to suffer if your instruction fails to focus on tested information.

We by no means are suggesting that you should take a purely reactive stance when confronted with a situation when standardized test scores are considered to be very important. It may be that the tests being used are not doing an adequate job of sampling important kinds of content. As a professional educator, you have an obligation to participate in the process of enlightening the general public about the limitations of standardized test scores. Professional educators today work for the adoption of student assessment programs that go beyond standardized testing to embrace diverse measures of student learning.

CRITICAL INCIDENT

Teaching to the Test

On a Monday afternoon, Betty Lewis waited with her math colleagues in the faculty lounge for a mathematics department meeting with Ms. Walker, the high school principal. Ms. Walker called this special meeting on short notice, and there had been a good deal of talk all day about what it might be about.

When a grim-faced Ms. Walker entered the room, it became obvious that she was in no mood for pleasantries. She got right down to business:

> "We just received our standardized test scores from the state for the mathematics test our students took in the spring. Our school's average score is down six points from last year. To make it worse, average scores in the other high schools in the district went up. The superintendent has called me on the carpet. He was blunt. He said the scores were an embarrassment to the district, and that members of the school board want to know what is wrong with our math department.
>
> "The superintendent let me know in no uncertain terms that he expects some immediate action to be taken. In response to his request, I am going to require that each of you teaching students who will be taking the test this year spend a minimum of 15 minutes in each class period drilling students on material likely to appear on the test. I have files of tests from previous years in my office. I want you to study them carefully and identify sample test items you can use to help your people practice for the test they will take in the spring. I will expect a weekly report from each teacher identifying precisely what has been done in every period to focus students' attention on content likely to be included on the standardized test."

Betty Lewis and the other teachers were stunned as they heard this announcement. One veteran teacher looked at Ms. Walker and commented, "Don't you think this policy is a somewhat drastic reaction to a one-year dip in our students' scores? Besides, if we do what you're asking, how will we cover the required course content?"

Another teacher said, "What about our academic freedom? As certified professionals, isn't it *our* responsibility to teach students what we consider to be important?"

Still another teacher protested, "I question the ethics of taking items from past tests and teaching the students to respond to them correctly. This is 'teaching to the test,' not teaching students how to understand the subject matter. It seems to me this is just plain wrong."

In response to these questions, Ms. Walker said:

"I hear what each of you is saying. Let me make some particular comments about the issue of ethics. I would ask you whether it is ethical for our school to be evaluated on the basis of one standardized score. That is precisely what our community is doing to us. We depend on our community for support. We may not like the game that is being played, but that is the reality we are faced with. Basically, the curriculum is what the community demands. If this means that your academic freedom sometimes has to be compromised, that is just how it is. None of us is happy about all this. But I assure you, the superintendent and board of education members are extremely concerned about the decline in our scores. If our students don't do better next year, some even more drastic changes may have to be made."

■   ■   ■

How do you respond to the issue of teaching to the test to raise scores? What are pluses and minuses of this practice? What are some values expressed in Ms. Walker's comments? What are some reflected in reactions of some of the teachers? Are there ways in which these divergent views about what teachers should do might be reconciled?

What would you do if you were a member of this mathematics department? Do communities unfairly judge schools based on standardized test scores? If so, what might be done about this situation? What is the proper course of action when there is a conflict between community desires and decisions that teachers as professionals want to make?

Availability of Support Materials

The availability of instructional support materials will have an influence on your content decisions. If you have to make a choice between two topics, one of which is supported by abundant learning resources other than the textbook and one of which is supported by few such materials, you may well feel compelled to select the one supported by plenty of support resources. Because better-funded districts tend to have more money to spend on instructional support materials, you will typically experience fewer support-material-availability constraints if you are employed in a more affluent rather than a less affluent school or school district.

Though the kinds of materials available do represent a problem, you need to guard against a temptation to view instructional resources as being more limited than they really are. For example, you no longer need well-stocked school libraries to provide your students with access to large quantities of information to supplement what is provided in course textbooks. Modern computer technology, particularly the World Wide Web, makes it possible to draw information into schools in even in the poorest and most remote locations.

Content-Breadth and Content-Depth Decisions

When you prepare to make content-selection decisions, you face two distinct but related tasks. On the one hand, you must decide on the *breadth* of content to be covered. This refers to the range of information to be introduced. (Are you interested in teaching students about political, social, and economic events from 1900 to World War II, *or* are you interested in teaching students the same information from 1607 to 1993?)

On the other hand, you also have to make decisions related to content *depth*. Depth refers to the extent of coverage related to a single content element. A decision to treat a given topic in great depth implies a need to commit considerable class time to this effort. There is an accompanying expectation that your students will emerge from this experience with an ability to engage in quite sophisticated thinking about the topic.

In making content-selection decisions, you have to strike a balance between breadth and depth. Because time is limited, a decision to provide too much breadth at the expense of depth can lead to very superficial treatment of many important topics. An error on the side of depth can produce students who are eminently well prepared in certain areas and woefully inadequate in others. The basic idea is to achieve a compromise between breadth and depth of coverage that results in a program well suited to your students' abilities.

It is clear that an appropriate relationship between breadth and depth can affect students' learning. Researchers in one study found that learners in some classes mastered as little as 57 percent of the introduced content, and learners in others mastered as much of 98 percent of the material (Barr, 1987). Content in classes where individuals mastered high percentages of what was introduced was well matched to the special characteristics of individuals in the class.

In another study, researchers found that a content-selection decision that reduced breadth of coverage to allow students to spend more time on a smaller number of topics helped below-average junior high school mathematics students to greatly improve their final test scores (Barr, 1987). This finding is consistent with a recommendation of teacher effectiveness that sufficient time be allowed for slower students to complete their work (Good & Brophy, 2000). When the emphasis is on breadth and a hurried pace through the program, many of these students give up. This reinforces their feelings of inadequacy and, often, leads them to develop negative attitudes toward their teachers and the school.

Making good breadth and depth decisions is difficult. In every secondary school subject area, the volume of content that could be taught is enormous. Clearly you have to establish priorities and make choices. How should you do this? One approach focuses on a breakdown of academic content into the basic structure of knowledge. The next section introduces procedures you might wish to use.

The Breakdown of Academic Content

Textbook writers, developers of curriculum guides, and others who attempt to organize content for instructional purposes seek to break down subject matter in a systematic way. One approach they use derives from the work of learning theorists Jerome Bruner (1960) and Hilda Taba (1962). This *structure-of-knowledge* scheme allows different content types to be scaled in terms of their relative importance. It is based on the assumption that a content type such as a generalization, which includes information applicable to diverse situations, is more important than a content type such as a fact, which includes information relative to a particular situation. The structure of knowledge features three basic content types. From narrowest (and least important) to broadest (and most important), these are as follows:

- Facts;
- Concepts; and
- Generalizations, principles, and laws.

[See Figure 5–3, for a graphic depiction of the relationship among (1) generalizations, principles and laws, (2) concepts, and (3) facts.]

Facts

Facts refer to a specific circumstance or situation. They have limited transfer or explanatory power. For example, that Mexico City has more people than New York City is a fact that has some significance. It might suggest a reason for asking your students to seek an answer to a question such as "Why has Mexico City grown so large?" However, simply knowing this fact does not help a person understand the general reasons cities grow or the causes of economic, political, and social problems of cities.

The real value of facts in the curriculum lies in their ability to help students understand concepts and generalizations. Appropriate selection of facts has long been an issue of concern to curriculum developers. Curriculum specialist John Jarolimek (1990) has recommended that, in planning instruction, you should select from among these three categories of facts:

- facts that are likely to remain important over a long period of time,
- facts used frequently in everyday living, and
- facts needed to develop or elaborate on important ideas and generalizations.

Concepts

Concepts are major ideas or categories that help organize information. Sometimes concepts are referred to as *terms*. The defining characteristics of a concept are called *attributes*. Less complex and simpler-to-learn concepts have relatively few of these. However, an abstract concept such as *democracy* has a large number of attributes.

The fewer the number of attributes and the more concrete a concept is, the easier it is for students to learn. More complex concepts require more teaching time than less complex concepts. Often the extra teaching time can be justified because students need

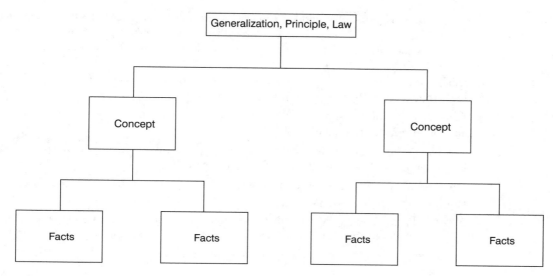

Figure 5-3
The Structure of Knowledge

to master complex concepts as a prelude to learning the broad explanatory generalizations that will enable them to transfer learning to varied situations.

One way you can help students learn a new concept is by presenting them with examples and non-examples of the concept. This helps them identify the concept's defining attributes. For this kind of lesson to succeed, the illustrations you select need to highlight the concept's key attributes, and you must ensure that your students pay attention to this information.

Concepts are organized in the mind into a hierarchy, or schema, that individuals use to store and retrieve information. Some concepts, such as *reptile* are broad terms that help organize vast quantities of subordinate information. These large-scale concepts help organize more narrow, related concepts such as *snake, turtle,* and *lizard,* which are much limited in scope. Awareness of concept hierarchies and the connections between broad and related, narrower concepts can help you plan and sequence material for students.

Generalizations, Principles, and Laws

The third type of content goes by several names, including *generalizations, principles,* and *laws.* Though they represent a common content type, there are some differences among these types. In general, laws and principles are based on somewhat stronger evidence and are more universally applicable than generalizations. Some academic disciplines tend to use one of these terms more frequently than others. For example, there are many laws in physics. Findings of social scientists often are reported as generalizations. Specialists in art and music often cite principles of composition.

Generalizations, principles, and laws are statements that summarize what the best available evidence has revealed to be true or correct. They are expressed as statements of relationships among concepts. Here are some examples selected from different subject areas:

- Inherited characteristics of living organisms do not occur randomly; rather, they follow predictable patterns.
- Increased specialization in production has led to interdependence among individuals, communities, states, and nations.
- Survival in the earth's environment depends on the ability of people to interpret various phenomena that come to them through their senses.
- Descending temperatures result in contraction of objects; ascending temperatures result in expansion of objects.
- Areas and perimeter measurements of polygons do not occur in a random pattern; they can be determined by computations involving linear and angle measurements.
- Measures regarded as radical in one generation often are considered moderate in the next.
- Compositions of chemical compounds follow predictable patterns that can be discerned through the application of appropriate analytical procedures.
- A force equal to the weight of the dispersed fluid buoys up a body immersed in a fluid.
- Because natural resources are limited and human wants are unlimited, every society has developed a method for allocating scarce resources.
- Different moods of paintings featuring common subjects and symbols result from differences in the sensory and compositional features of the individual work.

The "truth" of generalizations, principles, and laws is determined by reference to evidence. It is possible that what some experts regard as true today may be modified in the future when new evidence becomes available.

Scholars doing pioneering work in their individual specialties constantly challenge existing generalizations, principles, and laws. Therefore, they should not be introduced to students as definitive answers. Young people need to understand that the search for new knowledge continues and that many of them can look forward to active participation in this exciting process.

Because generalizations, principles, and laws summarize the work of leading specialists and organize tremendous quantities of information, they function well as content organizers. These broad explanatory statements encourage students to place facts in their proper context and to recognize the importance of understanding relationships among concepts.

Since generalizations, principles, and laws describe relationships among concepts, students must grasp the concepts before generalizations, principles, and laws can be understood. Consider this social science generalization:

As a society becomes more educated and industrialized, its birthrate declines.

If your students are unfamiliar with the concepts *society, education, industrialization,* and *birthrate,* this generalization will make little sense. You have to ensure that your students understand the concepts related to the generalizations you select as a focus for your teaching. You often can illuminate concepts by introducing students to specific facts. Your need to explain the concepts, generalizations, principles, and laws associated with them provides a justification for selecting certain facts for emphasis.

All of this suggests a central role for generalizations, principles, and laws when you plan for teaching. You begin your planning with a question like: "What generalizations, principles, or laws do I want my students to understand when this unit of study is completed?" Once these are identified, you can move on to identify key concepts and explanatory facts.

The Structure of Knowledge and Content-Selection Decisions

Focus generalizations, principles, and laws and related concepts can help you make content-selection decisions. They provide an important organizational framework for instruction. In a sense, they serve as targets toward which you can direct your teaching.

Facts, too, play an important role. They serve as important building blocks that help students to grasp important concepts and the generalizations, principles, and laws to which they relate. The most important consideration in selecting facts is their relevance for helping your students master concepts and focus generalizations, principles, and laws. When facts are selected with this purpose in mind, they can help students to develop understandings that have broad transfer value. This approach to fact selection can help you develop instructional programs that are internally consistent and that do not confront students with large quantities of fragmented and unrelated information.

For examples of the use of structure-of-knowledge components such as concepts and generalizations in formal instructional plans, see Chapter 7, "Preparing Units and Lessons."

Matching the Instructional Program to Students

When you make content-selection decisions, you need to consider characteristics of your students. The idea that content should be selected so that it fits students is a statement of good intentions. Within every class you teach, you will find great differences among learners' talents, interests, and motivations. Obviously, no content decision you make is going to result in a single program of study that is perfectly matched to each student. One of your important responsibilities is to take the general content that you have selected and adapt it, as necessary, so that each student in your class has a reasonable chance to master it. This suggests that, within your lessons, you often will introduce the same general content to different students in different ways.

MORE FROM THE WEB

Content Selection

The Web includes numerous sites that specialize in information of interest to teachers. We have selected some examples that feature content related to your responsibilities in selecting and sequencing content. As time permits, consider visiting some of these sites.

The History File

http://63.70.163.70/nche/file.html

- The National Council for History Education produces material available at this site. Among other things, you will find links to information related to content selection in world history and United States history courses.

English Units

http://english.unitecnology.ac.nz/resources/units/years12-13.html

- Educators throughout the world face content-selection challenges. The New Zealand Ministry of Education prepared material for this site. It includes content selection ideas for use in English courses taught to advanced secondary-school students. You will find ideas for performing *Julius Caesar*, analyzing *Heart of Darkness* and *Apocalypse Now*, studying *The Crucible*, preparing writing folios, and utilizing other kinds of content in English courses.

Science through Native American Eyes

http://www.cradleboard.org/cd.html

- Culture affects perception. This means people raised in individual culture groups tend to see and interpret reality in special ways. An organization called Cradleboard that is particularly interested in instruction that is responsive to the world view of Native American groups, sponsors this site. You will find a discussion here of a program that introduces science content within the context of Native American culture.

The Net Works—Constructing Web Lessons

http://www.feut.utoronto.ca/~rguilford/index.htm

- When you begin teaching, you probably will not find all the resource materials you need available in your building. Today, many teachers are constructing Web-based lessons. Material at this Web site can help you select and design Web-based content.

Designing, Implementing, and Sustaining Content–ESL Programs

http://www.ncbe.gwu.edu/miscpubs/cal/contentesl/c-esl2.htm

- Increasing numbers of students come to school speaking a language other than English as their first language. Materials at this site cover a broad range of topics related to helping these young people learn. Among other things, you will find ideas for selecting content and making curricular decisions that can help these students master content.

Towards an Ecozoic Curriculum

http://noisey.oise.utoronto.ca/osee/

- In selecting content, there may be occasions when you want to add a particular perspective to some traditional topics. Materials at this site, assembled by the Ontario Institute for Studies in Education, suggest ways of infusing environmental-education content into such subjects as business, English, French, geography, history, mathematics, and science.

Retanet—Resources for Teaching about the Americas

http://ladb.unm.edu/retanet/

- If you are interested in selecting content related to the nations of the Americas, this is a good place to begin. You will find a wide variety of resource materials. These include lesson plans, photos, links to embassies, and suggestions about where you might find additional information.

A commitment to make the instructional program responsive to student characteristics requires that you know your students well. Gathering diagnostic information about members of a class is not a particularly difficult or time-consuming task. For example, if you pay careful attention to what individuals have done on previous assignments, you will learn much about what particular students can do and about where their interests lie. Conferences you have with individual students can help you pinpoint problems they may be having and give you insight into their general levels of motivation.

Your aim is to make decisions that, when implemented, will help students master what is taught. Students who are successful develop better self-concepts and higher levels of self-confidence. These attitudes often translate into good motivation and high levels of achievement (Good & Brophy, 2000).

Sequencing Content

Decisions about what should be taught require more than simply selecting content. You also have to decide how selected elements of content need to be sequenced. Content can be sequenced in different ways. The following are some examples:

- Part-to-whole sequencing,
- Whole-to-part sequencing,
- Chronological sequencing,
- Nonsequential topic sequencing, and
- External constraint sequencing (Armstrong, 1989; Posner, 1987).

Part-to-Whole Sequencing

When you adopt this approach, individual content parts are sequenced in such a way that simple parts are taught before more complex wholes that demand an understanding of the individual parts. Some kinds of content lend themselves better to this kind of sequencing than others. Mathematics courses often are sequenced in this way. The internal logic of the discipline of mathematics strongly supports this sequencing scheme. It simply is not possible for students to grasp more complex parts of the subject without having first mastered less complex parts. The part-to-whole approach is also sometimes referred to as the *simple-to-complex* approach.

Whole-to-Part Sequencing

This approach is the reverse of part-to-whole sequencing. Here, you begin an instructional sequence by presenting students with a broad overview of a new topic. After you help them see the big picture, you go on to introduce the parts that, collectively, make up the whole.

Some subject areas lend themselves more naturally to this arrangement than others, for example, geography. World geography courses often begin with an overview of the entire globe. Frequently continents are introduced, as are global wind systems, weather systems, and ocean current systems. Following this overview, lessons often narrow their focus to deal in depth with large global regions. These, in turn, may be followed by lessons focusing on countries within regions and, perhaps, of regions within individual countries.

Chronological Sequencing

When you use this approach, you organize content elements based on the variable of time. This scheme makes sense for some content areas, but not for others. History courses often are organized this way. When this is done, lessons focusing on earlier periods of time usually precede those focusing on later periods. (The chronological approach does not mandate an earliest-to-latest sequence, but it is more common than a chronological sequence running from latest to earliest.)

Subjects other than history sometimes also are organized chronologically. For example, some English courses arrange materials to be studied chronologically. A survey of American literature course may begin with a study of colonial era literature, proceed to a consideration of literature of the early republic, and use similar units of time to move students forward toward a concluding unit featuring present-day literature.

Nonsequential Topic Sequencing

In some content areas, individual topics do not build on others in the course. For example, suppose you are teaching a high school crafts course. In planning this course, you will realize that basic information presented in a unit on tooling leather is not a prerequisite for units on making candles or using the potter's wheel. In courses of this kind, your instructional units logically can be sequenced in many different ways. You might decide simply to base your sequencing decisions on your own interests and students' feelings about what order of presentation might best motivate them.

External-Constraint Sequencing

Sometimes your sequencing decisions will have little to do with a serious consideration of the substance of the content or of student needs. External constraints may require you to cover specific topics at certain times. For example, if you are teaching a high school biology course that includes a field ecology unit that must be taught in an outdoor laboratory facility serving many schools, the date this facility will be available fixes the time when you will be able to teach this unit.

Sometimes, availability of important support media also influences sequencing decisions. One of the authors once worked in a state with a small population where one educational film served every high school in the state. Teachers who wanted to use the film had to schedule it months in advance, and often the date of availability exercised considerable influence over their content-sequencing decisions.

 WHAT DO *YOU* THINK?

Identifying Content to Be Taught

Suppose you accepted a teaching position in a district that had no curriculum guides for your subject. Suppose, too, that a late-summer fire had destroyed all course textbooks and that no replacements would be available until the second semester. If the school principal asked you to design your own course, how would you respond to these questions?

Questions

1. What major topics would you cover? How would you justify their selection?
2. In what sequence would you teach these topics? Why?

3. Suppose you had 18 instructional weeks to work with. How much time would you devote to each topic? Why?

4. What two or three major concepts related to each topic would you expect students to learn? Are any of these more important than others? If so, which ones, and why?

5. Would you use some generalizations or principles to guide planning and teaching of the course? If so, what would they be?

 FOR YOUR PORTFOLIO

1. What materials, ideas you learned in this chapter related to *selecting and sequencing content* will you include as "evidence" in your portfolio? Select up to three items of information to be included in your portfolio. Number them 1, 2, and 3.

2. Think about why you selected these materials for your portfolio. Consider such issues as the following in your response:

   ■ The specific purposes to which this information can be put when you plan, deliver, and assess the impact of your instruction;

   ■ The compatibility of the information with your own priorities and values;

   ■ The contributions this information can make to your personal development as a teacher; and

   ■ The factors that led you to include this material as opposed to some alternatives you considered.

3. Prepare a written reflection in which you analyze the decision-making process you followed. Also, mention the INTASC Standard(s) to which your selected material relates. (First complete the chart below.)

Materials You Selected and the INTASC Standards

Put a check under those INTASC Standards numbers to which the evidence you have selected applies. (Refer to Chapter 1 for more detailed information about INTASC.)

Item of Evidence Number	INTASC Standards									
	S1	S2	S3	S4	S5	S6	S7	S8	S9	S10
1										
2										
3										

Key Ideas in Summary

- Selecting content is one of your most important responsibilities as a teacher. In making content-selection decisions, you need to consider the nature of your students, what you expect them to learn, the kinds of materials that are available, and special characteristics of your instructional setting.

- In secondary schools, one of the two basic content-organization patterns is the single-subject pattern. The single-subject pattern uses single established subjects as titles of courses. This pattern draws strength from the similar organizational scheme found in most colleges and universities. It also is a pattern familiar to many patrons of the schools and, hence, it does not engender much controversy. Because contents of similarly titled courses tend to be somewhat equivalent from school to school, some people believe this scheme makes it easier to make judgments about the relative quality of programs in different schools.

- The second basic content-organization arrangement is the integrated-subjects pattern. In the integrated-subjects pattern, courses are designed to represent broad areas. High school humanities courses are an example of this arrangement. Typically, thematic statements guide courses. Content is drawn from many different subject areas. Supporters of this approach argue that it breaks knowledge out of the traditional boundaries of single subjects and enables students to confront information in a more natural, realistic way. Critics counter with the argument that standards of practice for integrated-subjects courses are not nearly as well established as for single-subject courses. Hence, what is taught in a course such as humanities at school A may be quite different from what is taught in a similarly titled course at school B. This lack of school-to-school consistency sometimes makes it difficult to make meaningful school-to-school program-quality comparisons.

- You will face important constraints as you make content-selection decisions. In some places, state and local regulations require certain elements of content to be included in certain courses. The nature of content assessed on standardized tests also may influence your decisions. Test results, in many places, have assumed great political importance. Schools are under pressure to provide programs that give students the background needed to achieve high scores. Curriculum guides and text guides in some cases also act to limit your instructional choices. Availability of instructional material also may impose limits on the content-selection decisions you make.

- Among decisions you will make are those concerning breadth. Breadth is concerned with the range of information to be covered. Survey courses tend to have more breadth than courses that presume general knowledge and that are designed to develop more sophisticated information about certain topics within a broad content area.

- Another aspect of content decisions has to do with depth. Depth refers to the sophistication or extent of coverage of individual elements of content. When you make a decision to increase depth, you also commit to devoting more time to a particular element of content. Such a decision likely will also be accompanied by an expectation that your learners will develop more sophisticated levels of understanding than you expect when they study other elements of content elements in less depth. Good depth and breadth decisions require you to have a clear understanding of your instructional priorities.

- The structure of knowledge provides a framework that you may find useful in making content-selection decisions. It includes these three levels or layers of content: (1) facts, (2) concepts, and (3) generalizations, principles, and laws.
- Facts are content elements that refer to a specific circumstance or situation. They have limited transfer power. Facts should be selected in terms of their ability to help students grasp important concepts and focus generalizations, principles, or laws.
- Concepts are major ideas, terms, or categories that serve as major organizers for vast quantities of related information. For example, the concept *automobile* is a descriptive term under which enormous quantities of related information can be subsumed. The defining characteristics of a concept are called its *attributes*. Less complex concepts have fewer attributes than more complex ones.
- Generalizations, principles, and laws are succinct distillations of the truths that have been found by professional scholars and researchers. They are expressed as statements of relationship among concepts. To understand generalizations, principles, and laws, students must understand the concepts embedded within them. The truth of a given generalization, principle, or law is based on the best available evidence. As new information becomes available, it may be necessary to modify the generalization, principle, or law.
- Student characteristics must be considered when content-selection decisions are made. A key to fitting content to students is in-depth knowledge of the students who are to be taught. The more you know about your students, the more likely you are to make content-selection decisions that will meet your students' needs.
- There are many approaches to sequencing content. Part-to-whole sequencing arranges content from simplest to most complex. Whole-to-part sequencing reverses this process and introduces complex whole first; then, more intensive instruction is provided focusing on individual parts. Chronological sequencing uses calendar time as a sequencing mechanism. Usually, material is sequenced from oldest to newest. Nonsequential topic sequencing is used when individual topics are more or less free standing—that is, when topics do not build on one another in any systematic or predictable way. External constraint sequencing refers to situations that require you to teach specific elements of a course at a particular time because of some out-of-the-classroom situation that mandates when a certain topic be covered. For example, there may be only certain times of the year when certain resources needed to teach a topic are available.

Reflections

1. Why are content decisions so important, and to what degree should teachers be involved in them?

2. What are some basic issues you need to consider as you seek to make responsible content-selection decisions?

3. Why have people who want to make school-to-school comparisons of program quality sometimes expressed concerns about courses organized according to an integrated-subjects pattern?

4. What are some features of curriculum guides and textbook guides that might influence your decisions about selecting and teaching content? Why is it not a good idea to rely only on guidelines provided in these materials when you make these decisions?

5. What is meant by content *breadth* and content *depth*, and how do decisions related to breadth and depth influence the amount of time spent on a given topic in a course?

6. What is the structure of knowledge, and what does its use in content selection suggest about the proper role for facts?

7. What kinds of things contribute to the complexity of a given concept?

8. How can you use components of the structure of knowledge as you make decisions about what content to include and exclude from your programs?

9. Why is it important for you to consider student characteristics when you make content-selection decisions?

10. What are some alternative approaches to sequencing content?

Learning Extensions

1. Obtain a textbook in your subject area that is used in secondary schools. Analyze its content. Is the content consistent with what you think should be taught? Is material sequenced as you would sequence it? In general, how could the content selection and sequencing be improved? Present your reactions to your instructor in a short paper.

2. Ask your instructor for help in locating any guidelines or requirements for teaching your subject that may have been adopted either by your state or by a local school district. How constraining are these guidelines for the individual teacher? Do they pose any potential problems for you as you think about content decisions you might like to make? Share your reactions with others in a general class discussion.

3. Interview a secondary school teacher about how he or she selects specific content to be taught. Ask this teacher whether he or she places more emphasis on certain topics than others and, if so, why. Ask also where this person faces any troublesome rules, regulations, or guidelines that restrict the range of his or her content selection decisions. Share teacher reactions to your questions with others in your class in a brief oral report.

4. Interview a teacher who teaches an integrated-subjects course. Inquire about problems and challenges associated with selecting learning materials, identifying appropriate standards of student performance, and explaining the program to parents and other patrons of the school? What does this person see as major advantages of this approach? Does he or she see any disadvantages? Share your findings with others in your class.

5. Select several topics you would teach in your own subject area. Sequence them in two different ways. Base your sequencing on one of the approaches introduced in

the chapter. Share your plans with your course instructor. Be prepared to discuss the strengths and weaknesses of each approach.

6. Go to Merrill Education's Link to General Methods Resources site at this URL: http://www.prenhall.com/methods-cluster/ At the bottom of the page select "curriculum" as your topic and click the "begin" button. This will take you to the "Overview" page. On the left side, click on "Web Links." On the Web Links page click on "integrated disciplinary curriculum." Follow links that will give you information related to establishing school programs that draw content from multiple disciplines. Prepare an oral report based on your findings.

7. Go to Merrill Education's Link to General Methods Resources site at this URL: http://www.prenhall.com/methods-cluster/ At the bottom of the page select "curriculum" as your topic and click the "begin" button. This will take you to the "Overview" page. On the left side, click on "Web Links." On the Web Links page click on "scheduling patterns." Follow links that will give you information related to: "Pros and Cons of Various Scheduling Patterns in Today's Secondary Schools."

8. Go to Merrill Education's Link to General Methods Resources site at this URL: http://www.prenhall.com/methods-cluster/ At the bottom of the page select "curriculum" as your topic and click the "begin" button. This will take you to the "Overview" page. On the left side, click on "Web Links." On the Web Links page click on "outlines and guides." Follow links that will give you information you can use to prepare a short paper titled "Examples of State Guidelines for Secondary School Curricula."

References

Armstrong, D. G. (1989). *Developing and documenting the curriculum.* Boston: Allyn & Bacon.

Barr, R. (1987). Content coverage. In M. Dunkin (Ed.), *The international encyclopedia of teaching and teacher education* (pp. 364–368). New York: Pergamon Press.

Bruner, J. (1960). *The process of education.* Cambridge, MA: Harvard University Press.

Burns, J. (1996, January 19). Learn from the teachers. *The Houston Chronicle,* pp. 1C, 4C.

Good, T., & Brophy, J. (2000). *Looking in classrooms* (8th ed.). New York: Longman.

Jarolimek, J. (1990). *Social studies in elementary education* (8th ed.). New York: Macmillan.

Posner, G. (1987). Pacing and sequencing. In M. Dunkin (Ed.), *The international encyclopedia of teaching and teacher education* (pp. 266–272). New York: Pergamon Press.

Pursuing excellence: A study of U.S. fourth-grade mathematics and science achievement in international context (1997). Washington, DC: National Center for Education Statistics.

Pursuing excellence: A study of U.S. eighth-grade mathematics and science teaching, learning, curriculum, and achievement in international context (1996). Washington, DC: National Center for Education Statistics.

Pursuing excellence: A study of U.S. twelfth-grade mathematics and science achievement in international context (1998). Washington, DC: National Center for Education Statistics.

Taba, H. (1962). *Curriculum development: Theory and practice.* New York: Harcourt, Brace and World.

TIMSS: The third international mathematics and science study (1999, March). Washington, DC: National Center for Education Statistics.

Walberg, H. J. (1998, July). *Spending more while learning less: U.S. school productivity in international perspective*. Fordham Report.
[http://edexcellence.net/library/walberg.html]

Whitford, S. (1996, January 19). Help us out, parents, you're needed most. *The Houston Chronicle*, pp. 1C, 4C.

6

Accommodating Diversity

This chapter will aim to

- recognize the importance of responding to the special needs and perspectives of students from diverse cultural backgrounds;

- identify some planning perspectives that can be helpful in developing instructional programs well suited to needs of African-American, Latino, native American, Asian, and other minority group students;

- describe some teacher actions that can help students with different kinds of disabilities succeed in the classroom;

- explain changes in approaches to working with students who have disabilities and their implications for regular classroom teachers; and

- describe characteristics of gifted and talented students and suggest ways that the needs of these young people can be accommodated in the classroom.

Introduction

Diversity among students in schools today is greater than it has ever been. Present trends suggest that you will find even more differences among your students in the years ahead. In part, these changes result from alterations in the make-up of the general population. In part, they have come about because of legislative actions. The one certainty is that you will work with students from different cultural, ethnic, and language groups and who may be characterized by one or more "exceptionalities." *Exceptional students* are those whose behaviors and/or talents deviate from the norm to the extent that special needs are present and additional service or support may be warranted (Patton, Blackbourn, & Fad, 1996).

The school population is more diverse than the population as a whole. In a recent year, African-Americans, Latinos, native Americans, Asians, and members of other minority groups made up about 28 percent of the U.S. total population (U.S. Census Bureau, 1999). This compares with about 36 percent of students in public schools who are members of minority groups. This figure is up from a total of 24 percent in 1976 (*Condition of Education*, 1999). This increase has come about primarily because of the tremendous growth in the numbers of Latino students. Today one of every four students enrolled in U.S. public schools is of Latino heritage. In 1972, only one of every 10 students was Latino (*Condition of Education*, 1999).

Exceptional students are found among all groups of learners in the schools. In a recent year, these students accounted for nearly 12.5 percent of the total school population (National Center for Education Statistics, 1997). These students include those with a variety of personal circumstances including specific learning disabilities, speech or

Figure 6-1
Graphic Organizer

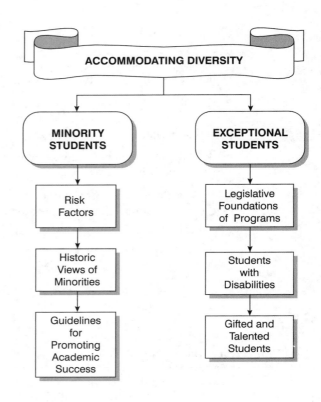

language impairments, mental retardation, hearing impairments, visual impairments, physical and health impairments, emotional disturbance, and other conditions. Increasingly, these learners are being served as members of regular classrooms. Over the past 25 years, there has been an increase of over 50 percent in the number of students participating in federal programs for learners with disabilities (*Condition of Education, Indicator 45,* 1998).

Minority Students

Whether you are a member of the cultural and ethnic majority or a member of a cultural or ethnic minority, as you prepare to work with students you need to recognize that there are no generalizations about teaching people from different personal backgrounds that are universally applicable. You will have to take the time to learn about the cultural backgrounds of the individual students enrolled in your classes. If you fail to do this, problems can arise. For example, some teachers have erroneously assumed that all Asian students are "model minorities" who are bright, psychologically secure young people who are motivated to do well at school. Differences among individual Asians are as significant as between Asians and other groups. If you stereotype these young people as members of a model minority who need only a minimal amount of your special attention, you may find that Asian students in your class who experience academic difficulties develop negative self-images. If you express public support for the model minority view, you may also unwittingly prompt non-Asian students to give Asian students in your class a hard time. Your other students may act irresponsibly toward these students out of a mistaken belief that the Asians are dull, academic grinds whose outstanding school performance requires others in the class to work too hard to keep up (Pang, 1995).

Risk Factors

Many minority students have not done well in school compared with the achievement of white students. Experts who have studied achievement of students in schools have identified a number of risk factors that characterize many individuals who do not do well. Among these risk factors are the following:

- lives in a single-parent family,
- family receives public assistance,
- primary language other than English,
- brother or sister who dropped out of school,
- mother not a high-school graduate,
- has attended five or more schools during lifetime,
- less than one hour per week spent on homework,
- spends no time each week reading for fun,
- watches television more than five hours a night,
- little communication with parents about things studied at school, and
- is overage for grade level by at least one year (Gleason & Dynarksi, 1998).

Individuals having a single risk factor may not necessarily experience difficulty in school. Researchers, however, have determined that students having two or more risk factors are particularly likely to do poorly. Minority students are much more likely than white students to be in this situation.

Historic Views of Minorities

An early explanation for minorities' failures to excel in school was the *genetic deficit* view (Savage & Armstrong, 2000). The premise of this position was that students from minority groups lacked the necessary intellectual equipment to do good work in school. This lack was ascribed to their status as sons and daughters of individuals who were not particularly bright. Hence, it was argued, an insufficient capacity to learn was passed on to their children. This mistaken belief provided a perfect rationale for schools to do little or nothing to improve instruction directed at minority students. Why, it was argued, should the schools commit scarce resources to programs designed to serve individuals who lacked the capacity to learn from them?

 MORE FROM THE WEB ━━━━━━━━━━━━━━━━━━━

Meeting Diverse Learners' Needs

Challenges educators face in providing instruction that is responsive to the needs of an increasingly diverse student population have prompted the development of many Web sites with practical information for teachers. We have selected a few you might want to visit.

Defining Multicultural Education

http://curry.edschool.virginia.edu/go/multicultural/initial.html

- Not all educators agree on components and purposes of multicultural education. At this site, you will find information related to this issue from a number of leading authorities in the field. You will find details related to definitions of the term *multicultural education* and to components, assumptions, goals, and principles of multicultural education programs.

Bilingual Education: Focusing Policy on Student Achievement

http://www.ascd.org/issues/language.html

- This site is maintained by the Association for Supervision and Curriculum Development (ASCD), a group dedicated to improving school programming for all learners. You will find information here about various approaches to meeting needs of bilingual students, particularly with respect to some controversies they have engendered and to some research-based findings about approaches that have worked well with students whose first language is not English.

The VENN View of Diversity: Understanding Differences Through Similarities

http://www.iteachnet.com/April97/VennDiversity_JackLevy.htm

- This article, prepared by Jack Levy of George Mason University, provides an overview of a series of research projects. The premise of this work is that people from different groups need to appreciate that they share certain commonalities before they can began to understand and appreciate their differences.

Teaching Diversity: People of Color

http://www.theaha.org/pubs/diversity.htm

- Some members of the American Historical Association (AHA) have been concerned that many studies of American history have failed to include references to contributions of certain racial and ethnic groups. In response to this situation, the AHA's Committee on Minority Historians has commissioned an essay series. At this site, you will find references to available essays, including topics such as "Teaching U.S. Puerto Rican History," "Teaching Asian American History," "Teaching Asian American Women's History," "Teaching African American History," and "Teaching American Indian History."

ERIC Clearinghouse on Disabilities and Gifted Education

http://ericec.org/

- This site is maintained by the ERIC center with responsibility for disseminating information about students with disabilities and students who are gifted. You will encounter a huge number of links here to sites with useful information about students in both of these categories.

The Council for Exceptional Children

http://www.cec.sped.org/

- The Council for Exceptional Children (CEC) is a leading professional organization for educators with interests in serving the needs of students with disabilities. You will find much information here about useful approaches to inclusion and to many other topics related to serving these students well in the classroom.

Federation for Children with Special Needs

http://www.fcsn.org/resource.htm

- The Federation for Children with Special needs is an advocacy group dedicated to supporting efforts to serve students with disabilities well. You will find links to information sources maintained by state and federal agencies. This is a good source for details about inclusion and other topics related to students with disabilities.

National Association for Gifted Children

http://www.nagc.org/home.htm

- The National Association for Gifted Children (NAGC) advocates in support of programs for gifted and talented students. There are good links at this site to other Web locations where information is available related to meeting the educational needs of these students.

The genetic deficit view had fallen from favor by the middle of this century. In the 1960s, a new deficit view enjoyed some currency for a time. This was the *cultural deficit* position (Erickson, 1987). Individuals who were impressed by this idea felt that school problems of minority group students could be traced to their homes. It was alleged that their homes provided an intellectually sterile background that failed to give them attitudes and aptitudes needed for success in school. The cultural deficit argument allowed school leaders, who were reluctant to commit serious resources to programs designed to help minority students, to blame the home for failure of these young people to learn. Because many minority students came from impoverished home backgrounds, some argued that the hope that special programs for minority students might improve their performance in school was illogical.

Still another variant on the blame-the-students, the-schools-can-do-nothing theme was the *communication process* position. This view blamed poor minority student performance on language differences separating students and their teachers. It was alleged that these differences were so profound that minority students could not understand what was said in the classroom and what was expected of them at school. Their failure was attributed to this communication gap. Critics of this position pointed out that some minority students did extremely well in school despite economic and social backgrounds very similar to those of minority students who did poorly.

Though you may occasionally hear support for the genetic deficit, cultural deficit, and communication deficit positions, most educators now reject these views. All three arguments have been recognized as weak attempts to excuse the school from being accountable for minority students' learning. Today, the view is that minority students' failures in school have often resulted from the lack of a serious commitment on the part of educators to plan and deliver programs designed to help these young people learn. The rhetoric of concern has been there for many years, but a willingness to develop an intellectual and a financial commitment to help minority students in schools is relatively recent.

Guidelines for Promoting Academic Success

A number of guidelines have been suggested to promote better learning and better attitudes toward school on the part of minority group learners. We have included here some recommendations that are reflected in many of these proposals:

- Assume all students can learn,
- Provide good teachers,
- Insist that teachers become aware of their own cultural perspectives,
- Encourage teachers to avoid favoritism in the classroom,

- Include students from varied ethnic and cultural backgrounds in each group when members of a class are divided into groups for instruction,
- Vary teaching methods to accommodate different learning styles,
- Develop close working relationships with students' families,
- Emphasize development of higher-level thinking skills, and
- Use conversations to uncover ways to contextualize instruction.

Assume All Students Can Learn

As a teacher, you will find minority group students (and, indeed, students in general) very sensitive to how you view them. If you feel that you have little confidence in their abilities to learn, minority group students will be inclined to "live down" to your expectations. Under the best of circumstances, the middle school, junior high school, and senior high school years are emotionally trying for young people. The last thing you want to do is to reinforce any feelings of personal inadequacy your students might have. Your students will not be motivated if you fail to convince them of your sincere belief in their ability to learn.

In addition to the negative impact on students' self concepts that can result if your actions suggest to them that they cannot learn, such an attitude can affect how you interact with these young people. There is evidence that teachers' beliefs about the learning potential of students influence their commitment to prepare good lessons and deliver high-quality instruction. In other words, your conviction that your instruction can make a difference motivates students to do their best. In the absence of this motivation, the quality of your instruction is likely to suffer and, as a result, your students will not achieve a high level of academic success.

When you think about your students, remember that there is great diversity within *any* group of people. You want to avoid concluding that information that may well describe certain individuals who are African-American, Latino, native American, or Asian generalizes to all people who belong to one of these groups. This kind of stereotyping distorts reality.

For example, your African-American students are likely to be descendants of people who came from widely separated areas in Africa, from the Caribbean, or from South America. Families of some of these students may have come to this country relatively recently. Others may be descendants of African-Americans who have lived here for generations (Lee & Slaughter-Defoe, 1995). Characteristics of your African-American students may also vary depending on socio-economic levels of their families, religious orientations, rural versus urban family backgrounds, and many other factors.

These differences imply a need to understand students well and to vary your instruction to meet their needs. You need to keep in mind the folly of searching for a single teaching approach that will respond well to the characteristics of every student you teach. This mistaken approach is akin to a futile search for an instructional holy grail. "It risks becoming a sacred calling that consumes resources in the search for an illusory panacea for complex social and educational ills" (Lomawaima, 1995, p. 342).

Provide Good Teachers

Good teachers help students develop better attitudes toward school and learn more than do mediocre teachers. It is particularly critical that minority students be taught by individuals who are sensitive to their special ethnic and cultural perspectives, respectful of them as individuals, and strongly committed to the view that they can and should learn. Regrettably, individuals who lack these important characteristics teach large numbers of minority students.

In many places with large minority-student enrollments, turnover rates of teachers are high. This means that many minority students are taught by teachers who are either relatively new to the profession or relatively new to the school where they are presently employed. Many of these teachers also are people who are teaching outside of their major field of preparation. Minority students, further, have a higher than average probability of being taught by teachers holding only an emergency teaching credential.

Teachers Must Be Aware of Their Own Cultural Perspectives

If you are a member of the white majority, you may well live in a world where perspectives of your own group are so dominant that you may fail to recognize that you have a worldview that may differ from that of members of other cultural and ethnic groups. In truth, all people are to a great extent conditioned to make sense of the world in ways consistent with the perspectives of the people with whom they interact. If you have had few relationships with people from cultures other than the dominant white majority, you may not immediately understand that some of your minority group students come from groups whose ideas about how the world is and how people should behave vary from your own. This means that you need to think clearly about your own assumptions and to reflect on how actions you take might be viewed by students in your classes with different views about how the world operates. You need to consider answers to such questions as these:

- What are my views about what the curriculum ought to be?

- How do I think individuals learn in the classroom?

- What do I consider to be appropriate behavior in the classroom?

- What assumptions am I making about the previous experience and the background my students bring to school?

- To what do I attribute lack of school success of students who are members of certain groups?

- Where did I get my ideas about good educational practice?

- How are my ideas influenced by the community I lived in and the schools I attended when I was a student?

Honest answers to these questions can help you think about the appropriateness of decisions you make about working with students from cultural and ethnic groups that differ from your own. To be successful, you have to operate in ways that draw on some practices of cultural anthropologists. You have to become a participant-observer in the community where you teach. You need to note carefully the worldviews, the values, the norms, the cultural practices, and the rituals of the individuals you teach. You can use this information to develop programs that will provide a culturally responsive education for your students.

If you fail to recognize that there are multiple perspectives on these issues and erroneously assume that your own worldview is the only one (or at least the only "correct" one), you may have difficulty communicating with people from other social and cultural orientations. This has proved to be particularly true if you are a white teacher and find yourself teaching large numbers of minority students. For example, as a member of the dominant white culture, you may conclude that a person who avoids eye contact with you when being addressed is "shifty," "guilty," or "ashamed." Your conclusion would make sense, given the cultural orientation of the white majority.

CRITICAL INCIDENT

"Mr. Hobbs, Your History Is Irrelevant."

Nolan Hobbs teaches United States history at Lee High School. He also occasionally is called on to teach economics classes and sociology classes. Recently, he shared these comments with Rafaela Sanchez, Lee High School's vice principal for academic programs.

"Things have gone just great this year. Well, that's generally the case, but there is a student in my fifth period class who has become a bit of a thorn in my side. I'm talking about Cassiella Birdsong. You'll remember she was in talking to you a few weeks ago about getting some bulletin board space in the hall for the African-American Students Association.

"Well, anyway, Cassiella has convinced herself that I have absolutely nothing to teach her. She told me this morning that our history book was 'filled with a bunch of junk about dead white guys.' Even though I go out of my way to include information about contributions of African-Americans, she still has it in her head that my whole course is dedicated to imposing a point of view she wants no part of.

"I know she's bright, and I am concerned that she's just not working up to her potential. I'm getting pretty frustrated with her telling me every day how 'irrelevant' everything in my course is. Her attitude is beginning to have a bad influence on some of the other students as well."

■ ■ ■

How might you explain Cassiella's point of view? What do these views tell us about her values? Is her reaction something Mr. Hobbs should be concerned about? What does Mr. Hobbs believe to be important? What should he do next? In addition to the vice principal, who else might he consult for advice? What specific advice would you provide to Mr. Hobbs and/or to Cassiella?

However, not all cultures view eye contact in the same way. In some minority cultures, young people are taught that it is not polite to look adults in the eye. Hence, a student who looks away from you when you are speaking may feel he or she is politely recognizing your position as a high-status, intelligent adult. You would be making an error if you concluded this behavior was an indication of a student who "has something to hide." Over time, errors of this kind can strain your relationships with students, thereby negatively affecting students' attitudes and motivation to do assigned work.

Avoid Favoritism in the Classroom

By the time they arrive in secondary schools, minority group students are aware that American society has different racial and ethnic groups. Some of them may have had experiences in school and elsewhere that have led them to conclude that sometimes members of minority groups are treated differently than members of the white, non-Latino majority. Additionally, nearly all students are concerned about the general issues of consistent and appropriate treatment. Your credibility definitely will be at risk if your students suspect you are not fair.

One way to demonstrate fairness is to avoid favoritism in the classroom. It is particularly important that minority group students sense that, as individuals and as a group, they are being treated as well as others in the class. If your minority students suspect that you single out individuals for negative treatment or comments in a way that seems tied to ethnicity or race, you may find it difficult to maintain their interest and cooperation.

Students often measure fairness by looking at how teachers handle episodes of misbehavior. The general rule you should follow is to respond to a given kind of misbehavior in the same way, regardless of who the offender is. That is, your high-achieving students shouldn't get off more lightly than your low-achieving students, your white students shouldn't get off more lightly than your minority group students, and so forth. When students feel that you dispense justice equitably and hold all to the same standard, their motivation levels increase, your discipline problems diminish, and students' achievement levels improve.

Include Students from Varied Ethnic and Cultural Backgrounds in Each Group

When you plan group work, it is important that your groups not serve as a vehicle for re-segregating students on the basis of race or ethnicity. For one thing, individual groups sometimes are asked to do different things (for example, you may assign some groups to work on more challenging academic tasks than others).

There is evidence that some groups are organized by teachers so that racial minorities are concentrated within a few groups (Rist, 1985). This is a mistake. Learners must not see group instructional techniques as subtle covers for an instructional program designed to provide different (and perhaps lower quality) instruction to minority group students.

Additionally, a key purpose of secondary education is to help students adjust to living in a multicultural society. Given this priority, it makes sense for you to organize groups to encourage personal contacts among students from varying cultural and ethnic backgrounds. Such practices break down group-to-group isolation and provide a way for students to become more familiar with perspectives different from their own.

Students in this group of middle schoolers reflect some of the racial and ethic diversity found in today's schools.

Respond to Varying Learning Styles

Students vary in terms of their preferred learning styles. This means that some individuals learn better when they read about new information. Others learn better when they listen to someone explaining new content. Others are visual learners—people who master new content best when they are presented with examples they can see. Still others need opportunities to touch, handle, and otherwise manipulate physical objects. Kinds of preferred learning settings also vary. For example, some individuals prefer to learn alone. Others do much better when they are organized into groups.

Researchers have found that students' cultural backgrounds affect their learning styles (Grant & Sleeter, 1994). This does not mean that individuals with similar cultural backgrounds do not vary. Rather, it suggests that more people from one cultural group may have a given learning style than people from another cultural group.

There is evidence that students from African-American and Latino backgrounds do better when they are presented with a broad general overview of a situation first and then asked to think about how specific information relates to the general situation (Bowman, 1991). (For example, it would be better for you to provide general information about the Civil War and then go on to ask about the relationship of the Battle of Gettysburg to the war in general.) Non-Latino white students, however, have been found to do well when complex situations are first broken down into small parts. These small parts are learned one at a time, and only in the end does a general picture emerge. (Given this orientation, you might have your class study individual battles of the Civil War one at a time and conclude with a description of their cumulative effective on the war in general.)

Develop Close Working Relationships with Students' Families

To the extent possible, you should establish relationships with members of minority group students' families. Although many relatives of minority students are positively disposed toward the school and its programs, this attitude is not universal. Some of them did not have particularly good experiences in school themselves and may be inclined to lump educators into a category that includes indifferent city hall bureaucrats, law enforcement officials, and other establishment figures that, in their view, have not always treated minorities fairly. People with these views may be reluctant to come to the school on open house nights or on other occasions, and you need to make special efforts to contact them.

Students' priorities and general attitudes are strongly influenced by those of their parents, grandparents, and other relatives, especially those living in the same household. If you can establish a common ground with a student's family members that results in a consensus regarding what the student ought to be doing in school, the student may benefit. It has been found that "school learning is most likely to occur when family values reinforce school expectations" (Ogbu, 1973, p. 27).

Emphasize Development of Higher-Level Thinking Skills

If you have some minority-group students in your classroom who are not doing well, you need to avoid the temptation to lower your instructional expectations. Their academic performance may result from circumstances having little or nothing to do with their real ability levels. Students gain nothing when they are provided with unchallenging classroom instruction. What you need to do is fit instructional tasks to students in such a way that they will be intellectually "stretched" but not to the extent they will be unable to succeed. Over time, instruction that pushes students to develop sophisticated thinking skills gives them the tools needed for dealing with more complex subject matter. These academic successes build students' confidence and stimulate their interest in the school program.

Use Conversations to Uncover Ways to Contextualize Instruction

As you seek to "connect" with your students, you need to develop instructional activities that members of your class see relate to their own lives, their families, and their communities (Tharp, 1999). Your aim is to *contextualize* your instruction. This kind of teaching ties closely to the personal experiences of the people who will receive it—your students. Providing good contextualized instruction requires you to know your students well. One useful approach for gaining insights into your students' personal backgrounds involves engaging them in conversations. If you listen carefully and respectfully to what students say, they will reveal a great deal about their personal, family, and community backgrounds. All of this information can be useful to you in designing lessons that are responsive to the individual circumstances of your students.

Exceptional Students

There are great differences among exceptional students. Sometimes the term *special education student* is used as a general descriptor for individuals who have learning disabilities, physical problems, or emotional and behavioral difficulties that deviate markedly from the norm. Exceptional students also include so-called *gifted-and-talented* learners whose intelligence and/or skill levels have been found to be well above those of their age or grade peers.

Legislative Foundations of Programs

Recently, a caller to a talk show complained about the disrupting presence of a special education student in one of her child's classrooms. The host immediately took up the issue and started blaming the "education bureaucracy" for what he described as this "ridiculous and unsound" educational practice. Later in the program a teacher called and explained that there were laws that governed these actions. The host, no fan of professional educators, responded that teachers were always looking for excuses to support decisions to engage in inappropriate professional practices.

This uninformed talk show host clearly failed to understand that there are complex regulations governing the education of exceptional students. Among these laws are (1) the Education for All Handicapped Children Act, which was first passed in 1975 as Public Law (P.L.) 94–142 and renamed the "Individuals with Disabilities Education Act" in 1990 (P.L. 101–476); (2) the Individuals with Disabilities Education Act of 1997 (P.L. 105–117); and (3) the Jacob K. Javits Gifted and Talented Students Act of 1994 (P.L. 100–297).

When the Education for All Handicapped Children Act was enacted in 1975, both supporters and critics predicted that it would change the face of education in the United States (Heward, 1996). This proved to be true. The updated version of this legislation, the Individuals with Disabilities Education Act, mandates the following six basic principles first enunciated in the original 1975 legislation.

- *Zero rejects.* Schools must enroll every child regardless of the nature or severity of the disability. Implementing this principle has been expensive. Many school districts have had to increase their budgets to provide funds to provide educational services for some students who, previously, were excluded from schools.
- *Nondiscriminatory testing.* Multiple indicators must be used to determine whether an individual has a disability and whether special services are needed.
- *Appropriate education.* Schools must develop and implement an Individualized Education Plan (IEP) for each student with a disability.
- *Least restrictive environment.* A student with a disability is to be educated in the setting that is the least restrictive for that individual. Often this has involved placement of students with disabilities in regular classrooms for at least part of the school day. This is often called *mainstreaming.* This provision has changed the nature of the student population served by regular teachers in traditional classrooms. Students with

disabilities, who formerly were segregated into special education classrooms, now are interspersed with so-called regular students in traditional classrooms.

- *Due process.* The rights of students and their parents in planning and placement decisions must be protected by due process procedures.
- *Parental participation.* Parental participation in the decisions made regarding the education of the student are mandated.

The Individuals with Disabilities Education Act of 1990 added an important new principle. It required schools to provide *transition services* for students with disabilities (Heward, 1996). Transition services are identified as a coordinated set of services designed to help the student make the transition from high school to post-school activities such as college, vocational training, employment, and independent living or community participation. This addition to the original legislation was adopted in response to studies that revealed educational programs were doing a poor job of preparing students with disabilities for life after high school.

Public Law 105–117, The Individuals with Disabilities Education Act of 1997, tremendously broadened existing requirements to serve learners with disabilities in regular classrooms. In part, this expansion stemmed from a strong legislative support for the principle of *inclusion*. Inclusion represents a commitment to the idea that students, regardless of unique personal characteristics (including, for example, disabilities of all kinds), not only have a legal right to services in a regular classroom but that they are welcomed and wanted as members of these classes. Some schools now pride themselves on being *full inclusion* environments. In these schools you will find almost a total absence of special classrooms for learners with disabilities. Virtually all services are provided to these students in regular classrooms.

Advocates of inclusive education claim several key advantages for this approach (Smith, Polloway, Patton, & Dowdy, 1996). Among their points are the following:

- It is possible for special education students to receive an education in the regular classroom that is appropriate for their needs.
- Educating special students in the regular classroom reduces the stigma that sometimes has been attached to them when they have been taught in separate "special education" classes.
- Because teachers in regular classrooms expect students to have varied abilities, there is less likelihood of any individual student being *permanently* mislabeled as a "special education" student and provided with an instructional program inappropriate to his or her needs.
- In a society that includes incredible diversity, there are benefits for both special education students and regular classroom students when they are taught together. This kind of association can promote tolerance of individual differences and recognition of the point that all people have personal strengths and weaknesses.
- All students benefit when teachers make efforts to individualize their instruction to meet individual student needs. When special education students are included in regular classrooms, there is a greater incentive for teachers to individualize their teaching.

The Individuals with Disabilities Education Act of 1997 put important new legal muscle behind the view that learners with disabilities should be taught, to the fullest extent possible, as members of regular school classes. Some important new requirements of this legislation include the following:

- A student's regular classroom teacher *must* be involved in the development of a student's Individualized Education Plan (IEP) and must participate in IEP planning.
- Parents and guardians have the right to be involved in *all* decisions regarding their children's eligibility for and placement in programs designed to serve them.
- Information about learners with disabilities' achievement must be included in regular public reports on test scores.

The Jacob K. Javits Gifted and Talented Students Act of 1994, unlike the others discussed in this section, did not mandate specific services but provides incentives for state and local education agencies to address the specific needs of individuals with this exceptionality. It allocates money for the identification of gifted students and the professional training of teachers. Money made available as a result of this legislation also supports the National Center for the Education of the Gifted. The Javits Act was adopted out of a recognition that gifted and talented students have special needs and that they may require additional support and services if they are to reach their potential.

Students with Disabilities

Students with disabilities include individuals having many different kinds of characteristics. In general, these are people who have a mental or physical condition that prevents them from succeeding in programs designed for people not having this condition (or these conditions).

Categories

Various schemes have been developed for categorizing disabilities. These schemes are discussed in the sections that follow:

- Mental Retardation
- Hearing Impairment
- Speech Impairment
- Visual Impairment
- Learning Disability
- Attention Deficit Disorder
- Physical and Health Impairment
- Emotional Disturbance

Mental Retardation

Mental retardation is a term that is difficult to define with any degree of precision. In general, people are described as mentally retarded when their intellectual development is (1) significantly below that of age-mates and (2) their potential for academic achievement has been determined to be markedly less than that of so-called normal individuals.

In the past, IQ scores were often used to determine whether a person could be categorized as mentally retarded. A problem with using IQ for this purpose is that people who may appear to be mentally retarded on the basis of an IQ test may be perfectly capable of functioning in a normal fashion under other conditions. For example, people with low IQ scores may succeed in some job roles after leaving school. Because of this, the American Association of Mental Deficiency (AAMD) has long advocated that mental retardation be identified using broader and more diverse measures than a simple IQ test score. The AAMD suggests that people who are mentally retarded cannot function within the typical range of life situations. Individuals capable of functioning within this range should not be classified as mentally retarded, regardless of their IQ test scores.

Several levels of mental retardation have been described. These include the categories of (1) educable, (2) trainable, and (3) severely or profoundly retarded. The type of student with mental retardation who is most likely to be assigned to spend part of the instructional day (or the entire instructional day) in a regular classroom is someone in the educable category.

It is difficult to speak authoritatively about what educable students can do. This is because there are tremendous differences among individuals in this category. In general, educable students can derive some benefits from the school program. It is your responsibility to diagnose specific characteristics of educable students and, in cooperation with parents and other school officials, devise appropriate learning experiences for them.

Educable students often have short attention spans. They may become easily frustrated. By the time they reach their secondary school years, many have a history of failure in school. Often they lack confidence as they begin a new task. Frequently they experience difficulty grasping abstract ideas or complex sequences of ideas.

Some of the following principles make sense as you plan instructional programs for educable students:

- Lessons should be short, direct, and to the point.
- Material should be introduced in short, sequential steps.
- Content introduced in prose form should be reinforced by additional visual and oral examples.
- It may be useful to assign a student who is not mentally retarded to work with the educable student as a peer tutor.
- Directions should be delivered clearly, using vocabulary words educable students understand.
- Lessons should not place educable students in highly competitive situations, particularly those requiring them to compete against non-mentally-retarded students.

In addition, educable students often require more time to complete tasks than do their non-mentally retarded fellow students. You need to avoid imposing tight, restrictive deadlines when giving them assignments. It is better for these students to succeed at completing fewer tasks than to fail a larger number of them. Successful task completion is an important builder of self-esteem for these young people.

Hearing Impairment

Students who are hearing impaired fall into two key categories: (1) students whose hearing loss is so profound as to greatly inhibit their ability to acquire normal use of oral language (classified as *deaf*) and (2) students whose hearing loss is serious, but not serious enough to prevent them from acquiring normal speech patterns (classified as *hard of hearing*).

There are great differences among students who are hearing-impaired. Some of them are unable to hear certain pitches. Others require different levels of amplified sound. Some have had a hearing loss since birth; others may have suffered a hearing loss after they were old enough to have acquired some oral-language proficiency. Despite individual differences, students who are hearing-impaired generally experience difficulty developing great proficiency with the spoken language. School programs for these students place a heavy emphasis on helping them improve their oral-language proficiency.

Many students who have severe hearing losses have been taught to pay close attention to visual clues. Many know how to read lips. Because of their dependence on visual signals, you need to provide students with hearing losses lessons that enable them to take advantage of their visual-learning skills. For example, you should face these students directly when you give directions and present new information. It helps if you write information on an overhead transparency rather than on a chalkboard. (When you write on an overhead, you face students, thus enabling hearing-impaired students to watch your lips. When you write on the chalkboard, students can't see your lips because you face away from them.) It is also a good idea for you to remain relatively stationary when speaking to hearing-impaired students. Trained lip readers find it difficult to understand a person who is in motion.

Assignments and other directions need to be provided in written form. (They can be oral as well, but the written information can help eliminate possible confusion among hearing-impaired students.) When you deliver a lecture, it helps to provide class members with a general printed outline that includes at least major topics and subtopics to be covered. Additionally, it is a good idea to provide students with lists of important (and potentially confusing) words before the lecture begins. This is particularly true when terms are to be introduced that have multiple meanings. (Consider the term *market* as it is understood in everyday conversation and how specialists in economics use it.) A discussion of special vocabulary before the lecture begins may help students who are hearing impaired (and other students as well) to better grasp the material.

All students do better when instruction is well organized and when point-to-point transitions are clear and smooth. Clarity in planning and delivering instruction is even more critical for hearing-impaired students than for the general population of secondary school learners. Students who are hearing impaired lack the multiple communication channels that other students sometimes use to make sense out of disorganized lessons.

Some hearing-impaired students wear hearing aids or other mechanical devices. You need to know how they work. For example, you should learn how batteries are replaced in hearing aids. It may be a good idea to keep a supply of batteries on hand. Many school districts employ specialists in the education of students who are hearing-impaired to provide additional guidance regarding how you can best serve these young people in your regular classroom.

Speech Impairment

Identifying students who have serious *speech impairments* is difficult. The process demands a great deal of personal judgment. In general, individuals are thought to suffer from impaired speech when their speech differs significantly from that of others in the same age group. Speech problems encompass a range of difficulties. These relate to such things as voice quality, problems in articulating certain sounds, and stuttering.

Because speech impairments do not represent the obvious obstacles to learning as hearing impairments and visual impairments do, you may not immediately appreciate their seriousness. You need to be aware of an important side effect of speech impairment, and one that occurs in a distressingly high number of students suffering from this problem—low self-image. Because of the frustration they feel at not being able to speak normally, some of these students conclude that they are inferior or even incompetent. The drop-out rate of students with speech impairments is high.

Often students with speech impairments profit from work with a trained speech therapist. Many school districts have these specialists on staff. There are also things you can do in your classroom to help these students. In general, students with speech impairments need emotional support. You need to avoid placing them in situations that call unnecessary attention to their condition.

In classroom discussions, it makes sense to call on students with speech impairments only when they raise a hand and indicate a willingness to volunteer a response. When such students begin to speak, they should be allowed to finish what they have to say without interruption or correction. Praise and other kinds of reinforcement should be provided when these students volunteer a remark in class.

You need to provide opportunities for speech-impaired students to speak with you on a one-to-one basis. These occasions allow you to boost students' morale by making sensitive, supporting comments to them. Additionally, these one-on-one discussions give students a chance to talk about course work (and other matters) without feeling that they will be embarrassed by a communication difficulty that might draw ridicule from others in the class.

Visual Impairment

The term *visual impairment* is used to describe a variety of conditions related to the sense of sight. Some visually impaired individuals have no sight whatever. However, most students in this category have some sight. Some see a world that is blurred, dim, or out of focus; others may see only parts of objects. About 1 percent of the school-aged population is visually impaired.

Whenever assignments are written on the chalkboard or written information is distributed, you need to make special arrangements to ensure clear communication with your students who are visually impaired. Sometimes oral explanations will suffice. At other times, you may find it useful to provide these students with audio recordings of information. Your students can play back the tapes later to ensure they have the needed information.

Personal mobility is an important problem for students who are visually impaired. Over time, many of these students develop good mental pictures of places they visit frequently. They require some experience in a new environment before a good mental picture develops. You need to make time for visually impaired students to visit classrooms when classes are not being held. This will give them an opportunity to become familiar with placement of furniture and with other room features. If you change room arrangements later, you need to give visually-impaired students time to become familiar with the new configuration.

Learning Disability

A student with a *learning disability* exhibits a disorder in one or more of the basic psychological processes involved in understanding or using spoken or written language. The problem may be revealed in such areas as listening, writing, reading, spelling, or computing. Sometimes learning disabilities are referred to by such terms as *perceptual handicaps, minimal brain dysfunction,* and *dyslexia.* Students who have learning disabilities have difficulty processing sensory stimuli.

People with learning disabilities often find it hard to follow directions. They may appear disorganized. You will often find that these students have difficulty getting started on assigned tasks. Often they have a low tolerance for frustration. They may become tense and appear incapable of doing anything when they feel you are pressuring them. Handwriting of these students often appears disorganized. Letters within words may be inconsistent in size, and there may be letter reversals. Some students with learning disabilities have unusual speech patterns. For example, words may be spoken out of their proper sequence.

Most students with learning disabilities need special help with organization. These students often find it difficult to distinguish between important and unimportant information. You need to take time to highlight key ideas for them and to provide ways of organizing information into meaningful patterns. In addition, learning disabled students often have a hard time dealing with alternatives. Sometimes they become anxious when they are forced to make choices. It makes sense for you to limit options available for these students.

By the time they reach their secondary school years, many students with learning disabilities have experienced years of frustration and failure in school. As a result, their self-esteem is low. You need to do whatever you can to help these young people develop more self-confidence. In a supportive classroom environment, these students *can* learn.

Attention Deficit Disorder

Attention Deficit Disorder (ADD) might be thought of as a specific type of learning disability. It bears special mention because students with ADD have been declared eligible for services under the Individuals with Disabilities Education Act "when ADD impairs educational performance or learning" (Lerner & Lerner, 1991, p. 1). Students with ADD have difficulty staying actively engaged on assigned tasks and in pursuing, paying attention to, and completing their school work. Sometimes they appear to be hyperactive, racing from one idea to another and producing extremely sloppy work as a result of a compulsion to finish quickly. At other times, these students give the impression that they aren't listening to what is being said (Lerner & Lerner, 1991). ADD is common. It accounts for fully half of all referrals of children to outpatient health clinics. More male students than female students suffer from ADD (Lerner & Lerner, 1991).

In working with these students, you need to modify the learning environment and the nature of assigned tasks. Students with ADD are easily distracted by noise. They have problems with tasks that are too difficult or when others in the class establish the learning pace. These students do better when tasks are self-paced.

In general, students with ADD require more structure in their lessons than other students. To help these students pay attention, it is a good idea to increase the potential for holding their interest by adding color, shape, and texture to learning materials. These students do better in small classes than in large ones, and they tend to profit more from direct instruction than indirect instruction (Lerner & Lerner, 1991).

Physical and Health Impairment

Physical and health impairment is a broad category. In general, it includes students who have limitations related to physical abilities or medical conditions that may interfere with their school performance. About half of the students in this group have suffered from a crippling disease.

The range of conditions in this category makes it impossible to provide recommendations appropriate for every student with a physical or health impairment. In working with these students, the first thing you should do is to gather complete information regarding the specific nature of the condition of each person who falls into this general category. Counselors and parents often are able to provide specific descriptions of each student's special circumstances. Once you have this information, you can decide on modifications of your programs that need to be made for each student with a physical or health impairment.

These modifications will vary greatly from case to case. For example, some conditions may make it impossible for affected students to complete tasks as quickly as others in the class. This may mean that you will have to adjust the time allowed for these students to complete the assigned work. To help learners who have physical problems requiring the use of walkers or crutches, you may find it necessary to rearrange classroom furniture to make it easier for these students to move about the room.

In general, students with physical and health impairments are fully capable of meeting the intellectual challenges of regular classroom instruction. Your major adjustment comes not in devising unique methods of instruction but in identifying appropriate responses to accommodate special limitations imposed by particular physical and health conditions of these students. When the special needs of these students are met, many of them do extremely well in the regular classroom.

Emotional Disturbance

Emotionally disturbed students are characterized by patterns of behavior that vary significantly from age-appropriate norms. These patterns negatively affect their personal and social development. Some emotionally disturbed students may be defiant, rude, destructive, and attention seeking. Others may be fearful and withdrawn.

Most emotionally disturbed students find it difficult to cope with their environments. As a result, they often experience difficulty making the kinds of adjustments needed to stay focused on school-related tasks. As a result, academic problems are common among these students and frequently lead to low self-concepts. Many of these students become caught up in a negative cycle featuring poor academic performance, leading to diminished self-esteem, and resulting in poor attitudes that contribute to additional academic performance problems and a renewal of the same distressing sequence.

You need to attend to four key principles in working with emotionally disturbed students:

- Activities must be success oriented. Students must sense that they have a reasonable chance of succeeding.

- Behavior expectations must be communicated with exceptional clarity, and they must be consistently enforced.

- Distractions must be minimized to reduce the probability of students' being distracted from their assigned work.

- Efforts need to be taken to ensure that students understand that there is a clear and definite relationship between their behaviors and consequences flowing from these behaviors.

A concern that has some connection to each of these four major principles is motivation. By the time many emotionally disturbed students enter their secondary school years, they have experienced so much failure that they doubt they can master anything that is taught in school. Additionally, many of them suspect that school learning isn't particularly useful. As a result, some of these students go to great lengths to avoid serious engagement with academic tasks. All of this means that you must work hard to convince these students that mastery of school subjects will yield important personal benefits. These benefits need to be characterized by immediacy. It does little good to tell an emotionally disturbed student to "do this because it will help you get a better job in 10 years."

Your instruction needs to be designed to maximize these students' potential for success. It helps to cut large complex tasks into smaller parts that appear less intimidating. As individual parts are mastered, you need to provide positive feedback to encourage students to stay on task. Additionally, you ought to take steps to help these students' develop appropriate self-regulatory behaviors. With help, these students can be taught self-monitoring techniques that will help them to behave in ways that will facilitate learning and assist them to develop more positive self-concepts.

In working with emotionally disturbed students, you need to understand that the problems these young people experience will not disappear overnight. In many cases, emotional disturbance is a condition that has developed over many years. Change may take months, or even years.

Action Requirements for Teachers

Suppose you find yourself with a number of students with disabilities in your classrooms. To help them learn, first of all, you must have an accepting attitude toward these young people. You don't want to approach teaching these students with a mistaken preconception that working with learners with disabilities will be a frustrating and unrewarding experience. On the contrary, you are likely to derive considerable satisfaction from helping these special young people as you see them begin to exercise self-control, make academic progress, and overcome emotional problems.

The world of teaching has changed dramatically in the past few years. As a secondary teacher, you are increasingly likely to be involved with groups of professionals. For example, your school may have specialists who work with language minority students as well as students with disabilities. In some schools, there are intervention-assistance teams whose members will be available to help you adapt and deliver instruction for exceptional students. You also may have available a resource teacher for some portion of the day who can assist you in working with students with disabilities. The increasingly common practice of deploying groups of professionals to help students means that you need to be prepared to work with others in team situations. You may well find yourself involved in such collaborative activities as the following:

- *Participating in the IEP meetings.* As a classroom teacher you will be expected to attend and make contributions during these meetings and to understand the specific objectives for the student as prescribed in the IEP.

- *Communicating with specialists in the education of students with disabilities concerning the objectives and the content of the classroom.* Discrepancies between expectations and the abilities of the students are a major cause of failure of students with disabilities who are taught in regular classrooms (Smith, Polloway, Patton, & Dowdy, 1996). Discussions you have with professionals who have special training in working with students with disabilities can help you work effectively with these young people.

- *Informing the special student about behavioral and academic expectations.* A lack of understanding on the part of students regarding the expectations and demands in the regular classroom is frequently the cause of much frustration and anxiety and can lead to acting out behavior. You need to take care that these students understand what they are to do.

- *Monitoring student progress.* It is especially important that you assess the progress of exceptional students frequently. This helps the team make adjustments in the delivery of services to the special education students. In addition, celebrating success is important in building students' self-esteem.

- *Communicating openly with specialists in the education of students with disabilities any concerns and fears you have about teaching these young people.* If you do not deal with these concerns and fears, you may communicate non-acceptance to the students with disabilities who are members of your classes.

- *Learning the unique characteristics of each student.* It is important to find out from specialists in the education of students with disabilities information about such issues as the distractibility of individual students, including details about such issues as learning rates, specific difficulties in processing information, and the nature of any special learning aids you need to provide.

Your objective is to provide opportunities for students with disabilities to succeed. This requires modifying your instruction so that these young people have a legitimate opportunity to learn and grow (Smith, Polloway, Patton, & Dowdy, 1996). At the same time, you need to guard against making too many accommodations. Many of these young people can do much of the work teachers ask of students without disabilities. You want to be sure that students with disabilities feel that they are a legitimate part of the regular classroom group. You should encourage them to participate and interact with regular students so they will not be isolated and separated from the normal activities of the classroom.

Your work with specialists in the education of students with disabilities should not be restricted to planning for classroom instruction. For example, together you may also want to spend time identifying appropriate post-high-school academic or vocational training opportunities for these young people. Students with disabilities represent a group that particularly benefits from adult support as they think about what to do with their lives. Teaching self-advocacy is a key to helping students with disabilities make the transition to life after high school.

Part of your efforts should be directed to helping special-needs students think about what they need to do to live independently. You can help them make this transition by pointing out practical applications of what you teach in the classroom. Helping students understand how to be organized, how to handle and solve problems, how to establish and maintain social networks, and how to deal with issues such as drug abuse are among the topics that you can deal with in the context of your lessons.

Gifted and Talented Students

In a status report prepared more than 20 years ago, the U.S. Commissioner of Education pointed out that only a few specific programs for the gifted and talented existed in the nation's schools. Stimulated by the considerable interest generated by this report, Congress established the Office of Gifted and Talented within the U.S. Office of Education. Some time later, the Jacob K. Javits Gifted and Talented Students Act of 1994 (P.L. 100-297) provided funds to support programs to identify gifted students and to prepare teachers to respond to their special needs. This legislation also established funding for a National Center for the Education of the Gifted.

At one time, students were selected for gifted and talented programs almost exclusively on the basis of their scores on standardized intelligence tests. Critics charged that gifted and talented people had a wide range of abilities and that intelligence test scores did not appropriately identify many of these. Further, fears that standardized intelligence tests were culturally biased and, hence, tended to screen out minority group students, drew additional negative attention to selection based only on test scores.

 WHAT DO *YOU* THINK?

Students Should Be Placed in Ability Tracks

A critic of present secondary school practices recently made the following comments:

"The presence of less academically able students in secondary classrooms results in a waste of academic talent. Teachers have to gear instruction to the lowest common denomi-

© 2000 Randy Glasbergen.
www.glasbergen.com

"ARE YOU TRYING TO AUCTION
YOUR BRUSSELS SPROUTS AGAIN?"

nator, which slows down the progress of brighter students and leads to boredom. If we want significant reform in education we need to remove this handicap and encourage our gifted and talented students. One way we can do this is to follow practices established in some other countries.

"Students could be tested as they enter high school and assigned either to a general track or a college track. Less able students would take general-track courses and not be asked to compete with brighter students in the college track. Students in the college track could be provided more challenging work. This system would simplify teachers' jobs. They would not have to plan for such a wide range of academic talent as they now must do in classrooms open to all."

Questions

1. Would everyone benefit from this plan? Why or why not?
2. Describe possible negative effects of this idea.
3. What track would you have been in if you had been assigned to either a general track or a college track at the time you completed the sixth grade? Point out any major flaws in this proposal.

Through the years, there has been a broadening of the conception of characteristics of gifted and talented people. The work of Renzulli (1978), a leading expert in the education of these students, was especially important in gaining acceptance for the idea that selection should be based on multiple criteria. Renzulli argued that evidence should be gathered in three distinct categories of student characteristics when decisions were being made regarding who should be admitted to gifted and talented programs. These characteristics are as follows:

- Intelligence,
- Task commitment, and
- Creativity.

Information related to intelligence should be gathered not just from standardized test performance. Other sources, such as grades and comments from individuals who have had opportunities to observe academic work of students, should be consulted.

The idea of task commitment refers to a person's ability to see through a project or activity to the end. People who are gifted and talented tend to finish things, even when there are frustrations along the way. They are not apt to bounce from one project to another, leaving a lot of loose ends along the way.

Creativity refers to the ability to engage challenges and solve problems in unusual ways. Gifted and talented students tend to look at dilemmas in nontraditional ways and to use innovative (and sometimes surprising) techniques to respond to them.

What are gifted and talented students really like? Certainly there are popular misconceptions. Consider, for example, how some films portray bright students as eccentric misfits. Contrary to this view, most studies have found that gifted and talented students are well accepted by their peers. It is true that these students face some special kinds of pressure from other students. In particular, they may be pressured to do less and thereby keep the teacher from setting expectations too high for the class as a whole (Brown & Sternberg, 1990).

Some gifted and talented students have parents who expect too much of them. This leads some of these students to set unrealistic expectations for themselves and to feel bad when they fail to live up to them. You can help these students by focusing them on their accomplishments, not their shortcomings (Baum, 1990). These students need to be taught that everybody has strengths and weaknesses and that there is nothing to be ashamed of when they are less than outstanding in a given area.

Enrichment and Acceleration

Enrichment and *acceleration* are the two basic orientations of programs for gifted and talented students. Enrichment programs assume students will remain in the same classes and go through school at the same rate as other non-gifted and talented students. However, there is an expectation that enriched programs will be provided for them that go well beyond the academic fare served up to the other students.

Acceleration programs increase the pace at which gifted learners complete their schooling. In an accelerated program, a gifted learner might complete the entire high school program in just two years. There is no attempt to keep gifted learners in classes with learners who are in the same age group. This often means that gifted learners are in classes where most of the others are older than they are.

Though there are loyal supporters of both, today enrichment programs are much more common than acceleration programs. This is true because enrichment programs can be implemented with fewer administrative changes. Also, the possibility that some gifted and talented students in accelerated programs will be in classes with students who are much older than they are is a source of concern to some parents and educators and, hence, is a force working against the popularity of the acceleration approach.

When you work with gifted and talented students, you have to take care to ensure that what these students are asked to do is truly different from what is required of other students. It is particularly important that you do not simply ask them to do more of the same. (For example, if you ask most of your students to do ten homework problems, it is a mistake to ask your gifted and talented students to do 15 problems from the same set.) If you do this, you will communicate to gifted and talented students that their condition is a burden for which you are punishing them by asking them to do more school work than their classmates. Students are likely to see this as unfair. One result can be a diminished interest in school and a disinclination to stretch academically.

It is important to encourage development of gifted and talented students' creativity. To accomplish this, you can do the following:

- Let your students know that you encourage risk taking.
- Suggest ways your students might put to use information they might gain as a result of taking risks.

You need to avoid placing unnecessary limits on gifted students' creativity by laying out hard and fast rules regarding how learning will be assessed. You should communicate to these young people that innovative, creative responses will be all right. You want to challenge them to develop unusual approaches that will stretch their imaginative and creative powers.

Establishing the Personal Importance of Learning

It is important to provide gifted and talented students with opportunities to pursue some issues they select themselves. They should be encouraged to redefine tasks you provide in ways that will make them more personally important. Gifted and talented students often are not motivated to stretch themselves in pursuit of arid academic goals that seem little connected to their own needs or interests. They may see such pursuits as "a stupid game" and simply refuse to play.

FOR YOUR PORTFOLIO

1. What materials, ideas you learned in this chapter related to *accommodating diverse learners* will you include as "evidence" in your portfolio? Select up to 3 items of information to be included in your portfolio. Number them 1, 2, and 3.

2. Think about why you selected these materials for your portfolio? Consider such issues as the following in your response:

- The specific purposes to which this information can be put to use when you plan, deliver, and assess the impact of your instruction,
- The compatibility of the information with your own priorities and values,
- The contributions this information can make to your personal development as a teacher, and
- The factors that led you to include this material as opposed to some alternatives you considered.

3. Prepare a written reflection in which you analyze the decision-making process you followed. Also, mention the INTASC Standard(s) to which your selected material relates. (First complete the chart below.)

Materials You Selected and the INTASC Standards

Put a check under those INTASC Standards numbers to which the evidence you have selected applies. (Refer to Chapter 1 for more detailed information about INTASC)

Item of Evidence Number	INTASC Standards									
	S1	S2	S3	S4	S5	S6	S7	S8	S9	S10
1										
2										
3										

However, when these bright young people are encouraged to play an active part in identifying (or at least redefining) the learning task, they often will commit their intellectual and emotional resources to it with great enthusiasm. This kind of commitment is essential. Without it, they may fail to fully develop their outstanding creative, imaginative, and intellectual powers.

Key Ideas in Summary

- Ethnic and cultural diversity among the population of secondary students are becoming more pronounced. In seeking to respond to particular needs of minority-group students, teachers need to guard against assuming that all students from a given ethnic, racial, or cultural group share common characteristics. There are important within-group differences, and the proper approach is to focus on the characteristics of the individual student, rather than the presumed characteristic of the group to which he or she belongs.
- A number of risk factors have been identified that commonly characterize students who drop out of school. These include (1) living in a single-parent home, (2) being a

member of a family receiving public-assistance funds, (3) speaking a primary language other than English, (4) having a brother or sister who dropped out of school, (5) having a mother who is not a high-school graduate, (6) having attended five or more schools during his or her lifetime, (7) spending less than one hour per week on homework, (8) spending no time each week reading for fun, (9) watching television more than five hours a night, (10) rarely communicating with parents about things studied at school, and (11) being overage for his or her grade by one year or more.

■ In times past, poor performance levels of minority students were attributed to such "causes" as *genetic deficit*. According to this now-discredited view, minority group children lacked the necessary intellectual resources to succeed academically; hence, it made little sense to worry too much about their failure to do well in school. Another outdated view suggested that minority students suffered from a *cultural deficit* (from intellectually sterile home environments) that failed to prepare them to do school work. Still another view was that minority students suffered a *communication process* problem. It was suggested that they had language characteristics that made it virtually impossible for them to grasp what teachers expected them to do. The genetic deficit, cultural deficit, and communication process views are now largely regarded as blame-the-victim excuses that allowed schools to avoid their responsibilities to provide quality educational services to minority group students.

■ A number of guidelines have been developed to help teachers promote better learning and better attitudes toward schooling among minority group students. These include: (1) assuming all students can learn, (2) providing minority students with good teachers, (3) insisting that teachers become aware of their own cultural perspectives, (4) encouraging teachers to avoid favoritism in the classroom, (5) including students from varied ethnic backgrounds in each group when students are divided into groups for instructional purposes, (6) varying teaching methods to accommodate different learning styles, (7) developing close working relationships with students' families, (8) emphasizing development of higher-level thinking skills, and (9) using conversations to uncover ways to contextualize instruction.

■ Provisions for meeting the needs of students with disabilities have changed in recent years. One approach has been that of defining a continuum of services and placing exceptional students in the least restrictive setting. Increasingly, there has been a commitment to the principle of *inclusion*. Inclusion presumes that (1) to the extent possible, these students should be taught in regular classrooms, and (2) their membership in these classrooms should be expected and welcomed.

■ Recent changes in the delivery of services require that secondary teachers collaborate with teachers who are specialists in the education of students with disabilities. Among other things, this cooperation can help students with disabilities make the transition to experiences they will face after completing high school.

■ There are several legislative mandates that must be followed in delivering instruction to students with disabilities. These mandates provide very specific guidelines that school authorities must follow in preparing, delivering, and assessing instructional programs for these students.

■ Teachers today encounter many students with disabilities in their regular classrooms. This means that all classroom teachers need to have some familiarity with various categories of student disability and be able to develop, in cooperation with others, programs of instruction that will be appropriate to the special needs of these learners.

■ Gifted students tend to be selected on multiple criteria. Often, these include measures of intellectual abilities, creativity, and task commitment (persistence). Despite some popular misconceptions, most gifted and talented students are well adjusted and get along well with other students. These students tend to be served either by enrichment programs or acceleration programs. Currently, enrichment programs are more common than acceleration programs.

Reflections

1. What does the term *exceptional student* mean? What are some categories of exceptional students found in secondary schools?

2. What are some risk factors associated with dropping out of school? Are these more or less common among minority-group students than among the school population as a whole?

3. What are some historic views of minority-group students, and how might they have influenced school practices in the past?

4. Why is it important for teachers to appreciate the cultural context minority-group students bring with them to school?

5. Why is it desirable for teachers to approach their instructional tasks with the assumption that all students can learn?

6. Open communication between regular classroom teachers and teachers with special training in the instruction of students with disabilities is critical to the development of lessons that will respond well to these students' needs. What are some kinds of information that regular teachers and these specialists need to share?

7. What is meant by *full inclusion*, and how is this concept changing what regular classroom teachers do?

8. What categories of mentally retarded students are you likely to encounter in your classes, and what are some things you can do to help these young people learn?

9. In what ways can you help students with (a) learning disabilities, (b) Attention Deficit Disorders, (c) physical and health impairments, and (d) emotional disturbance problems?

10. Why has selection of gifted and talented students sometimes posed problems? What are some criteria commonly used today to identify these young people?

Learning Extensions

1. Interview a central office administrator from a school district that enrolls a culturally and ethnically diverse group of students. Ask this person to comment on high school

graduation rate differences among the major cultural and ethnic groups enrolled. Also, solicit comments about any special programs the district has to encourage minority group students to stay in school. Share your findings in an oral report to your class.

2. Read some reports in professional journals (perhaps supplemented by other sources suggested by your instructor) that describe programs that have increased high school graduation rates of minority group students. From these articles, develop a list of features that seem associated with the success of these programs. Distribute these lists to others in your class, and use them as a basis for a discussion focusing on the topic: "Keeping Minority Students in Our Secondary Schools: What Works."

3. Many teachers who work successfully with students from diverse cultural and ethnic groups have taken time to familiarize themselves with how members of these groups see the world. Compile a list of journal articles, books, and other sources of information that might be helpful to non-Latino white teachers interested in learning more about the cultural perspectives of members of selected minority groups. Share your list with others in the class.

4. Invite a panel of five or six secondary school teachers to your class. Have them discuss experiences they have had in working with students with disabilities who are enrolled in their regular classes. In particular, urge them to share ideas about how instruction has been modified to meet these students' special needs.

5. Organize a class debate on this topic: "Resolved that programs for the gifted and talented divert scarce educational resources away from other, more deserving students."

6. Go the Merrill Education's Link to General Methods Resources site at this URL: http://www.prenhall.com/methods-cluster/ At the bottom of the page select "diversity in the classroom" as your topic and click the "begin" button. This will take you to the "Overview" page. On the left side, click on "Web Links." On the Web Links page click on "cultural/racial." Use these links to find information about classroom materials you can use that relate to cultural and ethnic diversity. Prepare a brief oral report for members of your class in which you describe some items you found and suggest how they might be used to support an instructional program.

References

Baum, S. (1990). The gifted/learning disabled: A paradox for teachers. *Education Digest, 55*(8), 54–56.

Bowman, B. (1991). Educating language minority children: Challenges and opportunities. In S. L. Kagan (Ed.), *The care and education of America's young children: Obstacles and opportunities* (pp. 17–29). Nineteenth Yearbook of the National Society for the Study of Education. Part I. Chicago: National Society for the Study of Education.

Brown, B. B., & Sternberg, L. (1990). Academic achievement and social acceptance. *Education Digest, 55*(7), 57–60.

Condition of Education. (1998). Education of students with disabilities. [http://www.nces.ed.gov/pubs98/condition98/c9845a01.html]

Condition of Education. (1999). Racial and ethnic distribution of elementary and secondary students. [http://www.nces.ed.gov/pubs99/condition99/indicator-46.html]

Erickson, F. (1987). Transformation and school success: The politics and culture of educational achievement. *Anthropology and Education Quarterly, 18*(4), pp. 335–356.

Gleason, P., & Dynarksi, M. (1998). *Do we know whom to serve? Issues in using risk factors to identify dropouts*. Princeton, NJ: Mathematica Policy Research, Inc.

Grant, C. A., & Sleeter, C. E. (1994). *Making choices for multicultural education: Five approaches to race, class, and gender.* New York: HarperCollins.

Heward, W. (1996). *Exceptional children: An introduction to special education.* (5th ed.). Upper Saddle River, NJ: Merrill/Prentice Hall.

Lee, C., & Slaughter-Defoe, D. (1995). Historical and sociocultural influences on African American education. In J. Banks & C. Banks (Eds.), *Handbook of research on multicultural education* (pp. 348–371). New York: Macmillan.

Lerner, J. W., & Lerner, S. R. (1991). Attention deficit disorder: Issues and questions. *Focus on Exceptional Children, 24*(3), 1–17.

Lomawaima, K. (1995). Educating native Americans. In J. Banks & C. Banks (Eds.), *Handbook of research on multicultural education* (pp. 331–347). New York: Macmillan.

National Center for Education Statistics. (1997). Children with disabilities. *Fast Facts*. [http://www.nces.ed.gov/fastfacts/display.asp?id=33]

Ogbu, J. H. (1973). *Minority education and caste.* New York: Academic Press.

Pang, V. (1995). Asian-Pacific-American students: A diverse and complex population. In J. Banks & C. Banks (Eds.), *Handbook of research on multicultural education* (pp. 412–424). New York: Macmillan.

Patton, J., Blackbourn, J., & Fad, K. (1996). *Exceptional individuals in focus* (6th ed.). Upper Saddle River, NJ: Merrill/Prentice Hall.

Renzulli, J. (1978). What makes giftedness: Re-examining a definition. *Phi Delta Kappan, 60*(3), 180–184, 261.

Rist, R. C. (1985). On understanding the process of school: The contributions of labeling theory. In J. A. Ballentine (Ed.), *Schools and society: A reader in education and sociology* (pp. 88–106). Palo Alto, CA: Mayfield.

Savage, T. V., & Armstrong, D. G. (2000). *Effective teaching in elementary social studies* (4th ed.). Upper Saddle River, NJ: Merrill/Prentice Hall.

Smith, T., Polloway, E., Patton, J., & Dowdy, C. (1996). *Teaching students with special needs in inclusive settings.* Boston: Allyn & Bacon.

Tharp, T. (1999). Vision of a transformed classroom. *Talking Leaves.* 3(3) 1–2. Santa Cruz, CA: Center for Research on Education, Diversity & Excellence, The University of California.

U.S. Census Bureau. (1999). *Population estimates.* [http://www.census.gov:80/population/estimates/nation/intfile3-1.txt]

7

Planning Units and Lessons

This chapter will aim to

- identify the three basic stages in instructional planning;
- describe the importance of unit and lesson planning;
- point out some variables that will influence what you do in planning instruction;
- explain differences between single-subject and interdisciplinary units;
- describe how you might go about initial planning for an interdisciplinary unit;
- explain some components of unit and lesson plans;
- describe components of several models for planning lessons;
- point out some basic issues that need to be addressed in preparing a lesson plan; and
- help you develop a usable format for preparing unit and lesson plans.

Introduction

When you look over tables of contents in secondary school textbooks or contents of school curriculum guides, you may conclude that most instructional planning has already been done. These resources *can* help you. However, because of the unique characteristics of your own teaching situation, you will find it necessary to assume responsibility for planning effective instructional programs for your own students.

Researchers have found that effective teachers spend considerable time planning for what they do in the classroom. One study found that outstanding teachers devote 10 to 20 hours a week outside of the classroom to instructional planning (Clark & Yinger, 1979). What you decide to do as a result of your instructional planning may vary from actions taken by other teachers in your building. For example, you may decide to write out highly detailed descriptions of what you intend to do each day. Others with whom you work may be comfortable with a few brief notes in a plan book, or even on a single sheet of paper.

In general, as a newcomer to the profession and as a teacher who may well have two or more separate subject preparations each day, your best initial course is to commit to providing considerable detail in your written plans for instruction. Careful planning of this kind can give you a good focus for your overall instruction and provide important cues that will help you move smoothly from point to point as you teach your students.

Planning Stages

Instructional planning can be divided into three basic stages. We label these stages:

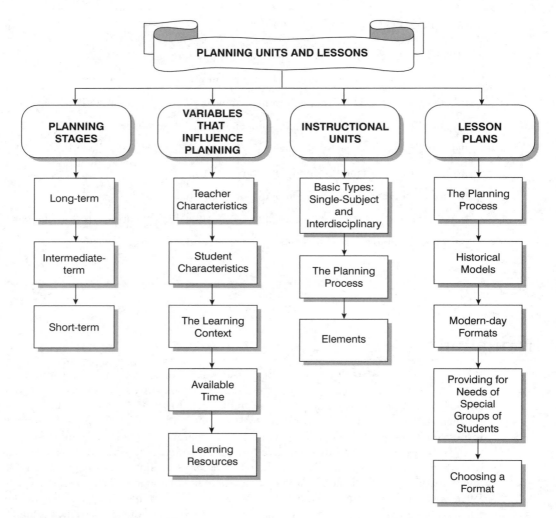

Figure 7–1
Graphic Organizer

- Long-term,
- Intermediate-term, and
- Short-term

Long-Term Planning

Long-term planning focuses on an extended period of time: a grading term of several weeks' duration, a quarter, a semester, or even an entire school year. It focuses on identifying and sequencing major topics or themes that you will teach during the period being planned. You may find that outsiders have made some of your long-term planning decisions. For example, local or state curriculum guidelines often specify what topics you must cover in a certain course during one semester.

Sometimes external influences will pressure you to emphasize certain kinds of contents at certain times. For example, some standardized-testing programs feature large numbers of questions about certain topics and relatively few about others. If you are in a district where improving standardized test scores is a high priority, your planning decisions may be influenced by a desire to provide learning experiences that will help students perform better on these assessments. Science fairs, history fairs, and other events that are scheduled at certain times of the year may also encourage you to focus students' attention on particular topics at specific times during the school year.

When long-term planning decisions are converted to written form, the resultant documents often do not contain much detail about how you will introduce content to students. Rather, the emphasis ordinarily is on broader issues. For example, long-term planning documents you prepare may include more general information and include such components as statements of philosophy, descriptions of overall goals and aims of individual courses, and listings of major topics you will be covering.

Intermediate-Term Planning

Intermediate-term planning begins to introduce more specificity into the planning process. Ordinarily, your focus here is on shorter periods of time that are embedded within the longer time periods that are the focus of long-term planning. For example, your planning might focus on four 4-week periods within a 16-week semester. The written expression of intermediate-term planning decisions often is a document called an *instructional unit*. Instructional units are designed for varying time periods; many organize instruction for a one- to five-week time period.

Sometimes school districts, state authorities, publishers, and others will provide you with unit plans. However, because conditions vary so much from place to place, you will need to modify these units to fit your own specific instructional environment. You must rework these externally developed units to take into account what your students already know, their interests and aptitudes, and the availability of learning resources you have available to support instruction. Because of the many special characteristics of individual students, classes, and schools, units you prepare yourself for use in your own classroom generally are better able to respond well to local conditions than those developed by outsiders.

Short-Term Planning

Short-term planning focuses on quite short periods of instructional time. The most common written expression of short-term planning is the *lesson plan*. Some lessons begin and end during a single instructional period. Others may cover a slightly longer period of time. Lesson plans function as a basic script for instruction. They contain information that helps you keep instruction on track and moving smoothly from point to point.

Lesson plans include more specific information than instructional unit plans. In addition to instructional learning intentions, they often provide details regarding instructional techniques used, how transitions are to be handled, specific learning materials used, and ideas for monitoring and assessing students. Lesson plans are context specific. Hence, they are best prepared by you personally.

Variables That Influence Planning

Several variables interact to influence planning decisions made by individual teachers, including the following:

Teacher characteristics,

Student characteristics,

The learning context,

Available time, and

Learning resources.

Teacher Characteristics

You and your teaching colleagues vary greatly in terms of your educational philosophies, beliefs about students and how they learn, academic background in the subjects taught, general interests, and mastery of individual teaching techniques. These variables interact to affect instructional decisions. Researchers have verified this observation. For example, there is evidence that teachers who have a poor personal academic grounding in the content they are expected to teach ask more low-level (recall and memory) questions and encourage fewer questions from students than teachers with better academic preparation in their subjects (Kauchak & Eggen, 1989).

To better identify personal characteristics that may unconsciously be shaping instructional decisions, it is useful to ask yourself self-diagnostic questions such as these:

How important do I think this content is?

How well am I prepared to teach this information?

What, in general, do I believe to be the most important outcomes of schooling?

What teaching approaches do I like, and which ones don't I like?

Student Characteristics

Students have vastly different interests, abilities, and academic backgrounds. Successful planning requires you to know your students well. Lessons that are based on unwarranted assumptions about students' mastery of prerequisite information (and about other critical student characteristics) will fail.

In thinking about the student-characteristics variable, you should consider asking yourself questions such as these:

What previous knowledge and background in this topic do these students have?

What are these students interested in?

Do some of these students have special needs? If so, how can they best be accommodated?

Are there ways to take instructional advantage of some special characteristics of students in this class?

The Learning Context

There are enormous differences among the nation's secondary schools. The character of individual schools is shaped by the general nature of the communities they serve, the characteristics of their students, the actions of school administrators, and state and local school policies. Taken together, these variables help give each school its own learning context.

Because of differences in the learning context, expectations of teachers sometimes vary considerably from school to school. For example, some administrators may be extremely sensitive to public reaction to students' standardized test scores and may pressure teachers to pay particular attention to content likely to be sampled on these tests. In other buildings, teachers may have to carefully document what they do, and administrators may require every teacher to submit detailed lesson plans for every class session that is taught.

The learning context in the school where you teach almost always will be more supportive of some kinds of teacher behavior than others. For this reason, in deciding whether to accept a position that has been offered to you, you should ask yourself questions such as these:

What does the community expect of teachers and the schools?

What will I need to do in this school to please administrators?

How are teachers evaluated in this school?

Is my teaching style compatible with what people expect here?

Available Time

Time affects planning in several ways. The most important time consideration in planning for instruction is the amount of time you have—days and class periods—actually available for instruction. You must make difficult decisions about how this precious time should be allocated among the many topics that may merit attention.

The planning process, itself, takes time. Do not be surprised if you feel some stress as you try to strike a balance between a need to plan new instructional experiences, correct student work, attend to committee obligations, and still maintain some semblance of a family and social life. Over time, your planning proficiency will grow, and you will find yourself better able to juggle unit and lesson planning and other aspects of your personal and professional life.

Learning Resources

You may find yourself in a teaching situation where the resources available to support your instruction will place limits on what you can plan and deliver to students. You need to take a realistic inventory of available learning resources before getting very far into the instructional planning process.

Learning resource problems sometimes pose serious difficulties when state regulations or even local administrative policies change suddenly. For example, a guideline requiring all science teachers to spend at least 40 percent of their time in class doing laboratory work will produce nothing but frustration if appropriate laboratory facilities and other materials are not in place to support this kind of teaching.

 CRITICAL INCIDENT

Challenges of the Web

Sam Buelton walked into Jody Chu's classroom shaking his head. As usual, Jody—the chair of the social studies department—was at her desk using time at the end of the day to deal with some administrative paperwork.

"Hello, Sam. How are things?" Jody asked, glad to be diverted from the memo she was reading with yet another warning from the principal's office about the excessive amount of copying paper the department was using.

"It's been one of those 'good news, bad news' days," Sam replied as he took a seat at a vacant student desk at the front of the room.

"How so?" asked Jody.

"You'll remember how I mentioned at the last department meeting that this semester I was going to insist that student term papers include citations to some sources on the Web."

"Yes, I remember we all thought that would be a good idea."

"Well," Sam continued, "the papers came in a couple of days ago, and I just began correcting them today during my planning period. You'll remember that I wanted them to choose some topic related to the American Revolution. To get them started, I gave them a list of some Web addresses. Apparently where I went astray was in telling them to look for links to other sites when they visited these sites."

"What happened?" inquired Jody. "It seems to me that instruction makes good sense. I mean, one of the advantages of the Internet is that it gives students a chance to access information in quantities that you and I never could have reached when we were in school."

"Well, you're certainly right about that," Sam acknowledged, "but, there was a downside to this I hadn't thought about. My list of Web sites included some impeccable sources of information such as the Library of Congress. What I hadn't counted on was students following links that led to other sites that led to more links that led to more sites, and on and on and on. What happened is that some of them found sites with information that, in some cases, goes beyond unreliable to simply outrageous."

"Such as?" asked Jody.

"Well, one of the papers I got has lots of beautifully footnoted references to 'information' put up on the Web by an outfit called Real Truth in History. From what I've been able to determine, this is a fringe group consisting of UFO aficionados and people who reject most mainstream historical scholarship. Among other things, there are assertions that extra-terrestrials who, for unexplained reasons, became progressively more angry with Great Britain in the late 18th century, were responsible for fomenting discontent among residents of the American colonies. According to this student's term paper, Sam Adams, Patrick Henry, George Washington, and the rest of the bunch were all getting advice from non-earthlings."

"Sam, that is just a hoot," said Jody, shaking her head and laughing. "That kid is breaking new scholarly ground!"

"I know at one level, it is just hilarious," acknowledged Sam. "But, Jody, this kid really believes this stuff. He told me that the authorities wouldn't allow inaccurate information to be put up on the World Wide Web."

"Now Sam, that's just another hoot, isn't it?" said Jody. "But, you *do* have a problem. It's what those of us who've been in the business refer to as the 'mysterious they' belief."

"Mysterious they?"

"Yes," Jody went on. "Lots of our students innocently believe in the existence of some 'mysterious they' who police publications and broadcasts to keep untruths from being disseminated. All of us in the profession continue to be amazed at how widespread this belief is. Listen carefully to discussions in your class and you're sure to hear comments such as: 'They won't allow it.' 'They always get the upper hand.' 'They keep people like us down.'"

"You're right," said Sam. "I've heard lots of comments like that."

"Well, to get back to the Web source problem, it seems to me you've got to deal with a couple of issues." Jody began gathering up her papers signaling to Sam that the conversation was about over. "You've got to deal with the 'mysterious they' issue and then you've got to provide some specific instruction on characteristics of reliable information sources."

"Makes sense," said Sam. "But, I'm not quite sure where to begin."

■ ■ ■

Do you think the situation Sam is encountering is a common one that secondary school teachers face? What are some alternative steps Sam might take? If you were Sam, how would you deal with the individual student who wrote the term paper he discussed with Jody? As you think about your response, remember that the student had done an excellent job of following citation-formatting guidelines and followed Sam's directions about using the World Wide Web to find information. What does this situation suggest to you about the level of detail that you need to provide in your instructions to students?

Instructional Units

Organizing instruction into well-planned units has several advantages. When you group lessons together and systematically sequence them in an instructional unit, each lesson can build on content you have introduced previously. Interrelated lessons can help you to develop an instructional scheme that promotes students' abilities to see relationships and to draw conclusions from analyses based on large quantities of information.

The process of unit planning will alert you to the need to gather certain kinds of learning resources. For example, as you plan a unit, you may determine that you need certain videotapes and maps. You may have to order these items from a centralized media facility several weeks in advance. Because usually you will plan a unit some time before you teach it, typically you will have enough time to obtain the learning materials needed to support your instruction.

When you plan units, you must be sensitive to the special characteristics of the learners you will teach. Information about students will help you identify an appropriate place for beginning instruction. This information can come from your personal knowledge of students' past performance and from other sources such as diagnostic test results.

Unit plans give you a sense of direction and security as you deliver instruction. They eliminate uncertainty about "what I should do tomorrow." They help establish a sense of order and routine that conveys to students that you know what you are doing.

Basic Unit Types: Single-Subject and Interdisciplinary

Many units treat topics that relate to a single academic subject, for example, American history, geometry, biology, or English. Others are interdisciplinary units. You may recall from Chapter 5 that integrated-subjects instruction featuring interdisciplinary teaching seeks to break down barriers separating individual subjects. The idea behind interdisciplinary units is to provide information in ways that help students grasp "the connectedness of knowledge and life" (Palmer, 1995, p. 55). Proponents of this approach believe that interdisciplinary teaching can help your students perceive reality as a whole, not as something that has been artificially divided into packages that bear names of the individual academic subjects (Pate, McGinnis, & Homestead, 1995).

The Planning Process

Some educational methods textbooks and teacher education programs recommend a *linear* approach to instructional planning. Linear planning begins by (1) identifying the unit generalizations and learning intentions, (2) identifying appropriate content for achieving the learning intentions, (3) designing and sequencing learning activities related to the learning intentions, (4) identifying and gathering needed learning resources, and (5) identifying evaluation procedures.

Though this approach seems to make certain logical sense, researchers have found that few teachers follow this sequence. When you teach, more typically you will find yourself moving back and forth among unit planning elements and continually making adjustments until all pieces seem to fit together (Yinger, 1979). Often you will begin your planning process by identifying examples of content that you need to teach. Once you have these in mind, you can move on to identify some guiding generalizations or some key questions. You are likely to make some modifications to your selected generalizations, content samples, and key questions as your unit planning process goes forward.

Figure 7–2 illustrates a basic planning framework for an interdisciplinary unit. Note that this unit is guided by a theme that is stated in the form of a question ("How 'Revolutionary' was the American Revolution?"). Themes, which may or may not be stated as questions, frequently provide a focus for interdisciplinary units. This unit proposes to draw content from eight separate subject areas. For each of these, the unit planner will identify a generalization, some content samples, and a key question.

Figure 7–3 suggests what the results of initial unit planning for this interdisciplinary unit might look like. Note the list of suggested resources at the end of this material.

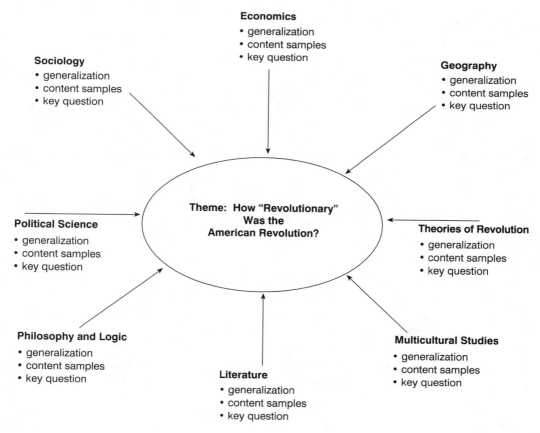

Figure 7–2
Planning Framework for an Interdisciplinary Unit

Economics

Generalization: Wars put financial strains on economies and require actions to divert more resources to military uses and to raise additional revenues, often through new taxes.

Content Samples

- Mercantilism
- Financial consequences for England associated with the defeat of France in French and Indian War and how these influenced policies toward the colonies
- Financial problems of the colonies in the war . . . the case of the hyperinflated "Continental"

Key Question: How did economic circumstances in both England and America contribute to the war, and how extensive were economic changes during and after the war?

Sociology

Generalization: The groups and classes to which people who lived in the former colonies belonged affected the levels of their interest in and support for the cause of the Patriots during the Revolutionary War.

Content Samples

- The relative strength of personal identity as "English" or "Colonials"
- The relative strength of personal identity as "Virginians" or "New Yorkers" compared with their identity as "Americans"
- The degree to which political and social events surrounding the war affected the personal and economic lives of individuals and groups

Key Question: How were individuals in different social classes affected by conditions that led to the war, to what extent did these prompt them to become active participants? How changed were these people's lives as a result of the war?

Geography

Generalization: Issues associated with such variables as the relative location of a place, its human characteristics, and its special physical features affect its interactions with other places.

Content Samples

- Regional attitudes toward the war
- Demographic differences among the former colonies
- Cultural and economic priorities in various regions of the former colonies

Key Question: How did special characteristics of individual regions affect attitudes toward the war, and did the war itself act to bind these regions more closely together?

Political Science

Generalization: Decisions relating to the exercise of political power are often reflected in documents issued by formal bodies that presume they have the authority to make such decisions.

Figure 7–3
Examples of Generalizations, Concept Samples, and Key Questions for an Interdisciplinary Unit on "How 'Revolutionary' was the American Revolution?"

Content Samples

- Declaration and Resolves of the First Continental Congress (1774)
- Declaration of Causes and Necessity of Taking Up Arms (1775)
- Virginia Declaration of Rights (1776)
- Declaration of Independence (1776)
- Political arrangements in the former colonies during the war
- Legacies of British governance systems and the impact of the war on oligarchic power

Key Question: What arguments were made in official documents asserting American authority over British authority, and what political arrangements were sought during and after the war that either were (1) consistent with traditional British practices or (2) changed from traditional British practices?

Theories of Revolution

Generalization: Revolutions are puzzling phenomena; various theories have been developed that have tried to identify the defining characteristics of a revolution.

Content Samples

- Crane Brinton's theory
- Martin Lipset's theory
- Theda Skocpol's theory
- Louis Gottschalk's theory

Key Question: What criteria should be applied to determine whether a given set of events is truly revolutionary, and do these criteria suggest that the American Revolution was a "real" revolution?

Philosophy and Logic

Generalization: Different rules for identifying assumptions, framing arguments, and otherwise building a case in support of a particular position are associated with specific philosophical and logical orientations.

Content Samples

- The Age of Reason as a context for thinking at the time of the American Revolution
- The Declaration of Independence as an example of Age-of-Reason logic
- Categorical syllogism as a framework for arguments in the Declaration of Independence
- The power of the categorical syllogism form to make arguments in the Declaration of Independence appear strong to educated eighteenth-century Europeans

Key Question: Is it true that the organizing and sequencing of an argument can add strength to the specific evidence that is presented, and did the special kind of logic used in the Declaration of Independence make a compelling case in support of revolution?

Figure 7–3, *continued*

Multicultural Studies

Generalization: Members of minority ethnic and cultural groups chose their sides based on such things as their status as free persons or slaves, their perceptions of the relative long-term benefits of becoming aligned with one side or the other, and their emotional ties to such enemies of Britain as Spain.

Content Samples

- In 1777, Lord Dunsmore promised freedom to any slave who would fight for the British.
- African Americans fought on both sides during the Revolutionary War.
- The status of African American troops depended heavily on whether they had been slaves or free people at the time of their enlistment.
- Latinos were heavily involved in actions in areas along the Gulf of Mexico and the lower Mississippi River, particularly under the leadership of Marshall Bernardo de Galvez, Governor of Spanish Louisiana.

Key Question: To what extent did experiences of cultural and ethnic minorities during the Revolutionary War lay the groundwork for actions taken in later years to achieve more widespread involvement in our nation's economic, social, and political affairs?

Literature

Generalization: Themes reflected in particular literary works often reflect social, economic, and political events of the times in which they are written.

Content Samples

- John Dickenson's *Letters from a Farmer*
- Philip Freneau's "The Northern Soldier" and "To the Memory of Brave Americans"
- Patrick Henry's "Speech before the Virginia Convention of 1775"
- Thomas Paine's *Common Sense*

Key Question: How did selected literature of the Revolutionary War period reflect conditions of the time, and to what extent did these works contribute to change?

. . .

Examples of Resource Materials

American Revolution: Resources at the New York public library. Available on the World Wide Web of the Internet: http://www.nypl.org/research/chss/subguides/milhist/rev.html

Bragdon, H. W., McCutcheon, S. P, and, Ritchie, D. A. (1996). *History of a free nation*. New York: Glencoe/McGraw-Hill.

Brinton, C. (1965). *The anatomy of revolution*. New York: Vintage Books.

Brookhiser, R. (1995). *Founding father*. New York: Free Press.

Cole, R. (1995). The role of African Americans in the American Revolution. Available on the World Wide Web of the Internet: http://www.ilt.columbia.edu/k12/history/blacks/blacks.html

Figure 7–3, *continued*

Dickenson, J. (1767, 1926). *Letters from a farmer. Letter III.* In F. L. Pattee (Ed.), *Century readings for a course in American literature.*(pp. 81–84). New York: The Century Company.

Dickenson, J. (1768). The liberty song. In F. L. Pattee (Ed.), *Century readings for a course in American literature.*(p. 73). New York: The Century Company.

Draper, T. (1995). *A struggle for power.* New York: Times Books/ Random House.

Forbes, E. (1943). *Johnny Tremain: A story of the Boston revolt.* Boston: Houghton-Mifflin.

Freneau, P. (1781, 1926). To the memory of the brave Americans. In F. L. Pattee (Ed.), *Century readings for a course in American literature.*(p. 148). New York: The Century Company.

Freneau, P. (1782, 1926). Arnold's departure. In F. L Pattee (Ed.), *Century readings for a course in American literature.*(p. 149). New York: The Century Company.

Freneau, P. (1786, 1926). The northern soldier. In F. L. Pattee (Ed.), *Century readings for a course in American literature.*(p. 145). New York: The Century Company.

From revolution to reconstruction.(1994). [http://grid.let.rug.nl/~welling/usa/]

Gottschalk, L. (1971). Cause of revolution. In C. T. Paynton & R. Blackey (Eds.), *Why revolution? Theories and analyses.* Cambridge, MA: Schenkman.

Henry, P. (1775, 1926). Speech before the Virginia Convention of 1775. In F. L. Pattee (Ed.), *Century readings for a course in American literature.*(pp.88–89). New York: The Century Company.

Hispanics in the American Revolution. (1995, 1996). [http://www.clark.net/pub/jgbustam/galvez/galvez.html]

Lee, S. P., & Passell, P. (1979). *A new economic view of American history.* New York: W. W. Norton.

Lipset, S. M. (1991). *Continental divide: The values and institutions of the United States and Canada.* New York: Routledge.

Medvedev, S. M.(1995). American Revolution: A revolution? [http://grid.let.rug.nl/~welling/usa/revo1.html]

Meltzer, M. (1987). *The American revolutionaries: A history in their own words.* New York: Crowell.

Miller, J. C. (1959). *Origins of the American Revolution.* Stanford, CA: Stanford University Press.

Olson, K. W. (1995). An outline of American history. [http://grid.let.rug.nl/~welling/usa/]

Paine, T. (1776, 1975). *Thomas Paine's* Common Sense: *The call to independence.* Woodbury, NY: Barron's Educational Series.

Ritchie, D. A., & Broussard, A. (1997). *American history: The early years to 1877.* New York: Glencoe/McGraw-Hill.

Snow, R. (1976). *Freeland Starbird.* Boston: Houghton Mifflin.

Ward, H. M. (1991). *The American Revolution: Nationhood achieved, 1763–1788.* New York: St. Martin's Press.

White, L. M. (1975). *The American Revolution in notes, quotes, and anecdotes.* Fairfax, VA: L.B. Prince.

This is a list that will be expanded and modified as the unit planning goes forward. Information displayed in Figure 7–2 is used to guide decisions that result in a complete unit, including components such as those introduced in the next subsection.

Elements

Instructional units can be formatted in many ways. Many of them include these parts:

unit title,

rationale and major goals,

major generalizations and concepts,

instructional learning intentions and a tentative time line for teaching content related to each,

instructional strategies for each learning intention,

plans for the beginning and ending,

evaluation procedures, and

list of needed learning resources.

The Unit Title

Your unit title should communicate the essence of the content you propose to cover. Unit titles ordinarily are short. Sometimes even one word suffices. Examples of unit titles include: "The Halogens" (chemistry), "The Lake Poets" (English), "Factoring" (mathematics), and "The Progressives" (history).

Rationale and Goals

A *unit rationale* is a statement designed to establish your unit's importance. Writing the rationale helps you explain why the unit's content needs to be taught. The rationale can be used to convince others that the material you propose to cover is important.

Goals in unit plans are statements that describe general learning outcomes. Sometimes they describe relationships between unit content and the entire school subject of which they are a part. Goal statements provide other teachers, administrators, parents, students, and others with an appreciation of the basic purposes of instruction associated with the unit. Suppose you were teaching high school English and were preparing a unit titled "The Epic Hero Theme." You might produce a goal statement something like this:

> *This unit seeks to introduce students to the form, extent of use, and the purposes of "epic hero themes" as vehicles for communicating a culture's values.*

Major Generalizations and Concepts

Generalizations in instructional units succinctly summarize the key ideas your students should master as a result of their exposure to unit content. (Chapter 5 provides more information about generalizations.) Recall that concepts are terms. Generalizations take the form of a statement of relationship among concepts. Hence, to understand a generalization, students must also grasp the concepts associated with it. Consider this generalization from sociology:

> *When urbanization occurs rapidly in a country, differences in status among people in various social classes become more pronounced.*

This generalization would be impossible to comprehend by a student who did not know the meaning of such concepts as *urbanization, country, status,* and *social class.* One of your tasks in planning units is to identify concepts associated with guiding generalizations that your students are unlikely to know. Instructional experiences need to be included that will help them grasp meanings of these concepts.

Instructional units containing large numbers of generalizations with complex concepts require more instructional time than those dealing with less complex concepts. This reality requires you to consider the sophistication of the content you expect your students to learn and think about how much instructional time you should allocate to teaching the unit.

Learning Intentions and Suggested Time Lines

Learning intentions describe what competence your students are expected to gain as a result of their exposure to instruction. They tie in closely to the generalizations and related concepts you select to guide overall unit planning. Numbers of learning intentions vary from unit to unit. You need to strike a balance between providing too many learning intentions (which means each covers a very restricted range of content) and too few (which may stretch a single learning intention across an excessively large and complex body of information). In a unit designed to cover about three weeks, there might be between six and ten learning intentions.

You have several approaches available as you think about how to write your learning intentions. Some people write them as broad statements that suggest little beyond the general kinds of information or skills they want students to acquire. A learning intention of this type might look something like this:

> *Students will describe basic causes of the American Revolution.*

Others prefer writing learning intentions that describe their expectations in much more specific language. Often these take the form of *performance objectives.* These are statements that indicate not just what students should be able to demonstrate as a result of their exposure to instruction, but also the kinds of tests they should take and the proficiency levels they should achieve. A learning intention of this type might look something like this:

> *On an essay examination, students will compare and contrast American and British advantages at the time the Revolutionary War began. Each essay must include references to at least two American advantages and two British advantages.*

The time you will allocate for instruction associated with each learning intention will vary with its sophistication. If the learning intention calls on your students to demonstrate only low-level knowledge and comprehension levels of thinking, you will need to

It isn't easy to select good unit titles. Each unit represents a segment of a course. The unit should bring together content elements that share common features. Often unit titles reflect a theme that functions as a useful organizer. If too much content is included in one unit, students may be overwhelmed. On the other hand, if information is divided into too many units, content can become excessively fragmented. This, too, poses difficulties for students.

Suppose you were assigned to prepare units for one semester's work in a middle school, junior high school, or senior high school. (You choose the course.) There are about 16 instructional weeks in a semester. Identify titles of five or six units you would use, and indicate how much time you would devote to each.

1. How did you decide on unit titles?
2. What are other ways you might have divided the semester's work into units?
3. How did you decide on time allocation?
4. What might be some alternative time recommendations?

Unit Titles	Time Allocation

Figure 7–4
Selecting Unit Titles

schedule relatively short periods of instructional time. On the other hand, if one of your learning intentions proposes to have students engage in sophisticated analyses of complex information you will have to commit considerable instructional time preparing students to succeed at this challenging task.

Time required to teach an individual unit also varies for reasons other than complexity of the learning intentions. The nature of students in your class will influence your pacing decisions. In addition, there often are differences depending on the time of the school year the unit is taught. Often units introduced early in a school year, when your students are getting re-acclimated to doing school work, will take up more of your instructional time than those you introduce later in the year.

Instructional Strategies

An instructional strategy consists of systematically organized instructional techniques that are directed toward helping students master a learning intention. You need to identify an instructional strategy for each unit learning intention. Because some learning intentions are intended to develop more sophisticated student thinking than others, some of your instructional strategies will be more complex than others. The "worth" of any instructional strategy is determined in terms of its ability to help students master the learning intention to which it relates.

Typically, instructional strategies are not described in great detail in instructional unit plans. A sentence or two describing the general instructional approach to be taken for each learning intention will suffice. You will describe your instructional strategies in much greater detail in your lesson plans. Lesson plans provide guidance for what you intend to do in the classroom on a given day, and it is appropriate that you include detailed information about instructional strategies you plan to use in these important documents.

Suppose you were teaching a high school physics course. When referring to a learning intention focusing on student comprehension of the coefficient of expansion principle, you might write the following information about an intended learning strategy in a unit plan outline:

Conduct an inquiry lesson on the unequal rate of expansion in response to heat of different metals using the bimetallic knife.

You would develop this strategy into a series of clearly defined steps in a related daily lesson plan.

Plans for the Beginning and Ending

Your unit plans often will feature detailed descriptions of how you intend to introduce the unit to students. The introduction is critically important to the success of the unit. If your initial activity captures your students' interest, it will be easier for you to sustain their enthusiasm as you go on to introduce the new body of content.

Good unit introductions accomplish several purposes. They stimulate initial student interest and give students a general overview of unit content. They also provide them with a clear idea about what you expect them to do.

Conclusions or suggested culminating activities often are written into instructional unit plans. Their purpose is to help students pull together the key ideas that have been introduced. Often these activities will ask your students to engage in application activities that require them to use some of the information they have learned. A good culminating activity can build students' confidence by providing them with opportunities to verify for themselves that they have mastered challenging new material.

Evaluation Procedures

It is necessary to include information about your approaches to evaluating student progress in your instructional unit plan. You need to think about evaluation procedures not just for the culminating assessment at the conclusion but also for interim assessments that you will make from time to time as you teach the material.

It is important that selected evaluation procedures be consistent with the unit's learning intentions. For example, if the language of your learning intention implies that students should be able to engage in analysis-level thinking, you must select an evaluation procedure that has the capacity to assess this kind of thinking.

Many evaluation procedures are available. For more information about the general issue of assessment of students, refer to Chapter 12, "Assessing Student Learning."

List of Needed Learning Resources

Well-designed units are supported by a variety of learning resources. You need to identify these resources as you plan your units. You may wish to reference such items as supplemental readings, software, video and audiotapes, World Wide Web addresses, compact disks, maps, laboratory equipment, and resource people who may be invited to the class. You may also want to list learning materials you have designed yourself that will supplement the text and other basic instructional resources.

Today, budgets, rather than materials' availability, place more limits on the kinds of learning resources you can obtain. Catalogs containing an incredible variety of support

This media specialist points out useful websites to two teacher colleagues who are beginning work on a new instructional unit.

materials regularly arrive at school district offices, at individual buildings, and in faculty mail boxes of classroom teachers. These catalogs taken together with district- and building-level library, media, and instructional resource centers will help you develop a feel for the range of available materials. If you are fortunate enough to be employed in a well-funded school district, you may be allowed to purchase substantial quantities of instructional-support materials for units you develop. If you work in a less affluent setting, it is probable that budgetary limitations will severely restrict your purchases of these materials.

Figure 7-5 introduces an example of a single-subject instructional unit that includes these basic components.

Lesson Plans

Instructional unit plans describe the general flow of instructional activity over a period of several weeks. Shorter-range instructional decisions are expressed in lesson plans. A lesson plan might be looked at as a script you can follow while teaching students during a given period (or, in some cases, over one, two, or three successive periods—some individual lessons take more than one day to teach).

Typically, you are likely to put more detail into your lesson plans earlier in your career than you will after you have taught for several years. Once you gain experience, you will be able to keep details related to your lesson in your head, and you will not require as many written prompts as you will as a beginner who is still getting used to managing students and moving smoothly from one instructional point to another.

There are no precise rules governing how much detail a "good" lesson plan should contain. In general, there should be enough information to enable a substitute teacher to deliver your lesson without too much difficulty.

The Planning Process

As is true for unit planning, the process followed in developing lessons varies from individual to individual. You may decide to begin by focusing on learning activities; some of your colleagues may begin by thinking first about the learning intentions they are trying to achieve; still others on your faculty may start the lesson-planning process by thinking about the kinds of evaluation tools they will be using. Regardless of where you decide to begin the planning process, you have to answer some key questions. Among them are the following:

What is the lesson learning intention? The answer to this question is important. For one thing, it requires you to weigh the importance of what you are contemplating and to determine that the purpose is a worthy one. Thinking about the learning intention sometimes also prompts ideas about possible teaching approaches.

What is a good entry point for instruction? To answer this question, you must have good information about the students to whom you intend to teach the lesson. The entry point of any lesson should tie in clearly to prior lessons and to what students already know.

Title

The American Revolution

Rationale and Unit Goal

The American Revolution was a key event in American history. An understanding of the Revolution helps explain the nature of Americans' basic beliefs and values. The goals of this unit are to help students grasp forces that led the American colonists to band together and to help students appreciate American values, beliefs, and institutions that, in large measure, are traceable to the American Revolution.

Focus Generalizations

Revolutions often occur when people believe that legitimate authority is insensitive to and unresponsive toward their needs.

Related Concepts

- Revolution
- Legitimate authority
- Wants and needs
- Responsive government

Revolutions challenge people to rethink their assumptions about the nature of the proper relationship between citizens and their government.

Related Concepts

- Role of citizenship
- Individual rights
- Role of government
- Governmental rights
- Loyalty
- Rebellion
- Independence

The values and beliefs of a given group of people have their roots in the pivotal events in the history of the people.

Related Concepts

- Values
- Beliefs
- Continuity and change over time
- Pivotal event
- Historical antecedents

Learning Intentions and Suggested Time Allocation

- Each student will identify events leading to the American Revolution. *Suggested time allocation*: 1 day

Figure 7–5
A Sample Unit

- In an essay, each student will compare and contrast American and British advantages and disadvantages at the time of the outbreak of hostilities. At least two advantages and two disadvantages should be cited for each side. *Suggested time allocation*: 2 days
- Each student will identify American approaches to financing the war. *Suggested time allocation*: 1 day
- Each student will identify key military developments of the Revolutionary War and explain their importance. *Suggested time allocation*: 3 days
- Each student will analyze the results of the war with specific reference to its (1) political effects, (2) social effects, and (3) economic effects. *Suggested time allocation*: 4 days
- Students working in groups will identify values and beliefs that became important during the time of the American Revolution that are still highly valued and influential in the United States today. *Suggested time allocation*: 2 days
- Each student will profess an interest in learning more about the American Revolution. *Suggested time allocation*: No specific allocation. The instruction of the entire unit should be directed toward this learning intention.

Suggested Teaching Strategies

Beginning the unit. Bring in newspaper accounts of an ethnic or civil conflict occurring somewhere in the world. Ask students questions such as these:

- What do you think causes people to become so angry that they will fight and kill one another?
- What happens to a country when this kind of conflict occurs?
- Are there circumstances when it is right for people to rise up against the legal government?
- What about our own Revolutionary War? Did the colonists have legitimate reasons for rebelling against England, or were they just trying to serve their narrow, personal interests?
- In what ways do you think the Revolution might have changed ways people thought and acted?

Show parts of the filmstrip series *The American Revolution: Two Views.* Point out to students that questions noted previously and those raised in the filmstrip will be investigated by the class over the next three weeks. Explain that the basic purpose will be to identify some reasons revolutions take place and to think about the nature of the proper relationship between a government and the citizens it serves. *Suggested time allocation*: 1 day

Recommended Teaching Approaches for Each Learning Intention

Learning intention 1: Divide the class into several groups. Ask members of each group to conduct research and to report on how each of the following events contributed to the eventual outbreak of the Revolutionary War:

- Proclamation of 1763
- Sugar Act of 1764
- Stamp Act of 1765
- Declaratory Act of 1766
- Townshend Acts

Show the film *Prelude to Revolution.*

Learning intention 2: Divide the class into four groups. Assign each group to develop one of these lists:

- List of British advantages and disadvantages
- List of American advantages and disadvantages
- List of possible British arguments in support of and against going to war
- List of possible American arguments in support of and against going to war

Each group will share its list with the whole class. Allow students to work with the computer-based lesson titled "Revolutionary War: Choosing Sides." Discuss.

Learning intention 3: Write the following information on the chalkboard: "It costs a great deal of money to conduct a war. How can this money be raised?"

Involve students in a brainstorming activity designed to provide answers to this question. Debrief. Go on to discuss ways money has been raised for recent conflicts (Desert Storm, Vietnam War, Korean War, and so forth). Assign students to read material explaining problems Americans faced in raising money to pay for the Revolutionary War and how money was actually obtained.

Learning intention 4: Lay out a time line for the years 1775 to 1781 in the front of the room.

- Assign groups of two or three students to conduct research on key events of the Revolutionary War.
- Ask them to place the event at its proper place on the time line and to write a description explaining what occurred and why the event was important.
- Ask students to view the videocassette titled, *The American Revolution.*
- Discuss key events of the war.

Learning intention 5: Provide students with information about the Treaty of Paris of 1783. Divide class members into four teams. Ask each team to gather information about one of these questions:

- What were the issues of interest to France, and how did the treaty affect France?
- What were the issues of interest to Spain, and how did the treaty affect Spain?
- What were the issues of interest to Americans, and how did the treaty affect the former colonies?
- What were the issues of interest to the British, and how did the treaty affect Britain?

Figure 7–5, *continued*

218

Conclude with a discussion of benefits and losses conferred by the treaty on the parties involved.

Learning intention 6: As a concluding activity, conduct a brainstorming activity in which students are challenged to identify basic values and beliefs held by the colonists during the Revolutionary War.

- Discuss the list generated by the class.
- Then, ask groups of students to take one of the identified values or beliefs.
- Find examples of how it still influences the behaviors of present-day Americans.

Learning intention 7: Administer an interest survey on the last day the unit is taught to identify which aspects of the unit topic were most interesting to students. The survey should also elicit information about how students feel about learning more about the American Revolution.

Suggested Evaluation Procedures

Procedures for Individual Learning Intentions

Learning intention 1: Use a matching test. Students will be required to match events leading up to the Revolution with a description of the event (knowledge- and comprehension-level evaluation).

Learning intention 2: Each student will be asked to prepare a written speech that might have been delivered by a colonist before the outbreak of the Revolutionary War. The speech may make a case either in support of or opposing going to war with the British. The written speech will be evaluated in terms of the quality of the arguments made, the correct identifications of potential advantages and disadvantages for each side, and its general persuasiveness (analysis- and synthesis-level evaluation).

Learning intention 3: Each student will respond correctly to 8 of 10 true-false items focusing on American attempts to finance the Revolutionary War (knowledge-level evaluation).

Learning intention 4: Each student will respond correctly to at least 80 percent of multiple choice items on a series of short examinations focusing on key events and other important developments associated with the Revolutionary War (knowledge- and comprehension-level evaluation).

Learning intention 5: Each student will prepare an essay focusing on social and economic consequences of the Revolutionary War. Each paper must include specific references to at least two social and two economic results of the war. Evaluation of the essay will take into account the quality of information cited and evidence that thinking goes beyond a recitation of material covered in class (analysis-level evaluation).

Learning intention 6: Each student will participate as a member of a team of four on a group activity that results in a product of some kind that illustrates and explains issues and values raised during the Revolutionary War that continue to be relevant for us today. These products or projects can take many forms, including art work, original plays, panel discussions, radio or television scripts, debates, and symposiums.

Learning intention 7: Administer a simple attitude inventory on which students are asked to respond on a 1 to 3 scale (1 being highest or most positive and 3 being lowest or least positive) that asks them to record their interest in or feelings about various topics covered during the unit. Students need to be informed that their responses on the attitude inventory will have no bearing on their grades. Some teachers may prefer to give the same attitude inventory both at the beginning and the end of the unit. This will allow the teacher to look for shifts in interest in individual topics that may have resulted because of what students experienced as the unit was taught.

Suggested Learning Resources

General Reference Books

Bliss, G. A. (1980). *The American Revolution: How revolutionary was it?* New York: Harper & Row.

Fritz, J. (1981). *Traitor: The case of Benedict Arnold.* New York: Putnam's.

Gephard, R. E. (Ed.). (1984). *Revolutionary America.* Washington, DC: U.S. Government Printing Office.

Meltzer, M. (1986). *George Washington and the birth of our nation.* New York: Watts.

Meltzer, M. (1987). *The American revolutionaries: A history in their own words.* New York: Harper & Row Junior Books.

Meltzer, M. (1988). *Benjamin Franklin: The new American.* New York: Watts.

Meltzer, M. (1991). *Thomas Jefferson: The revolutionary aristocrat.* New York: Watts.

Miller, J. (1959). *Origins of the American Revolution.* Stanford, CA: Stanford University Press.

Student Texts

Boorstin, D. J., & Kelley, B. M. (1986). *History of the United States.* Lexington, MA: Ginn.

Bragdon, H. W., McCutcheon, S. P., & Ritchie, D. A. (1996). *History of a free people.* New York: Glencoe/McGraw Hill.

Paine, T. (1776, 1975). *Thomas Paine's* Common Sense: *The call to independence.* Woodbury, NY: Barron's Educational Series.

Patrick, J., & Berkin, C. (1987). *History of the American nation.* New York: Macmillan.

Ritchie, D. A., & Broussard, A. (1997). *American history: The early years to 1877.* New York: Glencoe/McGraw Hill.

Ward, H. M. (1991). *The American Revolution: Nationhood achieved, 1763–1788.* New York: St. Martin's Press.

Figure 7–5, *continued*

The World Wide Web

American Revolution: Resources at the New York public library. (1995). [http://www.nypl.org/research/chss/subguides/milhist/rev.html]

Cole, R. (1995).The role of African Americans in the American Revolution. [http://www.ilt.columbia.edu/k12/history/blacks/blacks.html]

Hispanics in the American Revolution. (1995, 1996). [http://www.clark.net/pub/jgbustam/galvez/galvez.html]

Medvedev, S. M. (1995). American Revolution: A revolution? [http://grid.let.rug.nl/~welling/usa/revo1.htm]

Olson, K. W. (1995). An outline of American history. [http:/grid.let.rug.nl/~welling/usa/]

Fiction

Collier, J. L., & and Collier, C. (1976). *The bloody country.* New York: Scholastic.

Forbes, E. (1943). *Johnny Tremaine: A story of the Boston revolt.* Boston: Houghton Mifflin.

Snow, R. (1976). *Freeland Starbird.* Boston: Houghton Mifflin.

16mm Film

Prelude to revolution. 13-minute film available from Encyclopedia Britannica Educational Corporation, 425 N. Michigan Ave., Chicago, IL 60611

Videocassette

The American Revolution. Available from Guidance Associates, Communications Park Box 3000, Mt. Kisko, NY 10549

Filmstrip

The American Revolution: Two views. Four-color filmstrips and accompanying cassette tapes available from Social Studies School Service, P.O. Box 802, Culver City, CA 90232-0802

Computer Software

"Revolutionary war: Choosing sides." Computer-based role-playing exercise. One diskette available in either Apple or MS-DOS format from Social Studies School Service, P.O. Box 802, Culver City, CA 90232-0802

Posters

"American patriot posters." A set of ten color posters of Revolutionary-era patriots available from Social Studies School Service, P.O. Box 802, Culver City, CA 90232-0802

How can I gain students' attention? This question prompts you to think about how students can be motivated at the beginning of a lesson. If an initial interest can be established, your students are more likely to stay with you for the duration of the lesson.

What is the best way to sequence lesson content and activities? This is a difficult question because there is no answer that is right for all situations. In some cases, logic of the subject matter dictates the response. For example, in a mathematics lesson less complex content must precede more complex content. In other subjects, however, the sequencing decision is much more a matter of your personal professional judgment.

How can students become actively involved in the lesson, and what should they do to demonstrate they have learned? Lessons requiring students to actively manipulate the new content tend to be more successful than those that require them only to read or listen passively. Additionally, learning theorists say that new information is better remembered when people have had an opportunity to use it in some way. For this reason, it is important to include application activities in lesson plans, whenever possible (Good and Brophy, 2000).

How should students be grouped during the lesson? You need to decide whether your students will be taught as members of one large group or as members of a number of small groups. If the decision is to have them divided into groups, specific thought must be given to deciding how group members will be selected and how students will move smoothly (quickly and quietly) from the large group into the small groups. If it is important for groups to have leaders, you must decide how they are to be selected and how they will report to you. You also must plan ways to distribute materials quickly and efficiently to all group members.

How can needs of students at different ability levels be met, and what should be done to monitor the progress of individual students? Because all classes have individuals with vastly different levels of ability and interest, your plans must assume that some students will need different learning materials than others and that some will finish more quickly than others. You also should devise a system for keeping track of how individual students are doing.

What kind of practice assignments need to be developed? It is important to think carefully and to prepare in advance lesson assignments that call on students to apply what they have learned. Good assignments of this kind almost never can be created on the spur of the moment. You need to design them carefully before starting to teach your lesson.

How should the lesson be concluded? It is as important to plan a sound lesson conclusion as well as a highly motivating lesson beginning. Your conclusion should help students draw together major points that have been introduced. It is particularly important for you to build in time for the conclusion phase of a lesson. You do not want to just stop. Your ending needs to be a carefully executed component that you treat as an essential feature of the lesson.

What materials are needed? Some lessons fail because teachers have not thought about needed materials. Books, handouts, paper and pencils, and other needed items are not available for students to use. You should consider preparing a "needed-materials checklist." When you have such a list, you can check off the availability of individual items as you prepare to teach the lesson. This ensures that any problems you experience with the lesson will not be caused by lack of available materials.

What rules and management guidelines should be adopted for this lesson? Some lessons include activities that are designed to promote very active student involvement. To ensure that students maintain a focus on the planned academic activity, you have to think through your expectations regarding what kinds of student behaviors are appropriate and about how your expectations will be communicated to students. Additional thought needs to be given to possible actions that will ensure student compliance with these expectations.

How much time should be allocated to each part of the lesson? Time is a scarce commodity in the classroom. This resource needs to be expended wisely to ensure the maximum possible learning benefit for students. Some parts of lessons clearly deserve more attention than others. Careful planners take time to make decisions about how much time they intend to devote to each part of a lesson.

 MORE FROM THE WEB

Units and Lessons

A tremendous number of Web sites include information about instructional units and lesson plans. You will find instructions about different formatting approaches as well as numerous examples of completed units and lessons. You should have little difficulty in finding material related to the subject(s) you will be teaching. Here are some sites that are representative of what the Web has to offer if you are looking for information related to units and lessons.

Academic Learning Units

http://www.ide.mat-su.k12.ak.us/instrmdl/alubasic.htm

A school in Alaska made a decision to develop a common unit format for all teachers in the building. The format is explained in considerable detail at this Web address.

Frank's Teachers' Software

http://www3.sympatico.ca/frank.e.stokes/

More and more software is becoming available to help you construct units and lessons. At this site, you will find information about something called "Frank's Unit Maker," an inexpensive software package that will help you write instructional units on your computer.

EMT 669 Sample Instructional Units

http://jwilson.coe.uga.edu/emt669/units.html

> This site is one of many that feature examples of instructional units related to a specific academic subject. Here you will find a number of examples of instructional units for mathematics. Examples of titles are (1) Projective Geometry Unit, (2) Transformational Geometry, (3) Maximum and Minimum Values of a Function, and (4) Circles: Their Lines and Segments.

Lesson Plan Outline

http://www.geneseo.edu/~stuteach/lesplan.html

> There are many existing lesson-plan formats. You will find one example in this chapter. Here is another.

Outta Ray's Head Lesson Plans

http://www3.sympatico.ca/ray.saitz/lessons3.htm

> Many teachers have contributed to the supply of lesson plans included at this site. Most focus on language-arts related areas such as literature, writing, and poetry.

Teacher's Room: Lesson Plan Search Results

http://www.globefearon.com/teachers/search_handler.cgi

> Today, commercial firms that market materials of various kinds to teachers often make lesson plans available on their Web sites. The collection here has been gathered together on a site maintained by Globe Fearon. You will find lesson plans for a large number of school subjects available here.

Providing for the Needs of Special Groups of Students

Students in today's classrooms are more diverse than they have ever been. You need to prepare lessons that will meet the needs of exceptionally bright students as well as students with any one of a number of special conditions that range from emotional problems, to physical challenges of various kinds, and to mild and moderate mental retardation. Today, federal and accompanying state legislation requires all students to spend as much of the school day as possible in regular classrooms rather than in isolated classrooms where they have little contact with "typical students." This means that your lesson plans must make provisions to meet the special needs of a variety of students. A single approach to teaching a class of 20 to 30 students will not do.

For example, in making provisions for gifted and talented students you might decide to suggest additional reading, independent study projects, and special research projects. Most students in this category have well-developed reading skills. By way of contrast, many less able students in your classes will not be good readers. Your lesson plans should include alternative ways for students in this group to obtain essential information. You may decide to include such options as use of films or filmstrips or listening to audio tapes. It often also makes sense for you to provide them with some easy-to-read information sources dealing with content that more proficient readers can obtain from the text or from other printed material that is too difficult for less able students.

There are often language minority students in today's classroom. To assist these young people, you may decide to have some learning materials available that are written in the language they speak at home. For information about approaches to working with these students, write to:

National Clearing House for Bilingual Education
1300 Wilson Boulevard, Suite B2-11
Rosslyn, VA 22209

Another category of learner you are likely to find in your classroom includes the physically impaired student. Some excellent ideas for responding to the varied needs of students in this general category are available from the following:

National Library Service for the Blind and Physically Handicapped
Library of Congress
Washington, DC 20542

You may need to have large-type print materials and materials in Braille for any blind or visually impaired students you may have in your classes. For information about learning materials available for these students, write to:

American Foundation for the Blind
Consumer Products Department
15 West 16th Street
New York, NY 10011

There also may be deaf or hearing-impaired students in your classes. These students need visual reinforcement of any information you present orally. For more specific information about their needs and for a description of some useful products that are available, write to:

Gallaudet University
800 Florida Avenue, NE
Washington, DC 20002-3695

Choosing a Format

There are many acceptable ways to format a lesson plan. What is important is that you give serious thought to the organizational scheme and to prepare your plan carefully once you decide on an arrangement. The scheme you adopt should allow you to refer quickly to the completed plan to keep on track and to ensure that no planned parts of the lesson inadvertently are omitted. Because of the need to use lesson plans while instruction is being delivered, you do not want them to be too long. In addition, you want to avoid formats that make individual items difficult to find. (See Figure 7-6 for an example of a lesson-plan format.)

FOR YOUR PORTFOLIO

1. What materials, ideas you learned in this chapter related to *instructional units and lesson plans* will you include as "evidence" in your portfolio? Select up to 3 items of information to be included. Number them 1, 2, and 3.

2. Think about why you selected these materials for your portfolio. Consider such issues as the following in your response:

   - The specific purposes to which this information can be put when you plan, deliver, and assess the impact of your instruction,

   - The compatibility of the information with your own priorities and values,

   - The contributions this information can make to your personal development as a teacher, and

   - The factors that led you to include this material as opposed to some alternatives you considered.

3. Prepare a written reflection in which you analyze the decision-making process you followed. Also, mention the INTASC Standard(s) to which your selected material relates. (First complete the chart below.)

Materials You Selected and the INTASC Standards

Put a check under those INTASC Standards numbers to which the evidence you have selected applies. (Refer to Chapter 1 for more detailed information about INTASC)

Item of Evidence Number	INTASC Standards									
	S1	S2	S3	S4	S5	S6	S7	S8	S9	S10
1										
2										
3										

Lesson Plan Number _____

Unit Title _____

Lesson Title _____

Learning Intention _____

_____

_____

Needed Prerequisite Knowledge or Skill _____

_____

New Terms and Key Ideas _____

_____

_____

Procedures for Accommodating Students with Special Needs _____

_____

Time	Lesson Sequence	Materials
	1. Gaining attention/informing students of learning intention	
	2. Presenting new material	
	3. Checking understanding/monitoring	
	4. Eliciting behavior/practice/feedback	
	5. Providing for independent practice/application/extension	
	6. Providing for closure/evaluating learning	

Teacher Evaluation of Lesson Effectiveness

_____

_____

Figure 7–6
An Example of a Lesson Plan Format

Key Ideas in Summary

■ Because of the unique characteristics of individual teaching settings, you need to do much of your own instructional planning. Researchers have determined that effective teachers devote a great deal of time to planning.

■ As you prepare for instruction, you will engage in long-term, intermediate-term, and short-term planning. Long-term planning embraces a time period of a semester or a full academic year. Intermediate-term planning focuses on time periods ranging from about two to six weeks in length. Instructional unit plans represent the written expression of intermediate planning. Short-term planning focuses on what goes on during one (and sometimes two or three) class periods. Short-term planning decisions are written in the form of lesson plans.

■ Many variables affect specific decisions you make as you prepare instructional plans. Among variables that must be considered are (1) your own personal characteristics, (2) characteristics of your students, (3) the general learning context, (4) available time, and (5) available resources to support learning.

■ Some instructional units draw content from a single academic subject. Others are inter-disciplinary in nature. In planning interdisciplinary units, you often will begin by identifying relevant generalizations associated with each source subject, samples of content associated with each source subject, and a key question related to each source subject.

■ There are different ways to format instructional units. Many of them contain these key content categories: (1) unit title, (2) rationale and major goals, (3) major generalizations and concepts, (4) instructional learning intentions and an indication of time to be devoted to instruction related to each, (5) instructional strategies for each learning intention, (6) plans for beginning and ending the unit, (7) evaluation procedures, and (8) a list of needed learning resources.

■ Lesson plans include details regarding instructional decisions that will guide teaching for a relatively short period of time. They might be thought of as scripts teachers follow during a given period, sometimes a time as short as a single class period. Many different lesson plan formats have been developed.

Reflections

1. As a teacher, why do you have to do so much instructional planning of your own when so much excellent information is available in curriculum guides, textbooks, and other learning materials?

2. What are some characteristics of long-term planning?

3. What are some similarities and differences between intermediate-term and short-term planning?

4. What is the importance of the learning context in instructional planning?

5. What are some typical components of instructional units?

6. How might you go about the process of constructing an interdisciplinary unit?

7. Why is it probable that you will include more details in your lesson plans early on in your teaching career than during your later years in the profession?

8. What are some questions you should ask yourself as you plan lessons?

9. Why is it important to carefully plan conclusions for your lessons?

10. What are some sources of information that can be helpful to you in planning meaningful lessons for special groups of students?

Learning Extensions

1. Review some district- or state-level curriculum guides. How many parts of the instructional unit format introduced in this chapter are included in the guides? What would need to be added to this material to make an instructional unit complete?

2. Interview a teacher about the process he or she follows in preparing an instructional unit. How does this person start this task? What goes into his or her decisions about sequencing content? Where is information about available materials found? What kind of format is used?

3. Visit two or more schools and compare how teachers in each approach a common subject. What differences are attributable to teacher variables and student variables? What differences seem to be caused by differences in the teaching context?

4. Get together with several others who are preparing to teach the same secondary school subject. Develop an instructional unit following the format introduced in this chapter. Share your unit with your instructor and request a critique. Be prepared to participate in a class discussion focusing on special difficulties you encountered and how you overcome them.

5. Write a lesson plan focusing on a topic you would like to teach. Be prepared to share answers to these questions with others in the class: How long did it take you to prepare the lesson? Do you think you would be able to accomplish this task more quickly were you to prepare another lesson? How comfortable would you feel in teaching this content?

6. Go to the Merrill Education's Link to General Methods Resources site at this URL: http://www.prenhall.com/methods-cluster/ At the bottom of the page select "discipline-specific resources" as your topic and click the "begin" button. This will take you to the "Overview" page. On the left side, click on "Web Links." On the Web Links page click on a category that includes a subject you would like to teach. (Your choices here are "art and music," "foreign language," "language arts," "math," "physical education," "science," "social studies," and "vocational.") Follow links that will give you information you can use to prepare a short paper in which you explain kinds of information you found that you can include in lessons and units you might develop.

7. Go to the Merrill Education's Link to General Methods Resources site at this URL: http://www.prenhall.com/methods-cluster/ At the bottom of the page select

"discipline-specific resources" as your topic and click the "begin" button. This will take you to the "Overview" page. On the left side, click on "Lesson Plans." On the Lesson Plans page click on a category that includes a subject you would like to teach. (Your choices here are "Comprehensive," "Elementary," "Middle School," "Arts and Music," "Foreign Language," "Language Arts," "Math," "Science," and "Social Studies.") Go to some sites that include lesson plans appropriate for a subject you might be teaching. Print two or three of these lessons. Prepare a short paper for your instructor in which you compare and contrast design features of these lessons with the general format depicted in Figure 7–6.

References

Clark, C., & Yinger, R. (1979). *Three studies of teacher planning* (Research Series No. 55). East Lansing, MI: Michigan State University, Institute for Research on Teaching.

Good, T. L., & Brophy, J. E. (2000). *Looking in classrooms* (8th ed.). New York: Longman.

Kauchak, D., & Eggen, P. (1989). *Learning and teaching: Research-based models.* Boston: Allyn & Bacon.

Palmer, J. M. (1995). Interdisciplinary curriculum—Again. In J. A. Beane (Ed.), *Toward a coherent curriculum* (pp. 55–61). 1995 Yearbook of the Association for Supervision and Curriculum Development. Alexandria, VA: Association for Supervision and Curriculum Development.

Pate, P. E., McGinnis, K., & Homestead, E. (1995). Creating coherence through curriculum integration. In J. A. Beane (Ed.), *Toward a coherent curriculum* (pp. 62–70). 1995 Yearbook of the Association for Supervision and Curriculum Development. Alexandria, VA: Association for Supervision and Curriculum Development.

Yinger, R. (1979). *A study of teacher planning: Description and theory development using ethnographic and information processing methods.* Unpublished doctoral dissertation. East Lansing, MI: Michigan State University.

III

Instructing

8

Models of Direct Instruction

This chapter will aim to

- describe components of several direct-instruction models;

- point out features of direct instruction that explain some of the popularity of this approach among teachers, school leaders, and parents;

- identify kinds of learning intentions for which direct instruction is appropriate;

- describe situations for which direct instruction has been found to be a useful instructional approach; and

- apply the direct instruction model to specific instructional situations.

Introduction

What types of teaching do you remember as most common when you were a student? Chances are that what you recall as typical teaching falls into a category called *direct instruction*. Direct instruction is teacher centered. When you use it in the classroom, you act as the major provider of information. You maintain direct control over the content to be learned, the delivery of the content, the patterns of classroom interaction, the pace of instruction, and the evaluation of what is learned. Content is delivered in a systematic, step-by-step fashion. You work with students until they master one idea before you introduce another. The approach features whole-class or large-group instruction rather than individualized or small-group learning.

Several different names have been applied to this approach, including *explicit teaching, systematic teaching, target teaching, active teaching, clinical teaching,* and *mastery teaching.* Some variants of this approach have been used in classrooms for many years.

There are several reasons why this approach has achieved popularity. It doesn't ask you to do anything in the classroom that radically departs from what you observed many of your own teachers doing. In addition, procedures for implementing direct instruction are easy to learn, and the approach has been found to be especially effective in teaching students the kinds of basic information often evaluated on standardized tests. The current emphasis on accountability and the use of test scores for evaluating school districts, schools, and even teachers has made any approach that promises to help students score well on standardized tests attractive to school leaders. Finally, parents remember this kind of teaching from their own school days. Because they have experienced direct instruction, many of them presume this approach is both logical and legitimate.

In this chapter, we make suggestions about appropriate and inappropriate uses of direct instruction. We also introduce basic components of a direct instruction model in our presentation of this chapter's contents. After you finish reading this material, you may wish to revisit various sections to see how parts of our direct-instruction model have been incorporated.

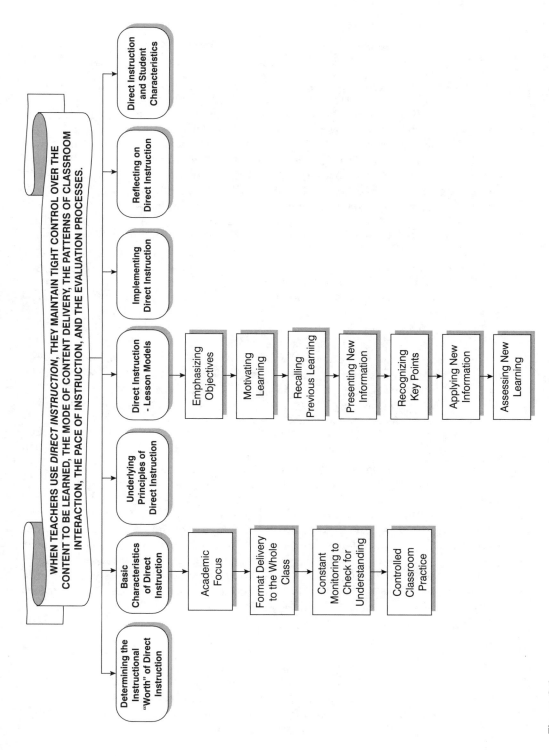

WHEN TEACHERS USE *DIRECT INSTRUCTION*, THEY MAINTAIN TIGHT CONTROL OVER THE CONTENT TO BE LEARNED, THE MODE OF CONTENT DELIVERY, THE PATTERNS OF CLASSROOM INTERACTION, THE PACE OF INSTRUCTION, AND THE EVALUATION PROCESSES.

- Determining the Instructional "Worth" of Direct Instruction
- Basic Characteristics of Direct Instruction
  - Academic Focus
  - Format Delivery to the Whole Class
  - Constant Monitoring to Check for Understanding
  - Controlled Classroom Practice
- Underlying Principles of Direct Instruction
- Direct Instruction - Lesson Models
  - Emphasizing Objectives
  - Motivating Learning
  - Recalling Previous Learning
  - Presenting New Information
  - Recognizing Key Points
  - Applying New Information
  - Assessing New Learning
- Implementing Direct Instruction
- Reflecting on Direct Instruction
- Direct Instruction and Student Characteristics

Figure 8-1
Graphic Organizer

Determining the Instructional "Worth" of Direct Instruction

If you visit some Web sites with information about direct instruction, you probably will encounter a pattern that we have always found troubling. That is, much material written about specific approaches to delivering instruction lacks balance. Particularly on the Web, you will find materials about "approach A" that fall into two major categories. Some of them will suggest that the approach is the answer to every teacher's dream and that its use in the classroom will excite, motivate, and thrill *all* students. Others will attack the approach as being totally beyond redemption and hint that true professional teachers would rather perish than be caught using it in their own classrooms. Perhaps our examples are a bit overdrawn, but you definitely will find yourself occasionally longing for a discussion of an instructional approach that features a dispassionate consideration of pluses and minuses rather than heavy-handed assertions of its "absolute excellence" or its "complete lack of redeeming qualities."

Why is there so much strident opinion-mongering in discussions of instructional methodologies? Doubtless many variables contribute to this pattern. One key point is that teachers work within large bureaucracies. It is difficult to win support for a dramatic expansion in the use of a proposed new instructional approach unless it generates enough strong feelings to overcome the inertia of established tradition. Hence, proponents more often feel pressed to "oversell" its benefits. Similarly, they also often feel compelled to engage in open attacks on alternative approaches as a way of attracting support for what they are espousing. You need to consider these realities of the public school setting when you read information about alleged benefits and shortcomings of a given instructional approach.

Fortunately, there are some research-based findings related to the effectiveness of direct instruction. In general, studies have found this approach to be particularly good for such purposes as teaching basic facts, concepts, procedures, and skills (Borich, 1992). Research on direct instruction and other instructional approaches typically points out that individual approaches have varying degrees of value for achieving particular purposes with certain kinds of students. The most important threat that runs through research on instructional techniques can be summed up as follows: *No single approach is most appropriate for all situations.* Your obligation as a professional is to vary what you do depending on the content to be taught, the nature of your students, the specific learning intentions you have established, your personal comfort and familiarity with a particular instructional approach, and the availability of needed instructional support materials.

Basic Characteristics of Direct Instruction

When some people hear the phrase *direct instruction*, they immediately think of the lecture method. It is true that lecturing features many elements of direct instruction, but there is much more to this approach than simply telling. In a typical lecture, teachers stand in front of the class and deliver information the students are supposed to remember. The communication is generally one way, from the teacher to the students, with occasional interjections of student questions. A fully developed direct-instruction approach involves more. It is faster paced, includes more student involvement, contains a highly organized set of interactions under the control of the teacher, and focuses more on student learning than on teacher performance.

An elaboration of some of the basic characteristics of direct instruction will indicate how direct instruction goes beyond what you might do in a typical lecture. In fact, in some direct-instruction lessons, you won't be involved in anything resembling a lecture at all. For example, you may choose to do demonstrations, show slides and provide comments, or present new content in other ways. The key to direct instruction is not lecture; rather, it is the presence of your control, as the teacher, over the flow of new information. In general, a complete direct instruction lesson includes these basic characteristics:

- Academic focus,
- Formal delivery to the whole class,
- Constant monitoring to check for understanding, and
- Controlled classroom practice.

MORE FROM THE WEB

Direct Instruction

Direct instruction has advocates as well as critics. Widespread interest in the topic has prompted development of much related information on the Web. Here are some sites you might wish to visit.

ADA—Association for Direct Instruction

- This is the home page of a national group dedicated to promoting the use of direct instruction in schools. You will find many links to useful information. For example, if you follow the "Who We Are" link, you will learn of the existence of a journal produced quarterly by the Association for Direct Instruction titled *Effective School Practices* that prints articles on direct-instruction research and practice.

Slavin's QAIT Model

http://www.valdosta.edu/~whuitt/psy310/QAIT.html

- At this site, you will find information related to work that instructional design specialist Robert Slavin has done to update an earlier mastery-learning model. Slavin argues that a successful mastery learning program depends on (1) the quality of instruction, (2) delivering instruction at a level students can understand, (3) the nature of incentives that are provided, and (4) the time allotted for students to learn the material being taught.

Direct Instruction: A Transactional Model

http://www.valdosta.peachnet.edu:80/~whuitt/psy702/instruct/instevnt.html

- At this site, you will find a useful listing of research-based information on how to increase students' attention during phases of direct instruction including those devoted to establishing initial motivation, introduction of new material, application of what has been learned, and review.

Direct Instruction (DI)

http://www.uncwil.edu/people/kozloffm/aftdi.html

- This material has been assembled by the American Federation of Teachers (AFT), one of the major national teachers' organizations. You will find an excellent overview of features of direct instruction as well as a comprehensive list of schools where direct instruction models are being used.

What Direct Instruction Is and Is Not

http://www.uncwil.edu/people/kozloffm/whatdiis.html

- As we note in this chapter, much that is written and said about individual instructional approaches lacks balance. Material available at this site tries to strike a reasoned middle ground, advocating for direct instruction, while, at the same time, not engaging in strident attacks on other approaches.

Academic Focus

Academic focus means that the lesson concentrates on teaching academic content or skills. This focus is maintained throughout the lesson. Explicit instructional objectives guide your planning and teaching. Your decision-making as the lesson is taught centers on keeping the lesson on target so that students master the objectives. You should seek to avoid digressions from the content focus, and, when these occur, act quickly to get students to refocus on content associated with the lesson purpose. Independent seat work activities should follow your presentation of information, and these activities should relate clearly to content you have introduced.

Formal Delivery to the Whole Class

Direct instruction features systematic and formal presentation of information to the whole class. You instruct in a logical, step-by-step fashion. Typically, you ask students to demonstrate their understanding of each step before they go on to the next. You control classroom interactions and the rate at which content is introduced. Under optimal conditions, you maintain as brisk a pace as possible consistent with students' ability to grasp what is presented. It is important to note that your control of the classroom does not mean an absence of active student participation. On the contrary, when direct instruction is effectively implemented, there is a high degree of student involvement associated with actions you take to ensure they are understanding the new material.

Direct instruction lessons feature many teacher-to-student questions. A large number of these tend to be recall questions. When your instruction is effective, students are able to respond to a high percentage of them (Rosenshine & Stevens, 1986). Questions often focus either on a request for specific answers or a request for an explanation of how a student arrived at an answer (Rosenshine, 1987). The general pattern that is followed has been described as factual question-student response-teacher feedback (Stallings & Kaskowitz, 1974).

The large number of questions asked during a direct instruction lesson gives you opportunities to interact with many of your students. This tends to keep all students in the class alert and actively involved. Your questions give them opportunities to repeat and practice what they have learned. This condition facilitates student learning of the new content.

Constant Monitoring to Check for Understanding

During a direct instruction lesson, you regularly ask questions and take other actions to ensure that students are understanding the material. Students' responses provide cues you can use to adjust the pace of the lesson and to spend more time dealing with content aspects that students find difficult. You want to make sure that the students have mastered each subsection of the lesson before moving on to the next subsection. Sometimes it is necessary to reteach some material in order to ensure mastery.

Controlled Classroom Practice

Effective direct instruction lessons feature substantial opportunities for students to engage in controlled practice. The key word here is *controlled*. Before students are allowed to engage in application activities requiring the use of presented information, you need to ensure that they have the necessary understanding to successfully complete the application exercises.

■   ■   ■

Take a minute to review what you have just read to this point. What accounts for the popularity of direct instruction? How is direct instruction similar to and different from a lecture? What would you need to do to change a traditional lecture format to make it more consistent with characteristics of effective direct instruction? What questions do you have about direct instruction? Summarize the basic characteristics of direct instruction.

Underlying Principles

Rosenshine and Stevens (1986) identify the basic principles underlying the direct-instruction model. These principles are taken from research and theory related to how individuals process information. The first principle states that individuals can only process a limited amount of new information at one time. If too much information is presented at once, students' abilities to process it are hindered. When this happens, they become confused, make faulty associations, and fail to attend to some key points of information. In frustration, students may turn off the processing altogether.

To prevent these kinds of problems, you have to avoid overwhelming students with too much information at once. New materials should be presented in the form of small steps. As you introduce material, you need to check frequently to ensure that your students are adequately grasping key points.

Another principle underlying direct instruction concerns the importance of prior knowledge. What people already know establishes a framework for helping them process new information. This means that you need to take time to find out what your learners already understand about a topic that you want to introduce. When you are armed with this kind of information, you can take appropriate action to help your students establish a learning set, or framework, that will help them correctly process the new information. To ensure that students have a good understanding of important prerequisite information, it makes sense for you to review with them what they have already learned and to point out how it connects to the material you are about to introduce.

A third principle of direct-instruction learning relates to the transfer of sensory perceptions from short-term memory to long-term memory. Short-term memory is the memory storage system where bits of information received by our sensory perceptors are stored for a brief time—a period up to about 30 seconds (Slavin, 1994). Unless something is done with the information, it will be lost and cannot be recalled. You need to find ways to help students retain important information for longer periods of time. To do this, you have to facilitate a shift of information from short-term to long-term memory.

A movement of information into long-term memory requires the brain to review, practice, summarize, and elaborate on the information received. You have to give your students opportunities to engage in active practice of what they have learned. They need to respond to questions, summarize information in their own words, and, in general, do something with the new information. There are considerable benefits when these actions result in a shift of information into long-term memory. Some experts believe that nothing is ever permanently lost from long-term memory. There are times when the information cannot be readily retrieved; but, when conditions are right, details stored in long-term memory can be recalled and used.

The interest in moving information into long-term memory provides a rationale for another basic principle of direct instruction—the emphasis on practice. Information is most readily recalled when it has been acquired through processes involving what sometimes is referred to as *overlearning*. Overlearning occurs when students practice using the new information to the point that little effort is required to give a correct response. When students can readily recall overlearned prior information, their information processing systems are free to devote full attention to the task of comprehending new information you are presenting to them. Because new learning builds on old, it makes sense for you to give students opportunities to overlearn by providing them numerous opportunities to rehearse and repeat what they have learned. Overlearning experiences that provide students with opportunities to rehearse and review material in a variety of settings are particularly effective.

■   ■   ■

This section has reviewed the basic principles that form a foundation for direct instruction. Stop your reading at this point. How do these principles fit with the way you think people learn and remember? Briefly write each principle in your own words. Give an example of short-term memory and long-term memory. Compare your responses with those of another person who is reading this chapter.

Direct Instruction: Lesson Models

Several variations of direct instruction approaches have been developed based on these basic principles (Hunter & Russell, 1977; Denton, Armstrong, & Savage, 1980; Slavin, 1999). As indicated in Figure 8–2, there are great similarities among components of these models. (Though each of the three models illustrated in Figure 8–2 features seven phases, this is simply a coincidence. It is quite possible for direct instruction models to have either smaller or larger numbers of components.)

Note that the reference to parts of the model has been to *components*, not to *steps*. The term "steps" would suggest that users of direct instruction should follow a rigid, mechanistic sequence while delivering lessons to students. This kind of by-the-numbers teaching is not what proponents of direct instruction espouse. Rather, the models seek to provide you with information about instructional responsibilities that you need to discharge as you engage students in new material. The way you decide to accommodate each of the responsibilities should be based on the following:

- the type of content you are teaching,
- what you expect your students to be able to do, and
- specific modifications you decide to make based on your professional reactions to how students are performing as you engage them with the new content.

Suppose you reviewed various models and decided to work with the one developed by Denton, Armstrong, and Savage (1980). In using the model, you need to make decisions about what you would do in these seven areas:

1. *Emphasizing Objectives.* Students need to have a clear answer to the "what-am-I-supposed-to-be-learning?" question. This component of the model requires you to decide how you will provide students with information they need to answer this question.

Hunter & Russell Model (Hunter & Russell, 1977)	Denton, Armstrong, and Savage Model (Denton, Armstrong, & Savage, 1980)	Slavin Model (Slavin, 1994)
1. Anticipatory Set 2. Teaching to an Objective 3. Presentation of New Material or Academic Input 4. Modeling 5. Checking for Understanding 6. Guided Practice 7. Independent Practice	1. Emphasizing Objectives 2. Motivating Learning 3. Recalling Previous Learning 4. Presenting New Information 5. Recognizing Key Points 6. Applying New Information 7. Assessing New Learning	1. Stating Learning Objectives and Orienting Students to Lesson 2. Reviewing Prerequisites 3. Presenting New Material 4. Conducting Learning Probes 5. Providing Independent Practice 6. Assessing Performance and Providing Feedback 7. Providing Distributed Practice and Review

Figure 8–2
Components Included in Three Direct-Instruction Models

2. *Motivating Learning.* This component of the model highlights your response to "build interest" in what you will be teaching. Actions you take to motivate students need to occur throughout an instructional sequence, not only at the beginning.

3. *Recalling Previous Learning.* Decisions you make that relate to this component seek to help students recall previous information they have learned, particularly information that ties in closely to new content you are about to introduce.

4. *Presenting New Information.* Your responsibility in this area is to decide how best to present new information to your students in a comprehensible and interesting manner.

5. *Recognizing Key Points.* When students are presented with new information, the volume of what has been presented may overwhelm them. Decisions you make that relate to this component of the model seek to reduce confusion and promote a focus on the most important parts of the newly introduced material.

6. *Applying New Information.* If students are to master new information, you must do more than simply expose them to it. They must have opportunities to use it. Decisions you make in this category identify ways in which students will be asked to put new learning into practice.

7. *Assessing New Learning.* To improve your instructional practices, you need to develop procedures that will provide you with a flow of information about (1) how each individual student is doing and (2) how the class, in general, is responding to

your instruction. Decisions you make related to assessing new learning identify procedures you will follow to obtain this information.

■ ■ ■

Jot down the seven components of direct instruction as outlined in the Denton, Armstrong, and Savage (1980) model. See if you can give an example of each component. Share your example with someone else who is reading this chapter.

Emphasizing Objectives

Instructional purposes expressed as objectives establish an academic focus for direct-instruction lessons. They provide you with targets you can use in planning instruction and adjusting what you do as you teach. They also can help you keep on track and avoid temptations to dwell too long on unimportant or minor details.

Giving the objective to the students helps establish a framework for what they are learning. You do not have to do this using the somewhat stilted language you might employ in a formal lesson plan. It is perfectly acceptable to provide students with a simple statement that lets them know what you want them to learn. More information on establishing learning intentions and providing worthwhile objectives is found in Chapter 7, "Planning Units and Lessons."

CRITICAL INCIDENT

This Is the Way We Teach

Rosa Garcia has just finished her teacher preparation program. She had a delightful student teaching experience with a very creative master teacher. Overall, she feels pleased with her preparation and is anxious to begin her teaching career. She has been hired to teach in a school district near her hometown. She knows little about the district other than that students there typically score below state averages on standardized achievement tests.

She was somewhat surprised by what she learned at the district's three-day orientation session for new teachers. During the first morning of the orientation session, the superintendent mentioned the lower-than-average scores of the students in the district. She noted that the scores are published in the newspapers across the state. This has harmed the reputation of the school district and has led to enormous pressure by the local community to correct this situation. Therefore, the school district has implemented a series of workshops covering a teaching approach that all teachers are expected to use. The superintendent went on to point out that this approach has been found to be the most effective approach to teaching. It includes seven steps that must be included in every lesson that is taught regardless of the subject or the grade level.

A district-wide lesson plan format including these seven steps has been developed, and all teachers are expected to use this lesson plan model and to turn in lesson plans on Friday for the following week. Furthermore, the school district has revised the teacher evaluation forms for the district. The evaluation form focuses on these seven steps and includes a rating for how well a teacher performs each of them. Continued employment in the district will be based on teacher performance on this evaluation form.

The superintendent went on to observe that, because many new teachers were prepared in teacher-education programs that did not stress this model, the remainder of the three-day new-teacher orientation would be spent teaching them how to implement the seven-step lesson model. This would prepare them for success in the district.

Rosa was shocked to hear these words. It was as if the superintendent were telling everyone that their preparation was worthless. She began to wonder how the interesting approaches she had learned in her student teaching could be applied. She sensed that the superintendent's final comments seemed to be an uncanny answer to what she was thinking.

"I know that there are some teachers who believe that this approach limits their creativity," the superintendent said. "Well, we believe there is plenty of room for teacher creativity *within* this approach. If your lesson is so creative that it doesn't fit within this model, then it is probably inappropriate for our students. Education is a serious business here. We expect to see student learning take place, and we won't tolerate cute lessons that don't result in observable student learning."

■ ■ ■

How would you react to this superintendent's approach to teaching? What are some positive aspects of this approach to improving education? What do you see as problems with this approach to school improvement? When you hear that an approach has been found to be the most effective *method of teaching, what should you ask?*

What are the superintendent's priorities? How are these priorities reflected in the policy requiring all teachers to adopt a common approach to planning and delivering instruction? How might Rosa's views (or those of other teachers) differ? What might their priorities suggest about their values? What do you think you would do if you were Rosa? Would you feel comfortable in this situation? Because this is an approach that is mandated by the school district and is the focus for evaluation, what course of action should Rosa pursue? From what you know about this approach, do you think that there is room for her to use some of the creative approaches she has learned?

What could Rosa have done to avoid finding herself in this situation? What implications does this have concerning your future job hunting?

Motivating Learning

Secondary students enter your classroom with a number of agendas. They have recently left another classroom, have been engaging in social conversation with peers, and may be anticipating future events. In short, they do not usually come into class thinking seriously about the forthcoming content of the class. In addition, they have been away from the class for a day (sometimes more) and have had lots of other events intervene since you last taught them. Finally, the topics you wish to introduce may not initially be of great personal interest to members of your class. To respond to these circumstances, you need to think through ways of capturing and maintaining student interest in what you want them to learn.

Ideally, you should do something that communicates information to students about the importance of what is to be learned and why it may be of special interest to them. Ideas for motivating students need to be planned not just at the beginning of a lesson but for use at various times throughout the entire time you are teaching the material. You need to develop a sense for when students' attentiveness begins to flag and then do something to rekindle their interest in what you are presenting.

In planning your motivational strategies, you might find it useful to consider how you might respond to questions students might ask themselves. Here are some examples:

- What personal use will I make of information in this lesson?
- Do people I respect other than the teacher have any interest in this material?
- Can this new information help me in my other classes?
- Will I have the necessary background to master this new content?

Recalling Previous Learning

Daily reviews are a common feature of direct instruction lessons. The idea is for you to provide students with opportunities to practice information they have learned previously. A daily review can help students understand that they have the background needed to master the content you are about to introduce. Information you gather from students when you engage them in recall of previous learning can provide you insights regarding some mistaken information or ideas that need to be corrected before you introduce the new material.

Rosenshine and Stevens (1986) recommend some of the following ideas for making the recall-of-previous learning experiences effective:

- Administer a short quiz on previously introduced material,
- Have students correct one another's homework,
- Ask students to summarize the main points of content introduced during the previous lesson,
- Assign students to prepare questions for each other based on previously introduced content, and
- Require students to review content of the previous lesson in small groups.

Presenting New Information

Presenting new information (sometimes called *input*) is central to all teaching. Your aim is to present new material to students so they will understand it. There is no single way to do this that has proved to be universally effective. To accomplish this task successfully, you have to know your students, your subject, and other characteristics of your instructional setting. Both artistry and technical skills are required as you develop presentation techniques that are well-fitted to your unique instructional circumstances.

Planning for presentation begins with a careful analysis of the content you want to teach. You have to make decisions about sequencing the new information and about breaking it into logical chunks. For example, if your students are easily distracted and are not especially task oriented, then you should present content in small steps and allow time for yourself to make frequent checks on student progress. If, however, they are interested in the topic and more mature, then it makes better sense for you to give them larger chunks of content at a time so that they don't become impatient and frustrated.

If good instructional resources are available, you want to use them to support your introduction. For example, you might choose to present some information using a computer or a videocassette player. However, you have to keep in mind that, even when you use alternative means to transmit information, you still need to incorporate the basic components of a direct-instruction lesson. You cannot expect success if you show a film without taking time to adequately prepare students to profit from this experience. You also have to engage in some serious checking-for-understanding instruction at the conclusion of the film. In other words, alternative presentation modes do not excuse you from exercising your professional responsibilities.

In deciding how to introduce material clearly and logically, you need to ask yourself questions such as these:

- How should the material be sequenced?
- How rapidly should information be presented?

Answers to these questions will vary depending on the nature of students in your class, the kind of content to be introduced, and the nature of the lesson's instructional objectives.

As you introduce new information, you need to think about what you will do in four important areas:

- Providing an overview or structure,
- Establishing a step-by-step progression,
- Highlighting main points, and
- Modeling what students should do.

Providing an Overview or Structure

A lesson structure or overview helps students see relationships among various parts of a lesson. You can present this kind of information in several ways. For example, you might project an outline on an overhead transparency, list main topic headings of the lesson on the chalkboard, or provide students with an incomplete lesson outline to fill out as new information is provided to them.

The outline or structure of the lesson can be presented as the lesson develops. You might write key words on the board or use simple diagrams that show interrelationships among isolated pieces of information. This can be an especially important aspect of direct instruction because of the focus on step-by-step progression. When you emphasize the importance of students' mastering each part of the lesson before moving forward, some individuals in your class may focus on the parts and miss the big picture. Diagrams and outlines can help them see how the pieces go together.

Establishing a Step-by-Step Progression

Good direct-instruction lessons proceed one step at a time. These steps should be presented at a pace sufficiently rapid to maintain student interest, but not so rapidly that they fail to keep up. You have to watch individual students carefully and alter your pace as needed to maintain levels of motivation and maximize learning.

You can start this process by identifying individual steps of your lesson before instruction begins. This requires you to think about all the things the students must be able to do to master the new material. Once you have identified this information, arrange content into a sequence that is logically consistent and compatible with students' characteristics. The process of doing this is sometimes referred to as *task analysis*.

Highlighting Main Points

Students retain critical information better when it is highlighted for them during presentations. Students' attention can be drawn to key points in a variety of ways, including writing main points on the chalkboard, repeating important information several times, and using marker phrases such as "now pay attention to this—you will need to use this material."

Modeling What Students Should Do

Many students fail, not because of lack of effort, but because they fail to understand what is expected of them. Similarly, if students see examples of what you want them to produce or do, the probability of their mastering the material you want them to know increases. Good modeling features frequent use of concrete examples, illustrations, or demonstrations.

Providing models or examples can take several forms. For example, you might simply show an example of a finished product. Sometimes you may be interested in helping students master a process of some kind. To help students better understand what you want them to do, you can talk them through the process as they engage in it themselves. This kind of demonstration reassures students that they will be approaching your assignment in a manner that is consistent with your expectations.

■   ■   ■

What should you consider when you are planning to present new information to a group of students? How would you apply the direct instruction approach when using media to present new material to a class? How does teacher creativity enter into planning?

Recognizing Key Points

When you introduce new material, students may experience problems that run counter to your expectations. If you find that they have trouble responding to questions you ask during the lesson, it is easy to conclude that they have not been exposed to sufficient

"Class, I've got a lot of material to cover, so to save time I won't be using vowels today. Nw lts bgn, pls pn t pg 122."

new information. This doesn't happen often. Students are more likely to suffer from what we call temporary information overload. The new information may have come at them faster than they have been able to absorb it. Actions you take to help them recognize key points can help them overcome this problem.

Use of *internal summaries* and *marker expressions* can help students identify aspects of new content that are important. When you use internal summaries, you break the flow of presentation of new content to briefly recapitulate what you have introduced so far. This allows you an opportunity to underscore for students the key ideas you have introduced that you particularly want them to master. You can also use marker expressions. These are phrases you use to draw the attention of your students to key points. Some examples of marker expressions include:

- "Write this down."
- "Pay attention to this point. It's important."
- "I want you to remember this."

Applying New Information

Practice promotes permanence of learning. You need to give your students sufficient experience in working with new content so their responses will become quick and automatic. For example, you can provide opportunities for them to "do something" with newly introduced content during the latter part of a lesson.

To gain the maximum benefit from providing students with opportunities to work with new information, you have to actively monitor them during this phase of instruction. It is important to move through the room to ensure that your students are engaging lesson content. You need to be easily accessible. You want students to feel free to ask you any questions they have about the new information with which they are working. Applying new information facilitates learning only when your students have a good grasp of the information they will be asked to use. If they do not, the practice activity can reinforce mistaken impressions and can be a barrier to appropriate learning.

Your students need to experience a high degree of success as they apply new information. To optimize their learning, researchers have found that students should respond to questions and perform other guided practice activities with about 80 percent accuracy before teachers introduce additional new information (Rosenshine & Stevens, 1986).

■ ■ ■

What are the purposes of actions you might take during the "applying new information" phase of a lesson? Why is a high rate of student success during this part of a lesson considered to be important? What are some things you might do to maximize students' learning when they are applying content you have just introduced?

Assessing New Learning

Actions you take during this phase of the instructional process give you information you can use in deciding whether to move forward with new content or to reteach and reinforce what you have already introduced. Assessing new learning may initially sound like nothing more than a recommendation to give students a test at the end of a lesson. While such assessments are important, your obligation to assess new learning requires you to check for student understanding after each part of your introduction of new information. Actions you take to assure that students are grasping what you are teaching give you confidence that students *do* understand what you *think* they understand before you go on to introduce additional material. You have several options when you consider actions to take to assess new learning.

One approach you can take is to ask students questions about what has been covered and to think carefully about the nature of their responses. When you do this, it is important to sample answers from a broad range of students. This practice will give you good ideas regarding (1) how individual students are grasping the material, and (2) how the class, as a group, seems to be mastering the material.

One of your obligations during this phase of a lesson is to provide feedback to students and correct their mistakes. This is what is termed *inferential diagnosis*, which means that you make diagnostic inferences based on your students' responses. As you work with individual members of your class, you need to ask yourself: "What does this response tell me this student is understanding and thinking?" The inferences you make in response to this question inform instructional decisions you will make about what kind of feedback you should provide or what actions you need to take to correct a student's mistakes.

This teacher assists students who are working on an assignment that requires them to apply new information that they have learned.

Your feedback and corrective options are varied. What you do should be in reaction to the kinds of responses you are getting from your students. Rosenshine and Stevens (1986) have identified these categories of student responses:

- A correct and quick student response,
- A correct but hesitant student response,
- An incorrect student response due to carelessness, and
- An incorrect student response due to lack of knowledge or skill

A Correct and Quick Student Response
If you get this kind of a student response, you should take it as a signal that students have properly understood the material. Your reaction should be aimed at keeping the lesson moving along at a brisk pace. Ordinarily, a brief comment to students affirming the appropriateness of their answers will suffice. What you do should take place quickly so your actions do not interrupt the momentum of the lesson.

A Correct but Hesitant Student Response
In some situations you will get student response that is correct, but that comes so slowly and hesitantly that you will suspect the person has doubts about the accuracy of what he or she is saying. Your response should be directed at removing the student's uncertainty. For example, you might affirm the accuracy of the student's answer and

briefly review reasons the response is correct. All of this must be accomplished relatively quickly so you can maintain the basic flow and pace of the lesson.

An Incorrect Student Response Due to Carelessness
Over time you will develop a feel for when a student's mistake is simply a careless slip and not evidence of misunderstanding. Asking a student to explain his or her answer often will reveal whether the mistake resulted from a lack of understanding or from carelessness. A quick comment or two from you before formal instruction resumes ordinarily will be enough to help the student who has made this kind of error.

An Incorrect Student Response Due to Lack of Knowledge or Skill
When a student mistake clearly reflects a lack of understanding, you need to do some reteaching. If only a few students are having difficulty, you may be able to continue with the rest of the lesson content, make assignments to the entire group, and call together students having difficulty and reteach them the aspects of content they are finding difficult to understand. Sometimes you may want to put students who have mastered the content to work as peer tutors to work with those individuals who are having difficulty grasping it. Peer tutoring works well so long as you and members of the class have confidence in the abilities of the students selected to work as tutors. Use of student tutors allows you to monitor the work of others in the class while the tutors provide assistance to students who need some additional help mastering basic information that most class members have already learned.

■ ■

What purposes are served by actions you take during the "assessing new learning" phase of the instructional process? What is the relationship between the assessment process and instructional actions you take once you have gathered and thought about information related to students' understanding of material you have introduced? What are some approaches to assessing new learning that you might use in teaching your own subject?

Implementing Direct Learning

The individual components of direct-instruction models can help you when you plan for instruction. However, there are other dimensions of teaching that need to be applied that can make your use of direct instruction more efficient. Some additional variables you should consider include:

- Teaching at the appropriate level of difficulty,
- Conducting appropriate task analyses,
- Attending to lesson closure, and
- Conducting periodic reviews.

Teaching at the Appropriate Level of Difficulty

It is obvious that for your teaching to be effective it must be at a level that is not too easy nor too difficult for the students. Something that is too difficult for them will go over their heads. Material that is too easy will bore them.

The issue of teaching at an appropriate level of difficulty has grown in importance in recent years with the increased diversity of students in classrooms. Many students in secondary schools come from homes where the primary language is not English. In addition, many students reach secondary schools without the necessary prerequisites for success. It is no longer reasonable to assume that students at a given grade level come to school with the prerequisites they will need to complete instructional tasks successfully. The movement toward full inclusion of students in regular classrooms who, in the past, would have spent their school years in special education classrooms, further emphasizes the importance of teaching at the appropriate level of difficulty.

Teaching at the appropriate level of difficulty is not easy. It requires that you constantly diagnose the ability levels of your students. This means that careful analysis of students' present levels of knowledge and general interests should be an integral part of your instructional planning. As you consider what you want students to learn, you need information about what individuals in your class may already know or be able to do. This information enables you to begin the instructional sequence at an appropriate entry point. It also helps you decide what approaches to take in introducing material and in involving students in meaningful applications of the new content.

Analyses you perform as part of your planning process may be formal, informal, or both. Sometimes you may wish to administer formal pretests to determine students' entry-level understanding. On other occasions, you may find that a review of students' previous work is sufficient. Of course, after you have worked with a class for a while, you will be able to make inferences about what individuals know and do not know simply by observing their daily performance in class.

Teaching at the appropriate level of difficulty requires you to look at student work not just as a means of assigning a grade but as a source of useful diagnostic data. This information can help you decide what to teach next and how you might introduce new material. A diagnostic mind-set will lead you to regard performance of students that is below your level of expectations as an opportunity for analysis and reflection. The result of this kind of thinking can help you design new instructional approaches with potential to respond more effectively to students' needs.

Conducting Appropriate Task Analyses

Teaching to the correct level of difficulty and performing sound diagnosis is facilitated by *task analysis*. Task analysis is the breaking down of complex learning into smaller components and then sequencing those components in a logical manner. Hunter (1994) identifies task analysis as an essential component of all instructional planning. Task analysis can help you deal with the special needs of diverse learners. For example, when you are teaching students with a primary language other than English you may have to begin at a different place than when you work with students who are native speakers of English.

To illustrate how you might use task analysis, consider this example. Suppose you were teaching English and wanted your students to learn how to write a three-paragraph essay. The purpose of your task analysis would be to find out what basic information students already have that will enable them to complete this assignment successfully. You might decide that the proposed activity assumes that: (1) students understand what a paragraph is, (2) they understand how to punctuate sentences correctly, and (3) they will be able to deal adequately with the proposed subject you want them to write about in an essay that is just three-paragraphs long.

If you determined that students were deficient in any of these areas, you would want to spend time teaching whatever might be needed to fill in any identified knowledge gaps. Additional thought about students' levels of understanding might also lead you to identify places where it would be wise to pause and check for understanding once you began teaching the new material.

Attending to Lesson Closure

Another important support for the direct instruction model is something called *lesson closure*. Lesson closures refers to a lesson's culminating activity or conclusion. It requires you to do more than simply inform your students that it is time to stop or that the lesson is over.

During lesson closure, you help students draw together the pieces of what they have learned so that they can make sense out of what they have been doing. Actions you take at this time help students organize what they have learned. They also allow you to re-emphasize the major points of the lesson. The thinking students do during lesson closure enhances their levels of comprehension and helps ensure that they process new information so it can be moved into long-term memory (Shostak, 1994).

Conducting Periodic Reviews

It is important for you to provide periodic reviews when you teach direct-instruction lessons. These allow you to help students recall critical aspects of new content that you have introduced. You should schedule regular times for periodic-review activities. For example, you might choose to set aside the first few minutes of class periods on Mondays to review what was learned the previous week. Such periodic reviews reinforce learning and help students maintain levels of expertise. They also help your students see that they are making progress. This kind of evidence enhances their self-images by allowing them time to reflect on their academic accomplishments.

■   ■   ■

Review what you have read about some important instructional actions that you can take to make your direct-instruction lessons more effective. What are the purposes of these actions? Think about a particular lesson you might teach. Specifically, what might you do to make sure you will be teaching the appropriate level of difficulty? What kinds of task analyses might you perform? How would you attend to the need to provide for lesson closure? How would you accommodate the need to provide periodic reviews?

Reflecting on Direct Instruction

Direct instruction has several advantages. Because lessons are presented to the class as a whole, planning is simplified. One lesson plan suffices for the entire group; hence, planning time is less than when you must develop alternative plans for individuals or small groups. (Of course, this single lesson plan may have several tracks or options that allow you to differentiate what you do to meet needs of inclusion students, students who are non-native speakers of English, and other students with special learning requirements.) Direct instruction puts you in a controlling position.

Direct instruction's focus on transmitting important elements of teacher-selected content allows you to prepare students well for tests. This is viewed as a particular advantage in schools and districts where there are pressures for students to achieve high scores on standardized achievement tests. (For more information about standardized tests in the schools, see Chapter 12, "Assessing Student Learning.") Researchers have found that students score well on achievement tests when they have been exposed to direct instruction in their classrooms. Direct instruction seems to increase the amount of student engagement with the kind of content that is featured on tests (Good & Brophy, 2000; Rosenshine & Stevens, 1986).

In a more general sense, direct instruction has been found to be effective when students are asked to master a well-defined body of content or a skill that can be broken down into parts and taught one step at a time (Rosenshine & Stevens, 1986). Basic skills instruction of all kinds is facilitated by direct instruction (Savage, 1989). These studies suggest that direct instruction makes sense when teachers are interested in providing students with basic information they will need as a prerequisite to engaging in complex higher level thinking and problem-solving activities.

There are also negatives associated with direct instruction. For example, it tends to work best when your intent is to transmit specific content items to students. Direct instruction may be less effective when you seek to develop students' abilities to reflect on complex problems and develop solutions of their own. Successful direct instruction also requires you to have excellent presentation skills. You must be well organized, able to identify an appropriate pace, and quick to gauge levels of student interest and adapt instruction, as needed, to maintain students' attention.

 WHAT DO *YOU* THINK?

Appropriate Uses of Direct Instruction

No single instructional approach is best for promoting the wide range of learning outcomes expected in the schools. The direct instructional model is more appropriate for some than for others.

It is more appropriate for the content that can readily be divided into parts, teaching basic skills, teaching students with an external locus of control, introductory material, and a prescribed body of content. It is less appropriate for content for which constituent parts are difficult to define, teaching higher-level thinking, teaching students with an internal locus of control, affective outcomes, and learning demanding creative thinking.

Questions

1. Why do you think direct instruction is less appropriate for some students and some outcomes?

2. What are some specific outcomes in your teaching areas for which direct instruction would be most appropriate?

3. What parts of the direct instruction model (and supplements to it introduced in this chapter) do you feel will be easiest for you to master? Most difficult? What might you do to prepare yourself better to do a good job with those components that, at this point, seem most troublesome to you?

Because so much content can be disseminated in a relatively short period of time during a direct-instruction lesson, if you fail to pay attention to students' reactions you may overwhelm them with too much information. This can lead to high levels of frustration and undermine students' confidence. When this happens, both their motivation and achievement levels may decline.

■ ■ ■

At this point, stop and take a minute to write your own brief definition of direct instruction. Compare your version with that of another person in your class who is also reading this chapter. How are they alike? How are they different? What questions do you have about implementing direct instruction?

Direct Instruction and Student Characteristics

Direct instruction has been found to be particularly effective with younger students, students who are having academic difficulty, and students who are in the introductory phases of learning a specific body of content (Rosenshine & Stevens, 1986). Direct instruction works well with students from lower socioeconomic backgrounds and with those who have an *external locus of control* (Savage, 1989). (Students with an external locus of control tend to attribute their successes and failures in school to chance factors or to factors they perceive as being beyond their personal ability to control.)

Approaches other than direct instruction seem to be more effective with high-achieving, task-oriented students who have an *internal locus of control*. (Students with an internal locus of control perceive school failures and successes to be directly connected to their own, controllable behaviors.) These students seem to benefit from instructional approaches that give them more choices in the classroom and that feature an instructional pace that is less subject to direct teacher control.

■ ■ ■

In summary, what questions do you have about general characteristics of direct instruction? Write down your questions and share them with several others. Present a master list of questions from your group to your instructor, and ask your instructor to react to them.

This Chapter as an Example of Direct Instruction

We attempted to use some elements of direct instruction in organizing content in this chapter. The direct instruction approach calls on instructors to provide students with information about learning intentions or objectives as well as with an overview and structure for the new learning. We began this chapter with a list of chapter purposes. That is followed by a formal introduction to the content. (This same approach is followed throughout the text.)

Direct-instruction lessons break content into small pieces or steps. Content in this chapter is broken down into major sections as well as subordinate subsections. At the end of many of these chapter divisions, we checked for understanding by asking you to reflect on what you had read by responding to questions, summarizing the content, checking your reactions with someone else, or generating questions of your own.

Direct-instruction lessons often feature examples, illustrations, or models. Illustrations are provided at various points throughout this chapter, and the general layout of the chapter is consistent with a direct instruction format.

Authors of a text are not really in a position to see that guided practice takes place (because we are not with you in the classroom, we cannot listen to you, watch what you do, and react to your comments in person). However, it is hoped that some of the practice activities scattered throughout the chapter as well as those at the end will allow your instructor to monitor your progress as you engage in various guided-practice activities.

FOR YOUR PORTFOLIO

1. What materials, ideas you learned in this chapter related to *direct instruction* will you include as "evidence" in your portfolio? Select up to 3 items of information to be included. Number them 1, 2, and 3.

2. Think about why you selected these materials for your portfolio. Consider such issues as the following in your response:

   ■ The specific purposes to which this information can be put when you plan, deliver, and assess the impact of your instruction,

   ■ The compatibility of the information with your own priorities and values,

   ■ The contributions this information can make to your personal development as a teacher, and

- The factors that led you to include this material as opposed to some alternatives you considered.

3. Prepare a written reflection in which you analyze the decision-making process you followed. Also, mention the INTASC Standard(s) to which your selected material relates. (First complete the chart below.)

Materials You Selected and the INTASC Standards

Put a check under those INTASC Standards numbers to which the evidence you have selected applies. (Refer to Chapter 1 for more detailed information about INTASC.)

Item of Evidence Number	INTASC Standards									
	S1	S2	S3	S4	S5	S6	S7	S8	S9	S10
1										
2										
3										

Some of the end-of-the chapter activities are designed to provide you opportunities for independent practice. They call on you to apply what you have learned and to extend your understandings of the material. Ideally, an independent practice experience related to direct instruction would be for you to prepare and deliver a direct instruction lesson to a group of students.

To summarize, we hope the way we have introduced direct instruction in this chapter has helped you to grow in your understanding of this approach. Its success is something you will have to evaluate for yourself. If you feel more comfortable about your knowledge of the essentials of a direct instruction lesson and have confidence in your ability to design and deliver this kind of instruction, we will have met our own aims. We hope you think we have succeeded.

Key Ideas in Summary

- There is no one best method for teaching. Various approaches are appropriate for helping students master different kinds of objectives. For some purposes, direct instruction has proved to be a desirable way to organize and deliver instruction.
- Direct instruction is a teacher-centered approach in which the teacher controls selection and delivery of content, mode of presentation of content, pace of lesson development, and patterns of classroom interaction. Continuous monitoring throughout the lesson ensures student understanding. The focus is on transmission of academic content. Instruction is provided to the class as a whole, not to individual groups of stu-

dents. Complex content is broken down into parts, and each part is introduced sequentially, one step at a time. The teacher takes pains to ensure that students grasp information associated with one step before going on to the next.

■ The underlying principles that support the direct instructional model are taken from information processing theory and research. Among these principles are (1) an individual can only process a limited amount of information at one time, (2) prior knowledge influences how a person processes new information, (3) information must be transferred from short-term to long-term memory for retention to occur, and (4) overlearning through rehearsal or practice is necessary to facilitate comprehension of future information.

■ A number of direct-instruction models are available, including those developed by Hunter and Russell (1977), Denton, Armstrong and Savage (1980), and Slavin (1994). These models present components that should be included in complete direct-instruction lessons.

■ In addition to accommodating components enumerated in formal direct-instruction models, there are other things teachers can do to increase the probability their students will learn. They can also take actions related to (1) teaching to an appropriate level of difficulty, (2) task analysis, (3) lesson closure, and (4) periodic reviews of newly presented information.

■ There are claimed advantages of direct instruction. Because the teacher works with the whole class, planning is somewhat simplified. Planning assumes that all students will be exposed to basically the same instruction. The teacher is very much in a central, controlling position during direct instruction lessons. Direct instruction allows for a clear focus on specific academic content. Some people feel the approach functions well as a means of preparing students for standardized tests.

■ Some criticisms of direct instruction have been made. Although the approach has merit as a way to help students recall specific information, it is less effective in helping students develop higher-level thinking skills that require them to reflect on complex issues and generate solutions of their own. Some teachers, too, lack the ability to diagnose needs of their students and student reactions as instruction is being delivered. This is a particular problem when direct instruction is being used. Because it is so teacher centered, an unaware teacher can overwhelm students with content and undermine their interest in what is being taught.

■ Direct instruction is more appropriate for meeting some kinds of instructional objectives than others. It works best when the content to be covered lends itself to be broken down into small parts that can be presented in sequential steps. Researchers have found that direct instruction works particularly well when the intent has been to teach skills. However, it has been found less appropriate when lesson objectives call on students to engage in higher level thinking and problem-solving activities. It also is not a favored approach when instructional plans are guided by affective objectives.

■ Some kinds of students seem to profit more from direct instruction than others. It has been found especially effective with younger students, students who are having academic difficulty, and students who are just beginning to work with a new content area. Studies have found that direct instruction lessons often are effective in working with students who have an external locus of control.

Reflections

1. What are some reasons for the popularity of direct instruction?
2. What are some basic characteristics of direct instruction?
3. What advantages and disadvantages have been claimed for direct instruction?
4. What is meant by the statement "direct instruction lessons feature a strong academic focus"?
5. How would you explain the phrase *controlled classroom practice*?
6. For what kinds of learning outcomes does direct instruction seem most appropriate?
7. What elements would you expect to see in a complete direct instruction lesson?
8. Some people argue that direct instruction is rigid, cold, and likely to create negative student attitudes. How do you react to this contention?
9. How would you feel if an administrator told you that he expected you to be using a direct instruction approach every day?
10. What problems, if any, do you envision as you think about implementing direct instruction in your own teaching?

Learning Extensions

1. Review your content field. Identify three or four topics that might be appropriately delivered using a direct instruction approach. For each topic, identify a series of parts or steps you would use in presenting information to students. Share your ideas with your instructor, and ask for a critique of your work.
2. Take time to look over parts of one of the direct-instruction models introduced in this chapter. Observe a teacher in a secondary school who is using a direct instruction approach to introduce information. To what extent did you find each of the elements of a formal direct-instruction model being used? Write up your findings in the form of a brief report, and submit it to your instructor.
3. Organize a debate on this topic: "Resolved that too much direct instruction occurs in today's secondary schools." Hold the debate during a regular class session. When it is over, engage the entire class in a discussion of this issue.
4. With assistance from your instructor, identify some summaries of what researchers have found about the effectiveness of direct instruction. Prepare a short oral report for class members in which you summarize what researchers have found.
5. For a topic in your own subject area, prepare a complete lesson plan based on direct instruction. Share it with others in your class, and ask them to suggest places your plan might be improved. You might also solicit reactions from your instructor.
6. Go to the Merrill Education's Link to General Methods Resources site at this URL: http://www.prenhall.com/methods-cluster/ At the bottom of the page select

"instructional strategies" as your topic and click the "begin" button. This will take you to the "Overview" page. On the left side, click on "Web Links." On the Web Links page click on "motivation." Follow links to gather information you can use as a basis for an oral report to your class that focuses on approaches to motivating secondary school students.

References

Borich, G. (1992). *Effective teaching methods* (2nd ed.). Upper Saddle River, NJ: Merrill/Prentice Hall.

Denton, J. J., Armstrong, D. G., & Savage, T. V. (1980). Matching events of instruction to objectives. *Theory into Practice, 19*(1), 10–14.

Good, T., & Brophy, J. (2000). *Looking in classrooms* (8th ed.). New York: Longman.

Hunter, M. (1994). *Enhancing teaching.* New York: Macmillan.

Hunter, M., & Russell, D. (1977). How can I plan more effective teaching lessons? *Instructor, 87*(2), 74–75; 88.

Rosenshine, B. (1987). Direct instruction. In M. Dunkin (Ed.), *The international encyclopedia of teaching and teacher education* (pp. 257–262). New York: Pergamon Press.

Rosenshine, B., & Stevens, R. (1986). Teaching functions. In M. Wittrock (Ed.), *Handbook of research on teaching* (3rd ed.) (pp. 376–391). New York: Macmillan.

Savage, M. K. (1989). The impact of different instructional models on teacher performance scores as measured by the Texas teacher appraisal system. College Station, TX: Unpublished doctoral dissertation.

Shostak, R. (1994). Lesson presentation skills. In J. Cooper (Ed.), *Classroom teaching skills* (pp. 90–113). Lexington, MA: D. C. Heath.

Slavin, R. (1994). *Educational psychology: Theory and practice* (4th ed.). Boston: Allyn & Bacon.

Slavin, R. E. (1999). *Educational psychology: Theory and practice* (6th ed.). Boston: Allyn & Bacon.

Stallings, J., & Kaskowitz, D. (1974). *Follow-through classroom observation evaluation, 1972–1973.* Menlo Park, CA: Stanford Research Institute.

9

Small-Group and Cooperative Learning

This chapter will aim to

- describe a rationale for using small-group learning;

- identify conditions that facilitate small-group learning;

- define *competitive, individualistic* and *cooperative goal structures;*

- describe some techniques you can use to prepare students for small-group learning;

- point out some examples of popular small-group learning techniques;

- identify features that distinguish *cooperative learning* from other small-group approaches; and

- explain purposes and procedures associated with several cooperative-learning techniques.

Introduction

Consider these points: (1) young people in secondary schools love to socialize and (2) learning is primarily a social act (Putnam, 1997). In planning your instruction, you can take advantage of these two principles to organize effective lessons that require your students to work in small groups in ways that encourage mutually supportive cooperative patterns of behavior. This kind of instruction promotes learning by providing a context for students to learn as they watch, listen, talk to, and support others.

There is evidence that teaching oriented in this way facilitates student achievement (King, 1999). Why is this so? One explanation is that student motivation increases when students are allowed to work with each other and when there are group goals and rewards rather than individual goals and rewards. Another explanation is that, through interaction with others, students find they are better able to clarify, reflect, reformulate, and elaborate on material more effectively than when they work alone. This intensive engagement with new content promotes development of the kinds of cognitive changes that are necessary for learning to occur. Further, many small-group and cooperative learning techniques feature *modeling.*

Modeling involves actions taken by the teacher or, occasionally, someone else who seeks to provide learners with examples or demonstrations of competencies associated with a lesson. For example, when modeling approaches are used in small-group and cooperative-learning lessons, students often gain tremendously in terms of their ability to apply problem-solving skills effectively as they wrestle with challenging situations and issues (King, 1999).

There is also evidence that small-group learning approaches can help you and your students develop a positive working relationship. Lessons organized in this way give

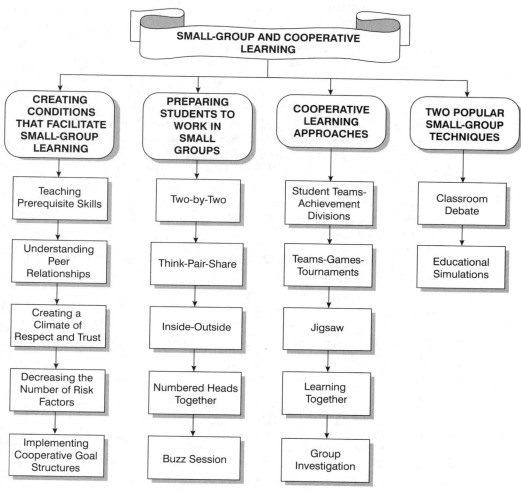

Figure 9–1
Graphic Organizer

you and your students opportunities to work together more personally than when you are teaching a more traditional lesson to an entire class of students. Because this kind of instruction keeps you closely involved with individuals, you ordinarily are able to spot and respond quickly to difficulties that particular students might be having. Any assistance you provide to promote students' success adds to their sense of self-confidence and tends to promote favorable feelings toward you and your teaching.

Learning occurs when students become active participants in lessons. In traditional large group instruction, some individuals in your classes simply do not get very involved. In a group discussion, there will be some students who rarely speak up, either because they are shy or for other reasons. Small-group learning lessons provide contexts that encourage all students to become actively engaged in lessons. The increased student-to-student and student-to-teacher interactions these instructional experiences provide help develop students' oral-language proficiencies, increase the probability they will acquire new content, and add to their sense of personal competence.

You may face potential difficulties when you begin using small-group approaches with a new group of students. For example, they may not know how to work together productively in small groups. If this happens, you may find individuals arguing about what they should do or abandoning academically related work in favor of a spirited social chat. You also may find that a few individuals in small groups may be inclined to sit back and let others do the work. Finally, it is possible you will encounter some students who simply do not like small group work. It may be that these students have always experienced high levels of academic success when they have been involved in classes featuring traditional large-group instruction. It could be, too, that they have had unfortunate experiences on previous occasions when they have been involved in poorly structured small-group lessons.

To remedy these problems, you need to know your students well, diagnose what obstacles may be standing in the way of their commitment to small-group learning approaches, and develop a response that seems appropriate for individual members of your class. In general, the best remedy is to plan small-group lessons carefully. If you do, you will greatly increase the probability that students will enjoy their experiences and look forward to occasions when you ask them to work in small groups. In this chapter, you will find information about some things you can do to create conditions that will facilitate small-group work and some examples of small-group learning techniques that many secondary school teachers have used successfully.

Creating Conditions That Facilitate Small-Group Learning

As is true of all instructional techniques, small-group learning operates within the context of the individual classroom. Some classroom characteristics are more compatible with certain instructional techniques than others. For example, you are likely to have more initial success with small-group learning if your students have some knowledge about how to work productively in this type of instructional setting.

One of the most important requisite conditions is that your students understand the purposes of the activity and what they are going to learn from it. You want to point out the specific personal benefits that they can derive from their participation in small-group lessons. For example, you might explain that a major reason people are dismissed from jobs is because they cannot work productively with others. You can let students know that, in addition to learning new content in a pleasing way, their involvement in small group learning will add to their level of comfort in working in close proximity with others who may have personalities and perspectives quite different from their own.

Many teachers who have not used small-group learning techniques express concerns that some students they put into groups will not work productively in this type of instructional setting (Joyce & Weil, 1996). To be sure, if a group task is poorly structured, the purposes of the activity are unclear, and there is little individual or group accountability, then group learning approaches are likely to be ineffective. However, the reality is that most of your students will have no problem working well together if you provide them with an appropriate orientation. This implies a need to give them clear guidelines regarding what they are to do and what the expected outcome of the lesson should be (Joyce & Weil, 1996). You will find it particularly helpful to require group members to produce some kind of tangible "product of learning" at the end of the lesson. This will provide both you and your students with tangible evidence that something worthwhile has been accomplished.

Teaching Prerequisite Skills

It makes sense for you to provide students with some initial instruction that focuses on specific skills that will help them work together. These skills involve such things as active listening, giving clear explanations, resolving conflicts, avoiding put-downs, and asking for clarification (Slavin, 1994). Your students should have little difficulty mastering these competencies. During initial small-group learning lessons, you might give students opportunities to practice them by organizing members of the class into groups of two or three students and assigning each group to perform simple tasks. As students become more comfortable with these skills, then you can start assigning them to larger groups of up to about six people (Joyce & Weil, 1996).

Understanding Peer Relationships

How well your students know one another, the norms of their peer group, the feelings individuals have about how well others in the group accept them, their general levels of interest in your subject, and how students in the group assess their relative chances of succeeding in your class help shape the general character of every student you will teach. As you prepare for a career in secondary education, you might want to see these variables in action. To do so, make arrangements to visit a secondary school classroom and follow a few students as they pass from class to class throughout the school day. Don't be surprised if you observe that students who are uncooperative in one class demonstrate completely different behaviors in another. The special dynamics of the group and the psychological climate created by the teacher often account for these differences.

All of this underscores the importance of taking time to learn something about your students every time you get a new group. What you find will vary somewhat depending on the particular setting of your school. For example, in small, rural secondary schools in areas where there is not much moving in and out of the area, students may know each other very well. However, this does not necessarily guarantee they will all get along well in your classes. If past relationships have not been positive, this interpersonal relationship history may carry forward year after year. Over the years, some of your students may have been labeled in ways that diminish their expectations of success and otherwise introduce tensions into the overall classroom-learning environment.

If you find yourself teaching in a large urban school, you may find that only a few students in your classes know each other before the school year begins. Initially, this can inhibit their willingness to participate actively in classroom discussions. You may need to take action to make class members comfortable with one another and more willing to become active participants in classroom activities. In particular, you will want to identify and help students who seem to be generally isolated from others in the class and who are particularly reluctant to become fully engaged in assigned activities that require students to work together.

Creating a Climate of Respect and Trust

Productive group work demands mutual respect and trust. If your students do not respect one another, they will have difficulty accepting the contributions of all members of the class. Under such conditions, your efforts to promote cooperative learning may well fall short of their goal, and students may develop antagonistic attitudes. This is especially likely to happen if some of them feel they are being asked to do more than their share of the work. If you suspect that some students are concerned about this issue, you need to take action to assure that each student is carrying part of the load.

In addition to working to distribute the workload equitably, you also need to help students involved in small-group work develop attitudes of mutual respect. This will not happen simply by telling students that this is your expectation. Respect has to be earned. What you can do is assign individuals to complete tasks for which they have a particular aptitude. When they complete these tasks successfully, others in the group see clear evidence of their contributions. This, in turn, leads others to respect and appreciate their value as group members.

Decreasing the Number of Risk Factors

One of the greatest risk factors for students is their fear of failure. In order for individuals to cooperate, they must feel that they are in a safe environment. This requires you to take action to lower the risks of participation and active involvement. For small-group learning lessons to be effective, your students have to believe that working together will enhance their opportunities for success. Sometimes academically talented students fear that working in small groups puts them at risk. They may be convinced that they can do better work working alone rather than as members of a small group that has collective responsibility for a task. If you are confronted with this situation, you must assure these students that there will be real benefits for them as a result of their participation in small-group lessons.

Many of your students are also likely to be concerned about the issue of grading. Some students fear any approach that alters the way grades are given. They often feel that a change will put them at a competitive disadvantage. When you introduce small-group learning, you have to take care to explain how students will be assessed and to make a case in support of the idea that the evaluation scheme will not increase the risk that they will receive bad grades.

WHAT DO *YOU* THINK?

"I Don't Need Their Help"

Suppose you are teaching a group of high school sophomores and receive this reaction from a student after you announce plans to involve class-members in a small-group learning exercise that will require them to work closely together and to assist one another to master the new content.

> "Why do we have to do this? I don't need help from these people. I work hard, and I get good grades. I know that when we start this small-group thing that I'll end up carrying the load for everybody. It just isn't fair."

Questions

1. How legitimate are the concerns of this student?
2. Is the student really distressed about the issue of fairness, or is something else a likely cause of this person's concern?
3. What would you say to this person in response to this statement?
4. Given the concerns raised by this student, what special directions might you give to members of the groups about their individual responsibilities?

Implementing Cooperative Goal Structures

The way you structure goals of small-group work can affect students' learning. The term *goal structure* refers to the way individuals relate to each other in accomplishing a particular goal (Woolfolk, 1995). There are three basic types of goal structure. Each requires a different relationship between an individual and the group. The three types are as follows:

- competitive goal structure,
- individualistic goal structure, and
- cooperative goal structure.

Competitive Goal Structure

In a competitive goal structure, students are placed in competition with each other. This means that the only way an individual student can succeed is by beating or finishing ahead of others. Ranking students according to their scores on tests and grading on the curve are two examples of how competitive goal structures have often been implemented in the classroom. Goals of this variety traditionally have been more common in secondary school learning programs than either of the other two basic types.

One of the reasons that competitive goal structures have been dominant is the belief that competition has motivational value and leads to higher achievement. Today, critics of this approach reject this claim. They point out that grades in a competitive-goal-structure environment tend to be based on tests that measure a narrow range of abilities. These tests tend to favor students with specific abilities over students who may have strengths in other areas. By the time many students who have been in classes featuring competitive goal structures reach the secondary level, they have given up. They do not believe that they have a real chance to surpass other students. For these students, competition is not motivating; rather, it is discouraging.

To illustrate this point, suppose that grades were based on a narrow range of ability, such as being able to run a mile in under five minutes. There would be some students who would see this as possible, and they would be motivated to accomplish this goal. However, there would be many others who would despair of their ability to reach this goal. They would simply drop out. An inappropriate application of competitive goal structures leads some students to commit to the idea that the "cards are stacked" against them. They may refuse to play the game entirely. When this happens, there is an increased probability that their attitudes will take a turn for the worse and that they will develop unproductive patterns of classroom behavior.

Competitive goal structures can have a negative influence on several other conditions necessary for cooperation in the classroom. For example, if class leaders are not in the academically talented group (e.g., the group of students who have traditionally done well on tests), other students in your class may conclude that academic success is not important. They may choose to identify, instead, with the class leaders whose interests and abilities are not connected to what you are trying to accomplish at school. This situation does not comport well with your objective of establishing a congruence between the enthusiasms of class leaders and the objectives of your academic program.

Individualistic Goal Structure

Individualistic goals structures do not require students to perform at better levels than others. In this arrangement, attaining success is purely an individual endeavor that is unrelated to the efforts of others. An individual performance standard for each student is set. You judge an individual student based on how well he or she does relative to this standard, not relative to the performance of someone else.

Although individualistic goal structures can lead to programs that build students' self esteem, there are also negatives associated with this approach. Though they decrease risk factors associated with competition, they do little to increase group cohesion or acceptance of others. They also overlook the fact that your students will not live their lives as isolated individuals; instead, they will be part of an interdependent culture. Individualized goal structures ignore the human need for belonging and socialization.

Cooperative Goal Structure

To achieve success in classes featuring cooperative goal structures, your students have to know how to work productively together. The cooperative goal structure recognizes that different individuals have unique skills and abilities. When these are joined together, greater accomplishments are possible. For example, the success of an orchestra, a choir, or an athletic team requires individuals with different abilities to work together to achieve a goal. In fact, the goals of these groups cannot be achieved by any one person. In a cooperative setting, risk factors often are reduced. This is true because others involved in the common effort become resources who share in the risks associated with the task of accomplishing a prescribed goal.

Cooperative goal structures in the classroom respond well to the interpersonal dimension of learning. They help your students recognize that they can learn from each other. They also capitalize on peer influences and the interests of students in working together. Many students find cooperative goal structures to be motivating.

Preparing Students to Work in Small Groups

There are simple techniques you can use to help students develop their abilities to function well in small-group learning situations. Committing some class time to this kind of preparation will enhance the likelihood your students will derive important benefits from lessons featuring this organizational pattern.

Two-by-Two

You can use an approach called *two-by-two* to break the ice with a new group of students. You begin by asking each student to find out something specific about one other person in the class. Once this has been done, ask students to join together to form groups of four. Tell students in each group that their task is to remember information about all four group members. Give them a little time to do this, and then ask individuals in each group to stop and tell what they can remember about each person. Follow the same general procedure as you go on to organize the groups of four into groups of eight, and then the groups of eight into groups of 16.

You will be amazed at how many students will be able to remember information about nearly every group member, even at the stage where groups feature 16 students each. This activity helps student become more comfortable with each other. When you later organize them into small groups for academic work, they will be comfortable in engaging in the intense person-to-person interaction that small-group lessons feature.

Think-Pair-Share

Think-pair-share is a technique that you can use to introduce small-group learning by beginning with a focus on dialogue between two students. You begin this approach by giving members of your class a question or problem to consider. In the first phase, each student thinks individually about the focus issue you have selected. Next, you ask students to work in pairs for the purpose of sharing their responses to the question or the problem. You follow this step by asking each pair of students to share their responses with the entire class.

Think-pair-share helps students learn how to discuss and share their ideas with others and to understand that "two heads are better than one." To enhance the probability that this approach will be effective, you want to select a focus question or problem that will be of interest to a large number of your students. To ensure that no student will feel in any way diminished at the end of the exercise because of a position he or she has taken, the question or problem you select should be one where there is no single "correct" or "right" response. Your intent is to encourage a diversity of answers and respect for a diversity of opinions. Think-pair-share can help students recognize that (1) it is possible to develop many reasonable responses to complex problems, (2) individuals of integrity may take different positions on these issues, and (3) a willingness to think, consider, and sometimes compromise are characteristics that contribute to the successful functioning of small groups.

Inside-Outside

Inside-outside helps students develop skills that help them to be more productive as members of small groups. In this approach, you organize members into two circles. People in one circle are located inside a larger, surrounding outside circle. You assign the "outsiders" (members of the outside circle) to observe behaviors of "insiders" (members of the inside circle). Each "outsider" is given one "insider" to watch. At this point, you give the "insiders" a problem to discuss or a task to complete. Members of the "outsiders" observe how the "insiders" go about their assigned work. You allow this phase of the lesson to continue for 10 or 15 minutes.

Next, you ask students to reverse their positions. Members of the former "insider" group now become members of the "outsider" group, and members of the former "outsider" group become members of the "insider" group. Following the same procedure as before, you assign each person in the "outside" group to observe one person in the "inside" group. Next, you give the new group of "insiders" a task to complete. The "outsiders" observe the "insiders" as members of this group begin doing what you asked them to do.

After 10 or 15 minutes have passed, you bring the entire class together again as a group. You ask individuals to share what they observed their "insider" doing. Ask them to comment especially on those contributions that helped the whole group complete the assigned task. You might also conduct a general discussion of some kinds of behaviors of individuals that were not especially helpful to the entire group. The purpose of the exercise is to help students recognize and commit to kinds of behaviors that facilitate completion of small-group tasks.

Numbered Heads Together

You can use the *numbered-heads-together* approach to introduce students to the idea of group scoring and individual accountability. You begin by organizing members of the class into groups of about four students each. (You can vary this number slightly, if you wish to do so.) You give every student in each group a number ranging from 1 to 4. Next, you provide each group a question or a problem. You explain that the group must develop an answer and share it among group members in ways that will assure that every member of the group knows it. You give groups sufficient time to develop answers. At this point, you ask groups to stop. You announce one of the numbers you have assigned ("1," "2,", "3," or "4"). Students in each group with the number you have called out raise their hands. If the person you identify to respond knows the answer, all members in his or her group get a point (Kagan, 1989). (If the answer is incorrect, you can go on and call on another volunteer). You repeat this process several times. Members of the group with the most points are declared to be the winners.

Numbered-heads-together allows you to set up conditions that ensure that each student in every group will be involved. Further, there is an incentive for every person in the group who has information relevant to solving the problem or answering the question to share what he or she knows with all group members. In addition, the expectation that every group member will be able to respond correctly when called upon encourages students to listen carefully to what others in the group are saying. In summary, the technique promotes the development of student behaviors that characterize effective, contributing members of small groups.

Buzz Session

Another technique you can use to build effective small-group participation skills is the *buzz session*. You begin a buzz session by organizing members of your class into small groups. Each group is given a focus topic. You choose one student to be a recorder. You provide this person with a piece of chart paper with three columns. This heading is written at the top of the first column: "What we already know about the topic." This heading appears at the top of the second column: "What we would like to know about the topic." The heading at the top of the third column reads: "How we might go about finding out what we would like to know."

The buzz session begins by group members generating as much information as they can related to what they already know about the topic. (The recorder writes information under the appropriate column heading.) Next, the group goes on to develop some ideas related to what group members would like to know. (The recorder writes ideas that are generated in the second column.) The group goes on to consider how they might find out what they would like to know. (The recorder adds this information in the third column.)

The buzz-session technique helps students think about how they might get started on a group task. It also tends to make new tasks somewhat less intimidating as group members learn that some students may already know quite a bit about the assigned topic. Finally, this approach provides opportunities for students to think carefully about how they might proceed to get needed information. This kind of preplanning can add an important dimension of efficiency to their work once they actually go about the business of responding to the assigned task.

Two Popular Small-Group Techniques

Secondary teachers use many kinds of small-group techniques. In the subsections that follow, you will find two examples. *Classroom debates* and *educational simulations* can be used in a variety of subjects and at varying levels of sophistication depending on the subject taught and interests and abilities of individual students.

Classroom Debate

Classroom debates are organized differently than the familiar high school debating tournament. You can use them when teaching a variety of subjects, and you can adapt them to fit different time periods. Classroom debates feature two teams of students who prepare positions on different sides of an issue. You can structure these in various ways. Here is one format that many secondary teachers have found useful.
You take action to assign:

- three students to the pro position,
- three students to the con position, and
- one student to the role of critic.

You ask the three students on the pro side to gather as much information as possible that supports a proposal. You direct the students on the con side to gather as much evidence as possible to attack the position. You ask the critic to learn as much as possible about both sides of the issue and to ask questions toward the end of the debate that will highlight weaknesses of both positions. Each member of the team is expected to participate actively.

In preparation for the activity, select an issue that clearly has two sides. For example, if you are teaching English, you might choose an issue related to a selection of literature such as the consistency of actions taken by one or more of the main characters. If you are teaching a social studies class, your focus issue might center on a historic event or on actions of some historic figure. If you are teaching science, you might choose a topic related to a threat to the environment.

Once you have identified a topic, you need to gather as much support material as possible for the students to use as they prepare for the debate. You may need to allow several class periods for them to develop an adequate background on aspects of the topic that will be considered during the actual debate. You will need to do considerable monitoring during the preparation phase to assure that students are doing the necessary work to build the knowledge backgrounds they will need to make a credible case as they participate in the debate.

When the teams are ready, you can use a sequence such as the following. This example presumes that the debate will be completed during a single, 50-minute class period:

1. Each member of each team speaks for two minutes. Pro and con speakers alternate. Approximate time: 12 minutes
2. Members of the pro team cross-examine members of the con team for a team total not to exceed six minutes. The members of the con team cross-examine the pro team for a team total of not more than six minutes. Approximate time: 12 minutes
3. Members of each team make a final statement. The total time for each team is not to exceed three minutes. Approximate time: six minutes

4. The critic questions members of both teams. His or her questions are directed to the team as a whole or to individual team members. The critic's purpose is to ask probing questions that point out the weak spots of the arguments. Approximate time: 8 minutes.

5. The whole class votes to determine a winner. Approximate time: two minutes.

6. You debrief the whole class. Your comments should be as supportive as possible and should highlight the important issues. During the debriefing stage you might ask questions such as:

   ■ What were the best arguments you heard?
   ■ What made these arguments effective?
   ■ What other points would you have brought up?
   ■ What are some other questions the critic might have asked?

Classroom debates often generate high levels of student interest. They can help you teach students such important skills as cooperating, speaking in front of a group, mustering evidence to support a position, listening, and learning how to analyze and synthesize information.

Educational Simulations

The terms *games* and *simulations* are often used interchangeably. However, they do have somewhat different meanings. Games usually involve some sort of competition within a set of rules and where there is an element of chance. Simulations, on the other hand, are designed to place participants in situations that parallel reality. Simulations simplify reality in order to highlight important skills and ideas. They do not necessarily involve winners and losers. In some simulations, it is possible for everyone to accomplish their objectives. When you use a simulation, what you are trying to do is place your students in circumstances that give them experience in making decisions and, then, experiencing the consequences of these actions.

There are many educational simulations designed for use in secondary school classrooms. These range in sophistication from relatively simple board games that have an element of chance and involve game-like situations to complex computer-based activities that focus on such complex activities as building a city or simulating complex science experiments. Simulations featuring complicated designs and focusing on multiple variables often require several class periods to complete.

If you decide to use a simulation with your students, you must plan thoroughly. Your planning needs to focus on these four phases:

■ Overview
■ Training
■ Activity
■ Debriefing

Overview

During this phase, you introduce students to the simulation. You will explain the purpose of the simulation, and you will explain and assign students to specific roles. You will also point out rules associated with the simulation as well as any classroom rules that will be in force during the time the simulation activity is taking place.

Training

During the training phase, you essentially will involve your students in a "walk-through" of the processes they will follow when the simulation begins. If often works best to select a few class members, assign them a role and then illustrate how they will be involved once the simulation begins. You should invite students to ask questions that will help them to better understand what they are to do.

Following your introduction, you will want to give students time to review their roles. If the simulation involves different groups of students, you need to make arrangements for groups of students to meet and discuss their roles and plot their strategy.

Activity

The action component of a simulation takes place during this phase. During this time, you play the role of coach, referee, and discussant. At times, your students may lose sight of the purpose of the simulation, and you may need to stop the action and help students think about their decisions and refocus their attention on the purposes of the activity. Some students may not know how to respond to some developments. You can coach them as to their options and choices. As your students gain confidence in their roles, they will require much less of your help.

You will find that new and unexpected circumstances arise during simulations. For example, it is common for disputes to arise over situations that are not directly covered in the rules. You have to be ready to make some interpretations and decisions when

This teacher gives two boys in her class instructions about the roles they will be playing in an educational simulation.

problems of this kind develop. In general, you want to make rulings that are generally consistent with the overall purpose of the simulation activity.

Debriefing

A well-planned debriefing is essential to the overall success of a simulation. This is the phase of the activity where you can bring closure to some important new learning that has emerged as a result of students' involvement. During the debriefing, you will review what happened and engage students in discussions related to why different things occurred. As you involve students in the debriefing, you provide them opportunities to think about their decisions, why they took them, their consequences, and their conclusions from having been involved in the exercise. A good debriefing discussion helps students grasp the key ideas and skills that the simulation was designed to teach.

Cooperative Learning Approaches

In recent years, there has been a growing interest in *cooperative* learning approaches. It is a technique that features "students working together in groups, with group goals but individual accountability" (Willis, 1992, p. 1). Each student's evaluation depends, in part, on the collective success of the entire group in completing an assigned task. This feature helps students develop a prosocial commitment to helping others (Slavin, 1990), and it replicates the kind of productive group work featured in the adult workplace (Willis, 1992). Though some cooperative learning approaches involve sophisticated planning, this is by no means the case with all of them. Many ordinary class assignments can be enhanced through the use of cooperative learning (Woolfolk, 1995).

Johnson, Johnson, Holubec, and Roy (1984) identified four characteristics that distinguish cooperative learning from other small-group approaches. The first characteristic is *positive interdependence*. This means that your students must depend on each other in order to accomplish a given task. This interdependence might be accomplished through a division of labor, a division of resources, the assignment of different roles to each individual within the group, or the establishment of goals that cannot be reached unless everyone works together.

 CRITICAL INCIDENT

Cooperative Learning Blues

"I went to this cooperative learning workshop last summer. It was great. There were teachers there who were using cooperative learning in their own classrooms, and they talked us through some of the pitfalls. I left pumped up and ready to try some of the ideas myself."

The speaker was Nora Bennington, a second-year English teacher at J.V. Ortonsen High School. Rene Wu, Nora's former college roommate and herself now also a high school teacher, listened attentively.

"So how has it gone?" Rene asked.

"I got off to a smoother start than I really had expected," Nora responded. "Having those teachers work with us helped a lot. I picked up good tips, and I managed to avoid stupid mistakes I probably would have made otherwise. Also, I decided to start with Learning Together, one of the techniques that isn't a killer when it comes to planning."

Nora continued, "The students were a bit reluctant at first, but now they're really into it. I tend to mix it up a bit. We do Learning Together a while, and then we do a day or two of large-group work. By and large, I think I'd have a revolution on my hands if I went back to using large-group work all the time."

"No real problems, then?" Rene asked.

"Well," replied Nora, "there *has* been a glitch. I've had one parent on my back constantly since I started using Learning Together. She's come to see me, and she's complained to the principal."

"What's her problem—an unhappy son or daughter, or what?" Rene inquired.

"No, that's not it at all. Her son, Eric, is really bright. He has gotten into the swing of things, and he tells me he likes the small-group work. His mother has a real problem with the grading thing. You know, each student in the group gets the same grade."

"And, I suppose," put in Rene, "that she's convinced that her Eric is doing everybody else's work."

"Yes, that's part of it. But there's a bit more. Every time she calls me I get this lecture about how competitive the world is and that this kind of learning just isn't preparing students for reality. She also makes pointed remarks about how each student has to take the Scholastic Achievement Test *alone* and that his or her personal score is what will be evaluated. She says this small-group work will make our students too dependent on others. She thinks the lazier ones will find somebody bright to carry the load and never really develop their own talents."

"Did they give you any information from the research this summer that you might use as ammunition?" asked Rene.

"As a matter of fact, they did," Nora replied. "And I've shared some of this information with her, but she's not impressed. I think she feels the researchers were people with a vested interested in cooperative learning. Since the results don't square with her biases, she questions the researchers' real motives."

"Rene, I don't mean to ramble on so long about this, but I'm in a quandary. I just don't know how to respond to this person. I hate to abandon a program I believe in and the students like. But, I am afraid Eric's mother is going to make my professional life very uncomfortable unless I give up on Learning Together."

■   ■   ■

What does Nora Bennington's commitment to Learning Together tell us about what she thinks is important in teaching and learning? How do her values differ from those of Eric's mother? What should Nora Bennington do next? Can you think of some other arguments that might make sense to Eric's mother? To what extent should other professionals be brought into the picture? What might these people do? Is it fair that one parent's concern might lead Nora to change her instructional program? Or, should she change only if a number of parents complain? Do you think the complaints of all parents would be equally weighed by school administrators? If not, which parents would be listened to most? What would you do if you were faced with this situation?"

A second characteristic of cooperative learning is its requirement of *face-to-face interactions.* In other words, your lesson cannot be properly labeled as an example of cooperative learning if (1) it requires students to be physically separated, (2) each student works completely independently, and (3) you simply combine results of this totally independent work at the end into something called a "group product." There must be some interconnectedness among your students throughout the activity, even though specific individuals may have some specialized responsibilities.

The third characteristic is *individual accountability.* This means that each member of the group is held accountable for a particular contribution to the overall effort. The purpose of cooperative learning is to enhance the learning of all of your students, not just a few. Therefore, the term does not apply appropriately to situations when one or two of your students do all of the work and the rest sit and watch. *All* class members must be actively involved and appreciate that their contributions are vital to the success of the work of the entire group and that they will be held accountable for them.

The fourth characteristic of cooperative learning is that it requires students to use *interpersonal and small group skills.* Indeed, one of the basic purposes of the approach is teaching students how to cooperate and work with others.

Researchers have found that cooperative learning lessons result in higher levels of student achievement than more traditional approaches from grades 2 through 12 (Slavin, 1994). The approach has been found to be effective when the learning task involves complex learning and problem-solving, especially for lower ability students (Woolfolk, 1995). In addition to its value in promoting desirable academic achievement, cooperative learning also has been determined to have a positive impact on other outcomes such as race relations, self-esteem, attitudes toward school, and acceptance of students with disabilities (Slavin, 1994).

These are some examples of widely used cooperative-learning strategies:

- Student Teams-Achievement Divisions,
- Teams-Games-Tournaments,
- Jigsaw,
- Learning together, and
- Group investigation.

Student Teams-Achievement Divisions

The Johns Hopkins Team Learning Project developed Student Teams-Achievement Divisions (Slavin, 1980). If you are interested in trying a cooperative-learning approach, you will find Student Teams-Achievement Divisions to be one of the easiest to implement. It can be used in many different kinds of secondary school classrooms.

General Background

This approach involves students in a learning format designed to promote cooperation and active participation by all. The scoring system used gives students a vested personal interest not only in their own learning, but in the learning of all group members as well.

Implementing

You begin by assigning students to learning teams consisting of four or five members. Each team has a mix of high, average, and low achievers. If your class has a diverse ethnic makeup, you want to make an effort to achieve a reasonable ethnic balance among members of each team. You should also try to have a gender mix on each team that closely approximates the percentages of males and females in the whole class.

Ordinarily, you will begin by introducing some new content using traditional whole-group instruction. Then, the Student Teams-Achievement Division teams go to work using task sheets. The tasks sheets provide students with directions regarding what they are to do. You design the tasks so that they relate to the content you introduced during the whole-group-instruction phase of the lesson. Students will work on the tasks as a team. You give students directions that tell them what team members are to take responsibility for, ensuring that each student understands the content. Students on the teams continue to work until they are convinced that every member has a good grasp of the material. Then you test them on the material. During testing, team members may not help one another.

You use a special system of scoring that is designed to emphasize the importance of cooperation and active participation of all group members. This system yields test scores for each student and, in addition, each student's score also plays a role in the process used to develop a score for the entire team.

An individual team member, depending on how well he or she does on the test, may add from 0 to 10 points to the total team score. To determine how much an individual student's score will add to the team score, you look to see how well this person did on the previous test. For example, suppose one of your students scored 15 points (out of 30 possible) on the previous test and 20 points (out of 30 possible) on this test. The difference between 20 and 15 (new test score minus old test score, or base score) is 5. Five points would be added to the team score as a result of this student's performance.

Each student may provide a maximum of 10 points to the overall team score. There are two ways this 10-point maximum can be earned. Ten points are awarded if the student scores 10 or more points higher on the present test compared with the last test. Ten points are awarded for any perfect paper regardless of what the student received on the last test. This is an incentive to maintain the active participation of brighter students.

Figure 9–2 illustrates an array of scores for one group of students in a biology class where a Student Teams-Achievement Divisions approach was used. Notice that Joyce R., who received the lowest grade on the quiz, still contributed the maximum of 10 points to the total group score. This occurred because her quiz score of 55 was significantly higher than her base score of 40.

Student Teams-Achievement Divisions encourages less-able students. These students have an incentive to do as well as they can. Even though their individual scores may not be high, they can make important contributions to the total score of their team. Brighter students are encouraged to help less-able members of their group because all

Figure 9–2

Example of a Group's Score in
Student Teams-Achievement
Divisions

Student	Base Score	Quiz Score	Team Points
Raoul A.	57	64	7
LaShandra C.	63	60	0
Joyce R.	40	55	10
LaRue T.	83	88	5
Samuel W.	75	95	10
		Team Total = 32	

group members benefit when they exceed the expectations reflected in their base scores. Each member of a group has a stake in the learning of every other member. Thus, every student has a reason to want to help all group members to learn, and improvement of all team members becomes the goal as team members strive to increase overall team scores. You might want to arrange for some special recognition for high-scoring teams at the end of a regular grading period.

Debriefing

During your debriefing, you will want to focus on the quality of interactions you observed among individual team members. You can share team scores with the group, making a special point of emphasizing how the contribution of every group member contributed to the group's overall score. The debriefing phase will also give you an opportunity to single out for special recognition those students who did very well themselves and who you observed to be especially helpful in assisting others to master the content.

Teams-Games-Tournaments

The Johns Hopkins Group also developed Teams-Games-Tournaments (Slavin, 1980). It requires somewhat more time to plan and implement than Student Teams-Achievement Divisions. Teams-Games-Tournaments can be used in a wide variety of secondary school classes.

General Background

Teams-Games-Tournaments is basically an extension of Student Teams-Achievement Divisions. When you use this technique, you organize students into groups that participate in academic tournaments.

Implementing

Your first task is to assign each student to become a member of a four-to-six member team. To the extent possible, you will want each team to include students representing both males and females and students who vary in their ethnicity and ability levels. Once you have your teams organized, you assign members to spend time studying some assigned material together. You will instruct students to help one another to master the content. Members of individual teams will compete for "team points" by participating in weekly academic tournaments.

The format for the tournaments requires you to re-organize students from the individual teams into "tournament groups." Three students of approximately the same ability level, each from a different team, constitute a complete tournament group. Once you have made student assignments to tournament groups, your next step is to direct each group to sit at its own table. For example, if you have 27 students in your class, you will need nine tables to accommodate each of the groups of three. Because students have been organized into tournament groups according to ability level, this means you will have nine different gradations of ability levels represented in your nine groups, ranging from a group that includes the three highest-ability students to the group including the three lowest-ability students.

Next, you draw out questions related to the content students have studied as members of their original teams. You ask these questions to the whole class. Points are awarded to a student's original team based on how many questions his or her team member answers correctly as compared to other people who are seated at this person's tournament-group table. The same questions are drawn and directed to the entire class. A high-achieving student sitting at a table with two other high-achieving students will probably have to answer a large number of questions correctly to be the top person at the table and, hence, earn points for his or her team. On the other hand, a low-achieving student seated with other low-achieving students may be the table winner by answering correctly a smaller number of the questions you ask.

After several tournament rounds, you may wish to reassign students to different tournament groups based on how they have performed. Suppose you wished to do this. If you had a class of 27 students, you might begin in the usual way by assigning your three highest-achieving students to table 1, your next three high-achieving students to table 2, continuing this pattern until reaching table 9, the table where the three lowest-achieving students would constitute a group. For subsequent tournament rounds, you might decide to assign students to tournament groups based on how well they performed during the previous round. If you followed this scheme, in preparation for your second tournament, you would assign the three students who had the highest scores in round one to table 1, the three students with the next highest scores to table 2, and you would follow this pattern in such a way that the students you would assign to table 9 would be the three students with the lowest round one scores.

The Teams-Games-Tournament approach combines cooperative and competitive activities. You will find that this activity will develop your students' abilities to work actively in groups. This is true because the design of the approach makes it personally advantageous for individual group members to help others to master the assigned content. In addition, the format tends to keep competition among students at approximately the same level, and your students will tend to feel the reward system is fair. Teachers who have used Teams-Games-Tournaments report that even reluctant learners become interested in school when the approach is used (Slavin, 1990).

Debriefing
During the debriefing phase, you will want to focus on the processes the students have followed in their groups to learn content. You need to emphasize the importance of

mutually supportive, collaborative behavior. Finally, the debriefing phase gives you an opportunity to respond to students' questions.

Jigsaw

Jigsaw is a cooperative learning method that can be used in many different kinds of secondary school subjects. This approach is appropriate when you want to teach a topic that can be conveniently divided into several major components. It is also helpful if information related to each component can be organized under a common set of headings. For example, if you were teaching the Latin America Unit in a geography course, the components might be the individual countries. Information about each might be organized under the common headings of (1) physical features, (2) population size and ethnic makeup of the population, (3) major languages, (4) major economic activities, and (5) education and literacy.

General Background

You prepare for a jigsaw lesson by identifying a topic and preparing a list of major headings under which students can organize information gathered about each subtopic. The technique can be used to help your students work productively with others to master a complex set of content elements.

Implementing

Suppose you are teaching English to a class of 30 students and have decided your focus topic will be: "A Comparison of the Literary Work of Selected Twentieth-Century American Writers." You may decide to have students gather information related to these major writers: (1) Theodore Dreiser, (2) Eudora Welty, (3) F. Scott Fitzgerald, (4) Ernest Hemingway, (5) Willa Cather, and (6) Joyce Carol Oates. Your next step is to divide students into five *home teams*, each of which will have six members. You will assign one student from each home team to become an "expert" in information related to one writer. In this situation, each six-person team would include one Theodore Dreiser expert, one Eudora Welty expert, one F. Scott Fitzgerald expert, one Ernest Hemingway expert, one Willa Cather expert, and one Joyce Carol Oates expert.

Once you have individual experts for each of these home teams, these teams break up. Members from each home team who have been assigned to become experts on a particular writer meet together as members of *expert teams*. For example, all of Theodore Dreiser experts meet together. (There will be five of these people, one from each home team of six.) You will give members of the expert teams directions about learning resources to use. For example, you might suggest they use their own notes and recollections from previous class sessions as well as books and other materials you may be able to furnish. Members of each expert group will organize information under common headings you provide such as: (1) novels written and major themes treated, (2) short stories written and major themes treated, (3) poetry and other writings and major themes treated, and (4) general reactions of critics to this person's work. Figure 9–3 provides an example of how home groups and expert groups can be organized.

When the expert teams have finished their cooperative study, you direct students to regroup in their original home group. You ask experts on each writer to teach what they

Focus: A Comparison of the Literary Work of Selected American Writers

Home Groups

GROUP 1

Anna (Dreiser)
Rodney (Welty)
Juan (Fitzgerald)
LaRue (Hemingway)
Spencer (Cather)
Agnes (Oates)

GROUP 2

Paul (Dreiser)
Sondra (Welty)
Norman (Fitzgerald)
Sally (Hemingway)
Nora (Cather)
Raoul (Oates)

GROUP 3

Yu (Dreiser)
Monica (Welty)
Lee (Fitzgerald)
Helmut (Hemingway)
Rene (Cather)
Roy (Oates)

GROUP 4

Sarana (Dreiser)
Ming (Welty)
Kara (Fitzgerald)
Renaldo (Hemingway)
Price (Cather)
Travis (Oates)

GROUP 5

Tasha (Dreiser)
Karl (Welty)
Courtney (Fitzgerald)
Toshi (Hemingway)
Rocky (Cather)
Cole (Oates)

Expert Groups

DREISER GROUP

Anna
Paul
Yu
Sarana
Tasha

WELTY GROUP

Rodney
Sondra
Monica
Ming
Karl

FITZGERALD GROUP

Juan
Norman
Lee
Kara
Courtney

HEMINGWAY GROUP

LaRue
Sally
Helmut
Renaldo
Toshi

CATHER GROUP

Spencer
Nora
Rene
Price
Rocky

OATES GROUP

Agnes
Raoul
Roy
Travis
Cole

Figure 9–3
Organization of Home and Expert Groups for a Jigsaw Lesson

have learned to all members of the home group. In this way, members of each home group receive information about all six authors. Because students know you will be giving everyone a criterion test at the end of the lesson, there is an incentive for all students in the home groups to listen carefully to presentations by experts related to each writer and to insist that the experts share all of their information.

Jigsaw requires you to monitor the work of expert teams carefully. Members of each expert group must understand all of the necessary information. Each expert group student must know the information well enough to pass it along successfully to members of his or her home group. You may encounter difficulties in using jigsaw if a student is absent and misses important information being studied and shared in this individual's expert group. When this happens, you must step in to provide the missing information to the home group. This problem can be avoided if you design the entire jigsaw lesson in a way that will allow it to be completed during a single class period.

Debriefing

You will typically debrief students following their participation in a jigsaw lesson by organizing them into a single, whole-class group. In your discussion, you will review all information that has been introduced. You will want to encourage your students to take notes during the discussion to record any new information that did not come out during their own group meetings. The debriefing session gives your students an opportunity to fill in any remaining information gaps. In addition, the session allows you to engage them in analytical thinking that will help them make interpretations beyond a simple knowledge-level understanding of the new content.

Learning Together

Some cooperative learning approaches include strong incentives for each student to help all others assigned to the same small group. *Learning Together* places an especially high premium on students helping students (Johnson, Johnson, Holubec, & Roy, 1984).

General Background

Learning Together can be used in many secondary school subject areas. Unlike Jigsaw, Learning Together does not require content that can be easily broken down into a set of parts or subtopics.

Implementing

Your first step in implementing a Learning Together lesson is to organize students into teams that include a cross-section of ability levels and talents. You give each team a task or project to complete. Individuals on each team assume responsibility for completing a part of the overall project that is compatible with their own interests and abilities. The idea is to maximize strengths of individual students to get a better overall group effort.

Roles of individuals in Learning Together teams can vary. For example, if the final product is to be a short play, one or more students might assume roles such as (1) head writer, (2) manuscript editor, (3) manuscript production chief, (4) set designer, and (5) sound and light planner.

Each team is responsible for gathering the information and materials needed to complete its assigned task or project. Your final assessment is based on the quality of the team's performance. Each student on a team receives the same grade. This encourages individuals to pool their talents in such a way that each student's work adds the greatest possible contribution to the effort.

Is it appropriate to give each team member the same grade? This issue has been researched. Johnson and Johnson (1985) report that, though students tend to favor competitive grading before they engage in cooperative tasks, after they have completed a cooperative learning project they commit to the idea that awarding every group member the same grade is a fair approach.

Debriefing

During this stage, you work with students to help them focus on the processes they used in their groups to respond to their assigned task. You want to ask questions that will encourage your students to think about what they learned from their experience and what they might do differently another time to improve levels of understanding of all group members.

Group Investigation

You can use *Group Investigation* when you want to give your students considerable freedom in deciding what they are going to do and how they are going to do it. You do not assign students to specific groups as you do when you are getting ready to involve students in Jigsaw or Learning Together lessons. You encourage them to form into groups that include members of their own choosing. You want to ensure that each group represents the diversity present in the class (Leighton, 1994).

General Background

The basic ideas incorporated in the Group Investigation technique derive from the work of the eminent American educational philosopher, John Dewey (Joyce & Weil, 1996). In this approach, you establish conditions that allow students to organize themselves into democratic problem-solving groups. Members of each small group follow the methods of inquiry as they investigate a significant topic of interest. (For more information about inquiry instruction, see Chapter 11, "Higher-Level Thinking.") This approach is designed to help your students learn how to define a task, search for and synthesize information, and present it in an interesting and coherent way to others.

Each group ordinarily investigates a different topic or question. However, all these topics are usually subsumed under the umbrella of a broad issue or question. Because interaction and trust among group members are critical to the success of Group Investigation and because each member will have to assume considerable responsibility, you will want to use this approach with students who have already demonstrated some skill in small group work and who trust one another (Leighton, 1994).

Implementing

You will begin by presenting your students with a broad topic, question, or puzzling event (Joyce & Weil, 1996). For example, if you are teaching science, you might pose questions to your students related to how pollution in the local region might be reduced. If you are teaching world history, you might ask students to consider what happened to the Maya civilization of Central America. If you are teaching English, you might decide to ask students a question involving common literary themes. Sometimes, you may decide to leave choice of a focus topic up to members of your class (Leighton, 1994).

MORE FROM THE WEB

Small Group and Cooperative Learning

Small-group and cooperative learning techniques have long been popular at the elementary-school level. In recent years, secondary school teachers have also been embracing these approaches. Given these increased-levels of interest, it is not surprising that supporters have established numerous Web sites with information regarding small-group and cooperative-learning programs. You may be interested in visiting some of the sites listed here.

Maximizing Learning in Small Groups

http://www.cs.ukc.ac.uk/national/CSDN/edu_resources/small_group_learning.html

■ At this site you will find a guide prepared by Igor Kusyszyn of York University in Toronto, Canada, that contains many useful suggestions for preparing students to work productively in small groups. In addition to highly detailed recommendations about instructions you want to give students, there are useful references to important principles that provide a rationale for your patterns of interaction with members of your classes.

Cooperative Learning in the Secondary School

http://www.ncbe.gwu.edu/ncbepubs/pigs/pig12.htm

■ As the title suggests, material at this site provides specific information about implementing cooperative leaning at the secondary-school level. Authors Daniel Holt, Barbara Chips, and Diane Wallace provide excellent guidelines related to such issues as (1) working with culturally and linguistically diverse students, (2) promoting students' social development, (3) maximizing content learning, and (4) implementing successful cooperative learning lessons.

Cooperative Learning: What Is It?

http://www.ilt.columbia.edu/k12/livetext/docs/cooplern.html

■ Stephen Balkcom, who prepared this information, provides a succinct explanation of basic features of cooperative learning. He organizes information about cooperative learning in the form of responses to questions such as (1) What is it?, (2) How does it work?, and (3) What are some examples of specific programs?

Enhancing Student Thinking through Collaborative Learning

http://www.ed.gov/databases/ERIC_Digests/ed422586.html

- Karen Yeok-Hwa Ngeow prepared this material that was released by the ERIC Clearinghouse on Reading, English, and Communication. It provides excellent information on topics including (1) Critical Aspects of Group Learning and (2) Instructional Phases of Collaborative Learning. You will also find a useful bibliography here.

Jigsaw

http://www.wcer.wisc.edu/nise/cl1/CL/doingcl/jigsaw.htm

- This site features basic descriptive information about the Jigsaw method. There are useful links to additional details regarding how this approach can promote "positive interdependence" (the idea that group members need one another to succeed) among students while, at the same time, supporting the principle of "individual accountability."

Once a focus has been established, you ask students to think about the topic individually, to list any questions they have, and to develop speculative hypotheses that might provide useful explanatory information. For example, if you are teaching science, you might ask, "What can be done to reduce pollution in our region?" If you are teaching social studies, you might inquire, "Why did the Mayans seem to just lay down their tools and walk away from the great cities they had created?" If you are teaching English, you might say, "Why do you think these themes have been written about by many writers at different times? Are there other themes that you would expect to find in literature?"

You organize students into small groups to develop responses to your questions. After they have had adequate time to generate some responses, you instruct members to reassemble as a whole group. You ask students in each small group the group's conclusions. You list important questions, hypotheses, perspectives, or issues that arise out of this phase of the lesson on the board or on an overhead transparency. Next, you will work with the class to organize responses into categories. These categories become the topics for the group investigations that comprise the next phase of the lesson.

At this point, you will organize learning teams, based on students' interests. To do this, you will ask your students to look at the focus questions and decide which one they want to work on. People with similar interests will join together and form a group. If more than one group wants to pursue a single question or topic, you can divide it into several parts, with one group assigned to work on each. Each group meets, and members begin working on the topic they have selected. As they begin, you need to help them understand the focus of their work, list important questions, and identify some resources they will need to complete their investigation. As they begin, members of groups have to decide what each person is going to do and how group findings will be presented to the rest of the class. In practice, different students end up doing different things. Some may seek the data, others may organize it, and still others may organize findings for the group's presentation to the whole class.

FOR YOUR PORTFOLIO

1. What materials, ideas you learned in this chapter related to *small-group* and *cooperative learning* will you include as "evidence" in your portfolio? Select up to 3 items of information to be included in your portfolio. Number them 1, 2, and 3.

2. Think about why you selected these materials for your portfolio. Consider such issues as the following in your response:

   ▪ The specific purposes to which this information can be put when you plan, deliver, and assess the impact of your instruction;

   ▪ The compatibility of the information with your own priorities and values;

   ▪ The contributions this information can make to your personal development as a teacher; and

   ▪ The factors that led you to include this material as opposed to some alternatives you considered.

3. Prepare a written reflection in which you analyze the decision-making process you followed. Also, mention the INTASC Standard(s) to which your selected material relates. (First complete the chart below.)

Materials You Selected and the INTASC Standards
Put a check under those INTASC Standards numbers to which the evidence you have selected applies. (Refer to Chapter 1 for more detailed information about INTASC.)

Item of Evidence Number	INTASC Standards									
	S1	S2	S3	S4	S5	S6	S7	S8	S9	S10
1										
2										
3										

As your students work in groups, your task is to circulate and help students think about aspects of the topic they may have overlooked, find resource materials, settle group disputes, and, in general, facilitate other aspects of group work. You may want to provide worksheets for students to use to keep track of information they uncover as they pursue their investigations. When this phase is complete, ask members of each group to make a presentation to the entire class. These presentations can take many forms. For example, some of your students may want to use a computer-based presentation, others may make a traditional oral report, still others might choose such presentation options as videotapes or student-written and acted dramas.

Debriefing

During the debriefing stage, you concentrate on helping students focus on the process of inquiry and their patterns of working together. You want to help them review the steps they followed as the lesson unfolded. One of your purposes is to encourage students to consider how they can apply inquiry processes they used to other settings and situations. What students learn about these useful thinking processes by participating in Group Investigation lessons may be every bit as important to their long-term development as the specific content they learn as a result of their involvement.

Key Ideas in Summary

- Small-group learning capitalizes on students' interests in working together. It promotes supportive student-to-student interaction and encourages students to learn from one another.
- Success in small-group work is not automatic. To profit from this kind of instruction, students must be prepared. Conditions that facilitate group work include teaching students necessary skills for group work, understanding the peer group dynamics at work in a particular group, creating a climate so students respect and trust one another, decreasing the fear of failure, and implementing cooperative goal structures.
- It is useful to introduce small-group work gradually by first involving students in some introductory activities that will teach them prerequisite skills and the necessary attitudes of respect and trust.
- Among small-group approaches that have been successfully used in secondary classroom are classroom debates, educational simulations, and cooperative learning.
- *Cooperative learning* is a general term used to describe small-group learning techniques that base each student's evaluation, in part, on the overall level of performance of his or her group. Researchers have found cooperative learning approaches to (1) have positive effects on students' self-esteem, (2) generate peer support for academic achievement, (3) increase the amount of time students spend on academic tasks, (4) improve students' attitudes toward the class where cooperative learning has been used, and (5) help students develop more positive attitudes toward others in their class.
- There are many cooperative learning techniques. Among those that are widely used are (1) Student Teams-Achievement Divisions, (2) Teams-Games-Tournaments, (3) Jigsaw, (4) Learning Together, and (5) Group Investigation.
- *Student Teams-Achievement Divisions* and *Teams-Games-Tournaments* are similar in that they feature some competitive elements. However, the competition is between and among teams. There is an attempt to make competitive aspects fair by ensuring that they take place between and among individuals of similar ability levels.

- *Jigsaw* is best used for content that can be broken into separate but related components. Jigsaw involves expert groups, where students learn about one aspect of the topic, and home groups, where those from the expert group teach the rest of their group about their specialty topic.
- *Learning Together* is best used when the task requires a diversity of skills. Students are grouped together and each is given a specific role in the group that best matches his or her talents. The group then produces a product that is generated through the collective work of all group members.
- In *Group Investigation*, students are presented with an opportunity to select a general focus issue, problem, or topic. Individual students join with others to pursue an investigation of a topic of common interest. Findings ultimately are shared with members of the entire class. Two of the purposes of Group Investigation are (1) developing higher level thinking skills such as how to learn and (2) synthesizing large quantities of information. Supporters of this approach argue that what students learn about the processes of productive inquiry is just as important as what they learn about the content they study.

Reflections

1. What are some variables that you would consider in deciding whether or not to use small-group learning in your classroom?

2. What are some conditions you need to create before you can expect small-group or cooperative learning approaches to function well in your classroom?

3. What do you think you need to learn in order to successfully implement small-group techniques in your classroom?

4. What distinguishes an educational *simulation* from a *game*?

5. What is the difference between a *competitive goal structure* and an *individualistic goal structure,* and why is this distinction important when you are considering using a cooperative learning approach?

6. Some cooperative learning approaches award the same grade to each member of a group. How do you feel about this practice?

7. Can you think of examples from your own experience when a group activity was tried and failed because characteristics of the classroom environment did not support this approach? What could have been done to change these circumstances?

8. What do you see as the strengths of the various cooperative learning approaches?

9. Can you think of a topic in your subject area that you would like to teach using the Jigsaw technique? If so, what would be the focus of students' work both in the home groups and the expert groups?

10. Proponents of some cooperative learning approaches argue that insights students develop about the processes of learning are as important as the content they master. Is this a defensible position? Why, or why not?

Learning Extensions

1. Observe a secondary school classroom. What opportunities do you see for implementing small-group or cooperative learning approaches? What might be some challenges teachers you observed would face in implementing these kinds of lessons?

2. Robert Slavin, David Johnson, Roger Johnson, and Edyth Johnson Holubec have written extensively about cooperative learning. Use a Learning Together format to involve members of your class in gathering information about articles or parts of books each of these authors has written about cooperative learning. Working together, prepare a large chart summarizing perspectives of each of these cooperative learning experts.

3. Are educational simulations good ways to transmit academic content to secondary school students? Do some research on this topic, and prepare a paper in which you discuss your findings.

4. Using content in this chapter as a focus, organize a Jigsaw scheme that members of your class can use to review chapter content. Share your design with your course instructor and, if he or she agrees, implement the technique during one of your class sessions.

5. Identify a topic in your subject area that could be the focus for a Group Investigation. Break the broad topic into some specific questions or subtopics that might be used as a research focus for different groups.

6. Go to the Merrill Education's Link to General Methods Resources site at this URL: http://www.prenhall.com/methods-cluster/ At the bottom of the page select "discipline-specific resources" as your topic and click on the "begin" button. This will take you to the "Overview" page. On the left side, click on "Web Links." On the Web Links page click on a category that includes a subject you would like to teach. (Your choices here are "art and music," "foreign language," "language arts," "math," "physical education," "science," "social studies," and "vocational.") Follow links that will give you information you can use to prepare a short paper in which you explain kinds of information you found that you can include in lessons and units you might develop.

7. Go to the Merrill Education's Link to General Methods Resources site at this URL: http://www.prenhall.com/methods-cluster/ At the bottom of the page select "instructional strategies" as your topic and click on the "begin" button. This will take you to the "Overview" page. On the left side, click on "Web Links." On the Web Links page click on "icebreakers." These are techniques you can use to help students feel more comfortable with one another when you are planning to involve them in lessons involving small group work. As you work with material at these sites, take notes. Use them as a basis for an oral report to your class on this topic: "Tips for Breaking the Ice: Helping Students to Know and Understand One Another Better."

References

Johnson, D. W., Johnson, R. T., Holubec, E., & Roy, P. (1984). *Circles of learning: Cooperation in the classroom.* Alexandria, VA: Association for Supervision and Curriculum Development.

Johnson, R. T., & Johnson, D. W. (1985, April). Structuring conflict in science classrooms. Paper presented at the annual meeting of the National Association of Research in Science Teaching, French Lick, IN.

Joyce, B., & Weil, M. (1996). *Models of teaching* (5th ed.). Boston: Allyn & Bacon.

Kagan, S. (1989). The structural approach to cooperative learning. *Educational Leadership, 47*(4), p. 13.

King, A. (1999). Teaching effective discourse patterns for small group learning. In R. Stevens (Ed.), *Teaching in American schools.* Columbus, OH: Merrill.

Leighton, M. (1994). Cooperative learning. In J. Cooper (Ed.), *Classroom teaching skills* (5th ed.) (pp. 282–325). Lexington, MA: D.C. Heath.

Putnam, J. (1997). *Cooperative learning in diverse classrooms.* Upper Saddle River, NJ: Merrill/Prentice Hall.

Slavin, R. E. (1980). *Using student team learning.* Baltimore: Johns Hopkins Team Learning Project, Center for Social Organization of the Schools, Johns Hopkins University.

Slavin, R. E. (1990). *Cooperative learning: Theory, research, and practice.* Upper Saddle River, NJ: Prentice Hall.

Slavin, R. (1994). *Educational psychology* (4th ed.). Boston: Allyn & Bacon.

Willis, S. (1992). Cooperative learning shows staying power. *Association for Supervision and Curriculum Development Update, 34,* pp. 1–2.

Woolfolk, A. (1995). *Educational psychology* (6th ed.). Boston: Allyn & Bacon.

10

Individualizing for Learning

This chapter will aim to

- describe some alternative views of *individualized instruction*;

- identify variables that can be altered to accommodate individual differences;

- explain some assumptions made by proponents of the *mastery learning* approach, and describe features of the *Personalized System of Instruction*;

- point out some arguments for and against attempting to individualize instruction in ways that accommodate individual learning styles;

- describe typical features of a *learning contract*;

- explain components that you might find in an *activity package*;

- identify some types of *learning centers* and explain purposes of each;

- describe features of *learning stations*;

- suggest ways in which computers can be used to support individualized instruction programs; and

- distinguish between the two major types of *peer-tutoring* programs.

Introduction

Now that you know that students from many backgrounds will be on your class rosters when you start teaching, what should you do? Rule number one is: "Avoid panic." Teachers throughout the country face and respond to the student-diversity challenge every day. The rich variety of young people in your classes provides a context that allows you to introduce individual students to perspectives that, absent the ethnic, language, and cultural diversity common in secondary schools today, would not be possible. To exploit this opportunity, you need to know something about *individualized instruction*. This general term refers to the idea that you need to vary lesson approaches in every class you teach in ways that will both accommodate and take advantage of the student-diversity variable (Lefrancois, 1994).

Instructional specialists for years have promoted the use of individualized instruction (Good & Brophy, 2000). In practice, teachers in elementary schools have been quicker to adopt various individualized instruction approaches than teachers in secondary schools. In one study, Larry Cuban (1984), an influential scholar who specializes in education, found that fewer than one fifth of secondary teachers made any attempt to individualize their teaching.

Why have relatively few secondary school teachers committed to individualized instruction? For many, there are probably personal reasons or reasons connected to

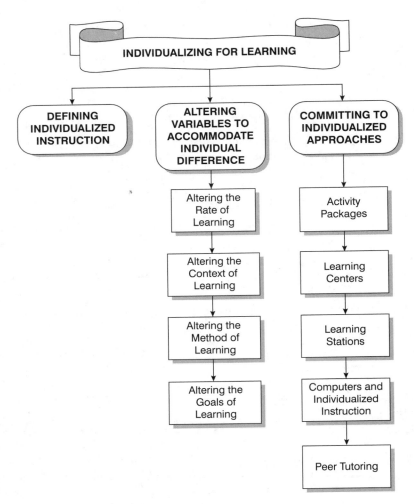

Figure 10–1
Graphic Organizer

some special features of their school and students. However, it may also be that proponents of individualized approaches sometimes have talked in global terms about the
benefits of this kind of teaching without providing detailed information about how to
implement it. Sometimes, too, enthusiasts have provided overblown descriptions of the
alleged benefits of individualized instruction and have raised doubts among experienced teachers who are appropriately wary when panacea-like qualities are claimed for
any instructional methodology.

The reality is that individualized instruction works best when it is used judiciously.
Individualized or differentiated approaches are appropriate when you want to teach
some aspects of curriculum, to certain students, under certain sets of conditions. At

other times, you will serve your students better when you provide the same lesson to a small group or a large group of individuals in your class. As you reflect on your options, you need to give careful consideration to your own teaching context and to think about your answers to questions such as these:

- Who are the students?

- What do you expect them to do when they have mastered the new material?

- Given the nature of the lesson you want to teach, what constraints are imposed by the kind of content you will be treating?

- What materials are available?

- What is the level of your own knowledge about the topic and about procedures for "packaging" information in a way that will individualize the lesson for different students in the class?

Reflection on these questions can help you make a decision regarding the appropriateness or inappropriateness of selecting an individualized approach to introduce specific content to specific students. In this chapter, you will find material that will broaden your understanding of processes and procedures associated with individualized instruction. This information will help you make informed decisions about individualized instruction as you consider adapting the approach to your own purposes.

Defining Individualized Instruction

The term *individualizing instruction* can be interpreted by different people in various ways. For some, *individualization* suggests a program where all students work independently on the same assignment. In this type of situation, every person does the same thing; only the rate of progress varies. This view of individualization is sometimes labeled *continuous progress learning*. The words *continuous progress* imply that the rate of academic development of one student will not be held up because others in the class may learn at a slower rate.

Others see individualization as focusing not on the rate of learning but on the content of instruction. These people see individualized programs as those where individual students study different topics, with the teacher acting as an overall learning manager. Individualized programs of this kind place a great deal of responsibility on students.

Another conception of individualization focuses on identifying modes of engaging students that are well suited to their individual characteristics. For example, there is considerable interest in *multiple intelligences* (Gardner, 1999). Individuals who subscribe to this theory contend that different individuals have varying forms of intelligence. As a teacher, you are most likely to succeed if you provide particular students with instruction framed in a way that capitalizes on the kinds of intelligence where they have particular strengths. This perspective underscores the folly of assuming any single learning activity will be universally appropriate for all students. For example, some of your students will do better when you introduce new content using a *narrational approach*—an entry point to instruction that features learning new information through stories of various kinds (Gardner, 1999). Others may do better if you use an *aesthetic approach*—a mode of instruction that focuses on students' receptiveness to artistic principles or to "materials arranged in ways that feature balance, harmony, and composition" (Gardner, 1999, p. 171). Still others may respond more positively to you if you use a *hands on approach*—an entry point to instruction that gives students opportunities to build or create something tangible (Gardner, 1999). If you would like to learn more about approaches related to the multiple intelligences theory, you might enjoy reading a recent book by Howard Gardner titled *Intelligence Reframed: Multiple Intelligences for the 21st Century* (1999).

Approaches to individualization based on multiple intelligences and on other theoretical underpinnings reflect a general orientation to teaching, not a specific set of procedures. When you say you are interested in "individualizing instruction" what you are committing to is an intent to think about teaching in a particular way. You are suggesting that you place a great deal of value on "personalizing" learning. In practice, this requires you to design your lessons in ways that will fit your teaching to the special needs of individuals in your classes and that will avoid forcing students to endure instructional approaches that are ill-suited to their personal attitudes and aptitudes.

Altering Variables to Accommodate Individual Differences

What does a commitment to individualizing instruction mean in practice? Among other things, it requires you to give serious thoughts to variables you can alter to accommodate individual student differences. As you plan instruction, you will be in a position to make changes associated with the following:

- the rate of learning,
- the context of learning,
- the method of learning, and
- the goals of learning.

Altering the Rate of Learning

The term *rate of learning* refers to the pace at which your instruction occurs. When you expose all students in a class to exactly the same instructional program, you assume that everyone is capable of learning at the same rate. This assumption rarely stands up to close inspection. Individuals learn at different rates. When your instruction fails to respond to these differences, students who generally learn faster often get good grades and those who learn more slowly get poor grades, and sometimes even fail.

Some experts contend that all students can learn or master the same educational goals if they are given sufficient time to do so (Lefrancois, 1994). They argue that students who fail often do not do so because of lack of aptitude for learning; rather, they fail because they are given insufficient time. They further suggest that "student aptitude" really refers to the amount of time a student needs in order to learn. Students with higher learning aptitude learn faster than those with lower aptitude. This means that, given enough time, all students can be successful.

When you manipulate the learning-rate or pacing variable, the basic content remains the same, as do basic assignments for students. What you alter is the time allowed for individual students to complete assigned tasks. You make arrangements that allow brighter students to move quickly through the material. This scheme permits your less able learners to use more time to finish their work.

Altering the learning rate makes the most sense in situations when you believe it is essential for all of your students to master a given body of content. This form of individualization is reflected in a number of formal instructional approaches, for example *mastery learning*. Mastery learning presumes that differences in students' levels of achievement result not from differences in student intelligence or aptitudes but rather from variations in time required by individuals to learn assigned content (Bloom 1976, 1980).

The *Personalized System of Instruction* (PSI) represents an example of an application of the mastery learning idea (Guskey, 1985). Similar to other mastery-learning programs, it features the following:

- Clearly specified learning intentions,
- Diagnosis of students' entry-level capabilities,
- Numerous and frequent assessment measures,
- Specification of mastery levels to be attained,
- A structured sequence of facts, principles, and skills to be learned,
- Frequent feedback to learners about their progress, and
- Provision of additional time that allows students who fail to achieve mastery to study some more and master the content.

Essentially, the PSI approach requires you to break down a course into small units of instruction with support materials provided for each. In PSI, your students take as much time as they need to learn each unit. You permit individuals to take a mastery quiz whenever they feel they are ready. Each quiz has a cut-off point (usually 80 to 90 percent correct) that is used to indicate mastery of the content. If a student does not pass the quiz, he or she is allowed more time to study the content with other students until the quiz can be passed successfully. When students are successful, they move on to the next small unit. At the end of the course, you administer an examination that covers all of the material. This means your unit quizzes are not used to assign grades to students. Instead, their function is to help individuals determine whether or not they need more time to learn the content. Students who pass the quizzes the first time spend less time on the material than do those who have to recycle (Slavin, 1994).

Mastery learning approaches such as PSI have positive as well as negative effects. On the positive side, researchers who have studied the impact of PSI at the college level have found the approach to be quite effective. In general, they have discovered that the mastery approach increases achievement (especially among less able students), results in less variation of achievement, and seems to have a positive impact on student attitudes toward school (Lefrancois, 1994).

PSI also has its critics. In certain situations, use of the approach has not resulted in increased student motivation and achievement. Some students don't like the format. Their complaints often center around the lack of opportunities to work with others. This may explain the finding that students in mastery learning approaches were observed to have lower completion rates in college courses than students who were enrolled in non-PSI versions of the same class (Lefrancois, 1994).

Other criticisms of mastery learning approaches have focused on procedural and contextual matters. For example, the additional time required to meet the needs of each student may not be available in most secondary schools. Schools operate within relatively fixed time constraints (Slavin, 1994). Any effort to implement mastery learning more widely probably would require restructuring of the school day and the school year. Perhaps those who learn quickly could leave school earlier in the day and would not have to stay in school for the 180 or so days that are usually required in a school year. When they mastered the content, their school year would be over. Other students who need more time to master the content might be in school for considerably longer than the present typical school day or the school year.

There is some question regarding whether the additional time required for the corrective instruction might be better spent covering more material. This concern arises because the amount of content covered is positively related to increases in achievement (Slavin, 1994).

Because mastery learning programs often divide large tasks into small pieces, if you adopt this approach, you will find yourself confronted with the need to keep on top of a great deal of paperwork. This feature, along with the frequent testing that goes on, often creates work for teachers that, in the view of some, goes beyond what they face in more traditional instructional programs (Good & Brophy, 2000). The potential for greatly increased record-keeping responsibilities has led many secondary teachers to steer clear of mastery-learning approaches. In addition, some secondary teachers have found that time spent monitoring students and keeping them on task increases when they use mastery learning.

Some critics of mastery learning have also challenged the assumption that frequent testing is desirable. They argue that frequent testing results in assessments that focus on isolated pieces of content. Such tests may encourage students to lose sight of the larger dimensions of the subject. Some teachers have found that students may do well on mastery tests but experience difficulty in applying what they have learned to different settings (Good & Brophy, 2000).

In summary, mastery learning programs work best when they focus on a relatively narrow band of content that is required of all students. They demand content that lends itself easily to division into numerous smaller pieces that can be organized for purposes of teaching and testing. Under these circumstances, mastery learning programs can motivate some of your students who have experienced chronic failure in more traditional instructional programs. Success will depend on your ability to monitor students carefully to assess levels of progress and encourage them to stay on task. It is particularly important that those students who have experienced only limited academic success in the past develop confidence in their own abilities to succeed. When you use a mastery learning approach, you have to work hard to ensure that this happens.

Altering the Context of Learning

Instead of focusing on the issue of pacing, you might want to individualize your instruction by *altering the context of learning*. When you do this, you do not change the goals of instruction. Rather, your focus is on identifying means for getting students to reach those goals in ways that are compatible with their own aptitudes and interests.

If you decide to alter the context of learning, you may wish to use an approach such as *orbital studies* (Tomlinson, 1999). In orbital studies, you assign students to follow different paths, based on their individual differences, that lead them to acquire information about a common topic or subject. For example, if you are teaching mathematics, you might assign students with interests in cars to study some topics in the context of how they are applied in car design. If you have others who are interested in urban design, you might ask them to study the same concepts as they might be applied in laying out city parks and other features of cityscapes.

Whether you use orbital studies or another approach to altering the context of learning, your basic assumption is that your students will be more motivated when they study materials that they find interesting. Supporters of this approach point out that many traditional programs fail to consider students' personal priorities. Content in traditional texts often contain examples that fail to connect with students.

From a management standpoint, there are some attractive features of individualizing by altering the context of learning. For one thing, you still maintain the focus of the entire group on a common set of skills or concepts. This means that you can be quite flexible in organizing your day-to-day instructional program. For example, on some days you may individualize content related to your major subject focus and assign students to work with different kinds of materials based on their particular aptitudes and interests. On other days, you may choose to have the entire class study work with the same learning materials.

Individualizing by altering the context of learning presents certain difficulties. For example, you may be challenged to find learning materials that are well suited to the diverse interests and aptitudes that may be represented among your students. Even if you can locate the kinds of materials you will need, the expense of acquiring them may be beyond what your school's budget can handle. In recent years, this problem has become less serious because of the proliferation of computers in the schools. Computers connected to the World Wide Web of the Internet can access almost unlimited information. In addition, more and more computers in schools now have multimedia capability. You can now find extensive learning materials available on fairly inexpensive CD-ROMs. These new electronic technologies make it easier for you to fill gaps in your on-site supplies of learning materials as you attempt to establish an appropriate "fit" between these items and the backgrounds of individual students.

It may take you some time to develop a high degree of comfort with an approach to teaching that regularly features altering the context of learning. The approach takes time to master, and time constraints during teacher preparation programs often mean

One variable you can manipulate in an individualized program is the context of learning. When you do this, all of your students seek to master a common set of learning intentions, but you provide them with means of doing so that take advantage of their individual strengths and interests. The idea is for you to provide options that are well matched to individual student interests.

As an exercise, identify a specific learning intention for a subject you would like to teach. Identify three separate interests that might be represented among students in your class. Suggest kinds of learning options that might help students with each of these interests to master the material.

Learning Intention: _____

    Interest A:

        Suggested Learning Experiences:

    Interest B:

        Suggested Learning Experiences:

    Interest C:

        Suggested Learning Experiences:

Figure 10–2
Altering What Students Study

that new teachers receive limited training in procedures for implementing instruction that is organized in this way. Initially, you may wish to try the approach in a single class, perhaps during instruction focusing on a topic that you will be teaching over a period of several weeks. This experience will help you to gain some insights into challenges associated with implementing and managing the approach. Once you have successfully altered the context of learning for a short period of time in a single class, you may want to implement it in other classes and for longer periods of time.

A force that sometimes militates against individualized programs that vary the context of learning is standardized testing. There is a trend for school quality to be assessed in terms of students' scores on these tests. When your students study material in contexts well suited to their personal needs, some of them may not come into contact with the kinds of contexts used to present items on standardized tests. This situation may cause you to feel pressured to expose all of your students to information in contexts closely paralleling those commonly assumed by developers of standardized assessments. There is no simple solution to this problem. In general, you need to seek a balance between your need to present content to students in ways they will find personally meaningful and your need to introduce it in a context that will not be startlingly different from what they will confront when they have to take standardized tests.

Altering the Method of Learning

Individualized programs that focus on *altering the method of learning* attempt to respond to different learning styles of students. These programs presume that people vary in their aptitudes for specific tasks and in their preferred modes of learning. This is what is called *attribute-treatment interaction.* The basic premise for this type of instruction is that your instructional methods should be matched to the particular learning styles of your individual students (Lefrancois, 1994).

Advocates of the learning-styles approach contend that just as individuals differ in personality, so too do they differ in the way they learn (Slavin, 1994). One approach to learning styles instruction focuses on the *modalities of learning.* Modalities refer to the sensory channels through which individuals receive and give information. These modalities include visual, auditory, kinesthetic, and tactile. Some people learn more efficiently when they are presented with visual material, others when they hear it, others when they touch or feel objects, and others when they are physically involved in doing something (Guild & Garger, 1985).

Another dimension that you will want to think about when considering learning styles relates to *field dependency* and *field independency.* Field-dependent individuals see patterns as a whole and have difficulty separating out specific aspects or parts of what they encounter. However, *field-independent* people tend to focus on the parts that make up the whole.

Learning styles also are sometimes classified according to an *abstract-concrete dimension.* Some people deal better with abstract than with concrete phenomena; others deal better with concrete than with abstract phenomena. Similarly, people vary in how they respond to *random versus sequential* information. Some deal better with information that appears in an ordered, sequential fashion. Others deal better with information that comes in a random, non-sequential way. Scholars who have studied the preference for abstract or concrete experiences and the preference for sequential or random information have found that (1) some people have concrete-sequential learning styles, (2) some people have abstract-sequential learning styles, (3) some people have concrete-random learning styles, and (4) some people have abstract-random learning styles (Gregorc, 1982).

In recent years, leading instructional specialists have done much to popularize approaches based on learning styles. They have identified four basic types of stimuli that influence learning: (1) environmental, (2) emotional, (3) sociological, and (4) physical. Rita Dunn and Shirley Griggs (1988) identified 18 different elements associated with these four sets of stimuli and devised a learning style inventory to help individuals identify their preferred learning style.

When you attempt to individualize by altering the methods of instruction, the learning intentions and content of learning remain the same for all students. Your task is to devise ways for students to process new information in ways that are compatible with their individual learning styles. To make this happen, you may decide to provide students with several options for learning new material. For example, some of your students might choose to read information from a textbook, and others might choose to view a sound clip from a CD-ROM with information about the same topic.

Altering the method of instruction based on learning style poses several problems. For one thing, a staggering variety of options are at least theoretically available to you as you attempt to accommodate different learning styles. Just diagnosing the learning styles of the number of secondary students taught in a normal day can be a formidable task. Current measures of learning style include many dimensions and often are lengthy and difficult to administer (Lefrancois, 1994). There is no standard test you can give that will reliably identify the preferred learning style of each of your students.

Some critics of this approach challenge the assumption that if you simply allow your students to choose a method of learning that seems right for them, they will choose one that is appropriate for their individual needs. They point to evidence that this might not be the case. For example, some research indicates that lower ability students tend to perform better when they are in highly structured classroom environments and that higher ability students tend to perform better in more loosely structured classroom environments. However, when students are asked for their preferences, lower ability students express a preference for permissive unstructured classes and high ability students express a preference for highly structured classrooms. These decisions run counter to what research suggests would be the "wise" choice for each group (Lefrancois, 1994).

In addition, the research base on learning styles and the effectiveness of matching teaching methods or styles to learning styles is thin. Existing studies have yielded inconsistent and contradictory findings (Slavin, 1994). Though the theoretical rationale for this practice is well grounded, research on matching instructional methods to individual student characteristics is in its infancy. In addition, there are practical issues to be addressed and resolved before altering the mode of instruction to fit individual student characteristics becomes a common feature of secondary school programs.

As a practical matter, you may find it difficult to implement a large number of different instructional approaches if you determine that your students have a wide range of preferred learning styles. For example, you may not know much about the kinds of instructional processes that are appropriate for students with some learning styles. In addition, you may lack access to some instructional resources you need to provide choices that are optimally suited to the learning styles of some members of your class. The bottom line is that you need to reflect on the nature of your students, the nature of your own background, and the nature of your particular instructional context as you decide how far you can (or want) to go down the path of altering the methods of learning.

Altering the Goals of Learning

In individualized instructional programs that feature *altering the goals of learning* the purposes of instruction are varied to accommodate characteristics of individual students. Such programs are controversial. They are also rare. Much of the debate about the approach results from the great latitude it can give to students. In a few altering-the-goals-of learning programs, students are permitted to make many decisions about what they want to learn. If you find yourself teaching in such a situation, your work will primarily be that of a facilitator. You will listen to students and help them clarify their personal goals. This approach presumes that your students are the best judges of their own educational needs. There also is an assumption that, when given the freedom to do so, your students will make intelligent choices.

Some examples of highly student-controlled programs of this type were implemented in a small number of schools during the late 1960s and 1970s in response to those who charged that schools were imposing too many restrictions on students. More recently, educational critics have been making quite a different argument. Many of them have suggested that schools provide students with too many electives and that authorities should require a larger number of core courses for all students. These recommendations have acted to eliminate most of the highly student-controlled individualized learning programs of the type that appeared in some schools 20 to 30 years ago.

Some more common examples of altering-the-goals-of-learning approaches to individualized instruction feature goals that are negotiated between teacher and students. One scheme of this type that has been used by many teachers is the *learning contract*. A learning contract is an agreement that you negotiate with an individual student. Its terms are variable. Typically, you as the teacher retain the final word as to what the contract will include. Often learning contracts specify a specific agenda of personalized tasks that a student must complete in a specified period of time (Tomlinson, 1999).

The following items illustrate contents often found in learning contracts:

- A description of what steps the student will take to accomplish the learning intention,
- A list of learning resources that will be used,
- A description of any product(s) the student will be required to produce,
- An explanation of criteria that will be used in evaluating the student's work, and
- A list of dates when different tasks are to be completed and submitted to the teacher for review.

CRITICAL INCIDENT

Success Is Killing Me!

LaShandra Pettybird, following a long-standing routine, settled into a comfortable chair in the faculty lounge at William Henry Harrison Middle School and opened the small bag containing her lunch. Her good friend Leticia Bennett, chair of the school's English department, joined her.

"LaShandra, how are things in the wild and wonderful world of seventh-grade science?" Leticia asked as she made herself comfortable.

"Mostly good news to report. But I'm still keeping total perfection at bay, thank you. In fact, some of this 'wonderful stuff' we've been doing is about to do me in," replied LaShandra.

"How so?" asked Leticia.

"Well, you might remember that I was getting nothing from Robin Coleman. Finally, I sat him down and we hammered out the details of a learning contract. Then he got busy. To the amazement, I think, of both of us, he has done just outstanding work on the assignments specified in the contract. His test scores have been excellent. He's even telling other people that 'science is pretty neat.'"

After pouring herself another cup of coffee, Leticia commented, "It seems to me you hit the right button. Is there really a down side to this story?"

"Well, yes and no," LaShandra replied. "Robin's good work has turned his mother into one of my biggest fans. In fact, she has been telling all of her friends about my 'outstanding learning contract system.' Lots of these people are parents of some of my other students."

"It sounds as though you are getting some wonderful public relations out of all this," said Leticia.

"Well," continued LaShandra, "that's true. But the problem is that I now have 23 parents begging me to set up individualized contracts for their children. I just can't do it. The time involved to lay out individualized objectives, find special learning material, and prepare tailor-made tests that will be different for 23 people would require me to work 30 hours a day, seven days a week. Some of these people are coming to see me on Thursday afternoon. I know they expect me to be enthusiastic about setting up all these individualized contracts. I'm afraid I am going to disappoint them if I say no, and I'm afraid I'll never survive the year if I say yes."

■　■　■

What should LaShandra say when she meets with the parents? Are there others from whom she should seek advice before they arrive? Would it be possible to develop learning contracts for these students without placing an irresponsibly heavy burden of work on LaShandra? How might school administrators feel about all this?

When you use a contract approach, both you and the student sign the agreement. Its provisions become the student's individualized curriculum. When its terms are satisfied, you and the student develop a new contract or agenda. Completed contracts document what the student has done and learned.

As a prelude to initiating a learning-contract approach, you need to become a proficient learning diagnostician. This means that you have to know your individual students well enough to recommend inclusion of learning experiences in any contracts you negotiate that are appropriate for the needs of the individual who will do the work. You also have to know a great deal about the kinds of support materials that are available for students to use. It makes little sense to negotiate contract terms that call on a student to work with learning resources that are not easily accessible.

Committing to Individualized Approaches

Successful implementation of individualized instruction requires you to make a serious commitment to this approach. In addition to the blocks of time you must allocate to preparing and monitoring individual instructional programs, you have to accept the responsibility of managing a huge volume of paperwork. Further, you have to be prepared for the reality that some of your students may not be pleased when they first encounter an approach to teaching that they may not have experienced before. This can be a particular problem if you make a common mistake: assuming that individualized instruction requires students to work alone. It does not. What you are trying to do is establish approaches that take advantage of students' individual strengths. Your analyses of student characteristics often will lead you to plan individualized lessons that require groups of students with similar interests and aptitudes to work together.

Teachers in today's secondary schools use many kinds of individualized approaches successfully. You may be interested in some of the examples introduced in the subsections that follow.

Activity Packages

One approach you might take in responding to the need to individualize your instruction involves preparation of *activities packages*. These are highly structured, self-contained guides to learning that break content into a series of small steps. Your students must accomplish each step before you allow them to go on to the next. Often you will develop a summary test that students will take after they have completed all material in a package.

Activity packages are an especially flexible format for delivering individualized instruction. You can construct packages to address possible needs to (a) vary the rate of learning, (b) vary the context of learning, (c) vary the method of learning, and (d) vary the goals of learning. Your decisions regarding an appropriate focus will be based on your own analyses of the needs of students in your classes. Regardless of what you decide to emphasize, your activity package probably will include components such as those discussed in the sections that follow:

- Title,
- General Description and Rationale,
- Learning Intentions,
- Pre-Measure of Understanding,
- Learning Program, and
- Post-Measure of Understanding.

Title

Titles play both a motivational and a descriptive function. Because you want to spark student interest in the content of the activity package, you need to think creatively about the title you select. For example, suppose you are teaching music and want to prepare a short activity package exposing students to some basic music theory principles. Simply titling the activity package "Music Theory" is unlikely to prompt much student excitement. You might decide on something a bit more evocative, such as "Beethoven to Heavy Metal: Explorations in Music Theory."

General Description and Rationale

This section of your activity package lets your students know what they must do to complete the work. You often will provide some indication of the approximate time required to do this. Often, too, you will briefly describe some important new terminology that students will be encountering as they work with the material. In addition, you will provide an explanation about why students should attach some importance to learning the new content.

Learning Intentions

In this part of the activity package, you will make clear to students exactly what it is they are expected to learn. You will include information that tells them what they will have to do to assure you that they have grasped the new material. The idea here is to give them some learning "targets" and to remove any misconceptions they might have regarding your expectations.

Pre-Measure of Understanding

Typically, you will want students to take a pretest or engage in some other kind of exercise to provide you information about what they know about the topic before they begin working with the instructional material in your activity package. Results on these pre-measures can tell you whether students have the needed prerequisite knowledge they might need to succeed on the tasks they must accomplish as they work through the activity package. In addition, this information can help you spot students who may already have mastered some of the material in the package. When this situation develops, you can direct these students to skip sections introducing material they have already mastered.

Learning Program

The heart of your activity package is the learning program. Often, you will divide this component into several sections. You will provide separate instructions for students regarding what they must do to complete each section. For example, you may include references to pages to be read, CD-ROMS to be viewed, software to be run, and papers to be written. You also will include any forms you want students to complete as they work with the new material.

   If you have divided the activity package into sections, you typically will provide assessment activities at the conclusion of each. For example, you may decide to include short practice tests. When students do well on tests associated with individual sections, typically they also do well on the more comprehensive post-measure of understanding they will take when they have completed the entire activity package. If your students do not perform well on a section test, they can go back and review the material again and retake the section test before moving on to new material.

Post-Measure of Understanding

You usually will develop some kind of post-measure of understanding for students to take once they have completed all work associated with a given activity package. You may decide to use short-answer or force-choice test items. You may decide to have students prepare a paper or a project of some kind. You will design the post-measure to reflect both the specific content of the activity package and the nature of students who will be working with the material.

Learning Centers

A *learning center* is a place you designate within your classroom where a student goes to pursue either required or optional activities related to a single topic. It functions as a self-contained environment for learning all required information about a given subject. Centers typically include these features:

- general information about the topic,
- a list of options students may pursue in mastering the material,
- needed learning materials, and
- information about tests or other assessment alternatives.

For example, if you were teaching a World History course, you could set up a center focusing on this topic: "Reasons for the Outbreak of World War I." Your center might allow students to gain information about this subject in a variety of ways. You could decide to include such options as:

- reading some material from one or two textbooks,
- reading a transcript of a lecture on this topic,
- working with an appropriate CD-ROM,
- listening through headphones to a discussion of this issue on a cassette tape, and
- reading items posted on Internet newsgroups that focus on World War I.

Sometimes you might decide to set up several centers in your classroom. Usually, when you do this, each center has an independent focus. Successful completion of work at one center is not a prerequisite for work at another.

You can make centers as simple or complex as you want. For example, you can do something as simple as setting up a bulletin board display in a corner of your room that features a topic title, an instruction sheet, and descriptions of activities students will complete prior to taking a test on the content. More complex centers you prepare may require space for media equipment such as computers, sound equipment, and electronic display panels. You may also find a need to provide special shelving for books, globes, reprints of articles, CD-ROMs, computer software, and other kinds of learning materials. A sophisticated center may require a considerable commitment of classroom space.

Learning centers can be used for different purposes. Among major types are:

- The Alternate-Materials Center,
- The Enrichment Center, and
- The Reinforcement Center.

The Alternate-Materials Center

The *alternate-materials center* focuses on content that you want all students in the class to learn. It responds to individual student needs by including a wide variety of learning materials related to the common topic. Your students are allowed to select materials that are consistent with their own interests and abilities.

In your classes, you may find that many of your students are not highly proficient readers. As a result, some of them may have a hard time dealing with information that is presented to them in the course textbook. An alternate materials center responds to this dilemma by providing other learning options for students who are not good readers. For example, you might provide less difficult reading materials, audio cassettes, relevant CD-ROMS, easy-to-use software and computers to run the programs, and other alternatives that treat information similar to that in the course text.

The Enrichment Center

The *enrichment center* is designed to challenge those of your students who are capable of doing more sophisticated work than many others in your class. Enrichment centers focus on a topic that is being studied by the entire group. However, only your more able students are assigned to work at centers of this type, and you include assignments that motivate them and encourage them to stretch their mental powers. Sometimes you may wish to use enrichment centers to maintain the interest of brighter students who finish regular assignments more quickly than others in the class and who need to be assigned to an additional productive learning activity.

The Reinforcement Center

Reinforcement centers focus on a topic all students in your class have been studying. Their primary purpose is to provide your students opportunities to review what they have learned. Hence, you will typically set up reinforcement centers toward the end of a given instructional unit. Activities provide your students opportunities to work again with difficult concepts that have been introduced and to practice new skills.

In preparing reinforcement centers, you will often want to focus on aspects of content that students have found difficult. Sometimes, when you have been working with a particularly large and difficult topic, you may wish to develop several reinforcement centers. You will design each of these to deal with a particular area of the general topic.

Learning Stations

Learning stations, unlike learning centers, divide a single topic into several components. Each learning station you prepare will provide experiences for students related to *one part* of a more general topic. Individual stations are interrelated, and your students must complete work at each of them.

In terms of their basic organizational features, individual learning stations are much like learning centers. They typically include general information, learning alternatives, needed materials, and details about what students must do to demonstrate what they have learned. Depending on the focus of the content, you may want your students to work through learning stations in a prescribed sequence. If you decide that it is important for teachers to complete the sequence in a particular order, you can assign numbers to each station and instruct your students to work through them in numerical order. In other cases, when the material does not have to be presented in a sequential fashion, you can begin the exercise by randomly assigning students to individual stations and telling them to work through them in any order.

Because this approach always requires you to develop several interrelated stations, you will find total preparation time is longer than what will be required of you when you develop a single learning center. In addition to deciding on which elements of a larger topic will be featured in each station, you also must think about how to manage student movement from station to station.

In planning a series of learning stations, your first task is to divide a proposed unit of work into a number of subtopics. Each of these becomes the focus for an individual station. Next, you need to decide on physical locations for each station and develop appropriate sets of instructions. You also have to gather together needed learning materials, support equipment, and assessment devices. Finally, you have to think through some important management issues, particularly procedures you want students to follow to signal to you they have completed work at a given station and are ready to move to another.

Planning for this last issue is important. Your rules should assure that individual stations do not become overloaded with students. To prevent this from happening, you might want to establish a no-more-than-four-students-at-one-station guideline. If such a rule is to succeed, you have to develop productive work for students who have completed work at one station and who are waiting for someone to vacate a position at another one. You might want to provide printed instructions to cover this situation that begin with this phrase: "If you have finished all work at this station and there are too many people at the next station, do this until there is a vacancy at the next station: [specific instructions follow]."

Successful learning-station instruction requires you to keep good records. These records help you keep track of the progress of individual students as they pass through the various stations. You can use this information to identify problems of individual students and to pinpoint any design deficiencies at a station that may be causing difficulties for a large number of your students.

Computers and Individualized Instruction

One of the fast-growing approaches to individualizing instruction in secondary schools is computer-based instruction. Over the past 15 years, numbers of computers in schools have increased at an explosive rate. Today, there are at least a few personal computers in virtually every middle school, junior high school, and high school in the nation. It is

English: Period 3

In this unit you will be required to do assigned reading, take two vocabulary tests, identify literary elements, and apply them in some creative writing. To accomplish these tasks, you will be assigned to work at one of the eight learning stations. The order of completion for the stations is unimportant. Go directly to the station to which you are assigned and begin work. You will find instructions at the station telling you what to do. [*Do not go to any other station until directed to do so by the teacher.*]

When you complete each assignment at each station, place it in this notebook. Raise your hand, and the teacher will come to you and check your work. If everything is in order, place the notebook in the box provided for your period on the shelf along the west wall. Then proceed to the next station as directed by the teacher.

As you work through the stations, keep track of your progress by completing this form.

Stations		Date Completed	Score
Station 1:	Test on "Sinking of PT 109"	_____	_____
Station 2:	Vocabulary Test #1	_____	_____
Station 3:	Short paper on imagery	_____	_____
Station 4:	Short story I wrote	_____	_____
Station 5:	Six examples of personification:		
	(1) _____ (4) _____		
	(2) _____ (5) _____		
	(3) _____ (6) _____		
Station 6:	Vocabulary test #2	_____	_____
Station 7:	Completed crossword puzzles	_____	_____
Station 8:	Six poems I wrote	_____	_____

Figure 10–3
Example of Student Instructions for Learning Stations

highly probable that you will find both computer laboratories in your school as well as several in your own classroom. Assuming your school's computers have an Internet connection, you and your students will be able to access a tremendous amount of information on the World Wide Web. This huge and diverse instructional resource opens up many possibilities to you as you work to develop instructional programs that are well fitted to the particular needs of individuals in your classes. For example, you might decide to include some Web-based options as you plan various kinds of learning stations or learning centers.

In addition to the Web, computers offer opportunities for you to take advantage of specialized software. Educational supply houses today sell programs that run the gamut from loosely organized general information about large topics to highly structured programs of study focusing on narrow issues. Some of the better software packages will allow you to alter most of the important variables associated with individualized instruction. For example, you can modify some programs to allow students to work at their own pace. Others allow for variations in how new content is introduced. Many of them provide alternative ways for your students to review content.

© 1997 Randy Glasbergen

"I forgot to make a back-up copy of my brain, so everything I learned last semester was lost."

Some software features *intelligent tutor programs*. These programs are designed to determine what a student already knows in relation to a particular learning outcome. Once this is determined, the program exposes the student to learning experiences that are designed to teach information he or she has not yet mastered.

The intelligent tutor program assesses what students already know by prompting them to respond to questions asked by the computer. Their responses are then compared to a data base built into the computer. As a result of the comparison, the computer program develops a unique student profile and goes on to establish a special sequence of learning experiences for the student. Once this step has been completed, the student begins moving through the planned instructional sequence. As this process goes forward, the program provides correctives, as needed, and provides other kinds of feedback related to the adequacy of the learner's performance.

One advantage of intelligent tutor and other computer-based individualized programs is that the computer has infinite patience. For example, a computer will allow students to recycle through difficult material as many times as they need to master the content. When your students use such programs, they are involved with an instructional process that truly allows them to progress at their own rate. In addition, many computer programs provide a useful record of student progress when they complete a learning session. This allows you to monitor this information at your own convenience. In addition, the information often will be stored and used when a student returns for additional work. Based on what they have done previously, the computer will provide an appropriate entry point for the students when they return to work again with the computer-based material.

Peer Tutoring

Another approach you can use to individualize your instruction is *peer tutoring*. This procedure requires you to assign students who have mastered certain new material to work with others who need additional help. There are two basic types of peer tutoring: *same-age peer tutoring* and *cross-age peer tutoring*. As the name suggests, same-age peer tutoring features tutors who are about the same age and who are in the same grade as those being tutored. On the other hand, cross-age peer tutoring features older, more advanced students working with younger, less advanced students.

MORE FROM THE WEB

Individualizing Your Teaching

In this chapter you have been introduced to a number of ways to meet needs of individual students The following Web sites contain information that you may find useful in applying the ideas of the chapter. Some of them contain lesson plans you can adapt to your classroom. Others provide rich resources that you can use in designing individualized learning instruction. Still others will provide opportunities to learn from other teachers who have developed individualized programs.

These students are helping one another as part of their work in a same-age peer tutoring program.

Educator's Tool Kit

http://www.eagle.ca/~matink/

- This site has an abundance of resources that can be valuable in helping you design individualized lessons. There are links to lessons plans, a whole section on students with special needs, and ideas on how to teach various subjects.

Designing Web-Based Learning Stations

http://www.essdack.org/stations/sld001.htm

- Tammy Worcester has made available at this site information that describes approaches you can use to develop learning stations that feature content from the World Wide Web. The information is introduced in the form of a 17-slide presentation and includes details that are helpful in developing an individualized instruction program featuring learning stations and Web content.

Plans for Individualized Instruction

http://www.coe.uh.edu/courses/cuin6373/idhistory/individualized_instruction.html

- If you are interested in historical developments related to individualized instruction, you will want to visit this site. Among other topics, you will find information about the Winnetka Plan and the Dalton plan. Both were forerunners of some individualized approaches that teachers use today.

Socrates—Style and Methods

http://www.san.beck.org/SOCRATES3-How.html

- At this site, you will find an extensive discussion of Socrates' approaches to teaching. One extensive section, titled "individualized instruction," explains how Socrates went about the business of discovering and responding to the special needs of his students.

Peer Tutoring

http://www.ncrel.org/sdrs/areas/issues/students/atrisk/at6lk20.htm

- The Northwest Regional Educational laboratory has posted information at this site. It features an extensive discussion of peer tutoring. In addition to descriptions of the approach, you will find excellent references to research studies that have been conducted to determine its effectiveness.

Concerns About Some Recent Criticisms of the Personalized System of Instruction (PSI)

http://www.lafayette.edu/allanr/concerns.html

- You will find a lengthy discussion here of the Personalized System of Instruction. This is a particularly good site for you to visit if you have an interest in research studies that have been undertaken to determine the effectiveness of this approach.

Researchers have found that both the person doing the tutoring as well as the person being tutored experience increased levels of learning. In fact, some studies indicate that the person doing the tutoring has the greatest achievement gain (Slavin, 1994). Given this information, you might occasionally choose students to serve as tutors who are not necessarily your brightest "academic stars." You will find that the responsibilities these students assume as tutors often will help them develop a better grasp of the content they are asked to teach. You might be interested to know that, in some places, high school students identified as being at risk of dropping out of school have been assigned to work as tutors in elementary schools. Their involvement gives the high school students an opportunity to revisit information they may not have learned well when they first encountered it. In addition, this arrangement often gives the older students a sense of responsibility that can lead to more positive attitudes toward school.

 FOR YOUR PORTFOLIO

1. What materials, ideas you learned in this chapter related to *individualizing for learning* will you include as "evidence" in your portfolio? Select up to 3 items of information to be included in your portfolio. Number them 1, 2, and 3.

2. Think about why you selected these materials for your portfolio. Consider such issues as the following in your response:

   - The specific purposes to which this information can be put when you plan, deliver, and assess the impact of your instruction;
   - The compatibility of the information with your own priorities and values;
   - The contributions this information can make to your personal development as a teacher; and
   - The factors that led you to include this material as opposed to some alternatives you considered.

3. Prepare a written reflection in which you analyze the decision-making process you followed. Also, mention the INTASC Standard(s) to which your selected material relates. (First complete the chart below.)

Materials You Selected and the INTASC Standards

Put a check under those INTASC Standards numbers to which the evidence you have selected applies. (Refer to Chapter 1 for more detailed information about INTASC)

Item of Evidence Number	INTASC Standards									
	S1	S2	S3	S4	S5	S6	S7	S8	S9	S10
1										
2										
3										

Regardless of the type of tutoring program you decide to implement, your tutors need training (Slavin, 1994). They have to learn how to provide assistance without doing the work for the person they are helping. In addition, you have to monitor tutors' work carefully. If you fail to do so, tutoring sessions can easily turn into opportunities for social conversation having little, if any, connection to academics. Tutors also are more confident as they approach their tasks when they know you are readily available to help them if they run into any difficulties.

Key Ideas in Summary

- The diversity of students in classrooms today means that teachers have learners with highly varied interests and aptitudes. This provides a context that is particularly appropriate for individualized instructional approaches that seek to take advantage of unique characteristics of individual students.

- One approach to individualizing involves *altering the rate of learning*. When this is done, all students are exposed to the same basic instructional program, but the speed at which individual students progress through the program varies. *Mastery learning* is an example of altering the rate of learning to individualize instruction. Mastery learning presumes that observed differences in students' levels of achievement have little to do with differences in their levels of intelligence or in their aptitudes. Rather, differences occur because individuals vary in terms of how much time they need to do the required work.

- Another approach to individualizing involves *altering the context of learning*. Goals pursued by all students may be the same, but the teacher seeks to identify areas in which students are particularly interested and to provide relevant instruction within the context of these enthusiasms. This approach assumes that students' levels of motivation increase when learning materials are closely matched to their interests.

- Individualized programs that attend to learning style differences of learners often involve teachers in *altering the method of learning*. Learning intentions and content remain the same for all students, but individuals are allowed to pursue different paths as they seek to learn the material. For example, some students may read about it, others may work with appropriate CD ROM disks, and still others may interview people and take notes.

■ A fairly unusual approach to individualizing, at least in public school settings, involves *altering the goals of learning*. In this approach, great latitude is given to students to select the goals of instruction and to make other important decisions about what they wish to learn. There is an assumption that, given the freedom to do so, students will make intelligent choices.

■ One approach to individualizing involves the use of *activity packages*. These are highly structured and self-contained guides that break learning content into a series of small steps. Students must successfully complete one step before going on to another. Activity packages represent a flexible format. They can be designed to respond to a variety of individual student needs.

■ A *learning center* is a designated place within a classroom where a student pursues learning activities related to a single topic. This self-contained environment for learning often provides general information about the topic, a selection of learning options for students, needed learning materials, and information about tests or other assessment alternatives.

■ *Learning station* approaches subdivide large topics into important subtopics. Each station focuses on one part of the general topic. Organizationally, each learning station is set up much like a learning center. Learning stations require more teacher time to prepare than learning centers. This is true because several of them must be set up at once, and complete instructions and support materials must be provided for each.

■ Emerging electronic technologies, particularly those based on computers, are providing more options for teachers who wish to individualize their instruction. In recent years, there have been great advances in software that can be used to generate instructional options suited to the needs of individual students. In addition, much material on the World Wide Web can be incorporated into individualized learning programs.

■ *Peer Tutoring* approaches feature students who have mastered new material working with other students who need additional help. Same-age peer tutoring uses tutors who are about the same age and in the same grade as the students they are helping. Cross-age peer tutoring features tutors who usually are older and more advanced than the students they have been asked to assist.

Reflections

1. What is your definition of individualized instruction? Which variables associated with individualizing learning do you think you would be most comfortable altering? Why?

2. What concerns do you have about altering each of the variables for individualizing instruction?

3. Some individuals see a conflict between recent state level efforts to mandate specific tests that all students must complete and the need to meet the needs of diverse students. What is your response to this issue?

4. Which approaches to individualized instruction do you see as most consistent with recent trends in education?

5. Which of the specific approaches to individualized instruction do you think would fit best with your beliefs and skills? Why?

6. Several approaches to individualizing instruction were introduced in the chapter. How would you rate your interest in each? Which do you think would be most difficult for you to implement, and why?

7. Some people suggest that the World Wide Web of the Internet offers an exceptionally rich resource for the teacher who wants to individualize. However, others argue that to use this resource requires considerable teacher control in order to prevent abuses. What is your opinion?

8. Suppose you decided to use peer tutors in one of your classes to assist students having difficulty mastering some new content you have introduced. How would you specifically prepare your tutors for their responsibilities?

9. Some critics of individualized instruction suggest that it is an impractical sham. They allege that the term "sounds good," but that, in reality, teachers simply lack sufficient time to plan programs uniquely suited to the needs of each student. What do you see as strengths and weaknesses of this argument?

10. As you reflect on your professional knowledge, what additional information do you think you need to acquire to better meet the needs of diverse students?

Learning Extensions

1. Observe in a secondary school. Look for ways the teachers individualize and adapt their instruction to meet the needs of diverse students. Using what you have learned in the chapter, identify places where these teachers have altered one of the four individualized-instruction variables introduced. Share your observations with others in the class.

2. Identify a specific topic you would cover in one of the courses you would like to teach. Develop a complete set of plans for a learning center devoted to this topic. Present your plans to your instructor for review.

3. Educational professional journals include many articles that report practical ideas for individualizing instruction. Begin an individualized instruction folder that includes reprints of at least ten articles. You might begin by looking at entries in the *Education Index*. Your instructor may have other suggestions to help with this project.

4. Identify a topic you may wish your students to learn. Suppose you wanted some students to gather as much information as possible about this topic using resources only available on the World Wide Web of the Internet. Develop a master list of URLs of Web sites with information that might help your students. Share this material with members of your class, and describe how you might use this information to individualize your instruction.

5. Re-read the material in the chapter that deals with *activity packages*. Choose a topic from your own field and prepare an activity package for students. Include alternate ways for students to do the work. Share your work with others in the class, and be prepared to discuss any special challenges you faced in assembling this material.

6. Go to the Merrill Education's Link to General Methods Resources site at this URL: http://www.prenhall.com/methods-cluster/ At the bottom of the page select "instructional strategies" as your topic and click on the "begin" button. This will take you to the "Overview" page. On the left side, click on "Projects on the Web." Follow links and prepare a short paper in which you describe how some of the ideas you encounter might be incorporated within a learning-stations approach built around materials available on the World Wide Web.

7. Go to the Merrill Education's Link to General Methods Resources site at this URL: http://www.prenhall.com/methods-cluster/ At the bottom of the page select "instructional strategies" as your topic and click on the "begin" button. This will take you to the "Overview" page. On the left side, click on "education resources." Follow some of these links and prepare a short paper identifying at least ten places where you might seek information on the Web that would be useful for planning individualized lessons for students.

References

Bloom, B. S. (1976). *Human characteristics and school learning.* New York: McGraw-Hill.

Bloom, B. S. (1980). *All our children learning.* New York: McGraw-Hill.

Cuban, L. (1984). *How teachers taught: Constancy and change in American classrooms, 1890–1980.* New York: New Press.

Dunn, R., & Griggs, S. (1988). *Learning styles: Quiet revolution in American secondary schools.* Reston, VA: National Association of Secondary School Principals.

Gardner, H. (1999). *Intelligence reframed: Multiple intelligences for the 21st century.* New York: Basic Books.

Good, T., & Brophy, J. (2000). *Looking in classrooms* (8th ed.). New York: Longman.

Gregorc, A. (1982). *Gregorc style delineator: Development, technical, and administrative manual.* Maynard, MA: Gabriel Systems.

Guild, P., & Garger, S. (1985). *Marching to different drummers.* Alexandria, VA: Association for Supervision and Curriculum Development.

Guskey, T. (1985). *Implementing mastery learning.* Belmont, CA: Wadsworth.

Lefrancois, G. (1994). *Psychology for teaching* (8th ed.). Belmont, CA: Wadsworth.

Slavin, R. (1994). *Educational psychology* (4th ed.). Boston: Allyn & Bacon.

Tomlinson, C. (1999). *The differentiated classroom: Responding to the needs of all learners.* Alexandria, VA: Association for Supervision and Curriculum Development.

11

Higher-Level Thinking

This chapter will aim to

- tell you how to implement metacognitive techniques that can help students learn how to direct their thought processes to higher levels;

- define discovery learning;

- describe the process of inquiry teaching;

- suggest how comparing, contrasting, and generalizing might be used in the classroom;

- explain how simulations can be used; and

- describe implementation procedures for and differentiate among purposes of creative thinking, critical thinking, problem solving, and decision-making.

Introduction

What do you want education to do for your students? Do you want them to take what they learn in school and apply it to real situations? If so, you are one of the many people who see education as dedicated to preparation for life. This orientation will lead you to help students develop sophisticated thinking processes such as comparing, contrasting, interpreting, generalizing, identifying assumptions, making valid inferences, criticizing, and summarizing. Educators use the term *higher-level thinking* to describe these abilities.

Teaching higher-level thinking processes is consistent with the constructivist view of learning. This orientation assumes that you, as a teacher, cannot simply give students knowledge. They must construct knowledge and meaning in light of their past experiences and their present interactions (Gennrich & Long, 1999). Methods that facilitate learning are those that (1) encourage students to experiment, discover, and apply things on their own, and (2) help students consciously monitor their own learning strategies (Slavin, 1994).

Constructivist learning assumes instruction should begin as close to the reality students experience as possible (Boudourides, 1998). You need to teach whatever basic skills are needed as part of lessons that emphasize resolution of complex, authentic problems. This kind of instruction focuses simultaneously on development of basic skills and higher-level thinking abilities. Some research indicates that this type of instruction is invaluable for those students who have experienced academic difficulties (Woolfolk, 1995).

A constructivist approach requires you to adopt a role that differs from what you might do in implementing instruction that is more traditional. You have to place more responsibility on students to control their own behavior and to take responsibility for their own learning. In addition, you have to be prepared for the possibility that at least some students will arrive at conclusions different from you own. You also have to accept that it is more difficult to evaluate what students have learned from lessons focusing on

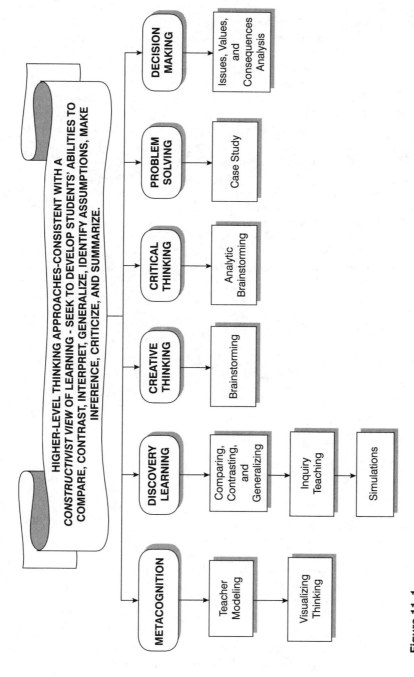

HIGHER-LEVEL THINKING APPROACHES-CONSISTENT WITH A
CONSTRUCTIVIST VIEW OF LEARNING - SEEK TO DEVELOP STUDENTS' ABILITIES TO
COMPARE, CONTRAST, INTERPRET, GENERALIZE, IDENTIFY ASSUMPTIONS, MAKE
INFERENCE, CRITICIZE, AND SUMMARIZE.

METACOGNITION

Teacher Modeling

Visualizing Thinking

DISCOVERY LEARNING

Comparing, Contrasting, and Generalizing

Inquiry Teaching

Simulations

CREATIVE THINKING

Brainstorming

CRITICAL THINKING

Analytic Brainstorming

PROBLEM SOLVING

Case Study

DECISION MAKING

Issues, Values, and Consequences Analysis

Figure 11–1
Graphic Organizer

323

higher-level thinking than those that focus on more basic thinking processes. Simple paper and pencil tests featuring objective items are not satisfactory. You must be willing to rely on essays, oral presentations, assessments of student products, and other kinds of evidence of learning that require considerable time to develop and to evaluate.

A special atmosphere permeates classrooms that feature an emphasis on developing higher-level thinking abilities. For example, you will need a wide repertoire of instructional techniques, a tolerance for considerable ambiguity, and a general sense of personal and professional security for these kinds of lessons. You have to be comfortable with turning a great deal of responsibility for learning over to students. You must know how to model higher-level thinking processes in ways that connect with students. In essence, you must be willing to act as a learning manager. Your obligation is to present students with the task to be accomplished, provide the basic information they will need to use as they work toward a solution, nurture their thinking processes as they engage the assigned problem, and challenge them to test their conclusions.

Interest in promoting higher levels of thinking has led many educators to advocate the direct teaching of specific thinking skills to students. They point out that instruction that emphasizes how to think is at least as important as instruction that focuses on learning traditional academic content (Beyer, 1987, 1988). However, this position does not imply an either-or dichotomy; it is necessary to teach *both* academic content and thinking skills (Joyce & Weil, 1996). Sound thinking skills help students achieve maximum benefit from the learning of academic subjects and prepares them to cope with challenges they will face throughout their adult lives (Ruggiero, 1988). This chapter introduces several strategies designed to promote higher-level thinking skills:

- metacognition,
- discovery learning,
- creative thinking,
- critical thinking,
- problem solving, and
- decision making.

Metacognition

Metacognition refers to knowledge about one's own learning or knowing how to learn (Slavin, 1994). It involves bringing to a conscious level the kinds of procedures people follow as they think. Metacognitive processes serve an important monitoring function. When people are aware of the steps they are taking as they think, they make more conscious choices about whether approaches they have selected for a given task are appropriate. The basic idea is to help develop conscious control over the process of learning. This is important because the student must actively be engaged if learning is to take place.

Instructional experiences can be provided that help students learn strategies for monitoring and modifying their patterns of thinking. Several approaches have been designed to achieve these purposes. Two that have been used by a number of teachers are teacher modeling and visualizing thinking strategies.

Teacher Modeling

Modeling has long been known to be a powerful instructional tool. As applied to metacognition, modeling seeks to help students recognize that people who successfully think about challenging topics carefully monitor their own thinking processes. They engage in a type of silent personal dialogue as they confront pertinent issues. They may speculate about alternatives, consider numerous responses, evaluate available evidence, weigh the relevance of competing views, and get deeply involved in other considerations related to the issue at hand. To help students understand how such thinking processes operate, you will find it useful to model these processes by thinking aloud as you and members of your class attack an issue together.

In doing this, the idea is to prompt your students to use thinking patterns that are appropriate for accomplishing a similar task. As students observe you, they will note general approaches to the issue that have proven to be productive. They will see the importance of thinking carefully about their own approaches to the task. If you have done a good job in thinking aloud with them, you will find that your students often perform better on an assigned task than if you simply assume that they already know how the task should be approached.

Suppose you are a teacher in an English class and are about to introduce a unit on descriptive writing. You might ask each student to write a two- to three-page paper on tourist attractions of a selected world place. Your intention might be for students to prepare an initial draft, think about it, and then prepare a revised version. If your directions to students go no further than a statement such as "prepare a draft, think about it, and then rewrite it," you will not cue students to the kinds of thought processes that should be used as they approach the task of revision. A more productive way to get them successfully started on the revision task would be for you to model what they should do.

For example, you might prepare an overhead transparency from a first draft of the same assignment prepared by a student from a previous semester. Then, you could think aloud with students in this way:

> All right, now look at this draft of a paper on Easter Island. Now, if this were my paper and I were about to revise it, these are some of the things I would want to do.
>
> First of all, people are going to be reading literature about lots of different places. They will be turned off by anything that has been written hastily without careful attention to spelling and grammar. The first thing I'll want to look for is spelling errors. Then, I'll want to be sure that verb tenses are correct and consistent throughout.
>
> I will want to hold the attention of my reader. I don't want to lose anyone with long, complicated sentences. As a quick check on this, I'll read the paper aloud. Anytime I run out of breath before I finish a sentence, I am going to mark that sentence. Later, I will go

back and cut these long sentences into shorter ones. Also, as I read I will try to spot any places where I am using the same word too frequently. If I find any excessive repetition, I will make a note to correct this situation in a revision.

As I read through the material, I will mark every sentence that has as its main verb some part of the verb "to be." This tends to be a very weak, dull verb for the reader. As I rewrite the material, I will try to replace these verbs with more action-oriented words.

Look at this sentence: "The giant statues are visited by many tourists." There are two serious problems here. First of all, the verb is in passive voice, a weak, uninteresting construction. Second, the reference to the statues simply being "visited" is not particularly exciting. I would rewrite the sentence to eliminate the passive voice and to add some color. One possibility might be a sentence something like this: "The giant statues of Easter Island challenge tourists' views of so-called primitive peoples."

As students listen to you think aloud about the thought processes involved in revising the sample paper, they have a model to follow as they begin to work on their own revisions. Modeling can also plant the idea that thinking about what the task requires is an essential prerequisite to beginning to address the task. This perspective is one that you want them to adopt as a result of your thinking aloud demonstrations.

Visualizing Thinking

Visualizing thinking encourages students to monitor their own thinking processes. This technique helps students think about the nature of an assigned task, consider the kinds of thinking they will be required to engage in, and identify the nature of the information they will need to gather. Once students decide on their responses to these issues, they are encouraged to develop diagrams. The diagrams help them to take and organize notes consistent with the requirements of the assigned task.

Suppose that you decided to have class members read the following material from a text:

Early Spanish Explorers of the Caribbean

In the year 1492, the Spanish explorer Christopher Columbus landed on San Salvador Island, a rather small island in the West Indies. San Salvador is in the group of islands that we know today as the Bahamas. Columbus later explored many other Caribbean islands. He set up a fort on one of the largest islands in the region, Hispaniola. Today, the countries of Haiti and the Dominican Republic occupy Hispaniola.

Another well-known early Spanish explorer was Nicolas de Ovando. In the year 1502, he was sent out from Spain to become Governor of Hispaniola. He brought a large number of colonists with him. These colonists sought to make their fortunes in two ways. Some of them attempted to strike it rich in gold mining. Others started large plantations. A common problem all of these early Spanish colonists faced was a lack of a large supply of local workers.

In response to this situation, the colonists initially tried to make slaves of the local Indians. This was not successful. The Indians did not take to slavery, and many of them died. Once the local supply of Indians on Hispaniola had been exhausted, the Spanish for a time tried bringing in Indians from other Caribbean islands. They, too, died. Later, slaves from

Africa were brought to the island. Though many of these slaves survived, Hispaniola continued to have a need for more workers than could be supplied.

As a result of this labor shortage, many Spanish colonists began moving from Hispaniola to other islands in the region. One of the other large islands that attracted a number of Spanish settlers was Puerto Rico. The first settlers arrived there in 1508 under the leadership of Ponce de Leon. The Spanish moved into Jamaica in 1509 when Juan de Esquivel led a group of settlers there. Spanish settlers reached Cuba, the largest island in the region, in 1514. In time, it became the most prosperous of Spain's Caribbean territories.

Because of differences in ability levels of students, you might wish some students to focus on different aspects of this material than others. For example, you might want some of your students to read with this learning task in mind:

Task: Who were four famous Spanish explorers who made discoveries in the Caribbean between 1492 and 1514, and what large islands did Spain occupy during this period?

To help them focus on this task as they read the material and take notes, you might prepare a visual-thinking diagram something like the one in Figure 11–2.

Leaders and Islands

Leaders   Islands

Figure 11–2
Example of a visual-thinking diagram

You might want others in the class to read for the purpose of accomplishing this somewhat different task:

Task: What actions were taken by the early Spanish settlers of Hispaniola to solve the labor shortage, and what happened as a result?

To help students focus on this task as they read the material and take notes, teachers might prepare a visual-thinking diagram something like the one in Figure 11–3.

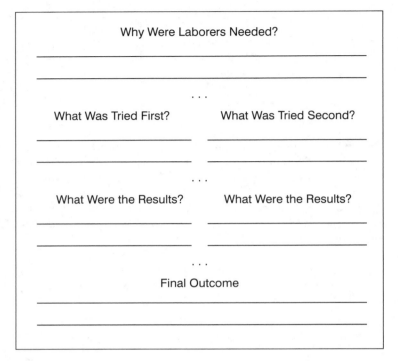

Figure 11–3
Example of a visual-thinking diagram

Note that, although the students were assigned the same material to read, the thinking task assigned to some students differed from the thinking task assigned to others. These differences are reflected in the visual-thinking diagrams. Use of such diagrams can help students focus on information that is relevant to a specific assigned task.

When you try this approach for the first time, you will want to provide members of your class with the blank diagrams. Once your students get used to working with them, you can ask them to develop visual-thinking diagrams of their own. The process of constructing the diagrams forces them to think about the nature of the task and about the nature of thinking that will be required in responding to it.

Use of the diagrams helps students to monitor and adjust their own thinking processes as they work with assigned materials. As a result, their work is likely to be more productive and their levels of achievement and self-satisfaction higher.

Discovery Learning

Discovery learning refers to learning that requires students to identify key ideas and principles themselves rather than be taught directly by teachers. Discovery learning has been given considerable support by the work of Jerome Bruner (1960). Bruner emphasized the importance of students' understanding the structure of a subject, that is, the basic concepts and principles that form its foundation.

If a student is to grasp the structure of a subject, Bruner believes that he or she must be actively engaged in the learning process. This kind of activity requires students to identify the concepts, the principles, and their relationships for themselves (Woolfolk, 1995). Good discovery learning lessons demand extremely careful teacher planning. In part, to emphasize this point, some proponents of the approach use the term *guided discovery* to indicate that the teacher has an important guidance function in creating conditions that help students discover meaningful concepts and principles.

One of the primary tasks in a guided discovery lesson is to identify and present activities or examples that will stimulate and facilitate students' search for information. For example, if you are teaching a social studies class, you might give students a blank map of a country and ask them to mark places where they think cities might be located. Once they have done this, you can encourage them to compare their guesses with a printed map. As they seek to explain the reasons for their correct as well as incorrect guesses, students move toward identifying some basic concepts and principles related to urban location and growth. You can go on to provide additional information and to ask good questions as you guide students through the processes of evaluating their responses and seeking deeper understanding. (Review Chapter 8 for information on questioning.)

Discovery teaching presents several challenges. You must have a solid academic understanding of the subject in order to identify its basic concepts and principles. You also need to have available good examples or situations that will stimulate student discovery of the basic concepts and principles. Asking good questions, providing additional information, and guiding students require you to have both excellent content knowledge and good teaching skills.

Today's electronic technologies make it easier to implement discovery approaches. A major condition for the effective use of discovery learning is the availability of information and data. The ready availability of data on the World Wide Web makes it possible for students to access tremendous quantities of information. No longer are they limited to what is available in the school library. Once students have learned how to ask the right questions and how to connect to the available sources, discovery learning activities can be taken to levels that were unimaginable only a few years ago.

Discovery learning is based on the inductive reasoning process. This process proceeds from the specific to the general. A simple example will illustrate the general procedure. Suppose you want to teach a group of learners the concept *fish*. You might begin by providing them with photographs of different fish. Through a series of questions, you would encourage students to identify common features of the things in the individual photographs. To conclude the exercise, you would urge students to develop their own description of the concept *fish* and would ask them to describe its necessary defining characteristics.

In summary, discovery learning can take many forms. The following are some variations of discovery approaches:

- comparing, contrasting, and generalizing;
- inquiry teaching; and
- simulations.

Comparing, Contrasting, and Generalizing

One effective way of helping students discover basic concepts and principles is by presenting individual pieces of information in ways that allow them to be easily compared and contrasted. By then looking at the data, patterns can be noted and generalizations or principles formed.

One approach to organizing data for learning activities requiring students to compare, contrast, and generalize involves use of the *retrieval chart*. A retrieval chart is basically a matrix that includes concept categories under which relevant information can be listed.

A lesson using a retrieval chart might develop along these lines. Suppose you were teaching English and decided to have your students read a novel called *Mines and Dreamers*. This novel features many interactions among the five major characters: Joe Carmody, Luella McPhee, Tony Marino, Gordon Duffy, and Selma Steele. In planning lessons designed to promote students' abilities to compare, contrast, and generalize, you might develop a chart that students could use to organize basic information from the novel. The chart might call for information about each character under these major headings:

- family background,
- education,
- occupation, and
- basic motives.

You could ask students to gather information individually. Or, you might have members of the class develop the information as part of a group discussion focusing on the novel. In either case, the result would be a completed data chart. This could take the form of a large chart in the front of the room, a chart prepared on an overhead transparency and projected on a screen, or individual charts that would be printed and distributed to each student. An example of such a chart with data filled in might look something like Figure 11–4.

The completed chart can be used as a basis for a discussion designed to prompt students to compare, contrast, and generalize. You might begin such an exercise by asking students to look carefully at the information on the chart and to respond to this sequence of questions:

1. What are some similarities you see among these characters?

   Possible responses:
   - Joe Carmody, Luella McPhee, and Gordon Duffy were reared in one-parent homes.
   - Joe Carmody and Luella McPhee have less than a high school education.
   - Tony Marino and Gordon Duffy are attorneys.
   - Joe Carmody and Tony Marino are both interested in improving the lot of the working poor.

   (These are examples. Students may identify additional and different responses.)

	Family Background	Education	Occupation	Basic Motives
Joe Carmody	Divorced parents; reared by mother	Grade 8	Union organizer; former coal miner	Improving lives of the working poor
Luella McPhee	Divorced parents; reared by mother	Grade 10	Owner of successful real estate firm	Personal social advancement; wants to hide nature of her family background
Tony Marino	Upper middle class; reared by both parents	College graduate	Attorney	Betterment of the condition of the working poor
Gordon Duffy	Upper middle class; divorced parents; reared by father	College graduate	Attorney	Promotion of his own economic self-interest; insensitive to needs of others
Selma Steele	Upper class; reared by both parents	College graduate	Business manager	Believes that what is good for business is, in the long run, good for everyone

Figure 11–4

2. What are some differences you see among these characters?

   Possible responses:

   - Their educational levels are different.
   - They come from a variety of home backgrounds.
   - Some of them are basically out for their own interests.
   - Some of them are interested in improving the lot of others.

   (These are simply examples. Students may identify additional and different responses.)

3. From looking at this information, what general statements can you make about what the author may believe to be true?

   Possible responses:

   - There is not necessarily a connection between a person's occupation and his or her sensitivity to the needs of others.
   - The kind of home a person grows up in as a child does not necessarily predict the kinds of attitudes toward others he or she will have as an adult.

   (These are simply examples. Students may develop different and additional generalizations from the information in the chart.)

The generalizations that students develop in this exercise result from consideration of a very limited amount of information. You would need to remind them that these conclusions should be regarded as only tentatively true. As you involve your students in the study of additional material, you can have them test the accuracy of these generalizations in the light of new information.

Inquiry Teaching

Inquiry teaching is a specific form of discovery learning that emphasizes use of the scientific method. When using an inquiry approach, you engage students in hypothesizing, gathering data, and verifying or modifying their conclusions.

Inquiry thinking involves students in the process of knowledge creation. This is true because students develop their own conclusions after considering independent pieces of evidence. Many students enjoy the process of knowledge generation. In addition to its high potential to motivate students, inquiry teaching helps young people develop the kinds of rational thinking abilities they will be called on to exercise throughout their adult lives. In short, supporters of inquiry thinking are as much interested in students mastering the scientific process as in their mastering the academic content that provides the focus for a given inquiry lesson.

Basic Steps in Inquiry Teaching

Inquiry teaching in American schools traces back to a famous book published by the eminent American educational philosopher, John Dewey. In *How We Think*, originally published in 1910, Dewey suggested basic steps for sequencing inquiry instruction. With some variation, the following steps, derived from Dewey's work, are featured in many inquiry lessons:

- Identify a focus and describe the essential dimensions of a problem or situation.
- Suggest possible solutions to the problem or explanations of the problem or situation.
- Gather evidence related to these solutions or explanations.
- Evaluate possible solutions or explanations of the problem in light of evidence.
- Develop a conclusion that is best supported by the evidence.

The first step is the establishment of a focus for the inquiry. Your function at this step is to present a puzzling situation (sometimes called a *discrepant event*) to students. This ought to be something that challenges their present conceptions. For example, you might conduct a science demonstration where something unexpected or surprising occurs. One that social studies teachers sometimes use begins with this question: "Why do cities grow up in some places but not in others." Often many students comment that many cities seem to grow up near a river, large lake, or ocean. When this idea surfaces, the teacher presents them with the example of Mexico City, located in the south central highlands of Mexico, a considerable distance from large and important bodies of water. The puzzle presented by the inland location of one of the world's largest cities becomes a point of departure for further development of the lesson.

The second step in the inquiry process requires students to develop hypotheses or possible explanations for the puzzling event. This is usually done as a group, and students are asked to generate as many explanations as possible. When you work with students during this phase of an inquiry lesson, your role is to help them clarify their hypotheses and encourage them to state these ideas clearly so that others understand the relationships they are establishing.

The third step in the process requires students to gather specific information relating to the guesses or the hypotheses that were made. During this part of the lesson your task as a teacher is to challenge students to think about the type of information or evidence that they would need to help them determine whether or not their guesses or hypotheses are correct.

At this point there are two ways you can proceed. One option is for you to function as a data source. If you do this, students will ask you questions, and your answers will help them arrive at conclusions. This approach requires you to take time to teach students to phrase questions clearly so that your answers will be responsive to the kinds of information they need. In general, you want them to ask questions that elicit information about facts that will help them arrive at a supportable conclusion. Formal models have been developed that feature the teacher-as-information source. Some of these place limitations on the kinds of questions students can ask. For example, the inquiry approach developed by Suchman (1962) in science requires that students ask only questions that can be answered with a *yes* or a *no*.

Another alternative at this point in the lesson is for you to direct your students to seek information about their tentative hypotheses elsewhere. If you decide to proceed in this fashion, you will need to help students identify appropriate questions and direct them toward the type of information they need to gather. Then you'll need to make arrangements for them to access appropriate information sources. These may include such options as the World Wide Web, documents, books, CD-ROMs, software, and films. After students have gathered data, your role is to encourage them to review and evaluate hypotheses they formulated in light of the new information. This results in their accepting, rejecting, or modifying their original hypotheses.

Finally, you need to bring the lesson to a close by summarizing the explanation and the evidence supporting it. It also is useful to review the steps that students followed to arrive at their conclusion. This step is important because helping students master rational thinking processes is one of the main purposes of inquiry instruction.

When a class is involved in an inquiry lesson, often individual students will arrive at different conclusions. If you find yourself confronted with this situation, you will have a marvelous starting point for engaging the class in a follow-up inquiry lesson. This lesson can help class members test the relative merit of each of the alternative conclusions.

An Example of an Inquiry Lesson

Let's see how an inquiry lesson might develop. Suppose you wanted students in a high school humanities class to probe the relationship between urbanization and life expectancies of American women. An inquiry lesson with this focus might develop along these lines:

Step 1

Focus: You might begin by writing the statistics* shown in Figure 11–5 on the board.

You: Look at this information. What trends do you see? Notice that women seem to be living longer in each of the three years. Notice, too, that more people seem to be living in cities. Now, I want you to think about two questions. First, what might be the connection between longer lives for women and the trend toward living in cities? Second, are there other possible explanations for women living longer in the later years?

Percentages of Females in Three Age Groups

Year	Under 30 (percent)	30 to 50 (percent)	51 or Older (percent)
1850	71	20	9
1910	61	25	14
1970	50	23	27

Median Age of U.S. Females in Three Years

Year	Median Age (in years)
1850	18.8
1910	23.9
1970	27.6

Percentages of U.S. Urban and Rural Population in Three Years

Year	Rural (percent)	Urban (percent)
1850	84.7	15.3
1910	54.3	45.7
1970	26.5	73.5

Figure 11–5

*Data are adapted from U.S. Bureau of the Census. (1975). *Historical statistics of the United States, Colonial Times to 1970*, Bicentennial Edition, Part I (pp. 11–12, 16, 19). Washington, DC: U.S. Bureau of the Census.

Step 2

Students provide answers to each question.

Question 1:   What might be the connection between longer lives for women and the trend toward living in cities?

A Sample of Possible Student Responses

- People in cities might have earned more. Women may have eaten better and stayed healthier in the cities.

- Women in cities may have had better access to newspapers. They may have read more about good health standards.

- There may have been better access to doctors in the cities. Thus, women may have begun to live longer because they were more likely to get treated when they were sick in cities than when they were sick in rural areas.

- Cities tended to bring more medical scholars and researchers together. This resulted in an explosion of new information about health and medicine. This new information increased the life spans of all people in the later years.

Question 2:   Other than the move from rural areas to the cities, what other things might have led to higher percentages of women in older age groups in the later years?

A Sample of Possible Student Responses

- Women could have started having fewer children. If this happened, fewer would have died in childbirth, and more would have lived to an older age.

- In the earlier years, a high percentage of women could have been immigrants. Immigrants tend to be younger. This would account for higher percentages of younger women in the earlier years.

- There could have been some fatal diseases that killed women in their twenties and thirties for which cures became available in later years.

- In earlier years, society may not have cared as much for older women as it did in later years. There could have been a deliberate failure to care for older women in the earlier years.

Step 3

During this phase of the lesson, you direct students to gather evidence supporting or refuting each of the possible explanations they had generated in response to the two questions. You will want to direct them to additional resource materials containing information. Students proceed to gather as much relevant information as possible.

It is important to have specific sources of information readily available for student use. Directions to students to "go to the library and find it" are a sure prescription for

These students look over data the teacher has asked them to use as they work on an inquiry lesson.

failure. Many will give up. Even those who do will be frustrated. These kinds of negative attitudes can undermine the motivational potential of a good inquiry lesson. This is a good place to use classroom computers. Students can access numerous databases through the World Wide Web, from CD-ROM discs, or from other sources.

Step 4

During this phase, the responses to the focus questions are reexamined in light of the additional information that has been gathered. The nature and reliability of the evidence is discussed. Once all information related to a given explanation has been considered, the class decides whether to accept, reject, or revise the explanation.

You conclude this phase of the activity by writing on the board those explanations for which the most evidential support has been found.

Step 5

Students are asked to look at the explanations for which they have found good support. The teacher may ask questions such as these:

- Given all of the evidence you have seen supporting these explanations, what do you think is the single best explanation for more women living longer in 1910 than in 1850 and in 1970 than in 1910?
- Why do you make this choice?
- How confident are you that it is correct?

When the students make a final choice, you review the supporting evidence. You remind class members that this conclusion should not be regarded as final. It may be revised should additional information become available.

This description has been compressed for purposes of illustration. Good inquiry lessons require time, and issues addressed are often complex. It takes time for students to master skills associated with logical thinking. If time is at a premium and the primary objective is content coverage rather than teaching the inquiry process, an inquiry approach may not be the best choice.

Simulations

Another powerful form of discovery learning involves the use of *simulations*. These are often called *simulation games* because they include a goal that is to be achieved by the player and some rules that must be followed in order to achieve the goal. The term *game* also captures the play-like environment that is often created when students are engaged in a simulation activity. Simulations are really complex forms of role playing that can be taken to quite sophisticated levels.

The goal of the simulation is to simplify reality and place the participant in a situation where the consequences of choices can be experienced. Thus, the consequences of different actions and hypotheses can be tested. An analysis of the actions and the results can help students discover principles and higher-level thinking processes as well as help them apply learning in ways that will facilitate transfer to real world problems. Because of the realistic setting, students often find simulation activities motivating and interesting.

The increased availability of technology and computers in the classrooms has greatly amplified possible uses of simulations in the school classroom. Today, excellent educational simulation software is available from educational materials supply houses. Computer-based simulations utilize a technology that makes it possible for students to immediately experience the results of their actions. This feature allows them to try multiple approaches as they test the adequacy of their initial solutions to problems.

An important step in all simulations is debriefing. When you use a simulation with a group of students, some of the most important learning occurs in a discussion at the end of the exercise. This phase of the simulation lesson gives your students an opportunity to analyze their actions and begin to develop concepts and principles based on what they experienced. This also provides them with an opportunity to share their experiences with others and formulate statements that explain the cause and effect linkages they found.

The basic steps in using a simulation in the classroom are the following:

- Assign roles to the students;
- Explain the objective for each role;
- Explain the rules and the operating procedure;
- Conduct a demonstration;
- Conduct the simulation activity;
- Debrief the activity, discuss what happened, and identify principles; and
- If needed, repeat the activity.

Creative Thinking

The world has a never-ending supply of serious problems. Throughout history, solutions to problems often have come from people who have responded to them in unusual, creative ways. Problems would not be problems if conventional solutions could be easily applied. It takes someone who has the curiosity, insight, and emotional security to try a novel approach to a solution.

Often, creative solutions result when people make unusual associations between different kinds of things. For example, Ruggiero (1988) points out that the inventor of the fork-lift truck got the idea from watching mechanical fingers lift donuts out of an oven. He goes on to note that Gutenberg's invention of the printing press resulted, in part, from his observation of a wine press.

Creative thinking is stimulated when people are able to defer final judgment and when they do not have fear of failure (Ruggiero, 1988). The ability to generate creative new information is not widespread among students (Perkins, 1981). To remedy this situation, specific instructional techniques have been developed to enhance students' creative thinking powers. One that is widely used is *brainstorming*. Brainstorming is designed to stimulate original solutions to problems. It seeks to unleash mental power in ways that discourage students from relying on ordinary and conventional responses. It places a premium on the ability to generate large numbers of creative responses.

Brainstorming developed in the world of business. Concerned leaders noticed that junior-level managers shied away from proposing novel solutions to problems. Often, they simply parroted positions of senior executives. As a result, insights of these younger executives rarely got a hearing. The brainstorming technique was developed to encourage a broad sharing of innovative ideas. The technique ensures that all ideas will be heard and considered.

Rules for conducting a brainstorming exercise are simple:

- Students are provided with a problem to consider. ("Suppose all books were printed with an ink that would disappear after six months. What would happen if that were true?")

- Students are invited to call out their ideas as rapidly as possible. A student is free to speak whenever an opening of silence occurs. The idea is to generate a rapid outpouring of ideas. Students are told to say whatever comes to their minds so long as it is relevant to the problem.

- Students are cautioned not to comment positively or negatively on any ideas suggested by others. All ideas are accepted. This rule helps break down students' fear of "saying something stupid."

- The teacher or a designated record keeper writes down every idea. This person should not be concerned about neatness. He needs to be someone who can write fast. Student ideas come at a very rapid rate.

- The exercise should be stopped when there is a noticeable decline in the rate of presentation of new ideas.

- A general discussion of the ideas concludes the exercise.

Brainstorming can be applied in a number of secondary curriculum areas. It is an effective technique for stimulating students to produce new ideas rather than rehash old ones or react to views of others.

Critical Thinking

Whereas the primary function of creative thinking is to generate ideas, the primary function of *critical thinking* is to evaluate ideas. Critical thinking always involves judgment. Critical thinking conclusions are based on more than uninformed opinion. Properly, judgments are made in terms of defensible criteria.

Sometimes you will be able to link activities that ask your students to engage in both creative thinking and critical thinking. When you do this, the creative thinking activity takes place first. During this phase of the lesson, you give your students directions that encourage them to produce ideas. During the second phase, you direct class members to use critical thinking approaches to evaluate these ideas.

A basic procedure for brainstorming was introduced in the section introducing creative thinking. Dunn and Dunn (1972) developed an analytic brainstorming approach that applies critical thinking to the initial creative results of the first part of a brainstorming activity. You might develop an analytic brainstorming lesson along these lines:

- You begin by posing a problem in the form of a statement about what an ideal solution to a problem might be: "The best thing we could do to prevent pollution of Gulf Coast beaches would be to. . . . " (Students brainstorm appropriate responses. You write down their answers so all students can easily see them.)

- With responses developed during the preceding step in full view, you next ask students why the best things mentioned have not already taken place: "What things are getting in the way of those 'best things' we could do to prevent pollution of Gulf Coast beaches?" (Students brainstorm responses.)

- The next phase features a question about what might be done to overcome obstacles noted in response to the question posed in the previous step: "How could we overcome difficulties that keep us from doing what we have to do to prevent pollution of Gulf Coast beaches?" (Students brainstorm appropriate responses.)

- Next, you ask students to point out difficulties of implementing ideas noted in the previous step: "What might stand in the way of our efforts to overcome difficulties that keep us from taking necessary action to prevent pollution of Gulf Coast beaches?" (Students brainstorm appropriate responses.)

- Now, you ask students to decide what should be done first to begin a realistic solution to the problem: "Considering all of our thinking, what steps should we take first? Be prepared to explain your choices." (Students respond and defend their choices by reference to appropriate criteria.)

In general, critical thinking involves approaches to making evaluative judgments that are based on logical consideration of evidence and application of appropriate criteria. Beyer (1988), a leading proponent of teaching thinking skills to students in the schools, points out that critical thinking does not result from following a specific sequence of steps. Rather, it involves the use of a number of mental operations, including the following:

- Distinguishing between statements of verifiable facts and value claims;
- Distinguishing relevant from irrelevant information, claims, or reasons;
- Determining the factual accuracy of a statement;
- Determining the credibility of a written source;
- Identifying ambiguous claims or arguments;
- Identifying unstated assumptions;
- Detecting bias;
- Identifying logical fallacies;
- Recognizing logical inconsistencies in a line of reasoning; and
- Determining the strength of an argument or claim. (Beyer, 1988)

Controversial issues often function well as stimuli for worthwhile lessons that feature critical thinking. Unfortunately, some teachers hesitate to bring such issues into the classroom. This is often due to fear of parent or community protests. Not wanting to stir up unnecessary resistance to school programs, these teachers steer the safe course and avoid discussing issues where there might be strong disagreement. We think this is the wrong response. Students need to know that there are responsible ways of dealing with controversial issues. In addition, the introduction of real-life disputes often motivates them. Students appreciate the importance of these issues, and they often commit enthusiastically to lessons featuring content that is relevant to the world they live in outside the school.

Lessons that feature controversial issues need not generate negative parental and community concern. In teaching this kind of content, you have to recognize that it is not your role to force students to arrive at a given conclusion. Rather, your purpose is to help students apply critical thinking to the process so that each person in the class can arrive at an intelligent and thoughtful position.

Problem Solving

Problem-solving approaches are used when students are asked to think about problems for which there is likely to be a best or correct solution. This does not necessarily mean that these solutions may not at some future time be challenged. However, they are considered best, correct, right, or appropriate, given the evidence that is available at the time the problem is considered. These are examples of issues that you might ask students to address when using a problem-solving approach:

- What is causing the leaves on my house plants to turn yellow and fall off?
- Why is it colder in the winter months in Minneapolis than in Juneau, even though Juneau is much farther north?
- Why do people in Maine and Alabama speak with different accents?
- Why don't armadillos live in California?
- What has caused twentieth-century English to differ more from seventeenth century English than twentieth-century French differs from seventeenth century French?

When you introduce students to problem solving, you teach them to follow certain steps:

- Step 1: Identify the problem.
- Step 2: Consider possible approaches to its solution.
- Step 3: Select and apply approaches.
- Step 4: Evaluate the adequacy of the conclusion.

Suppose you were teaching a high school algebra class and wished to apply this model. This is how your lesson might unfold:

Step 1

YOU: All right, class, I want each of you to solve this equation. (On the board, the teacher writes this equation: $2X^2 - 46 = 116$.) Now, does everybody understand what I want you to do? (Student raises a hand.) Ruby?

RUBY: You want us to solve for X, right?

YOU: Right.

Step 2

YOU: Now, before you start, I want someone to tell me how you're going to go about it. John, how about you?

JOHN: Well, we're going to have to get this thing down to a simpler form. The first thing I would do is get rid of the $2X^2$ by dividing both sides by 2.

YOU: Okay. That makes sense. What would need to be done next? Gabriella?

GABRIELLA: I think we'll need to arrange it so we'll have the X^2 on one side and all of the numbers on the other.

YOU: Fine. Now what do we need to remember about the sign of a number when we move it from one side of an equation to the other? I mean, if I had the equation X - 3 = 4, what would happen if I moved the minus three to the other side? Kim?

KIM: The minus three would become a plus three. So you would end up with X = 4 + 3, or 7.

YOU: Excellent. Remember the sign changes when we move from one side to the other. Now, once you moved all the numbers to one side, what would you have to do to solve for X? Jean?

JEAN: You would need to add all of the numbers together and then take the square root of the total.

Step 3

YOU: We seem to have the basic procedures well in mind. Now I want each of you to solve the problem. If you get stuck, raise your hand, and I will try to help you. (Students individually begin working on the problem.)

Step 4

YOU: I see that everybody has come up with an answer. Now let's check our work to see whether the answers are correct. Jennifer, tell me how we might do that.

JENNIFER: I'm not sure.

YOU: Anyone have an idea? Raoul?

RAOUL: We could substitute our answer for X in the original equation to see if it works.

YOU: Good idea. Let's try that. Raoul, what did you get as your answer?

RAOUL: 9.

YOU: Fine, now let's substitute 9 for X in our original equation. (You write the following sequence of substitutions on the board:)

$$2X^2 - 46 = 116$$
$$2 (9 \times 9) - 46 = 116$$
$$2 (81) - 46 = 116$$
$$162 - 46 = 116$$
$$116 = 116$$

Your answer seems to be correct. Does everybody see what I have done here? (Teacher goes on to answer questions and to emphasize the importance of checking the accuracy of answers to problems.)

You may also want to consider a *case study* as a vehicle for involving students in problem solving. For decades, the case study approach has been used in law schools and in many graduate schools of business. In recent years, case study instruction has been tried in many different subject areas. For example, if you were teaching a lesson involving geometry, you might try to liven up your instruction by presenting brief cases involving flight problems that pilots face. These cases can illustrate some practical applications of geometric principles.

When you use the case study method, you present the class with a fairly complete account of a situation that raises important questions. Students then identify the key issues and go about gathering information that will help them try to resolve them. Case studies are especially useful promoters of active student involvement. They help students understand that there are not always clear answers to problems.

Cases you select as a focus for this kind of instruction can be real or contrived. Actual cases bring an air of reality to the classroom but may have the disadvantage that some students will know the resolution and will, therefore, fail to take the problem-solving process seriously. Good cases focus on issues that the students see as important and for which there is not a simple right or wrong answer.

Decision Making

Not all problems have answers that are clearly right, correct, or appropriate. There are questions for which there are no best answers. In this situation, people often must make choices from among a variety of acceptable alternatives. This process involves a thinking skill known as *decision making* (Beyer, 1988). Because it involves choices from among a number of competing appropriate responses, decision making involves consideration of personal values and relevant evidence.

The thinking model for decision-making varies from that used in problem solving. The major reason for this difference is that value judgments play a much more important role in decision making than in problem solving. The following seven-step model is an example of an approach used in decision-making lessons:

1. Describe the basic issue or problem.
2. Point out alternative responses.
3. Identify evidence supporting each alternative.
4. Identify values reflected in each alternative.
5. Point out possible consequences of each alternative.
6. Make a choice from among available alternatives.
7. Identify evidence and values considered in making this choice.

CRITICAL INCIDENT

Why Don't Ms. Levin's "Good" Students Like Decision Making?

Naomi Levin, who teaches eleventh-graders in a high school in a medium-sized city in the Rocky mountains, is midway through her fourth year of teaching. Her subject is American history. Last summer, she attended a special institute on higher-level thinking skills, and she came back determined to use some of the techniques she learned in her own classes.

She decided to emphasize decision-making skills in a unit on the Great Depression. She selected these focus questions:

- What should the government have done (that it didn't do) to prevent the Depression?
- What should the government have done to end the Depression sooner?

To help students gather information about these questions and likely alternative responses, Naomi worked closely with the school librarian. A special shelf of resource materials was organized for members of Naomi's class to use. After she gave students a general orientation to the decision-making approach, students dug into the materials.

After students had had a chance to think about the questions, some possible responses, and some more-or-less final conclusions that made sense to them, Naomi led the class in a general discussion centered on the focus questions. She said that the intensity of student interest and the level of involvement was outstanding. She thought everything had gone very well. This view changed when some of her A students dropped by to talk after school.

These students reported that they had really enjoyed what was going on in class, but that they had some concerns. Most of them indicated that they were going on to college and that the class had spent a lot of time just on one topic. They indicated that they were worried about not covering other topics that they might need to know about to do well in college.

Also, they felt very uneasy about what kind of test they would be facing when "all this discussing and speculating ends." Though they didn't say so in so many words, they seemed to be indicating that they knew how to get As when content was taught in a more traditional way, but that they weren't sure about how their performances would stack up when they were evaluated on "this decision-making stuff." Several students strongly hinted that they would prefer to go back to a more familiar way of dealing with course content.

Naomi had always counted on her good students for support. She was disappointed that these class leaders expressed concern about an approach that, in her mind, works well. Now she is in doubt as to what she should do.

■ ■ ■

What values were implied by the reaction of some students to Naomi's new approach? Why were they concerned about this change? Did their values conflict with Naomi's? How might values of others (the principal, parents, community leaders, and other teachers) influence their reactions to Naomi's approach? How concerned should

Naomi be about this situation? Do you think it possible that any change from a familiar pattern will result in student concerns of this kind, or is there something attached specifically to the decision-making technique that brought it about in this situation? Is it acceptable to cover less content in more depth, or does such a decision irresponsibly deny students access to important information they should have? What kinds of assessment might be appropriate when the emphasis has been on developing students' decision-making proficiency?

An Example of a Basic Decision-Making Lesson

Step 1

A local school board has taken under consideration a proposal to require every student to take four years of mathematics. The issue or problem might be framed like this:

> "Should students be required to take four years of mathematics in high school?"

Step 2

In this case, there are just two basic alternatives. Alternative one is to support a requirement for all students to take four years of mathematics in high school. Alternative two is to oppose such a requirement.

Step 3

Some of the following evidence might be gathered to *support* a four-year mathematics requirement:

- SAT scores in mathematics have failed to reach levels achieved by students in the 1960s.
- The nation is facing an impending shortage of engineers and other technical people who must have sound backgrounds in mathematics.
- Students will begin college-level mathematics instruction at higher levels because of better high school backgrounds.
- The requirement will improve the general quality of the high school curriculum by making the whole program more rigorous.
- Some of the following evidence might be gathered to *oppose* a four-year mathematics requirement:
- The requirement will weaken existing math courses. This is true because all high school students do not have the talent for the math courses that, given the new requirements, they will be required to take.
- The requirement will result in an unfortunate reduction in the number of available electives.
- Not all high school graduates go to college.

- Not all occupational fields, even for college graduates, demand an extensive background in mathematics.

Step 4
Individuals who support a four-year mathematics requirement might cite these values, among others:

- Mathematics courses are difficult, and they provide a needed element of rigor to the high school program.
- Too much electivity in high school is not good.
- Society needs more technically trained people, and it is the school's job to provide them.
- The following values might be among those cited by individuals who *oppose* a four-year mathematics requirement:
- Individual choice is an important part of the high school experience.
- Mathematics is not necessarily more rigorous than other subjects it might displace.
- The society should not go overboard in imposing its priorities on individuals.

Step 5
A supporter of a four-year mathematics requirement might cite the following consequences as among those that might follow implementation of such a policy:

- Quantitative SAT scores may be expected to rise.
- High school graduates will be better prepared for college.
- The nation will be better able to compete with such technologically oriented nations as Japan.

An opponent of a four-year mathematics requirement might cite the following consequences as logically resulting from implementation of such a policy:

- The drop-out rate among high school students will increase as academic frustrations become too much for some students.
- Discipline problems will increase among students who remain because those who are not talented in mathematics will sense that they have been put in a no-win situation.
- Because vocationally oriented electives will decrease in number, some employers will begin to attack the schools for failing to provide relevant instruction.

Step 6
At this point, a decision is made. In this case, because there are only two alternatives, a choice would be made either to (1) support the decision to require four years of mathematics, or (2) oppose this decision.

Step 7

A person *supporting* the decision might identify the pieces of information and values relevant to his or her conclusion in this way:

> "I was impressed by the data showing the decline in quantitative SAT scores since the early 1960s. The growing shortage of engineers and technicians also impressed me. Thinking back on my own high school experience, I concluded that high school students lack the maturity to choose electives wisely. In the long run, they would be better served by a more prescriptive curriculum. Finally, I think the schools *do* have a responsibility to require students to take courses in areas where we have a critical national shortage."

A person *opposing* the decision might identify the pieces of information and values relevant to his or her conclusion in this way:

> "It is clear to me that requiring four years of mathematics will reduce the number of electives available to students. Many vocational electives in the high school program do a fine job of responding to the needs of students who will go to work once they graduate. We need to preserve these programs. Finally, I don't think we should allow needs identified by bureaucratic federal agencies to force content on students in the schools. Local control and freedom of choice are a cherished part of our educational heritage."

Issues, Values, and Consequences Analysis

Decision making applies to the affective or the values area of the curriculum as well as to the academic portion. One application of decision making to the values area is that of *issues, values, and consequences analysis.* The general steps that are followed are basically those usually used for decision making with the addition of components that require students to consider values related to the focus issue(s) as they move toward making a decision. These are the steps that you typically would follow in implementing this approach:

- Identify the general issue.
- Describe faction A, including basic beliefs and values.
- Identify relevant alternatives open to faction A.
- Identify possible consequences for each alternative.
- Identify what would be valued in choosing each alternative.
- Repeat the above steps for faction B (and any other remaining groups).
- Compare the values, alternatives, and consequences of all factions.
- Make a choice as to the best alternative in terms of what you consider to be the highest values.

Step 1: Identify the General Issue

During this step you work with the entire class to ensure that all students understand the issue. You may do this by introducing the students to a problem. (During the 1950s,

China was not a member of the United Nations. Some people thought it was strange that the world's most populous nation was not a member. Others feared that admitting China would give additional voting power to nations with Communist governments. There was much debate over whether China should be admitted to the U.N. What was the basic issue involved here? What was the basic disagreement? What are the two different groups that were involved?)

Step 2: Describe Each Faction

Decision making is needed in lessons such as this because there are two or more positions that are in conflict. Different groups have different opinions as to what should be done. During this phase, your intent is to have the students, working in groups, gain as much information about each one of the supporting positions. Who are they? What are their goals? What are their beliefs? What things are most important to them?

Step 3: Identify Relevant Alternatives Open to Each Faction

During this phase of the lesson, you ask students to work in groups to identify alternative courses of action open to members of the faction they are considering. Sometimes you will encourage students to brainstorm alternative answers to questions. For example, you might ask them to think about different answers to questions such as: "What are some of the things those opposed to admitting China into the U.N. might have done to prevent it?" "What are some things supporters could have done to gain China's admission?" "Were there options other than full admission or full denial?"

 MORE FROM THE WEB ▬▬▬▬▬▬▬▬▬▬▬▬▬▬▬▬▬▬▬▬▬▬▬▬

Higher-level Thinking

Much information today is available on the Web that relates to teaching higher-level thinking skills. The volume of information attests to the high interest both professional educators and the general public have in approaches to teaching that will prepare students to deal intelligently with the complex challenges they will face as adults. You may wish to visit some of these sites.

The WebQuest Page

http://edweb.sdsu.edu/webquest/webquest.html

- WebQuest, developed by Bernie Dodge and Tom March at San Diego State University, is a process involving inquiry-oriented lessons that use content available on the World Wide Web. When you reach this page, click on "Search." This will take you to a page titled "Matrix of Examples." Depending on your interests, click on either "Middle School or "High School." This will take you to a huge listing of individual school subjects. Under each, you will find links to complete lessons along with various kinds of learning tasks each incorporates. If you click on the name of one of these lessons, you will go directly to the complete lesson. These materials are nicely formatted. You will find WebQuest materials to be very professionally prepared.

Introduction to Creative Thinking

http://www.sccu.edu/Faculty/R_Harris/crebook1.htm

- This material, produced by Robert Harris of Southern California College, includes an excellent overview of creative thinking. Among topics addressed are: (1) creative methods, (2) negative attitudes that block creativity, (3) distinctions between creative thinking and critical thinking, and (4) mental blocks to creative thinking.

Critical Thinking: Primary and Secondary Information

http://www.criticalthinking.org/K12/default.html

- You will find numerous resources here that you can use in lessons that integrate critical thinking into your instructional program. This site is maintained by a number of organizations that are interested in promoting the development of critical thinking.

Problem Solving

http://mailer.fsu.edu/~jflake/probSol.html

- At this site you will find excellent links to sources where you can obtain useful sample problem-solving strategies.

Decision Making Strategies

http://scholar.coe.uwf.edu/pacee/steps/tutorial/DecisionMakingStrategies.htm

- This material was prepared by Monique O'Brien to assist Florida teachers in grades 4 to 12 who wanted information about instructional practices that would be consistent with a state mandate for teaching students' good decision-making strategies. You will find some good lesson ideas here.

Step 4: Identify Possible Consequences for Each Alternative

Alternative courses of action may produce different results or consequences. During this step, you encourage students to look at each alternative course of action and to consider the possible consequences of that action. For example, "What might have been the consequences of a massive information campaign to discredit China?" "What might have been the consequences of some sort of conditional admission?"

Step 5: Identify Values Associated with Each Choice
Once the alternatives and their possible consequences have been identified, the students should now identify what would be valued by choosing each alternative. For example, "What was most important for those who opposed admission?" "What was most important for those who favored admission?" "What would those who advocated a smear campaign have valued most highly?" "What would those who advocated partial admission have valued?"

Step 6: Compare the Values, Alternatives, and Consequences of All Factions
At this point the information gathered by the different groups investigating different factions can be brought together and compared. Your purpose at this point is to help

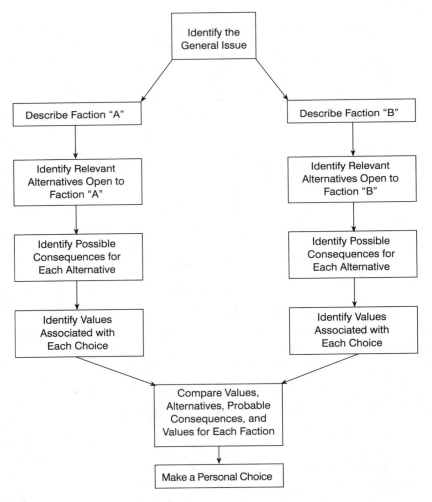

Figure 11–6
Format of the General Flow of an Issues, Values, and Consequences Analysis Lesson

students understand that many decisions involve a conflict of values and value priorities. For example, some people may have seen that their value of preserving democracy as a justification for opposing China's admission to the U.N. would have been in conflict with their value of honesty—particularly if smear tactics involving the use of false information had been used by some opponents of China's admission.

Step 7: Make a Choice

At this point you challenge students to make a personal decision about the issue that has been considered. You encourage them to consider which values they consider to be most important and then to reflect on which decision would be most consistent with their own values.

In summary, issues, values, and consequences analysis is designed to help students appreciate that decisions are not made just by dispassionate consideration of evidence. Individual values play a role. In addition, decisions frequently involve a conflict between two or more values. When people make decisions, they have to think about and weigh the importance of both their own values and those of others.

FOR YOUR PORTFOLIO

1. What materials, ideas you learned in this chapter related to *higher-level thinking* will you include as "evidence" in your portfolio? Select up to 3 items of information to be included in your portfolio. Number them 1, 2, and 3.

2. Think about why you selected these materials for your portfolio. Consider such issues as the following in your response:

   - The specific purposes to which this information can be put when you plan, deliver, and assess the impact of your instruction,
   - The compatibility of the information with your own priorities and values,
   - The contributions this information can make to your personal development as a teacher,
   - The factors that led you to include this material as opposed to some alternatives you considered.

3. Prepare a written reflection in which you analyze the decision-making process you followed. Also, mention the INTASC Standard(s) to which your selected material relates. (First complete the chart below.)

Item of Evidence Number	INTASC Standards									
	S1	S2	S3	S4	S5	S6	S7	S8	S9	S10
1										
2										
3										

Key Ideas in Summary

- There is much less centralized teacher control in techniques designed to develop students' higher-level thinking skills than in direct instruction lessons. The teacher functions as a manager who presents students with a problem and assists them, as needed, as they work toward a conclusion.
- *Metacognition* refers to thought about the process of thinking. Metacognitive instructional approaches seek to help students become conscious of their own thought processes and to select those that are relevant for solving particular problems and tasks with which they are confronted. Examples of these metacognitive approaches include teacher modeling and visualizing thinking.
- *Discovery learning* involves getting students to learn how to identify basic concepts and principles, or the structure of a subject, rather than having them taught directly by the teacher. Learning how to discover is at least as important as what is discovered. This develops thinking skills that will be useful in a variety of life situations. Contrary to some popular notions, effective discovery teaching requires teachers to spend more planning than is true when some other instructional techniques are selected.
- *Inquiry teaching* is based on inductive learning. Inductive learning proceeds from the specific to the general. This means that students first are presented with specific examples that they are asked to study. From this study, they derive general explanatory conclusions or principles. Inquiry teaching involves students in the creation of new knowledge. Approaches typically follow a logical, step-by-step sequence that is thought to develop students' rational thinking powers.
- *Simulation* is a powerful approach to helping students discover important processes and values as well as higher-level thinking skills. Simulations involve placing the students in situations that allow them to experience the consequences of their actions. An analysis of actions taken and the resulting consequences help students discover important principles and processes.
- *Creative thinking* frees people to develop unusual or novel solutions to problems. It involves unique insight. Creative thinking is thought to be stimulated when people are able to defer final judgment until many alternatives have been considered and when they do not fear failure. Brainstorming is an example of a classroom technique that is designed to elicit creative thinking.
- *Critical thinking* focuses on the evaluation of ideas. It aids students in making judgments based on consideration of evidence. The analytic brainstorming approach developed by Dunn and Dunn (1972) is an example of a classroom technique designed to encourage the development of critical thinking abilities.
- *Problem-solving approaches* are designed to help students consider problems for which a single best answer is thought to exist. This does not mean that this best answer will be

right every time. It simply implies that it is best, given presently available evidence. These steps are included in many problem-solving approaches: (1) identifying the problem, (2) considering alternative approaches to solving it, (3) selecting and applying one or more approaches, and (4) making a final judgment regarding the best approach (or solution).

■ *Decision making* refers to thinking sequences that are relevant when the problems that students confront have no generally agreed-on correct or right answers. A number of appropriate answers may be identified. The alternative selected reflects both a consideration of evidence and of values.

Reflections

1. Some scholars argue that teaching students how to engage in sophisticated thinking should be the primary mission of the school. Why might they take this position? Do you agree? Explain your response.

2. Teachers today feel obligated to cover much academic content in the courses they teach. Given this reality, should they devote class time to instruction designed to help students develop appropriate metacognitive processes? Why or why not?

3. Both the Suchman (1962) inquiry approach and visualizing thinking presume that students have trouble making sense out of the enormous volume of information that confronts them. Is this true? If so, are the Suchman technique and visualizing thinking sound approaches to helping them deal with it?

4. Why are relatively few people creative thinkers, and what might you do in the classroom to prompt more creative thinking from students?

5. What are some key features of approaches designed to elicit critical thinking?

6. How would you describe differences in the purpose of a traditional brainstorming approach and the variant called *analytical brainstorming*, developed by Dunn and Dunn (1972)?

7. Under what conditions would a problem-solving approach be an appropriate instructional choice?

8. Why do different people arrive at quite different conclusions when a decision-making approach is used to consider an issue?

9. In what ways do problem solving and decision making differ? Is it worthwhile for teachers to teach both approaches to students? Why, or why not?

10. What are basic steps followed in issues, values, and consequences analysis? Is it proper for school lessons to deal with issues involving values? Why, or why not?

Learning Extensions

1. Secondary teachers are pressed for time. Some people argue that time devoted to teaching students learning processes and thinking skills (e.g., metacognitive

approaches, creative thinking skills, problem-solving skills, critical thinking skills, decision-making skills, and so forth) takes valuable time away from content instruction. Find another student in your class to work with you on a project to prepare arguments related to this question: "Is taking class time to teach thinking skills to students responsible?" Make an oral presentation to the class in which one of you presents evidence supporting a *yes* answer and one of you presents evidence supporting a *no* answer.

2. Select a topic from a subject you are preparing to teach. Describe how you might incorporate one of the following into a lesson related to this topic:

- Inquiry teaching
- Problem solving
- Creative thinking
- Decision making
- Critical thinking

Present this information to your instructor in a short paper.

3. Interview teachers who have incorporated inquiry teaching into their instructional programs. Ask them to describe pluses and minuses of this approach. Share your findings with others in the class as part of a general discussion of inquiry in the secondary school classroom.

4. Prepare a collection of articles from professional journals or from Web sources that describe practical classroom applications of inquiry and creative thinking approaches. You may wish to use the *Education Index* to locate article titles and journals. A search engine will help you find items posted on the Web. Try to include at least ten articles. Present them to your instructor for review. Keep these materials as a resource to use when you begin teaching.

5. Invite several department heads from a local secondary school to visit your class. If this is not possible, try to get a director of secondary education, a director of secondary curriculum, or another central school-district office administrator to come. Ask about the relative emphasis on inquiry instruction and on teaching thinking skills to students. Specifically, ask whether teachers are encouraged to use these approaches and whether any effort is made to provide in-service training to help teachers become more proficient in implementing them.

6. Go to the Merrill Education's Link to General Methods Resources site at this URL: http://www.prenhall.com/methods-cluster/ At the bottom of the page select "instructional strategies" as your topic and click on the "begin" button. This will take you to the "Overview" page. On the left side, click on "Web Links." On the Web Links page click on "critical thinking skills." Follow links and gather information you can use as the basis for a brief oral report focusing on specific things you can do in your lessons to encourage development of students' critical thinking skills.

References

Beyer, B. K. (1987). Practice is not enough. In M. Heiman & J. Slomianko (Eds.), *Thinking skills: Concepts and techniques* (pp. 77–86). Washington, DC: National Education Association.

Beyer, B. K. (1988). *Developing a thinking skills program.* Boston: Allyn & Bacon.

Boudourides, M. A. (1998). *Constructivism and education: A shopper's guide.* Samos, Greece: International Conference on the Teaching of Mathematics, July 3–6. [http://www.duth.gr/~mboudour/mab/constr.html]

Bruner, J. (1960). *The process of education.* Cambridge, MA: Harvard University Press.

Dewey, J. (1910). *How we think.* Boston: D. C. Heath.

Dunn, R., & Dunn, K. (1972). *Practical approaches to individualizing instruction: Contracts and other effective teaching strategies.* New York: Parker.

Gennrich, D., & Long, L. (1999). *How does one develop tutor-led distance materials for use in collaborative learning groups, with an emphasis on constructivist learning?* Proceedings of the 8th Annual Teaching Learning Forum, The University of Western Australia, February 3–4. [http://cleo.murdoch.edu.au/asu/pubs/tlf/tlf99/dj/gennrich.html]

Joyce, B., & Weil, M. (1996). *Models of teaching* (5th ed.). Boston: Allyn & Bacon.

Perkins, D. (1981). *The mind's best work.* Cambridge, MA: Harvard University Press.

Ruggiero, V. R. (1988). *Teaching thinking across the curriculum.* New York: Harper & Row.

Slavin, R. E. (1994). *Educational psychology* (4th ed.). Boston: Allyn & Bacon.

Suchman, J. R. (1962). *The elementary school training program in scientific inquiry.* Report to the U.S. Office of Education, Project Title VII, Project 216. Urbana: University of Illinois.

Woolfolk, A. E. (1995). *Educational psychology* (6th ed.). Boston: Allyn & Bacon.

IV

Assessing and Managing

12

Assessing Student Learning

This chapter will aim to

- distinguish between *measurement* and *evaluation;*

- describe what is meant by *authentic assessment*, and point out some advantages of this approach;

- point out how *rubrics* are used;

- explain how *portfolios* can be used to document student learning;

- point out some uses of informal approaches to assessment, and describe how several informal techniques work;

- describe strengths and weaknesses of some traditional formal evaluation techniques; and

- explain techniques for formatting matching, essay, multiple-choice, completion, and true-false tests.

Introduction

"Is my program working well?" "Are my students learning?" When you start teaching, you will want answers to these questions. To get information about how well members of your classes are doing, you will need to use a number of measurement and evaluation techniques.

Though measurement and evaluation are related terms, they are not synonyms. Measurement refers to the process of gathering information and is, itself, nonjudgmental. Evaluation refers to the process of drawing conclusions after studying information gathered through various measurement processes. Unlike measurement, evaluation requires interpretation (Scriven, 1967). Measurements you take will almost never speak for themselves.

Your personal views about standards of student performance can influence your interpretation of measurements. For example, if you favor norm-referenced evaluation you may prefer to evaluate students in terms of how their work compares to that of others in the class. However, if you favor criterion-referenced evaluation you will be more concerned about how your students' work measures up to a pre-established standard of performance.

Educators today are being asked to do more frequent evaluations of students than they did in the past (Linn & Baker, 1999). Some of the pressures to do this are political. Citizens increasingly clamor for information about the quality of their schools. Often they insist on using comparisons of students' test scores to make their judgments. Many experts question the appropriateness of using test scores for this purpose, arguing,

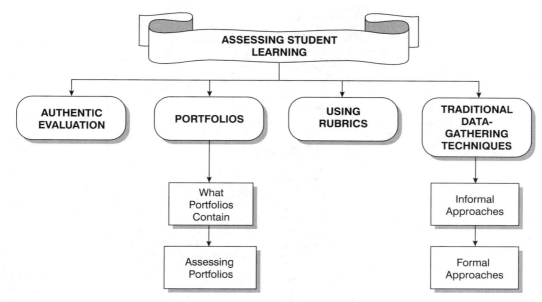

Figure 12–1
Graphic Organizer

among other things, that these scores may be affected by influences going well beyond what teachers and administrators can control.

Recent professional thought about evaluation has also encouraged an increase in the frequency of assessing students. In the past, experts in measurement were concerned primarily with gathering information about student learning only at the end of an extended period of instruction (Tyler, 1949). Since the 1960s, such experts as Scriven (1967) have proposed that it is appropriate to assess students at various times while a unit is being taught as well as at its conclusion. Scriven uses the term *formative evaluation* to describe the periodic evaluation that should take place while you are in the process of teaching new material. Formative evaluation gives you information you can use to provide continuous feedback to your students. It helps you to identify and respond to learning problems as they occur during the instructional sequence itself. Scriven uses the term *summative evaluation* to refer to the traditional testing that occurs at the end of an instructional sequence. Today, evaluation experts recommend that both formative and summative evaluation be used.

One of the challenges you face as you consider approaches to evaluating your students is ensuring that what you are evaluating ties clearly to what you want your students to learn. Critics of some traditional testing practices charge that often the behaviors that are evaluated are selected because they can easily be converted to items on tests and not because they are truly important (Wiggins, 1989a). To remedy this situation, a growing number of experts recommend assessment associated with authentic evaluation.

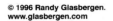

"I'm lousy at spelling because of my parents. They grew up listening to the Beatles, Monkees and Byrds!"

Authentic Evaluation

"You should not teach to the test" is a time-honored bit of folklore in education that rarely has been challenged. Proponents of *authentic evaluation* say that the problem is not teaching to the test but, rather, teaching to an inappropriate test. If you can design tests that truly require your students to demonstrate the kinds of learning you consider to be important, then it makes good sense for you to teach to the test, supporters of authentic evaluation argue.

Authentic tests are designed in such a way that students must demonstrate the kinds of learning that you have emphasized in class. Many traditional tests do not do this. Rather, they involve only samples of the total content that has been taught and require students to answer questions that do little beyond having them demonstrate their recall abilities. Only infrequently do traditional tests call on students to engage in complex performances that reflect sophisticated levels of understanding and competence.

Authentic tests require more. They ask students to perform in ways that are consistent with how experts in the subject area perform as they go about their work. The noted authentic assessment expert, Grant Wiggins (1989b), argues that "authentic assessments replicate the challenges and standards of performance that typically face writers, business people, scientists, community leaders, designers, or historians. These include writing essays and reports, conducting individual and group research, designing proposals and mock-ups, and so on" (p. 704).

Proponents of authentic testing see the test as the standard setter for the school. If tests are sophisticated and require students to engage in complex performances, then there will be incentives for students to work hard so they will be able to do well on these tests. However, if tests require students to engage in performances that require little academic effort and that fail to replicate the real demands faced by experts in the subjects they are studying, then students' development in school will fall short of what it might be.

Authentic assessment procedures require you to devote considerable time to test preparation. You can justify this time commitment because what students experience during authentic assessment activities is really an extension of your basic instruction. Authentic assessments seek to teach as well as reveal what students know. There is evidence that students find tasks associated with authentic assessment to be interesting and relevant. However, some teachers report that honor students, who have been successful performers on more traditional kinds of assessments, sometimes initially find it unsettling that there often are multiple correct answers or approaches when authentic assessment is used (Educational Testing Service, 1995). See Figure 12–2 for an example of an authentic assessment assignment.

Not everyone agrees that authentic assessment is a good idea. (See the critical incident for an example of what some teachers face when they begin to use it.) For one thing, it represents a change from what parents and other community members experienced when they were in school. Some people also worry that few standards presently exist to ensure the quality of authentic assessment procedures. They feel that a move away from more traditional ways of evaluating students might result in lower expectations of students and, hence, become an incentive for them to study less. Finally, traditional tests often yield scores that can be averaged together to suggest how well the general population of students in a given class or school is doing. Such scores sometimes are used to compare and contrast schools. (This is not something measurement specialists applaud, but it is done.) It is more difficult to make these kinds of comparisons when authentic assessment procedures are used.

Professionals at the Educational Testing Service have identified some other issues that deserve attention when authentic evaluation is being considered as an option:

- Authentic assessment tasks sometimes are difficult to develop.
- Teachers need to be involved in developing authentic assessment experiences, and they should have some training in how the approach works.
- Deciding how to score authentic assessment exercises can be a problem.
- Authentic assessment procedures often require more class time than more traditional approaches.
- Use of authentic assessment often also implies a commitment to use different kinds of instructional techniques.
- How to establish high levels of reliability when using authentic assessment is a continuing challenge (Educational Testing Service, 1995).

Using Rubrics

Engaging students in "authentic" learning experiences requires use of non-traditional assessment techniques. When your purpose is to make judgments about complex sets

The assignment that follows is an example of authentic assessment for a grade 7 social studies class. As you look over this material, consider how this kind of evaluation differs from what you experienced as a seventh-grader.

. . .

A STORY BASED ON LOCAL HISTORY:
ASSESSING A LESSON IN A GRADE 7 STATE HISTORY COURSE

Write a true story describing how some aspect of our community has changed from 1950 to today. Focus on any aspect you like. Some possibilities might include changes in the schools, changes in how people make a living, changes in where people do most of their shopping, changes in how the downtown area looks, changes in the places people live, and changes in what people do when they're not working. Interview long-time residents. Use microfilm copies of the local newspaper available in the school library. Write a two- to three-page paper describing your findings. You must also be prepared to tell others in the class what you found.

After you begin work, identify two major ideas about why changes have occurred. Then, develop three questions for each idea; try to answer the questions to test the accuracy of your ideas. Include your ideas, the questions you asked about them, and your findings in your paper.

EVALUATION GUIDELINES FOR THE TEACHER

In assessing work of individual students, consider the following:

- Whether the student identified two tentative ideas to explain the reported change
- Whether three questions were generated for each idea
- Whether the student drew on interviews and newspaper accounts to respond to these questions
- Whether the people selected to be interviewed had the necessary background to provide information related to the change the student was investigating
- Whether the student, in reflecting on what was said in interviews or what was read in newspaper accounts, was able to distinguish between fact and opinion
- Whether the student based conclusions on evidence that was clearly relevant to the position being taken
- Whether there was a logical, point-by-point development in both the student's written work and oral presentation to the class

Figure 12–2
An Example of an Authentic Assignment

of behaviors, familiar teacher-made true-false, matching, and multiple-choice tests will not do. When you face a need to assess a complex set of student behaviors, you will want to use a *rubric*. A *rubric* consists of a set of guidelines that tell you what to look at as acceptable evidence when you need to make judgments about the quality of learner performance on a given task or set of tasks. Often these judgments take the form of rating points. For example, you might use a rubric that rated student performance on a six-point scale, with a "6" being awarded for the highest level of performance and a "1" being awarded for the lowest, with other numbers being assigned to levels lying between the two extremes.

In a rubric, behaviors associated with each rating point are defined as clearly as possible. The purpose of these definitions is to provide some assurance that different raters would assign the same numbers to the same set of observed student behaviors. You may recall the example of the instructional unit introduced in Chapter 7 that focused on the American Revolution. You could devise a rubric to assess students' learning on this unit using a scheme such as the one depicted in Figure 12–3. Note that this rubric divides student behaviors into three categories: (1) quality of information, (2) quality of thinking, and (3) quality of written and/or oral communication. You would assign ratings to students associated with each of these categories.

CRITICAL INCIDENT

Do Parents and Administrators Really Want Authentic Evaluation?

Yesterday, Joe Plinney, who is in his second year of teaching journalism at Parson Weems Senior High School, talked about his work with Roy Lee, a long-time friend.

"When my students leave my class, I want them to be able to get the job done. After all, they're all juniors and seniors. I screened them before they came into this advanced journalism section. They're bright people. As far as I'm concerned, they should be able to go to work for a paper and even begin doing some real investigative reporting, right from the start."

Roy Lee nodded and said, "Sounds great to me. So what's your problem?"

"Well," Joe responded, "I've done a pretty fair job of analyzing what an investigative reporter has to do. And I've checked my ideas out with an editor or two. There's more to it than you might think. These people have to know what kinds of questions to ask. They have to figure out who to talk to and how to get them to open up. When something controversial comes up, they have to find someone reliable to corroborate what they have learned. And, of course, they've got to be able to stitch the story together so it not only is logical but also interests the general reader."

"That makes sense," Roy said. "How do you get the students to get a handle on all that?"

"It's both simple and difficult," Joe replied. "I've figured out that the way to get these students to really take seriously what investigative reporters do is to evaluate them on their ability to do all of these things. For all that we like to talk about 'learning for learning's sake,' most of these kids don't pay much attention to anything that's not connected to a grade. So, basically, all I have to do is give them an investigative reporting assignment and carefully check how well they execute it. That sounds easy, but it really takes a lot of time.

"Especially," continued Joe, "since to make the thing work I have to base each student's entire grade on how well his or her behavior compares to what real investigative reporters do. If I deviate from this and throw in some Mickey Mouse tests over basic terms, for example, students think the real purpose of the class is passing the test rather than learning how to operate as a reporter. Unfortunately, some of my parents and a couple of my building administrators don't agree with me."

"What's their concern?" asked Roy.

"A couple of things," answered Joe. "For one thing, basing a grade only on how well a student performs a complex activity such as investigative reporting is foreign to their experience. They remember pop quizzes, midterm examinations, questions from the text, and that sort of thing. What I want to do is quite different.

"And the administrators—though they won't come right out and say so—think my students won't score well on the standardized tests we give at the end of the year. They're afraid that, because these students won't have had exposure to traditional tests in my class, they'll freeze up when they have to take these exams. If our scores go down, I'll be in trouble. It will be especially bad if we don't stack up well against scores of other schools in the area. I'm sensing a lot of pressure to back off from what I want to do and to go back to more traditional tests."

"What do you think you'll do?" Roy asked.

Joe answered, "Right now, I'm on the fence. On the one hand, I think my priority should be to teach these young people how reporters function in the real world. On the other hand, I can understand that it will be bad for everybody if my approach angers parents and that the school may suffer a real public relations disaster if my students' standardized test scores take a dive."

■　■　■

What do Joe's arguments tell you about what he considers to be important in working with students? What problems does he see with traditional evaluation approaches and what benefits does he expect from the alternative he has selected? What do we learn about priorities of administrators in this school (at least as Joe sees them)? How might Joe's approach conflict with values of parents? What should Joe do next? What positives and negatives will result if he decides to base all of his evaluation on students' abilities to discharge the role of an investigative reporter? What positives and negatives might result from a decision to go back to a more traditional testing and grading procedure? From whom should Joe seek additional advice? Might anything be done to convince parents and others that traditional ways of evaluating and grading students may not have served students' long-term interests well?

Portfolios

Authentic assessment presumes that students will be graded on their abilities to demonstrate sophisticated behaviors that have relevance for real life, not just for school courses. This aim is not well served by many traditional testing practices. Short answer tests and sets of questions featuring multiple-choice, true-false, completion, and match-

Quality of Information	
Rating	Descriptors
1	• Student fails to identify and appropriately describe major concepts and ideas • Student fails to include appropriate facts and other supporting details
2	• Student identifies only a few major concepts and ideas • Student fails defend conclusions with facts and other supporting details • Student provides information that is mostly inaccurate or irrelevant
3	• Student provides some major concepts and ideas • Students provides only a small number of facts and other supporting details • Student's content contains a mixture of correct and incorrect information
4	• Student provides some concepts and ideas, but many of them are only partially defined and described • Student provides a modest amount of facts and other supporting details • Student's information is mostly accurate, but there are some mistakes
5	• Student's concepts and ideas, for the most part, are well defined and described • Student provides appropriate facts and other relevant supporting details • Student's work is characterized by only minor errors of fact
6	• Student's concepts and facts are carefully defined and appropriately described • Student provides and abundance of supporting facts and other relevant details • Student's work is characterized by an absence (or almost a total absence) of factual errors.

Figure 12–3
Example of a Rubric for Assessing Students' Products and Performances for a Unit Focusing on the American Revolution

Quality of Thinking Rating	Criteria
1	• Student fails to identify key evidence that relates to the issue • Student's work does not reflect application of critical thinking skills • Student fails to provide conclusions or provides conclusions that are unclear or unsupportable
2	• Student inappropriately applies critical thinking skills in assessing evidence and making conclusions • Student mentions little relevant evidence in support of conclusions • Student's conclusions do not flow logically from evidence presented
3	• Student does not consistently apply critical thinking skills in assessing evidence and making conclusions, and some critical thinking skills are not applied at all • Student's use of evidence is uneven; some is relevant, some is irrelevant, some is omitted. • Student's conclusions are not complete, given the evidence presented
4	• Student uses critical thinking skills to make some conclusions, but their application is not applied at all when arriving at others • Student identifies some of the evidence relevant to the examined issue • Student's conclusions generally follow logically from the evidence
5	• Student selects and applies appropriate critical thinking skills in almost every case during the process of arriving at conclusions • Student identifies, organizes, and uses evidence that is relevant to the examined issue • Students' conclusions are well-reasoned and clearly supported by relevant evidence
6	• Student selects and applies appropriate critical thinking skills in virtually all cases during the process of arriving at conclusions • Student identifies, organizes, and uses relevant evidence in ways that maximize the power of each piece of supporting information • Students' conclusions are based on clearly-analyzed, logical thought about evidence that, in every case, bears a clear relevance to the examined issue

Figure 12–3, *continued*

Quality of Written and/or Oral Communication Rating	Criteria
1	• Student presents nearly all ideas in ways that are unclear to readers/listeners • Student fails to stick to an identifiable point or theme; there is no central focus • Student fails to develop ideas in an organized, point-by-point way
2	• Student presents a clear majority of ideas in ways that are unclear to readers/listeners • Student's focus is illusive; it is there some of the time, not there for much of the rest of the time • Student's organization is erratic
3	• Student presents a small number of ideas clearly, but most are presented in ways that are unclear to readers/listeners • Student's focus appears to have been planned, but presentation drifts at many points from the focus, making it unclear to readers/listeners • Student's organization is adequate in places, but there are many places where the student fails to follow an established pattern
4	• Student presents some ideas clearly and in ways that reflect clear reasoning processes; others do not meet this standard • Student's focus, with a few lapses, remains generally consistent throughout • Student follows a generally consistent organizational scheme
5	• Student presents most ideas clearly and in ways that reflect clear reasoning processes • Student's focus is consistent and is maintained with few lapses throughout the written/oral presentation • Student follows a clear, coherent organizational scheme with only a few deviations from this standard
6	• Student presents all ideas clearly and in ways that reflect clear reasoning processes • Student's focus on a consistent thesis is evident throughout the written/oral presentation • Student follows a clear, coherent organizational scheme throughout the written/oral presentation

ing items tend to focus on narrowly defined content. They are not designed to provide a picture of how well individual students can put it all together to engage in a competent, professional performance. In recent years, more and more teachers have been using portfolios of student work to assess the degree to which they can perform in authentic and sophisticated ways.

A *portfolio* is a systematically organized collection of a student's work that covers a specific period of time. Artists, actors, models, and photographers have used portfolios for years to display their previous work when they have sought new commissions and other employment opportunities. In secondary school settings, English and language arts teachers, particularly in programs emphasizing development of students' writing skills, were among the first secondary-school instructors to make extensive use of portfolios. The portfolio format proved to be an excellent vehicle for gathering together student writing and displaying changes in proficiency over time. Today, secondary teachers in many subject areas use portfolios.

Portfolio-based evaluation avoids potentially dysfunctional interruptions of instructional processes that you may be using to promote the development of complex learning proficiencies. For example, if your purpose is to develop students' proficiencies as writers, traditional testing over writing mechanics (identifying when to use "who" instead of "whom" and so forth) will not engage students directly in the process of writing (Strzepek & Figgins, 1993). Indeed, time spent by your students preparing for these kinds of tests may divert considerable time and attention away from your longer-term objective of developing their writing skills. However, if you assess students by using portfolios, there is an incentive for them to continue a strong focus on the writing process itself. As they continue to develop, you can gather samples of students' work in individual portfolios, provide comments to them about their progress, ask probing questions, and otherwise make comments designed to encourage students to (1) reflect on what they are doing and (2) engage in self-evaluations as they look at the progress they made from their early papers to those produced later in the term or year.

Portfolio evaluation blends the instructional and evaluation processes. The portfolio is not a static collection of a student's work. The key to its effectiveness is ongoing dialogue between you and individual students and, often, between individual students and others in the class or among students and parents, friends, and other adults.

What Portfolios Contain

Components of portfolios vary depending on the subject being taught and the preferences of teachers and students. Some examples of what portfolios can contain include:

- Completed assignments;
- Journal entries (reflections by the students about content that has been learned);
- Reflections on discussions that have been held in (or out of) class;
- Bookmarks (Porter & Cleland, 1995). These are pieces of paper students have slipped into specific pages of books they are reading and on which they have written specific reactions to or questions about information on that page;

- Prompt questions provided by the teacher;
- Responses to prompt questions provided by the teacher;
- Photos, sketches, and other visuals;
- Summary statements made at different points regarding what has been learned; and
- Self-assessment statements regarding new areas of strength and areas needing additional work.

Use of portfolios is consistent with reflective teaching. Comments you make on students' portfolios will prompt them to think about what they have done, consider alternatives, and speculate about new issues. Writing in portfolios establishes a pattern of ongoing dialogue with students. These exchanges help to personalize your relationships with students, and they encourage you to focus carefully on the development of each learner. Gathering materials in portfolios also provides your students with tangible evidence that they are learning. Periodically, you will ask them to look over their portfolios and to self-validate their learning by citing specific examples of how more recent work represents growth and improvement over that done earlier (Porter & Cleland, 1995).

The evidence gathered in a portfolio also provides opportunities for you and individual students to engage in one-on-one discussions at grading time. When you have a student's portfolio in front of you, you are in a position to look at quite tangible evidence about what a student has done and to discuss individual strengths and weaknesses. This allows you to be quite precise in pinpointing areas needing work.

Proponents of portfolios argue that students who prepare them recognize that grading is data-based and, hence, they tend to accept the grades they receive. Supporters also argue that portfolio-based evaluation awards grades based on an uninterrupted focus on significant learning. This feature contrasts with more traditional assessment schemes where instruction periodically stops while students take tests that may be only loosely tied to the authentic, complex behaviors you are seeking as a teacher.

Many teachers find that students commit so much of themselves to constructing portfolios that they want to keep them as mementos of their school experience. If students keep their portfolios, you lose the ability to review them over the summer (or at a later date) to identify areas that posed learning problems for students that you might wish to approach in different ways when teaching new groups of learners. Some teachers electronically scan at least parts of student portfolios so they can refer back to them after the original copies have been returned to the students. There are also software packages available that prompt students to prepare their entire portfolios electronically—making it easy for you and your students to maintain complete copies of the materials.

Assessing Portfolios

Because the content and complexity of portfolios varies, approaches to evaluate them vary as well. Various rubrics may be used to award a quality scores to various parts of a complex portfolio. (Review Figure 12–3 for an example of this kind of alternative assessment rubric.) You may choose to use a summary rubric to assess a portfolio as a whole.

Ordinarily, when this is done, there is an attempt to provide a series of ratings on various categories that may be relevant to the focus of the portfolio. Various descriptors are used to describe rating points. One scheme might use terms such as "outstanding," "meets standard," "unacceptable." Another might vary the language a bit and use phrases as "Excellent," "Acceptable," or "Not Ready—Yet." Figure 12–4 provides an

Portfolio Assessment

Name _____

Date _____

Use this form to assess the portfolio as a whole. Since individual items in the portfolio have likely already been evaluated, it is important to evaluate the strengths and weaknesses of the entire portfolio and to focus on progress.

	Exceptional	Commendable	Acceptable	Unsatisfactory
Variety				
Understanding of the content				
Evidence of critical thinking and problem-solving ability				
Effectiveness of communication				
Evidence of creativity				
Knowledge of concepts and topical relationships with other content areas				
Overall progress in the course				

Comments _____
_____
_____
_____
_____

Figure 12–4
An Example of a Rubric for Assessing an Entire Portfolio

example of a framework for assessing the overall quality of a portfolio. You will note that it features four rating categories you can use in assessing a student's level of performance in each of the listed areas. The categories are "exceptional," "commendable," "acceptable," and "unsatisfactory." Note, too, the provision for open-ended comments. If you were to use this scheme, this feature would allow you to make additional written comments about some of the categories listed on the left side of the form and also to comment on other issues you want to bring to the attention of the student.

In summary, interest in portfolio use is growing. However, you need to be prepared for some challenges when you use them to assess students' work. Use of portfolios as data sources for grading is new. Many parents are unfamiliar with this approach, and you need to assure them that their use in place of more traditional tests will in no way impede their children's progress toward graduation and toward qualification for the world of work or college and university study. Specific criteria regarding what should go into portfolios and what constitutes excellence are still evolving. The requirement for you to write comments and prompt questions in each student's portfolio can be time consuming. Finally, some students who have seen themselves as winners in a system featuring more traditional testing procedures may not initially commit enthusiastically to a portfolio-based approach.

Despite these challenges, more and more secondary-school teachers are using portfolios. This is not to suggest that portfolio evaluation is likely to completely displace more traditional evaluation approaches. However, it does seem likely that portfolios will become at least a part of the evaluation repertoire of significant numbers of your secondary-school colleagues.

 MORE FROM THE WEB

Assessing Authentic Performances

Because so many people today are interested in authentic learning and alternative ways of assessing students, many Web sites have sprung up featuring information related to these topics. We have selected a few here that will provide you with excellent additional material related to assessment rubrics and to the general area of performance assessment.

Resources for Alternative Assessment

http://www.district44.dupage.k12.il.us/assess.html

- At this site you will find an outstanding list of links to Web locations that feature information related to alternative assessment. Among sites listed are those maintained by The National Center for Research on Evaluation, Standards, and Student Testing; the Wisconsin Education Association Council; The Annenberg Institute for School Reform; and The Center on Learning Assessment and School Reform.

Assessment Terminology: A Glossary of Useful Terms

http://www.newhorizons.org/assmtterms.html

- As the title suggests, this site features a glossary of terms associated with assessment terminology. Definitions provide long, detailed explanations of each term on the list. We highly recommend that you visit this site if you are unclear about the meaning of assessment-related terms.

Performance Assessment

http://www.weac.org/resource/may96/perform.htm

- This document provides a comprehensive overview of performance assessment. There are excellent sections dealing with standardized tests (and criticisms of them), authentic instruction and assessment, and development of performance criteria.

Standards, Rubrics, Portfolios, and Assessment

http://www.pasd.com/PSSA/WRITING/porthand/asssre.htm

- You will find an excellent discussion of such topics as content standards, performance standards, indicators, and benchmarks. Descriptions of both holistic rubrics and analytic rubrics are particularly good.

Assessment

http://www.nauticom.net/www/cokids/teacher16.html

- This site provides a compendium of links to sites with content focusing on various aspects of assessment. For example, you will find directions to Web addresses featuring information related to such diverse topics as using portfolios to communicate to parents about their children's progress, sources of online tests, and building rubrics.

Traditional Data-Gathering Techniques

Though support is growing for more authentic testing and use of portfolios, many traditional techniques for gathering assessment data and judging students are still in use. These can be divided into two broad categories: informal approaches and formal approaches.

Informal Approaches

When you hear references to gathering assessment data, you might first think of multiple-choice tests, true-false tests, or other formal testing approaches. Certainly pencil-

and-paper tests are important, but by no means are they the only kinds of traditional measures teachers use. For example, depending on what you are teaching, you might wish students to demonstrate their proficiencies by doing things as diverse as baking a cake, playing a difficult selection on a French horn, or rebuilding a carburetor and installing it in an automobile.

The choice of the assessment procedure depends largely on what kind of information you are seeking about your students. Often, informal procedures will provide you with useful insights about students' attitudes and levels of proficiency. Results of informal evaluation can give you information you can use to identify and respond to problems your students experience as they attempt to master new content.

There are many kinds of informal evaluation procedures. The ones presented here are just a small sample of the various things you can do to keep track of students' progress.

Teacher Observation

Teacher observation refers to a number of things you might do to ensure students are performing assigned tasks properly. For example, if you are teaching a math class, you may decide to walk systematically through the classroom once you have given your students a problem to work on for the purpose of identifying and helping students who are experiencing difficulty. If you are teaching art, you may observe students who are learning to use the potter's wheel and make helpful comments as they try to center the clay properly. If you are teaching English, you might want to listen carefully to the words used by a student during an oral presentation to determine the extent of his or her vocabulary. If you are instructing students in a physical education class, you probably will spend some of your time observing students to ensure they are performing required exercises correctly.

Your informal evaluations often will prompt you to give specific directions to a student about what needs to be done to complete a task successfully. Sometimes, you will want to make notes about specific difficulties individual students have been experiencing. These observation notes serve several purposes. For example, they can provide you with a continuing record to see whether a student is improving over time. A review of these notes can also help you identify problems being experienced by a number of students. When several students have failed to understand a lesson, you may decide that your instructions were not well understood and that you need to do something to clarify your expectations.

Headlines and Articles

This informal technique is an appropriate procedure for assessing students' abilities to describe essential features of a large body of information. A good newspaper headline provides a concise summary of the article that follows. A writer of effective headlines must be thoroughly familiar with the article's content.

For example, you might assign students to write headlines for a hypothetical article focusing on content they have studied. The headlines provide an informal assessment of students' understanding of general points raised in materials they have been working with. For example, a member of a social studies class that had been studying what has happened to Hong Kong since the territory reverted back to Chinese control after many years as a colony of Britain might prepare this headline: "Brits Out—Chinese In:

Hong Kong's Economy Barely Misses a Beat." Or, a student in a biology class might write: "Keeping Fit: Darwin's Theory a Survivor in Scientific World."

Student-produced headlines provide only general indications that basic information has been understood. They are not intended to provide you with insights about students' grasp of content specifics. However, a headline-writing activity can be a good choice for the limited purpose of informally assessing students' abilities to summarize information accurately.

You may wish to have your students prepare short articles to accompany their headlines. This kind of assignment will give them an opportunity to say more about the focus content.

Teacher-Student Discussion

You will often find yourself making informal judgments based on information gleaned from personal discussions with students. These conversations often reveal a great deal about your students' understandings, interests, and feelings. Information you gain from engaging in discussions with class members allows you to check the accuracy of your assumptions about how individuals are grasping the material you are introducing.

There are some important limitations to the teacher-student discussion approach. As a practical matter, you cannot engage in frequent one-on-one conversations with each student regarding all issues that are raised in class. There simply is not enough time. Hence, the levels of understanding of individual students cannot be sampled frequently. You have to augment information you get from informal evaluations with information gathered in other ways.

Student-Produced Tests

By the time students begin their secondary school years, they have taken hundreds of teacher-prepared tests. Few of them will ever have had the opportunity to prepare a test of their own. Some students enjoy assuming the role of the teacher and preparing test items over what they have been studying. To give students a sense that work they do in preparing tests is important, you might agree to use a selection of student-produced items on a real test covering the material. You will want to retain the right to add and modify items to ensure your test adequately samples the content.

Student-produced tests provide a good indirect measure of what students have learned. Such tests also reveal which elements of content different members of a class have deemed important. This information can help you identify students who need additional help with some content areas and others who may have faulty understandings of material you introduced.

Other Techniques

The informal procedures introduced here represent only a few of your available options. Among others that are widely employed are sorting activities of all kinds. Frequently, these activities provide opportunities for students to identify major content categories and to point out elements of content properly associated with each category.

Observations you make of students during a classroom debate can be used as an informal evaluation technique. Positions taken by individual students in classroom discussions and their skill in using evidence to support points can reveal much about what they have learned. At times you may wish to use crossword puzzles and other simple vocabulary exercises to collect general information about students' grasp of key concepts.

Formal Approaches

Formal approaches seek to make judgments about students' progress based on evidence gathered through the use of carefully planned measurement devices. Formal evaluation techniques take many forms. Multiple-choice tests, true-false tests, matching tests, completion tests, essay tests, rating scales, and checklists are among the types commonly used in secondary schools.

Formal evaluation tests fall into two broad categories: (1) standardized tests and (2) teacher-made tests. Professional evaluation specialists prepare standardized tests for use with large numbers of students. Some of these tests are designed to assess general aptitudes of students. Others assess student understanding of content related to subjects—for example, United States history.

The Scholastic Achievement Test (SAT), taken by many high school seniors and used by colleges and universities in their admissions screening process, is a well-known example of a standardized test. The National Assessment of Educational Progress administers standardized tests throughout the country to determine average levels of

These students are taking a standardized test. Increased public interest in holding schools and teachers accountable for students' performance has been accompanied by an increase in the number of standardized tests given to secondary students.

subject matter mastery of students at different grade levels. Some states require teachers to administer standardized tests that focus on basic skills and, in some cases, on individual academic skills. The results provide general indications of the effectiveness of school programs and sometimes point to curricular areas that need special attention.

Standardized tests are designed to measure the performance of a single student as it compares to the performances of all other students in similar circumstances. For example, a standardized reading test given at the seventh-grade level provides a score for each student that indicates how the student's performance compared with reading achievement of all seventh-graders.

You will rarely use students' scores on standardized tests for grading purposes. This is true because items on these tests often do not accurately sample the content introduced in your own classroom. Tests you prepare yourself are much more likely to feature items that tie closely to the content you have taught.

You need to know appropriate procedures for teacher-prepared tests because you will use them frequently to assess the progress of individual students. Guidelines for using several of these techniques are introduced in the following subsections.

Rating Scales

Some instructional objectives require students to engage in tasks that cannot be easily assessed with paper-and-pencil tests—using laboratory equipment, delivering speeches, completing art projects, and turning finials on a lathe are examples. A *rating scale* is a measurement tool you can use to record information about student proficiency on tasks of this type.

Typically, a rating scale identifies a specific set of characteristics or qualities. Indications along the scale make it possible for you to note the degree to which the indicated qualities are present. You must take care to ensure that the qualities identified on your rating scale are consistent with those referenced in your instructional purposes. In addition, you need to provide clear descriptions of the kind of performance implied by each point on the rating scale. Otherwise, you will have difficulty deciding exactly which rating to choose to indicate the quality of an individual student's performance.

Suppose you were teaching music and wanted to know how well a student could sight-read a given piece of music. You might develop a rating scale including the following directions and sample item:

Directions: Circle the appropriate number for each item. The numbers represent the following values:

5   =   outstanding
4   =   above average
3   =   average
2   =   below average
1   =   unsatisfactory

To what extent does the person play the appropriate notes?

5   4   3   2   1

This rating scale would not give you much specific information about what is implied by each rating. For example, what specifically separates "outstanding" from "above average," "above average" from "average," and so forth? The item might be improved somewhat by changing the descriptors for each rating point as follows:

        5 = always
        4 = frequently
        3 = occasionally
        2 = seldom
        1 = never

This modification certainly does not clear up all confusion about which rating you should award after an observation of a given student's performance, but this set of descriptors is more informative than the original one. (For example, you are unlikely to have difficulty distinguishing between "always" or "never." You may have problems making clear separations among "frequently," "occasionally," and "seldom," but these problems probably pose fewer difficulties than distinguishing among "above average," "average," and "below average.")

Sometimes it is helpful to add descriptive phrases at various points along the scale to indicate behaviors that students should demonstrate to earn a given rating. Suppose you were evaluating performances of students who were giving speeches. You might use a rating scale something like this:

5	4	3	2	1
Demonstrates a continuous unity of thought. Points are clear and related to the topic.		Demonstrates a generally logical flow. There are occasional drifts from the main topic.		Rambles consistently. Presentation lacks coherence. Topic never comes into focus.

Inclusion of these descriptors contributes to the accuracy of the rating process. Also, if you share them with students before they give their speeches, these descriptors will provide them with useful cues as they prepare for their presentations.

In summary, rating scales are useful for making judgments about the kinds of student performance that cannot be assessed by pencil-and-paper tests. A particular challenge for you in developing them is providing clear descriptions of the performance associated with each rating point.

Evaluative Checklists

Evaluative checklists share some characteristics with rating scales. Both are used to evaluate students on behaviors that do not lend themselves readily to traditional pencil-and-paper testing. Both require the focus behaviors to be clearly observable. (You must be able to see or hear what the student is doing to make a judgment and note information on the rating scale or checklist.)

A major difference between rating scales and checklists is that rating scales allow more flexibility in determining the degree of adequacy of a given student's performance. Nearly all rating scales allow you to make judgments at any one of a number of points along a scale (for example, on a 5-point scale, we might choose to mark any one of the following: 5, always; 4, frequently; 3, occasionally; 2, seldom; 1, never). By way of contrast, most checklists permit only a yes/no decision. You typically will use them only when you have an interest in noting the presence or absence of a given behavior. The checklist format does not allow you to make judgments regarding the relative quality of the behavior.

Suppose you wanted to monitor the progress of individual students on a term-paper project. You might put together a checklist looking something like this:

Essay Items

Essays are powerful because they can be used to assess students' thinking at many levels of sophistication. However, as a practical matter, they are best suited to assessing thinking at the higher levels—levels that call on students to apply, analyze, synthesize, or evaluate. Other procedures—for example, multiple-choice, matching, and true-false tests—are available to assess students' abilities to perform tasks requiring less sophisticated thinking.

You may experience problems with content coverage when preparing essays. Because of the time required for your students to respond to essay questions, you can include only a few essay items on a single examination. This can result in a very limited sampling of content unless you take great care in selecting the essay questions you will provide to your students.

Maintaining a consistent pattern of scoring when correcting essays is difficult. Correction takes a long time, particularly when large numbers of students are involved. Fatigue can interfere with grading consistency, even when you intend to apply the same standards to the last paper as to the first.

Though problems of content selection and correction consistency are difficult, you can overcome them. First, you need to take care in structuring the essay task for your students. This means that your directions regarding what must be included in the essay have to be as precise as possible. Notice the differences in the two following sets of instructions:

A. Write an essay in which you discuss the chromosome hypothesis and the gene theory.
B. Write an essay, about five pages in length, in which you compare and contrast the chromosome hypothesis and the gene theory. In your answer, provide specific references to

STUDENT'S NAME	yes	no
Topic has been selected and approved	_____	_____
Rough outline turned in	_____	_____
Final outline turned in	_____	_____
Note cards turned in	_____	_____
First draft turned in	_____	_____

Figure 12–5

(1) essentials of each position, (2) modifications that have been made to each position since it was initially adopted, and (3) strengths and weaknesses that have been attributed to each view by leading experts.

A student receiving instructions similar to those in A may be inclined to ramble. The language used to describe the task is imprecise. (The word discuss, for example, provides only a hazy guide to students regarding what they should write about.) Further, there are no references to how long the response should be. One student may write only a single paragraph. Another might write eight or nine pages. In light of these imprecise instructions, you probably will receive papers that are difficult to evaluate because individual students interpret the assignment in different ways.

The set of instructions in B is better. Students get a clear idea of what subjects should be covered in their response. In addition, a length condition is imposed ("about five pages"). Because of the specificity of these guidelines, students receiving the B instructions are not forced to do nearly as much guessing about what is expected as students receiving the A instructions.

In addition, correcting the set of papers received from students receiving the B directions should be easier. You should be able to check each paper to see whether the student has (1) compared and contrasted the chromosome hypothesis and the gene theory, (2) outlined essentials of each, (3) noted changes in each position since it was first postulated, and (4) described experts' views of strengths and weaknesses of each position. These "must-be-included" features enable you to look at each essay in the same way. They help you to maintain a consistent correction standard from paper to paper.

Completion Items

Like essays, *completion items* require students to write responses in their own hand-writing. (Sometimes students are allowed to use personal computers or typewriters.) However, completion items are much less powerful in terms of the kinds of thinking they can assess. Generally, they are most useful for assessing relatively unsophisticated levels of student thinking.

You will find that completion items are easy to construct. They can be used to sample a broad range of content. Individual items do not require much time to correct. Hence, you will be able to include several completion items on a given test or examination.

However, there is a problem in scoring completion items. It is difficult to construct items for which a single answer is the only one that is logically correct. You may find it particularly difficult to decide what to do about student answers that are partially correct. To get some perspective on this issue, look at the following completion-type item:

The person who succeeded John Major as Prime Minister of the United Kingdom was_____.

Probably, the answer the teacher had in mind was "Tony Blair." Other plausible alternatives exist, however. For example, students might have included answers such as "a member of the Labour Party" or even "a man."

To avoid correction problems, you need to write completion items in such a way that students clearly understand the type of response you are looking for. For example, the item above could easily be rewritten to narrow the range of plausible answers. A revised version might look like this:

> *The name of the individual who succeeded John Major as Prime Minister of the United Kingdom was _____.*

It is important that an individual completion item have only one blank. This blank ought to come toward the end of the item. This arrangement gives the student time to pick up relevant cues regarding the nature of the expected response. An item with many blanks that are placed at random is almost certain to result in confusion. Consider this faulty example:

> *_____ affects _____ independently of _____ except on those occasions when _____ and _____ are inversely related.*

To eliminate scoring problems, you may want to provide your students with a selection of answers, some correct and some incorrect, from which they are to draw their responses. When you do this, instruct students to select answers only from words on the provided list. This arrangement allows you to hold students accountable both for correct word choice and for spelling. (The word is there; the student has only to copy the word correctly to spell it right.)

Though this revision of the traditional completion format will help you to maintain a consistent grading pattern, it also turns the format of the completion item into a modified matching item. Further, it introduces the possibility that students may be able to guess at the right item. However, you may be willing to accept this potential problem as a price you are willing to pay to make your correction chores simpler and less subjective. An example of this kind of modification is provided in Figure 12–6.

In general, completion items do not represent a particularly good technique for assessing students' proficiencies. In most cases, multiple-choice, true-false, and matching items are preferred. These items have the capacity to assess similar levels of thinking and are much easier to correct than completion items.

Matching Items

Matching items are typically used to measure less sophisticated levels of student thinking. They are easy to construct, they can be corrected quickly, and there is little danger that one student's test will be graded according to a standard different from that used for another student's test.

Difficulties associated with the use of matching items usually have to do with item construction. You can overcome these problems by following a few basic guidelines as you design these tests.

Students become confused when they are confronted with a matching item containing a mixture of unrelated terms and definitions. To remedy this possible difficulty, all terms in a given matching item should focus on a single topic or theme. For example, if you decided to prepare a test including names of Confederate generals on one side and

---

STUDENT'S NAME _____

Completion Item

Directions: A number of blanks appear in the following short paragraph. Below the paragraph you will find a list of terms. Select appropriate terms from this list and print them carefully in the proper blanks. Include only terms in the list at the bottom of the page. You will be expected to spell these terms correctly.

In recent years, there has been a trend for people to move away from the core of a city toward the surrounding suburbs. Sociologists call this movement _____. Another urban phenomenon involves movement of people from one social class to a part of the city occupied by people in another social class. This is termed _____. When a new group in a society succeeds in taking over a neighborhood, a situation termed _____ results. When minority members of a community are removed by majority members, the situation is called _____. When this causes married couples to move to a locale where neither set of parents is resident, their new family residence is said to be _____. The group an individual interacts with over time on a more or less continuous basis is called a(n) _____.

List of Terms

recurrent	suburbanization	succession
allotropic	invasion	concession
neolocal	separation	expulsion
patrilocal	segregation	deviance

Figure 12–6
Example of a completion item with a provided list of terms.

a number of exploits associated with them listed on the other, you should provide a label something like this: "Matching Quiz: Confederate Generals."

As a rule of thumb, the list on the right-hand side (the one providing alternative descriptions or definitions from which students are to select answers) should contain approximately 25 percent more items than the list on the left-hand side. For example, if there were 10 items on the left side, there might be 12 or 13 alternative choices on the right side.

The practice of placing more options on the right makes it possible for a student to miss one question without being forced, as a result, to miss another. When you have an identical number of items in both left- and right-hand lists, the double penalty for a missed question comes into play. (For example, a student who incorrectly identifies term e as the response to item 1 instead of the response to item 3, which is correct, will end up having wrong responses both to item 1 and item 3.)

The entire matching test should be printed on one page. It is unacceptable for any portion of either the left-hand list or the right-hand list to be carried over to a second page. When this formatting error occurs, many of your students will fail to realize that part of the test is on another page, and they will make mistakes as a result.

Your directions must be clear. You need to let students know exactly where they are to place the letter identifying a particular alternative in the right-hand column in the blank before the appropriate item in the left-hand column. When explicit directions are not given, students often draw lines connecting items in the two columns. This results in a confusing spider web of lines that makes correction difficult. In addition, your directions should make clear to students that only one correct response is provided in the right-hand column for each item in the left-hand column. (See the sample matching test provided in Figure 12–7.)

Multiple-Choice Items

For more than a century, evaluation experts have shown a strong preference for *multiple-choice items* (Hattie, Jaeger, & Bond, 1999). Multiple-choice items can be adapted to a variety of subject matter content. They can be scored easily. They have the capacity to test not only for knowledge and comprehension but for some higher-level thinking abilities as well.

Example of a Properly Formatted Matching Test

MATCHING TEST: YOUR NAME: _____
TENNIS TERMINOLOGY

Directions: Find the term in the right-hand column that is defined by the definition in the left-hand column. Place the letter identifying this term in the blank space provided before its definition. Only one term is correct for each definition. Please do *not* draw lines connecting definitions to terms.

_____ 1. The point that, if won, wins the match for a player

_____ 2. The area between the net and the service line

_____ 3. Hitting the ball before it bounces

_____ 4. Stroke made after the ball has bounced, either forehand or backhand

_____ 5. The line that is perpendicular to the net and divides the two service courts

_____ 6. The initial part of any swing. The act of bringing the racket back to prepare for the forward swing

_____ 7. A ball hit high enough in the air to pass over the head of the net player

_____ 8. A ball that is served so well that the opponent fails to touch it with his or her racket

_____ 9. A shot that bounces near the baseline

_____ 10. Start of play for a given point

a. Ace
b. Backswing
c. Center service line
d. Deep shot
e. Forecourt
f. Set point
g. Lob
h. Match point
i. Serve
j. Volley
k. Dink
l. Ground stroke

Figure 12–7
Example of a Properly Formatted Matching Test

In terms of basic format, a multiple-choice item consists of two basic parts: (1) a stem and (2) some alternative choices, only a few of which (usually only one) are logically related to the stem. Among the alternative choices there are some correct answers and others that are called distracters. The difficulty of the item depends in large measure on the level of sophisticated thinking required to distinguish correct answers from the distracters.

You will find it challenging to prepare multiple-choice items featuring distracters that appear to be plausible answers. Carelessly written distracters tend to give away the correct answer, even to students who do not really know the content. Good ones take time to develop; hence, high-quality multiple-choice tests cannot be prepared hastily.

A number of principles guide development of sound multiple-choice items. First, it is important that the stem be clear and that you write all distracters in a way that ensures grammatical consistency with the stem. Consider this example:

Nils Johannsen, in his novel of the Canadian Prairies, *West from Winnipeg*, called trapping an

a. science.

b. art.

c. duty.

d. nuisance.

A student totally unfamiliar with this novel who read the question carefully would identify "b" as the correct answer simply because it is the only choice grammatically consistent with the article "an" at the end of the stem. To correct this problem, the writer of the item might have concluded the stem in this way: " . . . called trapping a(n)." This revision makes any of the four alternative answers grammatically plausible.

A stem that is too brief fails to cue students regarding what kind of information they should be looking for in the list of alternatives. Consider this example:

Roger Williams

a. sailed on the Mayflower.

b. established the Thanksgiving tradition.

c. founded the Rhode Island colony.

d. developed the New World's first distillery.

Because the stem is so incomplete, students are really faced with four true-false items to ponder rather than with one good multiple-choice item. A far better way of formatting this question would be as follows:

The founder of the Rhode Island colony was

a. Sir Walter Raleigh.

b. John Winthrop.

c. Roger Williams.

d. William Bradford.

As noted earlier, multiple-choice items can be designed to test quite sophisticated levels of thinking. Consider the example in Figure 12–8. It challenges students to make inferences based on their analysis of the prose.

As this example illustrates, it is possible to use multiple choice questions to assess students' abilities to engage in quite challenging levels of thinking. However, you will find that constructing multiple choice questions such as the one in this example takes time. You may decide that essay questions suit your needs better when you want to test your students' abilities to apply, analyze, synthesize, and evaluate.

True-False Items

True-false items, though most frequently used to assess knowledge-level thinking, do have some limited applications when you are interested in assessing your students' abilities to engage in more complex kinds of thinking. True-false items can be prepared

---

Directions: Read the passage, then circle the number before the answer you select.

Ellison had the flair of genius, but he was not a genius. Though pedestrian in his approaches, he was yet a phenomenon. His was a talent of concentration, not of innovation. No other man of his time rivaled his ability to shunt aside irrelevancies to focus on a problem's essentials. For him, noncritical considerations were a trifling bit of detritus to be swept away in a moment. His resolute attack on the nuggety essence of an unresolved issue obviated even the serious probability of egregious error. Contemporaries described his reasoning as "glistening." Only an audacious few ventured public challenges to his positions. It is not too much to say that he lived out his days surrounded by a nervously approving silence. Later generations have seen his conclusions as less than revolutionary. But, in his own time, Ellison's ability to "will" an impeccable solution to a complex issue made others seem small figures who were destined ever to walk lightly in the dark shadows of a giant.

One assumption revealed in the preceding paragraph is

a. Ellison was truly competent, but he had a flair for impressing people with the logical structure he built to support his solutions.

b. Ellison really was a genius whose "glistening" logic resulted in novel solutions to problems.

c. Today, people tend to be more impressed with Ellison than they were in his own day.

d. Ellison's form probably was a more significant contributor to his reputation than was the substance of his thought.

Figure 12–8
Example of a multiple-choice item intended to assess students' higher-level thinking abilities.

relatively quickly. They provide a format that ensures consistency of grading from student to student. Finally, you can correct true-false items quickly.

There are also some disadvantages of true-false items. For one thing, they encourage guessing. Because there are only two choices, your students have a 50:50 chance of getting an item correct even when they have no grasp of the content being tested. True-false items require you to prepare statements that are absolutely true or absolutely false. Much course content tends more toward gray areas than black or white. For this reason, you may feel constrained by the true-false format, which may require you to stay away from the main focus of your instruction to find the odd example that is absolutely true or absolutely false.

When you prepare true-false items, you have to provide instruction that directs students to record their answers in specific ways. Often, true-false tests are prepared with blank spaces in front of each item. Students are asked to write answers in the blanks. If you follow this approach, you need to instruct your students to write out the entire word "true" or "false" or the use symbols such as "+" for true items and "-" for false items. You do not want to tell students to write the letter "t" in the blank before true items and the letter "f" in the blank before false items. If you do this, some students will produce hybrid letters that, when looked at in one way, appear to be a "t" and, when looked at in another way, appear to be an "f".

You can eliminate some correction problems associated with true-false tests if you do away with the blanks. Instead, you can print the words "true" and "false" to the left of each item. When you do this, you can ask students simply to circle the correct word. An example of a properly formatted true-false test that asks questions about expected changes in numbers of employed teachers as projected by the National Center for Education Statistics (Gerald & Hussar, 1999) is provided in Figure 12–9.

FOR YOUR PORTFOLIO

1. What materials, ideas you learned in this chapter related to *assessing student learning* will you include as "evidence" in your portfolio? Select up to 3 items of information to be included in your portfolio. Number them 1, 2, and 3.

2. Think about why you selected these materials for your portfolio. Consider such issues as the following in your response:

   - The specific purposes to which this information can be put when you plan, deliver, and assess the impact of your instruction;

   - The compatibility of the information with your own priorities and values;

   - The contributions this information can make to your personal development as a teacher; and

   - The factors that led you to include this material as opposed to some alternatives you considered.

3. Prepare a written reflection in which you analyze the decision-making process you followed. Also, mention the INTASC Standard(s) to which your selected material relates. (First complete the chart below.)

Number of Individuals Expected to be Employed as Teachers*
(in thousands)

Year	Elementary	Secondary
1998	1,866	1,243
1999	1,885	1,260
2000	1,903	1,276
2001	1,920	1,291
2002	1,935	1,306
2003	1,943	1,325
2004	1,949	1,347

Directions: Use the data above as you respond to the following true-false items. If the statement is true, circle the word true. If the statement is false, circle the word false.

True   False   1. There will be an increase in both the number of employed elementary teachers and secondary teachers in each year from 1998 through 2004.

True   False   2. The number of additional elementary teachers added each year from 1998 through 2004 will be larger in years at the beginning of this time period than in years toward the end.

True   False   3. From this information, we can infer that numbers of secondary students will increase at a slower rate than numbers of elementary pupils in the years 1998 through 2004.

True   False   4. There will be a larger total increase in the number of secondary teachers than in the number of elementary teachers over the entire period from 1998 through 2004.

True   False   5. The smallest annual increase in the number of elementary teachers will occur between the same two years as the largest annual increase in the number of secondary teachers.

* Data are from D. E. Gerald & W. J. Husser. (1993). Projections of education statistics to 2004 (p. 72). Washington, DC: Department of Education, Office of Educational Research and Improvement, National Center for Education Statistics.

Figure 12–9
Example of a Properly Formatted True-False Test

Materials You Selected and the INTASC Standards

Put a check under those INTASC Standards numbers to which the evidence you have selected applies. (Refer to Chapter 1 for more detailed information about INTASC.)

Item of Evidence Number	INTASC Standards									
	S1	S2	S3	S4	S5	S6	S7	S8	S9	S10
1										
2										
3										

Key Ideas in Summary

- Measurement refers to the process of gathering information; evaluation refers to the process of drawing conclusions based on data gathered through measurement activities.

- Formative evaluation consists of the periodic assessment activities that occur as part of the instructional process. Formative evaluation occurs while new material is being introduced.

- Summative evaluation involves testing and other assessment activities that take place at the conclusion of an instructional sequence.

- Authentic evaluation refers to the idea that assessment should require students to demonstrate the important kinds of learning that have been emphasized in an instructional sequence, not just be required to work with samples of content that teachers select because they can be easily measured. Ideally, authentic assessment calls on students to perform in ways consistent with patterns used by experts in subjects students have studied.

- Assessment rubrics are often used to evaluate the quality of authentic performances. A rubric consists of a set of guidelines that tell you what to look for as acceptable evidence needed to support judgments about the quality of learners' performances. Often rubrics feature assign points to various, clearly defined descriptions about what students should be able to demonstrate as a result of your instruction.

- Teachers interested in authentic assessment often use portfolios. A portfolio is a systematically organized collection of a student's work that covers a specific period of time. Portfolios can include such things as completed assignments, student-produced journal entries, student reflections on discussions, prompt questions provided by the teachers, photos or sketches, and summary statements made about what has been learned. Use of portfolios is consistent with reflective teaching.

- Informal assessment techniques include a variety of approaches teachers use to gather information about what students have learned. Some of them are designed to provide insights about students' attitudes as well as about their abilities to perform academic tasks. Among informal options frequently used in the classroom are (1) teacher observation, (2) headlines and articles, (3) teacher-student discussions, and (4) student-produced tests.

- Formal approaches to evaluation seek to gather evidence by using carefully designed measurement tools. These tend to fall into two major categories: standardized tests and teacher-made tests. Professional measurement specialists prepare standardized tests. They are often used to provide information that is used to compare students in one place to those in other places. Individual teachers prepare their own teacher-made tests for the purpose of determining how well their students master specific content introduced in the classroom.

■ Formal approaches to evaluation include (1) rating scales, (2) evaluative checklists, (3) essays, (4) completion items, (5) matching items, (6) multiple-choice items, and (7) true-false items.

Reflections

1. What are the relationships between the terms measurement and evaluation?

2. What are the advantages for students of an instructional program that features carefully planned formative evaluation?

3. How might your use of authentic evaluation result in student learning that is more complex and sophisticated than would be the case if you did not use this approach?

4. What are some barriers to wider use of authentic evaluation?

5. Some people who advocate the use of portfolios suggest that the approach is consistent both with authentic assessment and with reflective teaching. To what extent is this true? What difficulties might you encounter as a first-time user of portfolios, and how would you cope with them?

6. What are some considerations you should think about in deciding which specific evaluation approach to use?

7. Are there any advantages to using informal evaluation? What do you see as some difficulties in developing your own assessment rubrics?

8. What is a basic characteristic of data-gathering procedures associated with formal approaches to gathering assessment information?

9. How can you ensure consistency of grading from student to student when you have used an essay to gather information about what students have learned?

10. How are standardized tests and teacher-made tests distinguished? Some people argue that standardized tests often are misused. What do they mean? What do you see as appropriate and inappropriate uses of standardized tests, and how do you defend your conclusions? Do your reactions tell us anything about your personal values priorities?

Learning Extensions

1. Do some additional reading on authentic evaluation. For periodical articles, consult the Education Index. Your instructor may also be able to direct you to some specific information sources. Design a complete authentic evaluation procedure for a lesson you would like to teach. Present it to your instructor for review.

2. Think about a topic that you would like to teach. Then, develop a folder of ideas that describes specific informal assessment procedures you might follow to gain insight into students' understandings and attitudes.

3. Prepare a position paper in which you take a stand in favor of or in opposition to this statement: "School tests irresponsibly direct students' attention to content that is easy to test but essentially trivial."

4. Seek out some teachers who regularly use portfolios of student work as part of their evaluation procedures. Invite one or more of them to visit your class. Ask them to describe how they format student portfolios and how they make judgments about the relative quality of the work of individual students. Ask also about some difficulties they faced (and how they overcame them) when they first started using portfolios.

5. For a subject you would like to teach, prepare examples of properly formatted (1) completion tests, (2) multiple-choice tests, (3) true-false tests, (4) matching tests, and (5) essay tests. Ask your instructor to critique your formatting of these materials.

6. Go to the Merrill Education's Link to General Methods Resources site at this URL: http://www.prenhall.com/methods-cluster/ At the bottom of the page select "tests and testing" as your topic and click on the "begin" button. This will take you to the "Overview" page. On the left side, click on "Web Links." On the Web Links page click on "general assessment information." Follow links that will give you information related to alternative and authentic assessment. Drawing on information you find, prepare a short paper titled "The Case For and Against Alternative and Authentic Assessment."

7. Go to the Merrill Education's Link to General Methods Resources site at this URL: http://www.prenhall.com/methods-cluster/ At the bottom of the page select "tests and testing" as your topic and click on the "begin" button. This will take you to the "Overview" page. On the left side, click on "Web Links." On the Web Links page click on "rubrics." Development of good rubrics is a continuing challenge for teachers interested in authentic assessment. Use the information you find as the basis of an oral report on some of the approaches to rubric construction available at the listed Web sites.

8. Go to the Merrill Education's Link to General Methods Resources site at this URL: http://www.prenhall.com/methods-cluster/ At the bottom of the page select "tests and testing" as your topic and click on the "begin" button. This will take you to the "Overview" page. On the left side, click on "Web Links." On the Web Links page click on "standardized tests." Work with several others and go to a number of the cited Web sites. Prepare a collective report to the class on purposes and appropriate uses of standardized tests.

References

Educational Testing Service. (1995). *Performance assessment: Different needs, different answers.* Princeton, NJ: Educational Testing Service.

Gerald, D. E., & Hussar, W. J. (1999). *Projections of education statistics to 2009.* Washington, DC: U.S. Department of Education, Office of Educational Research and Improvement, National Center for Education Statistics.

Hattie, J., Jaeger, R. M., & Bond, L. (1999). Persistent methodological questions in educational testing. In A. Iran-Nejan & P. D. Pearson (Eds.), *Review of research in education.* Vol. 24. Washington, DC: American Educational Research Association.

Linn, R. L., & Baker, E. L. (1999, Winter). Supporting schools' capacity to use information for improvement. *CRESST Line.* pp. 2–3.

Porter, C., & Cleland, J. (1995). *The portfolio as a learning strategy.* Portsmouth, NH: Boynton/Cook.

Scriven, M. (1967). The methodology of evaluation. In R. W. Stake et al. (Eds.), *Perspectives on curriculum evaluation* (pp. 39–83). AERA Monograph Series on Curriculum Evaluation, No. 1. Chicago: Rand McNally.

Strzepek, J. E., & Figgins, M. A. (1993). A polemic on evaluating writing. In K. Gill (Ed.), *Process and portfolios in writing instruction* (pp. 47–53). Urbana, IL: National Council of Teachers of English.

Tyler, R. W. (1949). *Basic principles of curriculum and instruction.* Chicago: The University of Chicago Press.

Wiggins, G. (1989a). Teaching to the (authentic) test. *Educational Leadership, 46*(7), pp. 41–47.

Wiggins, G. (1989b). A true test: Toward more authentic and equitable measurement. *Phi Delta Kappan, 70*(8), pp. 703–713.

13

Management and Discipline

This chapter will aim to

- define the terms management and discipline;

- list the key areas that lead to success in management and discipline;

- explain how you can go about establishing authority in the classroom;

- describe elements of the physical environment that need to be considered when organizing the room for instruction;

- explain how time needs to be managed in order to prevent problems;

- define principles to be followed when responding to behavior problems;

- state the importance of dialogue and negotiation in the classroom;

- describe some approaches to conflict resolution in the classroom; and

- list a range of responses that can be used when responding to misbehavior.

Introduction

As a teacher, you play two key roles: instructing students and managing the classroom. The second of these responsibilities is regarded as one of the most important challenges that new secondary teachers face (Williams, Alley & Henson, 1999). Few beginning teachers fail because of a lack of content knowledge. Most often their lack of success is associated with an inability to manage and control the classroom. To avoid problems of this kind, you need to work toward creating an environment that facilitates learning. Among other things, you will need to plan possible responses to incidents of misbehavior.

If your teacher-preparation program is typical of those found around the country, you will have spent a good deal of time acquiring content knowledge and learning how to transmit it effectively to students. It is probable that you have received much less information about your management role in the classroom. Though refinements in your expertise as a manager will come through direct experience you will have in your own classroom, we believe that there are concepts and skills associated with management and control that you can learn in your preparation program.

However, you need to understand that there is no universally applicable set of "quick fix" remedies that you can learn that will readily resolve every potential management difficulty you may face. If there were easy solutions, worries about classroom management would not be a topic of such serious concern among teachers, parents, and students.

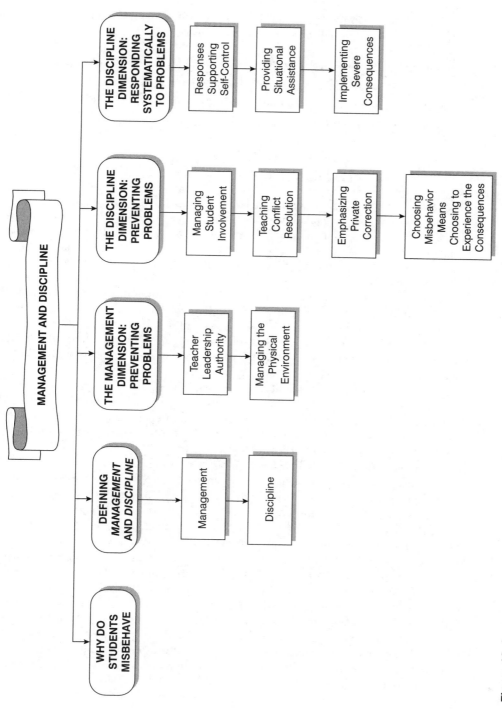

Figure 13–1
Graphic Organizer

395

The key to developing a program that results in successful and effective classroom control is in knowing something about these four areas:

- Actions you take in the classroom that are designed to prevent control problems,
- Actions you take to establish your credibility and authority,
- Actions you take to motivate and engage pupils, and
- Actions you take in response to inappropriate student behaviors.

Why Do Students Misbehave?

Recent acts of violence in secondary schools across America have prompted a search for causes. Secondary schools, regardless of their location, enroll some students who are frustrated, angry, alienated, and disengaged. Though these students represent a minority of the school population, you need to understand conditions that can lead to misbehavior problems and to master responses that are useful and productive.

As with any complex issue, there are multiple causes for acts that educators view as discipline problems. For example, some conditions that students experience outside the classroom influence their behavior at school. If there is violence in society, it is only logical to expect some violence in classrooms. Due to circumstances they must live with, a few students daily confront examples of young people and adults who respond to problems with violence. Some of these young people come to school with no knowledge of how to respond to problems in any other way.

Many students confront frequent change in their lives. Such changes, particularly in family circumstances, mean that some students you will teach come to school without the benefit of a history of ongoing family support and encouragement. Many of these young people lack a strong sense of self-identity and an accompanying sense that they have the ability to succeed at school-related tasks.

Your students do not leave their personal histories at the classroom door. Their diverse backgrounds provide you with an opportunity to learn more about each of the individuals in your classes and adapt your teaching methods in response to their personal circumstances. For example, there are things you can do to help students who do not have a history of responding to frustrations and conflicts in productive ways acquire patterns of behavior that will allow them to meet these challenges in more acceptable ways.

Secondary students are at an age when they are searching for meaning and purpose in life. They are drawn to people and places that offer opportunities for these needs to be met. If you implement fair and consistent management and discipline practices, your students will see you as someone who cares about them and who can provide reliable guidance when they face difficult situations. Your goal should be to establish a learning environment based on mutual respect, where your students feel safe from emotional and physical threat, and where your rules are logical and consistently applied.

As you begin to search for answers to the question of why students misbehave, you need to ask yourself these questions:

- Are you creating educational environments that respect students and value their input?
- Do your students feel a sense of power and control?
- Is the curriculum culturally relevant and worthwhile?
- Does your school provide opportunities for success rather than pose threats of failure? Do your students feel they really belong in your classroom?
- Does the educational experience offered to students by your school offer them opportunities to simply have fun?

Defining *Management* and *Discipline*

Before proceeding any further, you need to have clear definitions in mind of the terms *management* and *discipline*. How people define terms influences how they react in situations where these terms have relevance (Slee, 1995). Both *management* and *discipline* are examples of concepts that have often been misunderstood. These misunderstandings sometimes have led to inappropriate reactions when problems associated with these issues have arisen in school settings.

Management

Management includes the part of your role as a teacher that focuses on creating an environment and establishing conditions that facilitate student academic and social success. It involves your exercise of classroom leadership, facilitation of student motivation, arrangement of the physical environment, and management of time and lessons.

You may find yourself put off by the idea of management, imagining it to be characterized by autocratic teacher behaviors. We do not endorse this view. Indeed, this conception of management today also is rejected by many business leaders who have embraced an understanding of management that focuses on development of collaborative, democratic, and humane patterns of interaction (Kouzes & Posner, 1987). As you consider contemporary management in schools, you need to think about it in terms of your responsibilities for organizing what goes on in the classroom and for nurturing student behaviors that will allow them to have productive interpersonal relationships with a wide variety of people.

Your responsibilities as a classroom manager require you to establish priorities as well as an environment that will allow students to achieve worthwhile and important goals. William Glasser, in his book *The Quality School* (1990), defines this type of management in detail. He points out that it is the role of the manager to behave in ways that encourage students to see the connection between what they are being asked to do and the satisfaction of basic needs. Glasser describes teachers who exercise management in this way as functioning as *lead managers*. If you function as a lead manager, here are some things you will do. The teacher involves the students and gets their input in discussions of the work to be done and the conditions under which it is to be completed.

- You communicate expectations clearly and model tasks you assign. You continually solicit input from students.
- You ask students to inspect and evaluate their own work for quality, and you willingly listen to students and accept that they know a good deal about how to produce high quality work.
- You function as a facilitator who provides students with the tools they need to learn in an environment that is non-coercive and non-adversarial.

The importance of how you define management relates clearly to the issue of discipline. If your students do not feel a sense of ownership in the classroom, do not feel respected, and do not believe you are addressing their needs, then they may feel they have no choice but to engage you in a power struggle as they seek to get their needs met. They may end up seeking recognition in ways you find unacceptable. If, on the other hand, your students believe you are meeting their needs, behaving in ways that imply respect for members of the class, and helping them reach important goals, there is little incentive for your students to adopt disruptive behavior patterns.

Discipline

Some people view the terms *discipline* and *control* as synonymous. According to this view, the teacher's disciplinary role should center on enforcing conformity and obedience to a set of rules which, if followed, will minimize disruptions and allow academic content to be covered (Hoover & Kinsvatter, 1997). We reject this conception of discipline as inconsistent with an educational system designed to prepare students to become citizens in a democratic society. It unacceptably places teachers and students in unproductive adversarial roles.

We believe that *discipline* should be defined as the process of helping students develop self-control, character, orderliness, and efficiency. When you act on this conception of discipline, your interactions with students promote individual growth and the necessary acceptance of responsibility required of individuals living in a democratic society (McLaughlin, 1994).

WHAT DO *YOU* THINK?

Reflecting on Personal Experience

Your experiences as a secondary-school student can serve as a valuable source of information for teaching. However, you need to think seriously about specific experiences you remember. For example, consider how your own teachers handled discipline problems. Think about things they did that worked well and those that did not. What do you remember about teachers who seemed to have few discipline problems? About others who had difficulty in this area of professional responsibility?

Prepare a list of characteristics of both effective and ineffective managers of student behavior. How were students regarded and generally treated by teachers in each category? What are some things teachers in each category did when they had to respond to student behavior problems?

Questions

1. What differences do you remember about teachers in each category?
2. What do you think are the most important differences?
3. What are some principles that you might formulate based on your reflections about teachers in each category?
4. Share your principles with others in your class. How are yours similar and different from those developed by other class members?
5. Develop a master list of principles and compare them to ones outlined later in this chapter.

This view of discipline also gives you criteria for determining how to respond to classroom incidents. It encourages you to consider responses that will help your students move toward increased self-control. This perspective on discipline will allow you to see incidents of misbehavior as opportunities to teach students important lessons that will yield personal benefits to them throughout their lives. Your responses will be designed to promote students' development of patterns of self-control that are a key to productive and satisfying adult interpersonal relationships.

In summary, as a teacher, you have responsibility for both management and discipline. Your responsibilities for management should focus on organization and planning practices that can prevent problems. Your role in the area of discipline should focus on helping students develop responsible patterns of self-control. These patterns, once mastered, will serve students well throughout their adult lives.

The Management Dimension: Preventing Problems

Your management responsibilities require you to organize and manage time, materials, and space for the purpose of facilitating a smooth and efficient operation of your classroom. They also require you to take actions that will establish your leadership and motivate students.

Visitors to classrooms of teachers who are good managers often are unaware of specific decisions these teachers have made. These classrooms sometimes seem to run themselves. As skilled professionals, expert teachers make management look easy. In fact, these apparently problem-free classrooms are the result of hard work. They certainly are not chance occurrences that have come about because these teachers have been lucky enough to draw groups of unusually well-behaved students (Emmer, Evertson, & Anderson, 1980).

MORE FROM THE WEB

Management and Discipline

The following are a few of the many Web sites that provide information of interest to teachers regarding classroom management and discipline. Consider visiting some of these sites.

TITEN Preview

http://www.titen.net/preview/index.html

- This site provides useful information from Australia's Teacher in Training Education Network (TITEN). You will find links to such key topics as (1) diagnosing your own approach to discipline, (2) suggestions for beginning the school year, (3) models of discipline, (4) teaching tips with a view to maintaining good classroom discipline, and (5) developing a personal discipline style.

Classroom Management

http://www.teachnet.com/how-to/index.html

- You will find excellent links at this site to a number of topics related to the general theme of classroom management. These links direct you to information about such issues as dealing with late-arriving students and settling students down so you can begin productive work at the beginning of the period. There is also a link to some general classroom management tips.

Setting the Stage for High Standards—Elements of Effective School Discipline

http://www.aft.org/edissues/elements

- Material at this site was developed under the sponsorship of the American Federation of Teachers (AFT), a major national teachers' organization. Several years ago this group sponsored an initiative titled "Responsibility, Respect, Results: Lessons for Life." At this site, you will find recommendations for how teachers and school district policymakers can work together to establish policies that will allow better management of students and reduce the number of discipline problems.

Discipline Associates

http://jaring.nmhu.edu/classman.htm

- Issues associated with classroom management and discipline are widespread enough that several private companies around the country have been developed to provide consulting services to schools and teachers on these issues. One such company, Discipline Associates, maintains this site. You will find information here about seminars this group offers and publications they produce related to classroom management issues.

The Honor Level System

http://members.aol.com/churchward/hls/techniques.html

- At this site you will find 11 separate techniques for improving classroom discipline. Budd Ward has adapted them from some earlier work by Thomas R. McDaniel. They include (1) focusing, (2) direct instruction, (3) monitoring, (4) modeling, (5) non-verbal cueing, (6) environmental control, (7) low-profile intervention, (8) assertive discipline, (9) assertive I-messages, (10) humanistic I-messages, and (11) positive discipline.

Schoolwide and Classroom Discipline

http://www.nwrel.org/scpd/sirs/5/cu9.html

- Material at this site has been compiled as part of the Northwest Regional Educational Laboratory's School Improvement Research Series (SIRS). Author Kathleen Cotton provides excellent information related to such issues as defining *discipline*, research findings related to discipline, classroom discipline practices that have been found to work well, discipline approaches for different kinds of students, and formal discipline programs that have been adopted by schools around the country.

Teacher Leadership and Authority

Effective classroom management begins with you. Your philosophy, values, understanding of individual students, beliefs about learning, and leadership style all affect the social environment of the classroom and the presence or absence of problems. If you are to be effective, your students have to willingly accept you as a leader. In general, teachers who are viewed as leaders are secure, confident, and optimistic. This means that you should not be intimidated or fearful when you encounter people who know more than you do, and you should not be easily discouraged when you find your students initially unmotivated to learn what you want to teach them.

Your beliefs about your students will affect your personal leadership style (Clark & Peterson, 1986). For example, if you are a person who believes students are lazy and untrustworthy, you will develop management and control patterns different from those who trust and respect students. Students will quickly sense any negative attitudes you may have about them. If they believe you do not respect or trust them, they become very reluctant to accept you as a leader.

In preparing to work with secondary students, you need to remember that young people in this age group are striving to establish some sense of personal identity. As part of this effort, it is natural for them to engage in some testing of the limits of imposed authorities (parents, teachers, and others). Secondary students cannot be expected to defer quietly to every one of your demands, particularly if they sense an element of unfairness or if they feel you are challenging their self-respect.

There are many sources that will contribute to students perceiving you as having or not having leadership authority. French and Raven (1959) identified some perspectives you might consider as you develop your own approach to leadership in the classroom. They identified five sources of power or authority:

- Legitimate power,
- Reward power,
- Coercive power,
- Expert power, and
- Referent or attractive power.

Legitimate Power

Some roles in American society, including teaching, carry with them a certain power and expectation of leadership, regardless of who fills them. This is what is termed *legitimate power*. Your position as a teacher invests you with some power and authority. However, your legitimate power will not result in your students automatically respecting and following your leadership. Indeed, if you are foolish enough to tell your students to do something simply because you, as their leader, believe they should be enthusiastic about it, you will be disappointed. Some members of your class may even laugh. Simply put, authority power is not something you should put too much stock in as a way to motivate students.

Reward Power

As a teacher, you are going to be able to provide certain benefits to students. As a result, you will benefit from having some *reward power*. Rewards at your disposal include such things as grades, verbalized praise statements, certain privileges, and other actions in areas that individual students may see as having some personal importance.

However, there are limitations on your reward power. In some situations, all students may not value the kinds of rewards you are in a position to give. For example, if a given student attaches no importance or value to getting good grades, he or she will not be motivated to work hard or behave in order to get a high grade. A few students value the attention and praise they get from other young people more than the grades they receive. Many of them may have arrived at a point in their school careers where they have lost any confidence in their abilities to earn high grades. If you attempt to assert your leadership by making threats related to grades, these students may be quite indifferent to your approach.

Coercive Power

Individuals in positions of authority often hold the capacity to punish members of groups they lead. As a teacher, you are in a position to discharge some of this *coercive power.* Students who respond to coercive power accept certain patterns of behavior not because of a real commitment to them, but because they seek to escape punishment.

There are great limitations on coercive power as an approach to working with students. If you administer punishment of some kind, the result may be a temporary cessation of an objectionable student behavior. However, unless you provide support for an alternative, appropriate pattern of behavior, an even more unacceptable pattern may develop. Also, if you rely too much on punishment to assert your authority, you may encourage your students to view combat as the normal character of their relationship with you. They may feel challenged to outwit you and get by with breaking rules to show you that they are not intimidated by your behavior. Vandalism, truancy, and student anger frequently characterize classes taught by teachers who depend too much on punishment to maintain their authority.

Expert Power

Individuals perceived by a group to have superior knowledge or skill are accorded some leadership or authority. As a teacher you will enjoy some of this *expert power.* Leadership that comes to you because students appreciate your expert power can be effective. This is true because this authority is awarded to you out of respect, not because it is demanded. Researchers have found that students consistently report admiring teachers who know their content well and who are able to explain it clearly (Tanner, 1978).

There are two dimensions to the expert power you can have as a teacher. The first of these relates to your grasp of the subject material you will be teaching. The second has to do with your commitment to plan and execute lessons that enable students to learn. You cannot fake an understanding of content you do not have; you cannot teach off-the-cuff without preparation. Attempts to do either of these things will be quickly spotted by students and will undercut your expert power. If this happens, students may be prompted to challenge your authority.

Referent or Attractive Power

Individuals who are perceived to be trustworthy and interested in the well being of others are also accorded leadership status and authority. For instance, you probably are willing to listen to and entrust prized possessions to those friends and family that you believe have your best interests at heart. These are individuals who have what is referred to as *referent or attractive power.*

You should seek to develop relationships with students that will lead them to defer to your referent or attractive power. William Glasser (1990) considers this kind of leadership to be particularly important. He points out the need for teachers to create warm and personal classroom atmospheres where students believe they belong and where their needs are regularly met. This can be a difficult task for you as a secondary school teacher since you may see many of your students only once a day for less than an hour.

You can begin to build referent power by doing things such as learning students' names, encouraging them, and treating them respectfully. Fairness in testing and grading all play a role. Students are particularly troubled when they believe that the tests administered are unfair and seem more designed to trick them than to honestly measure what they have learned.

The most powerful combination of authority styles involves both expert and referent power. If your students see you as an expert who is interested in their welfare, you may well find that your legitimate, reward, and coercive powers are also increased. Rewards given by highly valued and trusted individuals are especially powerful. By the same token, reprimands or punishments meted out by someone who is valued and trusted are also very powerful. In fact, a simple reprimand by a highly valued teacher is often more powerful that a physical punishment administered by someone who is not trusted or respected.

Teacher Consistency

Another category of your behavior that can contribute to a smoothly functioning classroom is *consistency*. To be perceived as consistent, you do not have to engage in mindless and unthinking conformity to a set of procedures or rules. Rather, being consistent simply means that you will apply rules and enforce your expectations in ways that do not vary from situation to situation so dramatically that they are unsettling to students (Savage, 1999).

This means that student behavior you find unacceptable on one day should generally also be considered unacceptable on another. If you fail to be consistent, some of your students may come to class wondering, "What can we get away with today?" This may lead them to test you to see how far they can go. When you consistently apply your rules across time you will eliminate students' incentive to challenge the limits you have established.

You need to apply rules and regulations consistently to all students. This means you cannot simply overlook a situation when one of your "model" students breaks a rule. Selective enforcement will undermine your referent power and credibility and student hostility and disrespect may result. Consistency of follow-through is also important. This means that when you make a promise, you need to carry it out. If you make a threat, be prepared to implement it.

Managing the Physical Environment

Your classroom's physical environment influences how your students behave. In thinking about how to arrange furniture and other items in the classroom, you might consider your answers to questions such as these:

- Do I want to encourage interactions among students?
- Do I expect students to move from place to place during the class period?
- Do I want to focus students' attention on a specific part of the room?

As you go about the business of arranging your classroom, you will need to direct your attention to the following categories of concern:

- Classroom ambiance,
- Floor space,
- Time management,

- Establishing routines, and
- Providing assistance.

Classroom Ambiance

The *ambiance* of a place refers to its general atmosphere or feel. The ambiance of the classroom has been found to affect behavior patterns of both teachers and students (Weinstein, 1979). As the quality of the physical environment declines, teachers make more control statements and are less friendly. Students in such classrooms are less involved in lessons, and feelings of conflict among students increase. To create a positive ambiance, you need to work toward an overall orderly classroom appearance and to make good decisions regarding the nature of lighting, decoration of wall space, and control of temperature.

Floor Space

How desks and other classroom furniture are placed can cue students to your expectations. Arrangements need to vary to accommodate different kinds of learning activities. For example, different patterns may be helpful when you want students to listen to you, work individually, study together in small groups, or take part in a large-group discussion.

In determining a specific arrangement, you should begin by thinking about what your students will be required to do. When you plan to present new information, it is important that student desks be arranged in such a way that each student can see you without having to look around visual obstructions. Sometimes you may want to widen the spaces separating individual desks to discourage too much social interaction among students.

However, if your intent is for students to work individually on assignments, it makes sense to arrange classroom furniture so that you can move quickly to help any individual in the class. Ideally, you should be able to move easily to help anyone experiencing a problem. An arrangement that allows you to go immediately to any place in the classroom also promotes on-task behavior. (Students know you will arrive in a hurry if a disturbance breaks out.)

When you want students to work in small groups, you need to decrease spaces separating individuals in each group. This will allow all group members to see papers and other materials, and it will permit easy conversation among all participants. It is helpful if you can arrange chairs so that all group members can easily see one another. (This is difficult if your students are required to sit in rows.)

Managing Time

You will diminish the number of classroom control problems you experience if you develop good time-management practices. Researchers have found that there is much unproductive time in many classrooms (Good & Brophy, 2000). Effective teachers skillfully maximize the amount of time students spend on productive tasks. The operating principle here is that busy students don't have time to misbehave.

Two aspects of time management that can help you make productive use of classroom time are (1) establishing and using routines and (2) providing assistance to those students who need help.

Note the space separating clusters of student desks. The arrangement makes it easy for the teacher to move from place to place to monitor students and assist them with their work.

Establishing Routines

Many classroom events are routinely repeated. These include collecting and distributing materials, making announcements, responding to students' requests, using equipment, and taking attendance. Much time can be lost if you do not carefully plan and execute these routines.

For example, suppose you developed a practice of returning papers to students individually at the beginning of each period. This routine might be consistent from day to day, but it is a procedure that has the potential to consume a lot of class time. Students may want to ask you questions about comments you have written on their papers or about grades you have awarded. You easily might find yourself using up 15 minutes or more of classroom time to complete this task. In addition, if you spend part of this time responding to concerns of individual students, others in the class may have little to do. They may use this time to socialize, and you may find it difficult to settle the group down when you want to start the day's lesson.

You can avoid these problems by using a better time-management scheme. For example, you might establish a goal of returning all papers in no more than two or three minutes. To do this, you can select from among several approaches. For example, in advance of the class, you can organize papers by rows (if your classroom is organized by rows) and simply ask the person seated in front to pass them back. Alternatively, you may decide to pass them out to individuals during a part of the lesson when students are working quietly on tasks you have assigned. These approaches tend to reduce the number of opportunities for student comments to delay the beginning of instruction. In addition, these approaches help you get a routine task accomplished in a way that does not promote side conversations among students—something that can make it difficult for you when you want undivided attention as you begin teaching a lesson.

Providing Assistance

Assisting individual students can consume tremendous quantities of classroom time. Frederic Jones (1979), a scholar who studied this matter, concluded that many teachers spend more time than necessary working one-on-one with each student in their classrooms.

Jones suggests that you should begin helping an individual student by commenting positively about something he or she has done. Next, you need to provide a brief and direct suggestion regarding what the student should do next. This should be a recommendation that leads the student to act; it is important not to do the work for the student. As the student begins working in response to this suggestion, you should move quickly to assist another student (following the same process with this individual). If needed, you can check back briefly with students who have been helped to see that work is being done correctly and to provide a few additional suggestions, if needed. If you follow this pattern, Jones suggests that you will find you often need to spend no more than about 20 seconds working individually with each student (Jones, 1979).

You do not always have to be the one providing the help. One junior high school teacher created consultant badges that a few students earned and wore proudly. The teacher allowed these individuals to leave their seats to help other students who requested assistance. The teacher limited the number of consultants, and members of the class worked hard to win the honor of being among the "consultants of the week."

The Discipline Dimension: Preventing Problems

There are no sure-fire remedies or guaranteed fixes for behavior problems. What is effective in one setting and with one individual may not be effective in another. However, there are some things you can do to increase the probability that your management plan will be effective.

Maximizing Student Involvement

Productive learning in the secondary school depends on high levels of student engagement. You want to establish conditions that will allow students to be actively involved in their learning. Your purposes are to encourage them to develop a sense of ownership in the instructional program they are experiencing and to help them acquire a sense of solidarity with you and other students. Researchers have found that students become more engaged in learning subject matter content when they are involved in all aspects of classroom life and that there is merit in taking actions to give them a sense of ownership as early as the first day of class (Vars, 1997).

CRITICAL INCIDENT

How Do You Establish Control?

Loretta Carter remembers dreaming about becoming a teacher when she was in high school. She recalls the thrill of encountering new literature and applying the insights of the great writers to her own life. As an undergraduate student, her enthusiasm for her subject increased. She worked at perfecting the communication and planning skills she knew she would need to inspire high school students. She had great confidence in her ability to be a good teacher. She started her first teaching job this fall. Things have not worked out quite as she imagined they would.

For one thing, the students she is teaching are quite different from what she expected. She had wanted to teach advanced secondary students who were capable of appreciating good literature. Instead, she finds herself teaching ninth-graders. The students display little enthusiasm for academic pursuits and seem consumed by social and recreational interests. They view Loretta's classroom as a social gathering place where they can show off and challenge her authority. In addition, there are a number of students who have limited English proficiency. They have difficulty reading some of the literature selections she would like to use.

To remedy the situation, Loretta has tried several things, but nothing has worked. She started the year by being friendly with all of the students and hoped her enthusiasm would be contagious. She told the students that she trusted them and was sure that they didn't need a lot of rules. Instead of appreciating this expression of confidence, the students have taken this as an invitation to do whatever pleases them.

In thinking about this situation, Loretta has concluded that the students behave this way because they don't understand why it is important to know something about good literature. Yesterday, she took time to talk to the class about the importance of good literature. The students rejected her logic. One student made this comment: "Look, you may like this stuff, but we think it is *really* boring. We would much rather see a movie."

She has thought that she might try to use some literature that ties more clearly to students' interests. But the more she has pondered this approach, the less promising it has seemed. "How," she wonders, "can I build a responsible literature program around student interests that seem limited to film stars, sports, and sex?"

Recently, she's also been thinking about the advice experienced teachers sometimes give newcomers: "Don't smile until Christmas." She thinks she may have been demanding too little of her students. For the past several weeks, she has started lowering grades of students who misbehave or fail to do their work. This has only made matters worse. Many students laugh when they get a failing grade. Some actually seem to be competing to see who can get the most Fs.

At this point, Loretta is about to give up. She has been telling her friends that "students have really changed since we were in school." She is thinking about looking for a job where she can work with college-bound students. She commented recently, "I would do anything to work with some students who care."

■   ■   ■

What do you think are the key issues in this incident? What do you think about what Loretta has tried? Do you agree that students have changed a great deal in the past few years? What supports your view? What are Loretta's key values? Where did she acquire them? How might her values be different from those of the students? How might these differences affect what Loretta thinks is important and what the students think is important? Is there any way Loretta can bridge these differences, or do you think a move to another school would be the best solution for her? What do you think she needs to change? Where might she go to get help? What should Loretta's next step be?

Today there is an increased emphasis on the uses of dialogue and negotiation in creating an environment where the important issues of commitment and engagement can be addressed. Dialogue can help individuals understand the balance between rights and responsibilities. It can help your students redefine power relationships in schools that, when not examined or discussed, may appear oppressive and threatening to them (Gillborn, Nixon, & Rudduck, 1993). There is evidence that some negotiation with your students sends a strong signal to them that you are a caring teacher (McLaughlin, 1994). When you are perceived as caring, you begin to move into a relationship characterized by power *with* students as opposed to power *over* students. This sort of relationship contributes to students' sense of self-worth and helps them value their status as "belonging" members of your class (Glasser, 1990).

Including dialogue and negotiation in the classroom does not mean you turn everything over to students. Many things about school are not negotiable. For example, you have no authority to negotiate about such items as mandatory attendance, the length of the class period, and other aspects of school life that are governed by local and state regulations. When you set out to negotiate certain aspects of classroom life with students, you should explain these limitations up front so that students understand the context within which negotiation can take place. Though the list of limitations may seem long, there still are many aspects of the educational experience that you and your students can negotiate. These include setting the rules and the goals for the classroom, determining how conflicts are to be settled, identifying topics in the curriculum that center on student interests, organizing the classroom, setting class procedures and routines, and establishing and managing the physical environment.

Teaching Conflict Resolution

A valuable way of extending negotiation into the area of responding to discipline problems is to teach your students conflict resolution strategies (Dear & Advisory Panel on School Violence, 1995). It is important to recognize that conflicts are a natural part of life. They will inevitably occur in your classroom from time to time. Actions you initiate with your students related to conflict resolution will make life in your classroom better for both you and the young people you serve (Lee, Pulvino, & Perrone, 1998).

Schools that have adopted formal conflict-avoidance strategies tend to follow one of two basic approaches (Johnson & Johnson, 1995). One of these focuses on training groups of students who serve as peer mediators for the school. The other approach teaches all students in a school or a classroom how to manage conflict constructively. Johnson and Johnson (1995) point out that this involve-all-the-students model has proved the more effective of the two basic approaches in helping young people learn how to negotiate and mediate conflict.

Johnson and Johnson (1995) define the conflict resolution approach as involving six basic steps:

- Getting students to describe what each person wants,
- Having students describe their feelings,
- Explaining the reasons underlying their wants and feelings,
- Reversing perspectives in order to view the conflict from both sides,
- Inventing options that have mutual benefit, and
  Reaching a wise agreement.

You may find it useful to address conflict resolution by developing specific lessons that focus on the above steps. For example, you might develop lessons that include emphases on such issues as identifying conflicts, identifying different conflict-resolution styles, identifying emotions, practicing active listening, identifying problem-solving approaches, and evaluating resolutions. The conflict-resolution component of lessons can be embedded within large lessons that focus on your regular academic content. For example, if you are teaching English, you might choose to use a particular literary selection as a starting point for a discussion of an issue related to conflict resolution.

Content is best taught and learned when students have a need to know. Therefore, the best time to teach conflict resolution is when your students face a real conflict. In addition, you need to remember that a certain amount of repetition is needed for learning. You cannot expect one or two lessons taught at the beginning of the year to have much impact on your students' patterns of behavior.

Emphasizing Private Correction

Another important aspect of dialogue and negotiation in the secondary classroom involves how you respond to inappropriate behavior. When dealing with the issue of correction, you want to keep your conversation with the student involved as private as possible. By correcting misbehavior in private, you show respect for the student's dignity. Often it is helpful to work with a misbehaving student in a place where this discussion cannot be overheard by other students. This allows your conversation to take place in a setting that frees the student from trying to save face in front of others in the class. Private correction also affords opportunities for you and the student to improve your personal relationship. This arrangement gives you a chance to communicate your respect for the student while, at the same time, indicating your disapproval of a particular unacceptable behavior.

Choosing Misbehavior Means Choosing to Experience the Consequences

Focusing on dialogue and negotiation does not mean that there are no consequences for inappropriate behavior. It means that you give students some voice in negotiating the consequences. Part of this dialogue allows you to point out that when people choose to misbehave or violate the law, they also choose the consequences of their actions. Students must understand that you are not the one responsible for what happens to them when they misbehave. They need to understand that they will be held accountable for their own inappropriate actions. Some secondary students do not understand this connection.

To help your students grasp the tie between unacceptable behavior and consequences, William Glasser (1965) suggests that you use a series of questions when speaking to students about their behavior. The first question is, "What are you doing?" The intent is to get the student to focus on and describe the inappropriate behavior. If a student is unable to do this, you should explain carefully what the problem behavior is. The second question is, "What happens when people behave as you have done?" This begins to encourage students to think about the relationship between the behavior and its consequences. The final question is, "Is this what you want to happen to you?" This helps students reflect on what they have done and to begin thinking about whether they really want to face the consequences likely to befall them when they behave inappropriately.

Individual conferences you have with students will help them focus on the issue of consequences. During such a conference, you may ask the students to identify some things that might happen as a result of misbehavior. If student ideas are unrealistic, you can supply some acceptable alternatives.

The Discipline Dimension: Responding Systematically to Problems

Effective teachers anticipate typical problems that may occur and plan possible responses. You will find it useful to develop a range of responses that can be organized into two categories: (1) responses that are less intrusive to those than are more intrusive and (2) responses that allow students to exercise self-control to those where the teacher takes a more direct role.

Choice of a particular response in a specific situation depends on the severity of the problem and the probability that the student will be able to exercise self-control. In general, serious problems will require you to use more intrusive teacher responses than those that are less serious. In situations where an individual student persists in misbehaving over a period of time, you will want to begin with a less intrusive response and gradually escalate both the severity and intrusiveness of your reaction.

Responses Supporting Self-Control

Responses in this category are designed to be non-intrusive. The hope is that your actions will not interfere with the flow of your instruction and that students will self-correct their behavior when you give them an opportunity to do so.

Reinforce Productive Behavior

A commitment to reinforce desirable behavior is essential to any discipline plan. Students need to know that there are rewards for productive, acceptable patterns of behavior. Positive reinforcement helps them to become more self-controlled. It is important, too, that students recognize they will receive some attention when they behave properly.

Students sometimes feel that the only way to be recognized is by misbehaving. A student in such a classroom once made this comment to one of the authors: "In this school everybody knows me because I'm not afraid of the teachers. What do you get for being good?" In the minds of some students, "being good" earns contempt from other students, an occasional nod from the teacher, and an expectation that they will be asked to do more work than others in the class.

Praise can take many forms. Some secondary students will react negatively if you praise them excessively in front of other class members because they do not want to be seen as a teacher's pet. You will find that private comments, brief notes, and awards of special privileges are more effective. When the entire class has been working and behaving well, it also makes sense for you to provide the whole group with some positive reinforcement. Giving class members a few minutes to chat freely or inviting them to select a particular activity they enjoy are some examples of positive reinforcement.

Nonverbal Signals

Minor misbehaviors are much more common than serious ones. Often you can stop them through use of nonverbal signals. These include eye-contact (the famous "cold, hard stare"), nodding the head in the direction of the offending student, or using a hand gesture. All of these actions send a message to a student that you have noted a particular behavior and found it to be unacceptable. This kind of nonverbal notification often is sufficient to prompt the student to stop doing whatever has attracted your negative attention.

Proximity Control

Proximity control is another technique teachers can use that sends a message to a misbehaving student without interfering with the flow of a lesson. It involves nothing more than your moving closer to the student while continuing the lesson. Many of your students will find it difficult to continue misbehaving when they know you are close by.

Using the Student's Name in the Context of the Lesson

When efforts to gain student attention through nonverbal techniques fail, sometimes you can use a student's name in the context of a lesson to stop misbehavior and to refocus the student on what is being taught. The technique requires you simply to insert the name of the student as part of the general flow of information that is being presented. ("If John were a member of a scientific team, he would need to know. . . . ") Typically, a student will perk up when you say his or her name. The person you identify will recognize that you have been watching, have found something unacceptable, and that the behavior should change.

Self-Monitoring

Students who have difficulty in the area of self-control often benefit from direct instruction on how to monitor their own behavior. One way of doing this involves the student making a list of his or her own desirable and undesirable behaviors. Together you and the student can identify the kinds of reinforcers that might be employed to encourage the desirable patterns.

You may also find it useful to teach students to ask themselves a series of questions when they sense they may be about to lose control. Questions might include: "What will happen to me if I do this?" "Is it worth the risk?" "What should I be doing instead?" You can teach those students who frequently experience self-control problems to take other kinds of actions when they find themselves becoming upset, anxious, or angry. For example, you might encourage them to close their eyes, think of a favorite place or activity, and then refocus on their work.

Providing Situational Assistance

When responses designed to support student efforts at self-control are not effective, you need to become more involved. This means providing direct assistance to the student or restructuring the learning environment.

A Quiet Word

This response requires you to move to the classroom area where the misbehaving student is located and to provide a quiet reminder of what you expect his or her behavior to be. This needs to be done quickly and quietly. Your intent is to avoid distracting others in the class while drawing the attention of the offending student to exactly what is wrong and how it should be quickly corrected.

Implementing Logical or Natural Consequences

Sometimes nonverbal signals are not effective, a quiet word fails to get the job done, and a student contends that following rules is unimportant. When this happens, the student needs to experience negative consequences resulting from his or her failure to correct an inappropriate behavior. If a student destroys equipment, he or she should be required to make restitution. If a person cannot work productively in a group, he or she should be removed, required to work quietly at a desk, and carefully monitored. If an entire class is failing to stay at task during a lesson, you may insist that wasted time be made up later when, otherwise, the group would be engaging in an enjoyable activity.

Responding with Clarity and Firmness

When other techniques fail or when a given behavior is seriously disrupting an entire class, you need to take quick action. You need to make a specific reference to who is misbehaving, what this person is doing that is unacceptable, and what an appropriate alternative behavior might be. You might say something like this: "Susan and Jose, your whispering and note-passing are disrupting the class. Take out your lab manuals and begin the assigned work now."

Your messages need to be firm. This means they should be sent in an "I mean business" manner. You can accomplish this by using a steady, serious tone of voice, direct eye contact, an erect body posture, and by moving toward the offending student.

Removing the Student from the Situation

Students who continue to misbehave sometimes will develop more self-control when they are moved. This is particularly likely to be true if the problem involves a student talking to someone else in the class while you are trying to introduce a lesson.

Often it is helpful to move the student closer to your desk. This permits you to easily monitor the individual's behavior. Also, physical proximity to your own location in the classroom will prompt a misbehaving student to do a better job of managing his or her behavior.

Student Conferences

A personal conference with a student who continues to misbehave often yields productive results. During such a conference, you need to encourage a misbehaving student to do most of the talking and to make decisions regarding how the offending behavior might be changed for the better. You might also consider using conferences as opportunities to develop informal behavior contracts with students with unsatisfactory patterns of behavior. These specify what students are to do to improve their behavior, and they may reference some good things that will come to them as a result of positive changes in their behaviors.

Conferences need to be conducted in a firm, businesslike manner. Often students will be upset when a conference begins. If you fail to keep your own emotions under control, an unproductive exchange may result that features angry accusations and unproductive debates. One of your responsibilities is to cool the situation, explain exactly what is amiss with the student's behavior, and work calmly to lay out some possible solutions.

Implementing Severe Consequences

When a student's misbehavior is especially persistent or serious, it may be necessary for you to impose relatively severe consequences. They should be implemented rarely and only after other less-intrusive measures have been tried and found to be ineffective.

Removing the Student from the Classroom

When a student's misbehavior has not responded to other actions, you may find it necessary to remove the individual from the classroom. This can accomplish several things. First, it tells the student that you are serious about maintaining order. Second, because most students like to be with their friends and peers in the classroom, removing an individual takes him or her away from a rewarding social situation. Among other things, your action eliminates the possibility that the student will gain status in the eyes of others in the class by challenging you. Finally, removing a student from the class gives you and the student some cooling-off time.

When you remove students from the classroom, they need to be sent to a supervised area. Never tell them simply to go out into the hall or into any other kind of uncontrolled situation. If anything should happen to them or if they should act in ways that hurt people or damage property, you could face serious legal complications. What you want to do is send students you are removing from class to a counselor's office, the principal's office, or to a special designated area set aside by the school (staffed by adult supervisors) for students who have been asked to leave class for disciplinary reasons.

Once you have sent a student out of your classroom, you need to notify personnel in the school's central administrative office. They will alert individuals in the appropriate office that the student is expected. If a student fails to arrive in a timely manner, many schools have guidelines calling for someone to look for the student and to accompany him or her to the designated area.

Conference with Parents or Guardians

When students seriously misbehave, their parents or guardians must be reached. Often a telephone call or a note will initiate actions at home that will encourage the student to change an unacceptable pattern. If serious misbehavior persists, you should try to schedule a face-to-face conference with the student's parent(s) or guardian. In preparing for such a meeting, you should gather anecdotal records (brief summary accounts) of misbehavior. These should include dates and times of episodes of misbehavior and summaries of what you have already done to try to change this unacceptable pattern.

During the conference, you should try to make the parents as comfortable as possible, conveying to them that the purpose of the meeting is to solve the problem so their son or daughter can change an unproductive behavior pattern and do better in school. It is important for the parent(s) or guardian to share their perspectives on issues that are raised. If possible, the conference should conclude with a plan of action to which all agree. You may wish to prepare a written summary of the meeting and mail a copy to the parent(s) or guardian.

After several days have passed, you should initiate a follow-up communication with the parent(s) or guardian to bring them up to date on how the student is doing and solicit any further comments or reactions. The idea is to build a common team approach to helping the student. Often, when you and parent(s) or guardian work in support of a common plan of action, a misbehaving student will adjust behaviors into more productive patterns. This will not happen overnight. Unacceptable patterns often take a long time to develop. Logically, it also takes time for more acceptable patterns to displace them.

Involving Other Professionals

Because management of the classroom is seen as such an important aspect of being a successful educator, you may feel hesitant about seeking the advice of others. This is a mistake. Seeking advice is not a sign of incompetence; rather, it is a hallmark of a true professional. Everyone experiences difficulty at one time or another, and that is why other professionals are available to provide assistance, when needed.

There are several ways you can seek the assistance of others. One of these is through what might be called a *buddy system*. This is a system where teachers are teamed together to help each other in a time of crisis or need. If your school has such an arrangement, your assigned "buddy" probably will be a teacher assigned in a classroom located close to your own. If either of you experience a serious problem (perhaps an out-of-control student or a fight), the other person can be there in a matter of seconds to provide extra help. Pairs of "buddy" teachers frequently spend some time at the beginning of the school year laying out general plans for how they will react to crisis situations. If your school lacks a formal buddy system, you might want to work out your own arrangement for dealing with severe problems with an experienced teacher you trust.

Some secondary school principals, in recognizing the serious consequences of frequent misbehavior and its relation to school violence, have instituted a formal *on-call support system*. This system designates a member of the staff for each period of the day who will be available to render quick assistance to a teacher who needs it. This person can be an administrator or an experienced faculty member trained in conflict management and mediation.

FOR YOUR PORTFOLIO

1. What materials, ideas you learned in this chapter related to *management and discipline* are to be included? Number them 1, 2, and 3.
2. Think about why you selected these materials for your portfolio. Consider such issues as the following in your response:
   - The specific purposes to which this information can be put when you plan, deliver, and assess the impact of your instruction;
   - The compatibility of the information with your own priorities and values;
   - The contributions this information can make to your personal development as a teacher; and
   - The factors that led you to include this material as opposed to some alternatives you considered.
3. Prepare a written reflection in which you analyze the decision-making process you followed. Also, mention the INTASC Standard(s) to which your selected material relates. (First complete the chart below.)

Materials You Selected and the INTASC Standards

Put a check under those INTASC Standards numbers to which the evidence you have selected applies. (Refer to Chapter 1 for more detailed information about INTASC.)

Item of Evidence Number	INTASC Standards									
	S1	S2	S3	S4	S5	S6	S7	S8	S9	S10
1										
2										
3										

In extremely serious cases, a group of professionals may need to be brought in to develop a plan of action for a student with a particularly difficult and persistent misbehavior problem. These professionals might include school administrators, counselors, psychologists, other teachers, and even representatives from youth and community services agencies outside the school. When this is done, you need to present a well-documented case to the group so members will have a clear picture of the situation. This team can then recommend specific courses of action that might even include removing the student from the classroom or the school. Recommendations might include referring the parents and the students to outside community agencies for assistance.

Conclusion

Keeping issues associated with classroom management and discipline in a proper perspective is a challenge for those who are new to the teaching profession. On the one hand, it is important to recognize that the problems of discipline and violence in the school are important ones that cannot be ignored. On the other hand, you also need to understand that more than 90 percent of the problems that occur in classrooms are minor ones. We do not want to needlessly raise your level of anxiety about the problem of discipline in the schools or to give the impression that students in secondary schools are out of control. That simply is not the case.

In every secondary school across America, regardless of the community context, there are teachers who experience few problems. You, too, can be a part of this group. However, this will not happen automatically. It requires considerable thought and hard work. Some of the ideas introduced in this chapter will help you as you strive to develop effective management and discipline procedures.

Key Ideas in Summary

- Establishing and maintaining discipline in the classroom is one of the key elements of achieving success in teaching. Changing societal attitudes have made this a more difficult task for teachers. There are four key areas that teachers need to attend to in meeting this challenge: (1) managing the classroom environment, (2) establishing teacher authority and credibility, (3) motivating and engaging the students in learning, and (4) responding appropriately to incidents of misbehavior.

- The major purpose of classroom management and discipline is to help individuals learn self-control and the acceptance of responsibility. Therefore, discipline is connected to one of the central values of education and is critical to the development of effective citizenship.

- You, as a teacher, are the key player in establishing good classroom control. A vital part of the process is how you establish your authority in the classroom. Authority based on students perceiving you to be an expert and a trustworthy, dependable individual is the best type of authority. Your consistency will contribute importantly to your effort to establish credible authority with students.

- The physical environment of the classroom has an impact on students. You need to attend to how you organize the floor space, and where your desk is located. Having an attractive and inviting classroom also contributes to positive behavior patterns.

■ Establishing routines for recurring events and handling student requests for assistance are two ways of using time efficiently.

■ Involving students in classroom dialogues and in negotiation gives them a sense of shared power in the classroom and communicates that they are respected. Dialogue and negotiation not only help prevent problems but also are desirable steps to follow when problems do occur.

■ Teaching students that conflict is a naturally occurring part of life and helping them learn how to manage and respond to conflict are important tools in helping to defuse potentially disruptive situations in the classroom. This also involves teaching students verbal and nonverbal communication skills as well as specific steps in mediation and conflict resolution.

■ When students choose to misbehave, they need to realize that they are also choosing to experience the consequences of their actions.

■ Developing a range of responses to potential problems allows you to choose a response that will best help students learn how to exercise self-control. Responses can be organized on a continuum moving from those that are relatively nonintrusive to those that are more intrusive.

■ When serious problems occur, it is important to involve other professionals. Involving others is not a sign of poor teaching, but a signal of a good professional attitude. The seriousness of many problems may well go beyond your capacity to solve; hence, it makes good sense to involve others.

Reflections

1. What perceptions do you have about the problem of discipline in the classroom? Did they change as a result of reading the chapter? How can you check the accuracy of these perceptions?

2. What are some reasons students misbehave?

3. What do you define as the purpose of discipline in the secondary school? What are the implications of this purpose for the way you will respond to classroom incidents?

4. How can a teacher demonstrate respect for the dignity of all students and at the same time communicate that certain behaviors are unacceptable in the classroom?

5. How do you think teachers go about establishing credibility and authority in the classroom? What is your plan for doing this?

6. What aspects of a physical setting are especially bothersome to you as you attempt to learn? What are your ideas about the type of physical environment you want to create?

7. What are some of the recurring events in the classroom for which you will establish a routine? What are some examples of routines you will use?

8. What are some of the basic verbal and nonverbal communication skills that you think are important in teaching how to respond to conflict?

9. What do you think are some advantages and disadvantages of a formal "buddy system" as an approach to dealing with misbehaving students?

10. Does it really make sense to preplan responses to misbehavior? Is it ever possible to anticipate all the inappropriate student behaviors that might occur in the classroom? Does preplanning hold out a false hope of a sure-fire solution to potential problems that simply might not work in the real world of the classroom? How do you respond to these questions? Be prepared to justify your responses.

Learning Extensions

1. Take a few moments to list some of the concerns you have about classroom management and discipline. What worries you most? Brainstorm possible actions that you could take to address these concerns. Share your concerns and responses with others.

2. Research the seriousness of violence in the secondary classroom. Do this by reading articles in professional journals and then check that information by interviewing several secondary teachers. How serious is the problem for them? Are their perceptions similar to those found in the literature? What might account for any differences you find?

3. Visit a secondary school and pay attention to the physical arrangement of the classroom. What aspects of the physical environment might contribute to problems? How might they be altered?

4. Discuss with experienced teachers the routines they have established for recurring classroom events. Begin making your own list of routines and procedures you will implement. Follow this by developing your own range of possible responses to misbehavior. Develop them into a range of responses similar to the example presented in the chapter.

5. Do some research to see if any secondary schools in your area have implemented conflict resolution. Visit the schools and talk with students and teachers about the process. What are the steps that are used, and how are they implemented?

6. Go to the Merrill Education's Link to General Methods Resources site at this URL: http://www.prenhall.com/methods-cluster/ At the bottom of the page select "discipline/classroom management" as your topic and click on the "begin" button. This will take you to the "Overview" page. On the left side, click on "Web Links." On the Web Links page click on "secondary." You will find a link to a description of a classroom management plan developed by Dave Wiggins. Using information at this site, prepare a short paper in which you compare and contrast suggestions you find here with perspectives reflected in this chapter. Conclude by developing a discipline plan of your own.

References

Clark, C., & Peterson, P. (1986). Teachers' thought processes. In M. Wittrock (Ed.), *Handbook of research on teaching* (pp. 256–296). New York: Macmillan.

Dear, J., & Advisory Panel on School Violence. (1995). *Creating caring relationships to foster academic excellence: Recommendation for reducing violence in California schools.* Sacramento, CA: Commission on Teacher Credentialing.

Emmer, E., Evertson, C., & Anderson, L. (1980). Effective classroom management at the beginning of the school year. *The Elementary School Journal, 80*(5), pp. 219–231.

French, J., & Raven, B. (1959). The bases of social power. In D. Cartwright (Ed.), *Studies in social power* (pp. 118–149). Ann Arbor, MI: University of Michigan Press.

Gillborn, D., Nixon, J., & Rudduck, J. (1993). *Dimensions of discipline: Rethinking practice in secondary schools.* London: Department of Education, Her Majesty's Stationary Office.

Glasser, W. (1965). *Reality therapy: A new approach to psychiatry.* New York: Harper & Row.

Glasser, W. (1990). *The quality school: Managing students without coercion.* New York: Harper & Row.

Good, T., & Brophy, J. (2000). *Looking in classrooms* (8th ed.). New York: Longman.

Hoover, R., & Kinsvatter, R. (1997). *Democratic discipline: Foundation & practice.* Columbus, OH: Merrill.

Johnson, D., & Johnson, R. (1995). *Reducing school violence through conflict resolution.* Alexandria, VA: Association for Supervision and Curriculum Development.

Jones, F. (1979). The gentle art of classroom discipline. *National Elementary Principal, 58*(4), pp. 26–32.

Kouzes, J. M., & Posner, B. Z. (1987). *The leadership challenge: How to get extraordinary things done in organizations.* San Francisco: Jossey-Bass

Lee, J., Pulvino, C. & Perrone, P. (1998). *Restoring harmony: A guide for managing conflicts in schools.* Columbus, OH: Merrill.

McLaughlin, H. J. (1994). From negation to negotiations: Moving away from the management metaphor. *Action in Teacher Education, 16*(1), pp. 75–84.

Savage, T. (1999). *Developing self-control through classroom management and discipline* (2nd ed.). Boston: Allyn & Bacon.

Slee, R. (1995). *Changing theories and practices of discipline.* Washington, DC: The Falmer Press.

Tanner, L. (1978). *Classroom teaching for effective teaching and learning.* New York: Holt, Rinehart & Winston.

Vars, G. F. (1997). Student concerns and standards, too. *Middle School Journal, 28*(4), pp. 44–49.

Weinstein, C. (1979). The physical environment of the school: A review of the research. *Review of Educational Research, 49*(4), pp. 577–610.

Williams, P., Alley, R., & Henson, K. T. (1999). *Managing secondary classrooms: Principles and strategies for effective discipline and instruction.* Boston: Allyn & Bacon.

V

Teachers' Performance and Growth

14

Evaluating Teacher Performance

This chapter will aim to

- state the purposes of teacher evaluation;

- identify the strengths and weaknesses of different types of teacher evaluation;

- overcome some anxieties you may have about processes that will be used to evaluate your teaching performance;

- identify multiple data sources that can be used for evaluating your teaching;

- explain several observational approaches that can be used to gather information about your classroom performance; and

- describe how evaluators can use material in your teaching portfolio as evidence.

Introduction

As you work to improve your teaching, you will want to gather evidence about the effectiveness of your classroom performance. This information provides a data base you can use to reflect upon and make decisions about what you have done. You cannot rely on memory alone to guide your thinking, especially if you want to consider what has gone on over a number of teaching days (Good & Brophy, 2000). Your analyses will be better grounded if you take regular notes or otherwise gather information in a systematic way. For example, you might create a pool of reliable information by regularly posting information about what you have done and your related thoughts in a personal professional-development portfolio (Wolf, Lichtenstein, & Stevenson, 1997).

Evaluation data you gather yourself will not be your only source of information about your classroom performance. Today, school leaders increasingly are held accountable for how well teachers in their schools perform. Many school districts require principals and other supervisors to evaluate and provide feedback to teachers in their buildings. You may expect to see some of these people in your own classrooms several times each year. Information you receive typically will reinforce the good things you are doing and also suggest some areas you may wish to work on to make your lessons even more effective.

You may also find yourself benefiting from a trend to provide teachers with supportive feedback from other instructors through *peer coaching* programs. These typically feature classroom visitations from other teachers who will observe what you do and then engage you in a follow-up discussion. These sessions often provide highly useful feedback you can use as you seek to improve your instructional practices.

Regardless of the approach taken, sound judgments about your teaching depend on the quality of information available to those who will be making the assessment. In this

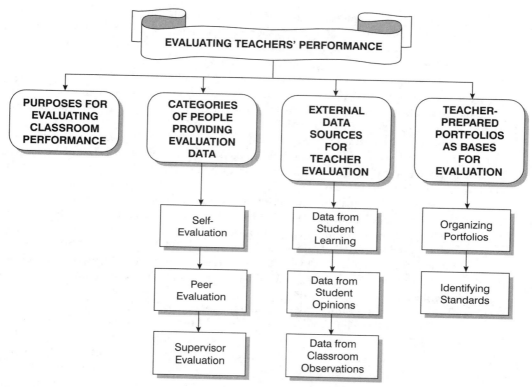

Figure 14–1
Graphic Organizer

chapter you will learn about some approaches to gathering data that can generate pertinent information related to the quality of your classroom performance. A familiarity with these approaches will put you in a position to provide suggestions to those who evaluate you, and give you tools to use later in your career should you be called upon to serve as a peer mentor for one or more new teachers.

Purposes for Evaluating Classroom Performance

There are two basic purposes for evaluating teachers. First, information gathered for developmental purposes helps you analyze what you are doing. A review of data that have been gathered during an observation can assist you as you make decisions about how to improve your own teaching (Barber, 1990). Your goal should be to modify and improve any patterns that are not as good as you would like them to be. This kind of assessment falls under the *formative evaluation* category introduced in Chapter 12, "Assessing Student Learning." Formative judgments may be based on data gathered through self-evaluation procedures, or they may result from examinations of evidence provided by an observer, such as another teacher, an administrator, or a supervisor.

Supporters of formative evaluation make this basic assumption: professional teachers constantly strive for improvement and, given credible evidence, they can and will modify their teaching (Barber, 1990). Notice that the emphasis is on *credible* evidence. This means that you, as a teacher, are unlikely to take results of this kind of evaluation seriously unless you are convinced that the information gathered to support the evaluative conclusions is reliable.

The second purpose for gathering data about instructional performance is to make a summary judgment of the teaching competence of the person who has been observed. This is what was described as *summative evaluation* in chapter 12. Often, your administrators and supervisors gather this kind of evaluation. They have professional and ethical obligations to ensure that you and your teaching colleagues perform at an acceptable level.

Summative evaluations of this sort can affect you in several ways. If they are well designed, they will communicate to you the norms and expectations of your school leaders. This kind of clarity, provided it is accompanied by a responsible set of data-gathering procedures, can provide you with a sense of security. Responsible summative evaluation processes act to assure you that your position is safe from arbitrary administrative decisions (Natriello, 1990).

In practice, many summative evaluation approaches fall short of the ideal, and, as a result, they generate much controversy. Part of the difficulty stems from problems professionals have had in agreeing on what constitutes "satisfactory" performance. There have been instances when judgments about teachers have been made on the bases of flawed data or biased judgments. Too great an emphasis on summative evaluation, when teachers lack confidence in the system, leads to low morale and a climate of fear (Duke, 1995). If "satisfactory performance" is defined too narrowly, there is also a danger that you may avoid pursuing challenging and ambitious instructional activities out of a concern that your "reward" for implementing these approaches will result in a negative summative evaluation (Duke, 1995).

The good news is that much work has been done to improve the quality of summative evaluations (Duke, 1995). School administrators increasingly recognize that teachers are less likely to react negatively to evaluation systems that clearly communicate what is expected of them. Better summative systems today feature carefully gathered information and are embedded with comprehensive evaluation programs that also provide teachers with frequent formative evaluation reports. When they have faith in the design and fairness of evaluation procedures, teachers have been found to want frequent evaluations (Natriello, 1990). This finding should provide some comforting assurance to you that, for the most part, you will be working with colleagues who truly are interested in improving the quality of their instructional performance.

Categories of People Providing Evaluation Data

When you teach, evaluation data may come to you from one of three basic sources: (1) you may engage in self-evaluation, (2) you might have another teacher observe your teaching and engage you in a peer-evaluation discussion, or (3) you may have a formal visit from a supervisor. As you think about particular features of evaluation data coming from each of these three sources, you need to keep in mind a key feature of evaluation: that is, *evaluation* involves judging the value of something based on a set of criteria. Making judgments based on *criteria* is what separates evaluation from mere opinion.

The appropriateness of the selected criteria is an important consideration. To be defensible, they must relate clearly to the purpose of the evaluation. Problems sometimes arise during teacher evaluation because of a mistaken assumption that there is a consensus regarding good teaching (Glass & Martinez, 1993). There is not. Difficulties are especially likely to occur when you and the person evaluating you have different views regarding the characteristics of sound instructional practice.

Even when views about specific aspects of effective practice differ, many people accept the idea that a major purpose of evaluation is to determine the extent to which your actions in the classroom promote student learning. If this is the priority and if criteria used in making judgments about your performance do not relate to this issue, you may well question the validity of results of the evaluation process.

Consider this example. Suppose an observer decided to focus attention on such issues as the attractiveness of your room, the quality of your bulletin boards, and the orderly arrangement of your student desks. Unless this evaluator has evidence of a connection between these criteria and student learning, focuses on these features make no sense as standards against which to judge the quality of your performance.

Not surprisingly, teachers frequently complain about evaluations based on what they believe to be inappropriate criteria. A teacher the authors know once received a negative evaluation because the observer felt the grouping of student seats into small circles in various parts of the room made the custodian's job difficult. With utter disregard for the highly effective small-group instruction this person was using, the evaluator sent a signal to this teacher that good teaching, by definition, featured whole-group instruction with all students seated in chairs arranged in neat rows.

Self-Evaluation

During *self-evaluation*, you can gather data, identify criteria to be used in making a judgment, and arrive at a conclusion about the quality of your teaching performance. If meaningful professional growth is to occur, you need to be open to the possibility that you will find areas in which you need to improve.

Self-evaluation data can come from several sources. For example, you might want to refer to some information you have included in a portfolio you have been keeping. Tools such as checklists and rating scales are other sources. Student achievement data and student attitudes and opinions may also play a role in the process. Occasionally, you might decide to make audio recordings as you teach and use them to revisit what you did during a lesson. Video recordings may also be used (although the equipment used to obtain them may introduce an unfamiliar element into your classroom and, hence, alter the typical classroom environment).

Reflective journals where you keep a record of classroom events and your reactions and thoughts can help you to identify recurring patterns of successes or problems that otherwise might be overlooked. You also may be able to draw on comments of other teachers who have observed your lessons. Often, exposure to their ideas can provide you with useful information you can use to challenge your own ideas and beliefs as you go about the business of examining your own practices (Airasian and Gullickson, 1997).

Several points support the importance of self-evaluation. First of all, it is something that you can do to generate information about your teaching more frequently than either peer evaluation or supervisor evaluation. This means you can use the approach to fill in any information gap resulting from infrequent peer or supervisor evaluation.

A second rationale for using self-evaluation is that you will be more inclined to change your behavior pattern when you personally identify something you do not like and have resolved to change (Airasian and Gullickson, 1997). When you make changes based on self-evaluation, you gain a sense of personal control over your needs and over how they should best be accommodated (Rodriguez & Johnstone, 1986).

Third, self-evaluation is a non-intrusive way of gathering information and making judgments about behavior. When you use it, you don't have to do anything that interferes with your classroom procedures. This distinguishes the approach from peer evaluation and supervisor evaluation, both of which introduce outside observers into the classroom. Because self-evaluation preserves a normal teaching environment, the information you gather may be a better reflection of how you behave under typical classroom conditions than information gathered by either peer observers or supervisors.

Finally, regular self-evaluation can build your confidence. Over time, modifications in your teaching behavior that you adopt as a result of your consideration of self-evaluation will be changes you believe in. If your self-evaluation information is compelling enough to commit you to make a change, it also typically will be a rationale you can use to explain modifications in your practices to others, for example administrators and parents or guardians of students.

There are a few negatives associated with self-evaluation. If you don't implement the approach carefully, you may be gathering haphazard and unsystematic information. If this happens, judgments you make about your performance will not be grounded in reliable evidence. Researchers have discovered that teachers who are unable to describe and defend procedures they have followed in gathering information about their teaching performances make conclusions about their teaching competence that correlate poorly with the findings of outside observers (Brown, 1983).

Sometimes it is difficult to make accurate records of what goes on during one of your lessons. Classrooms are fast-paced environments. So much happens that you will find it impossible to reconstruct from memory everything that happened. Using audio or video tapes to record lessons can help overcome this difficulty. Teacher-effectiveness specialists Good and Brophy (2000) report that researchers have found teachers' instruction to improve more from recording and evaluating their own lessons once every two weeks than from receiving feedback from an outside observer who watched them teach.

However, you need to remember that even audio and video recordings do not provide an absolutely complete record of what went on during a lesson. For example, audio recordings provide no information about nonverbal aspects of either your behavior or of your students' behaviors. Also, comments of some of your students may be hard, if not impossible, to hear on the tape. There is a particular problem when several students speak at the same time.

Video recordings often do not focus on the entire room. Behaviors that occur outside the range of the camera will not be recorded. Also, some of your students may not be in focus. Sometimes you will not be able to see the expressions of certain students as they react to different aspects of the lesson. Even with all of their limitations, however, audio recordings and video recordings can provide you with useful self-evaluation information.

Once you have decided how you will gather self-evaluation information, you need to decide what kind of information you are looking for. Questions such as these can help you develop an appropriate focus:

- How many different students did I involve in the discussion?
- Did my lesson follow a logical sequence?
- How often did I praise students, and whom did I praise?
- How long did I wait for students to respond after I asked a question?
- What did I do when I asked a question and nobody responded quickly?
- What did I do to highlight key points of the lesson?
- How often did I make control statements?
- How did I deal with misbehavior?
- What did I say to make a smooth transition from one part of the lesson to another?
- What did I do to accept students' ideas and feelings?
- What did I do to make sure students understood tomorrow's assignment?

Responses to the focus questions serve as the data pool you can consider as you decide whether anything you did during the lesson fell short of your expectations. If you are not satisfied, you can develop a personal action plan. For example, if one of your interests was to maximize the number of students participating in a discussion, and a review of what actually happened revealed that only a few took part, you can take action during future discussions to ensure involvement of more students. You can use recordings or other means of gathering data during subsequent lessons to verify that your hoped-for changes have occurred.

Peer Evaluation

Collaboration with a respected peer can help you gain insight into your behaviors and provide ideas about how your instruction might be improved. Collaborative work with other teachers often has an important psychological benefit as well, in that it breaks down the sense of isolation you may feel working alone in classrooms with no adult company. When a colleague observes your work, there is an opportunity for a rich debriefing discussion that allows you and another trained professional to share insights.

Several approaches to peer collaboration have evolved. Two common types are peer coaching and mentoring.

Peer Coaching

Peer coaching is defined as a situation in which two or more individuals voluntarily work together to help each other to solve problems and grow professionally. In peer-coaching, no individual is regarded as superior to another. All members of a peer coaching team are assumed to have abilities and skills that may be valuable to others.

Successful peer coaching groups require members to know one another well and to have a relationship based on mutual trust and respect. When you first get involved in such a group, you and other members will spend time sharing ideas about teaching and exchanging perspectives that help each member of the team to better understand the others. In time, members begin sharing and critiquing lesson ideas and instructional materials they are considering. Every effort is made to ensure that you and other members of the group make comments in ways that are as positive and supportive as possible. This approach helps others to build confidence in their own perspectives, and it enhances each member's sense of professional self-worth.

When individuals in the group feel quite comfortable with one another, they will begin observing each other's classroom teaching. Research has established that teacher anxieties about assessment diminish considerably when people they view as credible and trustworthy conduct the observations (Bang-Jensen, 1986).

When members of a peer-coaching group start observing members' classroom teaching, a formal supervision cycle often is followed that includes these elements:

- Pre-conference,
- Observation, and
- Post-conference.

During the *pre-conference*, you and the person who will be acting as your peer coach plan the observation experience together. You will provide this person with information about the purposes of your lessons and about any special features of your plan. Together you will discuss what you would like your peer coach to focus on as you teach the lesson as well as some approaches this person might use to get the information.

During the *observation*, your peer coach will gather appropriate data using procedures agreed to during the pre-conference meeting. This person may also take notes on other matters that he or she feels should be shared with you. Peer coaches are encouraged to prepare comments that are written in positive terms with a view to supporting your efforts.

During the *post-conference* phase, your peer coach shares information that has been gathered. Observations are presented to you in a nonjudgmental fashion, and you are invited to look for patterns and draw your own conclusions. Often your peer coach will affirm what you have done well and suggest a few ideas to try in the future. Ideally, the post-conference functions as a discussion involving equals.

There are some limitations on the use of peer coaching. First of all, the approach takes time. Schedules sometimes do not permit teachers to observe others, much less engage in needed pre-conferences and post-conferences. Also, peer coaching depends on mutual trust. If school administrators force you and other teachers to organize into peer coaching teams or require people who do not like or respect one another to be on the same team, nothing good will result (Bang-Jensen, 1986).

Mentoring

Mentoring involves the tutoring of a less skilled person by a more skilled person. The mentor serves as guide, adviser, role model, or consultant (Odell, 1990). There is a clear hierarchical relationship assumed in mentoring. One person is viewed as having more advanced knowledge than the other. This person uses this knowledge to assist the less skilled person. In teacher education programs, there is often a mentoring relationship between the supervising teacher and the student teacher.

If you take a teaching position in a school with a mentoring program, the benefit you derive will depend greatly on mutual trust and respect between you and your mentor. Ideally, mentoring relationships, like peer-coaching relationships, need adequate time to develop. This is particularly true when administrators assign someone to you as a mentor whom you, initially, do not know well. You both need to establish a high inter-personal comfort level for the relationship to work.

Supervisor Evaluation

Supervisor evaluation occurs when someone in a position of authority is given the responsibility of evaluating your performance. Results of evaluations by your school administrators have purposes going beyond those usually associated with self-evaluation or peer cooperation. Both self-evaluation and peer-cooperation efforts are almost uniformly focused on helping you to become a more proficient classroom instructor. This is also a key purpose of supervisor evaluation. However, supervisor evaluation has an additional purpose. Results provide data that can be used as a rationale for firing or retaining you, awarding you tenure, or assigning you to a higher salary category.

Supervisor evaluation can lead to high levels of anxiety. Relationships among individuals in the hierarchical organization of a traditional school contribute to this problem. Thomas Sergiovanni (1994), a scholar who has studied these relationships, points out that in these settings "those higher in the hierarchy are presumed to know more about teaching, learning, and other matters of schooling than those lower. . . . " (p. 216). If you do not have faith that your supervisor has these characteristics, it is natural that you might have some anxieties associated with your doubts about the credibility of the evaluator. Sergiovanni argues that the traditional supervisor-subordinate relationship often negatively influences administrator-teacher interactions and that it should be replaced by a conception of schools as communities. In such schools, status differences among people playing different roles would be minimized and interpersonal relationships would be less strained.

Even though you may have concerns about supervisor evaluation, researchers have found that, in general, teachers want and value this kind of assessment (McLaughlin & Pfeifer, 1988). One teacher who reflected on this finding indicated general agreement, but also noted an important condition: "We need people to come in and check on us just like anybody else. As long as it is done in a positive and constructive manner, all it can do is benefit education" (McLaughlin & Pfeifer, 1988, p. 63). When supervisors

An assistant principal speaks with two department heads about data-collection procedures that will be used during classroom observations of teachers.

provide positive and constructive feedback, they can help you overcome any fears you might have about the evaluation process.

Supervisor evaluation tends to be done in more systematic ways than self-evaluation or peer collaboration. For example, supervisors often use formal evaluation instruments that have been developed by trained specialists. Some evaluations are scheduled in advance so your supervisor can see you teach a particular lesson. At other times, this person may drop in to observe your classroom unannounced. Often, your supervisor will schedule a conference with you following the observation. This allows opportunities for the two of you to share comments and engage in a general discussion about the lesson.

In preparing for supervisor evaluations, you will find it useful to review the data-collection instruments your supervisor will use. This allows you to better understand the categories of behavior that will be assessed. If you disagree with the categories reflected on the instrument, it may be possible for you to discuss this situation in advance with the supervisor. As a result, you may be able to negotiate some kind of a compromise approach.

Whether supervisors ever see a truly representative sample of teachers' work is a matter of debate. When a supervisor comes into your room, the classroom environment is altered. Changes can be both positive and negative. On the one hand, sometimes your students will behave better and be more responsive than usual to your lesson. On the other hand, the supervisor's presence can make you a bit nervous, and this may change your typical patterns of behavior.

External Data Sources for Teacher Evaluation

Responsible teacher evaluation incorporates data from multiple sources. Each data source offers information that differs in some way from information provided by others. The chances that judgments will accurately reflect what you do in the classroom are greatly enhanced when evaluators consider data from multiple sources. Regrettably, some appraisals are made on the basis of extremely limited information. If this should happen to you, you would have reason to be concerned about the validity of observers' conclusions.

Data sources that are potentially useful for teacher evaluation fall into three categories:

- Data about student learning,
- Data from student opinions, and
- Data from classroom observations.

Data About Student Learning

Because promotion of learning is one of your fundamental obligations as a teacher, it is not surprising that student achievement information often will be of great interest to the people who evaluate you. Although information about student learning is important, there are reasons this kind of information should not be the only area of interest to those charged with appraising your effectiveness. For one thing, there is evidence that an exclusive emphasis on student achievement has the potential to encourage the use of questionable means to produce increases in student test scores. For example, a particularly stressed teacher might threaten students with punishments of various kinds if they failed to perform well.

In addition, some important educational objectives do not lend themselves conveniently to being measured on traditional kinds of tests. This particularly tends to be true for affective outcomes that focus on changes in students' attitudes and values. For example, you might believe that encouraging your students to use rational thinking processes is an important learning outcome. Measuring changes in this kind of a commitment directly is difficult. If you were evaluated only on how well your students performed on achievement tests, any good work you have done to help your students become rational thinkers would not be recognized.

Using student achievement data to evaluate your work also assumes your students have learned subject matter that is assessed from you. This is not always the case. For example, some bright students may well get high scores on tests because they have learned tested content on their own.

Despite these limitations, there is a place for student achievement data in teacher evaluation. However, achievement information must come from well-designed procedures. It is also important that tests or other data sources adequately sample information that students have been taught. You will find specific information about procedures for preparing good tests provided in Chapter 12, "Assessing Student Learning." In addition to data from well-designed tests, an evaluation scheme that includes information about student achievement should include more than test scores. For example, evaluators should also look at examples of daily work your students have completed and other products of student learning you have required them to complete.

Knowing that you will be asked to provide some evidence that your students have learned need not intimidate you. You should regard this expectation as an encouragement to assume professional responsibility for your students' performance. This realization can stimulate your thinking about ways to meet the needs of all the young people in your classes. Lessons arising out of this consideration can help students both master new content and feel better about themselves. Their improved performance levels, in turn, will help you to receive high marks when you are evaluated.

A focus on student learning can help you to reflect on what you are doing in the classroom. You might want to consider questions such as these as you think about what occurred when you taught specific lessons:

1. What did students learn, and what did they fail to learn?
2. What specific things did I do to promote learning in those parts of lessons most students learned well?
3. What specific things did I not do to promote learning in those parts of the lesson students failed to learn well?

Answers may prompt you to think of ways to modify your instructional approaches in subsequent lessons.

Data from Student Opinions

Your professional clients are your students. They come into contact with you every day they are in class, and they have a perspective on your teaching that cannot be duplicated by anyone else. For this reason, students' opinions sometimes will be included when you are evaluated.

At some time in your career, you may be involved in designing rating scales to be used by students as part of your school's teacher-evaluation process. If you are involved in such an effort, you need to consider difficulties associated with student ratings of teachers. For example, you want to be sure you ask students to rate only behaviors they are qualified to comment on. Some appropriate categories might be those that focus on teachers' organizational abilities, their willingness to highlight key points during lectures, and their skill in involving large numbers of individuals in discussions. On the other hand, few students have sufficient background to make meaningful judgments about such things as the depth of teachers' subject-matter knowledge or the quality of the teacher preparation programs in which their teachers at one time were enrolled.

Further, rating scales should feature items over which you, as a teacher, can exercise some personal control. Items related to acoustic quality of the classroom or the nature of overhead lighting are not appropriately included. Though these environmental variables may influence what your students learn, changes will require actions by others, and it is not fair for you to be held accountable for things you can do little about.

WHAT DO *YOU* THINK?

Are Student Ratings Worthwhile?

A teacher recently made these comments about student ratings of teaching:

"It makes little sense to include student ratings in a system that is designed to assess the relative excellence of my teaching performance. This approach can undermine my "good" teaching. It pits all of us who teach against one another in an unseemly popularity contest. It provides incentives for us to give easy assignments and to award lots of high grades. Immature students will respond to this unprofessional behavior by giving high ratings to those who demand little of them. From an educational standpoint, this makes no sense."

Questions

1. The person making this argument presumes that student ratings encourage irresponsible teacher behavior? Do you agree? Why, or why not?

2. Are students capable of knowing what their long-term interests are? Do they tend to favor teachers who they perceive as "easy graders," or do they appreciate teachers who hold them to high standards of performance?

3. If you were to make a comment to the person who made this argument, what would you say?

Interpreting ratings given by individuals can be difficult. Conclusions drawn from a review of rating scale responses should focus on what the majority of respondents have said. In any class, there are likely to be a few individuals with views that are at odds with the preponderance of opinion. Too much attention paid to these out-of-the-mainstream views may result in false conclusions about the adequacy of your performance.

Data from Classroom Observations

Formal classroom observations can provide useful information about the quality of your instruction. Various techniques provide data and shed light on such issues as students' attitudes, performance on assigned tasks, and levels of involvement.

Good classroom observation procedures require systematic data gathering. Typically, there is an emphasis on a specific set of focus behaviors. Data are collected that relate to these behaviors. This system allows the observer to focus on a relatively small sample of your classroom behaviors. Under these circumstances, it is possible for the observer to keep up with the rapid interchanges that frequently characterize classroom instruction. Without this kind of a limited focus, it is easy for observers to fall behind and get lost in a futile attempt to keep track of everything that happens.

The personal background of the observers may influence the accuracy of information obtained from classroom observations. Observers with little formal training in proper observation procedures sometimes bring perspectives to their work that they may not recognize. For example, they may have formulated impressions about what constitutes good teaching based solely on recollections from their own student days. It may well be that what appealed to them may not appeal to other learners; hence, their personal conceptions of "good teaching" may be at odds with findings of careful researchers. Clearly, observers who are familiar with findings of teacher-effectiveness research and who understand procedures to be followed in gathering information are prepared to provide more valid and reliable information about your teaching than observers who lack this background.

Trained observers often will use several approaches as they collect data about your teaching performance. Many formal observation instruments have been developed. In the following subsections, you will find some frequently used examples.

List of Focus Questions

Observers often develop a *list of focus questions* to guide their work. Sometimes they will work these out cooperatively with you prior to an observation. As you teach your lesson, the observer takes notes that include information related to each item on the list. Kinds of questions vary. For example, you might be interested in issues such as lesson pacing, the efficiency of transitions from one part of the lesson to another, the relative degree of participation by male and female students, and the amount of on-task behavior demonstrated by individual students during independent study.

A general guideline in preparing questions is to keep the list short. More useful information results when observers gather extensive information about a small number of focus questions. You will find an example of a list of focus questions in Figure 14–2.

Verbatim Record

Another approach observers sometimes use in gathering information is the *verbatim record*. In this procedure, a small number of teacher behavior categories are identified. Usually no more than three are selected for a given lesson. If you ask an observer to use this technique in your classroom, this person will write down everything you say that relates to each selected category. Sometimes the observer, alone, identifies the categories. Sometimes you and the observer will jointly agree on them before your lesson begins.

This approach also lends itself to self-evaluation. To use it in this way, you need to arrange to record your lesson. Later, you can play back the recording and note everything you said in each focus category. You will find an example of a verbatim record form in Figure 14–3.

The observer sometimes adds additional categories as a lesson is being taught. For example, the observer might note that you are overusing the word "good" when students respond correctly to a question. To point out this pattern to you, the observer might add a new category, *Specific Statements Made to Students Answering Correctly*, and write the word "good" under this heading every time you use the word for this purpose. The long string of "goods" that may result can be shared with you during a follow-up debriefing session.

When well-trained observers debrief you following a verbatim record observation, they try not to be judgmental. Ideally, they share information with you and ask whether

---

Teacher: _____   Date: _____

Lesson Topic: _____

Course Title: _____   Period: _____

Class Composition:

    Number of Males: _____   Number of English Language Learners: _____

    Number of Females: _____   Number of Students in Other Categories: _____

    Full Inclusion Students: _____

1. What routines were used to get the instructional phase of the class period started?
2. What did the teacher do to draw students' attention to the content of the lesson?
3. What was the sequence of activities?
4. How did the teacher check for student understanding?
5. How were students actively engaged in the lesson?
6. Was there evidence of re-teaching to help students having trouble with the content?
7. How were the special needs students accommodated?
8. Were key points highlighted? If so, how was this done?
9. If there was discussion, how many students participated? Were their answers responsive to the questions?
10. What appeared to be the intent of the lesson? Was it achieved?
11. What were general student reactions to the lesson?
12. How did the teacher handle episodes of inappropriate behavior?

Figure 14–2
Focus Questions for Lesson Observation

any revealed patterns are consistent with what you had intended to do. If you decide they are not, then you may wish to change certain things when teaching future lessons.

Frequency Count

Another easy-to-use procedure for gathering useful information during a classroom observation is the *frequency count*. It is basically a checklist that is used to note the number of times something occurs. Its appropriateness is restricted to kinds of behaviors that may recur several times during a lesson. A frequency count scheme might look something like the example in Figure 14–4.

A frequency-count checklist records only the number of times an individual behavior occurs. You cannot use this information to find out how long each of these episodes

Teacher: _____   Date: _____

Lesson Topic: _____

Course: _____   Period: _____

Number of Males: _____   Number of Females: _____

All comments of the teacher will be written down exactly as they are said so long as statements relate to one of these categories:

1. Motivating Students
   time   statement

2. Praising Students
   time   statement

3. Controlling Students
   time   statement

Figure 14–3
Verbatim Record

lasted. For example, an observer using a frequency count might find that in one of your classes you criticized students on ten separate occasions. In another, you may have criticized students only three times. This does not necessarily mean that you spent *more time* criticizing students in the first class. It is possible that, in the first class, each of your critical statements were very short. By the same token, in the second class, each of your three criticisms could have lasted a long time. Obviously, under these conditions,

Teacher: _____   Date: _____

Lesson Topic: _____

Course: _____   Period: _____

Number of Males: _____   Number of Females: _____

Directions: Tally the frequency of the following kinds of teacher behaviors:

1. Statements designed to motivate students to learn more about the lesson topic

2. Questions requiring factual recall

3. Questions requiring higher level thinking (questions above the cognitive levels of knowledge and comprehension)

4. Females called on by the teacher

5. Males called on by the teacher

6. Positive teacher comments directed toward females

7. Positive teacher comments directed toward males

8. Negative/critical comments directed toward females

9. Negative/critical comments directed toward males

Figure 14–4
Frequency of Selected Teacher Behaviors

a much higher proportion of total class time may have been taken up by your criticism of students in the second rather than in the first class.

Many kinds of items can be included on frequency-count checklists. New ones may be added if the observer notes a category of behavior you probably should know about. For example, if the observer notes that you have a pattern of calling only on students seated in the front of the room, focus categories labeled "students seated in front half of the room called on" and "students seated in the back half of the room called on" might be added.

Teacher-Prepared Portfolios as Bases for Evaluation

Throughout the text we have introduced ideas you might wish to include in portfolios. Taking time to collect and organize portfolio items makes little sense unless you have clear purposes in mind. In addition to serving as a repository for ideas about teaching, you can also include material you can use as you reflect on what you have done and think about how to improve your instruction. A portfolio with this kind of information can also serve as an important data source for others who are charged with evaluating your performance.

When you use a portfolio either as part of a self-evaluation process or as a data source for others who will be evaluating you, you need to pay particular attention to how you organize materials. At the same time, you need to keep in mind any expectations or performance standards that others who review the portfolio will want to see reflected in what you have assembled.

 ## CRITICAL INCIDENT

What is the Basis of My Evaluation?

"Got a minute?" Rick Rocheleau, an eighth-grade math teacher at Pioneer Heights Junior High School looked expectantly through the door at Sabrina Santayana, the chair of the math department. It was 4:30 in the afternoon. Nearly all of the students had left the building an hour ago. Even most of the teachers had gone home. Only a few remained working on paperwork and getting things in order for the next day's classes.

"Sure, Rick, come on in. I'm just completing yet another survey from those 'wonderful' folks down in the central administration building who think we love to spend our time filling out forms for them to file. I'd much rather talk to you than deal with this wretched paperwork." Sabrina gathered together what she had been working on and put the material into a briefcase for later attention at home.

"So how are things?" asked Sabrina.

"Well, generally OK, but you know, tomorrow's my day."

Sabrina looked momentarily puzzled, then remembered what Rick was talking about. "Ah yes, the annual visitation ritual from our revered vice principal and the follow-up formal evaluation conference. So, what's your concern? You've had two successful years here already. Your kids do just fine on our standardized tests scores. They like you. You relate well to parents. I know these evaluations aren't much fun, but, come on, you've been through them before."

Rick nodded his head. "True enough, but this is the *big* one for me. I'm in my third year here. If I get through with a positive evaluation and am rehired, I'll be tenured. I know tenure isn't an absolute guarantee of permanent employment, but I should have a job unless something really unexpected happens."

"Look, Rick," commented Sabrina, "let me give it to you straight. I played a role in your hiring. I wasn't the only one, but I was involved. There were lots of competitors for the vacancy we had at that time. We hired you because we thought you had the 'right stuff.' And you know what, we were right. Personally, I'm delighted that you'll qualify for tenure. It's good to get through the probationary years and have your competence recognized through the formal award of tenure. But, look, we never would have hired you if we had serious doubts that you would get bad evaluations and be sent on your way after a few probationary years. So, unwind my friend . . . it's going to be OK."

"Thanks for your thoughts," replied Rick. "But it just makes sense to me that they are going to apply a much higher standard this year. I mean, if I get a good evaluation, the school will be more or less "stuck" with me."

"*Stuck*! Rick, what a terrible choice of words." Sabrina put her face close to Rick's and said, "Now you just listen to me! If we get somebody good here as a tenured teacher, we regard that person as a wonderful 'professional catch,' not somebody we're 'stuck' with."

Rick smiled and shook his head. "I appreciate your position, but I'm not at all sure everybody sees it that way. I've been reading in the paper about how tight our school district budgets are going to be over the next five years. It's pretty clear that teachers' salaries are the most expensive part of the budget. The district could keep average salaries lower by tenuring fewer teachers and replacing them with lower-priced beginners. This has happened to some of my friends in other districts who received glowing evaluations their first couple of years and then were dismissed after a bad evaluation just before they were scheduled to receive tenure."

Sabrina shook her head. "Rick, in this life we can always find an example where something terrible and irresponsible has happened. But, it's not going to do you any good to go around with a Chicken Little, 'the-sky-is-falling' attitude. It's just not healthy to generalize from the most negative possible example. Don't do it. The bottom line here is that we want to improve instruction. To do that, we try to find and *keep* good people."

Rick took a deep breath. "OK, Sabrina, I hear you. But it's a bit easy, isn't it, for someone who is already tenured to tell those of us who aren't 'not to worry.' This is a real concern for me. It's late in the year. If I find I'm not going to be allowed to return here, I'm not sure that I'll be able to find another job. I *do* have to pay my rent and buy my groceries. And, I don't want to switch to some other kind of work."

■   ■   ■

How do you explain Rick's heightened concern for the evaluation procedure he will face this year as compared to those he's experienced in the past? What are Rick's assumptions about the priorities of school administrators? What do his concerns tell us about Rick's own values? What does he assume about the values of others involved in his evaluation? How accurate do you think Rick's assumptions are?

What kinds of past experiences might be affecting Rick's view of the upcoming evaluation? Sabrina suggests he may be generalizing too much from a few negative examples. Is he? Rick implies that Sabrina can afford to be unconcerned about bad experiences others have had when being considered for tenure because this is a problem she no longer personally has to face. Is Rick right?

How do you feel about Rick's concern? Is he overreacting? Are there others Rick should talk to about this situation?

Organizing Portfolios

Once material has been gathered for your portfolio you need to organize it in a manner that makes sense to you and that will allow you to identify patterns that reflect your growth and your professional developmental needs. Since each portfolio is a personalized collection of information and material, the organization should reflect your personal choices and needs. However, you may find an approach adapted from one suggested by Green and Smyser (1996) to be helpful. It involves collecting information related to five basic categories:

- *Personal background.* In this section you provide details about your educational and professional experiences. You should include information about your philosophy and beliefs, and the types of experiences you have had working with students. In your early years in the profession, it makes sense to include information about your preparation. Also note any conferences or workshops you have attended. If you have engaged in activities such as student teaching or substitute teaching, you should also give a brief description, combined with reflections, about these experiences.
- *Context information.* In this section you provide information about your own teaching context. How would you describe your students? What is the nature of your classroom? Is lighting adequate? Is noise a problem? Are there adequate teaching materials to work with? This kind of information will help to evaluate some of the constraints you work with every day in your classroom
- *Instruction-related information.* You will include information about unit and lesson plans, examples of materials you have prepared, and instructional aids in this section. These will serve as concrete evidence of what you know about teaching and learning. This part of the portfolio also often includes comments by others (classroom teachers, supervisors, and so forth) about your teaching and the materials you have created. Your own personal reflections about the adequacy of various instructional approaches, particularly as they relate to student learning, will also be included. Attempt to provide as much information as possible regarding your knowledge of teaching and learning and your ability to convey what you know to students. This important section often is the lengthiest in the portfolio.
- *Responses to special needs of individuals.* Students in your classroom will vary in terms of their ability levels and interests in your subject. One of your challenges is to adapt instruction to meet the needs of each of these people. In this section, include as much information as possible regarding what you adapted and altered to accommodate individual student needs. Evidence here should include examples of differentiated assignments, varied learning materials, and alternative assessments.
- *Contributions to the overall mission of the school.* This section provides you an opportunity to demonstrate how your efforts have contributed to the overall improvement of your school. You may choose to include some special projects that were undertaken that benefited students beyond your own classroom. Did you become involved in any extracurricular activities? Did you create any materials that were left with the school? Did you assist in planning any special events? If answers to these questions are "yes," include details in this section of your portfolio. Evidence of this kind communicates information about your ability to work with others in support of a larger, common goal.

Identifying Standards

Because they are personal documents reflecting individual styles and needs, not every portfolio contains exactly the same kinds of information. This circumstance contributes to the difficulty evaluators face in assessing them. The usual procedure is for them to look for internal consistency. For example, an evaluator might begin by looking for information that communicates your hopes and priorities. Then, this person goes through the portfolio seeking examples that confirm that your behaviors align consistently with the important purposes you have established. You will get a higher rating if the assessor finds abundant documentation of behaviors that are congruent with your professed priorities.

Portfolio evaluators often use clear sets of standards, or *rubrics*, to enhance their abilities to make consistent judgments. Often these rubrics are based on careful descriptions of features of "good teaching." What should good teachers know and be able to do, and how well should they be able to do it? Answers yield two types of standards. *Content standards* reference *what* teachers should know. *Performance standards* reference *how well* teachers can put what they know into practice (Wolf, Lichtenstein and Stevenson, 1997).

Content standards can be relatively broad statements based on basic principles and concepts of good teaching. For example, they might include statements such as "knows the subject being taught" or "relates subject to real world applications." Each one of these general statements can be modified to include a few "indicators" that provide more specific evidence about the presence or absence of behavior related to the standard (Wolf, Lichtenstein, and Stevenson, 1997). For example, what types of indicators might appropriately signal to an evaluator that you know your subject? Information about courses you took as a college or university student might be useful evidence. Additionally, you might want to provide examples in your portfolio of content-related generalizations and examples of how you provided clear explanations of key principles to your students. An evaluator reviewing this kind of material would probably see such information as acceptable evidence of your subject-matter knowledge.

When it comes to performance standards, the operating guideline is to "make them clear." Establishing this kind of clarity is not easy. For example, you probably have seen rating scales with performance standards that are described in such terms as "above average," "average," and "below average" or "adequate" and "inadequate." Such terms provide only an illusion of clarity. People vary enormously in terms of what they believe to be "average" or "adequate." As a result, different evaluators seeing the same evidence may come up with very different ratings when confronted with this kind of terminology on a performance standard.

One approach to resolving this problem and to making ratings of evaluators more reliable is to establish performance standards that reference the frequency of occurrence of the target behavior. For example, "half or more of the provided lesson plans included application activities for students that required them to engage in tasks demanding them to analyze, synthesize, or evaluate." This kind of a standard provides a clean decision rule for the evaluator.

Figure 14–5 illustrates how content and performance standards can be combined to facilitate evaluation of one dimension of good teaching, "knowledge of subject matter." In this figure, specific indicators of the broad category of knowledge of subject matter have been identified on one dimension. Performance standards have been identified on the other. It should be noted that, on any given day, you would not be expected to demonstrate all of the indicators. In addition, your evaluator may well consider other information before making a judgment about how well you know your subject.

KNOWLEDGE OF SUBJECT MATTER			
	Performance Standards		
Content Standards	In 50% or more of the cases investigated	In 30 to 49% of the cases investigated	In 0 to 29% of the cases investigated
Lessons and materials are accurate and free of factual errors			
Material is related to important concepts and principles			
Information clearly and logically presented			
Application of material is emphasized			
Content presented in more than one way to enhance understanding			

Figure 14–5
Rating of Content and Performance Standards

 MORE FROM THE WEB ▬▬▬▬▬▬▬▬▬▬▬▬▬▬▬▬▬▬▬▬▬▬▬

Understanding Teacher Assessment and Evaluation

You will have plenty of company if you have concerns about how your teaching will be evaluated. Information provided at some of these sites will give you a broader understanding of some issues associated with teacher evaluation and about some practices being followed in different parts of the country.

Developing Educational Standards

http://putwest.boces.org/standards.html

- This is a good place to begin. You will find links to educational standards for every state. There are also listings of standards for teachers. You will also be able to follow links that tie to subject matter groups, centers, and educational organizations. Various locations referenced at this site can help you better understand how teaching is being defined and assessed across the nation.

National Board for Professional Teaching Standards

http://www.nbpts.org/nbpts

- This is the home page for the National Board for Professional Teaching Standards (NBPTS), a group that is pushing an agenda that actively supports improved teaching in the nation's classrooms. NBPTS has developed national certification and some innovative ways of assessing teacher performance. You may be interested in how NBPTS defines "good teaching." You may wish to review information about NBPTS in Chapter 1, "The Changing World of Teaching."

NASSP

http://www.nassp.org

- At this Web address you will find the home page of the National Association of Secondary School Principals (NASSP). You will find a *search box* at the top left of the page when you go to this Web address. If you type in the words "teacher evaluation," you will be presented with links to a large number of articles and papers on such topics as teacher assessment, teacher rights, teacher portfolios, and student assessment of teachers.

ERIC Clearinghouse on Teaching and Teacher Education

http://ericsp.org

- At this Web address, you will find the homepage for the ERIC Clearinghouse on Teaching and Teacher Education. You can use a built-in site-search capability to look for information related to teacher assessment as well as topics related to teaching and teacher education.

CRESST: National Center for Research on Evaluation, Standards, and Student Testing

http://www.cresst96.cse.ucla.edu/index.htm

- At this Web address, you'll find the home page for the National Center for Research on Evaluation, Standards, and Student Testing. You will find numerous links to useful reports and articles. You may be especially interested in using CRESST's "Ask the Expert" service. In general, this site is a fine place for you to look for information about a variety of topics related to the general theme of assessment.

There are certain advantages to your being evaluated based on information contained in a portfolio you have assembled. More traditional schemes depend on data assembled by an evaluator during one or two classroom observations. Information in a portfolio, on the other hand, includes items you have gathered over a considerable period of time. You can include information of many types from many sources. In summary, your portfolio provides quite a comprehensive picture of what you do in the classroom. This feature gives evaluators an opportunity to consider information that is based on more than the kind of "snapshot" views that necessarily result from examinations of data obtained during a limited number of classroom observations. In addition, since you assemble the portfolio yourself, you are in a position to play an active role in the evaluation process by including portfolio materials that you believe provide an honest picture of what you do in the classroom. More and more school leaders are committing to portfolio-based teacher evaluation, and you may expect it to be used by even larger numbers of schools in the years ahead.

Key Ideas in Summary

- One reason you need feedback about your classroom performance is that the rapid pace and complex milieu of the classroom make it extremely difficult for you to recall accurately what went on during a given lesson.
- There are two basic purposes for evaluating your classroom performance. First of all, evaluation data help to identify specific actions you may wish to modify in subsequent lessons. Second, evaluation attempts to provide a summary judgment of your general levels of excellence at a particular time.
- Self-evaluation involves you in gathering data, identifying criteria to be used in making judgments, and drawing conclusions about your own teaching. Self-evaluation can be initiated as often as you wish. Engaging in self-evaluation can help you grow in terms of your sense of personal control over your own professional development. Finally, self-evaluation is non-intrusive. It does not introduce an outside observer into the classroom.
- *Peer evaluation* involves you working collaboratively with your fellow teachers to gather insights about their behaviors. It tends to break down the isolation you may feel as you work alone in your own classroom. In *peer coaching*, a popular form of peer evaluation, you and a group of other teachers voluntarily agree to work together to solve problems and help one another grow professionally. Each member of the peer coaching team is viewed as having abilities and expertise of value to the whole group. In *mentoring*, another form of evaluation, one person—the mentor—is perceived as having more knowledge than the other members of the group. Your mentor has an obligation to assist you to grow professionally.

- *Supervisor evaluation* occurs when someone in a position of authority over you conducts your evaluation. Results of supervisor evaluation sometimes go beyond providing data that you will use for self-improvement. Results in some instances are used to support dismissal and retention decisions or to support salary and promotion actions.

- Student achievement information may be part of the process your school leaders use to assess your instructional effectiveness. There are some limitations to relying too much on student test scores. For example, some tests may not adequately sample content you have taught. Further, some students may have learned information that is tested from sources other than the lessons you have taught. Student achievement information ought to include information from a variety of sources, including student essays, projects, and other products that reflect what they have learned.

- Data from student opinionnaires sometimes are used in teacher evaluation programs. Not everyone agrees that this practice is sound, but some research has supported a correlation between high student ratings of a teacher and high student academic achievement scores on tests over content taught by the teacher. It is not sound practice to ask for student opinions about subjects for which they lack expertise or an adequate experiential base.

- Classroom observational data of many kinds often will be included in your school's teacher evaluation procedures. Techniques have been developed that are capable of providing information about many dimensions of your classroom performance. Examples of these procedures include (1) lists of focus questions, (2) verbatim records, and (3) frequency counts.

- Teaching portfolios are increasingly being used in teacher evaluation. A teaching portfolio includes a variety of information about your performance. Evidence in a portfolio can provide a quite comprehensive picture of your patterns of behavior as a teacher. It is designed to demonstrate your work much as artists' portfolios show others what they have done. Your teaching portfolio may include (1) material you have prepared, (2) material gathered from others, and (3) examples of student work.

Reflections

1. Why is it desirable to collect information about what you do as a teacher in a systematic way rather than simply relying on your recollections of what went on in your classroom?

2. What are some key purposes of teacher evaluation?

3. What are some advantages and disadvantages of self-evaluation? Given these positives and negatives, do you think self-evaluation is worthwhile? Why, or why not?

4. What are similarities and differences between *peer coaching* and *mentoring*?

5. How do purposes of supervisor evaluation differ from those of self-evaluation or peer evaluation?

6. What are some limitations of relying exclusively on students' test scores to evaluate teachers?

7. If you decided to have your students complete opinionnaires focusing on their reactions to your teaching, what specific topics would you want them to respond to? Are there some issues you definitely would not wish to include? If so, what are they, and why would you exclude them?

8. If you decided to use focus questions as part of a self-evaluation process, what are some questions you would include?

9. What is a *verbatim record*, and how might information from this kind of observation tool help you improve your teaching?

10. What do you see as some advantages of a process for evaluating your teaching that would rely heavily on information you might compile in a portfolio?

Learning Extensions

1. Ask some administrators in several schools to share with you instruments used to gather information about teachers' classroom performance. Based on your analysis of these tools, what kinds of teacher behaviors seem to be of interest to users of these instruments? How important do you feel these behaviors to be? Prepare a short paper for your instructor in which you comment on these questions.

2. Use one of the instruments introduced in this chapter (or another provided by your instructor) to observe a class. Consider the information you gather. How useful is it for providing feedback to the teacher that might lead to improved teaching practices? Share your reactions in an oral report to the class.

3. Develop a rating scale that you think might be useful for your students to use to give you information about the quality of your teaching. Be prepared to defend the importance of items you include on your instrument. Share this material with others in your class, and request their reactions.

4. Interview a local administrator about the teacher evaluation schedule that is followed. How often is information collected? Are new teachers evaluated more often than teachers who have been employed for some time? What do observations emphasize? How is information shared with teachers? What kinds of problems have new teachers most frequently been found to have? Share this information with others in your class.

5. Develop a peer-coaching plan with one or two others in your class. Each person in the group should teach a lesson. Others should hold a pre-conference with the teacher before the lesson is taught and provide feedback after the lesson has been taught. How did you feel about this process? Share your reactions with others in the class.

6. Go to the Merrill Education's Link to General Methods Resources site at this URL: http://www.prenhall.com/methods-cluster/ At the bottom of the page select "professional development" as your topic and click on the "begin" button. This will take you to the "Overview" page. On the left side, click on "Web Links." On the Web Links page click on "professional portfolios." This will take you to a page with

numerous links to sites with information about preparing professional portfolios. Select several of these sites, and read the posted material. Then prepare a short oral report for your class in which you describe some recommendations for teacher portfolios you found at these sites and compare and contrast this information with this chapter's discussion of this issue.

References

Airasian, P. and Gullickson, A. (1997). Teacher self-evaluation. In Strong, J. (Ed.), *Evaluating teaching: A guide to current thinking and best practice*, pp. 215–241. Thousand Oaks, CA: Corwin Press.

Bang-Jensen, V. (1986). The view from next door: A look at peer supervision. In K. K. Zumwalt (Ed.), *Improving teaching*, pp. 51–62. 1986 ASCD Yearbook. Washington, DC: Association for Supervision and Curriculum Development.

Barber, L. (1990). Self-assessment. In Millman and Darling-Hammond (Eds.), *The new handbook of Teacher evaluation: Assessing elementary and secondary school teachers*, pp. 216–228. Newbury Park, CA: Corwin Press.

Brown, R. (1983). Helpful and humane teacher evaluations. In W. Duckett (Ed.), *Teacher evaluation: Gathering and using data* (pp. 9–26). Bloomington, IN: Phi Delta Kappa.

Duke, D. (1995). Conflict and consensus in the reform of teacher evaluation. In Duke, D. (Ed.), *Teacher evaluation policy: From accountability to professional development*, pp. 173–187. Albany, NY: State University of New York Press.

Glass, G. V., & Martinez, B. A. (1993). Politics of teacher education. *Proceedings of the CREATE cross-cutting evaluation theory planning seminar* (Appendix D), pp. 1–14. Kalamazoo, MI.

Good, T., & Brophy, J. (2000). *Looking in classrooms* (8th ed.). New York: Longman.

Green, J. E., & Smyser, S. O. (1996). *The teacher portfolio.* Lancaster, PA: Technomic.

McLaughlin, M., & Pfeifer, R. (1988). *Teacher evaluation: Improvement, accountability, and effective learning.* New York: Teachers College Press.

Natriello, G. (1990). Intended and unintended consequences: Purposes and effects of teacher evaluation. In Millman and Darling Hammond (Eds.), *The new handbook of teacher evaluation: Assessing elementary and secondary school teachers*, pp. 35–45. Newbury park, CA: Corwin Press.

Odell, S. (1990). Support for new teachers. In T. Bey & C. Holmes (Eds.), *Mentoring: Developing successful new teachers*, pp. 3–23. Reston, VA: Association of Teacher Educators.

Rodriguez, S., & Johnstone, K. (1986). Staff development through a collegial support group. In K. Zumwalt (Ed.), *Improving teaching: 1986 ASCD yearbook* (pp. 87–99). Alexandria, VA: Association for Supervision and Curriculum Development.

Sergiovanni, T. J. (1994). Organizations of communities? Changing the metaphor changes the theory. *Educational Administration Quarterly, 30*(2), pp. 214–226.

Wolf, K., Lichtenstein, G., and Stevenson, C. (1997). Portfolios in teacher evaluation. In Strong, J. (Ed.), *Evaluating teaching: A guide to current thinking and best practice*, pp. 193–214. Thousand Oaks, CA: Corwin Press.

15

Career-Long Growth

This chapter will aim to

- help you understand your need for career-long preparation and development;

- define characteristics of professionalism as they apply to teaching;

- identify teachers' professional growth stages;

- point out some alternative approaches you can use to seek additional expertise you will need as you work throughout your career to be a more effective teacher;

- distinguish between *general organizations* and *specialty organizations* for teachers;

- describe advantages for beginning teachers of affiliating with a professional group; and

- identify career options that may be open to you as someone who has a background in classroom teaching.

Introduction

Though you are almost at the end of this text, most likely you are still in the beginning phases of your professional preparation program. When you complete your studies, we hope you will be a highly talented beginning teacher. However, to reach a high level of professionalism and obtain the rich personal satisfaction that goes along with this kind of competence, you will need to engage in career-long professional growth.

When you survey the contemporary world of education, you may be struck by the complexity of changes taking place. You should take some comfort in knowing that these kinds of unsettled conditions have always characterized our profession. The likelihood is high that throughout your career you will confront proposals for change related to issues including:

- the nature of the curriculum,
- the degree of available school choice,
- basic processes of teaching and learning,
- use of technology to support instruction,
- amounts of required student testing,
- preparation and performance standards for teachers, and
- approaches to assessing teacher performance.

If what you want is a career that will change little during the next 10 to 20 years, you should consider a field other than teaching. Successful educators commit to the view

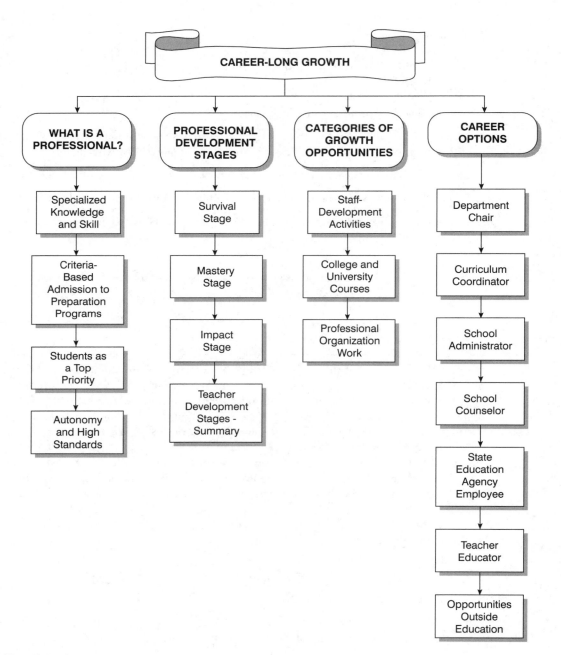

Figure 15–1
Graphic Organizer

that change is a constant professional companion. The expertise you leave with at the conclusion of your preparation program is something you should see simply as the end of your professional beginning.

Throughout this text we have emphasized the importance of reflective practice. This approach to teaching can provide you with the basis for establishing a career-long professional growth agenda. Reflective teaching encourages you to accept responsibility and be open-minded—attitudes that are essential if professional improvement is to occur.

You need to embrace the idea that what you do as a teacher makes a difference and that your actions have consequences. This means accepting responsibility for your actions and avoiding any temptation to blame difficulties on external factors, such as parental indifference, negative student attitudes, or administrative decisions that conflict with your beliefs. While certainly not all conditions you face will please you, it is important to avoid falling into the trap of assuming these circumstances can overwhelm your ability to adjust and respond in ways that provide sound educational experiences for your students. You need to remain open, flexible, and committed to responding proactively to the special situations you will face. That is what professionals do.

What Is a Professional?

As you consider a career in teaching, you may find it useful to reflect on the definition of the term *professional*. Education specialists John Jarolimek and Clifford Foster (1996) identify these general characteristics of professional teachers:

- They are people who possess specialized knowledge and skill.
- They are individuals who have been admitted to a professional development program after having met specified criteria.
- They act in ways that place students as their number one priority.
- They exercise a certain amount of autonomy and set high standards for their own professional practice.

Specialized Knowledge and Skill

How can you tell if a given occupation does not demand professional preparation? The basic measure is to look for answers to this question: Can a person be successful without specialized knowledge and formal preparation? A growing body of research attests to the fact that success as a teacher correlates highly with the content knowledge teachers bring to their positions and the systematic preparation they have had for their roles. The high dropout rate of individuals who enter the teaching profession without adequate professional preparation is further evidence of the need for teachers to have specialized knowledge.

Acquisition of specialized knowledge will not end when you meet qualifications for a degree or a teaching license, certificate, or credential. Because knowledge changes, you and your professional teaching colleagues will be involved in a career-long process of learning and development.

Criteria-Based Admission to Preparation Programs

Teacher preparation programs are "professional," in part, because candidates selected meet specified criteria. These criteria seek to identify people with the knowledge and attitudes that are necessary for successful professional practice. Not everyone meets these requirements; not everyone should be a teacher. As you will recognize, when you begin to work in the classroom you will need a depth of knowledge in the subjects you teach as well as sound professional knowledge related to instructional design and delivery issues. Specialized expertise you acquire in areas related to transmitting what you know (as opposed to simply acquiring this kind of knowledge yourself) has been found to highly correlate to the quality of instruction you are likely to provide your students (Darling-Hammond, 2000).

In addition to issues related to subject matter and pedagogical knowledge, professional teachers also need to have personality characteristics and emotional dispositions that allow them to succeed in the school environment. As a teacher, you will find yourself interacting with a wide array of people. You need to be able to establish good working relationships with students, other teachers, administrators, parents, and members of the general community. Some individuals simply do not have the skills required to facilitate the establishment of these important personal relationships.

Students as a Top Priority

Professionals in all fields accord a high priority to providing service to clients. As a teacher, your "clients" are your students. When you become a teacher, you accept responsibility for one of our society's most important obligations—educating young people. The importance of this role has been recognized for centuries. For example, the great Roman orator Cicero remarked that there is no nobler profession than teaching the youth of the Republic (Clark & Starr, 1996).

In practice, "putting students first" means that professional teachers place service to students higher than competing interests and obligations. This means that there will be occasions when you spend time with individuals far beyond the end of the regular school day. This means that you willingly listen to students' concerns even when you have stacks of paperwork to attend to. This means that you need to devote adequate preparation time outside of class to ensure that the lessons you provide are responsive to your students' needs. In summary, everything you do is framed by a commitment to helping the young people under your charge grow into secure, informed, and contributing members of our society.

An additional dimension of this priority requires you to express informed judgments about policies and practices that involve students. In the contemporary world, people often feel free to make proclamations and decisions regarding what should be done to educate our youth. Unfortunately, some of these proposals have the potential for harming the educational development of some students. Your role as a professional educator requires you to speak out against policies and practices that are potentially detrimental to students.

Autonomy and High Standards

As a professional, you will exercise a certain amount of autonomy and accept responsibility for setting high standards of professional practice. Though adopted curriculum requirements and other rules and regulations give some external direction to what you can do, you still have a certain amount of authority as a teacher to decide exactly what you will do each day. As a professional, you will not be subject to minute-by-minute scrutiny and your teaching methods are not likely to be prescribed by some external body.

Along with this autonomy comes responsibility. You need to be a thoughtful decision-maker who constantly seeks to improve your professional expertise. Teachers who resist change, are insensitive to the unique needs of a given class of students, and repeat units or lessons from year to year are simply behaving unprofessionally. This kind of behavior has the potential to diminish the profession and to invite intervention by dissatisfied external authorities.

Professional Development Stages

As you enter the field of teaching, you need to realize that there will be different stages you will experience as you continue to grow professionally. You need to understand the dimensions of each of these stages in order to cope with them. The sad fact is that many new teachers do not cope well. Current trends indicate that approximately 50% of new teachers leave within the first five years. Typically, about 15% leave after the first year and another 15% after the second year (Kronowitz, 1999).

Much of this high attrition rate can be ascribed to what is called *reality shock*. Reality shock is what happens when an individual experiences unexpected events during the early years at a job. Everyone experiences some unease upon undertaking a new responsibility. However, there is evidence that this problem is especially acute among new teachers. People who have studied this problem note that part of the difficulty is the disconnection between what new teachers remember about their own school days and what they encounter when they begin teaching (Ryan, et al., 1980). Consider your own situation. You spent many years sitting in school classrooms. You may have had contact with 50 to 100 teachers by the time you graduated from high school. Some were good, some not so good, and some probably fell somewhere in between. You have clear memories of the sights, the smells, and the pace of daily life in secondary schools.

You may well begin your work in the profession feeling confident that you really understand what your life as a teacher will be like. However, your confidence may be shaken once you have your own classroom and begin teaching. For the first time, you will be viewing education exclusively from the perspective of the teacher. In your former student days, you may have been largely unaware of those students who were not enthusiastic about school. You may have had only the vaguest understanding of the "behind the scenes" issues and problems your teachers were confronting.

Even the experiences you will have had as a student teacher may not prepare you for the fact that some (often quite a large number) of your students, initially at least, may be indifferent to the subjects you are teaching. You may also find that large numbers of students do not have as much background information as you imagined they would have had. You may also be surprised at how much work is required to motivate students and to maintain good order in the classroom. Finally, you may not initially be prepared for the huge time investment required to handle out-of school responsibilities, including lesson planning, correction of papers, attendance at meetings, and supervision of student activities.

Do not be surprised if some of these realities surprise and concern you when you accept your first teaching position. The good news is that thousands of teachers have successfully made the adjustment to their new professional roles and take great personal and professional satisfaction in their ability to promote the educational development of young people.

For years, researchers have been interested in how new teachers adjust to the profession. Experts who have studied this issue have identified three important teacher growth and development stages:

- the survival stage,

- the mastery stage, and

- the impact stage (Fuller, 1969).

Survival Stage

Given the above discussion, it should come as no surprise to you that the initial stage of development is called the *survival stage*. When you first begin teaching, you are likely to be worried about your adequacy as a teacher. You may well be concerned that problems will arise for which you are not prepared. It would not be unusual for you to worry about whether your students and professional colleagues will like and respect you. Initially, you are likely to focus on surviving each period, getting through the day, and making it to the next break in the school calendar.

The survival stage may vary in length. Some people quickly solve the survival problems and begin to develop confidence in their ability to handle the multiple dimensions of their teaching. You may be one of these individuals who develops a strong sense of teaching efficacy within a few months and completes your first year of teaching eagerly anticipating the next group of students. However, others who start at the same time as you do may struggle. They may have a difficult time adjusting and experience frustration and failure. By the end of the first year, some of these individuals may well decide to leave the teaching profession. Others will persist and return for a second year with the hope that things will surely improve. For many, the second year will prove to be more satisfying. Others, however, will continue to find it difficult to deal with all of the problems and frustrations involved in teaching and will remain in the survival stage. Many of them will leave at the end of the second or third year. A few people remain in the survival stage for a large portion of their careers and go on to become unhappy, even bitter, teachers.

CRITICAL INCIDENT

I Wasn't Prepared for This

Arlene Newby has been struggling through her first year of teaching mathematics to eighth-graders at King Middle School. She teaches a pre-algebra course to some of her students and a regular algebra class to the others. After a particularly difficult day, she made her way into the faculty lounge. Her friend, Latroya Birdsong, was sitting on one of the battered couches.

"So, another day in the bag, Arlene. Get some coffee and sit down. What's new with you?" asked Latroya.

"My day . . . my week . . . they've just been the pits," Arlene replied. "Even my best algebra kids have been on a tear. As for the rest of them, well, I just feel I'm barely keeping the lid on."

"Well, eighth-graders will be eighth-graders. Remember you've got all those surging hormones *and* the football game with Madison coming up tomorrow night. I mean the Pied Piper and Mother Theresa combined would have a hard time convincing these kids that quiet attention to mathematics should be their top priority."

"That's fine for you to say. You've been here for years. The principal thinks you're great. Parents support what you're doing. But what about me? I'm the new kid on the block. I feel I'm really under the microscope. I've had several parents make a big point of telling me that they expect their kids to become engineers or scientists and that they want them to 'really be prepared' for their high school math classes. If the kids thought math was half as important as their parents, my job would be a breeze."

"Anything else on your mind?" asked Latroya.

"Well, since you asked . . . yes. These pre-algebra classes are driving me nuts. The students just don't have the basics. I mean, some of them don't even know their multiplication tables. What did those elementary school teachers teach these kids? Not much. Sometimes I wonder why I struggled through all of those calculus classes only to be given a bunch of students who hate math and who can't even manage basic arithmetic. I just wasn't prepared for this."

"All right, so some of your kids don't think the sun rises and sets on math. And you think this wasn't true when you were in school? Give me a break." Latroya continued, "Do you think all my kids love English? Do you think Mr. Harmon's students turn hand-flips at the prospects of studying science? Are Ms. Knight's kids just lusting to study history? No way. That's not how the world is. Part of our job is seeing to it that kids tolerate our instruction. Beyond that, we try to motivate them to like it. Enthusiasm doesn't come from any inherent interest in the subject itself; it comes from what *we* do. You've got to get beyond this idea that these kids are just going to sit there and let you build on enthusiasm and interest that are already there. Won't happen."

"Well, thanks a lot, Latroya," sputtered Arlene, "you've just made my day. Now even you don't think I'm being professional. I'm so frustrated right now I can't believe it. I feel like a real square peg in a round hole. I'm working hard, getting by on less sleep than I need, and for what? I can't seem to please anybody . . . least of all myself. I just don't know what I'm going to do."

■ ■ ■

What do we learn about some things that are important to Arlene? What aspects of her teaching responsibilities seem to challenge some of her values? What are her assumptions about how students and schools ought to be? What discrepancies are there between these assumptions and what she encounters?

How do you explain differences in perspectives revealed in Arlene's comments and in Latroya's comments? What do these reveal about differences in values and in other priorities? What might account for these differences?

What kinds of personal responsibilities does Arlene have in trying to respond to the problems she feels she is facing? Has she assumed that professional development ceased before she began her first teaching job? Does she have an obligation to take specific actions that might lead to different patterns of behavior and to different expectations of students? Does she have a place in education, or should she pursue a different career option? What should her next steps be?

Your focus during the survival stage should be on mastering the basics of teaching. You need to work on ways to control and manage the classroom as well as develop systems for handling daily routines. You need to seek out "older hands" who have made necessary adjustments. You will find most of your colleagues to be highly sympathetic to the stresses and challenges you will be experiencing. Remember that even the most confident teachers in your building at one time were, themselves, newcomers to the profession.

When you begin teaching and are at the survival stage, there are several things you can do to make your life more manageable. First, have realistic expectations. Developing excellence in teaching takes time. Don't feel bad if every lesson does not work out well. Avoid negative self-judgments. You need to understand that even highly experienced teachers have forgettable days.

Second, if your school does not assign newcomers an official mentor, seek out experienced people on the faculty. They will likely remember the adjustments they had to make as newcomers to the profession. Many of these people will reach out and befriend a beginner. Their support can be invaluable as you work to retain and extend your self-confidence.

You also need to think about how people-intense the activity of teaching is. Prolonged interactions with others on a daily basis can produce stress. To counteract this situation, consider developing outside activities that you particularly enjoy. Many teachers find that exercise programs and other activities that free the mind from job-related concerns add a much-needed dose of psychological serenity.

Finally, remember that the first year of teaching is a unique time. Even if you were fortunate enough to have experienced an exemplary preparation program, much remains to be learned. You will find that much professional development occurs during your first year on the job. In fact, the benefits of this early, on-the-job learning are so great that we often counsel frustrated beginners who want to leave the profession to wait at least two years before making a decision.

Mastery Stage

After you solve survival-stage issues, you will move on to the *mastery stage*. Once you have arrived at this stage, you will have developed confidence in your ability to deal with your students and the curriculum. You will use successful routines and understand how to plan and use time wisely. Your concerns now will turn away from worrying about getting through the day or the week and become more focused on your skill as a teacher. You will pay more attention to mastering the fundamentals of teaching, and you are likely to develop new interests in approaches that promise to enhance your instructional effectiveness. You are also likely to look more carefully at the contents of the curriculum and to consider ways to augment basic information you have been sharing with your students.

If you are typical of teachers at this stage, you will be eager to seek out professional development opportunities. You will want to learn more about your subject area and about new approaches to teaching and learning. This phase of your professional development can last a long time. Learning new ideas and developing increased confidence in your teaching can generate great personal satisfaction. During this time of your professional life, you may well become interested in serving as a mentor for new teachers.

Impact Stage

The third stage that you are likely to enter as your career progresses is the *impact* stage. Once you have developed a strong repertoire of teaching skills and have developed confidence in your teaching abilities, your concerns are likely to turn from a focus on how to master more teaching approaches to an interest in the impact you are having on students. To be sure, you will have some concern about this issue even during the survival and mastery stages. However, it is at the impact stage that this issue assumes a position of primacy.

This priority will be reflected in several ways. For example, when a new teaching approach is promoted, you will not be inclined to adopt it simply to expand your repertoire of techniques. Rather, your first question will be: "What do we know about how this approach affects students and their learning?" Your acceptance or rejection of changed approaches will depend on your relative confidence that new ways of doing things have excellent potential to help members of your classes.

Your life as a teacher can be highly satisfying when you arrive at the impact stage. Seeing students grow and change and being able to adapt your instruction to meet the needs of individuals can be highly rewarding. At the same time, your concern for "impact" can produce some personal frustration as you witness adoption and implementation of policies that, in your view, may interfere with your ability to have a positive and lasting influence on students.

Teacher Development Stages—Summary

You need to understand that teachers do not necessarily move through these stages in lockstep fashion. At various times during your career, you may find yourself moving back and forth through the categories. In general, these changes occur when you face significant and unexpected personal and professional circumstances. For example, if you change schools at some point in your career and find conditions drastically different from where you previously were employed, you may shift back (initially, at least) to the survival stage. There can also be unexpected stresses in personal life that affect your abilities to cope with challenges at school, and these events can cause a backward developmental-stage shift.

Thinking about these stages can assist you in several ways. First, they can help you understand that these are stages that all teachers experience. At one time or another, every teacher in your building will have gone through the survival stage. Knowledge about these stages will help you appreciate that any feelings of being overwhelmed you may experience during your first year are not signs of personality flaws or professional failings. You are merely experiencing a normal stage of professional development. Further, you should understand that the survival phase will pass and that, in time, you will move on to professional stages you are likely to find more satisfying.

Secondly, you can use these stages to evaluate your own growth. If you are struggling to get through the day, you will know that you are in the survival stage. You may then turn your attention to different kinds of professional growth opportunities that will allow you to master tasks that are challenging to you and that will help you to move on to the next stage.

Finally, an understanding of the developmental stages can help you better understand your colleagues. Without understanding these stages, you might find yourself intimidated when you see some of your fellow teachers getting excited about a new program or growth opportunity while you are still struggling to get through the day. But, knowing what you now know about patterns of teachers' development, you should feel secure in understanding that these teachers have moved beyond the survival stage and have arrived at the point in their careers where they are concerned with expanding their instructional capacities and increasing their individual impact on students' lives.

Categories of Growth Opportunities

Regardless of the excellence of your teacher preparation and regardless of where you begin teaching, you are likely early in your first year of teaching to recognize that there are some gaps in what you need to know to become an effective teacher. This situation is inevitable, given the tremendous differences among students, physical facilities, materials availability, levels of parental involvement, and administrative support that vary from one school to another. You will have a number of options available to you as you seek to extend your levels of understanding. For example, you may wish to pursue some of these options:

- Staff-development activities (including meetings sponsored by the school or school district),
- College and university courses, and
- Professional organization work (including special programs sponsored by professional education associations).

Staff-Development Activities

Many school districts provide development activities for their teachers. These are part of a larger effort to improve the overall quality of educational programming. Sometimes staff-development activities for teachers are referred to as *inservice education*. In many districts, the school calendar is developed in such a way that students are dismissed from school on several days throughout the year to enable teachers to participate in professional development opportunities.

When you begin to teach, you may find that you are required to attend some staff-development sessions, or your attendance may be optional. In some places, teachers receive staff-development credits for their participation. When teachers accumulate enough of these, they qualify for salary increases.

Staff development takes a variety of forms. Sessions sponsored by school districts often feature speakers, workshops led by teachers with special expertise, and sharing sessions that allow teachers of common subjects to exchange ideas. As a newcomer to the profession, you may find these staff-development sessions an excellent source of information as you work to improve your instruction and your approaches to classroom management.

College and University Courses

You also may want to take some college and university courses while you are teaching. To serve this market, many institutions offer courses at night so local teachers can attend. In some places, Saturday classes are available. You may find yourself working in a school district that places limits on the numbers of courses teachers can take during the school year. This requirement has been adopted in some places out of a concern that teachers may not leave themselves enough time to plan adequately for their teaching responsibilities.

College and university courses, in addition to adding to your knowledge, may help you to move to a higher level on the salary schedule. In many places, salaries go up as (1) the number of years a teacher has taught increase and (2) the total number of academic credits the teacher has earned past the time of initial certification goes up. This scheme is built on the idea that your expertise will increase in tandem with years of experience and additional college-level study.

In addition to helping you become a more effective teacher, college courses you take may be applied toward an advanced degree. Teachers often qualify for a master's degree after taking courses for several years in the evening and attending several summer sessions. We caution against using applicability toward a degree as a reason for selecting any college courses you might take during your first year or two in the classroom. Advanced degree programs often prescribe specific programs of study. These courses may not meet the kinds of needs you face every day in your classroom. We think it makes much more sense for you to select courses that will be of immediate help in your day-to-day work. After these initial knowledge gaps have been filled, there will be plenty of time for you to enroll in a more formal program of study leading to an advanced degree.

Professional Organization Work

Professional organizations regularly sponsor events that include sessions designed to improve teachers' levels of expertise. They provide opportunities for teachers to interact with others who share similar interests. This is important in a profession where individual practitioners do not come into much direct contact with other professionals during the major part of the day when they are working with students in the classroom. An affiliation with professional groups can help you to appreciate the bonds that join all who teach.

This kind of involvement can give you access to information through several channels. Professional organizations sponsor meetings that almost always feature presentations and workshops that allow participants to gain up-to-date information about content and instructional methodologies. Many of them also publish journals and newsletters with helpful information. Simply coming into contact with others who share your professional concerns can be a confidence builder as you come to recognize that many others share an interest in issues that are important to you.

There are two broad types of professional organizations that serve educators: general organizations and specialty organizations. The two largest general organizations, the National Education Association (NEA) and the American Federation of Teachers (AFT), seek their members from the total national population of teachers. Members include teachers working at all grade levels and in all subject areas. Specialty organizations seek members from among teachers who are interested in specific subject areas or certain categories of learners. Both of these types of organizations provide professional growth opportunities for teachers.

General Organizations

The NEA and AFT are particularly interested in issues associated with teachers' working conditions. In many parts of the country, local affiliates of these groups represent teachers in negotiating salary and working conditions with representatives of the school board and administration. At the state and national levels, representatives of these organizations work to support passage of legislation of interest to teachers.

Representatives also serve as members of accrediting agencies that are responsible for examining and certifying the adequacy of practice within individual school districts. They sometimes also serve as members of bodies considering curriculum changes. In general, representatives of the major general professional organizations are involved in almost all situations when issues of great concern to teachers are considered.

Teachers who belong to these groups are in a position to keep informed about issues affecting the profession. For more information about these groups and their programs, write or go the Web sites of:

The National Education Association
1201 16th Street NW
Washington, DC 20036–3207
http://www.nea.org/

American Federation of Teachers
555 New Jersey Avenue NW
Washington, DC 20001–2029
http://www.aft.org/

Specialty Organizations

There are dozens of specialty organizations in the field of education. Affiliation with one will give you opportunities to exchange ideas and share perspectives with others who share your interests and who work with similar kinds of students. Thousands of teachers belong to these groups.

Specialty organizations provide numerous services to their members. Most of the large ones have annual meetings. These bring together educators from throughout the country to share ideas and discuss issues. Many national groups also have state and local affiliates that also sponsor meetings. Typically, these affairs include presentations that inform teachers about promising approaches to instructing and managing students.

Educators from throughout the country make their views known at annual meetings of such groups as the National Education Association and the American Federation of Teachers.

Most of the national specialty groups publish professional journals for their members. Articles often focus on up-to-date research findings, descriptions of innovative teaching practices, and discussions of other relevant issues. Many new teachers find these journals to be an excellent place to discover new teaching ideas.

Many specialty groups encourage people to join who are preparing to become teachers. We think this is a good idea. If you join and become active in one of these organizations, you will have opportunities to become acquainted with employed teachers and gain insights on some aspects of their professional lives that may not have received much attention in your education courses.

In the paragraphs that follow, we introduce a number of specialty groups. This listing is by no means comprehensive. We have selected these organizations to illustrate the broad range of those that invite secondary school teachers to join.

American Alliance for Health, Physical Education, Recreation, and Dance (AAHPERD). This group promotes the interests of educators who are specialists in health, physical education, recreation, and/or dance. Membership includes elementary and secondary teachers and administrators, college and university professors, and others interested in health, physical education, recreation, and dance.

For more information, write or visit the Web site of:

The American Alliance for Health, Physical Education, Recreation, and Dance
1900 Association Drive
Reston, VA 20191
http://www.aahperd.org/

Association for Career and Technical Education (ACTE). This large association includes among its members teachers, supervisors, administrators, and others with interests in improving educational programs that prepare young people and adults for careers. The group has a large number of affiliates at various locations throughout the nation. Prospective teachers are actively sought as members.

For more information, write or visit the Web site of:

The Association for Career and Technical Education
1410 King Street
Alexandria, VA 22314–2749
http://www.avaonline.org/

Council on Exceptional Children (CEC). This group is dedicated to promoting better education for students with disabilities and for students who are gifted. Membership includes teachers, administrators, college and university professionals, and others who share an interest in the group's focus.

For more information, write or visit the Web site of:

The Council for Exceptional Children
1920 Association Drive

Reston, VA 20191–1589
http://www.cec.sped.org/

International Reading Association (IRA).

The International Reading Association is one of the largest specialty groups in education. It has thousands of members and well over 1,000 local chapters. Teachers, reading specialists, administrators, consultants, educational researchers, college and university professors, and others interested in reading belong to this group.

For more information, write or visit the Web site of:

The International Reading Association
800 Barksdale Road
P.O. Box 8139
Newark, DE 19714-8139
http://www.reading.org/

International Society for Technology in Education (ISTE).

As its name suggests, this organization seeks to ensure that computers are being used effectively in the schools. The group promotes cooperation among various groups and individuals interested in improving instruction through appropriate applications of computer technology.

For further information, write or visit the Web site of:

The International Society for Technology in Education
480 Charnelton Street
Eugene, OR 97401-2626
http://www.iste.org/

Music Teachers National Association (MTNA).

This group seeks to improve music instruction, performance, and understanding. Members include people who teach music in the schools as well as music teachers who have their own private tutoring practices.

For more information, write or visit the Web site of:

The Music Teachers National Association
441 Vine Street, Ste. 505
Cincinnati, Ohio 45202–2814.
http://www.mtna.org/

National Art Education Association (NAEA).

The National Art Education Association promotes better instruction in the visual arts in schools. It is the nation's leading professional organization for art teachers. Membership includes anyone who has a direct connection to or an interest in art education in the schools.

For more information, write or visit the Web site of:

The National Art Education Association
1916 Association Drive
Reston, VA 20191-1590
http://www.naea-reston.org/

National Association for Gifted Children (NAGC).

As its name implies, this group serves individuals who are interested in improving the education of gifted students. Membership includes both educators and parents. It conducts training sessions for members and engages in lobbying activities in support of federal and state legislation that will provide better programs for gifted students.

For more information, write or go to the Web site of:

The National Association for Gifted Children
1707 L Street NW, Suite 550
Washington, DC 20036
http://www.nagc.org/

National Business Education Association (NBEA).

Members of the National Business Education Association include secondary and post-secondary teachers of business subjects. There are state and local affiliates scattered throughout the nation.

For more information, write or go to the Web site of:

The National Business Education Association
1914 Association Drive
Reston, VA 20191–1596
http://www.nbea.org/

National Council for the Social Studies (NCSS).

The National Council for the Social Studies is the largest specialty group serving the needs of social studies teachers. Members include classroom teachers, curriculum directors, state-level social studies specialists, college and university professors, and others who are interested in school-based social studies instruction.

For more information, write or visit the Web site of:

The National Council for the Social Studies
3501 Newark Street, NW
Washington, DC 20016–3167
http://www.ncss.org/

National Middle School Association (NMSA).

As the organization's title suggests, this is a group dedicated to issues having to do with development and learning of children in middle schools. This large and active organization includes numerous state and local affiliates. It hosts important conferences and produces materials of interest to middle-school-level educators.

For more information, write or visit the Web site of:

The National Middle School Association
4151 Executive Parkway
Westerville, OH 43091
http://www.nmsa.org/

National Council of Teachers of English (NCTE).

The National Council of Teachers of English seeks to improve the teaching of English in schools. This large group has many state and local affiliates. Membership is open to individuals who teach English or language arts at any grade level or who have an interest in this part of the curriculum.

For more information, write or visit the Web site of:

The National Council of Teachers of English
1111 W. Kenyon Road
Urbana, IL 61801–1010
http://www.ncte.org/

National Council of Teachers of Mathematics (NCTM).

The National Council of Teachers of Mathematics is a large group that includes more than 200 state and local chapters. It is dedicated to the improvement of mathematics teaching in the schools. Membership is open to anyone who shares this interest.

For more information, write or visit the Web site of:

The National Council of Teachers of Mathematics
1906 Association Drive
Reston, VA 20191–9988
http://www.nctm.org/

National Science Teachers Association (NSTA).

The National Science Teachers Association is the largest national group serving the interests of science teachers. It draws members from among teachers, administrators, curriculum specialists, state-level program supervisors, college and university professors, and others who are interested in improving science teaching in the schools. It has numerous state- and local-level affiliates.

For more information, write or visit the Web site of:

The National Science Teachers Association
1840 Wilson Boulevard
Alexandria, VA 22201–3000
http://www.nsta.org/

Organizations profiled here typify those that draw much of their membership from teachers. These groups help members build communities of shared concern. They function as catalysts for political action. Many federal and state laws that influence schools began as lobbying efforts of educational specialty groups. For example, present laws about serving students with disabilities can be traced to pressures first brought to bear on legislatures by organizations committed to better serving the needs of these young people.

WHAT DO *YOU* THINK?

Information from Specialty Organizations

Go to the Internet and find the *Educational Associations and Organizations* Web site at this URL: http://www.ed.gov/EdRes/EdAssoc.html

At this site, you will find links to a large number or organizations with interests in improving education. Go to links for any three of the following organizations:

- Education Commission of the States
- Education Policy Analysis Archives
- EDUCOM World Wide Web Server
- National Association of Secondary School Principals
- National Center on Education and the Economy
- Web66: A K–12 WWW Project

Review information at the three sites you select to visit.

Questions

1. How would you rate relevance of information at each of these sites as a valuable resource for a new teacher in a subject area you would like to teach?
2. To what extent might content at these sites be incorporated into (a) curriculum revision efforts and (b) planning of lessons for students?
3. Did you uncover some information you did not expect to see? If so, what was it?

You may wish to visit Web sites of some additional specialty organizations. The home page titled "Educational Associations and Organizations" is a good place to start. You will find links here to many public and private groups with interests in education. For example, you will find sites for groups such as Achieve (an organization that draws together governors, business leaders, and others interested in improving students' achievement levels), the American Educational Research Association (a group dedicated to promoting research on topics related to education), the Council of Great City Schools (a group dedicated to improving the education of inner-city youth), and the

National Rural Education Association (a group interested in improving education in rural areas). Here is the URL that will take you to the Web page with links to these and other education-related associations and organizations:

http://www.ed.gov/EdRes/EdAssoc.html

The U.S. Department of Education maintains another interesting Web site you may wish to visit—the *Education Resource Organizations Directory.* At this page, you can insert a topic in a simple search engine and it will provide you with a listing of education organizations that deal with it. If you type in the word "high school," you will get a listing of about 20 organizations, national- and state-level, with interests in improving education in grades 9 through 12. An additional feature at this site allows you to insert the name of your state to see whether any state affiliates of organizations concerned with your area of interest exist. Here is the URL for the Education Resource Organizations Directory:

http://www.ed.gov/programs/EROD/

Career Options

As you have been working to complete your preparation program, you may not have thought much about the wide range of career options in education. Many of these will be open to you only after you have spent some time actually working as a classroom teacher. A few of these roles would require you to leave classroom teaching entirely.

Department Chair

The department chair in a secondary school is the person designated to exercise leadership in a specific subject area (English, social studies, mathematics, science, and so forth). Duties vary, but often they include responsibilities in areas such as evaluating new faculty members, coordinating staff development opportunities, disseminating information about school policies, and ordering supplies for department members. In general, the department chair functions as a liaison between school administrators and faculty members in the department.

Typically, department chairs are selected from among the most experienced teachers in their respective departments. They tend to be individuals who have credibility both with their teaching colleagues and with school administrators. Often, department chairs teach a reduced load to allow them time to perform other assigned duties. They sometimes receive extra salary, and often they must work more days each year than regular classroom teachers.

Opportunities for people to become department chairs are limited. Only one chair is appointed for each department. In some schools, many years go by before a new chair needs to be appointed. One potential advantage of the department chair's role is that it allows an individual to assume some administrative and supervisory responsibilities while continuing to teach. Elevation to the position of department chair is one of the few promotions in education that does not remove a teacher completely from the classroom.

Curriculum Coordinator

This position often goes by one of a number of titles other than *curriculum coordinator*. Among them are *curriculum director, curriculum supervisor,* and *curriculum leader*. By whatever title it is known, this position requires the designated individual to assume leadership in such areas as curriculum planning, inservice planning, and instructional-support planning. In small school districts, the curriculum coordinator may have responsibilities for several subject areas and may even continue to teach part-time. In larger districts, curriculum coordinators do not teach. Typically, curriculum coordinators have their offices in the district's central administrative headquarters.

Curriculum coordinators are individuals with a great deal of knowledge about up-to-date trends in the subject area (or areas) for which they are responsible. They are in a position to influence the nature of the instructional program throughout the district in their areas of responsibility. Many curriculum coordinators hold advanced degrees. Curriculum coordinators often work a longer school year than teachers, and they are paid more. Their primary audience is teachers in the district. Especially in medium- and large-sized districts, curriculum coordinators only infrequently work with students in the classroom.

School Administrator

Nearly all school administrators begin their work in education as classroom teachers. By taking advanced courses, often including completion of at least a master's degree and relevant administrative certification requirements, they qualify for administrative positions. These positions exist both at the school level and at the central district administrative level. Some typical administrative positions at the school level are assistant principal and principal. Positions often found in central school administrative headquarters are director of personnel, assistant superintendent, and superintendent.

Administrators have responsibilities that require some skills that are different from those required of classroom teachers. Much of their work involves preparing budgets, scheduling plans, paperwork related to state and federal guidelines, and evaluation reports on teachers.

Administrators function as official representatives of the schools to the community; hence, they must have good public relations skills. School administrators almost always work a longer school year than classroom teachers and are paid higher salaries than teachers. Because demands of administration are quite different from those of teaching, some individuals who are outstanding teachers may not much care for administrative positions.

School Counselor

Many school counselors begin their careers as classroom teachers. In most parts of the country, school counselors must take additional graduate training to qualify for a counseling certificate. Many counselors obtain master's degrees with a school-counseling emphasis. Counselors usually work a longer school year than teachers, and they are paid more.

In addition to personal and academic counseling, many school counselors also are expected to perform a number of administrative tasks. Sometimes counselors are responsible for establishing the master teaching schedule for a school. Often they are in charge of all standardized testing. They must spend a great deal of time attending special meetings. Time available for working with individual students often is surprisingly limited.

State Education Agency Employee

All states have education departments or agencies that are largely staffed by professionals with backgrounds in education. State education agencies hire people with a variety of backgrounds and for diverse purposes. There often are subject area specialists who are charged with coordinating curriculum guidelines and inservice training throughout the state for teachers in specific subjects. There often also are assessment specialists who coordinate statewide testing programs. Teacher education specialists work with colleges and universities to ensure that teacher preparation programs are providing new teachers with appropriate backgrounds.

Employees of state education agencies often have had considerable prior experience working in the schools. Most of these positions require people to have at least a master's degree, and some of them require a doctoral degree. Considerable travel often is required. Employees of state education agencies work all year long. Levels of remuneration typically are considerably higher than those of classroom teachers.

Teacher Educator

Individuals who have taught successfully sometimes seek opportunities to share their expertise with future teachers. One way for them to do this is to become a teacher educator. Most teacher educators are faculty members of colleges and universities. A few are employed by large school districts.

Almost always, teacher educator positions require a doctoral degree. Because most teacher educators are members of college and university faculties, this degree is essential for the teacher educator to meet employment and tenure standards at most institutions of higher learning.

MORE FROM THE WEB

Professional Growth Opportunities

In this chapter you have been introduced to the idea that professional growth will be a career-long obligation. Today, much information is available on the Web that can be part of your personal development plan. We have selected some sites you might want to visit as you think about approaches to improving your abilities to serve students.

The New Teacher Page

http://www.new-teacher.com/

- This is an excellent source for new teachers or individuals interested in teaching. You will find specific information related to topics such as finding a job, substitute teaching, and becoming a professional in the classroom. In addition, there are links to other relevant education-related topics.

Recruiting New Teachers

http://www.rnt.org/

- This is a good place for you to begin a job search. As the home page of the nonprofit group Recruiting New Teachers, Inc., this site provides information for prospective teachers related to such topics as supply and demand statistics, information on certification, salaries, and current issues and trends. You might be particularly interested in downloading a copy of the group's electronic newsletter, *Future Teacher*.

Online Internet Institute

http://oii.org/index.html

- At this site you will find information about a concerted effort to improve education by making full use of resources available on the World Wide Web of the Internet. The site provides a link to a useful discussion forum.

The Global SchoolNet Foundation

http://www.gsn.org

- This outstanding site includes a wide array of online projects. In particular, you should visit the "professional development section." Other places provide excellent suggestions for using content from the World Wide Web in preparing your lessons.

Teachers Helping Teachers

http://www.pacificnet.net/~mandel/

- This site is a valuable one for acquiring insight into teaching. It includes subjects such as classroom management, lesson planning, and new approaches to teaching. You will also be able to discuss concerns with others by taking advantage of a link to a "teacher chat room" and the opportunity to discuss concerns with other teachers.

Educational Associations and Organizations

http://www.ed.gov/EdRes/EdAssoc.html

- This site, maintained by the U.S. Department of Education, provides links to a large number of public and private organizations with interests in improving education. You will find material of interest to teachers, administrators, legislators, and others concerned about teaching and learning.

The role of the teacher educator is more varied and complex than is sometimes imagined by those viewing it from the outside. Although exemplary teaching certainly contributes to success as a faculty member in teacher education, still more is necessary. Faculty members must also demonstrate initiative in improving preparation programs, keep up to date on findings of researchers, conduct research, write for publication, seek opportunities to make presentations at regional and national meetings, maintain good working relations with other departments and with the schools, serve on large numbers of committees, maintain good links with state education agencies, and counsel students. All of these obligations require processing of massive quantities of paperwork.

A person who enters a doctoral program must devote considerable time to intensive study. About three years of full-time study after the award of the master's degree is typical. Many institutions require that prospective doctoral students spend at least one full year as resident, full-time students on the campus. This means that a teacher interested in doing this must leave his or her teaching position for at least one year. Many who do decide to pursue a doctorate resign their positions to devote their full attention to their studies. Most universities have graduate assistantships and fellowships that provide modest financial support to individuals doing advanced doctoral work.

Teacher educators typically are employed for nine months out of the year. Many of them also have opportunities to work during the summer months as well. Salaries are not particularly high. In fact, some beginning teacher educators are paid less than some experienced public school classroom teachers. However, although beginning salaries of teacher educators tend to be modest, top salaries for experienced teacher educators tend to be higher than those paid to classroom teachers.

Individuals considering pursuing a doctoral program and becoming a teacher educator should seek information from reputable and accredited universities that offer doctorates. Some universities that offer doctorates are not widely respected, and an individual holding such a degree is going to have difficulty finding employment as a teacher educator. Discussions with practicing teacher educators can provide useful information. Once several possible universities have been identified, it makes sense to write to them for information about the specific features of their doctoral programs in education. There are important differences among institutions and someone considering advanced study should look for one that is compatible with his or her own objectives. For example, one university may have an outstanding program in mathematics education, and another may have special strengths in social studies education.

Opportunities Outside of Education

For a variety of reasons, some teachers decide to leave the classroom after teaching for just a few years. If you decide to do this, does it mean your time spent preparing to teach was wasted? Not at all. There are employment options outside of the public schools for individuals with backgrounds in teaching.

Many large private firms employ people with good teaching and curriculum-development skills to work in their employee training programs. Education in industry is becoming big business. Many large corporations have special training divisions. The term *human resource development,* often abbreviated to HRD, is frequently used to describe the corporate training function. There is a large national professional organization, the American Society for Training and Development (ASTD), that is devoted exclusively to promoting the interests of its members who are educators in industry. The group produces a fine journal titled *Training and Development.* People interested in the possibility of working as an educator in industry should look through several issues to get a feel for the kinds of things corporate trainers do.

In addition to working as educators in the private sector, teacher preparation provides individuals with the kinds of communication and interpersonal relations skills needed in many other fields. Educational materials salespeople, for example, often are individuals who once were classroom teachers. Many occupations that demand face-to-face contact with the general public have proved attractive to former teachers.

Final Comments

The teaching profession is complex. Changing student populations, federal and state education regulations, public expectations, and knowledge about what works in the classroom require you to commit to career-long professional development. It is a process that may take unexpected twists and turns but that, despite these surprises, promises to go resolutely onward. If you begin by embracing the idea that change is a regular feature of teachers' professional lives, you probably will be satisfied with your career choice. If you expect to be entering an ordered and predictable world, you will be disappointed.

When you teach, you will find yourself making dozens of decisions each day. Our intent in this book has been to provide you with some principles that have been followed by successful teachers. We hope some of these ideas will help you. We also recognize that not everyone should be a teacher. If it turns out that teaching does not suit you, we hope that you don't regret your time spent preparing for the profession. Many of the guidelines and ideas set forth in this book may serve you in a variety of other fields. We wish you well in whatever career path you ultimately choose to follow.

For those of you who do decide to teach, we hope you will enjoy some of the same exciting moments and rewards we have experienced as teachers. We are proud of what we do, and we look forward to welcoming you to one of civilization's proudest callings—teaching.

Key Ideas in Summary

- You will be involved in professional development throughout your career. Conditions change over time, as will your personal interests and needs. You cannot expect to have mastered everything you will need to know when you complete your initial teacher-preparation program.

- Teaching is a profession. This means you need to be prepared to accept special responsibilities. Professionals are individuals who have specialized knowledge and skill, have been selected for admission into the profession, place service to their clients as a priority, and have a high degree of autonomy and responsibility.

- At least three distinct growth stages have been observed in the professional growth of teachers. The first stage of growth is that of *survival* where your major emphasis will be on personal concerns and in getting through the day or week. The second stage is that of *mastery*. At this stage you will work to become thoroughly familiar with the techniques of teaching and will look forward to being seen as a "master" teacher. The third stage is that of *impact*. At this stage your priority concern will be how your teaching affects your students. Different people stay in these stages for different lengths of time and may move back and forth between these stages several times during their career.

- Many kinds of staff-development activities will be available to you as a teacher. If you work in a medium- or large-sized school district, you may find the district itself offers many inservice programs for teachers. For example, the district may provide opportunities for teachers to hear speakers, participate in workshops, and share ideas with others. In some districts, you will be required to participate in staff-development activities; in others they will be optional.

- Large numbers of teachers continue to take college and university courses while they teach. In many school districts, higher salaries are paid to teachers who have completed prescribed amounts of academic work. Courses often are offered in the evening so teachers can take them during the school year. Even more courses for teachers are available during the summer months. Some districts may place some restrictions on the number of courses you may take during the school year.

- Professional organizations regularly offer opportunities for teachers to improve their skills. Annual meetings regularly feature sessions where experts demonstrate techniques and share research findings. Many of these organizations publish journals that also are an important source of professional-development information.

- There are two basic types of professional organizations. General organizations such as the National Education Association and the American Federation of Teachers represent interests of the entire teaching profession. Members are drawn from all grade levels and subject areas. Specialty organizations such as the National Council for the Social Studies, the Council for Exceptional Children, and the Music Teachers National Association serve interests of teachers working within a given subject area. Affiliation with a group in your area of interest can help you develop a common community of interest with others in your field.

- In many secondary schools, each department has a chair. This person acts as the head of the unit. He or she may have responsibilities that include ordering materials, evaluating new faculty members, coordinating staff development opportunities, and disseminating policy information. The department chair acts as a liaison between department faculty members and school administrators. Often department chairs have a reduced teaching load. Frequently they work a longer school year than classroom teachers.

■ Curriculum coordinators ordinarily work out of central administrative offices. These specialists have responsibility for academic programming either for one or more subjects or for students in specific grades. Ordinarily, curriculum coordinators are individuals who have been teachers and who have taken advanced academic training. In many places, curriculum coordinators must hold at least a master's degree.

■ Nearly all school administrators begin their work in education as classroom teachers. They go on to take additional course work leading to administrative certification and, usually, to an advanced degree. They typically work a longer school year than classroom teachers.

■ School counselors are individuals who have taken special graduate-level training in counseling. Many of them are former classroom teachers. They typically work a longer school year than classroom teachers. In addition to personal and academic counseling, school counselors often perform some administrative duties related to such things as academic scheduling, standardized test scheduling, and administration.

■ State education departments and agencies employ large numbers of individuals with backgrounds in professional education. Many of these individuals have been classroom teachers, and they tend to hold advanced degrees. Many are subject-area specialists who are responsible for coordinating curriculum guidelines and inservice training throughout the state for teachers in their specialty areas. Many positions with state education departments and agencies require considerable travel.

■ Teacher educators usually are members of college and university faculties. Ordinarily, to qualify for a full-time faculty position in education at a college or university a person needs a doctoral degree. Many institutions will not hire people who have not had a certain minimum number of years working as a classroom teacher. Entry-level salaries of teacher educators are often lower than those paid experienced classroom teachers. However, experienced teacher educators tend to be paid more than experienced classroom teachers. Salaries vary considerably from place to place.

■ Today, many people with backgrounds in teacher education do not work in the schools. Some of them work in training and development departments in industry. People exiting teacher education programs often have the kinds of public relations and communications skills that make them attractive to employers in all kinds of businesses that require frequent public contact.

Reflections

1. A number of changes facing teachers today were mentioned at the beginning of the chapter. Which of these do you think will present you with the most personal challenges during your first years in the profession, and why?

2. What dangers for teachers are there in blaming students' failure to learn on external factors such as parental indifference, lack of administrative support, and so forth?

3. What kinds of specialized knowledge and skill will you have at the conclusion of your teacher preparation program that you lacked at the beginning?

4. What actions will you take if you find yourself stuck in the survival stage?

5. One of your obligations as a professional is to speak out against policy decisions that, in your view, might not be in the best interest of students. Are there some ideas for "improving" education you know about that you would actively oppose? If so, what are they, and what arguments would you use in support of your position?

6. What kind of an individual would you hope to have for a mentor, and in what ways would you like this person to assist you?

7. Why is it that teachers at the "impact" stage of development sometimes are more reluctant to embrace new instructional procedures than those at the "mastery" stage?

8. In thinking about your future professional development, are there some specific college or university courses you would like to take to add to the store of content and pedagogical knowledge you will have when you begin teaching? If so, what are they, and how would you expect these courses to benefit you?

9. What are some specialty organizations that, in your view, would be especially useful resources for you during your early years in the profession?

10. What are some career options both within and outside education for individuals who have followed a teacher preparation program?

Learning Extensions

1. Take a few minutes and write a response to the issue of what needs to be done to convince more people that teachers are professionals. Share your ideas with others in your class.

2. Interview some first- or second-year teachers. Ask them to describe their first year or their first few months of teaching. What surprised them? Did they experience any reality shock? How do their comments relate to the survival stage? How long did this stage last? What contributed to their growth out of this stage?

3. Take a few minutes to write down some ideas you have about characteristics of good teaching. Where did your ideas come from? How might you check to see whether others would support your ideas? Are your ideas based only on personal opinion, or do you have some other kinds of evidence to back them up? Share your views with your instructor.

4. Visit some administrators in a local school district. Ask if the district does anything special to help first-year teachers. Share your findings with others in your class.

5. Conduct some research on career opportunities outside of education for people who have completed teacher education programs. What do these positions entail? How do salaries compare to those of teachers? Organize your findings in a written report for your instructor.

6. Go to the Merrill Education's Link to General Methods Resources site at this URL: http://www.prenhall.com/methods-cluster/ At the bottom of the page select "professional development" as your topic and click on the "begin" button. This will take you to the "Overview" page. On the left side, click on "Education Resources." This will take you to a page with numerous links to sites with information about dealing more effectively with students in middle schools. Go to several of these sites. Note the Web addresses and take notes on kinds of helpful information each makes available. Prepare a short presentation to your class based on your findings.

7. Go to the Merrill Education's Link to General Methods Resources site at this URL: http://www.prenhall.com/methods-cluster/ At the bottom of the page select "professional development" as your topic and click on the "begin" button. This will take you to the "Overview" page. On the left side, click on "Web Links." This will take you to a page with a link to "Professional Standards." Click on this link. You will arrive at a page with links to a large number of groups and organization that have established various kinds of educational standards. Briefly visit each site. Briefly note kinds of material available at each listed Web site. Prepare a chart for distribution to others in your class containing the information you found.

References

Clark, L. & Starr, I. (1996). *Secondary and middle school teaching methods* (7th ed.). Columbus, OH: Merrill.

Darling-Hammond, L. (2000). Teacher quality and student achievement: A review of state policy evidence. *Educational Policy Archives*, 8(1). [http://epaa.asu.edu/epaa/v8n1/]

Fuller, F. (1969). Concerns of teachers: A developmental conceptualization. *American Educational Research Journal*, 6, 207–226.

Jarolimek, J. & Foster, C. (1996). *Teaching and learning in the elementary school* (6th ed.). Columbus, OH: Merrill.

Kronowitz, E. (1999). *Your first year of teaching and beyond* (3rd ed.). New York: Longman.

Ryan, K., Newman, K. K., Mager, G., Applegate, J., Lasley, T., Flora, R., & Johnston, J. (1980). *Biting the apple: Accounts of first year teachers*. New York: Longman.

GLOSSARY

Academic Freedom   Refers to teachers' rights to speak freely about their subject, experiment with new ideas, select materials they use in the classroom, and decide on teaching methods.

Academic Learning Time   That portion of total engaged time when the learner is experiencing a high degree of academic success while working on the assigned task. *See also* Allocated Time; Engaged Time.

Acceptable Alternative   As used in reference to compulsory schooling, a term used to describe a legal substitute for regularly authorized schooling.

Active Teaching   *See* Direct Instruction.

Activity Package   An approach to individualizing instruction that features highly structured, self-contained guides to learning that break content into a series of small steps that students are expected to master one at a time.

Administrator   *See* School Administrator.

Advanced Placement Program   A program sponsored by the College Entrance Examination Board that gives academically talented students opportunities to take rigorous, college-level courses while still in high school.

Allocated Time   Time that is assigned for the purpose of helping students to learn specific subjects or materials. *See also* Academic Learning Time; Engaged Time.

Alternate-Materials Center   A type of learning center where instruction is individualized by allowing students to choose from a variety of learning materials, all of which relate to a common topic. *See also* Learning Center.

Ambiance   *See* Classroom Ambiance.

American Alliance for Health, Physical Education, Recreation, and Dance   A specialty organization serving interests of educators who work in the areas of health, physical education, recreation, and dance.

American Educational Research Association   A specialty group dedicated to promoting research on educational issues and on disseminating research results to the national community of educators.

American Federation of Teachers   A general organization that represents interests of teachers at all levels and pursues a variety of issues relevant to education. *See also* National Education Organization.

American Society for Training and Development   A specialty organization that draws members from among people who work in training and employee development in private-sector enterprises of various kinds.

Analytic Brainstorming   A variant of brainstorming that applies critical thinking processes to results of an initial creative thinking exercise. *See also* Creative Thinking; Critical Thinking.

Aptitude-Treatment Interaction   A term from learning psychology that refers to the idea that an intervention (for example, a particular instructional approach) will vary in its impact on a person based on that person's predisposition to be influenced by characteristics embedded within the intervention.

Association for Career and Technical Education   A specialty organization for people interested in improving educational programs that prepare young people and adults for careers.

Attractive Power   *See* Reward Power.

Authentic Evaluation   Evaluation that calls on students to engage in complex performances that mirror the kinds of "real world" behaviors that parallel what people who are regarded as proficient in the use of these behaviors can do.

Boston English Classical School   This school, established in 1821, was the first public high school to open in the United States.

Brainstorming   A creative-thinking technique that seeks to unleash students' mental powers by encouraging the generation of large numbers of responses that are unrestrained by "conventional wisdom." *See also* Creative Thinking.

Breadth   As applied to school programs, this term refers to the range of information to be introduced. *See also* Depth.

"Buddy" System   A system that pairs teachers who will come to one another's aid in the event of a crisis situation, for example, a severe discipline problem.

Buzz Session   A small group technique responding (and recording answers) to a series of questions designed to help students develop some ideas about how they might begin their approach to a more complex group task that will follow this activity.

Cardinal Principles   The principles, promulgated in 1918 by the National Education Association's Commission on the Reorganization of Secondary Education, suggest that the senior high school should attend to issues associated with (a) health, (b) command of fundamental processes, (c) worthy home membership, (d) citizenship, (e) worthy use of leisure time, and (f) ethical character.

Case Study   Technique used to develop students' problem-solving abilities that involves them in (1) studying an account of a situation that raises questions, (2) identifying key issues, and (3) gathering information useful in framing responses to these issues. *See also* Problem Solving.

Certificate   *See* Teaching Certificate.

Charter School   A school that enjoys maximum flexibility of operation as a result of special state legislation that exempts it from many rules affecting other schools.

Chronological Sequencing   Sequencing of content based on the variable of time, typically with content related to earlier periods being taught before content related to later periods.

Clarity   A defining characteristic of effective teachers that includes variables such as the teacher's verbal and non-verbal style, lesson-presentation structure, and proficiency in providing cogent explanations.

Classroom Debate   A small group technique that allows students to debate a controversial issue in a format that features a group of approximately seven students who are assigned to (1) be members of a "pro" team, (2) be members of a "con" team, and (3) play the role of a critic.

Clinical Teaching   *See* Direct Instruction.

Classroom Ambiance   A term used to describe the particular atmosphere or feel of a classroom and how these features affect behaviors of both teacher and student.

Coalition of Essential Schools   An organization dedicated to promoting Theodore Sizer's ideas for redesigning the high school.

Coercive Power   A power given to someone who is in a position to administer punishment of some kind.

Competent Parties   Term used to refer to the requirement that people who sign a contract must be of legal age and must meet other requirements needed for the agreement to be valid.

Competitive Goal Structure   A kind of goal structure in which individuals are placed in competition with one another. *See also* Goal Structure.

Comprehensive High School   A term used to describe the most common model of the American senior high school. It developed from the work of the National Education Association's Commission on the Reorganization of Secondary Education in 1918 and promotes the view that the senior high school should promote multiple purposes.

Concepts   Major ideas, terms, or categories that help organize information. *See also* Structure of Knowledge.

Consistency   As applied to teachers, this term references behaviors that do not vary across times and situations in ways that students perceive to be unsettling.

Constructivism   A perspective that holds that knowledge is constructed in the minds of learners based on their prior knowledge and previous experiences.

Content Standards   Standards that describe what teachers are expected to do in the classroom to help their students master specific kinds of content. *See also* Performance Standards.

Context of Learning   A term that refers to the universe of attitudes and aptitudes that constitute a backdrop that students bring with them to the classroom that influences their general reactions to instruction. Instruction that comports well with a student's individual context has better potential to motivate him or her to learn than instruction that fails to consider the importance of this variable.

Continuing Contract   A contract that is automatically renewed at the end of each year unless the employing school district provides clearly specified legal reason for terminating the arrangement. *See also* Teacher's Contract.

Continuous Progress Learning   A result of teaching that permits each student to move ahead as he or she, individually, masters material with no delays imposed by the need to wait for other students to learn the provided information.

Contract   *See* Teacher's Contract.

Cooperative Goal Structure   A kind of goal structure that encourages individuals to support one another as they work toward a common goal. *See also* Goal Structure.

Cooperative Learning   A category of learning techniques that involve students working in groups, with *both* group goals and individual accountability.

Copyright Regulations   Laws and rules designed to protect the creative work of others.

Council of Great City Schools   A specialty group with a particular interest in improving education in inner city schools.

Council on Exceptional Children   A specialty organization that seeks to promote better educational experiences for students with disabilities and students who are gifted or talented.

Creative Thinking   Thinking that is characterized by novel, unconventional approaches.

Credential   *See* Teaching Certificate.

Criterion-Referenced Measurement   Measurement used when the purpose is to evaluate performance of an individual student against a pre-determined standard. *See also* Norm-Referenced Measurement.

Critical Thinking   Thinking that results in judgments being made in light of defensible criteria.

Cross-Age Peer Tutoring   A kind of peer tutoring that features older, more advanced students working with younger, less advanced students. *See also* Peer Tutoring.

Curriculum Coordinator   A title often assigned to a person in a school district with responsibility for curriculum planning, inservice planning, and instructional support planning for one or more parts of the overall district curriculum. Such a person sometimes also is known by such titles as *Curriculum Director*, *Curriculum Supervisor*, or *Curriculum Leader*.

Curriculum Director   *See* Curriculum Coordinator.

Curriculum Guide   A document that provides information about content and organization of instruction that may include such components as (1) units to be covered, (2) important generalizations, principles, and concepts to be taught, (3) suggested instructional approaches, and (4) suggested evaluation approaches.

Curriculum Leader   *See* Curriculum Coordinator.

Curriculum Supervisor   *See* Curriculum Coordinator.

Debate   *See* Classroom Debate.

Decision-Making   Thinking processes students are encouraged to use when they confront problems for which there are no clear "best" or "correct" solutions.

Deductive Thinking   A pattern of reasoning that begins with general conclusions and moves on to illustrate them with reference to specific examples. *See also* Inductive Thinking.

Department Chair   A title frequently given the person in a secondary school who leads an individual department and who serves as a liaison between school administrators and other teachers in the department.

Depth   As applied to school programs, this term refers to the extent of coverage given to a single element of content.

Digressions   As applied to teachers' explanations, an undesirable pattern characterized by wandering off the subject in ways that confuse students.

Direct Instruction   An academic-content-centered instructional approach that features the teacher working with an entire class of students and exercising considerable control over selection and delivery of content, mode of presentation of content, pacing of lesson development, and patterns of classroom interaction.

Discipline   As applied to the classroom, a term that refers to what teachers do to help students develop patterns of behavior associated with self-control, good character, orderliness, and efficiency. *See also* Management.

Discovery Learning   Learning that requires learners, themselves, to identify key ideas and principles rather than having them taught directly by teachers.

Distracter   Term applied to each of the incorrect answers in a multiple-choice item. The purpose is to "distract" a student who doesn't know the right answer and tempt him or her to select an incorrect response.

Dress Code   A requirement of a school or a school district that requires students to abide by certain dress guidelines when in school.

Due Process   A guarantee provided to United States citizens by the Fourteenth Amendment to the United States Constitution that requires that certain specified procedures be followed in any action that might put a citizen's rights in jeopardy.

Educational Game   An activity that typically involves some sort of competition within a set of rules and where there is a strong possibility that an element of chance will play some role in determining the final outcome. *See also* Simulation.

Educational Simulation   *See* Simulation. *See also* Educational Game.

Engaged Time   The part of allocated time when instructional activities actually related to the focus subject are occurring. *See also* Allocated Time; Engaged Time.

Enrichment Center   A type of learning center that features instruction geared toward talented students who are able to do more sophisticated work related to a topic than typical students in a class. *See also* Learning Center.

Evaluation   The process of drawing conclusions based on the analysis of information gathered through various measurement processes. *See also* Measurement.

Exhibitions   This term, as related to reform of the American high schools, refers to an assessment procedure that would replace traditional examinations with sophisticated student presentations of the products of learning that demonstrate to others in convincing ways that they can put to use knowledge they have acquired.

Expert Power   A power that is accorded someone who is believed to possess superior knowledge or skill.

Explicit Teaching   *See* Direct Instruction.

Expulsion   Term used to describe a permanent separation of a student from school. *See also* Suspension.

External Locus of Control   A condition characterizing individuals who attribute their successes and failures to chance factors or to factors they believe lie outside of their personal ability to control.

External-Constraint Sequencing   Sequencing that is driven by external influences such as needed teaching resources being available at only certain times during the school year.

Face-to-Face Interaction   A defining feature of cooperative learning lessons that requires a high degree of interconnectedness among students throughout the duration of the learning activity.

Facts   Isolated pieces of information, having little transfer value, that refer to a specific circumstance or situation. *See also* Structure of Knowledge.

Fair Employment Regulations   Regulations designed to prevent discrimination in the employment process.

Fair Use   A doctrine associated with copyright law that attempts to balance the rights of the copyright owner with the public's interest in having easy access to new ideas and information.

Family Educational Rights and Privacy Act   The 1974 legislation that requires schools to provide parents and guardians free access to their children's school records. Further, it grants rights to students to view their records and restricts access by unauthorized individuals to those records.

Feedback to Students   This term refers to actions teachers take to provide their students with information related to the appropriateness or correctness of their responses.

Field Dependent   A term used to describe people who understand things as they appear as part of a larger whole but who experience difficulty grasping them when they appear outside of the context within which they normally are expected to be found. *See also* Field Independent.

Field Independent   A term used to describe people who can readily grasp individual items even when they are encountered in situations outside of the context within which they normally are expected to be found. *See also* Field Dependent.

Fluid Plans   A term used to refer to flexible and responsive plans that a teacher modifies as a lesson unfolds to make instruction more appropriate for students given special conditions existing in the class on the day the lesson is taught.

Focus Questions   *See* List of Focus Questions.

Formative Evaluation   Evaluation that takes place as instruction goes forward for the purpose of providing continuous feedback to students. *See also* Summative Evaluation.

Foundation Program   As applied to school finance, this term refers to practices of states to provide additional funds to low-wealth school districts to assure that they have sufficient money to operate their programs at a minimally acceptable level.

Freedom of Conscience   This is the freedom guaranteed by the Constitution to be free from state interference in matters of religion and conscience.

Freedom of Expression   A right guaranteed to citizens that frees them, except in a small number of highly special situations, from governmental restrictions on what they can say.

Frequency Count   A term used to refer to a category of teacher observation instruments that feature an identification of behavior categories and a tallying of every occurrence of each listed behavior.

Full-Service School   A school that makes available to learners and their families a whole range of human-support-services that may include those designed to respond to health, emotional, social, and legal needs.

Game   *See* Educational Game.

Generalizations   Statements of relationship among concepts that summarize what the best-available information suggests is true or correct. *See also* Structure of Knowledge.

Goal Structure   A term that refers to the way people relate to one another as they seek to accomplish a particular goal. *See also* Competitive Goal Structure; Individualistic Goal Structure; Cooperative Goal Structure.

Goals of Learning   A term used to describe the purposes toward which instruction is directed.

Group Investigation   A cooperative learning technique that organizes students into democratic problem-solving groups who use scientific-inquiry procedures as they do their work.

Guaranteed Tax Base   A school financing scheme that pools all taxable property in the state, collects taxes centrally on all of this property, and distributes funding to schools in such a way that there is approximately the same amount dedicated to support instruction of students, regardless of where they live.

High-Stakes Testing   Term used to describe important kinds of testing where scores may have serious consequences for students whose proficiencies are measured and judged.

Higher-Level Thinking   Sophisticated thinking processes such as comparing, contrasting, interpreting, generalizing, identifying assumptions, making valid inferences, criticizing, and summarizing.

Homeschooling   Education of children by parents or guardians at home rather than in a public or private school classroom.

Human Resource Development (HRD)   A term, most frequently used in the private sector, to refer to the corporate training and development function.

"Imaginary Audience"   A term used by David Elkind to describe feelings of many adolescents that their every action is being observed and criticized by others.

Impact Stage   A stage in a teacher's professional development that focuses on how various approaches to teaching will exert a positive influence on students' learning and development. *See also* Mastery Stage; Survival Stage.

Inclusion   A term referring to commitment to the idea that students, regardless of unique personal characteristics (including, for example, disabilities of all kinds), not only have a legal right to services in a regular classroom but that they are welcomed and wanted as members of these classes.

Individual Accountability   As applied to small-group and cooperative-learning approaches, this term means that each member of a group is held accountable for a particular contribution to the overall effort.

Individualistic Goal Structure   A goal structure that encourages an individual to work toward a goal knowing that his or her accomplishment will be judged solely as a result of personal effort and will not be assessed in terms that relate to what others have done. *See also* Goal Structure.

Individualized Instruction   A general term that refers to teaching practices that seek to vary instructional approaches to meet the special needs of individual students.

Inductive Thinking   A pattern of reasoning that begins with specifics or particulars and moves on to explanatory generalizations or principles. *See also* Deductive Thinking.

Inferential Diagnosis   A process leading to judgments a teacher makes as a result of probing students' levels of understanding of new material.

Input   A term sometimes used to describe the phase of a lesson when new information is presented.

Inquiry Teaching   A specific form of discovery learning that emphasizes use of the scientific method, particularly hypothesizing, gathering data, and verifying/modifying conclusions. *See also* Discovery Learning.

Inservice Education   A general term used to refer to educational opportunities designed to improve the expertise of teachers who are already employed.

Inside-Outside   A technique designed to help students learn productive group behavior skills that involves people alternating roles between (1) working on an assigned task and (2) observing and commenting on those engaged in the assigned task.

Instructional Unit   A document containing quite explicit information about units in a course and that may include such components as (1) focus generalizations and concepts, (2) lists of learning intentions or objectives, (3) ideas for sequencing instruction, (4) lists of needed materials, (5) recommended instructional approaches, and (6) recommended assessment procedures.

Integrated-Subjects Pattern   A school course arrangement that features a focus on a theme that draws content from a variety of academic disciplines.

Intelligent Tutor Program   A kind of computer software used in individualized instruction programs that analyzes what a student knows about a given topic and then goes on to provide appropriate new learning experiences.

Interdisciplinary Teaching   A term sometimes applied to teaching courses organized according to an integrated-subjects pattern. *See also* Integrated-subjects pattern.

Interdisciplinary Unit   An instructional unit that draws content from two or more subject areas.

Intermediate-Term Planning   A kind of instructional planning that covers a period Lasting three to six weeks. *See also* Instructional Unit.

Internal Locus of Control   A condition characterizing individuals who believe their failures and successes to be directly connected to their own, controllable behaviors.

Internal Summary   An action taken during presentation of new information that involves the teacher stopping and briefly recapitulating what has been introduced to this point in the lesson.

International Baccalaureate   A structured program that allows students in different countries to pursue a secondary school curriculum which, if completed successfully, qualifies them for entry to top universities throughout the world.

International Reading Association   A specialty organization that draws members from people interested in improving reading in school programs.

International Society for Technology in Education   A specialty organization for people who are committed to improving instruction through appropriate applications of technology.

Interstate New Teacher Assessment and Support Consortium (INTASC)   An alliance of state education leaders, colleges and universities, and national groups with interests in promoting educational improvement by ensuring that new teachers meet high standards.

Issues, Values, and Consequences Analysis   An application of decision-making that includes consideration of values. *See also* Decision-Making.

Jigsaw   A cooperative learning technique that is appropriate when a teacher wishes to teach a topic that can be divided into several major components, each of which can be further subdivided into a set of common headings.

Laws   As used in the Structure of Knowledge, this term refers to summaries of information about what is true or correct that are based on exceptionally strong evidence. *See also* Structure of Knowledge.

Learning Center   A designated place within the classroom that functions as a self-contained environment where students can go to learn required information about a given topic.

Learning Context   The individual character of a school that is shaped by the nature of the community, the characteristics of its students, the actions of its administrators, and applicable state and local policies.

Learning Contract   An agreement negotiated between a teacher and student that specifies a series of learning tasks to be completed by the student to evidence learning of information described in the agreement.

Learning Station   An approach to individualized instruction that divides work among several stations, each of which requires students to do work related to one aspect of a larger topic.

Learning Style   A term used to refer to the contention that individuals vary in terms of how best they master new material and that successful instruction will adjust to accommodate these differences.

Learning Together   A cooperative learning technique that places a particularly high emphasis on the importance of students helping students.

Legitimate Power   The power and expectation of leadership accorded to individuals playing roles, including teaching, that invest them with a certain amount of authority.

Lesson Closure   A term that refers to a lesson's culminating activity or conclusion.

Lesson Pacing   The rate at which teachers introduce students to various elements in a lesson.

Lesson Plan   A plan that provides guidance for instruction for a short time span, often for a single class period.

Liberty Rights   Rights that prevent individuals from having restraints placed on their personal behavior.

Licensure   *See* Teaching certificate.

List of Focus Questions   Term applied to questions developed to guide note taking of an observer charged with collecting information about a teacher's classroom performance.

Logical Consequence   As applied to classroom management, a term that refers to consequences that bear a logical relationship to an inappropriate behavior; "making up time" is a logical consequence that might confront students who waste time.

Long-Term Memory   Memory storage system where new information is stored for considerable periods of time and where the information can be retrieved, when needed.

Long-Term Planning   A kind of instructional planning that covers an extensive period of time: several weeks, a quarter, a semester, or even a full academic year.

Long-Term Suspension   A suspension of more than 10 days. *See also* Suspension.

Malfeasance   A variety of negligence that occurs when a person deliberately acts in an improper manner and, thereby, causes harm to another. *See also* Negligence.

Malpractice   As applied to education, an action that is either unprofessional or an action that is inappropriate for the receiving individual and has some negative consequences for this person.

Management   As applied to teaching, a term that refers to actions a teacher takes for the purpose of creating an environment and establishing conditions that facilitate students' academic and social success. *See also* Discipline.

Marker Expression   A general term given to a phrase such as "this is a key point" that teachers use to draw students' attention to critically important information.

Mastery Learning   An approach to learning that assumes that achievement differences among learners result not from differences in their intelligence or aptitude but from variations in time that different students require to learn new material. For teachers, the implication is that, given sufficient time, nearly all students can learn what teachers seek to teach them.

Mastery Stage   A stage in a teacher's professional development that focuses on mastering fundamentals and adding new approaches that promise to enhance overall instructional effectiveness. *See also* Impact Stage; Survival Stage.

Mastery Teaching   *See* Direct Instruction.

Measurement   The process of gathering information through the use of tools designed for this purpose. *See also* Evaluation.

Meeting of the Minds   A phrase relating to a contract that indicates that all parties referenced are in agreement as to its contents.

Mentoring   The tutoring of a less skilled person by a more skilled person.

Metacognition   Mental activity associated with bringing to a conscious level those processes a person uses as he or she thinks and works through problems.

Method of Learning   A term used to describe approaches to teaching. Ideally, these should be suited to interests and aptitudes of individual students.

Misfeasance   A variety of negligence that occurs when an individual fails to act in a proper manner to prevent harm from coming to someone. *See also* Negligence.

Modalities of Learning   A term used to refer to the sensory challenges through which individuals receive and give information. *See also* Learning Style.

Modeling   Actions a teacher takes to illustrate for students a process or procedure they will need to follow to successfully complete an assigned task.

Multiple Intelligences   A theory that holds that different people have different kinds of intelligences and that good instruction should vary to accommodate the intelligences in which the person being taught has particular strengths.

Music Teachers National Association   A specialty organization dedicated to improving instruction in the area of music.

National Art Education Association   A specialty organization that draws members from among people who wish to promote better visual arts instruction in the schools.

National Association for Gifted Children   A specialty organization that serves people who wish to improve the education of gifted students.

National Board for Professional Teaching Standards (NBPTS)   A body that has developed a certification process that recognizes teachers who have met a rigorous set of professional standards with a special "National Board" certificate.

National Business Education Association   A specialty organization that draws together professional educators who are interested in business-related school subjects.

National Council for the Social Studies   A specialty organization that promotes good social studies instruction in the schools.

National Council of Teachers of English   A specialty organization dedicated to improving the teaching of English in the schools.

National Council of Teachers of Mathematics   A specialty organization dedicated to improving the teaching of mathematics in the schools.

National Education Association   A general organization that represents the interests of teachers at all levels and pursues a variety of issues relevant to education. *See also* American Federation of Teachers.

National Middle School Association   A specialty organization that is dedicated to studying and improving teaching and learning in the nation's middle schools.

National Rural Education Association   A specialty organization with particular interests in improving education in the nation's rural schools and school districts.

National Science Teachers Association   A specialty organization dedicated to improving the teaching of the sciences in the schools.

Negligence   A failure to use reasonable care and/or to take prudent actions to prevent harm from coming to someone.

Nonfeasance   A variety of negligence that occurs when an individual fails to act when there is a responsibility to do so. *See also* Negligence.

Nonsequential Topic Sequencing   A sequencing scheme in which individual topics do not build on one another in a systematic way and, therefore, can be taught in any order.

Nonverbal Signal   Term used to describe a nonverbal teacher behavior such as eye contact, a nod of the head, or a hand movement that is designed to communicate information to a student.

Norm-Referenced Measurement   Measurement used when the purpose is to evaluate performance of an individual student in terms of how it compares with those of similar students. *See also* Criterion-Referenced Measurement.

Numbered Heads Together   This is a small group technique that often is used to introduce students to the idea of group scoring and individual accountability.

On-call Support System   Name applied to a formal crisis intervention system in a school that features designated staff members being "on call" at certain periods during the day to respond to any developing serious problem.

Opportunity to Learn   A variable affecting student achievement that includes (1) a focus on a particular aspect of a subject that will be later tested and (2) sufficient time for students to master the new information.

Orbital Studies   An approach to teaching that attends closely to the *context of learning* variable. *See also* Context of Learning.

Pacing   *See* Lesson Pacing.

Part-to-Whole Sequencing   Instructional sequencing that proceeds from simple parts to complex wholes.

Pedagogical Assumptions   The basic values and beliefs that guide teachers' practices in the classroom.

Pedagogical Personality   A term used to refer to the ways in which a teacher's self-concept, confidence, and personal biases affect interactions with students.

Pedagogical Repertoire   A term used to refer to a teacher's knowledge of and appreciation for alternative ways of managing students and introducing content.

Peer Coaching   In education, a term referring to a process that features fellow teachers observing one another's teaching and otherwise working together in a supportive way with a view to improving the overall expertise of all participants.

Peer Tutoring   A process that features students who have already mastered new material working with students who are still in the process of learning it.

Performance Standards   Standards that identify levels of proficiency students are expected to attain. *See also* Content Standards; Standards-Based Education.

Personalized System of Instruction (PSI)   An example of a mastery-learning approach. *See also* Mastery Learning.

Portfolio   An organized collection of an individual's performance that covers a specific period of time.

Positive Interdependence   The idea that students must depend on and support one another to complete a task successfully.

Principles   As used in the Structure of Knowledge, this term refers to summaries of information about what is true or correct that are based on exceptionally strong evidence. *See also* Structure of Knowledge.

Problem Solving   Thinking process used when problems tend to have a clear "best" or "correct" solution.

Probable Cause   A high standard of evidence required before certain actions can be taken, including the issuing of search warrants. *See also* Reasonable Suspicion.

Profession   A term used to describe an occupation that includes individuals who (a) have specialized knowledge and skill, (b) have met specified criteria before being admitted to a preparation program, (c) act in ways that place their clients first, (d) enjoy a certain measure of autonomy as they work, and (e) who set and follow high performance standards.

Professional-Development Portfolio   A collection of information that is used to prompt reflection (for example, information about instructional techniques, descriptions of the teaching context, copies of lesson plans, examples of student work, comments of outside observers, and so forth) and written summaries of the teacher who has examined these materials, considered how various approaches to instruction have actually worked, and decisions about how future instruction might be improved.

Property Rights   Rights individuals have to enjoy benefits associated with their employment.

Proximity Control   A classroom control technique in which a teacher attempts to change an undesirable behavior by moving closer to the offending student.

Rate of Learning   A term referring to the pace at which individual students can "take in" and learn new material. Because individuals vary in their capacities to do this, teachers need to alter the pace of their teaching to accommodate these individual differences.

Reality Shock   A term used to describe reactions of first-year teachers to the many challenges and stresses they face as they begin their careers in the classroom.

Reasonable Suspicion   A less rigorous legal standard than probable cause that refers to evidence that is sufficiently compelling to convince a prudent and cautious individual that some criminal or illegal activity has occurred. *See also* Probable Cause.

Referent Power   A power or authority granted to someone who is perceived to be trustworthy and sincerely interested in the well being of people who may be affected by his or her decisions.

Reflective Teaching   A teaching approach, based on constructivism, that requires the teacher to reflect carefully on the condition he or she faces in the classroom and to respond flexibly and appropriately in ways that best serve the needs of individual students. *See also* Constructivism.

Reinforcement Center   A kind of learning center that features materials that help students review previously learned information. *See also* Learning Center.

Retrieval Chart   A matrix that includes concept categories under which relevant information can be listed.

Reward Power   A power that comes to someone because of his or ability to allocate benefits to others.

Rubric   Guideline or set of guidelines designed to tell an assessor what he or she should look at in making judgments about the quality of learner performance on a given task or set of tasks.

Same-Age Peer Tutoring   An approach to peer tutoring that features tutors who are about the same age and in the same grade as the students they tutor. *See also* Peer Tutoring.

School Administrator   A general title used to describe individuals playing major leadership roles at the school level, for example a principal or a vice-principal.

School-Based Management   *See* Site-Based Management.

School-Business Partnership   General term applied to cooperative work of businesses and schools to promote improvement of educational programs.

School Choice   A principle that establishes as a priority the rights of consumers of educational services (parents/guardians and students) to choose the schools that members of a family will attend.

School-to-Work   Term used to describe programs that attempt to smooth the transition from school to the workplace by carefully linking school programs to the kinds of knowledge and skills students will need when they leave school to become full-time employees.

Search and Seizure   Refers to the constitutional guarantee that citizens will not be subjected to unreasonable searches and seizures of their property.

Self Evaluation   A process whereby a teacher gathers and examines data with a view to making decisions about the adequacy of his or her performance and about changes he or she might make in the future.

Self-monitoring   Actions taken by an individual to monitor his or her own behaviors.

Service Learning   An instructional approach that seeks to enrich students' experiences by providing opportunities for them to use their skills and knowledge to provide service to and with their communities.

Sexual Harassment   A condition resulting when a hostile environment is created because of actions taken that relate to the gender of the individual.

Short-Term Memory   Memory storage system where bits of information received by the sensory perceptors are stored for a time period of up to about 30 seconds.

Short-Term Planning   A kind of instructional planning that covers a short period of time, often a single class period. *See also* Lesson Plan.

Short-Term Suspension   A suspension of less than 10 days. *See also* Suspension.

Simple-to-Complex Sequencing   *See* Part-to-Whole Sequencing.

Simulation   A powerful form of discovery learning that simplifies reality, places the individual in an environment where consequences of different decisions can be experienced, and that often features a game-like quality.

Single-Subject Pattern   A traditional school course arrangement that features a focus on a single academic subject, for example, biology.

Single-Subject Unit   An instructional unit that treats a topic related to one academic subject.

Site-Based Management   A school management approach that shifts power away from central school district authorities and places more power in the hands of leadership teams (teachers, administrators, community members, and others) at the individual building level.

Standardized Test   A test designed to measure the performance of a single student as it compares to the performances of all other students in similar circumstances. *See also* Norm-Referenced Measurement.

Standards-Based Education   Educational practices that include establishing clear, measurable descriptions of what students should come to know as a result of their educational experiences.

Structure of Knowledge   Scheme for breaking down knowledge that features three basic content types: (1) facts, (2) concepts, and (3) generalizations, principles, and laws.

Student Teams-Achievement Divisions   A well-known cooperative learning technique developed by Robert Slavin that promotes cooperation and active participation by all students involved in the lesson.

Summative Evaluation   Evaluation that occurs at the conclusion of a given sequence of instruction. *See also* Formative Evaluation.

Supervisor Evaluation   A kind of assessment process that features a person in a position of authority gathering information about and making a judgment concerning the adequacy of a subordinate's performance.

Survival Stage   A stage in a teacher's professional development, typically occurring early in his or her career, when concerns about getting through the day and handling the basic mechanical needs of teaching are of primary concern. *See also* Mastery Stage; Impact Stage.

Suspension   Term used to describe the temporary separation of a student from school. *See also* Expulsion.

Systemic Reform   The idea that improvement will not result from changing one or two components of the educational system. Rather, simultaneous attention to multiple components is required.

Systematic Teaching   *See* Direct Instruction.

Target Teaching   *See* Direct Instruction.

Task Analysis   The process of breaking down complex learning tasks into smaller units and sequencing these components in a logical manner.

Teacher Educator   A term used to describe a university or college faculty member with primary responsibility for preparing new teachers and for providing college- or university-based professional development experiences for teachers who are already on the job.

Teacher-Made Test   Test constructed by a teacher for use in his or her own classroom.

Teacher Observation   Term applied to a range of things teachers do in their classes to see that their students are performing assigned tasks properly.

Teacher's Contract   An official employment agreement between a teacher and a school district that includes information related to such issues as conditions of employment, salary, sick leave policies, insurance provisions, and grievance procedures.

Teaching Certificate   A license issued by a state authorizing qualified individuals to teach in its schools.

Teams-Games-Tournaments   An extension of Student Teams-Achievement Divisions that features organization of students into groups for the purpose of participating in academic tournaments.

Tech Prep   Term applied to describe school-to-work programs that typically involve two years of senior high school training and two additional years of training, often in community or junior colleges *See also* School-to-Work.

Tenure   A condition that allows a teacher who holds it to have a right to re-employment provided certain stipulated conditions are met.

Tenure Contract   A type of contract that stays in force from year to year unless the employing school district establishes that the employed teacher is guilty of violating state statutes governing teacher behavior. *See also* Teacher's Contract.

Term Contract   A type of contract usually presented to new teachers that offers employment for a fixed term, typically one school year. *See also* Teacher's Contract.

Textbook Guide   A document produced by a commercial publisher that contains suggestions for using a textbook.

Thematic Teaching   A term sometimes applied to teaching courses organized according to an integrated-subjects pattern. *See also* Integrated-Subjects Pattern.

Think-Pair-Share   A small-group technique in which the teacher presents the class a problem, organizes students in pairs to consider it, and asks a member from each pair to share conclusions with the entire class.

TIMSS   Acronym for the "Third International Mathematics and Science Study," an extensive and rigorous comparison of student achievement in different countries.

Tort   A civil wrong against another that results in either personal injury or property damage.

Two-by-Two   A technique to get students used to working with a new group that begins organizing them in groups of twos and, gradually, increasing the size of the group.

Unit   *See* Instructional Unit.

Verbal Mazes   An undesirable communication that features teacher explanations that meander in ways that are confusing to students.

Verbatim Record   An approach to obtaining information about a teacher's classroom performance that features identification of several categories and the writing down of everything the teacher says that falls within one of the listed categories.

Visualizing Thinking   A procedure involving the use of visual diagrams that help learners identify the kinds of thinking required to complete an assigned task and organize data in ways that will allow them to achieve success.

Voucher Plan   A plan that gives a voucher for funds needed to support the education of a child to his/her parent or guardian. This person can then choose a school for the student. When this is done, the voucher is turned over to the selected school. The school uses the funds to pay for educational services that are delivered to the student.

Whole-to-Part Sequencing   Sequencing that begins with an overview of a new topic and proceeds to introduce parts that go together to make up the whole.

Zero Tolerance Policy   A school policy that suggests that even a single violation of a particular rule will result in application of the severest penalty available.

AUTHOR INDEX

SUBJECT INDEX

intelligent tutor programs, 313
issues associated with cultural, racial, and ethnic
 minority students, 41–42
learning centers, 309
learning contracts, 305
mastery learning programs, 299–300
matching tests, 377, 382–384
measurement, 360
multiple-choice tests, 374, 377, 384–386
National Assessment of Educational Progress, 42,
 377
norm-referenced evaluation, 360
portfolios, 32, 95–96, 366–372
Personalized System for Instruction, 299
procedures used in a competitive-goal-structure
 environment, 270
rating scales, 377–379
recommendations embedded in instructional units,
 213–214
relationship between taught and tested content, 141
risk factors and achievement, 167
rubrics, 363–365, 371, 372–373
Scholastic Achievement Test, 377
sorting activities, 376
standardized testing, 15, 146–147, 199, 256, 363,
 366, 378
student-produced tests, 376
summative evaluation, 361
teacher observation, 375
teacher–student discussion, 376
teachers' performance, 426–448
traditional techniques, 374–388
true-false tests, 374, 377, 386–388
Association for Career and Technical Education
 (ACTE), 466
Attendance requirements, 104–105
Attention deficit disorder (ADD), 183–184
Attractive power, 403–404
Authentic evaluation, 361–363, 366

Bannister v. Paradis, 111
Bicentennial Commission of the American Association
 of Colleges of Teacher Education, 12
Board of Trustees v. Stubblefield, 128
Brainstorming, 338ñ340
Buddy system, 415
Buzz session, 273

Cardinal principles of secondary education, 50

Carnegie Forum on Education and the Economy, 29
Career-long professional growth, *See* Teachers'
 career-long professional growth
Career options, 471–476
 department chair, 471–472
 curriculum coordinator, 472
 human resource development professional, 476
 school administrator, 472
 school counselor, 472–473
 state education agency employee, 473
 teacher educator, 473, 475–476
Case study, 343
Center for Human Resources, 25
Center on Families, Communities, Schools, and
 Children's Learning, 27
Certificates, *See* Teaching certificate
Characteristics of schools, *See* School characteristics
Charter schools, 23–24
Checklists, *See* Evaluative checklists
Child-abuse reporting obligations of teachers, 123
Children's Defense Fund, 12
Chronological sequencing, 156
Clarity, *See* Teachers' clarity
Classroom debates, 273–275, 376
Classroom management, 394–407
 arranging floor space, 405
 attractive power, 403–404
 coercive power, 402–403
 establishing routines, 406–407
 expert power, 403
 lead managers, 397
 legitimate power, 402
 managing the physical environment, 404–405
 managing time, 405
 preventing problems, 399–407
 providing assistance to students, 407
 The Quality School, 397
 referent Power, 403–404
 reward power, 402
 teacher consistency, 404
 teacher leadership and authority, 401–404
 teachers' management responsibilities, 397–398
Clinical teaching, *See* Direct instruction
Classroom observation data, 437–441
 focus questions, 438
 frequency counts, 439
 verbatim record, 438–439
Coalition of Effective Schools, 51
Coercive power, 402–403